GUINNESS WORLD RECORDS 2015

Largest yo-yo

On Sep 15, 2012, Beth Johnson (USA) got her "Whoa-Yo" yo-yo to go-go to cheers from onlookers in LaRue, Ohio, USA. A record 11 ft 9 in (3.63 m) in diameter and weighing 4,620 lb (2.09 metric tons), the huge disk plunged 120 ft (36.5 m) on a rope attached to a 150,000-lb (68-metric-ton) crane before rebounding.

Diamonds

All the diamonds ever polished in history would fill just **one double-decker bus**

Actual Size

Largest brilliant-cut diamond

A 545.67-carat brilliant diamond known as the "Golden Jubilee Diamond" was purchased from the diamond speciality group De Beers by a syndicate of Thai businessmen and was presented to the King of Thailand in 1995 to commemorate his golden jubilee. It is now mounted in the Thai royal scepter.

Largest cut fancy black diamond

An unnamed fancy black diamond containing small red diamond crystals was polished into 55 facets over several years and finished in Jun 2004. It weighs 555.55 carats—the repetitive use of the number five is culturally significant in the Islamic world—and was inspired by Ran Gorenstein (BEL), who also commissioned it.

Most diamonds in one ring

The "Tsarevna Swan" ring, which was created by the Lobortas Classic Jewelry House (UKR), is white gold set with 2,525 diamonds. Fully wearable, it was presented and measured in Kiev, Ukraine, on Jul 21, 2011.

Most valuable casino chip

A casino chip designed by Gerald N. Lewy (CAN) was valued at CAN$450,000 ($436,500) on May 30, 2013. The 22-carat pink gold chip is set with 173 round brilliant-cut diamonds (17 of them around the rim) and 64 natural pink diamonds.

Most expensive diamond per carat

The diamond price record per carat is $1,375,938 for a 7.03-carat fancy vivid blue modified rectangular brilliant-cut diamond sold by Sotheby's on May 12, 2009. It was cut from an original stone that weighed 26.58 carats.

Most valuable boots

A pair of size-8.5 women's ankle boots made with 167 oz (4,738 g) of gold and covered in 39,083 natural

FACT

This scintillating Snoopy also features 783 black diamonds and a collar made from 415 red ruby gemstones!

Most valuable Snoopy

On Nov 13, 2009, to celebrate the 60th anniversary of Charles Schulz's cartoon-strip canine Snoopy, Tse Sui Luen Jewellery of Hong Kong, China, created a 5.5-in-tall (14-cm) "Diamond Snoopy" encrusted with 9,917 diamonds. Also known as "The Ever-Shining Star," the 207-carat creation went on sale with a price tag of HK$2,888,880 ($372,750).

Largest diamond in the universe

BPM 37093 is a white dwarf star 50 light-years from Earth in the constellation of Centaurus. In 2004, astronomers from the Harvard-Smithsonian Center for Astrophysics in Massachusetts, USA, deduced that the carbon white dwarf had crystallized into a diamond some 2,500 mi (4,000 km) across. The star has been nicknamed "Lucy," after The Beatles' song "Lucy in the Sky with Diamonds." Assuming the cost of $1,600 per carat, Lucy would set you back $16,000,000,000,000,000,000,000,000,000,000,000,000 ($16 undecillion).

Most valuable materials in a work of art

For the Love of God by Damien Hirst (UK) is a human skull encrusted with 8,601 flawless diamonds, including a 52.4-carat pink diamond in the forehead. The total 1,106.18 carats of diamonds were reported to cost a dazzling £12 m ($23.7 m).

ANATOMY OF A DIAMOND: THE "BRILLIANT" CUT

A diamond is "cut"—that is, shaped and polished—to enhance its beauty and brilliance.

Top view

Enlarged girdle

Side view

Bottom view

Upper girdle facet

Star facet

Upper main facet

Girdle

Lower girdle facet

Pavilion main facet

Table

Culet: Flattened apex of the lower facets (optional) *Enlarged culet*

Crown: Upper part of the cut diamond, usually with 33 facets

Pavilion: Lower part of the cut diamond, usually with 25 facets

"Baby" Williams

The latest fashion accessory for any self-respecting rapper is "grillz"—i.e., diamond dentures. The king of bling is undoubtedly Bryan "Baby" Williams (USA), who reportedly spent a record $500,000 on having his teeth permanently fitted with 18-carat white gold and platinum crowns set with asher-cut diamonds.

fancy colored diamonds weighing 1,550 carats was unveiled by Diarough/UNI-Design and A. F. Vandevorst (BEL) in Hong Kong in Dec 2013. The boots were valued at $3.1 m.

Most expensive diamond sold at auction

On Nov 12, 2013, the "Pink Star"—a flawless pink diamond—was sold to an anonymous bidder for 76,325,000 Swiss francs ($83.01 m) at Christie's in Geneva, Switzerland. The oval 59.60-carat diamond is mounted on a ring and measures 1.06 x 0.81 in (2.69 x 2.06 cm). It took two years to cut.

Most faceted diamond

Diamonds are cut with varying numbers of facets to enhance their sparkle (see below), the most common being the

57 or 58 facets of the "brilliant" cut found in most engagement rings. The "Brilliant Lady 21" cut, which was created by Louis Verelst (BEL), has 221 facets, producing a large number of reflections and resulting in increased brilliance.

Largest diamond pendant

The largest nonreligious pendant is "Crunk Ain't Dead," owned by hip-hop artist Lil' Jon (USA). With 3,576 white diamonds, it weighs 2 lb 2.4 oz (977.6 g) without its chain.

Most valuable necklace

"The Incomparable" contains a 407.48-carat flawless diamond and 102 "satellite" diamonds. Manufactured by the jewelers Mouawad, based in Switzerland, it was valued on Feb 13, 2013 at an incredible $55 m. The flawless diamond was discovered in the Congo some 30 years ago in a pile of kimberlite, a by-product of diamond mining.

First manmade diamond

In 1955, scientists in GE's laboratory in Schenectady, New York, USA, built an ultrahigh-pressure apparatus called the "Diamond Press." The press produced pressure of over 1.5 million lb/sq in (1 billion kg/m²) and up to 5,000°F (2,760°C). Metal and carbon were melted together, using an electrical current, and then cooled. The result: perfectly formed manmade diamonds up to 1/10th carat in weight.

The **largest manmade cut diamond** is a 2.16-carat synthetic marquis-cut diamond created by the Scio Diamond Technology Corporation (USA). The 0.5-in (13.42-mm) diamond was tested in Apr 2013 by the Gemological Institute of America.

FACT
The Incomparable appeared on eBay in 2002 with a starting price of $22.5 m but failed to sell.

Actual Size

Actual Size

First 100% diamond ring

On Mar 8, 2012, the jewelers Shawish (CHE) unveiled the first ring to be made entirely from a diamond. The 150-carat creation is reportedly worth a whopping $70 m.

Actual Size

Largest uncut diamond

The largest ever single, rough, uncut diamond was the "Cullinan," which weighed 3,106.75 carats when found in 1905 in South Africa. It was cut into nine smaller diamonds, the largest of which, the "Great Star of Africa," weighs 530.2 carats and tops the royal scepter (left) wielded by the UK's Queen Elizabeth II. The next largest fragment—the "Second Star of Africa"—sits in the Queen's Imperial State Crown.

Rock stars: diamonds defined

Diamond—the world's **hardest natural substance**—is a mineral formed 85–125 mi down in Earth's mantle. It is a form (allotrope) of the chemical element carbon (C) in which the atoms are arranged in a tetrahedral crystalline formation. Diamonds are measured in carats, with one carat equal to 200 mg. For each carat of diamond mined, 550,000 lb of earth is excavated.

Largest heist: the 90-second break-in

At lunchtime on Jul 28, 2013, an armed man entered the Carlton International hotel (right) in Cannes, France. His target: jewelry worth 103 m euros ($136.7 m). He single-handedly pulled off the biggest diamond heist ever in just one-and-a-half minutes. The diamond-encrusted watches, rings, and earrings he stole (left) belonged to Lev Leviev—a Soviet-born Israeli diamond and property mogul—and had been on display in an exhibition at the hotel.

British Library
Cataloguing-in-publication data: a catalogue record for this book is available from the British Library

ISBN 978-1-897553-37-4

This book is dedicated to Chris Bernstein

For a complete list of credits and acknowledgements, turn to p. 252.

Records are made to be broken—indeed, it is one of the key criteria for a record category—so if you find a record that you think you can beat, tell us about it by a making record claim. Find out how on p. 5. Always contact us before making a record attempt.

Check the official website—www.guinnessworldrecords.com—regularly for record-breaking news, plus video footage of record attempts. You can also join and interact with the Guinness World Records online community.

Sustainability
The paper used for this edition is manufactured by UPM Plattling, Germany. The production site has forest certification and its operations have both ISO14001 environmental management system and EMAS certification to ensure sustainable production.

UPM Papers are true Biofore products, produced from renewable and recyclable materials.

OFFICIALLY AMAZING

Editor-in-Chief
Craig Glenday
Senior Managing Editor
Stephen Fall
Layout Editors
Ian Cranna,
Rob Dimery,
Lucian Randall
Assistant Editor
Roxanne Mackey
Editorial Team
Theresa Bebbington (Americanization),
Marie Lorimer (indexing),
Matthew White (proofreading)
Picture Editor
Michael Whitty
Deputy Picture Editor
Fran Morales
Talent/Picture Researcher
Jenny Langridge
Picture Researcher
Laura Nieberg

VP Publishing
Jenny Heller
Director of Procurement
Patricia Magill
Publishing Manager
Jane Boatfield
Publishing Executives
Ebyan Egal,
Charlie Peacock
Production Consultants
Roger Hawkins,
Dennis Thon
Printing & Binding
MOHN Media Mohndruck GmbH, Gütersloh, Germany
Cover Production
Hololens Technology Co., Ltd;
Simon Thompson (API Laminates Ltd);
Bernd Salewski (GT Produktion)
Augmented Reality
Mustard Design Limited;
Anders Ehrenborg (Robert Wadlow modeling and texturing)

Design
Paul Wylie-Deacon, Richard Page, Matt Bell at 55design.co.uk
Original Photography
Richard Bradbury, Anne Caroline, Kimberly Cook, Matt Crossick, Daniel Deme, James Ellerker, Jarek Jõepera, Paul Michael Hughes, Shinsuke Kamioka, Ranald Mackechnie, Kevin Scott Ramos, Chris Skone-Roberts, Philip Robertson, Ryan Schude
Editorial Consultants
Mark Aston, Jan Bondeson, Iain Borden, Martyn Chapman, Nicholas Chu, Sammpa von Cyborg, Steven Dale, Joshua Dowling, Dick Fiddy, David Fischer, Mike Flynn, Justin Garvanovic, Ben Hagger, Ralph Hannah, David Hawksett, Eberhard Jurgalski, David Lardi, Glen O'Hara, Ocean Rowing Society, Paul Parsons, Clara Piccirillo, Dr Karl Shuker, Matthew White, World Sailing Speed Record Council, Stephen Wrigley, Robert Young

President: Alistair Richards
SVP Americas: Peter Harper
President (Greater China): Rowan Simons
VP Japan: Erika Ogawa
Country Manager, UAE: Talal Omar

PROFESSIONAL SERVICES
EVP Finance, Legal, HR, & IT: Alison Ozanne
Financial Controller: Scott Paterson
Management Accountants: Daniel Ralph, Shabana Zaffar
Assistant Accountant: Kimberley Dennis
Accounts Payable Assistant: Victoria Aweh
Accounts Receivable Manager: Lisa Gibbs
Head of Legal & Business Affairs: Raymond Marshall
Legal & Business Affairs Manager: Michael Goulbourn
Legal & Business Affairs Executive: Xiangyun Rablen
Director of IT: Rob Howe
Senior Developer: Philip Raeburn
Developer: Lewis Ayers
Desktop Support: Ainul Ahmed
Head of HR: Jane Atkins
Office Manager (UK): Jacqueline Angus
HR & Office Manager (Americas): Morgan Wilber
Office Manager (Japan): Fumiko Kitagawa
Office Manager (Greater China): Tina Shi
Office Assistant (Greater China): Sabrine Wang

TELEVISION
Director of TV Content & Sales: Rob Molloy
TV Distribution Manager: Denise Carter Steel

GLOBAL MARKETING
SVP Global Marketing: Samantha Fay
Marketing Director (Americas): Stuart Claxton
Marketing Director (Greater China): Sharon Yang
Senior PR Manager (Americas): Jamie Antoniou

PR & Marketing Executive (Americas): Sara Wilcox
Marketing Managers: Justine Tommey (UK), Tanya Batra (UK & EMEA)
Marketing Executives: Aurora Bellingham (UK), Christelle BeTrong (UK), Asumi Funatsu (Japan), Mayo Ma (Greater China)
PR Director (UK): Amarilis Whitty
PR & Sales Promotion Manager (Japan): Kazami Kamioka
PR Managers (UK): Tandice Abedian, Damian Field
PR Executive (UK): Jamie Clarke
PR Assistant (Greater China): Leila Wang
Director of Digital Content & Marketing: Katie Forde
Digital Manager: Kirsty Brown
Digital Video Producer: Adam Moore
Community Manager: Dan Thorne
Online Editor: Kevin Lynch
Designer: Neil Fitter
Design Executive: Jon Addison
Designer (Japan): Momoko Cunneen
Content Manager (Americas): Mike Janela
Digital & Publishing Content Manager (Japan): Takafumi Suzuki
Digital Manager (Greater China): Jacky Yuan

GWR CREATIVE
VP Creative: Paul O'Neill
Programme Manager, Attractions: Louise Toms

COMMERCIAL SALES
SVP Sales UK & EMEA: Nadine Causey
VP Commercial: Andrew Brown
Publishing, Sales, & Product Director (Americas): Jennifer Gilmour
Content Director (Greater China): Angela Wu
Head of Publishing Sales (EL): John Pilley
Sales & Distribution Manager (UK & international): Richard Stenning
Head of Commercial Accounts & Licensing (UK): Samantha Prosser
Licensing Manager, Publishing: Emma Davies

Commercial Director (Greater China): Blythe Fitzwiliam
Business Development Manager (Americas): Amanda Mochan
Head of Commercial Sales & Marketing (Japan): Kaoru Ishikawa
Senior Account Manager: Vihag Kulshrestha
Account Managers: Dong Cheng (China), Ralph Hannah (UK/Paraguay), Annabel Lawday (UK), Takuro Maruyama (Japan), Nicole Pando (USA), Lucie Pessereau (UK), Terje Purga (USA), Nikhil Shukla (India), Seyda Subasi-Gemici (Turkey), Charlie Weisman (USA)
Commercial Assistant (Greater China): Catherine Gao

RECORDS MANAGEMENT
SVP Records: Marco Frigatti
Director of RMT: Turath Alsaraf
Head of Records Management: Carlos Martinez (Japan), Kimberly Partrick (Americas), Charles Wharton (Greater China)
Database Manager: Carim Valerio
Adjudications Manager: Benjamin Backhouse
Team Leader, RMT (UK): Jacqueline Fitt
Specialist Records Managers (UK): Anatole Baboukhian, Louise McLaren, Elizabeth Smith
Records Managers (Americas): Alex Angert, Evelyn Carrera, Michael Empric, Johanna Hessling, Annie Nguyen, Philip Robertson
Records Managers (Greater China): John Garland, Lisa Hoffman
Records Managers (Japan): Mariko Koike, Aya McMillan, Mai McMillan, Justin Patterson, Gulnaz Ukassova
Records Managers (UK): Jack Brockbank, Fortuna Burke, Tom Ibison, Sam Mason, Mark McKinley, Eva Norroy, Anna Orford, Pravin Patel, Glenn Pollard, Chris Sheedy, Lucia Sinigagliesi, Victoria Tweedy, Lorenzo Veltri, Aleksandr Vypirailenko
Senior Project Manager (UK): Alan Pixsley
Project Managers: Samer Khallouf (UAE), Paulina Sapinska (UK)
Project Co-ordinator (UK): Shantha Chinniah

Be a record-breaker

Have you got a **record-breaking talent** to share?

Anyone can set a record and there are more ways of doing it now than ever before. It's free of charge and you can apply right away at **www.guinnessworldrecords.com**. When we started in 1955, record holders could only appear in the book—now you can get on TV, appear at live events, or get your attempt on our Web site.

Start

FACT

You can attempt a world record right now by visiting **www. guinnessworldrecords. com/challengers** and, once you get the green light, you can upload a video of your attempt. You'll soon hear—GWR adjudicate every week.

Register online

Head on over to **www.guinnessworld records.com** and click on "Register" at the top of the screen. It's a matter of minutes to set up your account and you're almost set. Have you got the guidelines yet?

Do you know which record you want to attempt?

If you think you've got what it takes to tackle an existing record, we want to hear from you. Want to try something new? We are equally excited by new ideas, so let us know right away.

YES

NO

Read, watch, browse

Keep reading the book! You'll find ideas there and in our TV shows and you can check out the latest action on the website at **www. guinnessworldrecords. com**. This will give you a sense of the records that we usually accept.

NO

YES

Record rules

If your chosen record already exists (or we like your idea), we'll send you the guidelines that anyone must follow when making an attempt. If you've submitted an idea and we don't accept it, we will tell you why.

Collect evidence

Make sure you give yourself plenty of time to practise your record attempt. When you're ready to go, you'll have to be careful to collect all the evidence we need to ensure your best chance of a successful attempt.

Just the facts

Gather your evidence and send it to us. Depending on the record, we'll need independent eyewitness statements, photos, video, and other proof outlined in the guidelines. Now just wait to hear ... Did you break your record?

Finish

NO   **YES**

You're a record-breaker!

If you've followed the rules and beaten an existing record or even set a new one, you'll receive a letter of confirmation. You will also be sent your official Guinness World Records certificate welcoming you into the family of record holders. Congratulations! If you're very lucky, you may even make it into next year's book.

Better luck next time

You may not be successful, but don't give up! Come back and try again or choose a different record for another chance to receive that world-famous certificate.

Inside 2015

What's new in the world's **best-selling annual book**?

All-new Augmented Reality!

Download our FREE "See It 3D" app now and see some of your favorite record holders come to life. Simply point your cell phone or tablet device at the pages where you see the "SEE IT 3D" icon and you'll be able to meet a giant, explore the depths of the ocean, and even battle with cheesy maggots in a fun new video game.

Augmented Reality (AR) software works by harnessing the camera of your tablet device or smartphone and using it to detect elements on the printed page. This triggers the device to display 3D images on the screen. Today, the technology behind it allows for virtual-reality environments, interactive 3D animations, and even games, such as the one below …

Augmented Reality alert!
3D ON THIS PAGE

PLAY THE AR GAME: Maggot Splat!

Try the **SEE IT 3D** experience now by downloading the app and playing this new game, inspired by the record for the **most dangerous cheese!**

Casu marzu is a Sardinian cheese that is deliberately left to rot, allowing flies to lay eggs and hatch thousands of maggots inside the cheese. This apparently improves the taste, although it can leave you with stomach pains. Your challenge is to splat the maggots as they ping themselves out of the cheese—just like they do in Sardinia. Register your high score and you could even win yourself an official Guinness World Records certificate! Good luck!

SEE IT 3D WITH THE FREE APP

① DOWNLOAD THE FREE "SEE IT 3D" APP

Download on the App Store
ANDROID APP ON Google play

GUINNESSWORLDRECORDS.COM/SEEIT3D

② LOOK FOR THE "SEE IT 3D" SYMBOL ON THE COVER OR INSIDE THE BOOK

SEE IT 3D WITH THE FREE APP

③ USING THE APP, VIEW THE BOOK AND WATCH THE RECORD HOLDERS APPEAR IN 3D!

#seeit3d

Share your AR experience with us:

f Facebook.com/GuinnessWorldRecords

Twitter.com/GWR

Youtube.com/guinnessworldrecords

g+ Plus.Google.com/+guinnessworldrecords

Instagram.com/guinnessworldrecords

CONTENTS

QUOTE

"When one thinks of Guinness World Records, automatically 'extraordinary' and 'remarkable' comes to mind. So for me to win, I am truly honored and delighted."
Usain Bolt

✕ Check out related and cross-referenced pages of records

NAVIGATE the Solar System

p. 20

Take a trip to Mars, Saturn, and the rest of the Solar System from the comfort of your armchair

EXPLORE the ocean depths

p. 42

Turn your device into a deep-sea explorer and encounter the creatures of the deep

ENCOUNTER the most venomous spider

p. 60

Get dangerously close to the Brazilian wandering spider ... without actually putting your life at risk!

MEET the performing Pomeranian

p. 66

Go for a walk with Jiff the dog and watch as the cool canine pulls off some of his trademark tricks

SIZE UP with the tallest man

p. 80

Get the exclusive chance to meet the most iconic record holder of all time. Robert Pershing Wadlow stood 8 ft 11.1 in (2.72 m) tall— how do you measure up?

#seeit3d

The SEE IT 3D app comes with a built-in camera feature, so snap yourself and your friends alongside the AR record holders and share your images with us.

Editor's letter

Globally, only 7.6% of claims became official world records last year

Welcome to this special diamond anniversary edition of the world's **biggest-selling annual book.** We may be entering our 60th year, but we're still a long way off from retiring and collecting our pensions! While this year's edition looks back over six ever-changing decades of record-breaking, we've still squeezed in every major new and updated record from the last year, so expect the usual mix of unrivaled sporting achievements, talented pets, cutting-edge scientific discoveries, and the most remarkable human beings on the planet ...

There's been no letup in the demand for record-breaking, with around 50,000 new claims, enquiries, and updates filling our inboxes and mail trays over the past 12 months. We've had claims from around the world, from Afghanistan (**longest chain of paper dolls**: a successful attempt, at 4.09 mi or 6.5 km) to Zimbabwe (**longest live DJ set**: TBC, but 168 hr is a tough record to beat!), as well as enquiries from as far afield as East Timor, Tongo, and Tajikistan.

Canada remains a strong country for record-breaking, with 1,700 claims registered. Thanks and congratulations to everyone who made it into our database as an official Guinness World Records title holder and went on to receive their official GWR certificate as proof.

As ever, the scope of record-breaking in Canada is impressive, ranging from the very Canadian **most people making maple taffy** (495 by Festival Beauceron de l'Érable in Saint-Georges, Quebec, on Mar 16, 2014) and **largest collection of maple syrup artifacts** (5,228 items amassed by Vernon Wheeler in McDonalds Corners, Ontario, as of Jan 17, 2014) to the sporty—the **highest total score in figure skating** (295.27 by Patrick Chan at the ISU Grand Prix Trophée Eric Bompard in Paris, France, on Nov 16, 2013; he won gold).

We've also had the strongest, such as multiple record holder Kevin Fast, who racked up another hit with the **heaviest sled pulled by Father Christmas** (35,163 lb, or 15,950 kg, in Cobourg, Ontario, on Nov 18, 2013). You can read more about the powerful pastor on p. 11 and in Show of Strength on pp. 104–5.

We've had schools getting involved (**most hunger relief packages assembled simultaneously**: 1,000 by Sandalwood Heights Secondary School in

Fastest marathon in a lacrosse kit

Paul Statchuk (CAN) ran the Scotiabank Toronto Waterfront Marathon in 3 hr 46 min 58 sec on Oct 20, 2013 in full lacrosse kit. As of Apr 2014, Paul holds two other sports kit records: **fastest marathon in an ice hockey kit** (4 hr 8 min 43 sec) and **fastest marathon in an American football kit** (3 hr 45 min 30 sec). For even more marathons, see pp. 230–31.

FACT

In 2009, Statistics Canada reported that consumers spend $6 bn on gift cards every year—but the average house has $300 in unused gift cards.

Largest fruit sculpture

Dairy Queen Canada and Orange Julius commissioned "fruit artist" Shawn Feeney of San Francisco's The Invisible Underground to sculpt a tree in Calgary on Aug 13, 2013. The tree—measuring 10 ft 0.47 in (3.06 m) tall—was crafted from pineapples, mangos, green apples, strawberries, oranges, and blueberries.

Largest collection of gift token cards

To make shopping trips with mom more interesting, brothers David and Aaron Miller (USA/CAN) started to collect gift tokens, and by 2013 they'd amassed 3,215 different cards. They're far from alone in hoarding with a passion—we've raided GWR's own massive archive of records to bring you the best hauls in Collections on pp. 90–91.

Fastest underwater escape from a straitjacket

Lucas Wilson (CAN) freed himself from a straitjacket in 23.16 sec while submerged at the gymnasium of École St. Patrick High School in Yellowknife, Northwest Territories, on Oct 5, 2013. Read more about his exploits and those of other escapologists, acrobats, contortionists and gymnasts, in Flexible Friends on pp. 106–7.

FACT

As of Oct 2013, David (right) had run 11 marathons (not all of them in fruit costume), including events in London, New York, Boston, Berlin, and Chicago. He said of the crowd, "It was fun waving at them all, especially the kids who couldn't quite work out what was going on."

Fastest half-marathon dressed as a fruit

The Scotiabank Toronto Waterfront Marathon on Oct 20, 2013 saw banana-clad Brit David Hiddleston record the best time for a half-marathon dressed as a fruit: 1 hr 25 min 45 sec. For more costumed antics, check out Mass Participation on pp. 116–17.

Brampton, Ontario, on Dec 18, 2013); businesses (**largest human power symbol**: 364 staff of easyhome Ltd. at Niagara Falls, Ontario, on Apr 9, 2014); theater companies (**longest-running annual musical theater production**: *Anne of Green Gables—The Musical*, staged 49 times since 1965 by the Confederation Centre of the Arts at the Charlottetown Festival); and simply groups of friends (**longest marathon playing table hockey**: 30 hr by Jason Kurylo, Robert Richard Tarzwell, Brent Corba, Jamie Macdonald, Chris Withers, and Derek Macdonald (all CAN) in Vancouver on Sep 20–21, 2013).

As well as all these new records, because it's our 60th birthday, we've decided to trace the evolution of some of your favorite

record categories. You'll find "Flashback" features at the beginning of each chapter. Each one explores a record-breaking topic—including 60 years of space travel (pp. 16–17), new discoveries in the animal world (pp. 44–45), and advances in telecoms technology (pp. 180–81)—and traces how the records have evolved in the years since our first book in 1955. We've also dipped into our earlier editions to bring you bite-size Flashbacks throughout the book, comparing records from the past to those of today. It's fascinating to see how much has changed since the 1950s … and how much has stayed the same!

One discovery we made this year while looking back through our archives is that the record for the absolute **heaviest weight lifted by a human** hadn't been updated. We're pleased to set the record straight and announce that the fully notarized record stands at 5,340 lb (2.42 metric tons) for two cars (plus drivers) on a platform backlifted by Canadian Gregg Ernst at the South Shore Exhibition in Bridgewater, Nova Scotia, set on Jul 28, 1993.

One of the reasons for the success of Guinness World Records over the past 60 years is that we've always tried to embrace any new habits, fashions, or technology. We're not a dusty reference book—we reflect what's happening around us. This year is no exception, which is why you'll find new categories for topics such as 3D printing (p. 206), Instagram and Twitter (p. 138), alternative transport (p. 190), and digital piracy (p. 174). Look out, too, for some 2013 "neologies" (newly coined words), such as "bitcoin" (p. 135) "twerking" (p. 117), and "selfies" (p. 207).

NEW DESIGN

We've also refreshed the design this year—riffing on the concepts of "diamonds" and "tablet typography"—courtesy of the creatives at 55 Design (UK). To that end, we've introduced a

A dog's dinner

Female Great Danes usually grow to 28–32 in (71–81 cm) tall. They must be at least 28 in (71 cm) high to qualify as one of the breed. Morgan eats about 10 cups of kibble a day and needs to be exercised for about 80 min daily.

Tallest female dog

A four-year-old Great Dane called Morgan was measured at 3 ft 2.6 in (98.15 cm) tall on Jan 9, 2013. She is owned by Dave and Cathy Payne in Melbourne, Ontario, although the question of who rules the home is subject to debate! For more on pets—including a Wolfhound from Canada with the longest tail—and to see how Morgan measures up against the **tallest male dog**, see pp. 64–65.

Most yards rushing in a Grey Cup game

Kory Sheets (USA) ran 197 yd while leading the CFL's Saskatchewan Roughriders to a win over the Hamilton Tiger-Cats, 45–23, in the 101st Grey Cup football game on Nov 24, 2013. His record eclipsed the previous Grey Cup mark of 169 yd, set by Johnny Bright in 1956. Sports fans should head to the packed sports section starting on p. 208.

(**fastest 5 meters on front paws**, p. 67), the QTvan from the UK (**smallest caravan**, p. 192), and the Fisarmonica Gigante from Italy (**largest accordion**, p. 97). Back by popular demand is our SEE IT 3D Augmented Reality (AR) feature. Check out how to access a wealth of 3D and interactive animations—and download the free app—on pp. 6–7. Among the amazing visuals on offer this year is an actual-size render of Robert Pershing Wadlow, the world's **tallest man ever** (p. 81), giving you the chance to have your photograph taken alongside this classic record holder. Many thanks to Mustard Design (UK) for their cutting-edge work on these added extras.

Most individual freestyle skiing Olympic golds

Freestyle skiing has been an Olympic sport since 1992, but it wasn't until Alex Bilodeau (CAN) won the moguls event at Sochi 2014 that an individual achieved more than one gold medal. His previous win came at Vancouver in 2010. For more Winter Olympics records, see pp. 244–45.

new element we're calling the Control Strip. You'll find this design feature along the bottom of most of the regular spreads. This space is dedicated to fact boxes, glossaries, the aforementioned Flashback panels, and infographics, giving you extra record data at a glance.

Yet another new feature for this book is the Gallery. These pages showcase some of the amazing photography that Guinness World Records has shot over the years. Picture Editor Michael Whitty and his team have once again been traveling the world to bring you the best new images, so look out for the likes of Jiff the dog from the USA

GWR ONLINE

Staying with digital matters, we were excited to welcome our 4-millionth Facebook fan in Apr 2014, and we've signed up to Instagram and Flickr to share some of the hundreds of incredible

photographs and videos that come into our offices every week. We're also closing in on our 500,000th follower on the GWR YouTube channel, and our Twitter following has reached 87.2K. Okay, we're a long way off Katy Perry (**most followers**

on Twitter) and Shakira (**most "liked" person on Facebook**)—see p. 166— but our job is to monitor and disseminate records, not to break them!

While we're in the digital realm, be sure to check out the Challengers section of our Web site. This gives wannabe record holders fast access to an official Guinness World Records adjudicator for a series of do-try-this-at-home record categories such as

Heaviest vehicle pulled over 100 ft by a female

All hail Toronto's Lia Grimanis (CAN), who pulled a 2014 International 8600 tandem axle cab weighing 17,820 lb (8,083 kg) over 100 ft (30.4 m) at the Toronto Convention Centre on Dec 12, 2013. Lia made the attempt on her 42nd birthday to show how strong women can be. She had also planned to haul it with a trailer but was thwarted by the Centre's slippery polished cement floor.

AE·76141

Longest chain of bracelets

On Aug 16, 2013, the Girl Guides of New Brunswick and Prince Edward Island linked together a chain of 19,953 bracelets at Snider Mountain Ranch, New Brunswick. The chain measured 6,001 ft 7 in (1,829.2 m)—more than three times the height of Toronto's CN Tower (1,815 ft; 553.3 m). For more on the world's largest and longest, see pp. 94–95.

FACT

Justine (right) was competing in the mogul freestyle event with her sisters Maxime and Chloe, with the latter winning silver—only the third time ever that sisters had finished first and second in an Olympic event. Including medals won by brothers in all Olympic individual events, it was the seventh time that siblings had scooped gold and silver.

Youngest Olympic freestyle skiing gold medalist

Justine Dufour-Lapointe (CAN, b. Mar 25, 1994) brought home a gold medal from the Winter Olympics in Sochi, Russia, at the age 19 years 321 days on Feb 8, 2014. Check out our record-breaking winter sports action—including more Sochi superlatives—on pp. 244–45.

Food & Drink, Sports & Fitness, and Video Games. Find out how it works at www.guinnessworldrecords.com/challengers.

The most exciting aspect of working at Guinness World Records is getting to meet the record holders face to face, and this year we've had some especially memorable encounters. We've had the honor of presenting certificates to some of sport's greatest legends, including Pelé (see p. 239) and Haile Gebrselassie (see p. 212), as well as welcoming adventurers to

First Olympic curling team to win every first-round game (female)

Canada is the only women's team to have won every first-round game in the round-robin format, with nine wins in Sochi from Feb 10 to 18, 2014. They faced strong competition from the likes of South Korea, who defeated the USA 11–2. It wasn't Canada's only clean sweep—both men's and women's teams won gold.

only about 10% of all the superlatives we have on file, and includes those classic records that have stood the test of time. So if you've achieved a record and you haven't been selected this year, better luck next time …

If you've made it your life's ambition to get your name in the *Guinness World Records* book, then apply now! Record-breaking is free and open to absolutely everyone—you'll find out how on p. 5. We need you

to keep on breaking those records. Sixty years ago, it wasn't possible to make a transatlantic phone call (p. 180), no human had set foot on the Moon (p. 16), and no one had ever thought of twerking! Imagine where we might be in 60 years' time …

Craig Glenday, Editor-in-Chief

Longest garlic bread

Étienne Thériault (CAN) and his team made a garlic bread measuring 54 ft 10 in (16.71 m) long in Bertrand, New Brunswick, on Jul 6, 2013. The bread used 22 oz (625 g) of garlic butter and was sold in pieces to raise money for a home for the elderly in Bertrand. There's more big food on pp. 100–1.

FACT

Rev. Kev (right) has made record-breaking pulls of aircraft, Santa sleds, fire trucks, and even an entire house mounted on a flatbed truck!

our offices (see pp. 142–57).

We're indebted, as always, to our countless record claimants and fans. Of course, we try to answer every e-mail and letter, although we can't find room for every single new record approved—our annual book features

Heaviest vehicle pulled in an arm-wrestling move

Kevin Fast (CAN) pulled a truck weighing 24,380 lb (11,060 kg) in Cobourg, Ontario, on Apr 26, 2013. The feat marked the third time that he had taken the record, having first set a mark of 16,997 lb (7,710 kg) in 2008 by "arm-wrestling" a fire truck.

Officially Amazing!

Celebrating the 60-year story of the **biggest-selling annual**

In the 1950s, Sir Hugh Beaver (left)—Managing Director of the Guinness Brewery—had the idea for a book of world records that might help settle arguments in pubs. Sixty years on, the idea of superlatives continues to fascinate and excite ... and inspires millions of people to strive for immortality by becoming record holders themselves.

"Turn the heat of argument into the light of knowledge." This was the remit of the first ever edition of *The Guinness Book of Records*, which itself had its origins in an argument. On Nov 10, 1951, during a shooting party at North Slob, by the Slaney River in County Wexford, Ireland, Sir Hugh Beaver (1890–1967)—MD of the Guinness Brewery—and his fellow fowl hunters failed to bag some golden plovers flying overhead. Could the plover be the fastest game bird in Europe? A debate ensued, but no answer could be found, not even in the well-stocked library of Sir Hugh's host later that evening.

It occurred to Sir Hugh that people across the UK and Ireland would be arguing over all kinds of topics, and that perhaps a book should be published to settle those

debates. If he could create such a book, he could even give it away to some of the 80,000 or so pubs in the UK as part of a promotion to sell more Guinness stout. To help him with his plan, he needed to locate a fact-finding agency, and, luckily, an underbrewer at the Guinness Brewery in Park Royal, London, had the answer: the McWhirter twins.

That underbrewer was Chris Chataway (1931–2014), an amateur athlete who acted as pacemaker for Roger Bannister, who on

1973 Broadcaster David Frost (second on left) acquires TV rights for GWR specials. The *Hall of Fame* special seen above appeared in 1986.

May 6, 1954 had broken the four-minute mile—a feat once thought to be impossible. The timekeeper for the race was Norris McWhirter (1925–2004), who, along with his identical twin Ross (1925–75), had recently set up a fact-finding agency in London.

1972 In the UK, the BBC produce a spin-off of TV show *Blue Peter* called *Record Breakers*, hosted by Roy Castle (right) and the McWhirter twins; it runs for nearly 30 years.

1998 *Guinness World Records Primetime* debuts on Fox TV on Jul 27, 1998, hosted by Mark Thompson, and runs for 53 episodes.

1955 Twins Ross (left) and Norris McWhirter publish the first edition of *The Guinness Book of Records* for the Guinness Brewery.

1954 Sir Hugh Beaver invites the McWhirter twins to start work on a book of superlatives

1956 The first US edition is published

1962 First French edition

1963 First German edition

1967 First Japanese, Danish, and Norwegian editions

1968 First Swedish, Finnish, and Italian editions

1971 First Dutch edition

1975 First GWR museum opens in the Empire State Building, New York, USA

1976 First Czech edition

1977 First Hebrew, Serbo-Croat, and Icelandic editions

1978 First Slovenian edition

1999 GWR launches its first UK TV show, named simply *Guinness World Records*, hosted by UK soccer star Ian Wright.

Sir Hugh commissioned the McWhirters to create his book of superlatives, and in 1954 the twins set up an office in a disused gym at 107 Fleet Street in London. Under the name Guinness Superlatives, they spent an intense few months researching and collating the first edition of *The Guinness Book of Records*, which was bound on Aug 27, 1955.

While it was initially intended as a promotional item, the book had a life beyond the bars, and when *The Guinness Book of Records* was offered up for the public to buy (minus the beer-proof coating!)

in October of that year, it became an instant best-seller, and it has remained at the top of the charts ever since. Within a year, it had launched in the USA—as *The Guinness Book of World Records*—and today is available in more than 100 countries in up to 20 languages.

In the years since its debut, the book has had a change of owner—it was sold by the Guinness Brewery in 1999—and a change of name

to its current title *Guinness World Records*, reflecting the fact that it's more than just a book; it also has TV shows, museums, Web sites, digital apps, e-books, and, most recently, live events.

RECORD ADJUDICATION

As the accepted global arbiter of record-breaking achievement, Guinness World Records now

processes around 50,000 claims a year, and has sent adjudicators as far afield as the bottom of the ocean and the top of the Burj Khalifa, the world's **tallest building**. We've expanded into larger premises in London, and opened new offices in New York (USA), Tokyo (JPN), Beijing (CHN), and Dubai (UAE), with more record representatives and

editorial consultants dotted all around the world.

As you'll see in this year's edition, we continue to evolve and adapt, reflecting the ever-shifting modern landscape and providing a snapshot of the universe in which we live. As long as humans continue to push the limits of what's possible, we'll be there with our stopwatches and counters, documenting and ratifying the achievements. And the next 60 years will undoubtedly be as fascinating and record breaking as the last.

Experience GWR live

Look out for the exciting new Guinness World Records Attractions, the first of which is scheduled to open in 2015. See records come to life using cutting-edge digital technology, and attempt your own records in front of official GWR adjudicators.

2006 Editor-in-Chief Craig Glenday welcomes the King of Pop, Michael Jackson, to the London offices on the eve of the 2006 World Music Awards, where Jackson's *Thriller* album is acknowledged as the **biggest-selling album of all time**.

2005 Her Majesty, Queen Elizabeth II, receives a copy of our 50th anniversary edition from GWR President Alistair Richards.

1996 GWR opens an office in New York, USA

2000 guinnessworldrecords.com launches

2003 The 100-millionth copy of the book is sold

2005 First annual Guinness World Records Day

2010 GWR app launches; Office opened in Tokyo, Japan

2012 Office opened in Beijing, China

2013 Office opened in Dubai, UAE

2015 GWR celebrates its 60th anniversary

2013 Hong Kong actor Jackie Chan accepts his two GWR certificates, for **most stunts by a living actor** (more than 100 movies) and **most credits in one movie** (15).

Space

This **gallery of galaxies** illustrates the beauty of our Universe ... *not* shown to scale!

1

3

2

4

5

1. Youngest galaxy
In Feb 2014, astronomers discovered galaxy Abell 2744-Y1, the light from which takes just over 13 billion years to reach Earth. Around 30 times smaller than the Milky Way, it is producing 10 times more stars.

2. Most common type of galaxy
Spiral galaxies, such as Messier 101—pictured here by the *Hubble* space telescope—account for 77% of all galaxies. Our Milky Way is also a spiral galaxy, characterized by spiral arms wound around a brighter core.

3. First discovered spiral galaxy
William Parsons, 3rd Earl of Rosse (IRL), identified M51 (the "Whirlpool Galaxy") as a spiral in 1845. He used the *Leviathan*, then the world's **largest telescope**, at Birr Castle, County Offaly, Ireland.

4. Closest galaxy to the Milky Way
The Canis Major dwarf galaxy lies an average of 42,000 light-years from the center of our galaxy. It was only found in 2003 because it was difficult to detect behind the plane of our own spiral galaxy as seen from Earth.

5. Most remote object visible to the naked eye
The Andromeda galaxy, known as Messier 31, is about 2.5 million light-years from Earth. Runner-up in this category is Messier 33, a spiral galaxy that can be glimpsed at a distance of 2.53 million light-years.

Contents

6. Densest galaxies
Ultra Compact Dwarf (UCD) galaxies, such as M60-UCD1 (pictured), contain around a hundred million stars squashed into a space measuring 200 light-years across.

7. Largest satellite galaxy
Of the 15 minor satellite galaxies orbiting the Milky Way, the largest and brightest is the Large Magellanic Cloud, some 160,000 light-years from the center of the Milky Way.

8. Fastest approaching galaxy
The Universe might be expanding, but M86, a lenticular galaxy around 52 million light-years away in the Virgo Cluster, is moving toward us at a rate of 260 mi/s (419 km/s).

9. Largest galaxy
IC 1101, in the Abell 2029 cluster, has a major diameter of 5.6 million light-years—80 times the diameter of the Milky Way—and a light output equivalent to 2 trillion times that of the Sun. It may be the result of many smaller galaxies merging.

10. Largest distant galaxy
"El Gordo" is the nickname of a galaxy cluster 7 billion light-years away. Discovered via a disturbance in the cosmic microwave background, El Gordo is actually two clusters colliding at a rate of several million mph.

Milestones in space

NASA's five Space Shuttles spent some 1,320 days in space

No human had crossed the edge of space when GWR started in 1955. It wasn't until 1961 that the milestone was reached, but the pioneers of space exploration went on to rack up achievements at a blistering pace—visiting the Moon, building space stations, and sending rovers to Mars and a probe beyond our Solar System.

It is testament to the power of human imagination that space flight quickly became an accepted part of everyday thought and discussion. Our concept of an expanding future for space exploration occupies much of our science fiction movies and television, and even cash-strapped nations compete to send probes to our sister planets.

The conquest of space was kickstarted as part of the increasingly bitter Cold War in the 1950s between the USA and the USSR. In 1955, both powers announced their intention to launch satellites, and the Soviets were the first to achieve the **first artificial satellite** with *Sputnik 1* in 1957. They were again the first to launch a man into space in 1961. Eager to catch up, US President Kennedy promised that the USA would be the first to get humans on the Moon. "We choose to go to the Moon in this decade," he said in 1962, "… because that challenge is one that we are willing to accept, one we are unwilling to postpone."

With that bold declaration, the space race became hotter than ever and the brightest and bravest ensured it changed humanity and the way we saw our planet and our place in the Solar System.

First untethered spacewalk: US astronaut Bruce McCandless II tests the Manned Maneuvering Unit (MMU) from the Space Shuttle *Challenger* on Feb 7, 1984.

1984

First flight between space stations: Mir EO-1 is the first expedition to the Soviet *Mir* space station. Its crew, Leonid Kizim and Vladimir Solovyov, launch from Earth on Mar 13, 1986, reach *Mir* two days later, and remain docked for six weeks. *Mir* deorbits some 15 years later on Mar 23, 2001. More than 100 people visit over its lifespan.

1986

First manned maiden space flight: John Young and Robert Crippen (both USA) launch the inaugural orbital mission of the Space Shuttle *Columbia* on Apr 12, 1981. It is the first time a new spacecraft system is piloted in space without a prior unmanned flight.

1981

1973

Farthest distance from Earth reached by humans: The crew of *Apollo 13* reach 248,654 mi above the Earth's surface on the "dark" (far) side of the Moon at 1:21 a.m. BST on Apr 15, 1970. They are 157.8 mi above the lunar surface.

Farthest distance traveled on another world: The unmanned Soviet *Lunokhod 2* rover travels 26 mi on the Moon between Jan 16 and Jun 23, 1973.

First men on the Moon: Neil Armstrong (USA), commander of the *Apollo 11* mission, takes his first small step at 2:56 a.m. GMT on Jul 21, 1969, followed onto the surface of the Moon by Edwin "Buzz" Aldrin Jr. (USA).

1969

1970

First manned space flight: Russian cosmonaut, Flight Major Yuri Gagarin, achieves an altitude of 203 mi in *Vostok 1* on Apr 12, 1961. Gagarin completes a single orbit of the Earth (still the **shortest orbital flight**) and ejects 108 min into the flight as planned.

1961

SPACE PIONEERS

1961

Yuri Gagarin:
First man in space
Gagarin's flight of Apr 12 (see above) hit a speed of 25,394.5 mi and made him a Soviet hero. Tragically, he was killed in a jet flight in 1968 at the age of just 34.

1963

Valentina Tereshkova:
First woman in space
Launched in *Vostok 6* from Kazakhstan on Jun 16, Tereshkova (USSR) flew for 2 days 22 hr 50 min. She went on to be politically prominent in the USSR.

1965

Alexey Leonov:
First spacewalk
Leonov (USSR) conducted the first ever extra-vehicular activity (EVA)—aka spacewalk—when he exited the *Voskhod 2* craft for 12 min on Mar 18, 1965.

1969

Neil Armstrong:
First men on the Moon
The commander of the *Apollo 11* mission was the first to walk on the surface of the Moon. He had learned to fly at 15 years old, before he got his driving license.

1969

"Buzz" Aldrin:
First men on the Moon
In 2013, Aldrin (USA) looked back: "Neil had an optimistic way of using the word 'beautiful.' But when I looked out, it wasn't beautiful. It was desolate."

1972

Eugene Cernan: Longest manned lunar mission
The US mission commander spent 74 hr 59 min 40 sec with Schmitt (see right) on the Moon on Dec 7–19. *Apollo 17* was the last manned Moon mission.

1995

First Shuttle docking:
On Jun 29, 1995, the Space Shuttle *Atlantis* connects with *Mir* as part of the Shuttle–*Mir* Program. This marks the 100th space flight launched by the USA as *Atlantis* brings Anatoly Solovyev and Nikolai Budarin to *Mir* and returns Vladimir Dezhurov, Gennady Strekalov (all USSR), and Norman Thagard (USA) to Earth.

1997

First Mars rover:
The 1997 *Sojourner* (USA) vehicle is landed by NASA's *Mars Pathfinder* spacecraft on Jul 4. A small mobile laboratory, *Sojourner* travels an approximate total of 328 ft and conducts such experiments as measuring the chemical composition of rocks.

FACT
Chris says there have been musical instruments in space since a US Project Mercury astronaut brought a harmonica—and the Russians had a guitar on a *Salyut* space station.

Chris Hadfield

On May 12, 2013, Commander Chris Hadfield (CAN) posted the **first music video filmed in space**, David Bowie's "Space Oddity," recorded on board the *ISS*. In an interview with GWR, Chris revealed that he had fronted bands for years but never covered Bowie, much less "Space Oddity." "The astronaut dies in it!" laughed Chris. "Why would I play that song, of all things?" Chris agreed—once his son Evan altered the words—and recorded vocals on his iPad. "It sounded way better than I thought it would, as if the track had soaked up a sense of place." Chord changes in zero gravity were a challenge because his guitar would float away when strummed, when it would sit in his hands on Earth. Other tracks were added and the video was mixed on Earth. For a father-son project, Chris was delighted at the song's success. "It bridged science fiction and science fact."

Largest space station:
The *International Space Station* (*ISS*) is a modular structure that launches in 1998. On Feb 24, 2011, the STS-133 Shuttle mission launches to dock the Leonardo Permanent Multipurpose Module with the *ISS*, bringing it to its current mass of 924,739 lb.

1998

First privately funded manned space flight: On Jun 21, 2004, *SpaceShipOne* reaches 328,490 ft, piloted by Mike Melvill (ZAF), built by Scaled Composites, and funded by Paul Allen (both USA).

2004

Most remote planetary landing:
Huygens lands on Saturn's largest moon, Titan, in Jan 2005. Data and images are sent back by the European Space Agency (ESA) probe from the moon that is at an average distance of 888 million mi from the Sun.

2005

Land speed record on Mars:
Twin NASA Mars exploration rovers *Opportunity* (shown left) and *Spirit*, landing in Jan 2004, are each capable of speeds up to 2 in per sec.

2014

First human-made object to travel in interstellar space:
On Sep 12, 2013, NASA announces that *Voyager 1* has crossed the heliopause, the boundary between the Solar System and interstellar space. As of Apr 9, 2014, it is 11.84 billion mi from the Sun on a mission begun in 1977 (see p. 25).

Closest flyby of Mercury:
On Jan 14, 2008, NASA's *MESSENGER* spacecraft performs a gravity-assist flyby to just 123.7 mi above the surface at closest approach.

2008

1972

Harrison Schmitt: Longest Moon walk
Along with Cernan (see left), the US geologist spent 7 hr 37 min on the Moon on Dec 12, the pair covering 12.6 mi and taking extensive samples.

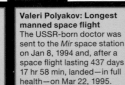
1994–95

Valeri Polyakov: Longest manned space flight
The USSR-born doctor was sent to the *Mir* space station on Jan 8, 1994 and, after a space flight lasting 437 days 17 hr 58 min, landed—in full health—on Mar 22, 1995.

1998

John Glenn: Oldest astronaut
The war hero, senator, and first American to orbit Earth (USA, b. Jul 18, 1921) made a 1998 space comeback on Oct 29 on the Space Shuttle, at 77 years 103 days old.

2004

Mike Melvill: First commercial astronaut
After piloting *SpaceShipOne* in 2004 (see above), the pioneer was awarded the first commercial astronaut wings by the US Federal Aviation Administration.

2005

Sergei Krikalev: Most time spent in space
The USSR-born cosmonaut notched up 803 days 9 hr in space, including stints on *Mir*, Space Shuttles, and the *ISS*. He retired from active space flight in 2007.

2007

Sunita Williams: Most spacewalk time (female)
The US astronaut has spent a total of 50 hr 40 min on spacewalks. In Sep 2012, she carried out external repairs to the power supply unit of the *ISS*.

Universe

Twin sunsets: the planet **Kepler-47b** is lit by two stars

GRB 130427A

FACT

Gamma-ray bursts are the Universe's most powerful events and thought to be the birth cries of black holes, as supermassive stars exhaust their fuel and collapse to a singularity.

of galaxies and other matter within the constellation Canes Venatici. Also known as the "Giant Void in NGH (Northern Galactic Hemisphere)," the "Canes Venatici Supervoid," or its more scientific designation AR-Lp 36, is the largest confirmed void to date in the visible Universe. With an estimated diameter of 300–400 Mpc (1–1.3 billion light-years), its geometric center is approximately 1.5 billion light-years away.

Highest-energy gamma rays from a gamma-ray burst

In May 2013, NASA announced that its *Fermi* gamma-ray space telescope had detected a burst measuring at least 94 billion electron volts (35 billion times the energy of normal, visible light). This explosion, known as GRB 130427A, came from a galaxy 3.6 billion light-years away.

Most massive black hole

On Dec 5, 2011, astronomers using the *Gemini North*, *Keck II*, and *Hubble* observatories reported a supermassive black hole in the center of elliptical galaxy NGC 4889, some 336 million light-years away. The black hole's mass is estimated at 20 billion times that of the Sun.

Densest known galaxy
M60-UCD1, announced in Sep 2013, is a type of galaxy called an Ultra-Compact Dwarf (UCD). This class was discovered in 1999 by astrophysicists led by Dr. Michael Drinkwater (UK). These galaxies are potentially leftover building blocks that once formed much larger galaxies. Half of the mass of M60-UCD1 is found within a radius of only 80 light-years, making the density of stars 15,000 times greater than our area of the Milky Way.

Most distant dwarf galaxy
In 2012, astronomers led by Dr. Simona Vegetti of the Massachusetts Institute of Technology announced the discovery of a dwarf galaxy orbiting a large elliptical galaxy some 10 billion light-years away. Undetectable by telescope, its gravity causes light distortion that gives it away. It's possible the galaxy is composed exclusively of dark matter, or it may contain stars that are too dim to be visible at this distance.

Largest cloud of primordial hydrogen
First discovered in 2000, LAB-1 is an astronomical object known as a Lyman-alpha blob. Measuring ca. 300,000 light-years across and 11.5 billion light-years from Earth, LAB-1 is a cloud of hydrogen gas that has yet to coalesce into galaxies. The blob is glowing—possibly due to the light from galaxies within that have already formed. Owing to its distance, we see LAB-1 as it was when the Universe was only around 15% of its current age.

Largest void
The Giant Void is a very large region of space with an abnormally low density

First sighting of an extragalactic planet

In 2009, astronomers announced that they had seen a planet in the Andromeda galaxy, 2.2 million light-years away. It became visible when it passed in front of a star, an event known as "microlensing," when the light of a star is magnified by an object passing in front. The Andromeda event was first seen in 2004, when it was believed to be owing to a binary star.

See Earth from space on pp. 34–35

Our very first record

We opened our first edition in 1955 with **"remotest known bodies."** The record went to an "extra-galactic nebulae at a distance of some 1,000 million light-years." In Mar 2014, the **most distant confirmed galaxy** is z8-GND-5296: its light takes some 13.3 billion years to reach us on Earth.

COSMOLOGICAL COMPOSITION

Astronomers once thought that the Universe was composed largely of "stuff"—i.e., stars and planets made of atoms and heavy elements. However, observations of how galaxies move suggest that most of the total mass of the Universe is invisible. It is currently understood that the majority of the Universe is "dark" energy and matter; the stars and planets, plus the interstellar hydrogen and other gases and dust, account for just ca. 5%.

KEY:
- Dark energy
- Dark matter
- Free hydrogen and helium, other gases, dust, stars, planets

<4.9%
26.8%
68.3%

We are all stardust

You're older than you might think—most of the elements in your body include atoms that arose during the Big Bang, 13.82 billion years ago.

The astronomer and influential science communicator Carl Sagan (USA, 1934–96), host of the original *Cosmos* TV show in 1980, famously wrote: "The nitrogen in our DNA, the calcium in our teeth, the iron in our blood, the carbon in our apple pies were made in the interiors of collapsing stars. We are made of star-stuff."

Most distant black hole

A supermassive black hole resides in the center of quasar ULAS J112001.48+064124.3. In terms of redshift (a light measurement—higher than 1.4 means the source is receding at more than the speed of light), it measures 7.085. This black hole was announced in Jun 2011 and emits radiation from superheated matter that surrounded it less than 770 million years after the Big Bang.

Oldest light

The Cosmic Microwave Background (CMB) is radiation that formed 380,000 years after the Big Bang. When the Universe was born, a tremendous amount of light was generated that remains all pervasive. The CMB can be seen as photons coming from all directions. The 2013 *Planck* map of CMB showed, among other things, that the Universe is older than thought, at 13.82 billion years.

Smallest extrasolar planet

Kepler-37b is a planet only slightly larger than the Moon. It orbits the star Kepler-37, around 210 light-years from Earth in the constellation of Lyra. Its discovery by NASA's *Kepler* space observatory—the mission launched to carry out research into habitable planets—was announced on Feb 20, 2013. Kepler-37b is only 1,199 mi (1,930 km) across, making it smaller than the planet Mercury.

Most magnetic object

If a magnetar flew within 100,000 mi (161,000 km) of Earth, it could strip the data off every credit card. Fortunately, there have been fewer than a dozen identified examples of these neutron stars (which come from the dead core of collapsed stars densely packed to the size of a city). Magnetars, thought to originate from the supernovae of massive stars, have magnetic fields that are up to a trillion times the size of, for example, a hospital MRI machine.

than 2 billion light-years away in a galaxy known as 3C303, the electrical current is measured at 1E18 amps (1 followed by 18 zeros). The scientists used the effect of the current on radio waves coming from the galaxy to measure this tremendous amount of electrical energy, which is most likely generated by magnetic fields from a black hole at the center of the galaxy. The resulting jet of matter extends into space to around 150,000 light-years—possibly the largest bolt of lightning ever seen.

Longest galactic jet

An energetic jet of matter emitted from a supermassive black hole in the center of galaxy CGCG 049-033 measures 1.5 million light-years long. Life on any planets in the path of the jet stream would be extinguished.

Highest electrical current

Scientists at the University of Toronto, Canada, have made the "shocking" discovery of the highest known electrical current in the Universe. Generated by a cosmic jet more

Most distant supernova

A Type IIn supernova some 11 billion light-years away was located using data from the Canada-France-Hawaii Telescope. In 2009, astronomers announced they had seen a galaxy that brightened momentarily with a spectrum characterized by a narrow color band of emitted light from hydrogen as it burns.

Largest structure

The Hercules-Corona Borealis Great Wall consists of a staggeringly huge cluster of galaxies and other normal matter measuring 10 billion light-years across and about 10 billion light-years from Earth. Superclusters are bound by gravity; this one was announced in Nov 2013 by astronomers who mapped it by charting gamma-ray bursts (pictured) in the region.

Deepest note

The Universe's lowest note is caused by acoustic waves generated by a supermassive black hole. It is in the center of the Perseus cluster of galaxies (above), 250 million light-years away. The sound—a B-flat note, 57 octaves below middle C—propagates through thin gas surrounding the black hole.

Nothing to see here: dark matter

Astronomers in the 1970s, particularly Vera Rubin (right), measured the velocities of stars in other galaxies and noticed that the stars at the galaxies' edges moved faster than predicted. To reconcile the observations with the law of gravity, scientists proposed that there is matter we can't see and called it "dark matter." This, the most common form of matter, neither emits nor absorbs light and radiation as stars and planets do. Measuring the effect of dark matter in gravitational terms, scientists have proposed that together with dark energy it makes up 95% of the Universe.

FACT

Light travels at 186,400 mi/s and a light-year measures how far light travels in a year.

The hole truth

Nearest distance between two black holes: Two orbiting black holes in quasar SDSS J153636.22+044127.0, separated by just one-third of a light-year

Closest black hole to Earth: V4641 Sgr, discovered 1,600 light-years away

Closest supermassive black hole to Earth: Sagittarius A*, center of the Milky Way, 27,000 light-years away

Solar System

The word "planet" derives from the ancient Greek for **"wandering star"**

Most tails for an asteroid

On Sep 10, 2013, the *Hubble* telescope found a bizarre asteroid with six distinct tails like a comet. The 1,570-ft-wide (480-m) asteroid P/2013 P5 probably has the tails due to the pressure of solar radiation, which has increased the asteroid's spin so much that mass is lost from its own rotation.

MERCURY

Largest impact basin on Mercury

The Caloris Basin has a diameter of ca. 950 mi (1,550 km) and is surrounded by 1.2-mi-high (2-km) mountains. It was formed 3.8–3.9 billion years ago when a 60-mi-wide (100-km) object struck.

Fastest planet

Mercury takes 87.96 days to orbit the Sun at an average distance of 35.9 million mi (57.9 million km), giving an average speed of 107,030 mph (172,248 km/h)—almost twice as fast as Earth.

VENUS

Brightest planet

With a maximum magnitude of -4.4, Venus is the brightest planet visible from Earth with the naked eye.

First thunder heard on another planet

On Dec 25, 1978, the USSR's *Venera 11* lander touched down on Venus. Among its instruments was an acoustic detector, which heard an 82-dB sound of unknown origin. A Venusian thunderclap is the most probable explanation.

EARTH

Densest planet

Earth is the densest planet, with an average density of 5.517 times that of water.

Deepest crater

Earth's Moon is home to the largest and deepest known

First caves on another planet

In Mar 2007, images from NASA's *Mars Odyssey* showed the discovery of what appeared to be seven circular pits on Mars' surface with entrances to underground caverns. In only one of the seven pits does a floor appear to be visible, at least 426 ft (130 m) below the surface.

Fastest trip to the *ISS*

The fastest time to reach the *International Space Station* (*ISS*) from launch to dock is 5 hr 39 min, achieved on May 29, 2013 UTC by the crew of Expedition 36 onboard the *Soyuz TMA-09M* (inset). They launched from Baikonur in Kazakhstan at 8:31 p.m. UTC and docked with the *ISS*'s "Rassvet" module at 2:10 a.m. UTC on May 30.

crater in the Solar System. The South Pole-Aitken impact basin on the far side of the Moon is 1,400 mi (2,250 km) in diameter and has an average depth of 39,000 ft (12,000 m).

MARS

Highest clouds

In Aug 2006, European scientists reported their discovery of clouds some 55–62 mi (90–100 km) above the surface of Mars. Detected by an instrument onboard the European Space Agency's *Mars Express* orbiter, the clouds are composed of carbon dioxide ice crystals. If the density of this upper atmosphere is greater than thought, it will mean more aerobraking for landing ships.

Crater walls

Central peak

-22.3   Elevation [km]   19.1

Tallest central peak for an impact crater

Rheasilvia is a 313-mi-wide (505-km) impact crater on asteroid 4Vesta between Mars and Jupiter. At its center is a peak rising a record 12 mi (20 km) above the crater floor (the central red feature seen on the satellite image above).

MAGNIFICENT MOUNTAINS: OLYMPUS, KEA, AND EVEREST

Olympus Mons on Mars is the **highest mountain in the Solar System**, with an elevation (peak height) of 15.5 mi—nearly three times that of Everest. However, Everest isn't Earth's highest mountain when Mauna Kea on Hawaii is measured from base to peak.

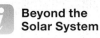

Olympus Mons elevation: 82,000 ft

Mount Everest elevation: 29,029 ft

Mauna Kea elevation: 13,796 ft (base to peak: 33,481 ft)

Sea level

For more on measuring mountains, see p. 36

⚡ Size matters

In our 1955 edition, the most remote planet was assumed to be Pluto, with a mean distance from the Sun of 3.6×10^9 mi. Pluto was discovered on Feb 18, 1930 by Clyde Tombaugh, an astronomer working at the Lowell Observatory in the USA. Today, Pluto no longer holds the record, because over the years astronomers raised doubts over its planetary status, citing its diminutive size and erratic orbit. In 2006, the International Astronomical Union offered a new definition of a planet; Pluto didn't qualify, and its status was revised to "dwarf planet."

FACT

You could fit one million Earths inside the Sun.

ℹ Beyond the Solar System

Voyager I, the **most remote manmade object**, is, as of 3:26 p.m. GMT on Feb 6, 2014, a distance of 11,827,492,990 mi from Earth. Having left the Solar System in Aug 2012, it is now traveling through interstellar space.

Largest area of surface ice
Almost all of the ice on Mars' surface is in the poles. The southern cap is the largest at around 260 mi (420 km) across, and contains enough water to cover the entire planet in a layer 36 ft (11 m) deep.

JUPITER

Most moons to a planet
As of 2013, 67 natural satellites of Jupiter have been discovered. Most are small, irregularly shaped bodies of ice and rock, and many are almost certainly captured asteroids.

One of the Jovian moons, Ganymede, has the **greatest mass of a moon in the Solar System**. It is twice as heavy as Earth's Moon and has a width of 3,273 mi (5,267 km).

SATURN

Least dense planet
Saturn is mainly composed of hydrogen and helium, the two lightest elements in the Universe. It would float on water if there was a bathtub large enough to hold it.

FACT
Saturn has the largest ring system: billions of tiny, orbiting particles of dust and ice, equivalent in mass to 30 million Mount Everests.

Tallest clouds
A massive vortex of clouds, about five times higher than Earth's hurricanes, was discovered to be at Saturn's south pole in 2006.

NEPTUNE

Farthest planet in the Solar System
Since Pluto's demotion from "planet" status in 2006 (see below left), Neptune is the farthest planet from the Sun. At a distance of 2.8 billion mi (4.5 billion km) away, it orbits at 3.38 mi/s (5.45 km/s) and takes 164.79 years to complete each orbit.

Fastest winds
There are no faster winds in our Solar System than those on Neptune. NASA's *Voyager 2* probe measured winds of around 1,500 mph (2,400 km/h) in 1989.

Largest hexagon
The largest hexagon in our Solar System is on Saturn's North Pole, where a massive pattern of hexagonal clouds, with sides measuring around 8,500 mi (13,800 km) in length, is located. It was first seen by the *Voyager* in the early 1980s and has since been studied in more detail, proving that it has lasted for at least 30 years.

SEE IN 3D WITH THE FREE APP

Augmented Reality alert! 3D ON THIS PAGE

Saturn

Uranus

Neptune

Jupiter

Largest planet
Our Solar System's mightiest body is Jupiter, with an equatorial diameter of 89,405 mi (143,884 km) and a polar diameter of 83,082 mi (133,708 km). Its mass and volume are around 317 and 1,323 times that of Earth respectively. Jupiter also has the **shortest day of any planet in the Solar System**, at just 9 hr 55 min 29.69 sec.

Earth

Mars

Venus

Mercury

Scaled up: the Sweden Solar System

When the Stockholm (now Ericsson) Globe Arena opened in Sweden in Feb 1989 as the world's **largest hemispherical building**, it gave two Swedish academics an idea. If the 360-ft-wide building was considered a scaled-down Sun, how far away would the planets lie, and what size would they be? Nils Brenning and Gösta Gahm went on to champion the **largest representation of the Solar System**—a 1:20-million-scale "model" that stretches 590 mi across the country, with planets, minor planets, and comets represented by scaled globes or artworks at their relative distances apart.

Mercury (9.8 in wide), 1.8 mi away

Earth (2 ft 1.5 in wide), 4.7 mi away

Sun (360 ft wide)

Glossary

Dwarf planet: a body with enough mass to form a spherical shape, but not enough gravitational attraction to clear its orbit of debris as it orbits the Sun.

Light-year: the distance that light travels in one year in a vacuum: some 5.87 trillion mi (5.87×10^{12} mi).

Mass: a measure of the quantity of matter in a body as well as its inertia.

Weight: the force of an object due to gravity.

Comets

Halley's Comet should make its next appearance in **2061**

00:01:12　11:59:36　11:57:00　11:56:00　11:51:36　11:49:48

Trajectory

Pictured here are snapshots from the last 10 min in the life of comet C/2011 N3 as it breaks apart and is vaporized by the Sun

First comet observed being destroyed by the Sun

On Jul 6, 2011, NASA's Solar Dynamics Observatory captured images of comet C/2011 N3's demise. The comet had a nucleus 29–147 ft (9–45 m) wide and got within 62,100 mi (100,000 km) of the Sun's surface, moving at about 1.3 million mph (2.1 million km/h), before breaking up and being vaporized.

Largest source of comets
Beyond Neptune's orbit lie the Kuiper Belt, the Scattered Disk, and the Oort Cloud, collectively known as Trans-Neptunian Objects. The Oort Cloud contains trillions of cometary nuclei. It surrounds the Sun at a distance of ca. 50,000 Astronomical Units (1 AU = distance from Earth to the Sun), around 1,000 times the distance from the Sun to Pluto. Scientists believe the cloud to be the source of most of the comets that visit the inner Solar System.

Comet up close

Nucleus: Dust, rocky debris, and frozen gas
Coma: Cloud of evaporated gases and dust around nucleus
Hydrogen envelope: Gets larger as comet nears the Sun
Dust tail: Follows comet's orbit; may be 93 million mi long
Ion tail: Made up of ionized gases flowing along the magnetic field lines of the plasma of the solar wind

Dust tail

Ion tail

Nucleus

Coma

Hydrogen envelope

Longest comet tail
The tail of comet Hyakutake measured 350 million mi (570 million km) long—more than 3 AU. The tail was discovered by Geraint Jones of Imperial College, London, UK, on Sep 13, 1999, using data gathered by the ESA/NASA spacecraft *Ulysses* on a chance encounter with the comet on May 1, 1996.

Closest approach to Earth by a comet
On Jul 1, 1770, traveling at 86,100 mph (138,600 km/h), Lexell's Comet came within 1,360,000 mi (2,200,000 km)—or just 0.015 AU—of Earth.

Most recent Great Comet

Great Comets are those that become extremely bright in the night sky. The most recent Great Comet was Comet McNaught, first discovered by Robert McNaught (AUS) in 2006. At its peak brightness, on Jan 12, 2007, its tail measured a maximum of 35 degrees long in the sky.

First cometary soft lander

Launched on Mar 2, 2004, the European Space Agency's (ESA) Rosetta mission will rendezvous with comet 67P/Churyumov-Gerasimenko in 2014. The spacecraft will study and map the comet then release the *Philae* lander, which will anchor itself to the surface of the 2.4-mi-wide (4-km) comet with harpoons and will survive for at least a week.

Smallest comet visited by a spacecraft
NASA's *Deep Impact* spacecraft, launched on Jan 12, 2005, was retasked as the EPOXI mission on Jul 3, 2007 with the goal of studying extrasolar planets and performing a flyby of comet 103P/Hartley. The flyby occurred

---

COSMIC PATH: A COMET'S JOURNEY THROUGH SPACE

A comet's coma and tails form during its journey around the Sun. One tail is composed of dust; the other is an ion (gas) tail. Solar wind and radiation angle the tails away from the comet

Dust tail is pushed out by sunlight

Ion tail is swept back by solar wind

Earth's orbit

solar wind

solar radiation

Coma forms when comet is about five times farther from the Sun than Earth is

Nucleus warms. Ice starts turning to gas

Tail points away from Sun

Coma and tail disappear as comet gets farther from Sun's warmth

⚡ Larger than we thought …

In 1955, *The Guinness Book of Records* said that it was estimated that no comet head contains "mass in excess of 20 miles in diameter" and that the longest tail "may trail out to 200 million miles." The **largest comet** now known is Chiron, which has a diameter of 113 mi and a tail that has measured up to 791 million mi long.

AZ Glossary

Asteroid: Inactive body of rock and metal orbiting the Sun.

Comet: Cluster of ice, dust, rock, and frozen gas left over from the birth of the Solar System. When it passes near the Sun, a coma and tail can often be seen (pictured above).

Meteor: Rock that enters the Earth's atmosphere and burns up into a "shooting star". See p. 32.

Largest recorded impact in the Solar System

From Jul 16 to 22, 1994, more than 20 fragments of comet Shoemaker-Levy 9 collided with Jupiter. The greatest impact was of the "G" fragment, which exploded with the energy of roughly 600 times the nuclear arsenal of the world, equivalent to 6 million megatons of TNT.

on Nov 4, 2010, as *Deep Impact* passed within 430 mi (700 km) of the nucleus. The comet is around 1.4 mi (2.25 km) long and has a mass of around 590 billion lb (300 million tonnes).

Most distant observations of a comet
On Sep 3, 2003, the European Southern Observatory in Paranal, Chile, released an image of Halley's Comet at 2,600 million mi (4,200 million km) from the

First comet sample returned

Encountering the comet Wild 2 (below) in early 2004, the *Stardust* spacecraft swept up tiny samples of cometary dust in an aerogel collector (above) and returned the material to Earth on Jan 15, 2006. Its ongoing analysis is providing insights into the chemical makeup of this icy, primordial body.

Sun. It shows Halley as a fuzzy dot with a brightness of magnitude of 28.2, nearly a billion times fainter than the faintest objects visible with the naked eye.

Largest observed coma
The coma of the Great Comet of 1811—discovered on Mar 25, 1811 by French astronomer Honoré Flaugergues— had a diameter of about 1.2 million mi (2 million km).

First comet discovered to be periodic

Halley's Comet, aka 1P/Halley, orbits the Sun every 75.32 years. Sightings of this comet go back to at least 240 BC, but it was English astronomer Edmond Halley who, in 1705, first realized that observations of this comet were of the same object and predicted its return for the year 1758. The main picture (below left) shows a Babylonian clay tablet from ca. 164 BC that mentions the comet. The inset, from the Bayeux Tapestry (made ca. 1100), depicts the comet along with Latin text stating: "These [people] are looking in wonder at the star."

First anticomet medication

Halley's Comet visited the inner Solar System in 1910. Earth passed through its tail, which included the toxic gas cyanogen. Needless panic buying of gas masks, "anticomet umbrellas," and "anti-comet pills" followed.

First impact on a comet

On Jul 4, 2005, a 770-lb (350-kg) copper "bullet" from NASA's *Deep Impact* craft hit comet Tempel 1 at 6.4 mi/s (10.3 km/s). The impact—equivalent to that of 10,360 lb (4.7 metric tons) of TNT—created a crater 330 ft (100 m) wide and 100 ft (30 m) deep.

Tail end: what happens to comets?

The "death" of a comet can come about in a variety of different ways. Not all comets are tied to an orbit around the Sun, and some of them simply fly out of the Solar System. Each time a comet passes the Sun, it loses samples of dust and ice; if all of the ice is lost, the comet can become an inactive, asteroid-like structure. Alternatively, complete loss of ice can result in the comet breaking up into dust clouds. Finally, comets can meet a violent end when their orbit results in them crashing into a moon or planet. Our own Moon (right) is pockmarked with impact craters caused by comets and asteroids crashing into its surface.

Comet watch

Closest comet flyby by a spacecraft: *Giotto* flew within 124 mi of Grigg-Skjellerup on Jul 10, 1992.

Most comet tails met by a spacecraft: *Ulysses* flew through the tails of Hyakutake (1996), McNaught-Hartley (2004), and McNaught (2007).

Most comets discovered by a spacecraft: *SOHO* (*Solar and Heliospheric Observatory*) had discovered 2,574 comets by Dec 2013.

SETI

SETI stands for the **Search for Extraterrestrial Intelligence**

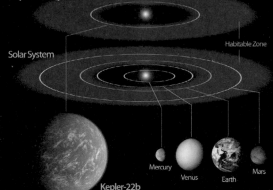

Kepler-22 System

Solar System

Habitable Zone

Mercury
Venus
Earth
Mars

Kepler-22b

First Earthlike planet

On Dec 5, 2011, Kepler-22b was announced as the first of more than 700 planets thought to reside within the habitable zone of its star, some 600 light-years away. At 2.4 times the size of Earth, the planet orbits its Sunlike star in around 290 days. If the planet has an Earthlike greenhouse effect, then its surface temperature could be 72°F (22°C).

First known pulsar

On Nov 28, 1967, British astronomers Jocelyn Bell Burnell and Antony Hewish spotted a radio signal from another star. All stars emit radio signals, but this turned on and off with perfect regularity: one pulse lasting 0.04 sec every 1.3373 sec. The pair playfully named the phenomenon "LGM-1" ("Little Green Men 1"). In fact, they had found what would be called a pulsar—a portmanteau of "pulsating star." Pulsars are the rapidly rotating remnants left by a supernova—and their behavior is entirely natural, if very precise. The first was later named CP 1919.

Largest planet-hunter space telescope

NASA's Kepler space telescope was launched on Mar 7, 2009 on a Delta II rocket from Cape Canaveral, USA. The spacecraft measures 8 ft 10 in x 15 ft 5 in (2.7 x 4.7 m) and follows an Earth-trailing heliocentric orbit. It can capture images of planets outside the Solar System, called exoplanets or extrasolar planets, using a mirror 4 ft 7 in (1.4 m) in diameter and a 95-megapixel camera. As of Feb 2014, it has identified 961 exoplanets—over half of the total discoveries of the past 20 years—and 2,903 unconfirmed candidates.

Most Earthlike exoplanet

The Earth Similarity Index (ESI) is a system devised to categorize and rate the increasing number of exoplanetary candidates. It rates how similar each is to Earth, based on size, density, escape velocity, and surface temperature. The ranking ranges from zero to 1, with Earth's value at 1. The exoplanet ranking highest on the ESI is KOI-3284.01, detected by the Kepler telescope in 2012 and given an ESI rating of 0.9. The planet may or may not be rocky, but it does have the potential for liquid water.

First physical message sent into deep space

Pioneer 10 is a NASA probe launched on Mar 3, 1972. A gold-strengthened aluminum plaque was attached to the outside showing a man and woman to scale with the probe, along with a map of the Solar System and the location of the Sun relative to pulsars in our galaxy. The probe's mission was to make the **first Jupiter flyby**, achieved on Dec 3, 1973.

Oldest unexplained extrasolar signal

On Aug 15, 1977, astronomer Jerry Ehman (USA) detected a radio signal using the *Big Ear* radio telescope at the Ohio State University, USA. The signal was monitored for 72 sec and closely matched the expected profile of an extraterrestrial signal. Ehman circled the readout and wrote "Wow!" It has never been detected again.

First digital time capsule chosen by public vote

A radio telescope at Yevpatoria in Ukraine sent a radio message on Oct 9, 2008 to the planet Gliese 581c, orbiting a star some 20.3 light-years from Earth. Images of landmarks and celebrities (such as singer Cheryl Cole, pictured) were sent, as well as 501 text messages from Bebo users. The message is due to reach Gliese 581c in 2029.

VOYAGER GOLDEN RECORD

Explanation of the *Voyager* Golden Record cover by NASA

Plan of record: Binary code defining speed around the edge

Elevation of record: Showing position of record cartridge

Sun location: Defined by 14 pulsars of known direction from the Sun

Wave form of video signals on recording: Binary code gives time of scan

Video image frame information: Decoded properly, first image is a circle

Two lowest states of hydrogen with spin moments of proton and electron: Clock reference for diagrams and decoded pictures

Lisa Vanderperre-Hirsch

Gray aliens are alleged extraterrestrial beings of wildly varying description, though they are often shown with oversize heads and black eyes. Lisa Vanderperre-Hirsch (USA) has the **largest collection of gray alien memorabilia**, with 547 individual items as of Nov 20, 2011 in Florida, USA. Her collection includes posters, calendars, and even alien-themed toilet paper.

Listening time

The amount of radio telescope capacity used for SETI is much less than is popularly assumed. Project Phoenix was given the **largest allocation for a single SETI project** at Arecibo to analyze patterns in radio signals. It used about 5% of the total observatory time (2,400 hr) from Sep 1998 to Mar 2004. Worldwide, just 30 or so scientists and engineers work full-time in SETI.

Most powerful radio signal aimed into space

On Nov 16, 1974, scientists at the Arecibo radio telescope in Puerto Rico sent a message containing basic data on humanity (right). The binary radio signal was broadcast to the M13 globular cluster in the constellation of Hercules and lasted 169 sec. It will arrive in 25,000 years at a strength 10 million times that of radio signals from our Sun. Any reply will take another 25,000 years to return to Earth.

Most remote manmade object
Voyager 1, launched on Sep 5, 1977, is a space probe whose primary mission was to make flybys of Jupiter and Saturn. As of Apr 9, 2014, it is 11.84 billion mi (19.06 billion km) from the Sun. *Voyager 1* and *Voyager 2* each contain a tougher version of a vinyl record: a gold-plated copper disk with stylus and instructions to alien life on how to play it (see *Voyager Golden Record*). The disk carries 116 images encoded in audio form and natural sounds of Earth, greetings in 59 languages, and music.

First report of a "flying saucer"
UFOs have been recorded for hundreds of years

in various forms, but it was the sighting by pilot Kenneth Arnold on Jun 24, 1947 that saw newspapers coin the term "flying saucer." Arnold didn't use the exact phrase to describe the nine objects he saw in the sky near Mount Rainier in Washington, USA, though he did say they were like saucers, disks, or pie plates.

First UFO landing pad
St. Paul in Alberta, Canada, is a prairie town with an official UFO landing pad, opened on Jun 3, 1967 by Canada's Minister of National Defence. The saucer-shape concrete platform sits above a pile

Longest-running SETI project

SETI@home, developed by the University of California, USA, is a crowdsourcing project that harnesses the power of PCs to process vast amounts of data. Signals from the Arecibo radio telescope were first made available for download on May 17, 1999 in a screen saver. The most intriguing discovery to date was a signal called SHGb02+14a, found in Mar 2003, that does not correspond to any known galactic phenomena.

of welcoming stones from each province of Canada. A sign declares the pad to be "a symbol of our faith that mankind will maintain the outer universe free from national wars and strife." Inside the pad is a time capsule to be opened on its centenary in 2067.

Largest civilian UFO investigative group
The Mutual UFO Network (MUFON) is an American-base organization that investigates UFO sightings. There are branches all over the world and more than 3,000 members. MUFON was started in May 1969.

Largest UFO convention
The 23rd International UFO Congress was held in Scottsdale in Arizona, USA, on Feb 12–16, 2014. An average of 1,500 people attended events throughout the week on topics such as official cover-ups, exopolitics, black projects, crop circles, and visitations.

First equation estimating intelligent life in our galaxy

In 1961, US astronomer Frank Drake devised an equation to give estimates of the number of planets inhabited by intelligent life:

$$N = R_* F_p N_e F_l F_i F_c L$$

While some of these variables (see glossary below) are extremely speculative, Drake himself estimated the number of advanced civilizations in our galaxy to be as high as 10,000.

$10,000,000.00 UFO ABDUCTION INSURANCE

First insurance against alien abduction

The UFO Abduction Insurance Co. (USA) offers an insurance policy costing $19.95 that pays out $10 m to abductees. Proof of abduction is all that the insurance company requires—an extraterrestrial signature will suffice.

Az The Drake equation

N Number of civilizations for possible radio communication

R. Average star formation rate in our galaxy

F_p Fraction of those stars with planets

N_e Average of planets that might support life

F_l Fraction of those planets that develop life

F_i Fraction of those planets that develop civilizations

F_c Fraction of civilizations that develop detectable technology

L Length of broadcast time of such civilizations

○ ○ ○

Life on Mars: examining the evidence

Astronomer Giovanni Schiaparelli (ITA) was the **first person to gather scientific evidence concerning life on Mars**. In 1877, he described telescopic observations of the planet that included *canali*, or channels, a network of lines across the surface. *Canali* was mistranslated as "canals" and later observers mapped them in detail, believing them to be structures built by a civilization instead of natural channels. As telescopes became more powerful, and space probes sent information from the surface, the "canals" were shown to be geological features.

Observatories

An **11,000-year-old site** in Turkey is thought to have been an early form of observatory

Largest array of radio telescopes

The VLA (Very Large Array) of the US National Science Foundation has 27 mobile antennae on rails in a Y-shape arrangement. Each arm of the Y is 13 mi (21 km) long, and each antenna has a dish that measures 82 ft (25 m) in diameter. The VLA, completed in 1980, is located 50 mi (80 km) west of Socorro in New Mexico, USA.

LARGEST ...

Primary mirror (nonsegmented)

The largest observatory mirrors are those in the dual-tube Large Binocular Telescope (see right), but the largest *single* primary mirror forms part of Japan's Subaru Telescope on Mauna Kea, Hawaii, USA. The 26-ft 10-in-wide (8.2-m) mirror is made from 8-in-thick (20-cm) glass weighing 50,265 lb (22.8 metric tons). With the help of 261 actuators to constantly keep the mirror focused, warping is limited to less than 0.1 microns (0.00001 millimeters).

Cosmic ray telescope

The Pierre Auger Observatory is a vast array of 1,600 particle detectors looking for very high-energy cosmic ray particles, which it is thought may be produced by supermassive black holes. Only one high-energy particle falls per 0.39 sq mi (1 km^2) in a century, so the observatory is arranged over a 1,158-sq-mi (3,000-km^2) area of Argentina—in an area larger than Luxembourg.

Highest astronomical observatory

The University of Tokyo Atacama Observatory (TAO) was established in Chile at an altitude of 18,500 ft (5,640 m)—double the height at which altitude sickness typically occurs. TAO perches on the summit of Cerro Chajnantor in the Atacama Desert. The observatory has an infrared telescope that was completed in Mar 2009.

Dish radio telescope

The Arecibo Observatory (see also p. 25) was considered impressive enough to star in the finale to the 1995 James Bond movie *GoldenEye*. The

Deepest observatory

The Sudbury Neutrino Observatory (SNOLAB) is 6,800 ft (2,075 m) down a mine in Ontario, Canada. There, shielded from cosmic rays that affect experiments into low-energy solar neutrinos, it searches for cosmic dark matter and supernova neutrino.

Largest robotic telescope

The Liverpool Telescope receives requests for data online and autonomously "decides" which observations to make. Located on La Palma in the Canary Islands with a 6-ft 6-in (2-m) mirror, the Liverpool reserves 5% of its observing time for use by schools.

HIGHEST OBSERVATORIES

Height	Observatory
18,500 ft	University of Tokyo Atacama Observatory (TAO), Chile
17,155 ft	Chacaltaya Astrophysical Observatory, Bolivia
17,060 ft	James Ax Observatory, Chile
17,025 ft	Atacama Cosmology Telescope, Chile
16,745 ft	Llano de Chajnantor Observatory (APEX), Chile
16,730 ft	Shiquanhe Observatory (NAOC Ali Observatory), Tibet
16,665 ft	Llano de Chajnantor Observatory (QUIET), Chile
16,400 ft	Llano de Chajnantor Observatory (ALMA), Chile
15,940 ft	Atacama Submillimeter Telescope Experiment, Chile
15,090 ft	Large Millimeter Telescope, Mexico

Sea level

⚡ Scope for improvement

The **largest reflector telescope** in our 1955 edition was the Hale Telescope of the California Institute of Technology on Palomar Mountain, USA, with its 16-ft 8-in unsegmented mirror. The record today—now categorized as the **largest unsegmented primary mirror**—is held by the 26-ft 10-in-wide Subaru Telescope on Mauna Kea (see above). The **largest land-base telescope** in *absolute* terms, though, is the segmented Gran Telescopio Canarias (right) at 34 ft 1 in wide.

Ａ-Ｚ Glossary

Actuator: Motor that moves the mirror or changes its shape in large reflecting telescopes.

Aperture: The opening in a telescope (or camera) that determines how much light enters and gets focused.

First light: Inaugural use of a telescope to record an astronomical image.

Primary mirror: The main light-gathering surface of a reflecting telescope.

Largest binocular telescope

The Large Binocular Telescope in Arizona, USA, comprises two identical telescopes, each with a 27-ft 6-in-wide (8.4-m) primary mirror. Working in tandem, they have an equivalent light-gathering power of a single mirror 38 ft 8 in (11.8 m) in diameter and are able to achieve the image sharpness of a 74-ft 9-in-wide (22.8-m) aperture.

ca. 2,000 mi (3,200 km) apart. The arms of these facilities are each 2.4 mi (4 km) long, providing LIGO with a high level of sensitivity. The detectors are currently being upgraded to continue the search for gravitational waves predicted in Einstein's general theory of relativity.

Liquid mirror
The Large Zenith Telescope (LZT), located east of Vancouver in Canada, uses a mirror made from liquid mercury. By spinning the 6,613-lb (3-metric-ton),

Largest movable motor-driven structure on land

The Robert C. Byrd Green Bank Telescope is a radio telescope at the National Radio Astronomy Observatory in West Virginia, USA. The dish measures 328 x 360 ft (100 x 110 m), and its highest point stands 480 ft (146 m) above the ground. The structure is fully steerable, and it can observe the whole sky from five degrees above the horizon.

distinctive design consists of a dish with a diameter of 1,000 ft (305 m), covering 18.5 acres (7.48 ha)—about the same as 14 football fields. The dish surface is covered by 38,778 aluminum panels. A steerable arm measuring 328 ft (100 m) is above the dish, allowing more of the sky to be seen.

Gravitational wave detector
The Laser Interferometry Gravitational Wave Observatory (LIGO) consists of two similar L-shape structures based in Louisiana and Washington (USA),

Largest concentration of high-altitude telescopes

Kitt Peak in Arizona, USA, is a 6,876-ft (2,096-m) mountain whose atmospheric clarity has attracted 24 major telescopes on its summit since 1958. Two are radio telescopes and the others are optical telescopes. The largest structure is the Nicholas U. Mayall Telescope, a 13-ft (4-m) mirror housed in a 187-ft-tall (57-m) building that can be seen from a distance of 50 mi (80 km).

19-ft 8-in-diameter (6-m) mercury mirror, the liquid forms a concave mirror shape. As a zenith telescope it is limited by looking straight up, but it is more economical because mercury is less expensive than glass mirrors.

Refracting telescope
Refracting telescopes use lenses to gather and focus light, as opposed to reflecting telescopes that use mirrors. The 1897 Yerkes Observatory in Wisconsin, USA, has a primary lens with a diameter of 3 ft 4 in (1.02 m).

Largest Cherenkov telescope

The H.E.S.S. II telescope, the newest part of the High Energy Stereoscopic System, has a diameter of 91 ft 10 in (28 m) and a total collecting surface area of 6,609 sq ft (614 m²). It detects faint Cherenkov radiation, which is produced by particles traveling faster than the speed of light. H.E.S.S. II saw its first light in Khomas Highland, Namibia, on Jul 26, 2012.

FACT
The H.E.S.S. II is larger than many telescopes but, as a Cherenkov detector, it is in a different category to true imaging telescopes.

Mirror call: largest telescope

The Gran Telescopio Canarias (GTC) is the **largest land-base optical telescope**, boasting a mirror with an effective aperture of 34 ft. This is also the world's **largest segmented primary mirror**, consisting of 36 hexagonal pieces, each of which can be moved separately to help counter the blurring effect of Earth's atmosphere on stellar light. The GTC, located at an altitude of 7,437 ft on La Palma in the Canary Islands, has produced images of the Milky Way at a resolution 60 million times greater than human vision.

FACT
Three big competitors in the next generation of observatories are the Giant Magellan Telescope (La Serena, Chile), the Thirty Meter Telescope (Mauna Kea, Hawaii), and the European Extremely Large Telescope (Cerro Armazones, Chile). Due for completion in the next decade or so, their budgets will average around $1.18 bn.

If all the oceans were combined into a single drop of water, it would be **851 mi** wide

Tallest illuminated icefalls

The waterfalls of Eidfjord in Norway plunge noisily some 1,640 ft (500 m) in summer. In the winter, when temperatures can drop to -15°F (-26°C), the water is frozen in its tracks. In Jan 2013, climbers Stephan Siegrist and Dani Arnold (pictured climbing, with Martin Echsner belaying), photographer Thomas Senf, and sports-equipment manufacturer Mammut captured images of these "icefalls" at night. Illuminations were provided by lamps, flashlights, and flares, and involved 2,300 ft (700 m) of cables.

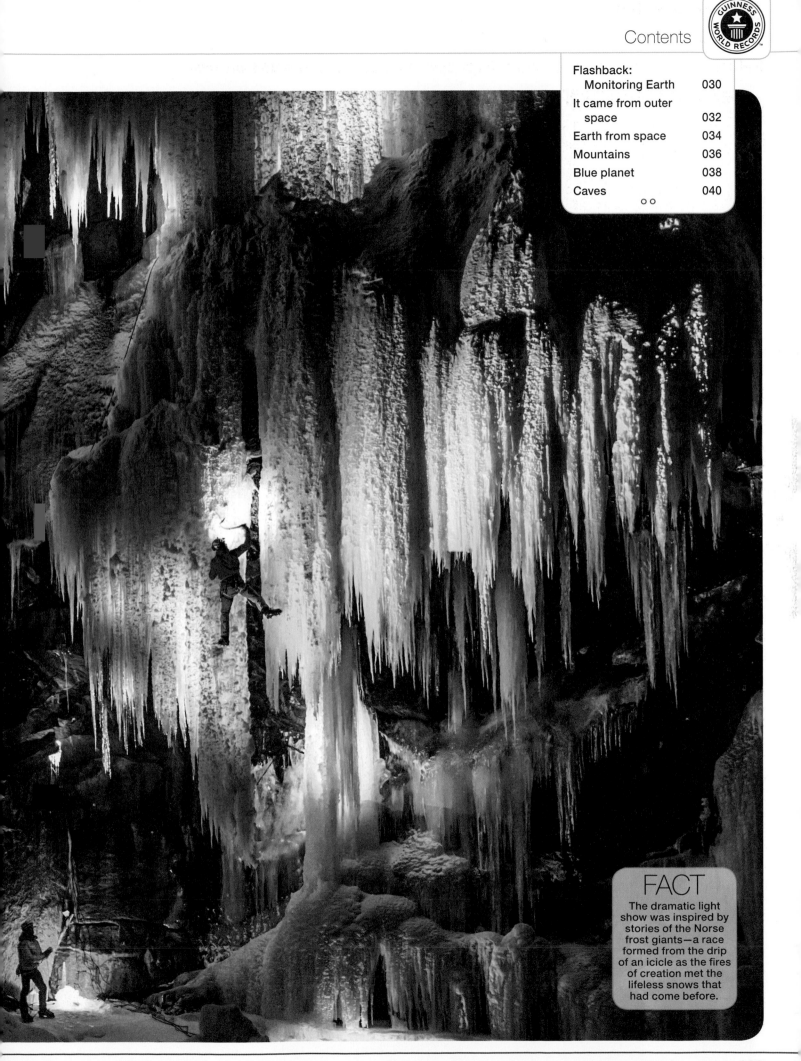

Contents

FACT

The dramatic light show was inspired by stories of the Norse frost giants—a race formed from the drip of an icicle as the fires of creation met the lifeless snows that had come before.

Monitoring Earth

The history of humanity is defined by our insatiable quest to explore and learn more about our planet. Ever since early explorers crossed the oceans in search of new lands, we have used the latest technology to watch the weather and monitored seas to predict storms. Today, technology is used by scientists to measure the health of the planet.

Our knowledge of the systems governing Earth has increased exponentially over the last 60 years, with increasingly more accurate sensors and comprehensive coverage in telecommunications to monitor the movement of the land and action of the seas. We are constantly seeking to understand the most intimate secrets of the powerful forces that sweep across our world.

Scientists are now able to make measurements of the magnetic properties of the planet. The strength of its gravity field has been mapped at all points to aid in construction projects, and we send robotic vehicles to test environments in which we could not survive.

More recently, advanced systems for data collection have helped us to chart the rate of climate change. Every year we are accumulating a more accurate picture of human processes, such as agricultural irrigation and deforestation. As we do so, we are discovering not only how our planet works but how better to respect and protect it.

The **longest-operating Earth-observation satellite** was *Landsat 5*, developed by NASA and launched on Mar 1, 1984 from Vandenberg Air Force Base, California, USA. Managed by the National Oceanic and Atmospheric Administration (1984–2000) and later the US Geological Survey (2001–13), it was decommissioned in 2013 after capturing more than 2.5 million images of Earth's surface during its 150,000 orbits.

The **first successful weather satellite** was the USA's *TIROS-1*, which was launched on Apr 1, 1960. "TIROS"—the "Television Infrared Observation Satellite"—remained operational for 78 days, during which time it employed its high- and low-resolution cameras to record images of cloud formations (inset) that were used by meteorologists worldwide to understand weather systems.

Magnetometers are sensitive instruments that measure magnetic fields in orbit. On May 15, 1958, the **first satellite magnetometer** was launched onboard the Soviet Union's *Sputnik 3*—a conical satellite 11 ft 8 in (3.57 m) long and 5 ft 8 in (1.73 m) wide at its base. It weighed 2,925 lb (1,327 kg) and possessed 12 scientific instruments (below). The satellite remained in orbit until Apr 6, 1960.

The **first geostationary weather satellite**—*GOES-1* (Geostationary Operational Environmental Satellite)—was launched from Cape Canaveral, Florida, USA, on Oct 16, 1975. The principal instrument onboard was the Visible Infrared Spin Scan Radiometer (VISSR), which provided day and night imagery of cloud conditions over the full-disk (inset). The satellite had the capability to relay meteorological data from more than 10,000 locations into a central processing center in order to build weather-prediction models.

The Argo program uses the **largest fleet of ocean sensors** to monitor global ocean current patterns. The 3,600 free-floating, robotic Argo sensors (mapped below) drift to 6,560 ft (2,000 m) deep and rise to transmit data via satellites. By Nov 2012, Argo had collected its millionth profile of temperature and salinity—twice the number obtained by all research vessels during the 20th century.

1955 · **1958** · **1960** · **1975** · **1984** · **2004**

60 YEARS OF WEATHER EXTREMES

1959

Greatest snowfall
From Feb 13 to 19, snow fell to a depth of 188.9 in on Mount Shasta Ski Bowl in northern California, USA.

1964

Driest place
From 1964 to 2001, the average annual rainfall for the Quillagua meteorological station in the Atacama Desert, Chile, was just 0.019 in.

1966

Highest annual mean temperature
Dallol in Ethiopia recorded a record annual mean temperature of 94°F for the six years between 1960 and 1966.

1970

Most intense rainfall
Basse-Terre, Guadeloupe, in the Caribbean, recorded 1.5 in of rain in one minute on Nov 26. This is the accepted highest figure, although scientists agree that it is difficult to assess exact rainfall readings over very short periods.

1983

Lowest temperature recorded on Earth
On Jul 21, temperatures at the Soviet Union's Vostok research station in Antarctica plunged to -128.6°F. The site was chosen for research with the aim of drilling into ancient ice.

On Jul 7, 2005, scientists were able to perform the **first accurate sea-level monitoring by satellite** using a number of different instruments (such as the *Gravity Recovery and Climate Experiment*—or *GRACE*—satellite, above). Satellite data was collected on changes in Earth's gravitational field, the mass of polar ice caps, and ocean topography and circulation (inset). Using this data, it was determined that, in the last 50 years, the rate at which the sea level is rising is 0.07 in (1.8 mm) per year—but in the last 12 years, this rate has increased to 0.118 in (3 mm) per year.

The **first satellite dedicated to monitoring climate change** was launched on Nov 2, 2009 by the European Space Agency (ESA). The Soil Moisture and Ocean Salinity (SMOS) mission surveys critical parts of the water cycle between oceans, air, and land by mapping the saltiness of the sea and monitoring water content in the planet's soil. The satellite works by measuring Earth's natural microwave emissions, which alter with the changing moisture levels on land or the salinity of the sea.

FACT
The radiometric temperature was measured by the amount of radiation (or lack of it) from the Antarctic Ridge.

The **lowest radiometric Earth temperature recorded by satellite** is -135.76°F (-93.2°C), on a high ridge in Antarctica, as preliminarily announced by NASA in Dec 2013. Data was collected by satellites including NASA's *Terra* (right) over 32 years, and it was found that the dry and clear air of the Antarctic allows heat to be efficiently radiated into space.

2005
2006
2009
2013
2015

The **largest-ever unmanned Earth-observation satellite** was *Envisat*, a European Space Agency satellite. It weighed 17,857 lb (8,100 kg), measured 85 x 32 x 16 ft (26 x 10 x 5 m), and orbited at an altitude of 487–491 mi (785–791 km). *Envisat* monitored Earth's land and oceans, ice caps (inset), and atmosphere with an array of instruments, before abruptly going silent on Apr 8, 2012, after 10 years in orbit.

The **fastest-melting Antarctic glacier** is Pine Island Glacier, which is dropping in height by up to 52 ft (16 m) a year, scientists discovered. Key data came from *Autosub* (below), an autonomous submarine that was sent under the vast glacier, which revealed it has become detached from an undersea ridge, allowing warm water to flow under it and increase the rate of melt.

From its launch in 2009 until its burn-up in 2013, ESA's *Gravity Field and Steady-State Ocean Circulation Explorer* (*GOCE*, above) was the **most accurate gravity-mapping satellite**, working to 1 milliGal (a unit used to measure the gravitational field).

The **highest-resolution maps of Earth's gravity field**, however, were created in 2013 by an Australian-German team using data obtained from the US Space Shuttle. The maps (right) improved the resolution of previous global gravity field maps by a factor of 40, and revealed that the pull of gravity is at its strongest at the North Pole; the lowest is at the top of the Huascarán mountain in the Andes.

1994

Longest-lasting cyclone
Hurricane/typhoon John formed on Aug 11 in the eastern Pacific Ocean. It lasted for 31 days, and it also traveled the **farthest distance for a tropical cyclone**: 8,251 mi.

1998
Largest coral reef die-off
In 1998, around 16% of all coral reefs were destroyed or damaged in a once-in-a-millennium event. The 1998 El Niño phenomenon may have triggered the disaster.

2008
Highest ocean temperature
In Aug 2008, scientists announced that they had recorded water at 867°F spewing from a hydro-thermal vent ("black smoker") on the ocean floor 9,842 ft deep at the Mid-Atlantic Ridge.

2013
Largest measured tornado
A tornado with a diameter of 2.59 mi was measured using Doppler radar by the US National Weather Service on May 31 in El Reno, Oklahoma, USA.

Greatest temperature range
Verkhoyansk, in the Siberian "Pole of Cold," is in the east of Russia. Temperatures have ranged 189°F: from a record low of -90.4°F to a record high of 98.6°F.

It came from outer space

Almost **220,400 lb of meteoroid material** enters Earth's atmosphere every day

Farthest sample-and-return mission

On Jun 13, 2010, the contents of Japanese space probe *Hayabusa* were retrieved in Australia after a sampling mission to the 25143 Itokawa asteroid some 65.6 million mi (300 million km) away. The probe had landed on Nov 25, 2005, and the samples it collected—1,500 tiny grains of dust—are the **first material returned from an asteroid**. The inset picture above shows Masaharu Nakagawa (left), science and technology minister for Japan, and *Hayabusa* project leader Junichiro Kawaguchi.

Fastest meteor shower

The Leonids are a shower of meteors entering Earth's atmosphere at around 44 mi/s (71 km/s) and begin to glow at an altitude of some 96 mi (155 km). The motion of the parent meteoroid stream, from comet 55P/Tempel–Tuttle, accounts for the speed. It is directly opposite to the orbital motion of Earth around the Sun, resulting in an almost head-on collision between the tiny particles and Earth annually on Nov 15–20.

Every 33 years, the Leonids look even more impressive as their parent comet swoops near the Sun. On Nov 16–17, 1966, the Leonid meteors were visible to lucky sky watchers between western North America and eastern Russia (then USSR), passing over Arizona, USA, at a rate of 2,300 per min for 20 min from 5 a.m.—the **greatest meteor shower** ever recorded.

First accurately predicted asteroid impact

Analysis of the orbit of asteroid 2008 TC3 indicated that it would hit Earth 21 hr after being discovered on Oct 6, 2008. At 2:46 a.m. on Oct 7, 2008, the asteroid—measuring a few yards across—exploded 23 mi (37 km) above Sudan with the force of 1 kiloton. Passengers traveling in a plane saw the flash from a distance of 750 nautical mi (863 mi; 1,389 km).

Heaviest manmade object to reenter the atmosphere

The Russian space station *Mir* came out of orbit during a successful controlled reentry of Earth's atmosphere on Mar 23, 2001. After 15 years in space, the 286,600-lb (130-metric-ton) laboratory broke into pieces that splashed down in the ocean east of New Zealand. The **largest space station** is now the *International Space Station*.

Greatest impact on Earth

The most widely accepted theory of how the Moon came into being is that it was part of Earth until 4.5 billion years ago. A planet the size of Mars is thought to have collided with the young Earth, shearing off much of the mantle and sending huge chunks of it into orbit. Over time, this debris collected under its own gravity to form the Moon.

Greatest recorded impact on Earth (unmeasured)

On Jun 30, 1908, the disintegration of an asteroid 6 mi (10 km) above the basin of the Podkamennaya Tunguska River in Russia resulted in a huge explosion. An area of 1,500 sq mi (3,900 km²) was devastated by the break up of the meteoroid, which released as much energy as up to

First identified impact crater

The Barringer Meteorite Crater, aka Meteor Crater, in Arizona, USA, measures around 0.74 mi (1.2 km) in diameter and 570 ft (173 m) deep. It was proposed in 1891 to be the result of a meteorite impact, and later determined to be the crater of an iron meteorite. Scientists believe that it landed some 49,000 years ago, with a force 150 times greater than that of the atomic bomb dropped on Hiroshima in 1945.

> GLOBAL IMPACT SITES

Meteorite impacts confirmed with shock waves or chemical evidence

Diameter (mi):
- ○ <6
- ○ 7–30
- ○ 31–60
- ● 61–185
- ○ Highly probable based on geological evidence

Source: www.impacts.rajmon.cz

AZ Glossary

Meteoroid: Metallic or rocky fragments, usually from a comet or asteroid and typically less than 3 ft 3 in wide; smaller fragments are known as micrometeoroids.

Meteor: A meteoroid that streaks through the atmosphere emitting heat and light; a "shooting star."

Meteorite: Meteoroid that survives Earth's atmosphere and lands on the ground.

○ ○ ○

Most people injured in a meteoroid explosion

There have been no confirmed human fatalities found in modern research into meteorite impacts. The worst effects recorded were on Feb 15, 2013, when a meteoroid exploded over Chelyabinsk Oblast in the Urals in Russia. Around 1,200 people were injured, mostly from flying glass caused by the shock wave following the fireball. Astronomer Alan Harris has calculated that the odds of being killed by an asteroid are 1 in 700,000. Scientists have suggested an asteroid bigger than 6.2 mi (10 km) across would kill most of humanity; fortunately, these only arrive once every 100 million years.

Largest meteorites
• **Overall:** Hoba meteorite—130,000 lb (59 metric tons), found in 1920 at Hoba West in Namibia.
• **Exhibited in a museum:** Cape York meteorite—68,085 lb (30,883 kg), found in 1897 near Cape York in the west of Greenland; now at the Hayden Planetarium in New York City, USA.
• **From Mars:** Zagami meteorite—40 lb (18 kg), found on Oct 3, 1962 near Zagami, Nigeria.

Largest tektite
Tektites are glassy pieces of rock formed by the melting and cooling of terrestrial rocks after meteor impacts. A tektite weighing 23 lb 13 oz (10.8 kg) was discovered in 1971 in Thailand.

A fragment from the Chelyabinsk Oblast meteorite (see left) recovered from Chebarkul Lake, placed in a local museum in 2013. Early analysis by scientists suggests that the meteor is of a common type known as ordinary chondrite.

Big Muley, aka sample 61016, came back with *Apollo 16* on Apr 27, 1972. At 25 lb 12 oz, it is the **heaviest rock returned from space**. All rock returned so far is lunar, from the Apollo and Luna programs (see below).

Of the roughly 50 known meteorites on Earth that have originated from the Moon, the **largest lunar meteorite** is Kalahari 009, with a mass of 29 lb 12 oz. It was discovered in the Kalahari Desert in Botswana in Sep 1999.

Northwest Africa 7325 (NWA 7325) was discovered in Morocco in 2012 and is thought to be the **first meteorite from Mercury**. Fragments, weighing 12 oz, are chemically consistent with data sent back from a Mercury-orbiting mission.

First person hit by space junk

The first and only person to be hit by a manmade object from orbit is Lottie Williams (USA). On Jan 22, 1997, in Tulsa, Oklahoma, USA, she was hit in the shoulder by a piece of blackened metal about 6 in (15 cm) long that NASA tests showed was probably from a *Delta II* rocket. Williams was unhurt.

five times that of all explosives used in World War II. While there are no exact figures on record from 1908, there are accurate measurements of the recent **greatest measured impact on Earth**. This was the Chelyabinsk impact of Feb 15, 2013 (see above).

Largest impact crater on Earth
The Vredefort crater, near Johannesburg in South Africa, may have lost the title of **oldest impact crater** to Greenland's Maniitsoq crater (see right), but it remains the largest crater, with an estimated diameter of around 186 mi (300 km). The crater was formed by an impact that occurred about 2 billion years ago.

Oldest impact crater on Earth

On Jun 29, 2012, scientists at the Geological Survey of Denmark and Greenland announced that they had discovered an impact crater in Greenland that could be 3 billion years old. Known as the Maniitsoq crater, the structure is around 62 mi (100 km) across. Much of it has eroded and it may once have been much bigger. If such a crater was formed in an impact with Earth today, most life would be wiped out.

Crash trash: NASA litter fine

On Jul 11, 1979, the defunct US space station *Skylab* (left) reentered Earth's atmosphere and disintegrated. Large chunks of the station survived to crash in Western Australia, and the Australian Shire of Esperance imposed a AUS$400 (now US$376) fine on NASA for littering, which NASA didn't pay. The bill was finally settled on their behalf in 2009 by US radio host Scott Barley, who raised the money from his audience for the 30th anniversary of *Skylab*'s demise. Pieces of *Skylab* are on display in Esperance's museum, as is a poster declaring the fine paid.

Sample-and-return

Numerous space missions have sought to return sample material to Earth:
• Apollo (1969–72): 2,415 samples of Moon rock weighing a total of 842 lb
• Luna (1959–76): Soviet robotic probe missions that collected 11.49 oz of lunar samples
• Orbital Debris Collector on *Mir* (1996–97) brought back interplanetary dust
• Genesis (2001–04): NASA project to collect solar wind molecules (**first material collected beyond the Moon**)

Earth from space

Approximately **2,500 manmade satellites**—both working and defunct—orbit Earth

First full-view color photograph of Earth
On Nov 10, 1967, NASA satellite *ATS-3* took a photograph of Earth while in geostationary orbit 23,000 mi (37,000 km) above Brazil.

First image of Earth from lunar orbit
NASA's Apollo precursor *Lunar Orbiter 1* snapped Earth on Aug 23, 1966 while orbiting the Moon (original shot, above right). Modern technology has allowed for the rendering of higher resolution images from the original sources and the result was unveiled in 2008 (below right).

First "Earthrise" viewed by humans

Apollo 8 was a manned spacecraft that orbited the Moon on Dec 23–24, 1968. On Christmas Eve, crew members Frank Borman, Bill Anders, and Jim Lovell (all USA) captured an iconic image of fragile beauty that became known as "Earthrise" and is credited with inspiring increased environmental awareness.

First image of Earth and the Moon in a single frame from space
On Sep 18, 1977, NASA's *Voyager 1* probe was on the way to Jupiter when it captured Earth and the Moon from a distance of 7.25 million mi (11.66 million km). The image of the Moon was far dimmer than Earth and had to be artificially enhanced by a factor of three to be visible.

Most distant image of Earth
The image called "the pale blue dot" was taken by *Voyager 1* on Feb 14, 1990 from almost 4 billion mi (6.5 billion km) away, on the request of astronomer Carl Sagan. "Every 'superstar,' every 'supreme leader,' every saint and sinner in the history of our species lived there," said Sagan, "on a mote of dust suspended in a sunbeam."

First image of Earth from space
A former Nazi V-2 rocket was launched by the USA on Oct 24, 1946 in New Mexico, USA, with a camera taking a frame every 1.5 sec. The rocket soared 65 mi (104 km) before crashing, with the film preserved in a steel enclosure.

Mars

Venus

Earth and Moon

First image from Saturn showing Earth, the Moon, Mars, and Venus

On Jul 19, 2013, NASA's *Cassini* spacecraft slipped into Saturn's shadow, where it compiled a panoramic mosaic of the planet, seven of its moons, and details of the inner rings. The image was taken 870 million mi (1.4 billion km) from Earth in a unique viewing geometry that meant the Sun's potentially damaging rays were eclipsed by Saturn itself.

Largest geological structure discovered from space

The "bull's-eye" of the Richat Structure in the Sahara of Mauritania was discovered from orbit by US astronauts Jim McDivitt and Ed White during the *Gemini IV* mission in Jun 1965. It has a diameter of 30 mi (50 km).

First Earth image from Martian orbit

On May 8, 2003, NASA's *Mars Global Surveyor* spacecraft turned its Mars Orbiter Camera back to Earth and captured it from 86 million mi (139 million km) away. The inset above shows Earth, with North and South America visible, and the Moon. At the bottom of the main picture (left) is Jupiter.

First high-resolution image of a total solar eclipse from lunar orbit

Earth looks like a diamond ring in this full solar eclipse series taken by Japan's unmanned *Kaguya*, aka the SELENE mission, on Feb 10, 2009.

Mountains

Every rise of 1,000 ft in altitude lowers the **boiling point of water** by 1.8°F

Highest polar ice cap

Dome Argus is a vast ice plateau near the center of East Antarctica. Its highest point is some 13,428 ft (4,093 m) above sea level. It is Antarctica's highest ice feature and overlies the 745-mi-long (1,200-km) Gamburtsev Mountain Range. For more on the formation of this record breaking range, see p. 37.

Tallest mountain

Measured from its submarine base in the Hawaiian Trough to its peak, Mauna Kea (White Mountain) on the island of Hawaii, USA, has a combined height of 33,480 ft (10,205 m), of which 13,796 ft (4,205 m) is above sea level.

Highest Arctic mountain

The summit of Gunnbjørn Fjeld in Greenland's Watkins Range reaches 12,119 ft (3,694 m) above sea level. It is a type of mountain known as a "nunatak," a rocky peak poking through a glacier or ice field. On the other side of the world, the **highest mountain in Antarctica** is Vinson Massif, one of the Seven Summits, whose peak reaches 16,050 ft (4,892 m) above sea level.

Highest mountain
The summit of Mount Everest, a Himalayan peak on the border between Tibet and Nepal, is at an altitude of 29,029 ft (8,848 m), higher than any other mountain. For more about the conquests of Everest, see p. 148.

Tallest mountain face
The Rupal face of Nanga Parbat, located in the western Himalayas, Pakistan, is a single rise of approximately 16,000 ft (5,000 m) from the valley floor to the summit. The mountain itself, which reaches an altitude of 26,656 ft (8,125 m), is the highest mountain in Pakistan and the eighth highest in the world.

Largest vertical extent
Both the highest and the lowest points on Earth's exposed surface are in the continent of Asia. Mount Everest, with its peak at 29,029 ft (8,848 m) above sea level, and the Dead Sea, with its surface at 1,384 ft (422 m) below sea level, make Asia the continent with the largest difference in vertical extent of 30,413 ft (9,270 m).

> **FACT**
> The Tibetan Plateau covers an area larger than Western Europe.

Largest plateau

The most extensive high plateau is the Tibetan Plateau, which covers 715,000 sq mi (1.85 million km²) of Central Asia. Its average altitude is 16,000 ft (4,900 m). The Himalayan mountain range, to the south of the plateau, is home to 30 of the world's tallest mountains.

MOUNTAIN RANGES

Largest
A mountain range is a series of mountains, or hills, that are connected in some way. The Himalayas, in Asia, is the largest mountain range, incorporating 96 of the 109 peaks measuring more than 24,000 ft (7,300 m).

Longest continental
The Andes in South America is 4,700 mi (7,600 km) long. It spans seven countries, from Venezuela to Argentina, and includes some of Earth's highest mountains. More than 50 of the Andes peaks

Highest mountain tabletop

Monte Roraima, on the border of Brazil, Guyana, and Venezuela, is a sandstone plateau measuring 9,220 ft (2,810 m) in height. Its harsh environment has deterred human presence and predators; as a result, around one-third of its plant species are unique to the mountain.

> **FACT**
> Monte Roraima is thought to have inspired Arthur Conan Doyle's novel *The Lost World*.

PEAK PERFORMANCE: COMPARING THE WORLD'S HIGH POINTS

ca. 13,615 ft

29,029 ft

Tibetan Plateau

16,023 ft

13,796 ft

Sea level

7,711 ft

ca. 15,419 ft

33,480 ft

27,711 ft

Highest island peak: Puncak Jaya, Indonesia, 16,024 ft above sea level

20,000 ft

19,684 ft

Highest underwater mountain face: Monte Pico, the Azores, 20,000 ft below sea level

Tallest mountain: Mauna Kea, 33,480 ft from its submarine base

Highest mountain: Mount Everest, 29,029 ft; average base elevation of ca. 15,419 ft, giving an average base-to-peak height of ca. 13,615 ft

Moving mountains

Sixty years ago, the height of Mount Everest changed overnight! The Great Trigonometrical Survey of India, a broad study that took place during the 19th century, calculated the height of the summit to be 29,002 ft in 1856. In 1955, however, this figure was adjusted to the present altitude of 29,029 ft. The mountain was given its present name in 1865, in honor of Sir George Everest (above). As British Surveyor General in India from 1830 to 1843, he had a major role in mapping the Indian subcontinent.

of the Cordillera Blanca. The mountain range contains 33 peaks of more than 18,000 ft (5,500 m) in addition to 80 glaciers and 120 glacial lakes.

Longest submarine

The Mid-Ocean Ridge runs 40,000 mi (65,000 km) from the Arctic Ocean to the Atlantic Ocean, around Africa, Asia, and Australia, and under the Pacific Ocean to the west coast of North America. Its peaks reach 13,800 ft (4,200 m) above the base ocean depth.

Fastest-rising mountain

Nanga Parbat in Pakistan is growing taller at a rate of 0.27 in (7 mm) per year. The mountain is part of the Himalayan Plateau, which was formed when India began colliding with the Eurasian continental plate between 50 million and 30 million years ago.

Greatest vertical drop

Mount Thor on Baffin Island in Nunavut, Canada, is a granite peak whose west face consists of a vertical drop of 4,101 ft (1,250 m). It is technically an overhang, with the average angle of repose of the cliff being at 105 degrees —or 15 degrees beyond the vertical.

reach at least 20,000 ft (6,000 m) high and for most of its extent the range is 200 mi (300 km) wide.

Highest coastal

The Sierra Nevada de Santa Marta is an isolated range of mountains located in Colombia, separated from the Andes. The range rises to an elevation of 18,946 ft (5,775 m) above sea level. Its considerable biodiversity led

UNESCO to designate the mountains as a biosphere reserve in 1979.

Highest tropical

Huascarán National Park in Peru's Cordillera Blanca ("White Range") mountain range has its highest point at 22,204 ft (6,768 m) above sea level. The protected area covers approximately 840,100 acres (340,000 ha) and covers almost the whole

Highest free-standing mountain

Mount Kilimanjaro in Tanzania, Africa, is 19,341 ft (5,895 m) above sea level. It is the fourth highest of the world's Seven Summits and the highest mountain in Africa. Standing independent of any range, Kilimanjaro is a dormant or extinct stratovolcano that last erupted around 200,000–150,000 years ago.

Oldest

The Barberton Greenstone Belt in South Africa, also known as the Makhonjwa Mountains, is formed of rocks dating back 3.6 billion years. It was here, in 1875, that the first gold in South Africa was discovered. The mountains rise some 5,900 ft (1,800 m) above sea level.

Smallest

The Sutter Buttes of California, USA, are the eroded remains of a volcano that was active around 1.6–1.4 million years ago. They are isolated within the flat floor of the Sacramento Valley and reach a maximum height of 2,060 ft (628 m), with a base diameter of around 10 mi (16 km).

Cold mountain: peaks under the ice

The Gamburtsev Mountain Range in eastern Antarctica extends for some 745 mi across the continent. It reaches 8,858 ft high but is permanently buried under more than 1,968 ft of ice, making it the world's **largest subglacial mountain range**.

Studies suggest that the Gamburtsev may date back 1 billion years, the result of mini-continents converging to form a supercontinent and forcing the land between them into a mountain range. In time, this range collapsed under its own weight and was eroded down to a residual root. Tectonic movement tore the land into separate continents and created a rift from present-day eastern Antarctica to India; the root, warmed by the rifting, forced up the land to form eastern Antarctica. As Earth cooled, this land became covered in an ice sheet the size of Canada.

Ice sheet

Gamburtsev Mountain Range

Root

FACT

Chimborazo, an inactive stratovolcano located in the Andes, is 20,564 ft tall—ca. 6,560 ft shorter than Mount Everest. Because it is located on the equator, however— which bulges outward more than the rest of the globe—scientists believe that its summit is the **most distant point on Earth from the planet's core**.

Blue planet

Oceans provide **190 times as much living space** as soil, air, and fresh water combined

Largest freshwater lake

Lake Superior is shared by Canada and the USA, bordered by Ontario and Minnesota to the north and west, and Wisconsin and Michigan to the south. The lake covers 31,700 sq mi (82,100 km²). Lake Baikal in Siberia, Russia, has the **greatest volume for a freshwater lake**, estimated at 5,500 cu mi (23,000 km³).

Largest bay

The Bay of Bengal in the Indian Ocean covers an area of 839,000 sq mi (2.17 million km²). One-quarter of the world's population of 7.2 billion live in the countries bordering it: Sri Lanka, India, Bangladesh, Myanmar, and Malaysia.

Chesapeake Bay is the **largest bay by shore length**, stretching 11,684 mi (18,804 km) along the Atlantic coast of Maryland and Virginia, USA.

Biggest rise in sea level since the last ice age

Meltwater Pulse 1A was an event occurring around 14,500 years ago, when sea levels rose by ca. 65 ft (20 m) in less than 500 years. Approximately 3,000 years earlier, as the ice sheets of the last ice age began to retreat, they added fresh water to the oceans. Global sea levels rose at an average of some 0.4 in (1 cm) per year until Meltwater Pulse 1A speeded things up, probably due to a partial collapse of the Antarctic ice sheets.

Oldest body of seawater

The US Geological Survey studied a body of groundwater more than 3,280 ft (1,000 m) below Chesapeake Bay in the USA. They reported that it dated from the early Cretaceous North Atlantic period, between 145 and 100 million years ago.

Lowest river

The Jordan River begins in Israel at an elevation of 9,232 ft (2,814 m) and flows 155 mi (251 km) south to the Dead Sea. Its lowest elevation here is 1,361 ft (416 m) below sea level.

This elevation makes the Dead Sea itself the **lowest exposed body of water**. Bordering Israel and Jordan, it is 50 mi (80 km) long and measures 11 mi (18 km) at its widest point.

Highest river

The Yarlung Zangbo has an average elevation of 13,100 ft (4,000 m). It rises in Tibet, runs for 6,550 mi (2,000 km) through China, and becomes the Brahmaputra River in India. It enters the ocean in the Bay of Bengal, where it meets the Ganges to form the **largest delta**, covering 30,000 sq mi (75,000 km²).

Largest desert lake

Lake Turkana, in the Great Rift Valley, Kenya, has a surface area of 2,472 sq mi (6,405 km²) —the equivalent of around 120 football pitches.

Oldest lake

Lake Baikal in Russia is up to 25 million years old. It formed following a tectonic rift in the Earth's crust.

Largest pink lake

A combination of microorganisms and minerals gives Lake Retba, or Lac Rose, in Senegal, its distinctive hue. At 2.7 sq mi (7.5 km²), it may be the biggest, but it's far from unique. Examples can be found in Canada (Dusty Rose Lake in British Columbia), Spain (two saltwater lakes near Torrevieja), and Australia (Lake Hillier). Lakes become pink through algae, or from organisms that produce carotenoids (as occur in carrots), such as the sea salt field *Dunaliella salina*.

WATER BODIES: LONGEST RIVERS, LARGEST OCEANS

Top 10 longest rivers

1. **Nile**, Egypt, 4,130 mi
2. **Amazon**, Brazil, 3,970 mi
3. **Yangtze**, China, 3,910 mi
4. **Mississippi**, USA, 3,900 mi
5. **Yenisei**, Russia, 3,440 mi
6. **Huang He**, China, 3,390 mi
7. **Ob–Irtysh**, Russia, 3,360 mi
8. **Paraná**, Brazil, 3,030 mi
9. **Congo**, Congo, 2,920 mi
10. **Amur–Argun**, Russia, 2,760 mi

Land area 34.2%

Arctic Ocean 2.8%
Southern Ocean 4.0%

Indian Ocean 13.4%

Atlantic Ocean 15.1%

Pacific Ocean 30.5%

Largest tidal bores

A tidal bore arises when the Sun, Moon, and Earth align to form dramatic tidal conditions. A solitary wave travels with great speed up a narrow river, forcing the flow upstream.

In 1955, the **largest tidal bore** was the Tsien Tang Kiang, attaining "a height of up to 25 feet and a speed of 13 knots." We later reported the 1993 incident in which one of these waves reached Hangzhou Bay, China. It rose to 30 ft, was 200 mi long, and pushed 2.3 million gal of water per sec to the shore, resulting in multiple fatalities.

Glossary

Acoustic doppler current profiler (ADCP, or ADP): A meter that measures the velocities of water currents across a range of depths by referencing the acoustic properties of sound waves.

Biome: A substantial community of flora and fauna that occurs naturally in a specific environment such as desert, grassland, tundra, forest, or ocean.

Delta: An area of land, created from sediment, that forms at the mouth of a large river.

Deepest river

In Jul 2008, scientists from the US Geological Survey and the American Museum of Natural History discovered that the Congo River, which spans 10 countries in Africa, has a maximum depth of at least 722 ft (220 m). The measurements were performed in the Lower Congo River using echo sounders, advanced GPS, and acoustic doppler current profilers.

OCEANS

Deepest point
Challenger Deep, located in the Mariana Trench in the Pacific Ocean, is 35,797 ft (10,911 m) at its deepest point. Mount Everest would entirely fit in it, with its peak 6,560 ft (2,000 m) below the surface.

Largest biome
The area in open ocean—away from both seabed and shore—is called the pelagic zone. Globally, its volume is 319 million cu mi (1.3 billion km³) and it supports life, making it by far the largest biome. It has many of the planet's larger animals, including whales.

Largest continuous ocean current system
The system of ocean circulation that transports cold and salty deep water is called the thermohaline conveyor belt ("thermo" from heat and "haline" from salinity). The water is slowly transported from the north Atlantic down to the Southern Ocean, where it travels east and north to the Indian and Pacific oceans. Here, it rises and becomes warm, traveling back west, where it sinks once again in the north Atlantic. The complete cycle can last for a thousand years.

WATERFALLS

Largest waterfall ever
Dry Falls, near Missoula in Montana, USA, is all that remains of a waterfall that stretched over 3.5 mi (5.6 km) and was 380 ft (115 m) high. It burst into life when the water from a massive glacial lake—formed 18,000 years ago—broke through the ice, causing a catastrophic flood.

Highest underwater waterfall
The Denmark Strait Cataract is underwater in the Denmark Strait, which separates Greenland and Iceland. The 2.17-mi (3.5-km) waterfall carries around 176.5 million cu ft (5 million m³) of water per sec. The Cataract, the **largest waterfall** of any

Largest area of bioluminescence

Legends of a "milky sea" date far back in naval history. In 2005, scientists at the US Naval Research Laboratory used satellite imagery to confirm detailed log reports made by the British ship SS *Lima* in 1995. They described an area in the Indian Ocean, near Somalia, measuring around 5,400 sq mi (14,000 km²). Vast amounts of bioluminescent bacteria, possibly *Vibrio harveyi*, are believed to be responsible.

kind, is formed as cold, denser seawater drops from the Greenland Sea into the slightly warmer Irminger Sea.

Largest plunge pool
Plunge pools form at the base of waterfalls as a result of water erosion. Perth Canyon is a plunge pool off the coast of Australia that measures ca. 1,000 ft (300 m) deep and 4.62 sq mi (12 km²) in area. The prehistoric pool was created when the region was above sea level.

Greatest waterfall flow
Boyoma Falls in the Democratic Republic of the Congo flows at a rate of 600,000 cu ft (17,000 m³) per sec. It has seven drops along 60 mi (100 km) of the Lualaba River.

Largest lake within a lake

Manitou Lake occupies an area of 41 sq mi (106 km²). It is located on the **largest island in a lake**, Manitoulin Island (see above), which covers 1,068 sq mi (2,766 km²) of the Canadian section of Lake Huron. Another geographical nesting doll is Vulcan Point, the **largest island in a lake on an island in a lake on an island**. The 130-ft (40-m) island sits in Crater Lake, the central crater of the Taal volcano in Lake Taal on the island of Luzon in the Philippines.

Tide of filth: a drop in the ocean

The **largest ocean garbage site** is in the North Pacific Gyre (right), a vortex of slowly revolving ocean water that naturally concentrates ever increasing amounts of floating litter in its center. Much of it is made up of plastic, which never degrades but breaks down into tiny fragments that pollute down to 32 ft below the surface. These tiny, toxic chunks enter the food chain and studies now suggest that waste outweighs nutritious plankton by a factor of six to one. Plastic bags account for more than 50% of all marine litter, the **greatest ocean pollutant** (left).

In deep water

Deepest lake: Lake Baikal, Russia, 5,370 ft deep

Deepest hypersaline lake: The Dead Sea, Israel/Jordan, 1,240 ft deep and more than eight times saltier than seawater

Deepest brine pool: Orca Basin, Gulf of Mexico, 7,200 ft below sea level, filled with water around eight times saltier than the Gulf

Caves

It typically takes **100,000 years** for a cave to grow large enough to accommodate humans

Longest sea cave

Matainaka Cave on New Zealand's South Island is 5,052 ft (1,540 m) long and is still forming through wave action from the sea. This length is more than three times that of its nearest rival, Mercer Bay Cave in New Zealand, which extends to 1,542 ft (470 m). The **largest sea cave** is in the Sea Lion Caves in Oregon, USA. One chamber is 310 ft (95 m) long, 165 ft (50 m) wide, and 50 ft (15 m) high, in a 1,315-ft-long (400-m) passage.

Longest cave system

It has taken some 25 million years for Mammoth Cave to form through the weathering action of the Green River and its tributaries. Situated in Mammoth Cave National Park in Kentucky, USA, the system is a network of limestone caves, of which 400 mi (644 km) have been explored so far.

Longest gypsum cave

Gypsum, a soft mineral, is used to make a type of plaster called plaster of Paris. A cave system called Optymistychna ("Optimistic"), near Korolivka, Ukraine, occurs in a layer of gypsum around 65 ft 7 in (20 m) thick. It has

Longest underground river

In Mar 2007, cave divers Stephen Bogaerts (UK) and Robbie Schmittner (DEU) announced that they had discovered a 95-mi-long (153-km) river beneath the Yucatán Peninsula in Mexico. The river, which has many twists and turns, spans around 6 mi (10 km) of land.

been mapped so far at 146 mi (236 km) in length, under an area covering 0.7 sq mi (2 km²).

Deepest blue hole

Blue holes are found at or just below sea level, and were once dry caves or shafts. They filled with seawater as the ice caps melted and the water levels rose during the last ice age. Dean's Blue Hole is 250 ft (76 m) wide, a vertical shaft that sinks for 662 ft (202 m) at Turtle Cove on the Atlantic edge of The Bahamas. It contains 11.8 million cu ft (1.1 million m³) of water.

Deepest ice cave descent

Janot Lamberton (FRA) descended to 662 ft (202 m) in a glacial cave

in Greenland. The cave, reached by Lamberton in 1998, was formed by a river of meltwater during the Arctic summer.

Deepest lava cave

Lava tubes are formed by streaming lava under the hard surface of a lava flow. While a volcano is erupting, the tubes drain lava away, before the rock cools and the process results in a long, cavelike channel. The deepest and longest example is Kazumura Cave in Hawaii, USA. It is 40.7 mi (65.5 km) long, and descends to a depth of 3,614 ft (1,101 m).

Largest cave chamber

A chamber is the largest order of space in a cave. It is often formed at a junction of passages, where erosion and collapse have exposed more rock, and its maximum size is dictated by the strength of the ceiling. The Sarawak Chamber in the Lubang Nasib Bagus cave of Sarawak, Borneo, is 2,300 ft (700 m) long. Its average width is 980 ft (300 m) and it is at least 230 ft (70 m) high. By way of comparison, that's nearly as long as seven football fields, and taller than Nelson's Column in Trafalgar Square, London.

Oldest caves

The Sudwala Caves in Mpumalanga, South Africa, are ca. 240 million years old. The series of caves is believed to have formed from Precambrian dolomite rock dating back 3.8 billion years. As well as providing shelter for prehistoric humans, it has been used in modern times for ammunition storage and as a concert venue. The bat guano (droppings) found there are used as fertilizer.

Longest explored cave system underwater

Sistema Ox Bel Ha ("Three Paths of Water" in Mayan), in the state of Quintana

LONGEST CAVES

1. **Mammoth Cave**, USA, 400 mi
2. **Sistema Sac Actun**, Mexico, 193 mi
3. **Jewel Cave National Monument**, USA, 166 mi
4. **Sistema Ox Bel Ha**, Mexico, 151 mi
5. **Optymistychna Cave**, Ukraine, 146 mi
6. **Wind Cave**, USA, 141 mi
7. **Lechuguilla Cave**, USA, 138 mi
8. **Hölloch**, Switzerland, 124 mi
9. **Fisher Ridge Cave System**, USA, 122.5 mi
10. **Gua Air Jernih (Clearwater Cave)**, Malaysia, 122.4 mi

Source:
www.caverbob.com

Deepest cave

The same year that we published our first edition, we said that six French speleologists discovered the Berger cave near Grenoble in France in Jul 1955. We called it the **deepest cave**, at 2,959 ft (902 m).

Today, Gouffre Berger is no longer quite the awesome challenge it once was, and is regularly explored by groups of up to 200. We also now know it is 3,681 ft deep and that Krubera Cave in Georgia is nearly twice as deep (see right).

Glossary

Cave: Natural chamber or series of chambers in the ground, hillsides, or cliffs.

Caving (or **spelunking** or **potholing**): Recreational exploration of caves.

Speleology: Scientific study of caves, including their structure, properties, history, occupants, and the process by which they form (speleogenesis).

○ ○ ○

Largest cave

Vietnamese farmer Ho Khanh found a cave in central Vietnam in 1991—and then forgot where it was. It wasn't until 2009 that he guided a UK team to Hang Son Doong ("Mountain River Cave"), which is 655 ft (200 m) high, 490 ft (150 m) wide, and at least 4 mi (6.5 km) long. Tourists with $3,000 to spare can now visit it—although they must first trek for over a day through jungle and abseil 260 ft (79 m) to the entrance.

Roo, Mexico, is a series of underwater passages accessed by surface lakes. As of Mar 2014, according to cave researcher Bob Gulden at caverbob.com, 151 mi (243 km) of the system has been mapped.

Greatest vertical extent for a flowstone cascade

Flowstone cascades form in sheets when limestone-saturated water runs down cave walls and floors, leaving behind calcite deposits that solidify over time. The largest vertical extent is 492 ft (150 m), in the Lechuguilla Cave in Carlsbad Caverns National Park, New Mexico, USA.

Longest stalactite

Stalactites form to hang from a cave ceiling. The longest free-hanging example is 92 ft (28 m) and hangs in the Gruta do Janelão in Minas Gerais, Brazil.

Tallest stalagmite

A stalagmite is the opposite of a stalactite. It is built up from the floor and the tallest is reported to measure some 230 ft (70 m). It is located in Zhijin Cave in Guizhou Province, China.

Tallest natural cave column

A column measuring 201 ft 8 in (61.5 m) in a cave at Tham Sao Hin, Thailand, was created by the merging of a stalactite and stalagmite. Where the two formations met they became one column.

Largest gypsum crystal

The Cave of Crystals, below Naica mountain in the Chihuahuan Desert, Mexico, contains translucent single crystals of gypsum measuring up to 36 ft (11 m) long and weighing up to 121,200 lb (55 tonnes). They began to form hundreds of thousands of years ago, when the cave was filled with warm, mineral-rich water.

Deepest unbroken vertical shaft in a cave

Straight, natural shafts are challenges for cavers—essentially, they are sheer drops without ledges. The Miao Keng Cave, near Tian Xing in China, has a continuous shaft 1,643 ft (501 m) deep that takes around two hours to abseil. The shaft is about two-thirds of the height of the **tallest building**—the 2,716-ft (828-m) Burj Khalifa in Dubai, UAE.

Get down: deepest cave gets deeper

It's not often that a geological feature breaks its own record, but that's exactly what happened with the **deepest cave**, Krubera Cave (left). Or rather, Gennady Samokhin (pictured right), a Ukrainian caver, extended the known depth of the cave on Aug 10, 2012 by 20 ft. The cave in the Arabika Massif, Georgia, now has an explored depth of 7,208 ft. The new area is in a sump (submerged section) called Dva Kapitana ("Two Captains") that Samokhin suspects may extend by as much as 6 mi, all the way to the Black Sea. Samokhin was also a member of the previous record attempt team in 2007.

Underground music

Deepest live radio broadcast: Two-hour CBC Radio Points North (CAN) show, 7,680 ft down in Creighton Mine in Ontario, Canada, on May 24, 2005

Largest natural underground musical instrument: The Great Stalacpipe Organ—stalactites covering 3.4 acres that produce tones when struck with mallets linked to a keyboard in Luray Caverns, Virginia, USA

Deepest concert underground: Agonizer (FIN), 4,170 ft below sea level at Pyhäsalmi Mine in Pyhäjärvi, Finland, Aug 4, 2007

Living planet

There are an estimated **7.77 million animal species** on Earth; to date, only 12% have been described

SEE IT 3D WITH THE FREE APP

Largest fish

The largest living fish is the rare, plankton-feeding whale shark (*Rhincodon typus*), which is found in the warmer areas of the Atlantic, Pacific, and Indian oceans. The largest scientifically recorded example was 41 ft 6 in (12.65 m) long—about the same length as three-and-a-half Mini Cooper cars—and measured 23 ft (7 m) around the thickest part of the body. It was captured off Baba Island near Karachi, Pakistan, on Nov 11, 1949, and weighed an estimated 46,000 lb (21 metric tons).

Contents

Augmented Reality alert!

3D ON THIS PAGE

FACT

A whale shark egg—the **largest of all fish eggs**—is typically the same size as a football!

New discoveries

It is a tragic but inescapable fact that animal species are becoming extinct all the time—in many cases, as a direct result of human activity. Happily, it is also true that even today a surprising number of previously unknown, entirely new animal species are coming to light: 15,000 each year, on average.

Many of the new species being discovered are small, inconspicuous creatures: mostly insects, worms, and other diminutive invertebrates. But quite a few much more sizable and very spectacular animals are also being uncovered, and on a global scale, not just in a few specific locations.

To demonstrate this heartening and ongoing revelation of previously unknown life forms, our expert Dr. Karl Shuker highlights some of the most notable new animal species that have come to light over the past six decades. All of these creatures have been found, formally described, and classified by scientists since the first edition of the *Guinness Book of Records* was published in 1955, and every one is a GWR record holder.

At the bottom of these pages we present 10 of the most recent, and most remarkable animal finds. Encouragingly, the evidence on these pages suggests that there are still plenty of new species waiting to be discovered!

Largest species of poison dart frog: South America's poison dart frogs have toxic skin secretions used by native Indian tribes to tip their blowgun darts. The largest species, the 1-oz (30-g) Colombian golden poison dart frog (*Phyllobates terribilis*), remained undiscovered by science until 1974.

1970s

1960s: During this decade, an extra-large brown spitting cobra was caught by herpetologist James Ashe in Kenya. In 2007, it was found to belong to a previously unknown species—at ca. 9 ft (3 m) long, the **largest species of spitting cobra**—which was formally named *Naja ashei*, or Ashe's giant spitting cobra.

1970s: In 1977, scientists onboard the US research submarine *Alvin* discovered an astonishing new ecosystem thriving around hydrothermal vents on the seafloor off the Galápagos Islands, Ecuador. Among the fauna were new species such as the giant tube worm (*Riftia pachyptila*), with huge, red, plumelike tentacles. It was the **first known ecosystem not to derive its primary energy from sunlight**, which can't penetrate down to it, but from chemical energy instead, released by bacteria.

1960s

Largest species of gerbil: Discovered in the 1960s, the great gerbil (*Rhombomys opimus*) can exceed 1 ft 3 in (40 cm) in length. It is native to Turkmenistan, Kazakhstan, Mongolia, and several other central and east-central Asian countries.

1950s

1950s: The year 1955 saw the discovery of the **most venomous jellyfish**, Flecker's sea-wasp (*Chironex fleckeri*), which is found in the waters off Queensland, Australia. Shown inset are sting wounds inflicted on the leg of a swimmer in Jan 2000.

Largest starfish: In 1968, a specimen of the very fragile brisingid *Midgardia xandaros* was collected in the Gulf of Mexico. It measured an astonishing 4 ft 6 in (1.38 m) from tip to tip. The species was formally classified in 1972.

TEN OF THE MOST RECENT ARRIVALS. NEWEST ...

Amphibian

2013
Botsford's leaf-litter frog (*Leptolalax botsfordi*) was formally described and classified in late 2013. It was discovered in the high elevations of Vietnam's Mount Fansipan, the tallest mountain in Indochina.

Ape

2010
The northern buff-cheeked gibbon (*Nomascus annamensis*) is native to the tropical rain forests between Vietnam, Laos, and Cambodia. It is distinguished from similar-looking species by its characteristic vocalizations.

Bird of prey

2010
Formally described and named in 2010, the Socotra buzzard (*Buteo socotraensis*) is native exclusively to the Socotra archipelago, a group of tiny islands forming part of Yemen in the Arabian peninsula.

Cat

2013
The selkirk rex is also known as the poodle cat because of its thick, curly fur, composed of three separate layers. The breed was developed from a spontaneous genetic mutation originating in Montana, USA, in 1987.

Freshwater cetacean

2014
Inia araguaiaensis, the Araguaian boto, was officially described and named in Jan 2014. It is a species of freshwater dolphin native to the Araguaia River basin of Brazil, and is the first such discovery for almost a century.

Most poisonous bird: hooded pitohui (*Pitohui [dichrous]*) of Papua New Guinea is one of the very few poisonous birds. Discovered in 1990, its feathers and skin contain the potent poison homobatrachotoxin, also secreted by the dart frogs of South America (see left).

2000s: The **newest species of big cat**, the Bornean clouded leopard (*Neofelis diardi*), was thought to be a subspecies until studies confirmed that its DNA and appearance were distinct. It was reclassified in Dec 2006 as a species in its own right.

2010s

1990s: The **newest genus of wild ox**, *Pseudoryx*, was created in 1993 to house a spectacular species first made known to science the previous year in Vu Quang, Vietnam. Now known as the saola or Vu Quang ox (*P. nghetinhensis*), this sizable species differs markedly from other oxen by way of its very long, slender, antelope-like horns and legs.

1980s

1980s: In 1983, scientists created a family of sharks, Megachasmidae, in order to accommodate a large and remarkable new species, the megamouth shark (*Megachasma pelagios*), which was first discovered in 1976 off Hawaii, USA. Megachasmidae remains the **newest shark family**.

2000s

1990s

Smallest sea horse: An adult pygmy sea horse (*Hippocampus denise*) is typically just 0.63 in (16 mm) long—smaller than an average human fingertip. The species was first discovered in 2003 in the delicate corals of the Flores Sea, off the coast of Indonesia.

Actual Size

2010s: The **newest species of monkey** to have been scientifically recognized is Vieira's titi (*Callicebus vieirai*). Native to the states of Mato Grosso and Pará in central-northern Brazil, it was officially described and named in 2012. It is readily distinguished from all other titis by its unique facial and pelage (hair) coloration.

Lemur

2013
The Marohita mouse lemur (*Microcebus marohita*) and Anosy mouse lemur (*M. tanosi*) are native to Madagascar, as are all lemurs. Each was distinguished from similar species of mouse lemur by sequencing its genes.

Marine cetacean

2012
The latest marine cetacean to have been scientifically recognized is the Burrunan dolphin (*Tursiops australis*), which was officially described and named in 2012. It is endemic to the coastal waters of southeastern Australia.

Owl

2013
The Seram masked owl (*Tyto almae*) was described and named in 2013, but it was first known to science in 1987, when a specimen was photographed (but not collected) in the wild. It is native to the Indonesian island of Seram.

Sea snake

2012
The mosaic sea snake (*Aipysurus mosaicus*) is known from a single specimen in Copenhagen's Natural History Museum. Caught in the 19th century in the seas between New Guinea and Australia, it was only made a new species in 2012.

Tapir

2013
Brazil's kabomani tapir (*Tapirus kabomani*) is one of the largest new mammals to have been discovered for a century, but it is the **smallest living species of tapir**, weighing on average a very modest 242 lb (110 kg).

Mammals

The rare **bowhead whale** (*Balaena mysticetus*) can live for longer than a century

Largest feline carnivore

The male Siberian tiger (*Panthera tigris altaica*) averages 10 ft 4 in (3.15 m) from nose to tail, stands 3 ft 3 in–3 ft 6 in (99–107 cm) to its shoulder, and weighs around 580 lb (265 kg). There are about 360 of the tigers in existence, a recovery from a low of 20–30 in the 1930s.

CARNIVORES

Largest bear ever
The tyrant polar bear (*Ursus maritimus tyrannus*) evolved from an isolated population of Arctic brown bears during the mid-Pleistocene epoch (250,000–100,000 years ago). With a body length of 12 ft 2 in (3.7 m) and a height to the shoulder of 6 ft (1.83 m), it could weigh more than a ton (2,200 lb). The tyrant was the first form of polar bear.

Oldest brown bear in captivity
On May 24, 2013, a 50-year-old European brown bear (*Ursus arctos*) named Andreas died in a sanctuary built by the World Society for the Protection of Animals (WSPA) in northern Greece. The average lifespan in the wild is 25 years.

Largest euplerid
Euplerids were once classed in the civet family and are also known as Madagascan civets. The largest of the 10 species is the fossa (*Cryptoprocta ferox*), which has the size and look of a small puma. It is 2 ft 3 in–2 ft 7 in (70–80 cm) long with a tail of 2 ft 1 in–2 ft 3 in (65–70 cm), and weighs 12 lb 2 oz–18 lb 15 oz (5.5–8.6 kg).

Oldest big cat fossil
In 2010, fossils from a previously unknown species similar to a snow leopard were unearthed in the Himalayas. The fossils of this species—named *Panthera blytheae*—have been dated to between 4.1 and 5.95 million years old, which supports the theory that big cats evolved in central Asia—not Africa—and spread outward.

Newest species of wild cat
Formally named in 2013, the southern Brazilian oncilla (*Leopardus guttulus*) inhabits the Atlantic Forest to the south of the country. They do not interbreed with oncillas elsewhere in Brazil.

Rarest fox
The island fox (*Urocyon littoralis*) is native to six of the eight Channel Islands in California, USA, each of which has its own separate subspecies of the species. In 2002, a total of 1,500 specimens was estimated (some of the subspecies numbered fewer than 100). Since then, the species has continued to decline, due in part to predation by golden eagles, disease parasites, and habitat destruction. The International Union for Conservation of Nature (IUCN) categorize it as "Critically Endangered."

Rarest raccoon
The Cozumel or pygmy raccoon (*Procyon pygmaeus*) is found on the tiny Cozumel Island, off Mexico's Yucatán Peninsula, which is 184.5 sq mi (478 km²) in area. The raccoon is classed as "Critically Endangered": only 250–300 specimens are believed to exist.

Most expensive species in captivity

The giant panda (*Ailuropoda melanoleuca*) indigenous population is owned by China. Four US zoos each pay an annual fee of $1 m to China to lease a pair. Cub births, bamboo production, and security all add to the cost, but it can be worth it. Edinburgh Zoo in the UK reported a 51% increase in visitors during the year after giant pandas Sunshine and Sweetie took up residence.

Fastest marine mammal

On Oct 12, 1958, a bull killer whale (*Orcinus orca*) an estimated 20–25 ft (6.1–7.6 m) in length was timed at 34.5 mph (55.5 km/h) in the northeastern Pacific. Similar speeds have also been reported for Dall's porpoise (*Phocoenoides dalli*) in short bursts.

Bear necessities

Largest home range for a land-base mammal: Polar bears (*Ursus maritimus*) cover Arctic areas of 11,500 sq mi—the size of Italy—in a year.

Most sensitive nose for a land mammal: Typically, polar bears can detect prey, such as seals, from more than 18.6 mi away and even when the prey is under ice.

Richest bear's milk: Polar bear milk contains up to 48.4% fat, which is as rich as cream and vital in order to build up the fat reserves in cubs, so that they can withstand the extreme conditions.

Fattiest diet: In the spring and summer months, polar bears dine on ringed seal pups, which have up to 50% body fat.

Blue whale: the biggest heart on Earth

Weighing up to 352,000 lb, the blue whale (*Balaenoptera musculus*) is the **largest mammal**, and the **largest animal** known to have existed. Pictured is a model of a blue whale's heart, made for Museum of New Zealand Te Papa Tongarewa by Human Dynamo Workshop. A blue whale's car-size heart weighs ca. 1,500 lb and is the **largest heart** of any animal. It beats 4–8 times a minute (**slowest heartbeat**).

Smallest family of land carnivores

Two families of land carnivores contain just one single species each. They are Nandiniidae, containing the nandinia (*Nandinia binotata*) of Africa, and Ailuridae, containing as its own living species the lesser or red panda (*Ailurus fulgens*) of Asia.

CETACEANS

Largest cetacean

A female blue whale (*Balaenoptera musculus*) killed at Twofold Bay in New

Largest cetacean family

The term "cetacean" describes whales, dolphins, and porpoises. Dolphins (*Delphinidae*) have 37 living species, not all of which are called dolphins. This diverse family also includes killer, false killer, and pygmy killer whales and pilot whales. They all breathe through a blowhole situated on top of their heads.

The **smallest species of baleen whale** (toothless but possessing baleen plates for filtering food from water) is the pygmy right whale (*Caperea marginata*), at 19 ft 8 in–21 ft 3 in (6–6.5 m) long and weighing around 6,600–7,700 lb (3–3.5 tonnes).

Deepest mammal dive

Scientists recorded a 6,500-ft (2,000-m) dive, lasting 1 hr 13 min, by a bull sperm whale (*Physeter macrocephalus*) off the coast of Dominica in 1991.

In 1989, a male northern elephant seal (*Mirounga angustirostris*) was recorded diving to 5,017 ft (1,529 m) off the coast of California, USA, the **deepest dive by a pinniped**.

Largest terrestrial carnivore

The polar bear (*Ursus maritimus*) weighs 880–1,320 lb (400–600 kg) and is 7 ft 10 in–8 ft 6 in (2.4–2.6 m) long. It feeds on the **largest prey**, killing walruses up to 1,100 lb (500 kg) and beluga whales of 1,322 lb (600 kg) to fill a stomach capacity of ca. 150 lb (68 kg), or 9 lb (4 kg) more than an adult human male.

South Wales, Australia, in 1910 measured 97 ft (29.57 m) long.

The **smallest cetaceans** are the Hector's dolphin (*Cephalorhynchus hectori*) and the vaquita (*Phocoena sinus*), both of which grow to a length of just 3 ft 11 in (1.2 m).

Largest carnivore

Male (bull) southern elephant seals (*Mirounga leonina*) weigh up to 7,720 lb (3,500 kg), with an average length of 16 ft 4 in (5 m). Also the **largest pinnipeds**, they dwarf even the polar bear (*U. maritimus*, left) and are found in the sub-Antarctic islands.

❌ For animals closer to home, try p. 64

CARNIVORE AND CETACEAN SIZES

Male Siberian tiger:
Length 10 ft 4 in, weight 580 lb

Polar bear:
length 8 ft 6 in, weight 1,300 lb

Adult human male:
Height 5 ft 8 in, weight 141 lb

Elephant seal:
length 16 ft 4 in, weight 7,720 lb

Killer whale:
Length 29 ft 6 in, weight 22,000 lb

Common dolphin:
Length 8 ft 6 in, weight 175 lb

Hector's dolphin:
length 3 ft 11 in, weight 90–130 lb

Blue whale:
Length 78 ft 8 in, weight 352,700 lb

🅰🆉 Glossary

Carnivore: Meat-eating animal (order Carnivora)

Cetacean: Aquatic mammal (order Cetacea). Divided into two main groups: toothed whales (dolphins, porpoises, smaller whales) and baleen whales (large filter feeders).

Pinniped: Carnivorous, semiaquatic marine mammal (order Pinnipedia). Comprises seals, sea lions, and the walrus.

Mammals

The cries of male howler monkeys can be heard from **3 mi away**

Largest monkey

The male mandrill (*Mandrillus sphinx*) of equatorial West Africa has a head and body length of 2 ft–2 ft 6 in (61–76 cm) and a tail measuring 2–3 in (5.2–7.6 cm). Males average 55 lb (25 kg) but can weigh 119 lb (54 kg). The mandrill's distinctive blue rump, red-stripe face, and yellow beard make it one of the most vividly colored mammals.

CHIROPTERANS

Largest bat colony
Up to 20 million female Mexican free-tailed bats (*Tadarida brasiliensis*) and offspring live in Bracken Cave in San Antonio, Texas, USA. Up to 500 baby bats occupy 1 sq ft (0.09 m²) of space. The colony's nightly flight out for food forms a column that can be picked up on the local airport radar.

Largest bat family
As of Nov 2013, there were 300 species of vesper bat (Vespertilionidae), with new ones described every year. Among the members are the common pipistrelles, the European serotine, the noctules, the tube-nosed, the mouse-eared, and the rare barbastelle.

Longest gestation period for a bat
The common vampire bat (*Desmodus rotundus*) has a gestation period of seven to eight months, and when the baby bat is born, it suckles its mother for an additional nine months and sometimes even longer. Native to Mexico, Central America, and South America, vampire bats feed solely on blood.

INSECTIVORES

Largest mammalian brain-to-body mass
Shrews have brains that constitute 10% of their total body weight.

Most dangerous insectivore
The solenodon is a small, innocuous-looking, ratlike Caribbean mammal. The Haitian solenodon (*Solenodon paradoxus*) and the rare Cuban solenodon (*Solenodon cubanus*) have toxic saliva that is potentially dangerous to humans.

Largest bat
Bats are the only mammals capable of true flight (i.e., by flapping wings) instead of gliding. The largest are the flying foxes or fruit bats (Pteropodidae), which can have a wingspan of 5 ft 7 in (1.7 m).

Smallest primate

The pygmy mouse lemur (*Microcebus myoxinus*) from Madagascar is about 2.4 in (62 mm) long with a tail of 5.3 in (136 mm) and an average weight of 1.1 oz (30.6 g). A white stripe runs from nose to forehead, and a black stripe runs down its back.

Heaviest tree shrew
Tree shrews resemble squirrels with pointed snouts and no whiskers. Fully grown male specimens of the Mindanao tree shrew (*Urogale everetti*), native to the Philippines, have been recorded weighing 12 oz (350 g).

Most sensitive animal organ
The star-nosed mole (*Condylura cristata*) takes its name from its 22-probed nose covered with 25,000 sensory receptors— five times the amount of touch-sensitive nerve fibers in a human hand.

FACT
Shrews have a big appetite: in just one day, they can eat their own body weight in bugs and worms!

Smallest monkey

Pygmy marmosets (*Callithrix pygmaea*) weigh 0.53 oz (15 g) at birth and grow to an average of 4.19 oz (119 g). They are 5.3 in (136 mm) long, excluding tail. Despite their size, pygmy marmosets can leap 16 ft 5 in (5 m) in the air.

CHIROPTERAN, INSECTIVORE, AND PRIMATE SIZES

Male eastern lowland gorilla: Height 5 ft 8 in, weight 360 lb

Mandrill: Height 2 ft–2 ft 6 in, weight 55 lb

Large and gigantic flying fox (fruit bat): Wingspan 5 ft 7 in, weight 3 lb 8 oz

Giant otter shrew: Head-to-tail length 2 ft 1 in, weight 2 lb 1 oz

Moonrat: Head-to-tail length 1 ft 5 in– 2 ft 4 in, weight 2 lb 3 oz–4 lb 6 oz

 Koala bears

Sleepiest marsupial: Because of its low-quality diet of eucalyptus leaves, koalas (*Phascolarctos cinereus*) spend up to 18 hr out of every 24 asleep.

Largest koala litter: Two—a pair of identical twins called Euca and Lyptus, born on Apr 10–11, 1999 in Queensland, Australia.

Oldest koala: Sarah, who died in 2001 at the age of 23 years, was born in 1978 and lived at the Lone Pine Koala Sanctuary in Queensland, Australia; koalas typically live for 16 years in captivity.

Oldest koala sanctuary: The Lone Pine Koala Sanctuary, where Sarah lived; it was established in 1927 by Claude Reid (AUS) and still operates today.

Largest insectivore

The moonrat (*Echinosorex gymnurus*) is neither a rat nor from the Moon! Found in southeast Asia, it is actually a giant relative of the hedgehog, but with thick fur instead of spikes. It is 10 in–1 ft 6 in (26–46 cm) long with a tail of 6–9 in (17–25 cm), and weighs 2 lb 3 oz–4 lb 6 oz (1–2 kg).

(163 kg) and has a typical bipedal height of up to 5 ft 9 in (1.75 m). The tallest recorded in the wild was a 6-ft 5-in (1.95-m) mountain bull shot in the eastern Congo on May 16, 1938.

Largest nocturnal primate

The aye-aye (*Daubentonia madagascariensis*) from Madagascar is rodentlike but closely related to lemurs. Under threat for being seen as an omen of death, the aye-aye weighs 5 lb 15 oz (2.7 kg) and averages 2 ft (65 cm) in length for the male, more than half of which is accounted for by its long tail.

Smallest loris

Lorises are small, nocturnal primates related to lemurs

Smallest mammal

Kitti's hog-nosed bat (*Craseonycteris thonglongyai*), aka the bumblebee bat, is 1.14–1.29 in (29–33 mm) long. Found in caves in Thailand and Myanmar, it was rated as "vulnerable" on the International Union for Conservation of Nature (IUCN) red list of threatened species.

and bushbabies. The smallest is the pygmy slow loris (*Nycticebus pygmaeus*), which measures 7.6–9 in (19.5–23 cm) in length, with a tail averaging 0.7 in (1.8 cm). It weighs 1–2 oz (36–58 g).

Smallest mammal on land

Savi's pygmy shrew (*Suncus etruscus*) is no bigger than a human thumb. Its body measures 1.4–2 in (36–53 mm) and its tail 0.9–1.1 in (24–29 mm). It weighs just 0.05–0.09 oz (1.5–2.6 g).

MARSUPIALS

Longest proportionate animal cecum

A cecum is a kind of pouch in the large intestine, which in herbivores contains bacteria that help to break down the cellulose present in plant material. The largest in the animal kingdom relative to body size belongs to the koala (*Phascolarctos cinereus*). It is 6 ft 7 in (2 m) long and 4 in (10 cm) in diameter, while the koala's own body length is just 2–2 ft 9 in (60–85 cm).

Most nipples

The female shrewish short-tailed opossum (*Monodelphis sorex*) has up to 27 nipples (or "mammae"), despite being tiny: 4–5 in (11–13 cm) with a tail of 2.5–3.3 in (6.5–8.5 cm).

Most northerly marsupial

The Virginia opossum (*Didelphis virginiana*) is the only species of marsupial that lives north of Mexico. It has been recorded as far north as southwestern Ontario in Canada.

PRIMATES

Largest primate

The male eastern lowland gorilla (*Gorilla beringei graueri*), found in the eastern Congo, weighs up to 360 lb

Largest mammal to build a nest

Male African gorillas (*Gorilla gorilla*) measure 5 ft 6 in–6 ft (1.7–1.8 m) and weigh 300–500 lb (136–227 kg). They create a new ground nest from the surrounding vegetation every day. The nests are circular and typically measure 3 ft 3 in (1 m) in diameter. Some lighter members of the troop build in trees and many make a separate nest during the day for a nap. These constructions are also the **largest nests built by a mammal**.

FACT

The **largest primate of all time** was *Gigantopithecus blacki*—a veritable King Kong, now extinct for 100,000 years—standing 9 ft 10 in tall and weighing 3,480 lb.

Largest marsupial: red kangaroo

There are nearly 60 species of kangaroo, the biggest being the red (*Macropus rufus*) from the dry center of Australia. The male red measures 5 ft 10 in tall and 9 ft 4 in long, and can weigh 200 lb. Reds arrive as the **largest newborn marsupial**, but because all marsupials are born very early, the reds weigh just 0.02 oz; it would take 36,000 newborns to equal their mother's weight. The **longest jump by a kangaroo** was in New South Wales, Australia, in 1951, when a female bounded 42 ft.

Glossary

Chiropteran: has forelimbs modified as wings; uses echolocation to navigate

Insectivore: insect-eating mammal

Marsupial: characterized by pouch in which mother carries her young

Primate: has large brain and flexible hands and feet; includes humans

Mammals

Giraffes give birth standing up, so newborn calves typically fall 5 ft to the ground

RODENTS

First domesticated rodent
The guinea pig or South American cavy (*Cavia porcellus*) was first bred as a food animal in the Andes in around 5000 BC. It is thought to be a domesticated version of the montane guinea pig (*C. tschudii*) native to the mountains of Peru.

Smallest ungulate
The lesser Malay mouse deer (*Tragulus javanicus*) has a body length of 1 ft 5 in–1 ft 9 in (42–55 cm), a shoulder height of 8–10 in (20–25 cm), and weighs 3 lb 4 oz–5 lb 8 oz (1.5–2.5 kg). Primarily nocturnal, this small ungulate is rarely seen.

Longest-lived rodent
Africa's naked mole rat (*Heterocephalus glaber*) spends its life in underground burrow systems located beneath East Africa's drier tropical grasslands, and can live for 28 years.

Smallest gliding rodent
The pygmy scalytail (*Idiurus zenkeri*) is also known as a flying mouse. Native to Central and East Africa, it has a maximum length of 7 in (18 cm), of which its long, featherlike tail accounts for more than half. It has a gliding membrane between the forelimb and hind limb on each side of its body, which it expands when leaping from a tree, enabling it to glide through the air.

Largest rodent ever
Josephoartigasia monesi was a 2-million-year-old fossil species that lived in what is today coastal Uruguay. It is currently known only from a single skull measuring 1 ft 9 in (53 cm) long, from which scientists estimate that the complete animal probably weighed 2,200 lb (1 metric ton).

Tallest mammal
Giraffes (*Giraffa camelopardalis*) are found in the dry savanna and open woodland areas of sub-Saharan Africa. An adult male giraffe typically measures between 15 ft and 18 ft (4.6–5.5 m) in height.

Largest jerboa
Jerboas are desert-dwelling rodents that jump and leap on their hind legs like miniature kangaroos. The suitably named great jerboa (*Allactaga major*) has an uppermost head-and-body length of 7 in (18 cm), with a tail that can grow to 10.2 in (26 cm). It primarily inhabits deserts in Russia, Kazakhstan, Turkmenistan, and Uzbekistan.

Largest squirrel
The Indian or Malabar giant squirrel (*Ratufa indica*) is endemic to deciduous and moist evergreen forests in peninsular India. It can grow to 3 ft 3 in (1 m) long, of which its long bushy tail constitutes two-thirds.

Fewest teeth for a rodent
Also known as the small-toothed moss-mouse, and native to Indonesia and Papua New Guinea, Shaw Mayer's shrew mouse (*Pseudohydromys ellermani*) has eight teeth—four incisors and four molars, with no canines or premolars.

The **most teeth for a rodent** is the silvery mole rat (*Heliophobius argenteocinereus*). Native to Central and East Africa, including Tanzania, Kenya, and the Democratic Republic of the Congo, it has no fewer than 24 grinding teeth (premolars and molars) plus four incisors: 28 teeth in all.

Largest rhinoceros
Restricted to southern Africa, the southern white rhinoceros (*Ceratotherium simum simum*) can grow to a length of 13 ft 9 in (4.2 m), with an uppermost shoulder height of 6 ft (1.85 m) and weight of 7,930 lb (3.6 metric tons).

Jumbo size: African elephant
The adult male African elephant (*Loxodonta africana*) is not only the **largest ungulate** but also the **largest land mammal**. It typically stands 9 ft 10 in–12 ft at the shoulder and, at 8,800–15,400 lb, can weigh more than 100 average-size men. The tallest in Africa are members of the endangered desert race from Damaraland in Namibia. A bull elephant shot near Sesfontein in Damaraland on Apr 4, 1978 was the tallest recorded example. It measured 14 ft 6 in in a line from the shoulder to the bottom of the forefoot—as tall as a London double-decker bus!

Glossary

Rodent: Largest order of mammals, found on every continent except Antarctica; characterized by their paired upper and lower incisor teeth ("rodent" means "gnawing").

Ungulate: Broadly defined as a mammal with hooves (enlarged, modified toenails that, unlike claws and nails, support its weight).

UNGULATES

Smallest rhinoceros

Once widespread across southeastern Asia but now confined to Sumatra, the Malay Peninsula, and Borneo, the Sumatran rhinoceros (*Dicerorhinus sumatrensis*) has a maximum head-and-body length of 10 ft 5 in (3.18 m), tail length of 2 ft 3 in (70 cm), and shoulder height of 4 ft 9 in (1.45 m).

Largest herd of white deer

Within the former Seneca Army Depot in Seneca County, New York, USA, is a herd of some 300 white

Least classifiable mammal

The African aardvark (*Orycteropus afer*) has cylindrical teeth unlike those of any other mammal and claws instead of the hooves of other ungulates. It has its own order—Tubulidentata ("tube teeth").

Largest deer

A male Alaskan moose (*Alces alces gigas*) standing 7 ft 8 in (2.34 m) tall and weighing an estimated 1,800 lb (816 kg) was shot in the Yukon territory of Canada in Sep 1897. The **smallest deer** is the northern pudu (*Pudu mephistophiles*), which grows to 1 ft 1 in (35 cm) tall at the shoulder and weighs up to 13 lb 3 oz (6 kg). It is found in Colombia, Ecuador, and Peru.

deer. Their species is the North American white-tailed deer (*Odocoileus virginianus*), and their white coat results from a recessive nonalbino mutant gene allele.

The **rarest deer** is the Bawean (*Hyelaphus kuhlii*), limited to the tiny Indonesian island of Bawean. Fewer than 250 mature individuals are believed to exist. It is categorized as "Critically Endangered" by the International Union for Conservation of Nature (IUCN).

Largest camel

The dromedary or one-humped camel (*Camelus dromedarius*) has a top head-and-body length of 11 ft 5 in (3.5 m), with a maximum shoulder height of 7 ft 10 in (2.4 m), and it can weigh 1,520 lb (690 kg). Native to the Middle East, it survives today as a feral animal only in Australia and Spain.

Largest wild pig

Central Africa's giant forest hog (*Hylochoerus meinertzhageni*) has a head–body length of 6 ft 10 in (2.1 m), a shoulder height of 3 ft 5 in (1.05 m), and can weigh 600 lb (275 kg).

Actual Size

Smallest rodent

Both the northern pygmy mouse (*Baiomys taylori*, above) of Mexico and the USA and the Baluchistan pygmy jerboa (*Salpingotulus michaelis*) of Pakistan have a 1.4-in (3.6-cm) head-to-body length and 2.8-in (7.2-cm) tail.

Longest hair for a domestic cattle breed

The domestic cattle (*Bos taurus*) with the longest hair is the Highland cattle. Originating in Scotland but subsequently exported worldwide, this famously hirsute breed has an average hair length of 1 ft 1 in (35 cm). This is measured from the length of the "dossan" (bangs) and also the length of hair in the ears.

RODENT AND UNGULATE SIZES

Giraffe:
Height 15–18 ft, weight 3,500 lb

Never forget ...
The largest land mammal (African elephant) is nearly 3 million times heavier than the smallest (pygmy shrew)!

Adult male African elephant:
Height 9 ft 10 in–12 ft, weight 8,800 lb–15,400 lb

Southern white rhinoceros: Length 13 ft 9 in, weight 7,930 lb

Capybara:
Length 4 ft 3 in, weight 175 lb

Lesser Malay mouse deer:
Length 1 ft 5 in–1 ft 9 in, weight 3 lb 4 oz–5 lb 8 oz

Pygmy mouse:
Height 1.4 in, tail length 2.8 in

FACT

The World Wildlife Fund (WWF) has five ungulates on its critically endangered list: saola (*Pseudoryx nghetinhensis*), Sumatran elephant (*Elephas maximus sumatranus*), Sumatran rhinoceros (*Dicerorhinus sumatrensis*), black rhinoceros (*Diceros bicornis*), and Javan rhinoceros (*Rhinoceros sondaicus*).

Birds

Longest-toed bird (relative to body)

The chicken-size northern jacana (*Jacana spinosa*) has four toes, each about 2.8 in (7 cm) long. When fully extended, they span 26 sq in (168 cm²), enabling the bird to walk on lily pads and other floating vegetation.

Largest owl

The European race of the eagle owl (*Bubo bubo*) has an average length of 2 ft 2 in–2 ft 4 in (66–71 cm), an average weight of 3 lb 8 oz–8 lb 13 oz (1.6–4 kg), and a wingspan of more than 5 ft (1.5 m).

Largest woodpecker

The imperial woodpecker (*Campephilus imperialis*) measures up to 1 ft 11 in (60 cm) long. It was formerly widespread across Mexico, but due to extensive habitat destruction its numbers rapidly plummeted. The last confirmed sighting was in 1956, but observations by locals continued into the mid-1990s. It is categorized as "Critically Endangered," possibly extinct, by the International Union for Conservation of Nature (IUCN).

Loudest parrot

Research conducted at San Diego Zoo in California, USA, recorded shrieks reaching 135 decibels by the Moluccan (salmon-crested) cockatoo (*Cacatua moluccensis*), native to the Moluccas in Indonesia.

Fastest wingbeat

During its diving courtship displays, the ruby-throated hummingbird (*Archilochus colubris*) has a wingbeat rate of 200 beats per sec, as opposed to the 90 beats per sec produced by other hummingbirds.

Smallest swan

The smallest swan—but largest species of South American waterfowl—is the black-necked swan (*Cygnus melancoryphus*). It grows up to 4 ft (1.24 m) long, with a wingspan of 5 ft 9 in (1.77 m). The coscoroba swan (*Coscoroba coscoroba*) is slightly smaller, but it is no longer thought to be closely related to true swans and may well be a swan in name only.

Smallest bird

Male bee hummingbirds (*Mellisuga helenae*) of Cuba measure 2.24 in (57 mm) long, half of which is the bill and tail. They weigh just 0.056 oz (1.6 g), generally regarded as the lowest limit for warm-blooded animals. Females are slightly larger.

Actual Size

Rarest heron

The global population of the white-bellied (imperial) heron (*Ardea insignis*) is estimated at no more than 400 birds and is thought to be decreasing. It is categorized as "Critically Endangered" by the IUCN. The species is native to the eastern Himalayan foothills of India, Myanmar, Bhutan, and possibly Bangladesh but is now extinct in Nepal.

Rarest kingfisher

The Tuamotu kingfisher (*Todiramphus gambieri*) is confined entirely to a very small area on the single island of Niau in the Tuamotu Archipelago of French Polynesia. As of 2013, only 125–135 birds still exist. It is threatened by non-native rats and cats, as well as by cyclone-induced habitat destruction.

FACT

Birds are closely related to dinosaurs. In the USA, there are plans to retro-engineer a dinosaur using chicken DNA.

Largest toucan

The largest species of toucan is the toco toucan (*Ramphastos toco*), which weighs up to 1 lb 14 oz (876 g) and grows up to 2 ft 1 in (65 cm) long—one-third of which is its huge bill. Males are larger than females. It is native to much of eastern and central South America, but particularly Brazil.

⚡ Brink of extinction

The North American ivory-billed woodpecker (*Campephilus principalis*) remains the **rarest bird**. Sixty years ago, we said that it "may even be extinct. It is believed that less than a dozen still exist in the Florida area." Today, our consultant Karl Shuker says, "I consider there to be good evidence that it survives, albeit very precariously."

Ostr-etch: tall story

The North African ostrich (*Struthio camelus camelus*) is the **largest living bird**. Males have been recorded at 9 ft tall and weighing 345 lb. It cannot fly, but the ostrich makes up for that by being the **fastest flightless bird on land**, reaching 45 mph. Its powerful strides can exceed 23 ft and are comparable to those of the **fastest land mammal**, the cheetah. It can also attack with a powerful kick. Because of its size, the ostrich is also the bird that lays the **smallest eggs relative to body weight**: only 1.4–1.5% of its total mass.

Fastest bird diving

The peregrine falcon (*Falco peregrinus*)—found on almost all continents—is thought to reach a terminal velocity of around 186 mph (300 km/h) in a diving stoop. At this point, it is the fastest animal on the planet. Bad news for any prey below.

Fastest bird in level flight

In a report published by French and British researchers working in the sub-Antarctic, the average estimated ground speed for a satellite-tagged grey-headed albatross (*Thalassarche chrysostoma*) is 78.9 mph (127 km/h), sustained for more than 8 hr while returning to its nest at Bird Island, South Georgia, in the middle of a storm.

Actual Size

Largest family of birds

The Tyrannidae family of tyrant flycatchers has more than 400 species, including the brown-crested flycatcher (*Myiarchus tyrannulus*, above left), lesser kiskadee (*Philohydor lictor*, below left), and vermilion flycatcher (*Pyrocephalus rubinus*, below). Highly diverse in form, these insectivorous birds live in North, Central, and South America.

Most airborne bird

After leaving its nesting grounds as a youngster, the sooty tern (*Sterna fuscata*) remains aloft for 3–10 years while maturing, settling on water from time to time before returning to land to breed as an adult.

The **longest bird migration** is that of the Arctic tern (*Sterna paradisaea*). It breeds north of the Arctic Circle, then flies south to the Antarctic for the northern winter and back again—a round trip of approximately 50,000 mi (80,467 km).

Smallest flightless bird

Found only on a small area of land in the South Atlantic, the Inaccessible Island rail (*Atlantisia rogersi*) weighs a mere 1.4 oz (40 g). First discovered in 1870, the birds are around the size of a three-day-old chicken.

The **longest time for a bird to learn to fly** is exhibited by the wandering albatross (*Diomedea exulans*), whose chicks take 278–280 days on average to make their first flight after hatching. Because it takes so long for the young albatross to get to this stage, the adults breed only once every two years.

Most expensive pigeon

On May 18, 2013, pigeon breeder Leo Heremans (BEL) sold his racing pigeon for 310,000 euros ($400,000) on www.pipa.be. The pigeon, Bolt, was named after world-record-holding Jamaican sprinter Usain Bolt and will be used for breeding.

Shortest bills

The shortest avian bills in relation to body length belong to the smaller swifts (Apodidae family), and in particular to the glossy swiftlet (*Collocalia esculenta*), whose bill is almost nonexistent.

Longest bills

The Australian pelican (*Pelecanus conspicillatus*) is the bill to beat, at 1 ft 1 in–1 ft 6.5 in (34–47 cm). But the **longest beak in relation to body length** is that of the sword-billed hummingbird (*Ensifera ensifera*) of the Andes from Venezuela to Bolivia. The beak measures 4 in (10.2 cm), making it longer than its body without the tail.

TOP OF THE BILL: BIRDS SEEDED

Black-legged falconet: Head-to-tail length 5.5–5.9 in, weight 1.23 oz

Bee hummingbird: length 2.24 in, weight 0.056 oz

Male wandering albatross: Wingspan 11 ft 11 in, weight 13–28 lb

Andean condor: Wingspan 10 ft 6 in, weight 33 lb

North African ostrich: Height 9 ft, weight 345 lb

Best of the nests

- **Highest nest:** Marbled murrelets (*Brachyramphus marmoratus*) nest as high up as 147 ft.
- **Largest ground nest:** Malleefowl (*Leipoa ocellata*) nests contain up to 8,100 cu ft of matter and weigh up to 660,000 lb.
- **Longest nest burrow:** Rhinoceros auklet (*Cerorhinca monocerata*) nest burrows typically measure 6–10 ft long.

Reptiles & amphibians

More than **6,000 species of lizard** are known to exist

Heaviest venomous snake

The eastern diamondback rattlesnake (*Crotalus adamanteus*) weighs 12–15 lb (5.5–6.8 kg), with the biggest on record at 34 lb (15 kg). Other contenders are the king cobra (*Ophiophagus hannah*), up to 20 lb (9 kg), and the gaboon viper (*Bitis gabonica*), weighing 18 lb 12 oz (8.5 kg).

Fastest lizard
The Costa Rican spiny-tailed iguana (*Ctenosaura similis*) can attain a land speed of 21.7 mph (34.9 km/h).

Highest frequency frog croak
The concave-eared torrent frog (*Odorrana tormota*) of eastern China croaks at a frequency of 128 kHz—an ultrasonic emission well beyond the range of human hearing (which cannot detect sound frequencies above 20 kHz).

The reason that this frog produces such a high-frequency croak is to overcome the very loud low-frequency sound of the waterfalls near which it lives in order to communicate with others of its species.

Largest caiman
Caimans are alligator-related crocodilians and, of their six species, the largest is the black caiman (*Melanosuchus niger*). Old males can sometimes exceed 16 ft 5 in (5 m) in length and 880 lb (400 kg) in weight. The black caiman is native to rivers and swamps in the Amazon basin.

Largest frog

The goliath frog (*Conraua goliath*) is 1 ft (30 cm) long on average, the same size as a rabbit. The largest individual specimen was captured in Apr 1889 in Cameroon with an overall length of 2 ft 10.5 in (87.63 cm). Classified as "endangered" by the International Union for Conservation of Nature (IUCN), the frog is found mainly in Central Africa.

Largest plant-eating lizard
Jim Morrison, singer with The Doors, called himself "The Lizard King." In his honor, an extinct species of iguana was named *Barbaturex morrisoni*. It was almost 6 ft 6 in (2 m) in length and inhabited what is now Burma during the Eocene epoch, some 40–36 million years ago. High temperatures may have helped the lizard evolve to its unusual size.

Most poisonous newt
The California newt (*Taricha torosa*) is poisonous all

Rarest tree frog

Rabbs' fringe-limbed tree frog (*Ecnomiohyla rabborum*) was only discovered by science in 2005, and just one living specimen is currently known to exist. The male lives at the Atlanta Botanical Garden in Georgia, USA.

Longest iguana species

The green, or common, iguana (*Iguana iguana*) can exceed 6 ft 6 in (2 m) in length. Found in an extensive range from Brazil and Paraguay to as far north as Mexico and the Caribbean, they are among the largest lizards in the Americas. Iguanas live near water and are excellent swimmers, feeding largely on leaves, flowers, and fruit.

⚡ Longest frog jump

A frog-jumping contest recorded in our 1955 edition produced the **longest frog jump** by an amphibian athlete named Can't Take It. On May 17, 1953 before a crowd of 30,000 in California, USA, it soared 15 ft 6.5 in. The record was leapfrogged with a stunning performance by a South African sharp-nosed frog (*Ptychadena oxyrhynchus*) named Santjie, who was competing in a triple jump. On May 21, 1977, Santjie flew 33 ft 9 in—about half the length of a basketball court.

REPTILE SCALES

Papuan or Salvadori's monitor: length 15 ft 7 in

Komodo dragon: length 10 ft

Galápagos giant tortoise: length 4 ft 5 in

Estuarine or saltwater crocodile: length 23 ft

Black-and-white tegu: length 4 ft 7 in

Reticulated python: length 32 ft 9.5 in (longest specimen discovered)

Largest tegu

The black-and-white or Argentine giant tegu (*Tupinambis merianae*) is native to east and central South America and can grow to 4 ft 7 in (1.4 m) in length and weigh 15 lb 7 oz (7 kg). Tegus are predatory, and they are popularly kept as pets by reptile fanciers.

over: its skin, muscles, and blood contain tetrodotoxin, a toxic and powerful nerve poison that is a hundred times more deadly than cyanide. It's the same stuff that makes the puffer fish (Tetraodontidae) the **most poisonous edible fish**. The newt itself is immune to the effects of venom.

Smallest crocodilian

Females of the dwarf caiman (*Paleosuchus palpebrosus*) of northern South America rarely exceed a length of 4 ft (1.2 m) and males often don't grow more than 4 ft 11 in (1.5 m). They are generally nocturnal and usually solitary.

Smallest lizard family

The Lanthanotidae family of lizards has just one member—the earless monitor (*Lanthanotus borneensis*). This is an evolutionary oddity known only in Sarawak, Borneo. It lacks external ears, and the nearest relatives of this small family are the true monitors and the venomous Gila monster and beaded lizards.

Most legs for a worm lizard

As their name suggests, worm lizards resemble earthworms and are generally limbless. But four of the 180-plus species—known as ajolotes (*Bipes* spp.) and confined to Mexico—possess a pair of small forelimbs with large clawed feet positioned behind the head. These limbs are sometimes mistaken for ears.

Actual Size

Most geographically restricted python

Liasis mackloti savuensis is confined to the tiny Indonesian island of Savu, south of Java, from which it gets its common name: the Savu Island python. Savu is the largest of the three Savu Islands, whose total area is only 178 sq mi (460.84 km²).

Smelliest species of frog

The skunk frog (*Aromobates nocturnus*) of Venezuela is well named. Measuring 2.44 in (6.2 cm) long, it is a member of the poison-arrow frog family (Dendrobatidae), yet its defensive skin secretion contains not toxin but the same stink-producing compound present in the anal emissions of mammalian skunks.

Most powerful species of vertebrate

In terms of watts of power generated per pound of muscle, the giant palm salamander (*Bolitoglossa dofleini*) of Central America is the strongest vertebrate species. Its tongue explodes outwards at 818 watts per lb (18,000 watts per kg) of muscle. It is believed that elastic collagen tissue in the salamander's tongue stores up energy prior to its explosive release, much like a stretched rubber band or a bowstring drawn back.

FACT

A typical Salvadori's monitor might have a body of 3 ft 11 in but a tail of more than double that: up to 8 ft 10 in. By comparison, the average Komodo dragon is 7 ft 4 in long.

Longest lizard

While the **largest lizard** overall may be the bulky Komodo dragon (*Varanus komodoensis*), Salvadori's monitor (*Varanus salvadorii*) has an impressive tail to tell. Its lengthy appendage brings the total length of the Papua New Guinean lizard up to a maximum of 15 ft 7 in (4.75 m).

Scaled up: long snakes

The reticulated python (*Python reticulatus*) of Indonesia, southeast Asia, and the Philippines is the world's **longest snake**. A specimen measured in Indonesia in 1912 was 32 ft 9.5 in long—equivalent in length to the outstretched arms of eight adult men.

Pictured is Si Belang, a 19 ft 10 in-long python adopted by the Toe family in Borneo. The 132-lb snake lives, sleeps, eats, and bathes with the family, including three-year-old Karim. Si Belang is not a threat to the Toes; he recognizes them as his own family and their home as his territory.

I toad you so

Largest toad: Cane toad (*Bufo marinus*), 5.8 lb; 1 ft 9.2 in long

Most paternal amphibian: Male midwife toad (*Alytes obstetricans*), carries eggs around its thighs until they hatch

Smallest toad: *Bufo taitanus beiranus* from Africa, 0.9 in in length

Fishes

The whale shark is **not a shark**; a starfish is **not a fish**; an electric eel is **not an eel**

Largest carp species

The Siamese giant carp (*Catlocarpio siamensis*), aka giant barb, is the largest of the cyprinid (carp) family. The longest specimens currently reported —such as the 225-lb (102-kg) barb above—are around 5 ft 10 in (1.8 m) in length, while the longest known specimen measured 9 ft 10 in (3 m).

long, almost twice the length of the whale shark, the **largest fish** alive today (see p. 42).

Largest freshwater fish

The largest fish that spends its whole life in fresh or brackish water is the Mekong giant catfish (*Pangasianodon gigas*), principally of the Mekong River basin, and *Pangasius sanitwongsei*, mainly of the Chao Phraya River basin, both native to southeast Asia. Both species are reputed to grow to 9 ft 10 in (3 m) and weigh 660 lb (300 kg). The *Arapaima gigas* of South America is reported to reach 14 ft 9 in (4.5 m) long, but it weighs only 440 lb (200 kg).

Smallest fish

The smallest adult fish—and indeed the **smallest vertebrate**—is a mature male *Photocorynus spiniceps* anglerfish, which is just 0.24 in (6.2 mm) long and is found in the Philippine Sea. The male's primary purpose is to facilitate reproduction. To do so, he permanently attaches himself to the larger female by biting her back, belly, or sides, in the manner of a parasite. The female is responsible for swimming and for eating.

The **smallest freshwater fish** is the dwarf pygmy goby (*Pandaka pygmaea*), a colorless and nearly transparent species found in the streams and lakes of Luzon in the

Actual Size

Slowest fish

The slowest-moving marine fish are the sea horses (family Syngnathidae), of which there are just over 30 species. Some of the smaller species, such as the dwarf sea horse (*Hippocampus zosterae*, above), which reaches a maximum length of only 1.6 in (4.2 cm), probably never attain speeds of more than 0.001 mph (0.016 km/h).

Largest fish ever

In 2008, two palaeontology students discovered a specimen of the marine fossil species *Leedsichthys problematicus* in clay pits near Peterborough in Cambridgeshire, UK. Dating back 155 million years, this particular specimen measured 72 ft (22 m)

Longest bony fish

The lengthiest of the bony or "true" fishes (class Pisces, aka Osteichthyes— see Glossary, below) is the oarfish (*Regalecus glesne*), or the "King of the Herrings," which has worldwide distribution. In ca. 1885, a 25-ft-long (7.6-m) example weighing 600 lb (272 kg) was caught by fishermen off Pemaquid Point in Maine, USA. The specimen pictured here was found dead in the water off Toyon Bay, California, USA, on Oct 13, 2013, by staff of the Catalina Island Marine Institute; it measured 18 ft (5.5 m) long.

FACT

An oarfish seen swimming by a team of scientists off New Jersey, USA, in 1963 was estimated to be 49 ft 10 in long!

✖ Longing for the sea? Turn to p. 38

> ## WHAT A WHOPPER! COMPARING FISH SCALES

Great white shark: length 14 ft 9 in, weight ca. 1,980 lb

Thresher shark: head-to-tip-of-fin length 16 ft 4 in, weight 500 lb

Oarfish: length 24 ft 11 in, weight ca. 600 lb

Actual Size

Photocorynus spiniceps: length 0.24 in

Whale shark: length 41 ft 6 in, weight ca. 33,000 lb

Ocean sunfish: length 9 ft 10 in, weight 4,400 lb

Glossary

Chondrichthyes: cartilaginous fish; have skeletons made of cartilage—a flexible but firm tissue less stiff than bone.

Osteichthyes: bony fish; have skeletons made from bone. There are ca. 28,000 species of Osteichthyes, accounting for 96% of all fish species. They also form the **largest class of vertebrates** (animals with backbones).

FACT
Thresher sharks are believed to use their tails to herd and then stun schools of milling fish ready for eating.

Longest fin

All three species of thresher shark (family Alopiidae) have a huge, scythe-shape caudal (tail) fin that is about as long as the body itself. The largest and most common species, *Alopias vulpinus*, found worldwide in temperate and tropical seas, grows to 19 ft 8 in (6 m) in length, of which almost 9 ft 10 in (3 m) consists of this greatly elongated upper tail fin.

Philippines. Males are only 0.29–0.38 in (7.5–9.9 mm) long and weigh just 4–5 mg.

Highest living fish
The Tibetan loach (family Cobitidae) is found at an altitude of 17,060 ft (5,200 m) in the Himalayas.

Longest fish migration
Many fish species undertake long annual migrations between their feeding grounds. The longest straight-line distance known to have been covered by a fish is 5,800 mi (9,335 km) for a bluefin tuna (*Thunnus thynnus*) that was dart-tagged off Baja California, Mexico, in 1958, and caught 300 mi (483 km) south of Tokyo, Japan, in Apr 1963.

The **longest journey by a freshwater fish** is some 3,000–4,000 mi (4,800–6,400 km), taking about six months, by the European eel (*Anguilla anguilla*). This species spends between seven and 15 years in fresh water in Europe, before abruptly evolving into breeding condition, changing color to become silver, and growing a longer snout and larger eyes. The much-altered animal then begins a marathon trek to the species' spawning grounds in the Sargasso Sea, east of North America.

Most venomous fish
Poisonous creatures contain poison within their bodies, which they pass on to any creatures that consume, or even touch them, while venomous creatures inject venom into their victims. The stonefish (family Synanceiidae) of the tropical waters of the Indo-Pacific are highly venomous. *Synanceia horrida* has the largest venom glands of any known fish. Direct contact with the spines of its fins, which contain a strong neurotoxic poison, can prove fatal.

The **most poisonous fish** is the puffer fish (*Tetraodon*) of the Red Sea and Indo-Pacific region, which produces a fatally poisonous toxin called tetrodotoxin. Its ovaries,

FACT
There are more fish in the Amazon River than there are in all of Europe.

Fastest fish
The cosmopolitan sailfish (*Istiophorus platypterus*) is considered to be the fastest species of fish over short distances, although practical difficulties make measurements extremely hard to secure. Trials at the Long Key Fishing Camp in Florida, USA, suggested a top speed of 68 mph (109 km/h).

eggs, blood, liver, intestines, and, to a lesser extent, its skin, contain tetrodotoxin. Less than 0.004 oz (0.1 g) is enough to kill a human adult in as little as 20 min.

Most ferocious freshwater fish
Piranhas are renowned for their ferocity, particularly those of the genera *Serrasalmus* and *Pygocentrus*, found in the large rivers of South America. Attracted to blood and frantic splashing, a school of piranhas can within minutes strip an animal as large as a horse of its flesh, leaving only its skeleton.

FACT
Technically, there is no such thing as a "fish"— the creatures on these pages are from many different animal families.

Heaviest bony fish

The ocean sunfish (*Mola mola*) has been recorded weighing 4,400 lb (1,995 kg) and measuring 10 ft (3 m) from fin tip to fin tip. *Mola mola*— named from the Latin for "millstone" in reference to its shape—is found in all oceans in tropical or temperate climates and feeds on zooplankton, small fishes, and algae. Sharks and rays, by contrast, are cartilaginous, not bony as in the case of the ocean sunfish.

Shark attack: great white shark

The **largest predatory fish** is the great white shark (*Carcharodon carcharias*, from the Greek for "sharp-toothed"). Adults average 14–15 ft in length—as long as a typical family sedan car— and generally weigh 1,980 lb. There are many claims of huge specimens up to 33 ft long, and plenty of circumstantial evidence suggests that some great whites grow to more than 20 ft in length. Pictured here is a lucky seal escaping the jaws of a great white, snapped in Jul 2013 off the coast of Seal Island, South Africa, by photographer David Jenkins.

⚡ Freshwater giant

In our 1955 edition, the **largest freshwater fish** was the 22-ft-long giant Russian sturgeon (*Acipenser*), found in the Volga River. "However, we now know that this is not an exclusively freshwater species," says our animal consultant Dr. Karl Shuker. "At 9 ft 11 in, the largest fish that spends its whole life in fresh water is Asia's Mekong giant catfish." (see p. 56)

Crustaceans

A female skeleton shrimp **consumes the male** shortly after mating

Most abundant animal

Copepods, found almost everywhere with water, comprise 12,000 species and form groups that can reach a trillion individuals. Most are less than 0.04 in (1 mm) long.

Deepest-living crustacean

In Nov 1980, live amphipods were found at a depth of 34,450 ft (10,500 m) in Challenger Deep, the **deepest point on Earth**, in the Mariana Trench of the western Pacific Ocean.

Longest journey by a crab

In Dec 2006, it was reported that an American Columbus crab (*Planes minutus*) had been discovered washed up but still alive on a beach in Bournemouth, UK—5,000 mi (8,000 km) from its home in the Sargasso Sea, east of Florida, USA. The 6-in (15-cm) crab is believed to have made its journey by clinging to barnacles on a buoy for three months, surviving storms, predators, and sharp changes in sea temperature.

Fastest-swimming crustacean

Henslow's swimming crab (*Polybius henslowii*), native to the eastern Atlantic Ocean, has been timed at 4 ft 3 in/s (1.3 m/s) in captivity. It is probable that it would be able to swim even faster under natural conditions in the wild.

First venomous crustacean

Xibalbanus (previously *Speleonectes*) *tulumensis* feeds upon other crustaceans. Its claws inject a cocktail of chemicals, including a paralyzing neurotoxin similar to rattlesnake venom. The toxin breaks down the victim's body tissues, turning it into liquid to be sucked up from its prey's exoskeleton. The blind crustacean inhabits underwater caves of the Caribbean, Canary Islands, and Western Australia. *Xibalbanus tulumensis* is a member of the remipede class and is the only crustacean that possesses venom.

Largest freshwater crustacean

The Tasmanian giant freshwater crayfish (*Astacopsis gouldi*) is also the **largest freshwater invertebrate** of any kind. Native to small streams in Tasmania, Australia, it can measure 2 ft 7 in (80 cm) and weigh 11 lb (5 kg). Overfishing and habitat loss have seen the species decline and it is listed as endangered.

Largest extent of color vision

Stomatopods, such as mantis prawns, have eight different types of color photoreceptor in their eyes (humans have three). These reef-dweller crustaceans can distinguish numerous shades within the electromagnetic spectrum's ultraviolet waveband—entirely invisible to humans. Their clear-eye vision is used to identify prey (which is often semi-transparent) and dodge predators.

FACT

Pictured inset is a 3-ft 3-in-long American lobster found off the coast of Maine, USA, on Feb 17, 2012. The 39-lb 10-oz beast was dubbed Rocky before being released back into the wild.

Heaviest marine crustacean

The American or North Atlantic lobster (*Homarus americanus*) is the heaviest marine crustacean. On Feb 11, 1977, a specimen weighing 44 lb 6 oz (20.14 kg) and measuring 3 ft 6 in (1.06 m) from tail fan to the tip of its largest claw was caught off Nova Scotia, Canada. It was sold to a New York restaurant owner.

CRUSTACEAN LENGTHS

Tasmanian giant freshwater crayfish: 2 ft 7 in

Purse crab: 3 ft 3 in

Giant spider crab: leg span 12 ft 1.5 in

Giant acorn barnacle: 2.76 in

Actual Size

Parasitic pea crab: 0.25 in

Common sea slater: 1.2 in

Water fleas (branchiopods): 0.009 in

Glossary

Arthropod: Animal from the phylum Arthropoda (meaning "jointed leg") that includes insects, arachnids, and crustaceans; arthropods account for 80% of all animal species.

Crustacean: A group (or sub-phylum) of arthropod comprising 67,000 described species, from the minuscule 0.003-in-long *Stygotantulus stocki* up to the giant spider crab (*Macrocheira kaempferi*) with its 12-ft 1.5-in span from claw to claw (see above right). They are distinguished from other groups of arthropods by their two-parted limbs and the form taken by their larvae.

Actual Size

Smallest crab
Parasitic pea crabs (*Pinnotheres pisum*) can measure 0.25 in (6.3 mm) across. They live in the organ cavity of bivalve mollusks, such as oysters and mussels, where they tuck into food collected by their molluskan host's gills.

Sharpest night vision for an animal
Gigantocypris is a marine crustacean living at depths of more than 3,300 ft (1,000 m) with almost no sunlight. But this genus of ostracod has eyes with an f-number (a measure of light sensitivity) of 0.25. In comparison, humans measure around f-2.55. Each eye possesses a pair of high-power parabolic reflectors that direct the dim light onto the retina.

Largest barnacle
The giant acorn barnacle (*Balanus nubilus*) stands up to 5 in (12.7 cm) high and measures 2.76 in (7 cm) across. It lives as far down as 300 ft (91 m) and its side plates withstand strong currents. The barnacle is food for whelk snails, which can drill into the shell.

Largest copepod
Pennella balaenopterae is a parasite living on the backs of fin whales (*Balaenoptera physalus*). It can attain a length of 1 ft 0.5 in (32 cm).

Largest wood louse
The common sea slater (*Ligia oceanica*) can grow to 1.2 in (3 cm) long and is twice as long as it is broad. Its speed when startled has earned it the nickname "sea cockroach." It is an aquatic species that breathes air and lives on rocky coasts of temperate waters.

Smallest crustacean
Stygotantulus stocki measures 0.003 in (0.094 mm), making it the **smallest arthropod** of any kind. It is an ectoparasite—a parasite on the surface—of crustaceans called harpacticoid copepods. The **smallest nonparasitic crustaceans** are water fleas (branchiopods) of the genus *Alonella*. These freshwater fleas measure less than 0.009 in (0.25 mm).

Largest marine crustacean
The giant spider crab (*Macrocheira kaempferi*), found off the southeastern coast of Japan, has a leg span of up to 12 ft 1.5 in (3.69 m). Pictured here is "Big Daddy," whose leg span of 10 ft 2.5 in (3.11 m) makes him the **widest crustacean in captivity**. The leggy crab—named after a famous British wrestler—was measured at Sea Life in Blackpool, UK, on Aug 8, 2013.

Rarest crayfish
The endangered Shasta crayfish (*Pacifastacus fortis*) is native to Shasta County in California, USA, where it is found along portions of the Pit River. It occurs in only 5 sq mi (13 km²) of the river, and its fragmented population probably numbers no more than 300 in total.

Fastest land crustacean
Tropical ghost crabs of the genus *Ocypode* can scuttle up to 6 ft/s (2 m/s)—not bad for sideways sprinters. This is equivalent to a human running at 201 mph (324 km/h).

Purse crab: island monster
The **largest** (and **heaviest**) **land-living crustacean** is the purse (or robber, coconut, or tree) crab (*Birgus latro*), which lives on tropical islands and atolls in the Indo-Pacific. It can weigh as much as 9 lb and has a leg span of up to 3 ft 3 in. This type of hermit crab feeds on rotting coconuts, but it will eat a variety of other food. It has been hunted almost to extinction on many islands in the Indian and Pacific oceans, due to its size and its use as a culinary delicacy. The young are hatched in the sea but return to land and lose the ability to survive in the water.

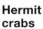
Hermit crabs
Hermit crabs (Paguroidea) aren't true crabs (they have three instead of four pairs of walking legs), but they are crustaceans. They don't have shells; instead, they reuse those that have been abandoned by other creatures. The hermit crab is the **animal with the most chromosomes** (the body's hereditary information), with 127 pairs, compared with just 23 pairs in humans.

Insects & arachnids

For every human, there are an estimated **1.4 billion insects** alive right now

SEE IT 3D WITH THE FREE APP

The **fastest insect wing-beat** under natural conditions is 62,760 beats per min by a tiny midge of the genus *Forcipomyia*.

Most venomous spider

The Brazilian wandering spiders of the genus *Phoneutria* are highly venomous, particularly the Brazilian huntsman (*P. fera*), which has the most active neurotoxic venom of any living spider. Just 0.006 mg of its venom is sufficient to kill a mouse.

Largest appetite relative to weight

The caterpillar of the North American silk moth (*Antheraea polyphemus*) eats more food relative to its own body weight than any other animal. Living on the leaves of oak, birch, willow, and maple trees, it eats up to 86,000 times its own weight during the first 56 days of its life.

Fastest insect

A speed of 3.36 mph (5.4 km/h), or 50 body lengths per sec, was registered by *Periplaneta americana,* the familiar American cockroach of the order Dictyoptera, in 1991.

The **fastest caterpillar** is the larva of the mother-of-pearl moth (*Pleuroptya ruralis*), which can travel at 0.8 mph (1.37 km/h).

The **fastest flying insect** is the Australian dragonfly (*Austrophlebia costalis*), at 36 mph (58 km/h) in short bursts. In 1917, a ground velocity of 61.3 mph (98.6 km/h) was recorded over 240–270 ft (73–82 m).

Least classifiable insect

A newly discovered nymph (juvenile) form of plant hopper resembles nymphs from at least four taxonomic families but has defied classification. It was found in the rain forest of southeastern Suriname.

Actual Size

Most toxic insect venom

Pogonomyrmex maricopa is a stinging species of harvester ant native to Arizona, USA. The LD_{50} value of its venom (the dosage required to kill 50% of mice subjected to it) is 0.0000019 oz/lb when injected intravenously into mice.

Actual Size

Longest insect tongue

Loudest insect

The African cicada (*Brevisana brevis*), discovered in 1850, produces a calling song with a mean sound pressure level of 106.7 decibels at a distance of 1 ft 7 in (50 cm). Songs play a vital role in cicada communication and reproduction.

Most times for an insect to molt

All insects molt several times during the course of their lifetime. Up to 60 molts have been recorded for the firebrat (*Thermobia domestica),* a primitive, wingless insect that is widely distributed in North America and other temperate regions worldwide. The firebrat molts throughout its life, whereas most insects do so only during their juvenile (nymph, or larval) stage.

Largest ant

The wingless queen of the fulvous driver ant *Dorylus fulvus* is native to South Africa. It grows to a maximum length of 1.9 in (5 cm), some 0.7 in (2 cm) longer than the male of the species. The term "fulvous" describes the ant's characteristic tawny brown coloration.

Actual Size

> ## OUTSIZE INSECTS, CENTIPEDES, AND ARACHNIDS

Fulvous driver ant (wingless queen): length 1.9 in

Giant centipede: length 10.2 in

Hercules beetle: length including horns 6.6 in

Titan beetle: body length 5.9 in

Giant water bug: length 4.5 in

Chan's megastick: length 13.9 in

Goliath bird-eating spider: leg span 11 in

Most aggressive butterfly
The powerful flier *Charaxes candiope* of Uganda actively dive-bombs people who invade its territory.

Most dangerous bee
The Africanized honeybee (*Apis mellifera scutellata*) will generally attack only when provoked but is persistent in pursuit. It is very aggressive and fiercely protective of territories up to a 0.5-mi (0.8-km) radius. Its venom is no more potent than that of other bees, but it attacks in swarms so the number of stings inflicted can be fatal.

Most bee stings removed
The greatest number of bee stings sustained by any surviving human subject is 2,443, by Johannes Relleke at the Kamativi tin mine, Gwaii River, in Wankie District, Zimbabwe (then Rhodesia), on Jan 28, 1962. All the stings were removed and counted.

Hardiest beetle
The most indestructible beetle is a small species known as *Niptus hololeucus*. Researcher Malcolm Burr has revealed that no fewer than 1,547 specimens were discovered alive inside a bottle of casein protein that had been stoppered for 12 years.

Actual Size

Most painful insect sting
In 1983, entomologist Justin O. Schmidt (USA) published a detailed pain index of insect stings, based on a four-point scale. The most painful sting, registering 4.0+ on his index, was that of the bullet ant (*Paraponera clavata*), native to Central

Heaviest moth
Native to Australia, the heaviest species of moth is the giant wood moth (*Endoxyla cinereus*). The weightiest specimen on record is an adult female that measured 1.1 oz (31.2 g). Females have a wingspan of approximately 9.8 in (25 cm), while males are only about half that size.

Actual Size

Augmented Reality alert!
3D ON THIS PAGE

(3.9 cm) long. The **smallest species of bee** is *Perdita minima* of south-western USA, measuring just under 0.07 in (2 mm) long and weighing only 0.333 mg (that's 3,030 bees to the gram, or 85,133 to the ounce).

Scorpion
A specimen of *Heterometrus swannerdami* found during World War II in the village of Krishnarajapuram, India, measured 11.5 in (29.2 cm) in length from the tips of the pedipalps (pincers) to the end of the sting.

Cockroach
A preserved female *Megaloblatta longipennis* in the collection of Akira Yokokura (JPN) measures 3.8 in (9.7 cm) long and 1.75 in (4.5 cm) across.

Actual Size

Fastest spider
The giant house spider (*Tegenaria gigantea*) is native to North America. An adult female studied during tests in the UK in 1970 attained a running speed of 1.18 mph (1.90 km/h) over short distances. This is equivalent to covering 33 times her own body length in 10 sec.

Lowest temperature endured by insects
The woolly bear caterpillar of the Greenland tiger moth (*Gynaephora groenlandica*) lives in the high Arctic. It can survive being frozen at -58°F (-50°C) for 10 months of the year.

Bee
Females of the king bee (*Chalicodoma pluto*) from the Moluccas Islands of Indonesia measure 1.5 in

and South America. Schmidt described its sting as "like walking over flaming charcoal with a 3-in [8-cm] rusty nail in your heel."

LARGEST ...

Wasp
A female giant tarantula-hawk wasp (*Pepsis heros*) found in Peru had a wingspan of 4.75 in (12.15 cm) and body length of ca. 2.25 in (6.2 cm).

Actual Size

Heaviest praying mantis
Native to India, Myanmar, Nepal, and Sri Lanka, the weightiest species of praying mantis is the giant Asian mantis *Hierodula membranacea*. The heaviest specimen on record was a well-fed female that was reliably weighed and found to tip the scales at 0.3 oz (9 g)—approximately the same as nine paper clips.

Longest insect tongue
The tongue, or proboscis, of Morgan's sphinx (hawk) moth (*Xanthopan morganii praedicta*) measures up to 1 ft 1 in (35 cm)—more than twice the entire length of the moth. It enables the moth to reach the nectar deep inside the star-shape flowers of the comet, or Darwin's, orchid. The insect is native to Madagascar.

Actual Size

Apian alert: bees at risk
Since around 2006, many bee populations have collapsed—a phenomenon known as colony collapse disorder. Possible causes include poisoning from pesticides, destruction of the bees' natural environments, and parasites that feed on bees' blood. The welfare of the bee impacts directly on our own food chain; with no bees to pollinate them, up to half of our fruit and vegetable plants would disappear, along with animal-feed crops.

Bee-suited: attracting a mantle
A "mantle" is an enormous cluster of bees that forms a protective layer around the queen bee. By wearing the queen in a locket around the neck, an individual can encourage a mantle of bees to form around their body. This rippling mass of bees can weigh many pounds, with the **heaviest mantle of bees** record currently standing at 134 lb 14 oz—about the same weight as an adult man—by Ruan Lianming (CHN) on May 6, 2012. Ruan used 56 queens to attract an estimated 621,000 bees in Fengxin County, Jiangxi Province, China.

What's the buzzzzz?
First use of apitherapy: The Greek physician Galen (AD 129–200) is said to have used honey and bee venom to treat baldness.

Largest bee house: A bee house measuring 42 ft 7 in x 4 ft 2 in x 1 ft 2 in was built in Barking, London, UK, on Jun 18, 2011.

Largest wasp nest: A nest measuring 12 ft 1 in x 5 ft 8 in and ca. 18 ft in circumference was found at Waimauku, New Zealand, in Apr 1963.

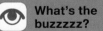

Mostly mollusks

Octopuses don't have eight legs—they have **two legs and six arms**

Deepest octopus
The dumbo octopus (*Grimpoteuthis*) lives as far down as 5,000 ft (1,500 m). Its body, 7.8 in (20 cm) long, is soft and semigelatinous, enabling the octopus to resist the great pressure found at this depth. It travels by moving its fins, pulsing its webbed arms (octopus limbs are called arms rather than tentacles), or pushing water through a funnel as a form of jet propulsion.

Most bioluminescent octopus
Squids include many bioluminescent species, but only *Stauroteuthis syrtensis* lights up the octopus world in a significant way. It uses a row of suckerlike structures that glow blue-green and emit light at 470 nanometers (a wavelength that travels well under water). Researchers believe the flashing entices prey within reach.

Smallest octopus
With an average arm span of less than 2 in (5.1 cm), *Octopus arborescens* is the smallest species. It is found in Sri Lanka.

First complete nervous system
In 2013, scientists announced a nervous system had been found in a 1.18-in-long (3-cm) fossil belonging to a previously unknown species of segmented marine arthropod. This creature is an ancestor of chelicerates (spiders, scorpions, and horseshoe crabs). Belonging to the extinct genus *Alalcomenaeus*, it lived more than 520 million years ago in the Cambrian period in the seas of southwest China.

Heaviest colossal squid
Colossal squid are shorter than giant squid, but they make up for it in weight. One specimen of adult male colossal squid (*Mesonychoteuthis hamiltoni*) weighed ca. 990 lb (450 kg) when caught by fishermen in the Ross Sea of Antarctica in 2007.

Rarest jellyfish
The Cookii Monster (*Crambione cookii*) of Australia is pink, 1 ft 8 in (50 cm) long, and very venomous. Recorded in 1910 in Cooktown, Queensland, the species disappeared until a specimen was caught in 2013 off Queensland's Sunshine Coast by Puk Scivyer of nearby UnderWater World, where it now resides.

Largest invertebrate
An Atlantic giant squid (*Architeuthis dux*) that washed up in Thimble Tickle Bay, Newfoundland, Canada, on Nov 2, 1878 had a body measured at 20 ft (6.1 m) long and one tentacle reaching 35 ft (10.7 m), giving a total of 55 ft (16.8 m). Pictured is a giant squid snapped in Feb 1996 in New Zealand.

Largest clam
The marine giant clam (*Tridacna gigas*) lives on the Indo-Pacific coral reefs. A specimen measuring 3 ft 9 in (1.15 m) and weighing 734 lb (333 kg) was collected off Ishigaki Island, Okinawa, Japan, in 1956. It was examined in 1984 when experts estimated that it weighed over 750 lb (340 kg) when alive.

Most venomous gastropod
Predatory marine shells called cone shells (genus *Conus*) deliver a fast-acting neurotoxic venom. While several species are capable of delivering enough toxin to kill humans, the geographer cone (*C. geographus*) of the Indo-Pacific is particularly dangerous and should never be handled.

Longest bivalve mollusk
Bivalves, such as clams and oysters, have a hinged shell. The longest bivalve is the giant shipworm (*Kuphus polythalamia*), a marine species that lives in a tubular shell. The longest specimen measured 5 ft (1.53 m).

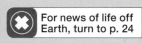

For news of life off Earth, turn to p. 24

Big suckers: giant octopus

The **largest octopus** is the Pacific giant octopus (*Enteroctopus dofleini*, right), the biggest specimen of which sported an arm span of 31 ft 6 in—the same arm span of eight adult men! Despite their size, they are not exempt from predators, but, like most cephalopods, they have a good defense mechanism: above left is a Pacific giant squirting a plume of ink in its wake as it evades attack. They are also masters of camouflage and can change color—and even texture—to match their surroundings (bottom left).

FACT
Centipedes don't have 100 legs but do have an even number of leg pairs.

Full of venom
All octopuses, cuttlefish, and some squid are venomous. Fortunately, only the venom of one—the blue-ringed octopus—is powerful enough to kill humans.

Largest snail

An individual African giant snail (*Achatina achatina*) was recorded at 1 ft 3.5 in (39.3 cm) when fully extended, with a shell length of 10.75 in (27.3 cm). Weighing 2 lb (900 g), this specimen was named Gee Geronimo and was kept in Hove in the UK after being collected in Sierra Leone in Jun 1976.

FACT

Gee Geronimo's owner, Chris Hudson (UK), got divorced after his wife complained that the house was too full of snails—and that he even had a bucket of them under their bed.

Actual Size

LARGEST ...

Centipede

The giant centipede (*Scolopendra gigantea*) of Central and South America is 10 in (26 cm) long. It preys on mice, lizards, and frogs—and one group was found in Venezuela hanging upside down from cave roofs to feed on bats. The centipede uses modified jaws to catch its food, delivering venom that feels like an insect sting in humans and can cause swelling and fever.

Millipede

A fully grown African giant black millipede (*Archispirostreptus gigas*) owned by Jim Klinger of Coppell, Texas, USA, measures 1 ft 3.2 in (38.7 cm) in length and 2.6 in (6.7 cm) in circumference, and has 256 legs. The average length for this type of millipede is 6–11 in (16–28 cm).

Oldest mollusk

In Oct 2007, at Bangor University in Wales, UK, scientists announced that the annual growth rings in the shell of a quahog clam (*Arctica islandica*) showed it to be 405–410 years old. This was later revised to 507. Alas, the clam was killed in dating.

Horseshoe crab

The Atlantic horseshoe crab (*Limulus polyphemus*) measures up to 1 ft 11.5 in (60 cm) in length, yet despite its name it is not a crab. An aquatic relative of arachnids, its appearance has been relatively unchanged for millions of years.

Marine snail

The largest marine gastropod is the trumpet or baler conch (*Syrinx aruanus*) of Australia. A specimen collected in 1979 had a shell 2 ft 6.4 in (77.2 cm) long, with a maximum girth of 3 ft 3.75 in (1.01 m). It weighed nearly 40 lb (18 kg) when alive.

Eye-to-body ratio

Vampyroteuthis infernalis—the "vampire squid from hell"—has a body measuring 11 in (28 cm) in length and eyes with a diameter of 0.9 in (2.5 cm). The ratio is almost 1:11—the human equivalent of eyes the size of table tennis bats! Squid also have the largest eyes in absolute terms (see below).

Newest slug

Science was already aware of the giant pink slug (*Triboniophorus aff. graeffei*) of New South Wales, Australia, but it was thought to be an unusual color variety of the red triangle slug (*Triboniophorus graeffei*). In Jun 2013, genetic results revealed it to be a species in its own right.

SIZING CEPHALOPODS, MYRIAPODS, AND MOLLUSKS

Ash-black slug: length 11.8 in

Atlantic horseshoe crab: length 1 ft 11.5 in

Giant centipede: length 10 in

African giant black millipede: length 1 ft 3.2 in

African giant snail: snout-to-tail length 1 ft 3.5 in

Atlantic giant squid: length up to 55 ft, has the **largest eye of any animal** (above), at 1 ft 3.7 in in diameter

Superlative squid

Smallest: 0.5-in-long *Parateuthis tunicata*.

Most bioluminescent: Firefly squid (*Watasenia scintillans*) emit flashes of light.

First video of giant squid in natural habitat: Jul 2012, filmed south of Tokyo in the Pacific Ocean.

First giant squid captured: Seven juveniles caught off the coast of New Zealand in Mar 2002.

Pets

There are **70 million** pet dogs and **74.1 million** pet cats in the USA

Oldest bearded dragon

Guinness (b. Jul 26, 1997), a bearded dragon owned by Nik Vernon (UK), was 16 years 129 days old when he died on Dec 2, 2013. Bearded dragons generally live to about eight years in the wild in Australia and typically a maximum of 14 years in captivity.

Largest breed of spaniel

Named after Clumber Park in Nottingham, UK, the Clumber spaniel has been a favorite of aristocracy and royalty. The breed standard specifies a weight of 86 lb (39 kg) and a height of 20 in (51 cm). The Clumber is loyal but a little demanding: its white coat sheds throughout the year, and the breed tends to slobber and snore.

Smallest breed of poodle

Poodles can be found in standard, miniature, and—the smallest—toy categories. To qualify, a toy poodle must have a maximum height to the withers of either 11 in (28 cm) or 10 in (25.4 cm), depending on the guidelines of different international bodies.

Oldest pig ever

Pig Floyd (b. Feb 17, 1992)—a potbellied pig owned by Kris and Tricia Fernandez of Baton Rouge, Louisiana, USA—was 21 years 166 days old when assessed on Aug 2, 2013.

⊗ More amazing animals: pp. 66–67

First pet hedgehog

A relative of the Algerian hedgehog (*Atelerix algirus*) was domesticated during the 4th century BC by the Romans. They were primarily raised for their meat and quills but were also kept as pets, as several different species are today. Modern popular breeds are the Egyptian long-eared hedgehog (*Hemiechinus auritus auritus*), the Indian long-eared hedgehog (*H. collaris*), and the African pygmy hedgehog (*A. albiventris*), which is a hybrid of the Algerian and the four-toed hedgehog.

Most intelligent breed of dog

The Border collie is the smartest pooch of all, followed by the poodle and German shepherd, according to Professor Stanley Coren (USA) of the University of British Columbia, Canada, and 200 professional dog obedience judges. Top dogs understand a vocabulary of 250 words—as many as a two-year-old human child. Bottom of the class are the bulldog, the Basenji, and, last of all, the Afghan hound.

Most expensive sheepdog

Shepherd Eddie Thornalley (UK) bought Marchup Midge (both above) from UK breeder and trainer Shaun Richards at an auction in Skipton in North Yorkshire, UK, on Oct 26, 2012. His winning bid was £10,080 ($16,216).

COLOSSAL COMPANIONS

Tallest horse: 6 ft 10.5 in, Big Jake, Belgian gelding

Tallest donkey: 5 ft 8 in, Romulus, American mammoth jackstock

Largest pet canary: 8.66 in, Parisian frill

Largest pony breed: 5 ft, Connemara

Tallest male dog: 3 ft 8 in, Zeus, Great Dane

Tallest female dog: 3 ft 2.6 in, Morgan, Great Dane

Tallest domestic cat: 19 in, Trouble, Savannah Islands

Largest domestic rabbit: 2 ft 11.75 in, Flemish giant rabbit

◉ Top cats

Most popular in politics: Socks was adopted by future President Bill and Hillary Clinton (USA) in 1991. During his eight-year stint at the White House, Socks was said to have received 75,000 letters and packages a week.

Most traveled: In Feb 1984, Hamlet escaped from his cage on a flight from Toronto in Canada and became caught behind airplane paneling for over seven weeks, accidentally traveling about 600,000 mi.

Wealthiest: In 1988, Ben Rea (UK) bequeathed his £7-million ($12.5-million) fortune to Blackie, the last of the 15 cats he shared his mansion with.

ℹ Nero the friendly lion

George Wombwell (UK, 1777–1850) had a successful traveling menagerie. It included Nero, a lion so docile that he refused to fight dogs when his owner arranged a bout. Wombwell's tomb is still viewable today; he was buried in London's gothic Highgate Cemetery, under a statue of sleepy Nero, lying with his head on his paws.

Tallest donkey

Romulus is an American Mammoth Jackstock who measured 17 hands (5 ft 8 in; 1.72 m) tall on Feb 8, 2013. He is owned by Cara and Phil Yellott of Red Oak in Texas, USA. His brother, Remus, was measured at over 16 hands (5 ft 4 in; 1.62 m). The minimum height for the big breed is 14.2 hands (4 ft 10 in; 1.47 m).

Shortest cat

Lilieput, a nine-year-old female Munchkin cat, measured 5.25 in (13.34 cm) from the floor to the shoulders on Jul 19, 2013. She is owned by Christel Young of Napa, California, USA. Gone but not fur-gotten is Colonel Meow (inset), the characterful **cat with the longest fur**, who passed away on Jan 30, 2014. His fur measured 9 in (22.87 cm) and his owner was Anne Marie Avey (USA).

Smallest breed of horse

Originally developed in Argentina in 1868, the smallest recognized breed of horse is the Falabella miniature horse, which has an average height at the withers of 8 hands (32 in; 81.2 cm). While miniature horses are shorter, they are also smaller—their limbs and body grow in proportion. The use of a "hand" (10.1 cm; 4 in) as a unit of measurement goes back to ancient Egypt.

Largest breed of horse

The English Shire horse is a type of draft horse. Stallions stand 17 hands (5 ft 8 in; 1.72 m) or even taller at maturity. It was one of these working animals that was the **tallest** and **heaviest** horse ever to be documented. Sampson (later renamed Mammoth) was a Shire gelding born in 1846. By 1850, he measured 21.2½ hands (7 ft 2.5 in; 2.19 m) and later weighed 3,359 lb (1,524 kg). Mammoth was bred by Thomas Cleaver of Toddington Mills in Bedfordshire, UK.

Largest breed of pony

The Connemara pony of North America ranges in height from 13 to 15 hands (4 ft 4 in–5 ft; 132–152.4 cm).

The **smallest breed of pony** is the Shetland pony. Often used by children learning to ride, its maximum accepted height is 3 ft 6 in (107 cm) at the withers, with a minimum of 2 ft 4 in (71 cm). Dwarf ponies have a genetic mutation that may make them smaller, but Shetland ponies are the smallest of the pure breeds.

Tallest dogs

Zeus (USA, left), a Great Dane, measured 3 ft 8 in (111.8 cm) tall on Oct 4, 2011. Owned by Denise Doorlag and family of Otsego in Michigan, USA, Zeus is both the **tallest male dog** and the **tallest dog ever**. The **tallest female dog** is also a Great Dane: Morgan, owned by Dave and Cathy Payne of Melbourne in Ontario, Canada, measured 3 ft 2.6 in (98.15 cm) to the shoulder on Jan 9, 2013. The two dogs met for the first time in Oct 2013.

Smallest dog

Vanesa Semler of Dorado, Puerto Rico, owns a female Chihuahua called Milly, who measured 3.8 in (9.65 cm) tall on Feb 21, 2013. As a puppy, she was fed using an eyedropper and was small enough to fit on a teaspoon.

First pets: domestic bliss

As our ancestors formed settlements, animals became domesticated for practical uses. They were used for food and clothing or would help us work. Dogs became the **first domestic animals**, around 13,000 BC in the Middle East. The bones of the **oldest known domestic cat** date back 9,500 years, and were discovered in a neolithic village on Cyprus next to its presumed owner. Records of the **first domestic elephants** tell of their use as beasts of burden at least 4,000 years ago in the present-day area covering Pakistan and India.

And finally ...

• **Longest tail on a dog:** Finnegan, from Calgary, Canada, is an Irish wolfhound with a 2-ft 4.46-in tail, as of Aug 15, 2013.

• **Largest donation of pet food in one week:** Full Stride Media (Pty) Ltd (ZAF) collected 22,066 lb of pet food for animal charities on Oct 6–13, 2013, in Johannesburg, South Africa.

Animals in action

GWR's human talent always faces fierce **furry or feathered competition** ...

Most treats balanced on a dog's nose
Despite his name, Monkey is a dog, and on Jul 2, 2013 he balanced 26 treats on his nose, appearing with handler Meghan Fraser (USA) on the set of *Guinness World Records Unleashed* in California, USA.

Most beverage cans opened by a parrot
Zac the macaw opened 35 cans using just his beak in San Jose, California, USA, on Jan 12, 2012. The talented bird also set the record for the **most slam dunks by a parrot in one minute**, with 22 dunks into a specially designed net on Dec 30, 2011.

Longest jump by a cat
Flying feline Alley cat-apulted himself to a record with a 6-ft (1.82-m) leap on Oct 27, 2013. Alley, a rescue cat owned by Samantha Martin (USA), is part of the Amazing Acro-Cats touring show.

Fastest 30 m on a scooter by a dog
Owner Karen Cobb (USA) didn't need to do much to encourage her enthusiastic four-year-old Briard, Norman, to scoot 30 m (98 ft) in 20.77 sec, at All-Tournament Players Park in Georgia, USA, on Jul 12, 2013.

FACT
Nifty Norman also rides bicycles (with training wheels, of course), skateboards, and surfboards.

Largest working rodent
The Gambian giant pouched rat (*Cricetomys gambianus*) measures 3 ft (90 cm) long and is used to sniff out land mines in Mozambique. The rats are trained to associate the scent of explosives with a food reward and identify the presence of explosives by grooming and scratching at the ground.

Highest-ranking penguin

Colonel-in-Chief Sir Nils Olav is the male king penguin mascot of Norway's Hans Majestet Kongens Garde (King's Guard) unit. He lives in the UK's Edinburgh Zoo, which received its first king penguin, from Norway, in 1913. In 1972, when the Norwegian King's Guard visited the zoo, a penguin was adopted and was named Nils Olav in honor of King Olav V. The current incumbent became Colonel-in-Chief on Aug 18, 2005.

▲ **Fastest dog to retrieve a person from water**
Search-and-rescue dog Jack, a black vom Mühlrad Newfoundland dog, is handled by Hans-Joachim Brückmann (DEU). On Jun 11, 2013, Jack retrieved one of his handler's aides from 82 ft (25 m) in 1 min 36.81 sec on the Kaarster See lake in Kaarst, Germany.

▲ **First dog to detect diabetic episodes**
Armstrong the Labrador was trained in 2003 by Mark Ruefenacht (USA) to detect, via scent, the chemical changes leading to hypoglycemia (low blood sugar)—a condition that can cause a diabetic to slip into a coma. The Dogs for Diabetics charity was founded in 2004, following Armstrong's success.

SEE IT 3D
WITH THE FREE APP

FACT

Jiff appeared in a Katy Perry video ("Dark Horse," 2013) and in the movie *Adventures of Bailey: A Night in Cowtown* (USA, 2013).

3D ON THIS PAGE
Augmented Reality alert!

Fastest 10 m on hind legs by a dog

Jiff the Pomeranian covered 10 m (32 ft) in 6.56 sec at TOPS Kennels in Grayslake, Illinois, USA, on Sep 9, 2013. The plucky Pom, who performs various tricks, can also walk on his front paws (inset), covering 5 m (16 ft) in a record 7.76 sec—the **fastest 5 m on front legs by a dog.**

Plants

A notch or limb on a tree stays the **same distance** from the ground

First use of spices in cooking

Garlic mustard plant seeds were used between 6,150 and 5,800 years ago (around 4000 BC). In 2013, archaeologists announced that the spice had been found in European pottery shards.

Largest cashew nut tree

Natal's cashew tree (*Anacardium occidentale*) in Rio Grande do Norte, Brazil, covers around 80,700 sq ft (7,500 m²) with a perimeter of around 1,640 ft (500 m). That's a lot of nuts—indeed, the yield is up to 80,000 fruit per year. Some estimate the tree to be up to 1,000 years old, although it is also said that it was planted in 1888 by local fisherman Luiz Inácio de Oliveira.

Largest corm

A corm is an underground plant stem that is used for storage by some plants to survive adverse surface conditions throughout the seasons. The largest is produced by the titan arum (*Amorphophallus titanum*) and commonly weighs around 110 lb (50 kg). The heaviest specimen weighed 257 lb 15 oz (117 kg) and was recorded in 2006 in the Botanical Garden of Bonn University in Germany.

The titan arum is also the **smelliest plant** when it blooms—which is fortunately relatively rarely. It releases an odor, comparable to that of rotten flesh, that can be smelled at a great distance to attract the carrion beetles and flesh flies that pollinate it. Like the **largest living flower** (right), its stench gives it the nickname "corpse flower."

Largest horsetail

One of the oldest plant genera to survive, horsetail is a living fossil. It is the only surviving member of the Equisetopsida class that once featured strongly in late Mesozoic period forests for up to 100 million years. Today, the Mexican giant horsetail (*Equisetum myriochaetum*) is the largest species, a primeval-looking plant reaching 24 ft (7.3 m) in height.

Shiniest living objects

Marble berry (*Pollia condensata*) is a 3-ft 3-in-tall (1-m) herb native to Ghana. Resembling Christmas ball decorations, its vivid fruit is approximately 30% as reflective as a silver mirror. This is the highest reported light reflectivity of any biological material.

Largest water lily

Native to freshwater lakes and bayous in the Amazon basin, the giant water lily (*Victoria amazonica*) has floating leaves measuring up to 10 ft (3 m) across and is held in place on an underwater stem 23–26 ft (7–8 m) long. The leaves are supported by riblike cross ridges that are said to have inspired the metal girders of Crystal Palace in London, UK, built in 1851.

FACT

If evenly distributed, a mature giant water lily leaf can support up to 100 lb of weight.

Largest branched inflorescence

A branched inflorescence is a cluster of flowers on a multibranched stem instead of on a single stem. The largest is that of the talipot palm (*Corypha umbraculifera*), which consists of up to several million creamy white flowers. The palm is native to parts of India and Sri Lanka. Its inflorescence grows at the apex of the tree's trunk and is 19–26 ft (6–8 m) long.

Largest poppy flowers

Coulter's Matilija poppy (*Romneya coulteri*) has silky white flowers around an eye-catching ball of golden stamens and grows to 5.12 in (13 cm) across. It grows in southern California, USA, and northern Mexico and its bold display of flowers makes it a popular ornamental plant.

LARGEST PLANT SIZES

Redwood: height 379 ft 1 in

Puya raimondii: height 35 ft

Talipot palm: length 19–26 ft

Raffia palm: leaf length 65 ft 7 in, stem length 13 ft

Rafflesia arnoldii: width 3 ft, weight 24 lb

Giant water lily: width up to 10 ft

Palmed off

Before the leaf of the raffia palm took the record, it was the giant water lily that was considered the **largest leaf**, in 1955 reported as 21 ft. Back then, it was called *Victoria regina* before the name *Victoria amazonica* became widely used. Its common name is the royal water lily.

ℹ️ Trees of the Amazon

The Amazon basin and Guiana Shield area of South America has an estimated 16,000 tree species, of which just 227 species (1.4%) account for half of all Amazon trees. The rarest 11,000 species account for just 0.12% of the total number of trees in the region. The study from which this data is extracted, published in *Nature* in 2013, suggests that there are a total of 400 billion trees alive today in the Amazon rain forest.

Most massive plant by area
A network of quaking aspen trees (*Populus tremuloides*) grows in the Wasatch mountains, Utah, USA, covering 106 acres (43 ha) and weighing an estimated 13,227,700 lb (6,000 metric tons), making it also the **heaviest organism**. The clonal system is genetically uniform and acts as a single organism, with all the component trees changing color or shedding leaves in unison. The network looks like a forest, but it is made up of plants that have grown from the root system of a single tree dating back at least 80,000 years.

Smallest bromeliad
While the best-known member of the bromeliad clan is the pineapple, its unlikely relation is Spanish moss (*Tillandsia usneoides*). Neither a moss nor Spanish, the beardlike growth is made up of the smallest bromeliads, with slender stems bearing tiny flowers and a series of leaves that cling together. It produces hanging threadlike chains that stretch up to 19 ft 8 in (6 m) long.

Tallest banksia
Banksias are Australian wildflowers of the genus Banksia, some of which are so large that they grow as tall as trees. The tallest species are the coast banksia (*Banksia integrifolia*) and the river banksia (*B. seminuda*), both of which can grow to 100 ft (30 m) in height.

Tallest cycad
Cycads can look like palm trees and are sometimes grouped with them, but they are coning plants (like pine trees). Hope's cycad (*Lepidozamia hopei*) from Queensland, Australia, is the largest, growing to heights of 49 ft (15 m).

Tallest moss
Dawson's giant moss (*Dawsonia superba*), a New Zealand native, can grow to 23.6 in (60 cm) tall, but its spores are no more than 0.00039 in (0.01 mm) in size.

i Assassin bugs
A trick employed by some carnivorous plants is to use "assassin bugs," which live unthreatened on the plant itself. The bugs feed off the trapped prey and the plant then absorbs what it needs from the bugs' excrement.

Actual Size

Largest living flower
Rafflesia arnoldii gets its nickname "corpse flower" owing to its smell of rotting flesh (see also **smelliest plant**, left). And there is a lot of flower to sniff—it measures up to 3 ft (91 cm) across and weighs up to 24 lb (11 kg), with petals that are 0.75 in (1.9 cm) thick. The rare flower is native to southeast Asia and grows as a parasite inside and upon jungle vines.

Largest prey of carnivorous plants
Of all the carnivorous plants, the ones that digest the largest prey belong to the Nepenthaceae family (genus *Nepenthes*). Both *N. rajah* and *N. rafflesiana* have been known to eat large frogs, birds, and even rats. These species are commonly found in the rain forests of Asia, in particular Borneo, Indonesia, and Malaysia. By using their color, smell, and nectar to attract prey, the plants then trap, kill, and digest enzymes, before absorbing what is needed for nutrition.

Vaulting ambition: seed storage
The Svalbard Global Seed Vault is an underground facility on the Norwegian island of Spitsbergen designed to store samples of the world's seeds as insurance against threats to biodiversity. Opened on Feb 26, 2006, it is the **largest seed vault**. The goal is to store a total of 4.5 million samples (about 2 billion seeds) from 100 countries and, as of 2013, more than 770,000 samples had been deposited. The vault cost $8.3 m and the location—426 ft into the permafrost of a mountain—was chosen for being the best suited to keeping the temperature of samples at a stable 64.4°F.

👁 Marine plants
Deepest: Algae at 882 ft, found by Mark and Diane Littler (both USA), The Bahamas, Oct 1984

Fastest growing: Giant kelp (*Macrocystis pyrifera*), growing 1 ft 1.3 in per day

Largest clonal colony: DNA-sharing colony of Neptune grass, aka Mediterranean tapeweed (*Posidonia oceanica*), 4.9 mi across, Mediterranean Sea, discovered 2006

Humans

The surface area of a human lung is equivalent to the **size of a tennis court**

Longest fingernails on a pair of hands

She's nailed it: Chris "The Dutchess" Walton (USA) has a set of fingernails measuring 11 ft 10 in (3.62 m) for her left hand and 12 ft 1 in (3.68 m) for her right hand—a total of 23 ft 11 in (7.3 m). Chris's twisting talons were measured in London, UK, on Sep 16, 2013.

Contents

FACT
Fingernails grow at around 0.1 in per month. And men's nails usually grow faster than women's.

Changing shapes

One constant in Guinness World Records' 60-year history has been the popularity of the Human Body chapter. It's the part of the book that most people flick to first, and many of the colorful characters who've filled the pages over the years have attained iconic status. Here, we look back at how some of these records have changed since our first edition in 1955.

Ask anyone to name a favorite record holder from the *Guinness World Records* book and the chances are they'll recall someone from the Human Body chapter. With visually striking record holders such as Robert Wadlow (**tallest man ever**), Lee Redmond (**longest fingernails**), and Robert Earl Hughes (**largest chest measurement**

and former **heaviest man**), it comes as no surprise. It helps that their stories are so memorable. Who could forget that Wadlow died as a result of a blister from ill-fitting footwear? Or that Hughes was buried in a coffin the size of a piano case?

In this Flashback, we examine a selection of iconic Human Body superlatives that appeared in our first

edition and identify who now holds the record. In some cases, such as the **tallest man ever**, the record hasn't changed in 60 years; in others, such as the **longest hair**, the current claimant has surpassed the original holder by a long way …

Longest mustache
Measured at 14 ft (4.29 m) on Mar 4, 2010, the face furniture of Ram Singh Chauhan (IND) earned him a place in the record books for the longest 'tache of all time. Ram started growing his facial hair in 1970 and, with his wife's help, grooms his whiskers daily with coconut and mustard oils.

Heaviest living male
Although his peak weight of 1,235 lb (560 kg) secured Manuel Uribe (MEX, pictured) the extant world record in 2006, he's not the **heaviest man ever**. That accolade goes to Jon Brower Minnoch (USA, 1941–83, see p. 80), whose weight was estimated by doctors at an unparalleled 1,400 lb (635 kg) in 1978.

Most children delivered at a single birth to survive
Nadya Suleman (USA) claimed headlines across the world on Jan 26, 2009, when she gave birth to six boys and two girls in Bellflower, California, USA. Dubbed "Octomom" by the US press, Suleman conceived with the aid of *in vitro* fertilization (IVF), swelling her family from 6 children to 14.

Oldest living woman
As we go to press, 115-year-old Misao Okawa of Japan is the oldest woman—and **oldest person**—alive on Earth (see p. 76). She's not the **oldest woman ever**, of course: the all-time holder, also a woman, is Jeanne Louise Calment (FRA), who died on Aug 4, 1997 at the remarkable age of 122 years 164 days.

2015
1955

| Most children | Oldest woman | Longest mustache | Heaviest man |

"Multiple births"
Our first edition mentions fanciful accounts of women having as many as 36 children in a single birth (illustrated right is "Dorothea," who reportedly had 11 babies in 1755). Turning to "medically more acceptable cases," however, we go on to discuss the five Dionne babies—then, one of only three examples of quintuplets to survive—born on May 28, 1934.

YVONNE EMILIE MARIE CECILE ANNETTE

"Oldest centenarians"
Longevity is a subject that has clearly always been controversial. "Few subjects have been so obscured by deceit and falsehood," we wrote in 1955. The oldest woman then on record "for whom there exists acceptable evidence" was vicar's daughter Katherine Plunkett of County Louth, Ireland, who lived for 111 years 328 days from 1820 to 1932.

"Longest mustache"
Our earliest edition makes reference to Mr. John Roy of Glasgow, UK, whose 16.5-in-long (41.91-cm) mustache is the "longest mustache owned by a member of Britain's 'Handlebar Club.'" Roy, a smoker, once tried to have his mustache insured because of the fire risk, but he couldn't afford the premiums.

"Heaviest heavyweight"
Now known as the man with the **widest chest measurement** (10 ft 4 in; 315 cm), Robert Earl Hughes' (USA) first appearance in GWR was as the **heaviest living man**, at 946 lb (429 kg). We also named the "heaviest man recorded in medical history" as Miles Darden (USA, 1799–1857), who peaked "slightly in excess of 1,000 lb" (453 kg).

Tallest living man
Towering 2 ft 8 in (81.2 cm) over GWR Editor-in-Chief Craig Glenday is Sultan Kösen of Turkey, who took the title of tallest living man—and human— in Feb 2009. Currently standing at 8 ft 3 in (251 cm), Sultan is one of just eight people over 8 ft (243 cm) to be ratified in the past 60 years.

FACT
As a teenager, Sultan was signed to play basketball for Galatasaray in Turkey but proved too tall to compete!

FACT
In 1955, we reported on a man claiming to be the world's tallest human at 9 ft 6 in (289 cm), but who turned out to be 7 ft 3.5 in (222 cm) when assessed medically!

Shortest living man and woman
Pictured here is GWR's Head of Records, Marco Frigatti, with the current shortest living humans. Jyoti Amge (IND, right) measured 24.7 in (62.8 cm) in Nagpur, India, on Dec 16, 2011, while two months later, at a clinic in Kathmandu, Nepal, on Feb 26, 2012, Chandra Bahadur Dangi (NPL, left) reached just 21.5 in (54.6 cm). Mr. Dangi is also officially ratified as the **shortest man ever measured** using modern medical equipment.

Longest hair (female)
The world's lengthiest locks (female) belong to Xie Qiuping of China at 18 ft 5.5 in (5.62 m). She has been growing her hair since 1973, from the age of 13. "It's no trouble at all. I'm used to it," she said. "But you need patience and you need to hold yourself straight when you have hair like this."

Greatest vocal range
Brazil's Georgia Brown has a vocal range that spans an incredible eight octaves (from G2 to G10), as verified at Aqui Jazz Atelier Music School in São Paulo on Aug 18, 2004—a record that has remained unchallenged for more than a decade!

FACT
Xie travels with an assistant to hold her hair and help her manage her plentiful tresses.

Longest hair	Greatest vocal range	Tallest man	Shortest man and woman

"Longest tresses"
The "longest recorded feminine tresses," we said in 1955, "appear to be those of the 19th-century exhibitionist named Miss Owens, which were measured at 8 ft 3 in [251.4 cm]." Millie Owens was the "Queen of Long Hair" and enjoyed a career showing off her tresses and selling picture postcards.

"Greatest range"
The singer with the greatest range in 1955 was named as Miss Yma Sumac (born Zoila Augusta Emperatriz Chávarri del Castillo, 1922–2008), an acclaimed soprano from Peru: "She is reputed to have a range of five octaves from A# to B."

"Tallest giants"
"The only admissible evidence upon the true height of giants is that of recent date made under impartial medical supervision." So said Norris and Ross McWhirter in 1955 before going on to dismiss the likes of Og, King of Bashan at 9 Assyrian cubits (16 ft 2.5 in; 494.03 cm) due to "confusion of units" from the Bible. They then name Robert Wadlow as the tallest man "of whom there is irrefutable evidence." Find out more on p. 81.

"Shortest dwarfs"
Sixty years ago, we named Miss Edith Barlow (below right) as the UK's "shortest living dwarf," at 22 in (55.8 cm), making her the world's **shortest living woman** by default. Only Walter Boehning, aka Böning (DEU, d. 1955, below) was shorter in absolute terms, claiming to be the "smallest dwarf in the world" at an unconfirmed height of just 20.5 in (52 cm). By 1964, Boehning was removed from the book due to a lack of supporting evidence for his claimed stature.

Senses & perception

The eyes can process around **36,000 pieces of information** every hour

FACT
Quieter V6 engines were introduced in the 2014 season—to the disappointment of many F1 fans!

Noisiest workplace

The cockpit of a Formula One car is the loudest place on Earth in which any human works for a sustained period. The noise level directly in front of the engine where a driver sits has been measured at 140 dB. All drivers wear tailor-made earplugs.

HEARING

Highest detectable pitch
The upper limit of human hearing is accepted to be 20,000 Hz (hertz, or cycles per second), although this figure decreases with age. By way of comparison, bats emit pulses at up to 90,000 Hz.

The average accepted **lowest detectable pitch** by the human ear is 20 Hz, although in ideal conditions a young person can hear frequencies down to 12 Hz. Inaudible infrasound waves in the range of 4–16 Hz can be felt by the human body as physical vibrations.

Smallest bone
The stapes, or stirrup bone, measures 0.1–0.13 in (2.6–3.4 mm) in length and weighs 2–4.3 mg. One of the three auditory ossicles in the middle ear, the stapes plays a vital role in hearing.

SIGHT

Farthest object visible to the naked eye
Gamma-ray bursts are the birth cries of black holes. At 2:12 EDT on Mar 19, 2008, NASA's *Swift* satellite detected a gamma-ray burst from a galaxy some 7.5 billion light-years away. Some 30–40 sec later, the optical counterpart of the burst was seen on Earth and captured by a robotic telescope. The explosion, known as GRB 080319B, was visible to the naked eye for around 30 sec.

Most active muscle
Scientists have estimated that human eye muscles move more than 100,000 times a day. Many of these rapid eye movements take place during the dreaming phase of sleep.

Most sensitive color vision
The average human eye can perceive approximately a million colors. Our powers of color vision derive from three types of cone cells in the eye, each responsive to different wavelengths of light. Our brains combine the signals to produce the perception of color. Work completed by neuroscientist Gabriele Jordan at the University of Newcastle, UK, proved that some people have four cones,

Quietest place

Tests performed on Oct 18, 2012 in the Anechoic Test Chamber at Orfield Laboratories in Minneapolis, Minnesota, USA, gave a background noise reading of just -3 dBA (decibels A-weighted). The term "dBA" denotes sound levels audible to the human ear—i.e., excluding extreme highs and lows.

Most valuable tongue

On Mar 9, 2009, Lloyd's reported that the tongue of Gennaro Pelliccia (UK) was insured for £10 m ($14 m). Pelliccia tastes every single batch of coffee beans made for Costa Coffee (UK) stores and has now learned to distinguish between thousands of different flavors.

enabling them to see more colors—about 99 million more, in fact. Jordan and her team created a test in which three subtle color circles flashed on a screen. Only one person was able to distinguish them every time—an English female doctor known as "cDa29"—who has the most sensitive color vision measured.

SMELL

Smelliest substance
The manmade foul-smelling substances "Who-Me?" and "US Government Standard Bathroom Malodor" have five and eight chemical

---

HOW MANY SENSES DO WE HAVE?

Conventionally, we think of ourselves as having five senses: sight, hearing, taste, touch, and smell. But if to "sense" something simply means to be aware of it, then we have many more than just these five "primary" senses. Here are a few others to consider:

Temperature: We can tell hot from cold and adjust accordingly

Kinesthetics: The brain's parietal cortex enables us to tell where every part of our body is in relation to its other parts. (Test this by trying to touch your nose with your eyes closed!)

Interoception: Our internal senses alert us when we are feeling hungry or tired

Pain: A mechanism for the body to sense damage

Time: We sense time passing

Balance: We are sensitive to body movement, direction, and acceleration

Listen up: the decibel scale

The loudness, or intensity, of a sound is usually measured in decibels (dB). Decibels are calculated according to a logarithmic scale, which increases by a set ratio.

Total silence would measure 0 dB; a sound 10 times greater would be 10 dB, but a sound 100 times louder than 0 dB would measure only 20 dB, and sounds 1,000 times louder than 0 dB would register just 30 dB.

Listed here are typical decibel readings, recorded from a distance of 32 ft away from the source.

DECIBEL (dB) READINGS

All readings from 32-ft distance

dB	Sound
150	Jet engine
114	Train whistle
110	Subway train
107	Pneumatic riveter
89	Power saw
64	City traffic from inside car
46	Normal piano practice

Most valuable nose

On Mar 19, 2008, Lloyd's reported that Ilja Gort (NLD) had his nose insured for 5 m euro ($7.8 m). Gort, the owner of the vineyard Château la Tulipe de la Garde in Bordeaux, France, insured his nose in an attempt to protect his livelihood.

ingredients respectively. Bathroom Malodor smells primarily of human feces and becomes incredibly repellant to people at a ratio of just two parts per million. It was originally developed to test the power of deodorizing products.

Smelliest molecule

The chemicals ethyl mercaptan (C_2H_5SH) and butyl seleno-mercaptan (C_4H_9SeH) have a distinctive smell reminiscent of a combination of rotting cabbage, garlic, onions, burned toast, and sewer gas.

TASTE

Sweetest substance

Thaumatin, aka talin, from arils (appendages found on certain seeds) of the katemfe plant (*Thaumatococcus daniellii*) found in West Africa, is 3,250 times sweeter than sugar when compared with a 7.5% sucrose solution.

Bitterest substance

The bitterest-tasting substances are based on the denatonium cation and have been produced commercially as benzoate and saccharide. Taste detection levels are as low as just one part in 500 million, while a dilution of just one part in 100 million will leave a lingering taste.

Actual Size

Mapping the senses

This oddly shaped figure is a "sensory homunculus." This is what you'd look like if your body parts were in proportion to the areas of the brain concerned with sensory perception. Based on a model at the UK's Natural History Museum, it shows which areas of our bodies are the most sensitive to touch.

TOUCH

Most touch-sensitive part of the body

Our fingers have the highest density of touch receptors in the body. The fingers are so sensitive that we can feel two points of contact just 0.07 in (2 mm) apart. They can also detect a movement of just 0.02 microns—that's 31-millionths of an inch (or 200-thousandths of a millimeter).

FACT

The term "homunculus" was coined by alchemists in the 17th century and means simply "little person."

Lips have many sense receptors—which is one of the reasons why babies put objects into their mouths to learn about them.

When it comes to detecting our world, the tongue is highly sensitive, with a very dense concentration of neural connections.

Our fingers feel the world in sensory high definition by containing the highest density of touch receptors in the body. Sense receptors are more concentrated in smaller fingers. As a result, women tend to have a more developed tactile sensitivity than men.

The calves are among the least sensitive body parts—the brain can only distinguish two points of contact around 1.77 in apart, compared with 0.07 in for the fingers.

The 100,000–200,000 sense receptors on the sole of each foot help stabilize the whole body. They are at their most effective when we walk barefoot.

Talking scents: our sense of smell

Smell accounts for around 80% of our sense of taste. The first sense to develop, it is functional before we are born and is generally most sensitive in childhood. We can detect some 10,000 odors, but prolonged exposure to a smell causes our awareness of it to reduce quickly. We are more sensitive to smells in spring and summer, because the air is more moist then; exercise also increases the moisture in our nostrils, improving our sense of smell. Women have a stronger sense of smell than men—it is particularly acute during pregnancy.

Smells enter the nasal vestibule (nostril), where small hairs filter out dust and other fine particles. At the top of the nasal cavity are ca. 40 million olfactory receptor cells, which detect the odorant molecules and send a message to the brain. When you eat, you "taste" the food using these same cells, which detect food odors in the mouth.

Receptor cells

Nasal cavity

Nasal vestibule

Mouth

And finally ...

- **Longest echo:** 1 min 15 sec by Trevor Cox and Allan Kilpatrick (both UK) inside a disused oil tank at Inchindown in Highland, UK, on Jun 3, 2012.
- **Fastest time to boil water by passing electricity through body:** 1 min 22.503 sec, to heat 5.28 fl oz of water from 77°F to 206°F by Slavisa "Biba" Pajkic (SRB) in Istanbul, Turkey, on Jul 13, 2013.

Oldest people

The number of people over 65 is expected to **double to 800 million** by 2025

Largest gathering of centenarians

On May 19, 2013, the Regency Jewish Heritage Nursing & Rehabilitation Center in Somerset, New Jersey, USA, hosted a gathering of 31 people at the age of 100 years or over—only two of whom were men. Their combined ages stretched back to about 1100 BC, when the ancient Phoenicians were inventing the alphabet.

television, the modern automobile, and airplanes. When asked on her 120th birthday what she expected of the future, she replied: "A very short one."

Parent-child (aggregate)

The highest combined age for a parent and child alive at the same time is 215 years in the case of 119-year-old Sarah Knauss (USA, 1880–1999) and her 96-year-old daughter Kathryn Knauss Sullivan (USA, 1903–2005). Knauss was the second-oldest human ever, reaching 119 years 97 days.

Adoptive parent

Frances Ensor Benedict (USA, 1918–2012) was 83 years 324 days old when she adopted her foster daughter Jo Anne

Oldest solo parachute jump (female)

Dilys Margaret Price (UK, b. Jun 3, 1932) made a parachute jump at Langar Airfield in Nottingham, UK, on Apr 13, 2013 at the age of 80 years 315 days. The **oldest solo parachute jump (male)** was made by Milburn Hart (USA, 1908–2010) in Washington, USA, on Feb 18, 2005. He was 96 years 63 days old.

Oldest competitive sprinter

Hidekichi Miyazaki (JPN, b. Sep 22, 1910) was 103 years 15 days old when he competed at the International Gold Masters in Kyoto, Japan, on Oct 6, 2013. He took part in the 100 m race, which he finished in 34.10 sec, shaving 2.67 sec off his previous best.

Longest separated twins

Twins Ann and Elizabeth were born to unmarried mother Alice Lamb in Aldershot, Hampshire, UK, on Feb 28, 1936. A decision was made to separate the twins for adoption, and Ann grew up unaware of her sister Lizzie, who now lives in Portland, Oregon, USA. The pair were finally reunited on May 1, 2014 after a record 77 years 289 days apart.

OLDEST ...

Person (ever)

The greatest fully authenticated age to which any human has ever lived is 122 years 164 days by Jeanne Louise Calment (FRA, Feb 21, 1875–Aug 4, 1997). She lived through two World Wars and the development of

Oldest BASE jumper

Donald Cripps (USA, b. Sep 12, 1929) was 84 years 37 days old when he parachuted off the 876-ft-high (267-m) New River Gorge Bridge near Fayetteville in West Virginia, USA, on Oct 19, 2013. BASE jumping—from Buildings, Antennas, Spans (bridges), and Earth (cliffs)—is the most dangerous form of parachuting, due to the short falls involved.

Benedict Walker (USA) on Apr 5, 2002 in Putnam County, Tennessee, USA. At 65 years 224 days, Jo Anne (b. Aug 24, 1936) is also the **oldest adoptee**.

Fashion model

Aged 85 years 295 days as of Apr 22, 2014, Daphne Selfe (UK, b. Jul 1, 1928) is the oldest professional fashion model. Her 60-year career includes appearances for Dolce & Gabbana and Gap, modeling in *Vogue* and *Marie Claire*, and posing for photographers David Bailey and Mario Testino.

Actor to win an Oscar

Christopher Plummer (UK, b. Dec 13, 1929) was 82 years 65 days old when he won the 2012 Best Supporting Actor Oscar for *Beginners* (2010).

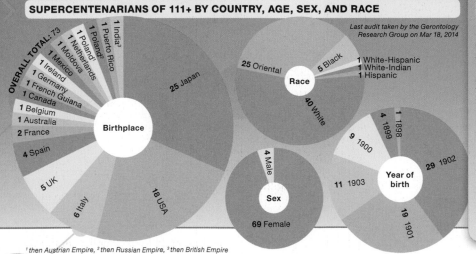

SUPERCENTENARIANS OF 111+ BY COUNTRY, AGE, SEX, AND RACE

Last audit taken by the Gerontology Research Group on Mar 18, 2014

OVERALL TOTAL: 73

Birthplace: 1 India[3], 1 Puerto Rico, 1 Poland[2], 1 Netherlands, 1 Moldova, 1 Mexico, 1 Ireland, 1 Germany, 1 French Guiana, 1 Canada, 1 Belgium, 1 Australia, 2 France, 4 Spain, 5 UK, 6 Italy, 18 USA, 25 Japan

Race: 25 Oriental, 5 Black, 1 White-Hispanic, 1 White-Indian, 1 Hispanic, 40 White

Sex: 4 Male, 69 Female

Year of birth: 1 1898, 4 1899, 9 1900, 11 1903, 19 1901, 29 1902

[1] then Austrian Empire, [2] then Russian Empire, [3] then British Empire

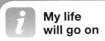

Lying about age is nothing new

In our first edition, we cautioned against "deceit and falsehood" encountered in claimed ages. Using information investigated by the Canadian government, we listed the greatest age reached by a male as 113, by Pierre Joubert, a French Canadian bootmaker (b. Jul 15, 1701, buried Nov 18, 1814). An investigation in 1990, however, established that Joubert was actually 82 at the time of his death, and that the person buried in 1814 was Joubert's homonymous ("same name") son, born in 1732.

FACT

Life expectancy has risen worldwide on average by four months each year since 1970.

My life will go on

The greatest age reached by a survivor of the *Titanic* was 104 years 72 days. Mary Wilburn, née Davis (UK, 1883–1987), was 28 when the ship sank in 1912.

Oldest living person

Misao Okawa (JPN, b. Mar 5, 1898) turned 116 in 2014. Misao, who lives in a nursing home in Osaka, Japan, became the **oldest living woman** on Jan 12, 2013 and **oldest living person** on Jun 12, 2013. She is also the ninth oldest verified person ever.

OLDEST SUPERCENTENARIANS

As of Apr 14, 2014, there were 74 people whose age had been verified as passing the 111-year mark. The estimated worldwide total of living supercentenarians is 300–450 persons.

Who	Born	How old?
Misao Okawa (JPN)	Mar 5, 1898	116 years 40 days
Jeralean Talley (USA)	May 23, 1899	114 years 326 days
Susannah Mushatt Jones (USA)	Jul 6, 1899	114 years 282 days
Bernice Madigan (USA)	Jul 24, 1899	114 years 264 days
Emma Morano-Martinuzzi (ITA)	Nov 29, 1899	114 years 136 days
Anna Henderson (USA)	Mar 5, 1900	114 years 40 days
Antonia Gerena Rivera (USA)	May 19, 1900	113 years 330 days
Ethel Lang (UK)	May 27, 1900	113 years 322 days
Nabi Tajima (JPN)	Aug 4, 1900	113 years 253 days
Blanche Cobb (USA)	Sep 8, 1900	113 years 218 days

Source: Gerontology Research Group

Oldest living man

Shortly before going to press, we heard of the passing of Arturo Licata (ITA, May 2, 1902–Apr 24, 2014), who had briefly been the oldest living man, aged 111 years 357 days at his death. His successor, Dr. Alexander Imich (POL/RUS, now USA, b. Feb 4, 1903), took the title at the age of 111 years 79 days. He is pictured here in his Upper West Side home in New York.

Oldest newspaper delivery person (female)

At 88 years 346 days old as of Mar 27, 2014, Beryl Walker (UK, b. Apr 15, 1925) was still delivering newspapers six mornings a week in Gloucester, Gloucestershire, UK. She has now given up her evening round.

The **oldest actress to win an Oscar** is Jessica Tandy (UK, 1909–1994), who won the 1990 Best Actress award at 80 years 295 days for the title role in *Driving Miss Daisy* (1989).

Newspaper delivery person

Ted Ingram (UK, b. Feb 14, 1920) delivered the *Dorset Echo* from the 1940s until Nov 9, 2013, when he was 93 years 268 days old.

Soccer referee

As of Apr 14, 2013, Peter Pak-Ngo Pang (USA, b. IDN, Nov 4, 1932) was still refereeing in the adult men's league in San Jose, California, USA, aged 80 years 161 days.

Convicted bank robber

On Jan 23, 2004, 92-year-old J.L. Hunter Rountree (USA, b. 1911) received 12 years 7 months for robbing a bank (unarmed) in Texas, USA.

Oldest dance troupe

The Hip Op-eration Crew (NZ) are hip-hop dancers whose ages range from 67 to 95, giving an average of 79 years 197 days (as of May 10, 2014). The 23 core members, from the small island of Waiheke, New Zealand, include 12 in their eighties and nineties. Their performances include a guest slot at 2013's World Hip Hop Dance Championship final in Las Vegas, Nevada, USA. Respect.

Theater actor

On Nov 29, 2013, Radu Beligan (ROM, b. Dec 14, 1918) was still performing at the National Theatre in Bucharest, Romania, at 94 years 350 days old.

Painter

Alphaeus Philemon Cole (USA, 1876–1988), whose work is in the permanent collections of the National Portrait Gallery (UK) and the Brooklyn Museum (USA), painted and exhibited his work up to the age of 103. A portraitist, Cole began his art career in the 1890s with Seurat and Signac as contemporaries.

Chess master

Zoltan Sarosy (HUN, b. Aug 23, 1906) was the Canadian Correspondence Chess Champion three times (1967, 1972, 1981) and, according to ChessGames.com, continues to play at 107 years of age.

Elder statesmen: current national leaders

Combining political power with staying power, Shimon Peres (right), the ninth President of Israel, is the **oldest living head of state**. Born Szymon Perski in Wiszniew, Poland (now Vishnyeva, Belarus), on Aug 2, 1923, he celebrated his 90th birthday in 2013.

Only six months younger is the President of Zimbabwe, Robert Mugabe (left, top), born on Feb 21, 1924. Almost exactly a year younger than Peres is Saudi Arabia's King Abdullah bin Abdulaziz al-Saud (left). Born on Aug 1, 1924, he has already outlived two of his crown prince heirs.

Longest careers

Professional hairdresser: Dorothy McKnight (USA, b. Feb 27, 1922) of Lake Worth, Florida, USA, since Jun 13, 1939.

Church pianist/organist: Martha Godwin (USA, b. Jan 17, 1927) in Southmont, North Carolina, USA, since Apr 1940.

Stuntman: Rocky Taylor (UK, b. Feb 28, 1945), since Mar 1961. He appeared in *World War Z* (released Jun 2013).

○ ○ ○

Body parts

Adults are made up of around **7,000,000,000,000,000,000,000,000,000** atoms

Farthest eyeball pop

Kim Goodman (USA) popped her eyeballs to a protrusion of 0.47 in (12 mm) beyond her eye sockets in Istanbul, Turkey, on Nov 2, 2007, beating her previous record of 0.43 in (11 mm) in 1998. Kim discovered her talent when she was hit on the head by a hockey mask, but can now pop her eyes out on cue.

Stretchiest skin
Garry Turner (UK) is able to stretch the skin of his abdomen to a distended length of 6.25 in (15.8 cm) due to a rare medical condition called Ehlers-Danlos Syndrome. With this condition, the collagen that strengthens the skin and determines its elasticity becomes defective, resulting in, among other things, a loosening of the skin and "hypermobility" of the joints.

Largest hairy family
Victor "Larry" Gomez, Gabriel "Danny" Ramos Gomez, Luisa Lilia De Lira Aceves, and Jesus Manuel Fajardo Aceves (all MEX) are four of a family of 19 that span five generations with a rare condition called congenital generalized hypertrichosis—excessive facial and torso hair. The women are covered with a light-to-medium coat of hair while the men have thick hair on approximately 98% of their body apart from their hands and feet.

Hairiest teenager
In 2010, trichologists (medical experts specializing in hair) used the Ferriman-Gallwey method to evaluate the hirsutism (hairiness) of Supatra "Nat" Sasuphan (THA, b. Aug 5, 2000). Ten areas of her body were scored from 1 to 4 according to the density of the hair. Nat received a score of 4 on four areas: face, neck, chest, and upper back.

Tallest Mohawk spike
Kazuhiro Watanabe (JPN) has a spike measuring 48 in (1.23 m), dwarfing even Eric Hahn's full Mohawk (see box on opposite page). The length was verified at Dwango Hanzomon Studio in Chiyoda, Tokyo, Japan, on April 23, 2014.

Longest tongue

Nick "The Lick" Stoeberl's (USA) lengthy licker measured 3.97 in (10.10 cm) from tip to closed lip when examined in Salinas, California, USA, on Nov 27, 2012. The bank teller and stand-up comedian has been known to use his tongue, wrapped in plastic wrap, to paint artworks!

Fellow American Chanel Tapper has the record for the **longest tongue (female)**, measuring 3.80 in (9.75 cm) when examined in California, USA, on Sep 29, 2010.

Longest fingernails on one hand
The aggregate measurement of the five nails on Shridhar Chillal's (IND) left hand was 23 ft 1.5 in (7.05 m) on Feb 4, 2004. His thumbnail was the longest, at 5 ft 2.2 in (1.58 m), and his index finger was the shortest, at 4 ft 3.5 in (1.31 m). Chillal stopped cutting his fingernails in 1952.

LARGEST ...

Human skull
The largest documented skull was that of an adult male with a 120-cu-in (1,980-cm³) cranial capacity. The average skull has a capacity of 57.9–109 cu in (950–1,800 cm³), depending on age and size.

Hands
Robert Wadlow's (USA) hands measured 1 ft 0.75 in (32.3 cm) from wrist to tip of middle finger—not surprising

TALLEST AND SHORTEST

Tallest (8 ft scale):
- Robert Wadlow — 8 ft 11.1 in
- John William Rogan — 8 ft 8.0 in
- John F. Carroll — 8 ft 7.7 in
- Väinö Myllyrinne — 8 ft 3.0 in
- Sultan Kösen — 8 ft 3.0 in
- Don Koehler — 8 ft 2.0 in
- Bernard Coyne — 8 ft 2.0 in
- Zeng Jinlian — 8 ft 1.7 in
- Patrick Cotter (O'Brien) — 8 ft 1.0 in
- Brahim Takioullah — 8 ft 0.9 in

Shortest:
- Chandra Bahadur Dangi — 1 ft 9.5 in
- Gul Mohammed — 1 ft 10.5 in
- Junrey Balawing — 1 ft 11.5 in
- Pauline Musters — 2 ft
- Jyoti Amge — 2 ft 0.7 in
- Madge Bester — 2 ft 1.5 in
- Younis Edwan — 2 ft 1.5 in
- Calvin Phillips — 2 ft 2.4 in
- Khagendra Thapa Magar — 2 ft 2.4 in
- Lin Yih-Chih — 2 ft 3 in

The skinny on weight loss

In 1955, we reported on a 31-in-tall dwarf as the "thinnest human": "The lowest recorded human bodyweight was the 12 lb [5.44 kg] of the Welshman, Hopkin Hopkins, at his death in Glamorganshire in March 1754. At no time in his 17 years of life did he attain a weight of more than the 17 lb [7.7 kg] he was at 14 years."

The record, since retitled **lightest person** and now open only to adults aged 18 or older, is held by 26.37-in-tall Lucia Xarate (aka Lucia Zarate, MEX, 1863–89), whose adult weight peaked (at 20 years old) at 13 lb.

Simmonds' disease

The lightest recorded adults of average height are those who have Simmonds' disease (hypophyseal cachexia)—brought about by a failure of the pituitary gland. Losses of up to 65% of the original bodyweight have been recorded in females, with a low of 45 lb documented in the case of Emma Schaller (USA, 1868–90), who stood 5 ft 1 in tall.

Widest tongue

At its widest point, Byron Schlenker's (USA) tongue measures 3.26 in (8.3 cm). Three separate measurements were made in New Hartford, New York, USA, on Oct 30, 2013—3.22 in (8.2 cm), 3.30 in (8.4 cm), and 3.26 in (8.3 cm)—with the average taken as the final record value.

given his status as **tallest man ever** (see pp. 80–81). The current **tallest man**, Sultan Kösen (TUR, see p.80), has the **largest hands on a living person**: 11.22 in (28.5 cm) long.

Feet
If cases of elephantiasis are excluded, the largest feet ever measured belonged to Robert Wadlow, who wore US size 37AA shoes—the equivalent of 1 ft 6.5 in (47 cm).

The **largest feet on a living person** are those of Brahim Takioullah (MAR)—at 8 ft 0.9 in (246.3 cm), the world's second tallest living human—whose left foot measured 1 ft 3 in (38.1 cm) and his right 1 ft 2.76 in (37.5 cm) on May 24, 2011.

Tonsils
The palantine tonsils (the lymphatic tissue at the back of the mouth) of Justin Werner (USA)

his existing tattoos and is now adding white designs on top of the black, and colored designs on top of the white. Maria Jose Cristerna (MEX) is the **most tattooed woman**: she had a total body coverage of 96% on Feb 8, 2011.

Piercings (lifetime)
Elaine Davidson (BRA/UK) had been pierced 4,225 times as of Jun 8, 2006. She also received the **most piercings in a single count** with 462 in one sitting on May 4, 2000.

Largest gape

A mouth gape stretches from the incisal edge of the maxillary central incisors to the incisal edge of the mandibular central incisors. J.J. Bittner (USA, right) is able to open his mouth to a gape of 3.30 in (8.4 cm). Meanwhile, Francisco Domingo Joaquim "Chiquinho" (AGO, inset) has the **widest mouth**, measuring 6.69 in (17 cm) on Mar 18, 2010 in Rome, Italy.

measured 2.1 x 1.1 x 0.7 in (5.1 x 2.8 x 2 cm) and 1.9 x 1 x 0.7 in (4.7 x 2.6 x 2 cm). They were removed at the ExcellENT Surgery Center in Topeka, Kansas, USA, on Jan 18, 2011.

MOST ...

Tattoos
Lucky Diamond Rich (AUS, b. NZ) has spent more than 1,000 hr having his body modified. Lucky had a 100% covering of black inked over

Rolf Buchholz (DEU) had the **most piercings in a single count (male)**, with 453 on Aug 5, 2010. As of Dec 16, 2012, Rolf had 516 modifications, including a split tongue, two subdermal horn implants, four ear expanders and five magnetic fingertips in his right hand, making him the **most modified person**.

Hair-raising: incredible coiffures

Joining the GWR family in 2013 was Alan Edward Labbe (right) of Waltham, Massachusetts, USA, whose hairdo—measured at 5-ft in circumference on Jul 26—earned him a certificate for the **largest male afro**. Alan joins the likes of Eric Hahn (USA, left), whose 27-in fan of hair was verified as the **tallest Mohawk** on Nov 14, 2008, and Xie Qiuping (CHN, bottom left), who has grown the **longest hair (female)**—her terrific tresses, last measured on May 8, 2004, stretch for 18 ft 5 in.

Hole again

Most piercings...
• **On a senior citizen (single count):** "Prince Albert," aka John Lynch (UK), 241, as of Oct 17, 2008
• **In the tongue:** Francesco Vacca (USA), 16, as of Feb 17, 2012
• **On the face:** Axel Rosales (ARG), 280, as of Feb 17, 2012

○ ○ ○

Extreme bodies

Kuwaiti citizens have the **highest body mass index**: 27.5 for men, 31.4 for women

Tallest living person

At 8 ft 3 in (251 cm), Sultan Kösen (TUR) had feared that he might be too tall to find true love. But on Oct 26, 2013, his dream of finding a soul mate came true when he married 5-ft 9-in-tall (175-cm) Merve Dibo in Mardin, Turkey.

FACT

Sultan is 2 ft 6 in (76 cm) taller than Merve, but the **greatest height difference in a married couple** is 3 ft 1 in (94.5 cm) for Fabien and Natalie Pretou of France.

Heaviest twins

Billy Leon (1946–79) and Benny Loyd (1946–2001) McCrary, alias McGuire (both USA), were average in size until the age of six. But by Nov 1978, Billy and Benny weighed 743 lb (337 kg) and 723 lb (328 kg) respectively. Each brother had a waist measuring 6 ft 11.8 in (2.13 m) in circumference.

Largest waist

At his peak weight of approximately 1,200 lb (544 kg), Walter Hudson (USA, 1944–91) had a waist measurement of 9 ft 11 in (302 cm).

Heaviest woman ever

Rosalie Bradford (USA) was claimed to have registered a peak weight of around 1,200 lb (544 kg) in Jan 1987. Although she had some success in controlling her size, it continued to be a problem throughout her life and she died from weight-related complications in Nov 2006.

Heaviest living man

In 2006, Manuel Uribe (MEX) peaked in weight at 1,235 lb (560 kg), but by Mar 2012 he had slimmed down to 980 lb (444.6 kg). He remains the heaviest living man weighed by GWR.

FACT

GWR discovered Manuel after he asked for help to lose weight on Mexican television.

FACT

The **heaviest man ever** was Jon Brower Minnoch (USA, 1941–83), whose weight peaked at an estimated 1,400 lb (635 kg).

Largest chest measurement
Robert Earl Hughes (USA, 1926–58) had a chest circumference of 10 ft 4 in (315 cm). In our first edition of 1955, he was listed as the **heaviest human**, with a weight of 946 lb (429.6 kg), although when he was weighed shortly before his death he had reached 1,067 lb (484 kg).

Shortest woman ever
Pauline Musters (NLD) was born in Ossendrecht, Netherlands, on Feb 26, 1876, measuring 12 in (30.5 cm). By the time she died of pneumonia with meningitis on Mar 1, 1895 in New York City, USA, at the age of 19, she had grown to only 2 ft (61 cm).

Shortest living woman
Jyoti Amge (IND) was measured at 2 ft 0.7 in (62.8 cm) on Dec 16, 2011—her 18th birthday. She towers over the **shortest living man** (and **shortest man ever**), Chandra Bahadur Dangi (NPL), who was measured at 1 ft 9.5 in (54.6 cm) tall on Feb 26, 2012.

GUINNESS WORLD RECORDS 2013
DISCOVER A WORLD OF NEW RECORDS

Tallest man ever

Robert Pershing Wadlow of Alton, Illinois, USA, was listed as the tallest man in our first edition and his record has never been beaten. When last measured, on Jun 27, 1940, he was 8 ft 11.1 in (2.72 m). He died less than a month later, on Jul 15.

Family matters

In Senegal, the average household has **8.9 family members**; in Germany, it's just 2.0

Highest combined age for nine living siblings
As of Jun 24, 2013, the nine Melis siblings born to Francesco Melis and his wife Eleonora Mameli of Perdasdefogu, Italy, had an aggregate age of 828 years 45 days.

Largest family reunion
On Aug 12, 2012 at Saint-Paul-Mont-Penit in Vendée, France, 4,514 members of the Porteau-Boileve family came together for a truly great reunion.

Largest proportion of children
Niger has the highest proportion of children, with 50% of the total population 0–14 years old in 2012.
The **smallest proportion of children** is that of the two Special Administrative Regions of China: Hong Kong and Macau. Just 12% of their respective populations were 0–14 years old in 2012.

Lowest birth rate
In 2011, Germany had the lowest crude birth rate—the number of babies born per 1,000 people—with 8.1 births. In the same year, Germany had the 16th-largest population in the world, at 82.2 million.
As of 2011, Niger remained the country with the **highest birth rate** with 48.2 births for every 1,000 people.

Greatest number of descendants
In polygamous countries, the number of descendants can become incalculable. In terms of documented cases, at the time of his death on

Most twins in one academic year at a school

A total of 24 pairs of twins were enrolled in fifth grade at Highcrest Middle School in Wilmette, Illinois, USA, for the academic year 2012–13. That's eight more pairs than the previous record holders!

Running in the family

The **most family members from multiple generations to complete a marathon** is eight, by the Shoji family (JPN, above) at the 40th Honolulu Marathon in Hawaii, USA, on Dec 9, 2012.
The **most siblings to complete a marathon** is 16, by the Kapral family (USA, inset) in Appleton, Wisconsin, USA, on Sep 20, 2009.

Oct 15, 1992, at 96 years old, Samuel S. Mast of Fryburg, Pennsylvania, USA, was known to have 824 living descendants. The roll call comprised 11 children, 97 grandchildren, 634 great-grandchildren, and 82 great-great-grandchildren.
The last Sharifian Emperor of Morocco, Moulay Ismail (1672–1727), was reputed to have fathered a total of 525 sons and 342 daughters by 1703 and produced a 700th son in 1721. However, it is impossible for these figures to be fully verified.

Most prolific mother
A total of 69 children were born to the wife of Feodor Vassilyev (1707–ca. 1782), a peasant from Shuya, Russia. In 27 confinements, she gave birth to 16 pairs of twins, seven sets of triplets, and four sets of quadruplets.

Most children delivered in a single birth
Nine children were born to Geraldine Brodrick (AUS) at the Royal Hospital for Women in Sydney, Australia, on Jun 13, 1971. All the children (five boys and four girls) died within six days.

MOST EXPENSIVE WEDDINGS

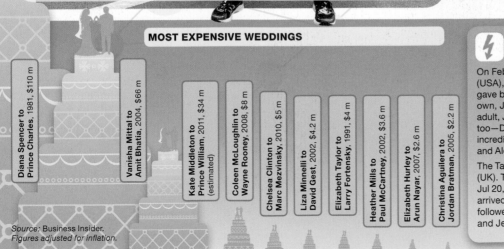

- Diana Spencer to Prince Charles, 1981, $110 m
- Vanisha Mittal to Amit Bhatia, 2004, $66 m
- Kate Middleton to Prince William, 2011, $34 m (estimated)
- Coleen McLoughlin to Wayne Rooney, 2008, $8 m
- Chelsea Clinton to Marc Mezvinsky, 2010, $5 m
- Liza Minnelli to David Gest, 2002, $4.2 m
- Elizabeth Taylor to Larry Fortensky, 1991, $4 m
- Heather Mills to Paul McCartney, 2002, $3.6 m
- Elizabeth Hurley to Arun Nayar, 2007, $2.6 m
- Christina Aguilera to Jordan Bratman, 2005, $2.2 m

Source: Business Insider. Figures adjusted for inflation.

⚡ Consecutive births of twins

On Feb 5, 1955, Gail Taylor (USA), a twin (of sibling Dale), gave birth to twins of her own, Janet and Joyce. As an adult, Janet gave birth to twins, too—Debra and Daniel—and, incredibly, Debra followed suit, giving birth to twins Nathan and Alexander: a record four generations of twins.

The Taylors (above) share their record with the Rollings family (UK). Twins Elizabeth and Olga were born on Dec 3, 1916. On Jul 20, 1950, their nieces Margaret and Maureen Hammond arrived, and their own nieces—Fay and Fiona O'Connor—followed on Feb 26, 1977. Finally, Fay and Fiona's nieces Kacie and Jessica Fawcett were born on Jan 12, 2002.

Oldest first-time grandmother

Marianne Wallenberg (DEU, b. Feb 7, 1913) was 95 years 81 days old when her first grandson, Joshua Fritz Wallenberg (CAN), was born at Sinai Hospital in Toronto, Ontario, Canada, on Apr 29, 2008. Joshua's twin, Karina Diana, was delivered at the same birth.

Lightest birth

The lightest birth for a surviving infant of which there is evidence is 9.17 oz (260 g) for Rumaisa Rahman (USA), born at Loyola University Medical Center in Maywood, Illinois, USA, on Sep 19, 2004, after a gestation period of just 25 weeks 6 days.

Rumaisa was born with her twin sister Hiba, who weighed 1 lb 4.4 oz (580 g). Together, they hold the record for the **lightest birth for twins**, with a total weight of 1 lb 13.57 oz (840 g).

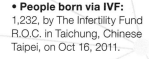

Longest marriage

Herbert Fisher (USA, 1905–2011) and Zelmyra Fisher (USA, 1907–2013) were married on May 13, 1924 in North Carolina, USA. They had been married 86 years 290 days at the time of Herbert's death.

On Jan 26, 2009, Nadya Suleman (USA) gave birth to six boys and two girls at the Kaiser Permanente Medical Center in Bellflower, California, USA—the **most children delivered in a single birth to survive**. The babies were conceived with the aid of in vitro fertilization (IVF) treatment and were nine weeks premature when they were delivered by Cesarean section.

Heaviest birth

Giantess Anna Bates (née Swan, CAN), who measured 7 ft 11 in (241.3 cm), gave birth to a boy weighing 22 lb (9.98 kg) and measuring 2 ft 4 in (71.12 cm) at her home in Seville, Ohio, USA, on Jan 19, 1879. The baby died 11 hr later.

Donna Simpson (USA) weighed 532 lb (241 kg) when she delivered daughter Jacqueline in Feb 2007, making her the **heaviest woman to give birth**.

Longest interval between birth of triplets

The greatest gap between the birth of a first and third triplet was 66 hr 50 min for the arrival of Christine, Catherine, and Calvin, children of Louise and Robert Jamison (all USA) in 1956. Christine was born at 3.05 a.m. on Jan 2, Catherine was born at 10 a.m. on Jan 3, and Calvin was born at 9.55 p.m. on Jan 4.

Peggy Lynn (USA) gave birth to a girl, Hanna, on Nov 11, 1995. Hanna's twin, Eric, was not delivered until Feb 2, 1996—84 days later—at the Geisinger Medical Center in Pennsylvania, USA—a delay that represents the **longest interval between the birth of twins**.

Largest gathering of ...
• **Multiple births:** 4,002 sets (3,961 pairs of twins, 37 sets of triplets, four sets of quads) amassed outside Taipei City Hall in Chinese Taipei on Nov 12, 1999.

• **People born via IVF:** 1,232, by The Infertility Fund R.O.C. in Taichung, Chinese Taipei, on Oct 16, 2011.

• **People born prematurely:** 386, by UNICEF in Buenos Aires, Argentina, on Sep 30, 2012.

• **People with the same birthday:** 228 people, all born on Jul 4, by Stichting Apenheul (NLD) in Apeldoorn, Netherlands, on Jul 4, 2012.

Most bridesmaids to a bride

Nisansala Kumari Ariyasiri (LKA) was attended to by a record retinue of 126 bridesmaids at her wedding to Nalin Pathirana at the Avenra Garden Hotel in Negombo, Colombo, Sri Lanka, on Nov 8, 2013. Around 700 guests were also present.

For more group records, see p. 116

High do: tallest married couple

On Aug 4, 2013, Sun Mingming—the world's **tallest active basketball player**—and handball player Xu Yan (both CHN) were married in Beijing, China, generating speculation that they had become the world's **tallest married couple**.

On Nov 14, 2013, Guinness World Records was able to confirm this as a record when the towering twosome were measured by doctors at the Oasis Healthcare Centre in Beijing in the presence of official adjudicators. Mingming and Yan reached 7 ft 9 in and 6 ft 1.7 in respectively, giving a record combined height of 13 ft 10.7 in and beating the previous record by 1.7 in.

FACT

The **tallest married couple ever recorded** in history was Anna Haining Swan (CAN) and Martin van Buren Bates (USA), whose combined height was 15 ft 8 in when they married in St Martin-in-the-Fields church in Trafalgar Square, London, UK, on Jun 17, 1871. Anna later gave birth to the **heaviest baby** (see main text above).

Medical bag

The 14th-century outbreak of the Black Death killed up to **200 million** people

Largest waiting mortuary

German physician Christoph Wilhelm Hufeland (1762–1836) designed "waiting hospitals" to avoid burying the living. The largest of these was in Munich around 1880, and had room for 120 corpses. "Patients" were tied to an alarm system triggered by movement.

First three-headed baby

In 1834, Dr. Raina and Dr. Galvagni (both ITA) described a stillborn, three-headed infant. This was the to Dec 26, 1898. He was an assistant to the coffin's inventor, Count Michel de Karnice-Karnicki (RUS). It had a periscope-like tube reaching above ground to let in air for the prematurely buried. Lorenzo said of his Christmas break that it had been "damned smelly down there."

Lightest person

Lucia Zarate (aka Xarate, MEX) weighed 2 lb 6 oz (1.1 kg) at birth and 4 lb 11 oz (2.1 kg) at the age of 17. By 1884, when she was 20, she weighed 13 lb (5.9 kg). Born with a variant of dwarfism, she reached a height of 2 ft 2 in (67 cm).

Longest human horn

There are many historical instances of humans growing large horns, usually from the head. Madame Dimanche (FRA), who lived in Paris, France, in the early 19th century, had a horn measuring 10 in (25 cm) in length and 2 in (5 cm) in diameter at the base.

First recorded case of congenital hypertrichosis

The hirsute covering of Petrus Gonzales (ESP, b. 1537) was caused by congenital hypertrichosis lanuginosa. Educated at the court of the French king Henri II, he married a wife who did not share his condition.

First recorded lithopedion

The 1582 autopsy on 68-year-old Madame Colombe Chatri (FRA) revealed an ossified child (lithopedion or "stone-child"). The fetus had died in pregnancy and was calcified by her body to prevent infection from the tissue.

First proven case of superfetation

Superfetation is the conception of twins from two different menstrual cycles—and potentially different fathers. A 1980 case of disputed paternity of twins in Germany used genetic testing to establish the putative father of Twin Two with 99.995% probability, while excluding him as the father of Twin One.

Smallest waist

Ethel Granger (UK, 1905–82) reduced her natural waist from 24 in (56 cm) to 13 in (33 cm) from 1929 to 1939 by wearing increasingly tighter corsets. The same measurement was matched by actress Mlle Polaire, aka Émilie Marie Bouchaud (FRA, 1874–1939).

First safety coffin

Duke Ferdinand of Brunswick-Wolfenbüttel (DEU) suffered from taphophobia (see below). Ahead of his death in 1792, he ordered a coffin with a window, an air hole, and a lid that was unlockable instead of nailed down.

Faroppo Lorenzo (ITA) underwent the **longest voluntary burial** in a safety coffin, from Dec 17,

First documented account of a pig-faced lady

Papers published by G.J. Boekenoogen (NLD) trace the legend of girls born with the face of a pig back to the 1630s. A Dutch print goes farther back, recounting the tale of a girl from 1621 who grew up to eat from a trough and talk in grunts. Such fanciful accounts were spread in pamphlets and ballads that were in general circulation during the 17th and 18th centuries.

TOP 10 CAUSES OF DEATH WORLDWIDE IN 2011

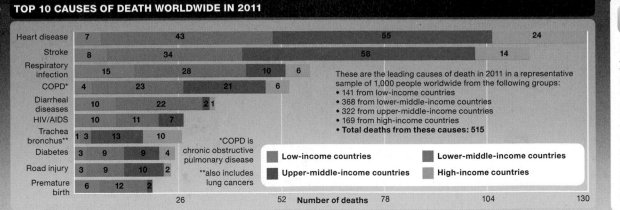

	Low-income	Lower-middle-income	Upper-middle-income	High-income
Heart disease	7	43	55	24
Stroke	8	34	58	14
Respiratory infection	15	28	10	6
COPD*	4	23	21	6
Diarrheal diseases	10	22	2	1
HIV/AIDS	10	11	7	
Trachea bronchus**	1 3	13	10	
Diabetes	3	9	9	4
Road injury	3	9	10	2
Premature birth	6	12	2	

| 26 | 52 | Number of deaths | 78 | 104 | 130 |

These are the leading causes of death in 2011 in a representative sample of 1,000 people worldwide from the following groups:
- 141 from low-income countries
- 368 from lower-middle-income countries
- 322 from upper-middle-income countries
- 169 from high-income countries
- **Total deaths from these causes: 515**

*COPD is chronic obstructive pulmonary disease

**also includes lung cancers

- Low-income countries
- Lower-middle-income countries
- Upper-middle-income countries
- High-income countries

Source: World Health Organization, 2013

Glossary

Hypertrichosis: Abnormal growth of hair; the condition can be congenital (from birth). Hairiness can be assessed using the Ferriman-Gallwey method (see p. 78).

Taphophobia: The fear of being buried alive. This was a pressing concern before doctors were able to reliably detect signs of life in people who might appear to be deceased.

First recorded asymmetrical conjoined twins

Lazarus Colloredo (ITA, b. 1617) had a parasitic twin complete with head and three deformed extremities growing from his chest. The twin was apparently considered to be a separate individual and was given the name Joannes Baptista. Lazarus toured to exhibit his twin, who displayed some reaction to stimulus, implying limited autonomous functionality.

Most tapeworms expelled

It is possible for more than one tapeworm to exist in the body. In 1883, Dr. Aguiel described an unnamed patient who expelled a 2-lb 3-oz (1-kg) lump containing 113 ft 2 in (34.5 m) of tapeworm. Three years later, Dr. Garfinkel saw a peasant with 238 ft (72.5-m) of tapeworm with 12 heads.

first reported instance of extreme conjoined twinning; one of the necks had two heads.

Longest human tail

Indian plantation worker Chandre Oram showed a tail measuring 1 ft 1 in (33 cm) in length to the world's media in 2008. Other notable cases include a 12-year-old boy in French Indochina who was said to have sported a 9-in (22.8-cm) tail. In 1901, anatomist Dr. Ross Granville Harrison described a baby boy with a 3-in-long (7.6-cm) tail that was examined by Harrison after amputation.

Most ascarides expelled

Ascarides are roundworm parasites that live in the small intestine. They sometimes appear by the hundreds, but in 1880, Dr. Fauconneau-Dufresne reported on the case of a Frenchman who had managed to expel around 5,000 ascarides in less than three years, largely through vomiting.

Most children born to unseparated conjoined twins

Chang and Eng Bunker (1811–74) were born in Thailand, then called Siam—the origin of the now-defunct term "Siamese twins." The two men fathered 21 children, the descendents of whom held their 24th annual reunion in Mount Airy, North Carolina, USA, in 2013.

Longest nose ever

Thomas Wedders (UK) was a traveling circus sideshow act in the 1770s, with a nose that was reputed to measure 7.5 in (19 cm) long.

Most deadly outbreak of listeriosis

Sources differ, but somewhere between 47 and 84 people were killed in California, USA, in the 1985 outbreak of listeriosis. It was caused by the bacteria listeria in cheese and, even at the lowest figure, it remains the instance with the highest number of fatalities. It is also the deadliest outbreak of bacterial food-borne disease in the USA.

Oldest dwarf

Hungarian-born Susanna Bokoyni of New Jersey, USA, was 105 when she died on Aug 24, 1984. Born in Apr 1879, she was 3 ft 4 in (101.5 cm) tall and is one of two centenarian dwarfs on record. The other was Anne Clowes (UK), who died on Aug 5, 1784 at the age of 103 and was 3 ft 9 in (114 cm) tall.

Oldest ever male conjoined twins

Giacomo and Giovanni Battista Tocci (ITA) were born on Oct 4, 1877 and lived to be 63. They were separate above the waist, but shared an abdomen, pelvis, and two legs. Having made money from touring Europe and the USA, they retired from public life.

Together: conjoined twins

Masha and Dasha Krivoshlyapova (both USSR, left) suffered from *dicephalus tetrabrachius dipus* (two heads, four arms, and two legs), a very rare form of conjoined twinning. They were born on Jan 3, 1950 and, until their death on Apr 17, 2003, were the **oldest living conjoined female twins**. The title then went to the craniopagus (joined at the head) twins born on Sep 18, 1961 as Lori and Dori Schappell (both USA, right). As of May 8, 2014 they were 52 years 232 days old. In 2007, Dori announced that he was transgender, identifying himself as a male called George.

FACT

The decision to separate conjoined twins is not taken lightly, and many twins—such as Lori and George (left) and Chang and Eng Bunker (above)—opt to stay together. Complications arise when twins share vital organs. In the case of the Bunkers, their livers were fused; the procedure to separate them would be relatively simple today, but not so back in the 1800s, hence their decision to stay together.

:Recordmania

Mania: noun, from the Greek, *be mad*; an excessive enthusiasm or passion

Largest collection of soft-drink cans

Davide Andreani's (ITA) mania for Coca-Cola cans began at the age of five, when he started collecting unfamiliar cans brought home by his father from European business trips. At the last count, confirmed on Aug 14, 2013, Coke addict Davide owned a record 10,558 unique single-brand cans from 87 countries.

FACT
Most of Davide's cans are unopened. He empties them by piercing a hole in the bottom so the cans don't explode!

Mr. Versatility

No sooner had work started on the first edition of *The Guinness Book of Records* in London than a boy was born in New York City, USA, who would go on to become the undisputed king of breaking records. His name was Keith Furman, but today he's better known by his spiritual name: Ashrita.

That the man who holds the Guinness World Records title for **most Guinness World Records titles held** was born within a month of the company is a coincidence, but it's a joyous one. Keith Furman was born on Sep 16, 1954. It would be 25 years before he set the first of many Guinness World Records,

but he has achieved more in 36 years than most people could do in 10 lifetimes.

The manager of a health food store, Furman was given the name Ashrita—Sanskrit for "Protected by God"—by his spiritual teacher Sri Chinmoy (IND, 1931–2007), who taught him self-transcendence and meditation. Using these lessons, Ashrita set his first record in 1979—achieving 27,000 jumping jacks—and he hasn't looked back. As of May 1, 2014, he had set 521 records, of which 182 are still current.

Come with us on a journey through just some of the records set by Mr. Versatility …

> **ℹ For the record**
>
> Ashrita set his 100th record on Sep 24, 2005, **spinning the largest hula hoop**—16 ft (4.8 m) in diameter—three times around his waist on the set of *Richard & Judy* in London, UK.

Ashrita … in his own words

"My teacher's philosophy of self-transcendence—of overcoming your limits and making progress spiritually, creatively, and physically using the power of meditation—really thrills me. If you can connect with your inner source and be receptive to a higher Grace, you can accomplish anything.

"Attempting records has become an inherent part of my spiritual journey. I scour the *Guinness World Records* book looking for categories I think will be challenging and fun. Many of the records involve childlike activities, such as juggling, hopscotch, unicycling, pogo-sticking, and balancing objects on my head and chin. I get joy not only in practicing the activity itself, but also in seeing my progress toward achieving a goal. The particular event is unimportant as long as it gives you the opportunity to dance on the edge of your capacity."

1986 **Most consecutive forward rolls:** 8,341

2003 **Fastest marathon skipping (no rope):** 5 hr 55 min 13 sec

2006 **Fastest mile spinning a whip top:** 25 min 13 sec

2004 **Fastest mile while hula-hooping:** 14 min 25 sec

1997 **Farthest distance jumped on a pogo stick:** 23.11 mi (37.18 km)

2007 **Farthest distance jumped underwater on a pogo stick:** 1,680 ft (512.06 m)

1979 1980 1981 1982 1983 1984 1985 1986 1987 1988 1989 1990 1991

1998 **Farthest distance walked with a milk bottle on the head:** 80.96 mi (130.3 km)

2007 **Fastest mile on a pogo stick while juggling three balls:** 23 min 28 sec

2004 **Fastest time to walk 8 km on stilts:** 39 min 56 sec

2007 **Most skips on spring-loaded stilts in one minute:** 106

1999 **Farthest distance carrying a 9-lb (4.08-kg) brick nonstop (male):** 85.05 mi (136.87 km)

2010 **Longest duration juggling three objects under water:** 1 hr 19 min 58 sec

FURMAN'S FAVORITES

Ashrita has broken records on all seven continents, including the **fastest mile on a pogo stick** in Antarctica and the **fastest mile on a kangaroo ball (spacehopper)** along the Great Wall of China. Here, he picks his most memorable records.

Most consecutive forward rolls	8,341
Farthest distance with milk bottle on head	80.9 mi
Pogo-stick jumping (in Mount Fuji foothills)	11.5 mi
Underwater pogo-stick jumping (in the Amazon River)	3,647 jumps 3 hr 40 min
Fastest sack race mile (against a yak)	16 min 41 sec
Most jumping jacks—Ashrita's first record!	27,000
Pool cue balancing (at the pyramids, Egypt)	7 mi
Fastest mile pushing an orange with nose	22 min 41 sec
Fastest 8 km on stilts	39 min 56 sec
Fastest 5 km skipped without a rope	30 min

Key

Record set then later lost

Still holds record

Current as of May 1, 2014

2011 **Most apples snapped in one minute:** 40

2011 **Most baseballs held in a glove:** 24

2009 **Fastest 10 m balancing a pool cue on the chin:** 3.02 sec

2008 **Fastest mile on stilts:** 12 min 23 sec

93 1994 1995 1996 1997 1998 1999 2000 2001 2002 2003 2004 2005 2006 2007 2008 2009 2010 2011 2012 2013 2014

2009 **Fastest mile balancing a book on the head:** 8 min 27 sec

2010 **Longest control of a golf ball with one club:** 1 hr 20 min 42 sec

2010 **Fastest one-mile piggy-back race:** 12 min 47 sec

2012 **Longest duration balancing a chain saw on the chin:** 1 min 25.01 sec

2010 **Fastest 100 m frog jumping:** 7 min 18 sec

2012 **Fastest mile bounce-juggling three objects:** 7 min 27 sec

2012 **Fastest 5 km joggling in swim fins:** 32 min 3 sec

:Collections

There are an estimated **five million stamp collectors** in the USA

Pizza boxes
When Scott Wiener (USA) orders a pizza, he's usually more interested in the box than the food. As of Oct 23, 2013, the pizza buff—who has even written a book about his passion, *Viva La Pizza!: The Art of the Pizza Box*—had amassed a collection of 595 boxes from 42 different countries.

These are the latest collections to be added to the GWR database:

Airline boarding passes
Having flown with 90 airlines in 28 years, João Gilberto Vaz of Brasilia, Brazil, had saved 2,558 boarding passes as of Jan 23, 2014. He flies an average of 91.35 flights per year.

Bagpipes
Daniel Fleming of Cleethorpes in Lincolnshire, UK, owned 105 sets of playable bagpipes as of Oct 24, 2013.

Coins from the same year
Rahul G. Keshwani (IND) has 11,111 coins from the year 1989. The collection, made up of the defunct 25-paise coin, was verified on Jul 28, 2013 in Mumbai, India.

Cookbooks
Sue Jimenez (USA/CAN) had 2,970 cookbooks as of Jul 14, 2013 in Albuquerque, New Mexico, USA.

Electronic calculators
Gerhard Wenzel (DEU) has no fear of wrongly counting his collection of calculators—not

Fake food
Plastic food replicas are a common sight in Japanese restaurants … and in the home of Akiko Obata in Sanbu-gun, Chiba, Japan. Obata's collection of 8,083 fake dishes—plus food-related keyrings, toys, and magnets—was verified on Jan 24, 2014.

with 4,113 examples to help add them up, as of Sep 7, 2013, in Solingen, Germany.

Ganesha-related items
Ram and Lalita Kogata (IND) own 10,631 items relating to Ganesha, the Hindu god with the head of an elephant. Their collection was counted on Sep 14, 2013 in Udaipur, Rajasthan, India. The couple also have the **largest collection of Ganesha statues**, with 2,930.

Gift cards (gift tokens)
In 2007, teenage brothers Aaron and David Miller (USA/CAN) wanted to make shopping with their mother more interesting, so they started to collect gift tokens. As of Aug 30, 2013, they had amassed 3,215 different cards.

Horse-related items
Equine enthusiast Edgar Rugeles (COL) had collected 2,762 models of

Doctor Who memorabilia
Ian O'Brien (UK) had acquired 1,573 unique items relating to everyone's favorite Timelord, as of Sep 6, 2013, in his home in Manchester, UK. He started his collection in 1974 with a yellow Dalek (a Louis Marx toy) and received *The Dr. Who Annual* every Christmas. His personal favorites are a TARDIS console released by Dapol and a very rare nursery toy Dalek by Selcol.

TOP 10 LARGEST CATEGORIES OF COLLECTIONS

Total: **12,558,180** as of Apr 22, 2014

1: Tobacco — 4.65 million items
2: Human body — 2.17 million items
3: Publishing — 1.65 million items
4: Food and drink — 1.45 million items
5: Clothing and accessories — 806,698 items
6: Leisure, games, and hobbies — 551,046 items
7: Travel — 459,249 items
8: Stationery — 381,101 items
9: Household — 237,006 items
10: Animal — 184,946 items

Stamps featuring …
Paintings: J. M. van der Leeuw (NLD), 19,284 stamps as of May 25, 2013 in Wageningen, Netherlands
Sea life: Samhar Moafaq Noori Ahmed (IRQ), 2,775 stamps as of Nov 16, 2013 in Leeds, Yorkshire, UK
First-day covers: George Vavvas (GRC), 7,215 stamps as of Apr 6, 2013 in Ioannina, Greece
Popes: Magnus Andersson (SWE), 1,580 stamps as of Nov 16, 2010 in Falun, Sweden

Glossary
Bibliophilism: Enthused book collecting
Cagophily: Key collecting
Cartophily: Cigarette- or chewing gum-card collecting
Labeorphily: Beer bottle-label collecting
Philately: Postage stamp collecting
Timbromania: Mania for collecting postage stamps

○○○

CHARACTER COLLECTIONS

Collection	Amount	Record holder	Date counted
X-Men	15,400	Eric Jaskolka (USA)	Jun 28, 2012
James Bond (see below)	12,463	Nick Bennett (UK)	Nov 21, 2013
Winnie the Pooh	10,002	Deb Hoffmann (USA)	Sep 14, 2013
Mickey Mouse	6,726	Janet Esteves (USA)	Nov 11, 2013
Conan the Barbarian	4,670	Robert and Patricia Leffler (both USA)	Apr 2, 2003
Hello Kitty	4,519	Asako Kanda (JPN)	Aug 14, 2011
Trolls	2,990	Sherry Groom (USA)	Oct 26, 2012
Donald Duck	2,775	Steffen Gerdes (DNK)	Jun 27, 2012
The Simpsons	2,580	Cameron Gibbs (AUS)	Mar 20, 2008
Batman	2,501	Kevin Silva (USA)	Oct 25, 2013
Doctor Who (see opposite page)	1,573	Ian O'Brien (UK)	Sep 6, 2013
Charlie's Angels	1,460	Jack Condon (USA)	Feb 6, 2007
Superman	1,253	Herbert Chavez (PHL)	Feb 22, 2012
Daleks	1,202	Rob Hull (UK)	May 14, 2013
Harry Potter	807	Jayne Gradel (USA)	Jun 13, 2013

1
2
3

horses, among other items of horse memorabilia, as of Aug 26, 2013, in Bogotá, Colombia.

Keys
Lisa J. Large of Kansas City, Missouri, USA, owned 3,604 different keys as of Nov 20, 2013.

Ozzy Osbourne memorabilia
As of Oct 18, 2013, Claus Solvig of Rødovre, Denmark, had acquired 1,811 items relating to heavy-metal legend Ozzy Osbourne.

James Bond memorabilia

Nick Bennett (UK) began his bond with Bond in 1995 and his collection of 12,463 items, as verified on Nov 21, 2013, is now housed in a warehouse in Warrington, UK. The collection includes Roger Moore's shoes from *The Man with the Golden Gun* (UK, 1974), a unique 007 doll worth in the region of £10,000 ($16,000), and a speedboat from *Live and Let Die* (UK, 1973).

Collect call: anything goes

Guinness World Records has at least 169 collection categories for which a record has yet to be awarded. Now's the time to check behind the couch— perhaps you have the **largest collection of ...** *Alice in Wonderland* memorabilia; Aloha (Hawaiian) shirts; autographed golf balls; autographed soccer memorabilia; baby bibs; baseball jerseys; basketball memorabilia; beauty pageant sashes; bedpans; boxed PC games; branded cans; Buddhist statues; camel-related items; candy canes; cleaning brushes; collie-related items; crotcheted items ... Find out how to register your claim on p. 5.

And finally ...

- **The Nightmare Before Christmas** memorabilia: William Wong (HKG) owns 2,020 items (Feb 18, 2014).
- **Star Wars** memorabilia: Steve Sansweet (USA) has 300,000 unique *Star Wars* items in California, USA. Of these, 92,240 had been catalogued by May 4, 2014.
- **Clothing labels:** Paul Brockmann (USA) has amassed 4,120 labels (Mar 11, 2014).

Model making

Airfix originally sold **inflatable rubber toys**; it didn't sell model-making kits until 1952

Largest toothpick sculpture
Michael Smith (USA) used more than 3 million toothpicks to create "Alley," a 15-ft-long (4.5-m) alligator that weighed 292 lb (132.4 kg) when measured in Prairieville, Louisiana, USA, on Mar 22, 2005.

Largest display of toothpick sculptures
A full miniature orchestra—comprising 62 musicians with their instruments, plus a conductor—was modeled by Go Sato (CAN) using 12,500 toothpicks and displayed in Ottawa, Ontario, Canada, on Jun 18, 2013.

Largest Plasticine model
Martin and Nigel Langdon (UK) have spent thousands of hours since the early 1960s painstakingly modeling their ideal city with more than 500 lb (226 kg) of Plasticine. The model, complete with Roman-style colosseum and American-inspired skyscrapers, now covers an area 15 ft (4.5 m) long by 4 ft (1.2 m) wide. The only things not made of Plasticine are the tree trunks, which are made of dyed matchsticks.

Largest model aircraft kit

In the TV series *Toy Stories* (BBC, 2009), presenter James May (UK) took part in the construction of a model aircraft from a fully scaled-up Airfix kit, resulting in a 1:1 replica of a Supermarine Spitfire Mk1 with a wingspan of 36 ft 9 in (11.2 m) and a length of 29 ft 11 in (9.12 m). It was built at the Royal Air Force Museum Cosford in Shropshire, UK.

Largest matchstick model
"Cathedrals of the Sea" is a North Sea oil production platform modeled from 4,075,000 matchsticks. It was made by David Reynolds (UK) and completed in Jul 2009.

Largest collection of military models
Francisco Sánchez Abril (ESP) started collecting miniature military vehicles in 1958 and, as of Feb 2012, had amassed 2,815 unique items representing the military might of 25 countries.

Largest model airport
Knuffingen Airport, located at Miniatur Wunderland in Hamburg, Germany, is built to a scale of 1:87. The 494-sq-ft (45.9-m²) model is based on the

Tallest toothpick sculpture

Stan Munro (USA) created a model of the Burj Khalifa tower in Dubai, UAE, the world's **tallest building**. The 16-ft 8-in-tall (5.09-m) sculpture was measured at the Phelps Art Center in Phelps, New York, USA, on Jun 22, 2013. It took Munro around six months to make and includes approximately 250,000 toothpicks.

Tallest matchstick model

A scale replica of the Eiffel Tower, built from matchsticks by Toufic Daher (LBN), stands at 21 ft 5 in (6.53 m) tall. It was unveiled at City Mall, Beirut, Lebanon, on Nov 11, 2009, in celebration of GWR Day.

> **HOW TO MAKE A SHIP IN A BOTTLE**

01 Choose a bottle with a fairly large neck and paint a sea effect inside the bottle.

02 Using wood, build the hull of the ship. Build everything except for the mast, sails, and the sail's support beams (spars). Make sure it can fit through the neck of the bottle. Paint.

03 Make the masts. Create a hinge using wire, which is used to bend the sails, in the base of each mast. Make the sails and spars.

04 Make holes in each mast and run a line of thread through them. Attach the masts and rigging to the hull of the ship; lay them flat along its length.

05 Push the ship through the bottle's neck. Color putty to represent the sea. When the putty sets, the ship should be stable.

06 Gently pull the thread running through the masts, so that they rise vertically on their wire hinges.

07 Fasten the masts by applying glue to their bases. Insert a cork to seal the bottle.

Pietro D'Angelo

Since 2008, Italian artist Pietro D'Angelo has been creating a series of sculptures made from paper clips—all handmade in his own home. Created in 2008, Pietro's *Pole Dance* is the **tallest paper clip sculpture** in the world, stretching 7 ft 5 in. Each sculpture takes Pietro two to three months to produce and includes 10–20,000 paper clips. The dextrous D'Angelo used iron paper clips at first, but now has stainless steel versions specially made for him by a paper clip factory.

Largest collection of dioramas

A diorama is a 3D model of a landscape or scene containing numerous elements, and the largest collection on record is owned by Nabil Karam (LBN). Among his 333 dioramas—which were counted in Zouk, Lebanon, on Nov 17, 2011—are famous battles, a train station, an airport, and scenes from classic movies.

Smallest ship in a bottle

In 1956, Arthur V. Pedlar (UK) constructed a ship inside a 1-cc glass phial measuring 0.9 in (2.38 cm) long and 0.3 in (0.9 cm) wide, with a neck of just 0.07 in (0.2 cm). The galleon had three masts, five sails, and three flags.

Largest display of ships in a bottle

Kjell Birkeland (NOR) owned a fleet of 655 model ships, as of Feb 15, 2013. The bottled boats are displayed at the Arendal Bymuseum in Arendal, Norway.

Largest ship in a bottle

"Nelson's Ship in a Bottle" is a scale replica of HMS *Victory* contained within a giant bottle. The artwork was made by Yinka Shonibare MBE (UK) and measures 15 ft 5 in (4.7 m) in length and 9 ft 2 in (2.8 m) in diameter. It was originally displayed on the Fourth Plinth in Trafalgar Square, London, UK, in 2010.

international airport serving Hamburg, and took seven years to complete.

Fastest rocket-powered model car

The Heathland School Rocket Car Club in Hounslow, UK, built "Möbius," a jet-propelled model car that reached an incredible speed of 204.95 mph (329.84 km/h) on Jun 14, 2013.

Longest model train

A model train measuring 925 ft 6 in (282.11 m) and comprising 31 locomotives and 1,563 carriages was constructed by the Wilmington Railroad Museum Model Railroad Committee. It was presented in Wilmington, North Carolina, USA, on Apr 23, 2011.

The **longest model train track** is the Great American Railway, which boasts a total of more than 9.5 mi (15.2 km) of HO (1:87 scale) track. Built by Bruce Williams Zaccagnino (USA), it is the star exhibit at the Northlandz attraction in Flemington, New Jersey, USA.

Most model rocket kits launched simultaneously

Boy Scout Jacob Smith (USA) launched 3,130 model rockets at the same time to commemorate the 100th anniversary of the Boy Scouts of America. The launch took place in College Station, Texas, USA, on Oct 9, 2010.

Largest Dalek sculpture

Snugburys Ice Cream (UK) has made straw sculptures for over 10 years and, in 2013, built a 35-ft-tall (10.6-m) Dalek. The sculpture, made in celebration of *Doctor Who*'s 50th anniversary, took 700 hr to complete and used 13,440 lb (6 metric tons) of straw and 11,200 lb (5 metric tons) of steel.

Mini-marvel: Queen Mary's Dolls' House

Built in 1921–24 by architect Sir Edwin Landseer Lutyens (UK) at a scale of 1:12, Queen Mary's Dolls' House includes plumbing, electricity, and a cellar stocked with drinkable wine. It is the **most visited dolls' house**, having been on display for many years at Windsor Castle in Windsor, UK, which attracted more than 9 million visitors between 2004 and 2013 alone. Its miniature library contains the **most works of literature made for a dolls' house**; the 206 unique literary works include a handwritten book of poetry by Rudyard Kipling and *How Watson Learned the Trick*, a story specially written by Arthur Conan Doyle.

i Diminutive domiciles

Also known as "baby houses," these dolls' houses date back at least to the 16th century. The early versions were usually replicas of grand houses of rich families instead of toys. By the 18th century, "doll cabinets"—miniature houses set in fine cabinets—were common. The Victorian era saw the birth of the dolls' house as we know it today: a beautifully crafted child's plaything.

:Big stuff

The **Great Wall of China** is big—but it's a myth that it is visible from the Moon

Largest poster

The boss of all posters is a poster to promote *Boss*, a 2013 Bollywood movie. It took 30 hr to print and had an area of 34,814 sq ft (3,234 m²), longer than 12 tennis courts. It was made by Team Akshay (IND) and Macro Art Ltd (UK) and unveiled on Oct 3, 2013.

Hot dog cart
Marcus Daily (USA) built a 12-ft 3-in-tall (3.72-m) cart that, despite its size, is mobile, although at 23 ft 2 in (7.06 m) in length, it moves with difficulty. Marcus plans to turn the cart—which set the record on Oct 28, 2013 in Union, Missouri, USA—into a permanent restaurant.

Knitting needles
Despite being 13 ft 0.75 in (3.98 m) long, needles made by Jim Bolin were used by Jeanette Huisinga (both USA) to knit a square of 10 x 10 stitches at Monroe Elementary School in Casey, Illinois, USA, on May 20, 2013.

Megaphone
Members of the public were encouraged to make their thoughts heard loud and clear with a massive megaphone measuring 8 ft (2.43 m) long. It was built by Bezoya (ESP) in Madrid, Spain, on Oct 10, 2013.

LARGEST ...

Envelope
Ajmal Khan Tibbiya College (IND) made an envelope measuring 58 ft 7 in (17.86 m) in length and 42 ft 11.7 in (13.10 m) in width in Aligarh, Uttar Pradesh, India, on Apr 3, 2013.

Model tooth
A massive molar measuring 27 ft (8.23 m) tall was made by Sensodyne (MEX) and displayed in Mexico City's Parque México on Nov 25, 2013 to raise awareness of tooth decay.

Longest golf club

Karsten Maas (DNK) made a 14-ft 5-in-long (4.37-m) golf club and drove a ball 542 ft 10 in (165.46 m) at the Golf in Wall course in Wall, Germany, on Apr 30, 2013. Karsten, who performs in his own trick golf shows, last set the record in 2009. Normal golf drivers are usually around 3 ft 9 in–4 ft (1.14–1.22 m).

Largest floor lamp

Fredrik and Martin Raddum (NOR) were the bright sparks behind a lamp measuring 30 ft (9.16 m) high in Oslo, Norway, in Feb 2013. The lamp shade is made of polyester and fiberglass and is 13 ft (3.98 m) in diameter. The supporting pole is made of steel.

Oil lamp
An oil lamp with a volume of 172.4 gal (652.8 liters) was commissioned by the municipality of Almócita in Almeria, Spain, as part of their celebrations for The Night of the Oil Lamps festival held on May 11, 2013.

Paintbrush
Indian artist Sujit Das made a paintbrush measuring 28 ft (8.5 m) long and weighing 48 lb 8 oz (22 kg). It was used at Nagaon Government Boys' High School in Nagaon, India, on Jun 19, 2012 to paint portraits of Mahatma Gandhi, Bhagat Singh, and Bishnu Prasad Rabha.

Longest board cut from one tree

Daniel Czapiewski (POL) cut a board measuring 152 ft 7 in (46.53 m) in Szymbark, Poland, on Jun 9, 2012. For more from Daniel, see Big Orchestra on pp. 96–97.

XL XMAS

Largest Christmas cracker: length 207 ft, diameter 13 ft

Largest Christmas star: height 103 ft 8 in

Tallest artificial Christmas tree: height 170 ft 7 in

Largest Christmas bauble ornament: diameter 13 ft 9 in

Largest nativity figurine: height 17 ft 4 in, diameter 11 ft 1 in

Largest candy cane: length 36 ft 7 in, diameter 4 in

Largest Christmas candle: height 12 ft 9 in, width 10 ft 2 in

Big news

In 1955, we reported on the "most massive single issue of a newspaper yet published": a 490-page edition of *The New York Times* from Sep 12, 1954. This has since been beaten by the Sep 14, 1987 Sunday edition of the *New York Times*—a single issue that contained 1,612 pages. At a back-breaking 11 lb 14 oz, it's also the **heaviest newspaper ever**.

Making it supersize

"Big stuff" records typically require claimants to recreate a scaled-up version of a regular-size object, maintaining proportions where possible and using the same construction materials. Although guidelines may vary, we expect the supersize version to be functional—a giant pencil should still be able to write, for example, no matter how big!

Largest clothespin

Karl Josef Biller (DEU, pictured right) devised a fully functioning wooden clothespin—just don't get your finger caught in it! It measured 11 ft 5 in (3.5 m) long and 2 ft (65 cm) high, and was unveiled on Sep 9, 2012 in Regensburg, Germany.

Mailbox
A 2,418.49-cu-ft (68.484-m³) mailbox was erected by Yamaguchi University's Choshu Enjoying Science Innovation Project in Ube, Yamaguchi, Japan, on Dec 27, 2012. A first-class effort all round!

Silver ring
A 201-lb 5-oz (91.32-kg) ring made from 99.99% pure silver was made by Valentine Diamond (TUR). The ring, which has an inner diameter of 3 ft (92 cm), was measured in Istanbul, Turkey, on Sep 27, 2013.

Sand castle
Ed Jarrett (USA) became king of the (sand) castle with his 38-ft 2-in-tall (11.63-m) effort at Point Pleasant Beach in New Jersey, USA, on Oct 29, 2013.

Playing cards
A pack of playing cards measuring 4 ft 3 in x 3 ft 1 in (1.295 m x 0.939 m) was unveiled by Viejas Casino & Resort in Alpine, California, USA, on Sep 12, 2013. The cards were played in a hand of blackjack on the world's **largest blackjack table**—a fully functioning gaming table covering an area of 2,226.51 sq ft (206.85 m²)—made to celebrate the venue's 21st anniversary.

Paper aircraft
It's one thing to make a paper plane with a wingspan of 59 ft 9 in (18.21 m); it's another to make it fly. Yet Braunschweig Institute of Technology (DEU) did just that in Braunschweig, Germany, on Sep 28, 2013. Launched from an 8-ft-high (2.47-m) platform, the aircraft flew 59 ft (18 m).

Wooden spoon
A traditional folk art spoon made by Centrul Cultural Mioveni of Romania measured 58 ft 4 in (17.79 m) long in Mioveni, Romania, on Jun 7, 2013.

Largest Santa Claus

Shopping Center Norte unveiled a Santa towering 65 ft 7 in (20 m) tall, 23 ft (7 m) wide, and 13 ft (4 m) deep in São Paulo, Brazil, on Nov 7, 2013. It was estimated that up to 5 million shoppers would pass through the mall over Christmas to admire the styrofoam and fiberglass giant. Next to Santa was a wrapped present that itself stood 13 ft (4 m) high.

Largest soccer shirt

The Nigerian national squad—the Super Eagles—had a shirt made by Guinness Nigeria plc. It measured 241 ft (73.55 m) wide and 294 ft (89.67 m) long in Lagos, Nigeria, on Jan 25, 2013.

FACT
In Brazil, Santa Claus is known as Papai Noel. He comes through the window and hides presents in shoes left out for him.

Knitty gritty: longest scarf

Helge Johansen (NOR) is no knit-wit: he's the proud creator of the world's **longest knitted scarf**. It's taken the nimble-finger Norwegian 30 years to knit his neck warmer to an incredible 14,978 ft—long enough to stretch the entire length of Central Park in Manhattan, New York, USA, or as long as 550 London double-decker buses. In order to measure his knitwear for Guinness World Records Day 2013, Helge unraveled his scarf—which he usually keeps in a ball (right)—in a sport center in Oslo, Norway, snaking the scarf in dozens of tight loops (left).

And finally …

- **Largest marquee:** 435,655 sq ft, erected by Barrett-Jackson Auction Company in Scottsdale, Arizona, USA, in Jan 2014.
- **Largest spade:** 14 ft 9 in tall with a 3-ft 1-in-wide blade, by Rollins Bulldog Tools in Harlow, UK, on Sep 27, 2013.
- **Largest flag (draped):** 1,097,682 sq ft, by Moquim Al Hajiri in Doha, Qatar, on Dec 16, 2013.

○ ○ ○

Big orchestra

The word "orchestra" comes from the ancient Greek *orcheisthai*, meaning **"to dance"**

Largest drum kit
The Drumartic (AUT) percussion group's kit list includes a bass drum at 9 ft 6 in (2.9 m), a floor tom at 6 ft 11 in (2.11 m), and a rack tom at 5 ft 2 in (1.57 m). The hi-hat cymbals are 5 ft 8 in (1.73 m) wide. Their huge creation is called Big Boom.

Largest electric guitar
Modeled on a 1967 Gibson Flying V, this 12:1-scale replica is 43 ft 7 in (13.29 m) tall, 16 ft 5 in (5.01 m) wide, and weighs 2,000 lb (900 kg). It was made by Scott Rippetoe (USA, above) and students from Conroe Independent School District Academy of Science & Technology in Texas, USA. It was first played on Jun 6, 2000, some seven months after work began.

Longest alphorn
Seven months in the making, "Corno vivo Oli" is 86 ft 9 in (26.46 m) long and weighs 203 lb 14 oz (92.5 kg). It was made by the Rottumtaler Alphornbläser (DEU) out of a single Douglas fir and was presented and measured in Bellamont, Germany, on Sep 16, 2012.

Largest piano
Constructed by Daniel Czapiewski (POL, below left), this very grand piano is 8 ft 2 in (2.49 m) wide, 19 ft 10 in (6.07 m) long, and 6 ft 3 in (1.9 m) high. It was played at a concert in the village of Szymbark, Poland, on Dec 30, 2010. Sadly, Daniel—a gifted woodworker and friend of GWR—died on Dec 3, 2013.

FACT
Pianos usually have 88 keys. This record-breaking behemoth has 156 of them!

Largest accordion

This 8-ft 3-in-tall (2.53-m), 6-ft 2-in-wide (1.9-m), and 2-ft 9-in-deep (85-cm) squeeze-box weighs about 440 lb (200 kg). Built by Giancarlo Francenella (ITA, above, with his daughter Laura), the instrument is named "Fisarmonica Gigante" and was completed in 2001.

Most pieces in a drum kit

In terms of individual elements, the largest drum set belongs to Dr. Mark Temperato (USA, above) and comprises 813 pieces. They were counted in Lakeville, New York, USA, on Mar 21, 2013. It takes a team of four people more than 20 hr to set up this colossal kit, and around 45 minutes to hit every piece of percussion in it. Beat that!

Largest violin

Created by the Vogtland masters of making violins and bows (DEU), this giant violin is 14 ft (4.27 m) long, has a maximum width of 4 ft 7 in (1.4 m), and is played with a 17-ft-long (5.2-m) bow.

Largest saxophone

With a tube length of 22 ft 1 in (6.74 m) and a bell diameter of 1 ft 3 in (39.1 cm), this supersize sax was created by J'Élle Stainer (BRA) for the company Below65-4hz.com (ITA) to mark the 200th anniversary of Adolphe Sax. It stands 8 ft 11 in (2.74 m) tall, weighs 63 lb 0.8 oz (28.6 kg), and was measured in Cerveteri, Italy, on Aug 3, 2013. Above, project coordinator Gilberto Lopes tries it out.

Fun with food

Americans eat **68 quarts of popcorn** a year—enough to fill a bathtub!

Most pancakes made in one hour

Ross McCurdy (USA) singlehandedly made 1,092 pancakes in Kingston, Washington, USA, on Aug 13, 2013. The **most pancakes made in eight hours by a team** is 76,382, by Batter Blaster (USA) on May 9, 2009.

Fastest field-to-oven-cooked loaf
Australian farmer Neil Unger had long wanted to take the "paddock-to-plate" challenge. The record had stood unbroken since 1999, but with a team of assistants he took wheat from a field to produce 13 loaves of bread (a "baker's dozen") in 16 min 30.83 sec. The feat took place in Cawdor, New South Wales, Australia, on Jan 11, 2013.

Fastest time to eat a bowl of pasta
Furious Pete, aka Peter Czerwinski (CAN, pictured on p. 99), ate a bowl of pasta in 41 sec on the set of *Abenteuer Leben* (Kabel eins) in Sankt Peter-Ording, Germany, on Jul 13, 2013.

Fastest time to eat a jam doughnut with no hands
Oli White (UK) used no hands and didn't lick his lips as he hoovered up a jam doughnut in 28.75 sec at Alexandra Palace in London, UK, on Aug 17, 2013. It was the third time in the space of a year that the GWR YouTube presenter managed to break the record.

Most bites in one minute while juggling apples

Entertainer and juggler Michael Goudeau (USA) took 151 bites from three apples while juggling for 1 min on the set of *Guinness World Records Unleashed* in Los Angeles, California, USA, on Jun 20, 2013.

Most Bhut Jolokia chile peppers eaten in two minutes

The Bhut Jolokia, or ghost chile, rates at approximately 1,000,000 on the Scoville scale (see below). On Jun 19, 2013, Jason McNabb (USA) ate 2.33 oz (66 g) of these chiles—more than 13 whole peppers— in Los Angeles, California, USA.

FACT
Ghost peppers can burn bare skin, so always wear latex gloves if handling.

MOST ...

Bananas sliced with a sword on a slackline in one minute
A slackline is similar in look to a tightrope, but it is slung much closer to the ground. Veteran record breaker Ashrita Furman (USA) balanced on a slackline as he was thrown 36 bananas, each of which he cut in two in New York, USA, on Aug 3, 2013.

Spice up your life: the Scoville scale

We have American chemist Wilbur Scoville to thank for the scale that rates the chiles we chomp. In 1912, long before high-pressure liquid chromatography tests in labs, he relied on taste alone. A grain of chile was dissolved in an alcoholic solution added to sweetened water until it could barely be noted by a panel of testers. The more dilution required, the higher the rating. See right for some ratings from the scale still used—although technology has replaced tasters.

Chile	Scoville rating
Peperoncini	100–500
Jalapeño	2,500–5,000
Cayenne	30,000–50,000
Tabasco	
Scotch bonnet	80,000–300,000
Bhut Jolokia	800,000–1.04 million
Naga viper	1.38 million
Carolina reaper (pictured left)	1.56 million (the **hottest chile**)

Egg-streme efforts

Fastest time to crush 10 eggs: 12.64 sec, Mauro Vagnini (ITA), Milan, Italy, Apr 28, 2011

Most standing jumps onto raw eggs without breaking them: nine, Lan Guangping (CHN), Beijing, China, Sep 9, 2013

Most eggs held in one hand: 27, Silvio Sabba (ITA), Milan, Italy, May 19, 2013

FACT

Champagne bottles sabered in one minute

"Sabrage" is a technique used to open champagne by holding the bottle at an angle and sliding a saber (sword) up the neck deftly enough to slice off the collar and cork. On Sep 8, 2013, Mitchell Ancona (USA) sabered open 34 bottles in a minute in Ridgefield, Connecticut, USA.

The **most champagne bottles sabered at once** is 277, by Centro Empresarial e Cultural de Garibaldi in Rio Grande do Sul, Brazil, on Oct 5, 2013.

Using the conventional method of opening, UK TV chef Gino D'Acampo (ITA) recorded the **most champagne corks popped in one minute**, with seven on Jul 29, 2013.

Cream-filled sponge cakes eaten in one minute

Competitive eater Patrick Bertoletti (USA) put away 16 creamy sponge delights in Los Angeles, USA, on Jun 26, 2013.

Eggs held unbroken on a roller coaster

Özgür Tuna held 110 eggs in a basket while Udo Baron (both DEU) gave him advance warning of the roller coaster turns. The pair were at Europa-Park in Rust, Germany, on Jun 21, 2013.

Hamburgers eaten in three minutes

Takeru Kobayashi (JPN) ate 11 hamburgers in Istanbul, Turkey, on Jun 5, 2013.

Ice cream scoops balanced on one cone

Dimitri Panciera (ITA) balanced 85 scoops at a festival of ice cream in Zoppè di Cadore, Italy, on Jul 21, 2013.

Most nuts crushed by sitting down in 30 seconds

Cherry Yoshitake (JPN) crushed 48 walnuts using his buttocks at the Wakamiya Hachimangu shrine in Kawasaki, Kanagawa, Japan, on Jan 15, 2013.

Fastest time to eat three éclairs

Furious Pete demolished three chocolate éclairs in 18.02 sec at MEATMarket in Covent Garden, London, UK, on Jul 10, 2013. That day he also set a gastronomic record for the **most hamburgers eaten in one minute**, with four. Fans follow his antics on YouTube, with his videos having notched up more than 115 million views by Feb 1, 2014.

Mustard drunk in 30 seconds

Denis Klefenz (DEU) consumed 10.37 oz (294 g) from a tube of Kühne Senf Mittelscharf German mustard on Jun 20, 2013.

Walnuts crushed by hand in one minute

Not content with crushing 131 walnuts in his hand in 60 sec on Dec 10, 2012, Ashrita Furman went on to set another nutty record, for the **most walnuts cracked against the head in one minute**: 44, on Jan 8, 2013. Both were set in New York, USA.

Fastest time to drink one liter of lemon juice

Michael Jenkins (USA) won a three-way, head-to-head challenge by drinking a liter of lemon juice through a straw in a record time of 54.1 sec in Los Angeles, California, USA, on Jun 20, 2013, beating the next fastest time by 10 sec.

100% Pure

Lemon Juice
Not From Concentrate

Trenchermen: eating to excess

A "trencher" was a medieval bowl carved out of a loaf of stale bread and, as the first edition of *The Guinness Book of Records* explained in 1955, "trencherman" was the name given to a glutton who enjoys food to excess, often setting records in the process. However, we went on to say that trenchermen records did not match "those suffering from the rare disease of bulimia (morbid desire to eat) and polydipsia (pathological thirst). Some bulimia patients have to spend 15 hr a day eating, with an extreme consumption of 384 lb of food in six days by Matthew Daking, age of 12, in 1743 ... Some polydipsomaniacs are unsatisfied by less than 96 pints of liquid a day."

FAST FOOD: FROM SWIFT SWALLOWERS TO NIMBLE NIBBLERS

- 61.46 sec, **eat 500 g of cranberry sauce**, Erkan Mustafa (UK)
- 54 sec, **eat three mince pies**, Robert Edward Lee (AUS)
- 50.08 sec, **wrap five portions of fries**, Stephanie Celik (UK)
- 41 sec, **eat a bowl of pasta**, "Furious" Peter Czerwinski (CAN)
- 36.10 sec, **eat three pickled eggs**, Kyle Thomas Moyer (USA)
- 18.02 sec, **eat three chocolate éclairs**, Peter Czerwinski (CAN)
- sec, **eat a slice of toast**, Anthony Falzon (MLT)

seconds: 50 40 30 20 10 0

And finally ...

- **Most cappuccinos made in one hour:** 289 by Suzanne Stagg (AUS) in Hobart, Tasmania, Australia, on Nov 29, 2013
- **Largest cream tea party:** 510 people in Buxton, Derbyshire, UK, on Nov 24, 2013
- **Most people dunking cookies:** 1,796 by Oreo India at I.I.T., Mumbai, India, on Dec 22, 2013

ooo

Big food

There are **more Indian restaurants** in London than in Mumbai and New Delhi combined

Largest samosa

On Jun 22, 2012, chefs and students at Bradford College in West Yorkshire, UK, cooked up a supersize Indian pastry weighing 244 lb 4 oz (110.8 kg) and measuring 4 ft 5 in (1.35 m) long, 2 ft 9 in (85 cm) wide, and 11 in (29 cm) high. The team dubbed their world beater "Big Bertha."

LARGEST ...

Bowl of apple sauce
Musselman's Apple Sauce (USA) produced a bowl of apple sauce weighing 716 lb (324.8 kg) at the Baltimore Running Festival in Maryland, USA, on Oct 12, 2013.

Cheesecake
Philadelphia Cream Cheese (USA) created a cheesecake weighing in at 6,900 lb (3,129 kg) in Lowville,

New York, USA, on Sep 21, 2013. It measured 7 ft 6.2 in (2.29 m) in diameter, and 2 ft 7 in (78.7 cm) tall.

Chewing gum stick
Japanese firm Lotte produced the biggest stick of chewing gum, in Sapporo, Hokkaido, Japan, on Oct 5, 2013. It measured

3 ft 6.7 in (1.85 m) long, 11.57 in (29.4 cm) wide, and 1.14 in (2.9 cm) deep.

Chocolate mousse
A mousse weighing 496 lb 12 oz (225.3 kg)—as heavy as three average men—was whipped up for charity at the Aventura Mall in Florida, USA, on Oct 6, 2012.

FACT
This titanic turkey meal is free for anyone who can eat it—solo—within 45 min!

Largest Christmas dinner

This 21-lb 2-oz (9.6-kg) festive feast for one comprises a turkey, carrots, parsnips, broccoli, cauliflower, roast potatoes, "pigs in blankets," and 25 Brussels sprouts. It was on the menu of The Duck Inn in Oakenshaw, UK, on Dec 24, 2013.

Cinnamon roll
Weighing the equivalent of five adult women, the largest cinnamon roll tipped the scales at 609 lb (276 kg) and was baked by the Second Floor Bakery in Holland, Michigan, USA, on May 4, 2013. The roll measured 6 ft (1.83 m) in diameter and was 7 in (17.8 cm) deep.

Largest macaron tower

Sebastien Laurent (FRA) created a 12-tier, 21-ft 11-in (6.7-m) display that comprised 8,540 macarons at Château de Montjoux in Thonon-les-Bains, France, on Jun 8, 2013.

Largest pizza commercially available

Big Mama's & Papa's Pizzeria's Giant Sicilian pizza measures 4 ft 6 in x 4 ft 6 in (1.37 x 1.37 m). Sold at six locations in Los Angeles, USA, it's large enough to feed between 50 and 100 people. The outsize snack will set you back $199.99 plus tax.

FACT
First made in Naples, Italy, pizzas originally used dough and tomatoes but no cheese.

Crab cake
Made from fresh Maryland blue crab meat, the largest crab cake weighed 300 lb (136 kg). It was made by Handy International Incorporated (USA) in Timonium, Maryland, USA, on Sep 1, 2012.

Rocky road
On Jan 25, 2013, Australian confectionery company Darrell Lea created a "rocky road"—a chocolate, nut, marshmallow, and cookie candy bar—that weighed 575 lb 13.5 oz (261.2 kg).

★ Big burger recipe ★

The Black Bear Casino Resort (USA) share their recipe for the **largest hamburger**. You will need:

2,014 lb beef (about 3.5 cows)
52 lb 8 oz tomatoes
50 lb lettuce
60 lb onions
19 lb pickles
40 lb American cheese
16 lb 8 oz bacon

Cook the beef for 4 hr on a 14-ft 9-in skillet, using a crane to flip the patty. Once it's done, add toppings and serve in a giant bun!

CAN I HAVE SOME MORE, PLEASE?

A standard bathtub holds about 21 gallons. So how long do you think it would take you to drink all these record breakers?

 = 25 bathtubs

Largest cocktail 10,500 gal

Largest bowl of soup 7,042 gal

Largest cup of coffee 3,487 gal

Largest cup of hot chocolate 880 gal

ⓘ Waste not, want not

GWR insists that the products of all "big food" record attempts must be consumed to avoid wastage. At most record attempts, food is eaten by participants or spectators, distributed to food banks or sold off to raise money for charity. If food is not eaten, or becomes inedible in the process of being prepared, it will not qualify as a record.

HUMONGOUS HELPINGS

Most of the records on these pages are for one huge item of food. But in the table below, you'll find records for the largest overall servings—ordinary food served in extraordinary amounts.

	What	Quantity	Who	Date
	Baked potatoes	3,784 lb 7 oz (1,716.6 kg)	Comité Organizador de Fegasur (PER)	Jun 9, 2012
1	Chili con carne	2,420 lb (1,097.7 kg)	Chris' Dream Chili Team (USA)	Jun 15, 2013
	Dumplings	1,510 lb 2 oz (685 kg)	A Chang Meat Dumpling Restaurant (TPE)	Nov 18, 2012
2	Fish and chips	105 lb 4 oz (47.75 kg)	Fish and Chips@ LTD (UK)	Jul 30, 2012
	Fries	987 lb 10 oz (448 kg)	Adventure Island (UK)	Jun 29, 2011
	Fruit salad	15,291 lb (6,935.88 kg)	University of Massachusetts Dining Services (USA)	Sep 2, 2013
3	Lobster	1,126 lb 8 oz (510.99 kg)	International Lobster Festivals, Inc. and San Pedro Fish Markets (USA)	Sep 14, 2013
	Mussels	10,798 lb 3 oz (4,898 kg)	Havfruen Fiskerestaurant (NOR)	Aug 3, 2012
	Papas rellenas	1,867 lb 1 oz (846.9 kg)	Municipality of Ventanilla, Sociedad Peruana Cebiche Más Grande del Mundo, and APRIEG (all PER)	Sep 29, 2013
	Pastries	39,550 pastries	2023 Metre Barış ve Kardeşlik Böregi (TUR)	Jun 3, 2012

Smoothie
More than 3,200 bananas were liquidized by the Cabot Creamery Cooperative in New York City, USA, on May 3, 2013 to make a 339.9-gal (1,514-liter) smoothie—enough to fill at least 16 average bathtubs!

LONGEST ...

Blood sausage
Created in Burgos, Spain, during the city's year as the Spanish Capital of Gastronomy 2013, a blood sausage was measured at 576 ft 5 in (175.7 m). Weighing in at 465 lb (211 kg), the *morcilla* was made by more than 450 volunteers, following the local recipe: pork, pork fat, horcal onion, bahia rice, lard, pork blood, spices, and salt, in a casing of tripe.

parked wing to wing—was made by Panaderia Schick at the Centro Comercial Managua in Nicaragua on Nov 17, 2013.

Garlic bread
Etienne Thériault (CAN) created a stick of garlic bread 54 ft 10 in (16.71 m) long at École Ola-Léger in Bertrand, New Brunswick, Canada, on Jul 6, 2013.

Hotdog
A hotdog measuring 668 ft 7 in (203.8 m) was created by Novex SA in the city of Mariano Roque Alonso, Paraguay, on Jul 15, 2011—long enough to fill 1,132 regular hotdog buns!

Cake roll
Starting on Apr 16, 2013, it took 66 pastry chefs from Japan's Kai Corporation two days to create a strawberry-topped cream sponge roll measuring 428 ft 8 in (130.68 m) in Tokyo, Japan.

Fruitcake
A fruitcake measuring 1,651 ft 4 in (503.34 m)—as long as nine jumbo jets

Ice cream dessert
On Aug 18, 2013, a 1,249-ft 11-in (380.97-m) line of ice cream scoops decorated with chocolate syrup, nuts, and sprinkles was served—in an array of (clean!) gutter pipes—by PGA National Resort & Spa and Luke's Ice Cream in Palm Beach Gardens, Florida, USA.

Largest serving of doughnuts

MEGA Alma-Ata shopping and entertainment mall in Almaty, Kazakhstan, fried up 1,470 lb (667 kg) of *baursaks* (sweetened fluffy dough) on Nov 2, 2013. A specially constructed wooden barrel was needed to hold the doughnuts.

Ham-made: grow your own burger

Professor Mark Post (left), a Dutch vascular biologist at Maastricht University in the Netherlands, demonstrated the **first laboratory-grown hamburger** during a launch event in London, UK, on Aug 5, 2013. The *in vitro* meat—the first example of what its creator says could provide an answer to global food shortages and help combat climate change—was fried in a pan and tasted by two volunteers.

The result of years of research by Professor Post, the meat in the burger was made by knitting together around 20,000 strands of protein cultured from cattle stem cells in his lab. Post and his team are working to show that meat grown in petri dishes might one day be a true alternative to meat from livestock.

And finally ...

- **Largest gingerbread house:** 1,452 cu yd (internal volume), built by Traditions Club (USA) on Nov 30, 2013.

- **Largest bag of potato chips:** 2,515 lb 7 oz, by Corkers Crisps (UK) on Sep 13, 2013.

- **Longest sandwich line:** 2.4 mi of chocolate and hazelnut spread sandwiches, by Nocilla (ESP) on Jun 1, 2013.

○ ○ ○

◉ Curious claimants

You don't need to be **Usain Bolt or Edmund Hillary** to be a record breaker … luckily for this heroic lot!

Silvio Sabba

With 48 current Guinness World Records to his name—all achieved in less than three years—Italy's Silvio Sabba is one of our most prolific claimants and king of the one-minute records. He's pictured here attempting the **most matchsticks stacked into a tower** (74), **most dice stacked using chopsticks** (44), and **most clothespins clipped to the face** (51).

28
Number of dice that Silvio stacked into a tower—using just his mouth—in a minute on Jul 3, 2013.

Simon Elmore
Here's a record that really sucks! Britain's Simon Elmore managed to stuff 400 regular drinking straws into his mouth at once on Aug 6, 2009. And, as per Guinness World Records guidelines, he held them in place for a full 10 sec. Unfortunately for Simon, he was two straws short of his personal goal, but he still did enough to earn himself the world record.

Gary Duschl
The latest surveyor's report on Gary Duschl's (USA) epic **longest chewing gum wrapper chain** gives a total of 14.8 mi (23.9 km)—that's almost 230 soccer pitches long! Gary has been linking gum wrappers since Mar 11, 1965, and as of Mar 2014 has made 3,743,076 links to 1,871,538 wrappers.

Nathan Dickens

There was plenty of bizarre behavior on American TV when *Guinness World Records Unleashed* aired in 2013. Among the records established was the **most targets hit by blindfolded tennis serves in two minutes** (15), by the USA's Nathan Dickens.

Stephen Kish
A regular in the first series of the BBC's *Officially Amazing* TV show, "Sizzlin'" Stephen Kish (UK) bounced his way to a record for the **most table tennis balls bounced into a beer glass in one minute** (six).

Michael Pericoloso

Putting the "breaking" into record breaking is Michael Pericoloso (USA), who earned his certificate for the **most yardsticks broken over the head in one minute** (37) on *Guinness World Records Unleashed* in Jun 2013. Ouch!

John Cassidy
When it comes to balloon-shaping, John Cassidy (USA) leaves the competition feeling deflated. John's records include the **fastest time to create a balloon dog sculpture** (6.5 sec), the **most balloon sculptures made in one minute** (13), and the **most made in one hour** (747).

Did you know?
Low-fat milk is best for this attempt—if you use whole milk, the fat tends to clog up the tear ducts!

Brandon Kee

Ever heard the phrase "Don't shoot 'til you see the whites of his eyes"? It could've been coined for Brandon "Youngblood" Kee (USA), holder of the record for the **fastest time to hit five targets by squirting milk from the eye** (34.9 sec). How does he get it there? He snorts it up his nose, then forces it out of his tear ducts. Eye caramba!

Take the challenge
Got a unique talent or record worthy party piece? If so, visit our Challengers website—**guinnessworldrecords. com/challengers**—where you can attempt a record of your own and upload a video to one of our adjudicators.

Show of strength

Danish strong man John Holtum could **catch cannonballs** fired straight at him

Most skillets rolled in one minute

Steve Weiner (USA) rolled 12 skillets, or frying pans, in Los Angeles, California, USA, on Jun 25, 2013. The **most skillets rolled by a female** is five, by Polish powerlifter Aneta Florczyk in Beijing, China, on Nov 14, 2008.

Fastest time to pull a train over 20 meters using rice-bowl suction
By pressing a bowl on his abdominal muscles, Zhang Xingquan (CHN) created enough suction to pull a train weighing 291,000 lb (132 metric tons), with two drivers weighing 330 lb (150 kg). It took him 1 min 18.92 sec to cover 20 m (65 ft 6 in) in Erlianhaote, Inner Mongolia, China, on Jul 24, 2013.

Greatest weight lifted in one hour by kettlebell snatch
On Dec 23, 2013, Sergey Trifanov (BLR) lifted 66,165 lb

(30,012 kg) by snatching kettlebells at the State Technological University in Vitebsk, Belarus.

Most baseball bats broken with the back in one minute
Matt Dopson (USA) was on the set of *Guinness World Records Unleashed* to snap 19 baseball bats over his back in Los Angeles, California, USA, on Jun 24, 2013.

Most wins of the Lumberjack World Championships
Jason Wynyard (NZ) won the Tony Wise

All-Around Champion title 15 times between 1999 and 2013. The nine events include standing chop, hot saw, springboard chop, and 60-ft (18-m) speed climb. The World Championships are held annually in Hayward, Wisconsin, USA.

The **most Lumberjack World Championships won by a woman** is nine, by Nancy Zalewski (USA). She won the title of Lady Jill (men are lumberjacks, women are lumberjills) in 2003–04 and 2007–13. The All-Around Lady Jill title is given to the woman who scores highest over the entire competition.

Heaviest weight lifted by pierced ears

Johnny Strange (UK) lifted a 32-lb 13.5-oz (14.9-kg) keg attached to a hook through his pierced ears in Doncaster, South Yorkshire, UK, on Oct 12, 2013. Along with Daniella D'Ville (opposite), Johnny performs as part of the Institution of Human Marvels.

Most apples crushed with the bicep in one minute

Mama Lou, aka Linsey Lindberg (USA), used muscle power to squash eight apples in Los Angeles, California, USA, on Jun 26, 2013. Once an accountant, she quit to be a performer and now blows up and pops hot water bottles and rips telephone directories in half.

HEAVIEST WEIGHT LIFTED BY ...

Nose (floss): Christopher Snipp (UK), May 11, 2013 — 34 lb 13 oz

Tongue: Thomas Blackthorne (UK), Aug 1, 2008 — 27 lb 8.75 oz

Beard: Antanas Kontrimas (LTU), Jun 26, 2013 — 141 lb

Nipples: "The Baron" (FIN), Jul 19, 2013 — 71 lb 14 oz

Fingernail: Chikka Bhanu Prakash (IND), Nov 20, 2011 — 19 lb 1 oz

Forehead (hooks): Burnaby Q. Orbax (CAN), Jun 21, 2013 — 9 lb 1 oz

Ears: Johnny Strange (UK), Oct 12, 2013 — 32 lb 13.5 oz

Cheeks (hooks): Sweet Pepper Klopek (CAN), Jun 21, 2013 — 9 lb 1 oz

Toes: Guy Phillips (UK), May 28, 2011 — 50 lb 11 oz

Pinkie fingers: Kristian Holm (NOR), Nov 13, 2008 — 148 lb 13 oz

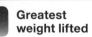

Pulling vehicles

Heaviest road vehicle pulled by teeth: Igor Zaripov (RUS), double-decker bus weighing 27,249 lb in London, UK, on Oct 15, 2012.

Heaviest train pulled by teeth: Velu Rathakrishnan (MYS), two trains weighing 287.4 tons in Kuala Lumpur, Malaysia, on Oct 18, 2003.

Heaviest vehicle pulled by nipples: "The Great Nippulini," aka Sage Werbock (USA), a wagon loaded with people weighing a total of 2,179 lb 4 oz in Milan, Italy, on Mar 25, 2011.

Greatest weight lifted

"The greatest weight ever raised by a human being," according to our first book back in 1955, "is 4,333 lb (1.84 tons) by the 25-stone [350-lb] French-Canadian Louis Cyr (1863–1912) in Chicago in 1896 in a back-lift (weight raised off trestles). Cyr had a 60½-in chest and 22-in biceps." Today, the fully notarized record stands at 5,340 lb for two cars (plus drivers) on a platform backlifted by Gregg Ernst (CAN) at Lunenburg, Nova Scotia, Canada, in Jul 1993.

FACT

Daniella's death-defying act includes a bed of nails, lying on broken glass, and charming snakes.

HEAVIEST ...

Boat pulled by a team of swimmers

A team of 73 people organized by lifeguard association SLRG Luzern (CHE) pulled a boat weighing 712,534 lb (323.2 metric tons) on Sep 14, 2013 in Lucerne, Switzerland. They took 4 min 34.72 sec to pull the boat 328 ft (100 m).

George Olesen (DNK) recorded the **heaviest boat pulled by an individual**. The boat was a ferry weighing 22.7 million lb (10,300 metric tons) and he heaved it 16 ft 8.8 in (5.1 m) in Gothenburg, Sweden, in Jun 2000.

Tire spun around the body

As well as breaking records with ordinary hula hoops, Paul Blair (USA) has shaken his stuff with a tire weighing 116 lb 10 oz (52.9 kg). Paul, who performs as Dizzy Hips, set his latest record on Sep 8, 2013.

For more physical feats, turn to p. 118

Fastest time to break 16 concrete blocks on the body (female)

Daniella D'Ville, aka Danielle Martin (UK), had 16 concrete blocks smashed on her body—one at a time—in 30.40 sec with a sledgehammer wielded by fellow performer Johnny Strange (UK) at the Tattoo Jam in Doncaster, South Yorkshire, UK, on Oct 12, 2013. Each of the slabs had a minimum density of 41 lb per cu ft (650 kg/m³).

Heaviest weight lifted by beard

Antanas Kontrimas (LTU) used his beard to lift 141 lb (63.8 kg)—in the shape of *Rekorlar Dünyası* presenter Gupse Özay'ın—in Istanbul, Turkey, on Jun 26, 2013. It was his 10th consecutive successful attempt at a record he first set in 2000, when he lifted 122 lb 11 oz (55.7 kg).

Vehicle pulled with an arm-wrestling move

Kevin Fast (CAN) challenged a truck to an arm-wrestling contest—and won! With his elbow on a table in an arm-wrestling position, the multiple record holder pulled a truck weighing 24,380 lb (11,060 kg) in Cobourg, Ontario, Canada, on Apr 26, 2013. Kevin also holds records for the **heaviest aircraft pulled by a man** (a Boeing C-17 Globemaster III weighing 416,299 lb; 188.83 metric tons), and the **heaviest house pulled by a man** (79,145 lb; 35.9 metric tons). You can also see him setting a new caber-tossing record on p. 112.

Yoke walk over 10 meters

The yoke is a metal bar carried over the shoulders with weights on either side. Patrik Baboumian (DEU, b. IRN) carried a weight of 1,224 lb (555 kg) in Toronto, Ontario, Canada, on Sep 8, 2013.

Heaviest vehicle pulled over 100 feet (female)

Lia Grimanis (CAN) dragged a 2014 International 8600 tandem axle cab weighing 17,820 lb (8,083 kg) across a distance of 100 ft at the Toronto Convention Centre in Toronto, Ontario, Canada, on Dec 12, 2013.

Weight lifted with one ear using a clamp

Rakesh Kumar (IND) used an ear clamp to lift 182 lb 1 oz (82.6 kg) in Istanbul, Turkey, on Jul 25, 2013.

Vehicle pulled with ears (female)

On Jun 20, 2013, Asha Rani (IND) used both ears to pull a 3,745-lb (1,700-kg) van in Leicestershire, UK. Back in Aug 2012, she had pulled a double-decker bus—at 26,678 lb (12,101 kg), the **heaviest vehicle pulled by a woman using her hair**—a distance of 56 ft 5 in (17.2 m).

Gym king: endurance weightlifter

Eamonn Keane (IRL) holds 22 records, as of Mar 2014, for endurance weightlifting. The champion lifter's most recent feat was the **most weight lifted by incline dumbbell flies in one minute** (in which dumbbells are held in each hand on an incline bench before bringing them together over the chest), with 4,761 lb in Louisburgh, Ireland, on Oct 16, 2013. His oldest record still standing dates back to 2003: the **heaviest weight lifted in one hour by bench press**, an astonishing 305,300 lb. He did 1,280 repetitions with 200 lb and 493 reps with 100 lb.

✋ And finally ...

• **Heaviest vehicle pulled 100 meters by a wheelchair team:** basketball wheelchair team Hannover United (all DEU) pulled three trucks with a total weight of 110,407 lb 8 oz over 100 m in Hörstel, Germany, on Jul 10, 2013.
• **Most kettlebell weight lifted in one minute with alternating floor presses:** Anatoly Ezhov (BLR) lifted 9,010 lb (170 reps of a 53-lb kettlebell lift) in Zurich, Switzerland, on Feb 27, 2014. ○○○

Flexible friends

Overall, **women are more flexible** than men of the same age

Fastest time to cram into a box (male)

Mr. Yogi Laser, aka Kenneth Greenaway (USA), took 5.35 sec to squeeze into a box measuring 20 x 20 x 17.5 in (50.8 x 50.8 x 44.4 cm) in California, USA, on Jun 27, 2013. The **fastest time to cram into a box (female)**—a space of just 20.4 x 17.7 x 17.7 in (52 x 45 x 45 cm)—is 4.78 sec, by Skye Broberg (NZ) on Sep 15, 2011.

Fastest escape from a straitjacket
Sofia Romero (UK) freed herself from a regulated Posey straitjacket in 4.69 sec at the Aylestone Leisure Centre in Leicester, UK, on Jun 9, 2011.

The **fastest escape from a straitjacket and chains while suspended** is 10.6 sec and was achieved by Lucas Wilson (CAN) at Holy Trinity Catholic High School in Simcoe, Ontario, Canada, on Jun 8, 2012.

Wilson also recorded the **fastest escape from a straitjacket underwater**— 23.16 sec —at École St. Patrick high school in Yellowknife, Northwest Territories, Canada, on Oct 5, 2013.

Most people belly dancing simultaneously
Danone Canarias (ESP) organized a mass belly dance that involved 842 performers at Playa de Las Canteras in Las Palmas, Gran Canaria, Spain, on May 29, 2011.

YOGA

Longest yoga chain
A chain of 696 students from the CK School of Practical Knowledge (IND) formed a yoga chain in Cuddalore, India, on Jan 30, 2013. They performed five different yoga poses, including: Cow's Face (Gomukhasana), Child's (Balasana), Half Lotus (Padmasana), and Easy Seated (Sukhasana).

Longest yoga marathon (female)
During a 32-hr marathon, Yasmin Fudakowska-Gow (CAN) completed 1,008 yoga positions at Om West Centre Holistique in Quebec, Canada, on Aug 2–3, 2010.

The **longest yoga marathon (male)** lasted 29 hr 4 min and was achieved by Michael Schwab (AUT) in Vienna, Austria, on Sep 26–27, 2009.

ACROBATICS

Longest backflip
Lukas Steiner (AUT) carried out a 13-ft 11.7-in (4.26-m) backflip in Milan, Italy, on Apr 28, 2011.

Most jackhammer hops in one minute

Bryan Nguyen (USA) performed 49 jackhammer hops—a staple break-dancing move—in a minute on the set of *Guinness World Records Unleashed* in Los Angeles, California, USA, on Jun 19, 2013. The guidelines require that the hand leaves the ground on each hop.

Steiner also recorded the **longest jump from feet to handstand (male)**. From a standing start, he leaped 8 ft 4.39 in (2.55 m), landed on his hands, and pressed himself into a handstand, held for 5 sec. The attempt was undertaken in Mittweida, Germany, on Nov 10, 2011.

Longest time to hold the Marinelli bend position

This extraordinarily demanding position requires the performer to sustain his or her entire body weight via a mouth grip on a short pole. Tsatsral Erdenebileg (MNG) maintained a Marinelli bend for 4 min 17 sec on the set of *Rekorlar Dünyası* in Istanbul, Turkey, on Jul 17, 2013.

LARGEST ACTIVITY EVENTS

Largest aerobics display: 50,420 participants, Aug 15, 2011

Largest yoga class: 29,973 students, Nov 19, 2005

Largest dance class: 9,223 participants, Apr 30, 2010

Largest Zumba class: 6,671 participants, Sep 15, 2012

👤 = 1,000 participants

Largest pilates class: 3,486 participants, Jun 2, 2013

Largest limbo dance: 1,208 children, Oct 1, 2011

Glossary

Parkour: The discipline of moving rapidly through a typically urban environment by means of performing acrobatic feats such as jumping, climbing, and flipping to negotiate obstacles. It began in France and was popularized by David Belle and Sébastien Foucan. Parkour practitioners are known as "traceurs"; they "trace" their way through their environment.

FACT
US gymnast George Eyser won six medals at the 1904 Olympics—despite his wooden leg.

Supple difference
Babies have a greater amount of soft cartilage than bone. In time, however, much of it hardens into bone—which is why adults are so much less flexible than babies.

Farthest arrow shot using feet

Nancy Siefker (USA) shot an arrow into a target 20 ft (6.09 m) away using only her feet on the set of *Guinness World Records Unleashed* in Los Angeles, California, USA, on Jun 20, 2013. The guidelines require that the target should be no more than 12 in (30 cm) in diameter. However, Nancy, a circus performer, hit a target measuring just 5.5 in (13.9 cm).

On May 24, 2010, Chase Armitage (UK) performed the **longest backflip off a wall**, measuring 11 ft 5 in (3.48 m), for *Zheng Da Zong Yi – Guinness World Records Special* in Beijing, China.

The **most backflips against a wall in one minute** is 29, by Miguel Marquez (ESP) for the same TV series in Beijing, China, on Jun 19, 2009.

Most circular jumps on a wall in one minute

To make a circular jump, performers use only their hands to spin the body 360 degrees against a wall. On Mar 24, 2010, Aung Zaw Oo (USA) carried out 11 circular jumps on a wall in Rome, Italy.

Longest forward-jump flip/somersault

Hasit Savani (UK) achieved a 19-ft 7-in (6-m) forward-jump flip at Talacre Community Sports Centre in London, UK, on Feb 15, 2012.

Most forward-roll front flips in one minute

Mathew Kaye (UK) managed 17 forward-roll front flips in a minute at Parkour Park in Chineham, Hampshire, UK, on Sep 8, 2010. On the same day, he also recorded the **most pistol squats on a scaffold pole in one minute**, with 29. A pistol squat is a bodyweight squat done on one leg to full depth. Mathew can be seen performing parkour in Coldplay's video for "Charlie Brown" (2011).

Most hula hoops spun simultaneously around the waist (team)

Marawa the Amazing (AUS) and her Majorettes whirled into the record books by spinning 264 hula hoops at once at the Shaftesbury Theatre in London, UK, on Nov 14, 2013, in celebration of Guinness World Records Day. For more Marawa, spin over to p. 112.

Oldest person to perform a backflip

Walter Liesner (DEU, b. Jan 14, 1913) was 94 years 268 days old when he backflipped into a swimming pool in Wetzlar, Germany, on Oct 9, 2007. Walter, a part-time gymnastics teacher for most of his life, shot to local fame at the age of 17 when he performed a handstand on the handrail at the top of the Wetzlar church tower, 137 ft (42 m) above the ground.

Joint session: pros and cons of hypermobility

People with extreme flexibility are often said to be double-jointed or even triple-jointed. There is disagreement about the accuracy of these terms, however, and some scientists prefer the term "hypermobility" to describe unusually unrestricted joint movements. For dancers or gymnasts, such flexibility can improve performance, but it can also give rise to problems, including dislocation of the joints, back pain, and damage to soft tissue. Superflexibility, however, can be helpful to contortionists such as Zlata, aka Julia Gunthel (DEU, left, **fastest time to burst three balloons with the back**: 12 sec), and Daniel Browning Smith (USA, right), who achieved the **fastest time to enter a locked straitjacket** (2 min 8 sec) on Aug 16, 1999.

Handcuff escapology

Fastest escape from handcuffs underwater: 3.425 sec, Thomas Blacke (USA), Oct 25, 2011

Fastest escape from double-locked handcuffs: 1.59 sec, Chad Netherland (USA), Jan 8, 2011

Most handcuff escapes in one hour: 627, Zdeněk Bradáč (CZE), Feb 12, 2010

Performers

"Circus" is from the Latin for "**ring**"—rounded arena for entertainment

Eichholz went 51 ft 4 in (15.66 m) in Beijing, China, on Sep 9, 2013.

Greatest height by a human cannonball
The Bullet, aka David Smith, Jr. (USA), was fired 85 ft (26 m) vertically on Jul 8, 2013 in California City, California, USA. He also holds the record for the **farthest distance for a human cannonball**, with 193 ft 8.8 in (59.05 m) in Milan, Italy, on Mar 10, 2011. Cannonballing began on Apr 2, 1877, when 14-year-old Zazel, aka Rosa Richter

Most soap bubbles blown inside one large bubble
Andy Lin, aka Kuo-Sheng Lin (TWN), blew 152 soap bubbles inside a larger bubble at the World Trade Center in Taipei City, Chinese Taipei, on Dec 23, 2011. On Apr 17, 2012, Kuo-Sheng also set a record for the **most bounces of a soap bubble**, with 195 consecutive bounces.

Greatest weight juggled
Ukrainian strong man Hercules, aka Denys Ilchenko, juggled three tires weighing a total of 59 lb 7 oz (26.98 kg) in Nairn in the Scottish Highlands, UK, on Jul 17, 2013. The tires stayed aloft for 32.43 sec on Denys's third attempt.

❌ More performance feats on p. 104

(UK), became the **first human cannonball**. She was shot a distance of 20 ft (6 m) at Westminster Aquarium in London, UK.

Farthest distance walked balancing a lawn mower on the chin
Multiple record holder The Space Cowboy, aka Chayne Hultgren (AUS), walked 93 ft 2 in (28.4 m) with an unpowered lawn mower on his chin in Sydney, Australia, on Nov 14, 2013. His other records include the **most**

hat flicks from foot to head on a unicycle in one minute, with 10 in London, UK, on Sep 28, 2012.

Greatest distance traveled on a slackline by unicycle
Slacklines are less rigid to cross than tightropes and German "extreme unicyclist" Lutz

Largest free-floating soap bubble
SamSam BubbleMan, aka Sam Heath (UK), made a bubble indoors with a volume of 117 cu ft (3.3 m³) on Jan 11, 2013 in London, UK, for *Officially Amazing* (Lion TV).

Most poi weaves in one minute
Poi is the art of swinging weights on lengths of material in different rhythmic patterns. Joe Dickinson (UK)

Most apples held in own mouth and chain sawed in one minute
Johnny Strange (UK) chain sawed eight apples in his mouth in a minute at Doncaster's Tattoo Jam in South Yorkshire, UK, on Oct 12, 2013. Teaming up with Daniella D'Ville (see opposite), Johnny also set a record for the **most apples held in the mouth and cut in half by chain saw in one minute**, with 12.

LARGEST ANIMAL CIRCUS ACTS

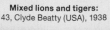

Lions: 40, Alfred Schneider (UK), Bertram Mills Circus, London, UK, 1925

Mixed lions and tigers: 43, Clyde Beatty (USA), 1938

Polar bears: 60–70, Willy Hagenbeck (DEU), Circus Paul Busch, Berlin, Germany, 1904

⚡ Circus animals
As the graphic to the left suggests, Guinness World Records has had a long and varied history of documenting records involving circus animals. Today, circuses are much more sensitive to the welfare of animals, and many have banned animal acts outright. Similarly, we no longer monitor records involving circus animals where we cannot be 100% sure of the animals' treatment and welfare.

Jeff Dunham
American ventriloquist and stand-up comedian Jeff Dunham holds the record for the **most tickets sold for a stand-up comedy tour**—his "Spark of Insanity" tour, which was performed in 386 venues worldwide from Sep 13, 2007 to Aug 21, 2010, sold an incredible 1,981,720 tickets, presumably leaving Dunham laughing all the way to the bank.

Most swords swallowed underwater

The Space Cowboy, aka Chayne Hultgren (AUS), swallowed three swords underwater at the Olympic Park Aquatic Centre in Sydney, Australia, on Nov 14, 2013.

13 changeovers—passing while leaping over each other—the **most complete changeovers juggling three objects in one minute**, on Jan 1, 2012.

Greatest distance on a slackline while juggling three objects
Carson Firth (USA) combined slacklining with juggling to walk a record 28 ft 4 in (8.65 m) in Florida, USA, on Aug 9, 2013.

Longest career as a ringmaster

Norman Barrett (UK) had been a ringmaster for 56 years, as of Mar 20, 2014. But he didn't need to run away to join the circus—his father owned one and he was born into the life on Dec 20, 1935. Norman was 12 when he first performed.

achieved 74 three-beat poi weaves in one minute at the Secret Garden Party in Cambridgeshire, UK, on Jul 22, 2012.

Youngest person to do a quadruple somersault
Michael Martini (ITA, b. Nov 17, 1999) performed a quadruple somersault when 13 years 196 days old at Circo Orfei in Massafra, Italy, on Jun 1, 2013. Michael is a professional performer; GWR does not otherwise monitor this category for under-16s.

JUGGLING

Fastest time for a pair to exchange costumes while juggling
Matt Baker and Joe Ricci (both USA) swapped outfits in 2 min 52 sec in Jiangsu, China, on Jan 8, 2014. The two men also recorded

Most rotations of a sword balanced on a dagger

Specialist circus sideshow performer Daniella D'Ville, aka Danielle Martin (UK), set a new record when she rotated a sword balanced on a dagger nine times in a minute at Doncaster's Tattoo Jam on Oct 12, 2013.

Most melons chopped on the stomach on a nail bed

Daniella D'Ville had 10 watermelons sliced on her stomach while lying on a bed of nails at Doncaster's Tattoo Jam on Oct 12, 2013.
The **most watermelons chopped on the stomach in one minute** (no bed of nails) is 48, sliced by Bipin Larkin on Ashrita Furman (both USA) in Jamaica, New York, USA, on Nov 30, 2012.

Most consecutive ax juggling catches
Having demonstrated the potency of his axes by chopping wood, Max Winfrey (USA) juggled three of them, making 163 catches, in Winter Garden, Florida, USA, on Jun 7, 2013.

Most objects juggled while sword swallowing
The Space Cowboy juggled five balls after swallowing a sword in London, UK, on Sep 14, 2012. Luther Bangert (USA) matched this feat in Iowa City, USA, on Jul 7, 2013. Luther kept

the balls aloft for 11.72 sec; The Space Cowboy kept them airborne for 6.5 sec.

Most juggling catches on a circus pole in one minute
Isabelle Noël (DEU), a performer and circus teacher, perched on a 160-ft (49-m) pole to make 179 catches at Europa-Park in Rust, Germany, on Jun 21, 2013.

Cirque du Soleil: circus maximus

Montreal-based Cirque du Soleil, cofounded and run by Guy Laliberté (CAN), is the **largest circus organization**, with 19 touring and resident global productions. The record-breaking company (see right) turns over more than US$1 bn annually and has 5,000 employees. Cirque du Soleil faces increased competition and tougher markets, but Laliberté still found the time and money to enjoy a $35-m break on the *International Space Station* in 2009—one of seven visitors since 2001 to experience the **most expensive tourist trip**.

Cirque du Soleil presents ...
Most people simultaneously stilt walking in multiple venues: 1,908 on Jun 16, 2009
Largest underwater stage hydraulic lift system: Handling Specialty Manufacturing (CAN) built a 3,650-ft stage in a pool of 1.47 million gallons of water in 1999 for Cirque du Soleil
Fastest 50 m hand walking on stilts: Carlos Rodriguez Diaz (CUB), 1 min 30 sec in Florida, USA, on Jun 16, 2009

:Indoor pursuits

A 3 x 3 Rubik's Cube has **43,252,003,274,489,856,000** permutations

Most people playing pinball simultaneously

On May 16, 2013, 100 paddle flippers amassed at First Canadian Place in Toronto, Canada, to play pinball. The free-to-play event was organized by the Stratford Festival to promote the Avon Theatre's production of *Tommy*, the musical that features the song "Pinball Wizard."

Largest plastic-cup pyramid in 30 minutes
Uri, Jonathan, Daniel, and Oded Ish-Shalom (all USA) built a pyramid using 652 plastic cups in 30 min in Jerusalem, Israel, on Feb 22, 2012.

Fastest sport stacking (individual cycle stack)
William Polly (USA) set an individual cycle stack time of 5.59 sec at the WSSA US National Sport Stacking Championships in Maryland, USA, on Mar 24, 2013.

board game in Tribeca Central Park, Jakarta, Indonesia, on Jun 16, 2013.

Longest board game marathon
Brett Carow and Sam Hennemann (both USA) played 116 back-to-back games of Strat-O-Matic Baseball for 61 hr 2 min in New York City, USA, on Jun 7–9, 2012.

CHESS

Fastest time to arrange a chess set
Ray Butler (USA) set up a chess board in 41.87 sec in Las Vegas, Nevada, USA, on Sep 18, 2013. The **fastest time to arrange a set by a team of two** is 41.24 sec, by Tyler Eichman and John Walker (both USA) in Oconto, Wisconsin, USA, on Nov 27, 2013.

Longest chess marathon
On Dec 17–19, 2010, Daniel Häußler and Philipp Bergner (both DEU) played chess for 40 hr 20 min in Ostfildern,

Most people playing a board game simultaneously
The Dokter Toy company (IDN) assembled 1,239 people to play the Crazy Birds

Most Scrabble opponents played at once

Chris May (AUS) won 25 of the 28 games of Scrabble he played simultaneously at Oxford University Press in Oxford, UK, on Jun 11, 2013. Then ranked No. 9 in the world at Scrabble, May took more than four hours to finish all the games.

Germany. Häußler won 191 to Bergner's 114 games, with 50 draws.

Most chess games played in one location
The Sports Authority of Gujarat (IND) ran 20,480 games simultaneously at the University of Gujarat Sports Grounds in Ahmedabad, India, on Dec 24, 2010.

Largest chess set
On May 27, 2009, the Medicine Hat Chess Club

of Alberta, Canada, unveiled a set measuring 19 ft 4 in (5.89 m) on each side. The king was 3 ft 10 in (1.19 m) tall and 1 ft 2 in (37.4 cm) wide at its base.

DOMINOES

Most dominoes toppled by an individual
Liu Yang (CHN) single-handedly arranged and then toppled 321,197 dominoes at CITIC Guoan Grand Epoch City in Beijing, China, on Dec 31, 2011.

Largest ball bath

On Oct 30, 2013, the swimming pool at the Kerry Hotel in Pudong, Shanghai, China, was drained and filled with one million green and pink balls as part of Breast Cancer Awareness Month. The balls, which covered a surface area of 3,397 sq ft (315.6 m²), were later sold to raise funds for charity.

HOW THE MIGHTY HAVE FALLEN: MOST DOMINOES TOPPLED BY A GROUP

= 15,000 dominoes

1,605,757 Netherlands 1998

2,472,480 Netherlands 1999

2,751,518 China 1999

3,407,535 China 2000

3,847,295 Netherlands 2002

4,345,027 Netherlands 2008

3,992,397 Netherlands 2004

4,491,863 Netherlands 2009

4,002,136 Netherlands 2005

4,079,381 Netherlands 2006

FACT
The current record for the **most dominoes toppled by a group** was set on Domino Day 2009, aka "The World in Domino—The Show with the Flow," on Nov 13. The dominoes were set up by 89 builders in the WTC Expo center in Leeuwarden, Netherlands.

Tallest domino structure

A domino tower 19 ft 9.2 in (6.02 m) high and consisting of 11,465 dominoes was erected and toppled by Yspertal Domino Team (AUT) in Yspertal, Austria, on Nov 3, 2013. Pictured is Marcel Pürrer, one of the team of four who built the tower.

FACT
The tower formed the final part of a 100,101-domino array built by 44 people over four days.

Most solves in Rubik's Cube competitions in a single year

In 2012, Sébastien Auroux (DEU) solved 2,033 Rubik's Cubes in official World Cube Association competitions. This equates to 5.5 competitive solves every day and doesn't include any cubes solved outside of formal events.

MOST SOLVES OF RUBIK'S CUBES IN ONE YEAR

Name	Solves	Attempts	Year
Sébastien Auroux (DEU)	2,033	2,122	2012
François Courtès (FRA)	1,651	1,780	2013
Zoé de Moffarts (BEL)	1,518	1,575	2012
Arnaud van Galen (NLD)	1,481	1,568	2012
Erik Akkersdijk (NLD)	1,477	1,609	2010
Jan Bentlage (DEU)	1,452	1,517	2012
Bence Barát (HUN)	1,349	1,392	2010
Clément Gallet (FRA)	1,213	1,249	2011
Tim Reynolds (USA)	1,205	1,281	2012
Laura Ohrndorf (DEU)	1,193	1,295	2013

Source: World Cube Association, as of Dec 31, 2013

Longest domino wall

Germany's Sinners Domino Entertainment holds multiple records for setting up and toppling dominoes. On Jul 6, 2012, at the Wolfgang Ernst Gymnasium School in Büdingen, Germany, Sinners erected—and then toppled—a 98-ft 5-in-long (30 m) wall built from 31,405 dominoes. On the same day, Sinners also set a record for the **most dominoes toppled in a pyramid**, with 13,486.

They were back in action on Oct 23, 2012, this time in Kefenrod, Germany, with the **most dominoes toppled in 30 seconds**, setting up and toppling 60 pieces.

Six months later, Sinners set another record for the **most toppled in a spiral**, with 55,555 on Jul 12, 2013.

Most toppled in one minute

Gemma Hansen (UK) set up and toppled 75 dominoes at Butlin's in Minehead, UK, on Aug 7, 2010. At the 2011 event, also on Aug 7, Andy James (UK) stacked 39 dominoes in a single pile: the **most dominoes stacked in one minute**. Paul Lusher (UK) equaled his record on Sep 4, 2011.

World Cube Association fastest single solves

2 x 2: Christian Kaserer (ITA), 0.69 sec

3 x 3: Mats Valk (NLD), 5.55 sec

4 x 4: Feliks Zemdegs (AUS), 24.66 sec

5 x 5: Feliks Zemdegs (AUS), 50.50 sec

6 x 6: Kevin Hays (USA), 1 min 40.86 sec

7 x 7: Bence Barát (HUN), 2 min 40.11 sec

Megaminx: Simon Westlund (SWE), 42.28 sec

Square-1: Andrea Santambrogio (ITA), 7.41 sec

Pyraminx: Oscar Roth Andersen (DEN), 1.36 sec

Skewb: Brandon Harnish (USA), 2.19 sec

Rubik's Clock: Sam Zhixiao Wang (CHN), 5.27 sec

Correct as of Feb 26, 2014

Captains of cup: sport stacking

The eighth annual STACK UP! was organized by the World Sport Stacking Association (USA) on Nov 14, 2013. They assembled more than half a million people to record the **most people sport stacking in multiple venues**. Speed stackers use special cups, which they arrange in specific sequences as fast as possible and then take them down again, often too quickly for a casual observer to follow. The 555,932 stackers represented 2,631 schools and organizations from 29 countries. Stacking fans claim that it improves hand and eye coordination with its emphasis on dexterity.

Pricey pastimes

Most expensive...
Toy model car: 1930s W. E. Boyce delivery van, £19,975 ($35,728).
Mickey Mouse toy: clockwork Mickey Mouse motorcycle, £51,000 ($83,466).
Toy soldier: 1963 prototype G.I. Joe, $200,000 (£124,309).
Doll: 1914 French doll by Albert Marque, $263,000 (£162,181).

:Outdoor pursuits

Skateboarding was **banned in Norway** from 1978 to 1989 because of the high accident rate

Most waterskiers towed by one boat

On Jan 27, 2012, a total of 145 skiers were towed behind a boat at the Horsehead Water Ski Club in Strahan, Tasmania, Australia.

BUNGEE

Highest dunk of a doughnut
Ron Jones (USA) dunked a doughnut by bungee from 198 ft 8 in (60.55 m) into a coffee cup measuring 3.5 in (8.89 cm) in diameter in California City, California, USA, on Jul 7, 2013.

Highest bungee jump dive into water
Raymond Woodcock (UK) was 72 years old when he bungee-jumped 380 ft (115.9 m) from a crane into water in Chepstow, UK, on Aug 18, 2013.

Fastest 100 m in high-heel roller skates

Marawa Ibrahim (AUS) glided 100 m (328 ft) in 26.10 sec in Regent's Park, London, UK, on Aug 21, 2013 while wearing her custom-made 5.1-in-high (13-cm) high-heel roller skates. "Marawa the Amazing," as she is known, manages a troupe of majorettes who perform in the UK.

Most jumps in one hour
Mike Heard (NZ) jumped 80 times under Auckland Harbour Bridge on Sep 16, 2011, using a cord measuring 31 ft 2 in (9.5 m).

The **most bungee jumps in 24 hours** stands at 105, by Kevin Scott Huntly (ZAF) at Bloukrans Bridge, Garden Route, South Africa, on May 8, 2011. His time was 7 hr 42 min—an average of one jump every 4.5 min, with a cord measuring 131 ft 3 in (40 m).

FLYING DISK (FRISBEE)

Fastest relay over 20 m
On May 6, 2012, a team of five threw a disk in 8.74 sec. Tim, Daniel, Lindsey, and Elyse Habenicht and Cliff West (all USA) were in College Station, Texas, USA.

Longest throw caught by a dog
Robert McLeod (CAN) threw a flying disk 402 ft (122.5 m) to Davy Whippet in Thorhild, Alberta, Canada, on Oct 14, 2012.

Another canine disk master is Beibei the border collie. His owner Liu Haiwang (CHN) helped him set the **most catches by a dog over 10 m in three minutes**, with 18 in Beijing, China, on Sep 7, 2013.

Longest throw to hit a target
Brodie Smith (USA) dunked a disk into a basketball hoop from 150 ft (45.7 m) in Patterson Park in Austin, Texas, USA, on Dec 3, 2013. Brodie was not allowed to hit the backboard in the attempt.

Most beverage cans hit in one minute
Robert McLeod (CAN) hit 28 cans at Edgemont World Health club in Calgary, Canada, on Jan 28, 2012. His other achievements include setting the **longest throw, run, and catch on ice skates**, with 240 ft (73.2 m) on Feb 24, 2013, and the **longest time for a disk to stay aloft thrown from ice skates**, with 12.03 sec in Edmonton, Canada, on Feb 23, 2013.

FACT
Marawa's flair and coordination with the hula hoop took her to the semifinals of *Britain's Got Talent* in 2011.

POGO STICK

Fastest mile dribbling a basketball
On Aug 9, 2013, Ashrita Furman (USA) pogo-sticked a mile—while controlling a bouncing basketball—in 23 min 2.91 sec in New York City, USA. Ashrita's eight pogo records include the **fastest mile**, set on Jul 24, 2001 at 12 min 16 sec.

Most caber tosses in three minutes

Kevin Fast (CAN) tossed 14 cabers in Quinte West, Ontario, Canada, on Sep 7, 2013. Kevin has been setting records for many years and currently holds eight records for feats of strength.

POGO POWER: BOUNCING INTO THE RECORD BOOKS

Fastest one mile: 12 min 16 sec, Ashrita Furman (USA), Jul 24, 2001

Most balloons popped in one minute: 57, Mark Aldridge (UK), Apr 1, 2010

Most consecutive front flips: 5, Jake Gartland (USA), Jul 28, 2011

Most consecutive backflips: 17, Fred Grzybowski (USA), Dec 19, 2013

Farthest distance underwater: 1,680 ft, Ashrita Furman (USA), Aug 1, 2007

Get your skates on

Fastest time to roller-skate across the USA: Russell "Rusty" Moncrief (USA), 69 days 8 hr 45 min, Mar 15, 2002.

Fastest time to roller-skate the length of the UK: Damian Magee (UK), 9 days 5 hr 23 min, Jun 19–28, 1992.

Tallest moving human pyramid on roller skates: NSA Roller Gymnastics Team (USA), four stories high, Pennsylvania, USA, 1985.

Longest journey by water jet pack

On Nov 8, 2013, TV presenter Pollyanna Woodward (UK) jetted off from Gozo Marina in Malta using a jet pack that draws in water and forces it out under pressure, providing lift. She covered a record 22.64 mi (36.45 km) in 4 hr 45 min.

Most consecutive jumps
James Roumeliotis (USA) recorded 70,271 consecutive pogo jumps, i.e., without a break and without falling off, at Pogopalooza 10 in New York, USA, on Jul 26, 2013.

James had previously set the record for the **most bounces in a pogo marathon**, with an ankle-crushing 206,864 jumps. His attempt took 20 hr 13 min at Pogopalooza 8 in California, USA, on Jul 29, 2011. James commented afterward, "My calves are killing me. My ankles are swollen. I can't actually feel my hands, my right thumb especially."

ROLLER SKATING

Longest forward jump
Jeff Dupont (USA) jumped 20 ft 3 in (6.18 m) without using a ramp at the Willamalane Center for Sports and Recreation in Springfield, Oregon, USA, on Feb 12, 2012.

Highest forward flip jump on a pogo stick
Biff Hutchison (USA) jumped 8 ft 2 in (2.49 m) in Tompkins Square Park, New York, USA, on Jul 27, 2013. The next day he set the **highest jump on a pogo stick** at 9 ft 7.5 in (2.93 m).

Longest cumulative abseil in one hour—team of 10

In a stunt organized by ECCO Shoes (DEU), ten abseilers—all wearing high heels—descended the 339-ft 2-in-tall (103.4-m) Park Inn hotel in Berlin, Germany, in one hour on Jul 6, 2013. A total of 32 descents were logged: a cumulative distance of 2.05 mi (3.3 km).

Most spins while carrying two people
On Dec 10, 2012, Liu Jiangshan made 17 consecutive 360-degree spins on roller skates while hanging onto Wang Chenyu and Yang Liangliang (all CHN) in Beijing, China.

SLINGSHOT

Longest slingshot
The greatest distance for launching an object from a sling is 1,565 ft 4 in (477.10 m), using a 4-ft 2-in-long (1.27-m) sling and a 2.25-oz (62-g) dart, by David Engvall (USA) at Baldwin Lake, California, USA, on Sep 13, 1992.

Most cans hit in one minute
Michael McClure (USA) used metal balls to strike 13 beverage cans with a slingshot—from 33 ft (10 m)—at the East Coast Slingshot Tournament in Alverton, Pennsylvania, USA, on Jun 8, 2013.

Longest chain of roller skaters

The Clyde 1 radio station and ScotRail (both UK) set in motion 254 participants in a roller-skating line in Glasgow, UK, on Sep 8, 2013. They were led by Clyde 1 DJ Diane Knox-Campbell.

Pie's the limit: flying disk history

As long ago as ancient Greece, the discus was in use (right), and a clay disk found in Utah, USA, suggests that Native Americans used something similar. In the 1870s in Connecticut, USA, a baker called Russell Frisbie started stamping "Frisbie's pies" on the bottom of his light, circular pans. Students at nearby Yale played throw and catch with the pans, shouting "Frisbie!" as an alert. In California, Wham-O adopted the name for its plastic disk, changed the spelling, and patented the Frisbee. More than 100 million Frisbees have now been produced, but the bakery itself closed in 1958.

FACT
Mountain biking was adopted as an Olympic sport in 1996. BMX followed in 2008.

Did you know?
In the late 1990s, the US Marine Corps experimented with skateboards in urban-military exercises, using them to detect trip wires in buildings and draw out sniper fire.

Wheelie good

The **skateboard ollie** is named after its inventor, Alan "Ollie" Gelfand

Longest vehicle drift

In a drift, a driver controls a vehicle through a sustained rear-wheel skid. Johan Schwartz (USA) maintained a 51.27-mi (84.13-km) drift at the BMW Performance Center in Spartanburg, South Carolina, USA, on May 11, 2013.

First double loop by a car
Gary Hoptrough (UK) conquered the "Deadly 720" by completing two 360-degree loops—each 26 ft (8 m) in diameter—in a Rage R180 buggy on *Top Gear Live* at Moses Mabhida Stadium in Durban, South Africa, on Jun 16, 2012.

Longest individual ATV side wheelie
On Oct 30, 2012, Daniel Adams (USA) executed a 16.89-mi (27.17-km) wheelie on the side wheels of an all-terrain vehicle (ATV) near Grantsville in Utah, USA.

Longest UTV ramp jump
Tanner Godfrey (USA) made a 105-ft 3-in (32.08-m) ramp jump in a utility terrain vehicle (UTV) at Eureka Casino Resort in Mesquite, Nevada, USA, on Feb 22, 2013.

BICYCLE

Most 180-degree jumps in one minute
The most 180-degree jumps on a bicycle in a minute is 43, by Daniel Rall (DEU) at Comtech Arena in Aspach, Germany, on Jul 13, 2013.

Highest vertical drop
Wayne Mahomet (UK) made a vertical drop of 13 ft 5 in (4.1 m) on his bicycle at the Dounby Show in Dounby, Orkney Islands, UK, on Aug 8, 2013.

Fastest 10-obstacle slalom (blindfolded)
On Jul 23, 2013, Juan Ruiz (MEX) negotiated his bicycle around 10 obstacles set randomly on a 66-ft (20-m) slalom course in 25.43 sec on the set of *Guinness World Records—Rekorlar Dünyası* in Istanbul, Turkey. Juan has been blind since birth and used echolocation to achieve the feat.

Fastest 100 miles
Ian Cammish (UK) took 3 hr 11 min 11 sec to cycle 100 mi (161 km) on Aug 10, 1993.
The **fastest 100 miles by a woman** is 3 hr 49 min 42 sec, by Pauline Strong (UK) on Oct 18, 1991.

Farthest wheelie on front wheel with feet off the pedals
Andreas Lindqvist (SWE) carried out a 1,036-ft 8-in

Longest wheelie by a skid loader

On Jul 28, 2012, Jake R. Hatch (USA) carried out a 71-ft 9-in-long (21.88-m) wheelie in a Bobcat skid steer at Taylor Rodeo Grounds in Taylor, Arizona, USA.

(316-m) front-wheel wheelie without his feet touching the pedals of his bike on the set of *Guinness Rekord TV* at Liljeholmshallen, Stockholm, Sweden, on Oct 6, 2001.
On the same show, Lindqvist also performed the **longest duration bicycle wheelie on the front wheel with feet off the pedals**, staying aloft for 2 min 20 sec.

Most BMX megaspins in 30 seconds
A BMX megaspin involves standing on a rear peg, holding onto the handlebars, and, with the front wheel raised, kicking the rear tire so that the bike spins. On Jul 19, 2013, Takahiro Ikeda (JPN) performed 45 spins in 30 sec in Kōtō, Tokyo, Japan.

MOTORCYCLE

Longest jump with backflip on a minimoto
On Oct 9, 2012, Ricardo Piedras (ESP) carried out a 48-ft 4-in-long (14.74-m) jump with backflip on a minimoto (minibike) in Barcelona, Spain.

Longest dirt-to-dirt motorcycle ramp jump

The greatest distance covered in a dirt-to-dirt motorcycle ramp jump is 297 ft 6 in (90.69 m), by Alex Harvill (USA) at the Horn Rapids Motorsports Complex in West Richland, Washington, USA, on Jul 6, 2013. He reached a speed of 96 mph (154 km/h) on the approach to the takeoff ramp.

GREATEST STUNT DISTANCES: LONGEST RAMP JUMP BY ...

Car in reverse:
61 ft 2 in, *Top Gear* stuntman (UK)

Skateboard: 79 ft, Danny Way (USA)

Rollerblades:
98 ft 5 in, Chris Haffey (USA)

Bicycle (assisted):
116 ft 11 in, Colin Winkelmann (USA)

Monster truck:
214 ft 8 in, Dan Runte (USA)

Car:
269 ft, Travis Pastrana (USA)

Motorcycle:
351 ft, Robbie Maddison (USA)

FACT
The 2011 film *Drive* (USA), starring Ryan Gosling, was directed by Nicolas Winding Refn, who has never owned a driver's license.

0 ft

Shortest braking distance by a vehicle on ice

On Jan 8, 2013, Fulda Reifen—a tire brand of Goodyear Dunlop Tires Germany—set a braking distance of 157 ft 11 in (48.132 m) for a car driven at 30.1 mph (48.5 km/h) on the frozen Schwatka Lake near Whitehorse, Yukon, Canada.

Longest stoppie

The greatest distance for a stoppie (aka endo or front-wheel wheelie) on a motorcycle is 1,320 ft 4 in (402.42 m). It was achieved by Jesse Toler (USA) at the Charlotte Diesel Super Show staged at the 7MAX Dragway in North Carolina, USA, on Oct 5, 2012.

Most switchback zero rotations in one minute

For this record, a rider must be seated back-to-front on a motorcycle ("switchback zero"), without touching it with his or her hands, and rotate the machine through 360 degrees. On Aug 22, 2013, British rider Mark Van Driel completed a total of 13 motorcycle switchback zero rotations in one minute on the set of Officially Amazing in Mildenhall, Suffolk, UK.

Most steps climbed by bicycle

Krystian Herba (POL) climbed all 2,754 steps of the World Financial Center in Shanghai, China, by bike on Mar 17, 2013. He did so, without touching the walls or putting his feet on the floor, in a time of 1 hr 21 min 53 sec.

SKATEBOARD

Fastest 110-m hurdles by hippy jumps

A hippy jump involves jumping off a moving board and over an obstacle while the skateboard passes beneath. Steffen Köster (DEU) hippy-jumped along a 110-m (360-ft) hurdle course in 29.98 sec in Rust, Germany, on Jun 19, 2013.

Fastest time to slalom 100 cones

On Aug 16, 2013, Jānis Kuzmins (LVA) slalomed his board through 100 cones in 19.41 sec on the set of CCTV Guinness World Records Special at the Asia-Pacific Experimental School of Beijing Normal University in Beijing, China.

Farthest distance in 24 hours

Andrew Andras (USA) traveled 261.8 mi (431.33 km) on his skateboard in 24 hr at the Homestead-Miami Speedway in Homestead, Florida, USA, on Jan 7–8, 2013.

On the same date and at the same venue, Colleen Pelech (USA) achieved the farthest distance traveled on a skateboard in 24 hours (female): 167.2 mi (269.08 km).

Fastest 400-m hurdles on a bicycle

On Aug 26, 2013, Austrian cyclist Thomas Öhler negotiated a 400-m hurdles course by bicycle in 44.62 sec in Linz, Austria.

Most ollie 180s in a minute

Eric Carlin (USA) performed 25 skateboard ollie 180s in 60 sec in Mount Laurel, New Jersey, USA, on Jul 2, 2013.

Longest stationary manual

Brendon Davis (USA) remained stationary on one set of wheels for 19 min 39.56 sec at the Society skate shop in San Carlos, California, USA, on May 11, 2013.

Most shove-its

On Sep 5, 2013, Gabriel Pena (USA) executed 33 shove-its (a 180-degree-or-more board spin) in 30 sec in Houston, Texas, USA.

Fastest motorcycle wheelie on ice

On Jan 27, 2013, Ryan Suchanek (USA) carried out a wheelie at a speed of 108.5 mph (174.6 km/h) across the frozen Lake Koshkonong in Wisconsin, USA. In doing so, he broke his own existing world record by 13.5 mph (21.7 km/h). The speed was measured over a distance of 328 ft (100 m).

FACT

Ryan Suchanek (left) rode a 2005 Kawasaki ZX10R. Its tires were studded to provide better traction on ice.

Monster feats: Bigfoot

It may have recorded the longest monster truck ramp jump with a leap of 214 ft 8 in, but Bigfoot 18 isn't the biggest in the Bigfoot family. Bigfoot 5, built in 1986, has the accolade of being the largest monster truck, standing 15 ft 6 in tall with 10-ft-high tires and weighing in at 38,000 lb. The man behind the monsters is Bob Chandler (USA), who began building them in 1975 as a way of publicizing his four-wheel-drive center in Missouri, USA.

Z Glossary

Caballerial: a 360° turn with the skater's back facing the ramp. Named for Steve Caballero.

McTwist: a 540° turn on a ramp.

Ollie: a jump in which the tail of the board is smacked ("popped") on the ground. In a "nollie," the nose of the board hits the ground.

Railslide: sliding the underside of the board along an object. ○ ○ ○

Mass participation

A gathering of 9,768 firefighters in Oct 2011 is almost **four times the population** of the Falkland Islands

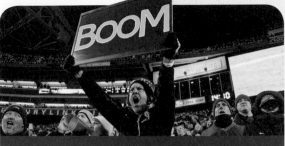

Loudest stadium crowd roar

Fans of the Seattle Seahawks (USA) achieved a 137.6-dB(A) roar at CenturyLink Stadium in Seattle, Washington, USA, on Dec 2, 2013, in a match against the New Orleans Saints. The term "dB(A)" denotes decibel levels audible to the human ear—i.e., excluding extreme highs and lows.

LARGEST ...

AED training session
Automated External Defibrillators (AED) diagnose and treat heart conditions. A training session for 2,109 participants on the machines was held by AED4all.com, Anne-Marie Willems and René Verlaak (all NLD) in Nijmegen, Netherlands, on May 29, 2013.

Baking lesson
Much dough was kneaded by 426 students of Green Grin Club Limited, Grin Kitchen Limited, and Ma On Shan Tsung Tsin secondary school (all HKG) in Hong Kong, China, on Sep 7, 2013.

Barbecue
Try to guess how much food you need for a barbecue for 45,252 people. Ingredients used by Estado de Nuevo León (MEX) included 34,000 lb (15.5 tonnes) of beef with 39,500 lb (18 tonnes) of onions, and 33,000 lb (15 tonnes) of corn tortillas, topped with 35,000 lb (16 tonnes) of salsa. It took place in Parque Fundidora in Monterrey, Mexico, on Aug 18, 2013.

Barefoot walk
The National Service Scheme Cell of Acharya Nagarjuna University (IND) took 7,050 people for a shoe-free stroll in Guntur, Andhra Pradesh, India, on Dec 12, 2012.

Largest horse race

The Federation of Mongolian Horse Racing Sport and Trainers registered 4,249 runners in an 11.18-mi (18-km) race in Khui Doloon Khudag, Ulan Bator, Mongolia, on Aug 10, 2013. The youngest rider was seven years of age and the oldest was 79.

Gathering of professional clown doctors
Clown doctors can ease difficult and frightening procedures in hospital for sick young people. On Jan 30, 2013, a group of 153 clowns marked the 20th anniversary of the clown doctoring work done by the Theodora Foundation, headquartered in Bern, Switzerland.

Largest gathering of people dressed as penguins

Children's hospice Richard House got 325 oversize penguins to waddle together in Wood Wharf, London, UK, on Guinness World Records Day on Nov 13, 2013.

> ## GREATEST GATHERINGS

Largest religious crowd: 30 million, India, 2013

Largest funeral: 15 million, India, 1969

Largest papal crowd: 4 million, Philippines, 1995

Largest antiwar rally: 3 million, Italy, 2003

Largest gathering of Sikhs: 3.5 million, India, 1999

⚡ Big banquets

In our 1962 edition, one of the earliest examples of a mass participation record was reported. "Lyons catered for the world's largest banquet at Olympia, London, on 8th August, 1925. A total of 6,600 guests were seated at 5 miles of tables served by 1,360 waitresses supported by 700 cooks and porters. The occasion was a War Memorial fund raising effort by Freemasons."

LARGEST GATHERING OF PEOPLE DRESSED ...

	Category	People	Organizer/Event	Location	Date
1	as Mohandas Gandhi	2,955	Sowdambikaa Group of Schools	Tiruchirappalli, India	Oct 11, 2013
	with false moustaches	2,268	City of Fairfield & Fairfield RAGBRAI Committee	Fairfield, Iowa, USA	Jul 26, 2013
2	as witches	1,607	La Bruixa d'Or	Sort, Lleida, Spain	Nov 16, 2013
3	as *Star Trek* characters	1,063	Media 10 Ltd.	ExCeL, London, UK	Oct 20, 2012
4	as Saint Patrick	882	Saint Brigid's National School	Castleknock, Dublin, Ireland	Mar 14, 2013
	as fairies	871	St. Giles Hospice	Lichfield, Staffordshire, UK	Jun 22, 2013
	as Superman	867	Escapade, Kendal Calling	Lowther Deer Park, Cumbria, UK	Jul 27, 2013
	in one-piece pajamas (onesies)	752	Henry Allen Onesie Angels	StadiumMK, Milton Keynes, UK	Nov 2, 2013
	as nurses	691	Dubai Health Authority	Dubai, UAE	Jan 24, 2014
	as trees	516	Ośrodek Kultury Leśnej w Gołuchówie	Gołuchów, Poland	Sep 30, 2013
	as cows	470	Chick-fil-A	George Mason University, Virginia, USA	Jul 2, 2013
	as monks	463	Ardfert Central National School	Ardfert, County Kerry, Ireland	May 11, 2013
	in Disney costumes	361	Walsgrave Church of England Primary School	Coventry, UK	Jul 12, 2013

Caroling
The Waukesha Downtown Business Association (USA) cajoled 1,822 carol singers in Waukesha, Wisconsin, USA, on Nov 22, 2013.

On a single bed
Leaving no room to roll over, 54 people were crammed on a single bed by Xilinmen Furniture in Beijing, China, on Sep 7, 2013.

Blowing bubble gum bubbles
Lester B. Pearson Public School in Aurora, Canada, organized 544 people to simultaneously blow gum bubbles on Jun 6, 2013.

Blowing up balloons
A different kind of blowing saw Bayer Yakuhin (JPN) organize 2,639 simultaneous balloon inflations on Jan 14, 2014, in Osaka, Japan.

Painting buildings at once
On May 18, 2013, Slovenian paint manufacturer Helios put 1,272 painters to work across nine venues.

Most people twerking
On Sep 25, 2013, GWR adjudicator Charlie Weisman witnessed 358 people twerking simultaneously in New York City, USA. The event was organized by hip-hop artist Big Freedia (USA).

MOST PEOPLE ...

On the same drum
Queen's "We Will Rock You" was an anthemic choice for 263 people playing a drum measuring 32 ft 9 in (10 m) in diameter and 5 ft 2 in (1.6 m) high. Organized by PLAY (POL), the event took place at Przystanek Woodstock in Kostrzyn nad Odra, Poland, on Aug 2, 2013.

Singing a national anthem simultaneously
A total of 121,653 employees from the Sahara India Pariwar company sang India's national anthem in Lucknow, India, on May 6, 2013.

Largest gathering of zombies
A brain-munching 9,592 members of the walking dead did the New Jersey Zombie Walk in Asbury Park, New Jersey, USA, on Oct 5, 2013. They shuffled their way to regaining the record from the Zombie Pub Crawl of Minneapolis, USA.

Hindu pilgrimage: Kumbh Mela festival
Between 80 and 100 million people attended the 55-day Kumbh Mela festival, which began in Allahabad, India, in Jan 2013. A Hindu pilgrimage to bathe in a sacred river is usually held every three years in one of four cities, but 2013 was a special version, the Maha Kumbh Mela, which occurs every 144 years. The city prepared for the onslaught—more than the entire population of the UK—with 14 temporary hospitals, 243 doctors on call, around 30,000 police and security staff on duty, and 40,000 restroom facilities. The cost was approximately 11.5 bn rupees ($182 m), but it was hoped that the festival would earn as much as 120 bn rupees ($1.9 bn).

And finally ...
- **Most people shaking cocktails simultaneously:** 1,710, Diageo (UK), Sep 18, 2013
- **Most people popping party poppers:** 743, Grey Court School (UK), Jul 17, 2013
- **Longest high-five chain:** 695 people, St. Francis of Assisi Primary School and Calwell High School (both AUS), Sep 27, 2013

○ ○ ○

No pain, no gain

Due to a genetic anomaly, **redheads** are more susceptible to pain

Longest time spent in full-body contact with ice

Wim Hof (NLD) spent 1 hr 53 min 2 sec immersed in ice in Naarden, Netherlands, on Oct 18, 2013. When it comes to withstanding sub-zero temperatures, Wim has consistently proved himself to be one cool customer: he has held this record 16 times in the past.

Longest time in full-body contact with snow

Oleksiy Gutsulyak (UKR) endured 60 min 8 sec of close contact with snow in the Kyrylo Tryliovski City Park in Kolomyia, Ukraine, on Jan 25, 2013.

Longest time to hold the breath voluntarily (male)

Stig Severinsen (DNK) held his breath underwater for exactly 22 min at the London School of Diving in London, UK, on May 3, 2012. The female record is held by Karoline Mariechen Meyer (BRA), who held her breath for 18 min 32.59 sec in the Racer Academy swimming pool in Florianópolis, Brazil, on Jul 10, 2009.

Most nails removed from wood with teeth in one minute

Tommy Heslep (USA) yanked 16 nails from a length of wood using just his teeth in a nail-biting 60 sec on the set of *Guinness World Records Unleashed* in Los Angeles, California, USA, on Jun 19, 2013. Around 300 lb (135 kg) of pressure was needed to remove each nail.

Longest full-body burn (without oxygen)

The greatest duration for a full-body burn without oxygen is 5 min 25 sec. The fiery feat was accomplished by Jayson Dumenigo (USA) in Santa Clarita, California, USA, on Mar 27, 2011.

The **most people to perform simultaneous full-body burns** is 21, achieved during an event organized by Ted Batchelor and Hotcards.com (both USA) at the Hotcards Burn in Cleveland, Ohio, USA, on Oct 19, 2013.

The **fastest time to run through 10 locked and burning doors** is 12.84 sec, performed by Chris Roseboro (USA) on

Most animal traps released on the body in one minute

On Oct 12, 2013, Johnny Strange (UK) set off six vintage animal traps on his body in a minute at Doncaster's Tattoo Jam, held at Doncaster Racecourse in South Yorkshire, UK. All of the traps were once used to catch rabbits. It's one of six GWR records that this sideshow entertainer extraordinaire currently holds.

GREATEST DISTANCES RUN ON A TREADMILL IN ...

- **1 week (female):** 517.6 mi, Sharon Gayter (UK), Dec 14–21, 2011
- **1 week (male):** 510.9 mi, Pierre-Michael Micaletti (FRA), May 13–19, 2012
- **48 hr (male):** 271.79 mi, Tony Mangan (IRL), Aug 22–24, 2008
- **48 hr (female):** 192.5 mi, Martina Schmit (AUT), Mar 10–12, 2006
- **24 hr (male):** 160.2 mi, Suresh Joachim (AUS), Nov 28–29, 2004
- **24 hr (female):** 153.6 mi, Edit Bérces (HUN), Mar 8–9, 2004
- **12 hr (male):** 76.67 mi, Eusébio Bochons (CHE/ESP), Dec 7, 2013
- **12 hr (female):** 60.14 mi, Theresa Dugwell (CAN), Mar 2, 2013

⚡ Lasting achievements

You might think that the human capacity for athletic endurance was fairly well set by now, but committed individuals have a way of confounding expectations. Back in 1998, Rory Coleman (UK) held the record for the **fastest time to run 100 miles on a treadmill (male)**, with a time of 23 hr 43 min. By 2003, Andrew Rivett (UK) was more than 7 hr faster (16 hr 23 min 16 sec). The current record, held by Suresh Joachim (AUS), is 13 hr 42 min 33 sec—around 10 hr faster than the 1998 record holder!

ℹ Dreading the tread

Treadmills were once a common feature in UK prisons. Engineer William Cubitt (UK) introduced them ca. 1818, variously to supply power, grind corn, and punish prisoners. They were abolished in 1898.

the set of *Guinness World Records Unleashed* in California City, California, USA, on Jul 7, 2013.

Most nails inserted into the nose in 30 seconds

Burnaby Q. Orbax (CAN) inserted 12 nails, into—then out of—his nose, one at a time, in 30 sec in London, UK, on Jun 22, 2013. Each nail was 4 in (10 cm) long.

Heaviest vehicle pulled using a hook through the nasal cavity and mouth

On Jun 5, 2013, Ryan Stock (CAN) pulled a 2,167-lb (983-kg) Volkswagen Beetle—with two women inside it—using a hook fed through his nasal cavity and out of his mouth for *Rekorlar Dünyası* in Istanbul, Turkey.

MOST …

Arrows broken by the neck in one minute

Fitness enthusiast Michael Gillette (USA) snapped 12 arrows by placing the sharp end of each one against his throat, in the

Most coconuts smashed with the elbows in one minute

On Jun 24, 2013, actor and martial arts expert Jeffrey James Lippold (USA) used his elbows to smash through 21 coconuts in one minute on the set of *Guinness World Records Unleashed* in Los Angeles, California, USA.

jugular notch, and forcing the other end against a wall in Los Angeles, California, USA, on Jun 27, 2013.

Ceramic slabs broken by the head by forward flips in one minute

In just 60 sec, Michael Gonzalez (USA) smashed 43 ceramic slabs with his head, following a forward flip, on the set of *Guinness World Records Unleashed* in Los Angeles, California, USA, on Jul 2, 2013.

Concrete blocks broken in one minute (male)

Ali Bahçetepe (TUR) smashed 1,175 concrete blocks by hand in Datça Cumhuriyet Meydanı, Turkey, on Nov 17, 2012.

Ali is something of a past master when it comes to concrete deconstruction. Over the years, he has also recorded the **most concrete blocks broken in 30 seconds** (683) and the **most concrete blocks broken in one stack** (36).

Ice blocks broken by a human battering ram

Uğur Öztürk (TUR) rammed through 14 ice blocks for *Rekorlar Dünyası* in Istanbul, Turkey, on Jun 26, 2013.

Most rope jumps on a bed of nails over a person

As if lying on a bed of nails isn't testing enough, Amy Bruney jumped 117 times on top of a bed of nails balanced over her husband Jon Bruney (both USA) on the set of *Guinness World Records Unleashed* in Los Angeles, California, USA, on Jun 25, 2013.

Pine boards broken with the elbow in one minute

Mohammad Rashid (PAK) broke 68 pine boards with his elbow in one minute at the Punjab Youth Festival in Lahore, Pakistan, on Mar 13, 2013. At the same event on the same day, 1,450 attendees also set the record for the **most people arm wrestling**.

The following year, perhaps looking for less painful records to attempt, the festival organizers formed the **largest human flag**, involving 28,957 participants at the National Hockey Stadium in Lahore on Feb 15.

Hard to beat: Paddy Doyle

If one man knows all about pushing the body to the limits of its physical capacity, it's Paddy Doyle (UK). This tough and tenacious character has been setting and breaking GWR endurance records for years—his oldest current record goes all the way back to 1989 (**most push-ups in 12 hours:** 19,325)! Along the way, he's also survived the **most competitive full-contact rounds** (6,324) and performed the **most push-ups using the back of the hands in one hour carrying a 40-lb pack** (663). See right for more examples of Doyle's derring-do.

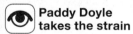

👁 Paddy Doyle takes the strain

Most jumping jacks in one minute carrying a 100-lb pack: 33, on Nov 10, 2013

Most step-ups in one minute carrying a 100-lb pack: 31, on Aug 17, 2013

Fastest cross-country half marathon carrying a 100-lb pack: 4 hr 18 min, on Jun 22, 2013

Most squat thrusts in one minute with a 40-lb pack: 21, on Mar 28, 2011

○ ○ ○

Modern world

There are **250 births** every minute ... and 105 deaths

Largest collection of US presidential memorabilia >

Ronald Wade (USA) owned 6,960 items of memorabilia with a US presidential theme as of Oct 14, 2013. Ronald started his collection with a badge at the age of 10 and, after graduation, he became a White House page during Richard Nixon's presidency (1969–74). He has also donated many items to the Bush Library outside Dallas and has had a replica of the Oval Office built in his house in Longview, Texas.

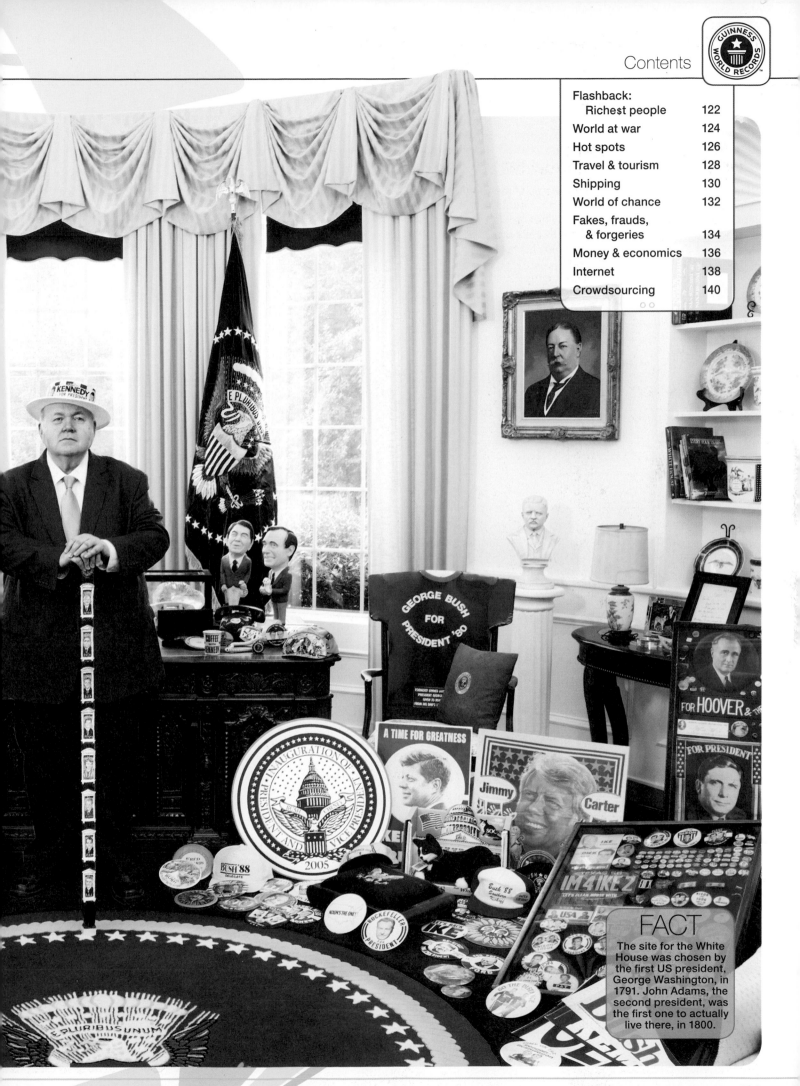

FACT

The site for the White House was chosen by the first US president, George Washington, in 1791. John Adams, the second president, was the first one to actually live there, in 1800.

Richest people

Even if he spent $1 m a day, it would still take the **richest man** nearly 200 years to spend all of his cash!

Meet the oil barons, retail magnates, and tech tycoons who are all members of the exclusive Guinness World Records Super-Rich Club—the 16 men (and yes, they're all men, and all but four of them American) who've held the record for the wealthiest living person over the past 60 years.

"The meek shall inherit the Earth, but not its mineral rights." So said Jean Paul Getty (USA), the oil baron who was the world's **richest person** for seven of the last 60 years. He was not alone in oil—one in four of our featured billionaires owed their megabucks to a vicelike grip on our natural resources.

Oil is no longer such a king. More recent entrants to the Billionaires' Club found their fortunes by trading in less tangible goods such as software and media rights, or have a near magical ability to read the stock markets.

In real terms, the richest man to emerge since we started publishing in 1955 is Bill Gates (USA). Adjusted for inflation, his software-base fortune via Microsoft reached an almost inconceivable $120 bn in 2000. It was built on the back of the dot-com boom, which, in the USA, saw the value of shares on the NASDAQ stock exchange more than double in the year up to Mar 10, 2000. Alas, all good things come to an end, and the wheel of fortune crushed many of those same companies: just 12 months later, most NASDAQ dot-coms had ceased trading.

Bill Gates survived, although, by the end of 2001, even he was down to his last $77.8 bn.

King Bhumibol Adulyadej

One surefire way to riches is to be born to them. Thailand's King Bhumibol Adulyadej, with assets of $30 bn, is the **richest monarch**. Here, he is with Brunei's Sultan Haji Hassanal Bolkiah (left), the second richest monarch with a mere $20 bn—but what's a few billion between royal friends?

FACT
The business card of gangster Alphonse Gabriel "Al" Capone read: "Secondhand furniture dealer."

Al Capone

Our 1960 edition records the belief that Chicago gangster Al Capone (USA, 1899–1947) held the record for the **highest gross income ever achieved in a single year by a private citizen.** Adjusted for inflation, in 1927 he earned $1.41 bn from a trade we said included "illegal liquor trading and alky-cookers (illicit stills)" as well as "dog tracks, dance halls ... and vice."

FACT
J. T. Williamson's wealth was never stated explicitly in the first *Guinness Book of Records*; his entry merely stated that his wealth "transcends all other personal fortunes."

FACT
Guinness World Records has been published every year since 1955, with the exception of 1957, 1959, and 1963. We have included the record for the **richest person** in every edition.

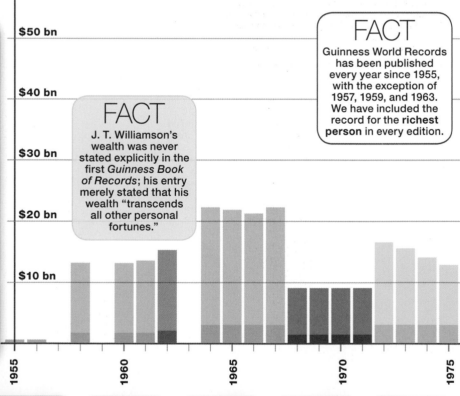

$100 bn
$90 bn
$80 bn
$70 bn
$60 bn
$50 bn
$40 bn
$30 bn
$20 bn
$10 bn

1955 1960 1965 1970 1975

THE GWR RICH LIST: HIGHEST ROLLERS, 1955–2015

John Thoburn Williamson
(CAN, 1907–58)
Record: 1955–56
Industry: Minerals, founded Williamson diamond mine
Peak: $60 m
Adjusted: $514 m

Jean Paul Getty
(USA, 1892–1976)
Record: 1958, 1960–61, 1964–67
Industry: Oil, building on empire of father George Franklin Getty
Peak: $3 bn
Adjusted: $22.2 bn

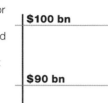

Haroldson Lafayette Hunt
(USA, 1889–1974)
Record: 1962
Industry: Oil empire based in Texas, after running cotton plantation
Peak: $2 bn
Adjusted: $15.2 bn

Howard Hughes
(USA, 1905–76)
Record: 1968–71
Industry: inherited father's tool business, moved into aviation, also movie production
Peak: $1.37 bn
Adjusted: $9 bn

Daniel K. Ludwig
(USA, 1897–1992)
Record: 1972–77, 1979–81
Industry: Shipping, oil, banking, cattle, insurance, property, hotels
Peak: $3 bn
Adjusted: $16.5 bn

John D. MacArthur
(USA, 1897–1978)
Record: 1978
Industry: Insurance (with wife Catherine), property, mainly in Florida, USA
Peak: $1.72 bn
Adjusted: $6 bn

Forrest Mars, Sr.
(USA, 1904–99)
Record: 1982–83
Industry: Food, building on father's Mars candy business, leaving company in 1969
Peak: $1 bn
Adjusted: $12.3 bn

David Packard
(USA, 1912–96)
Record: 1984–85
Industry: IT and computing, cofounding Hewlett-Packard with Bill Hewlett in 1939
Peak: $1.8 bn
Adjusted: $3.98 bn

Adjusted wealth estimated in 2014 using the consumer price list

TOP 10 RICHEST PEOPLE IN 2014

Of the **richest person** record holders over the last 60 years, only three feature in the current top 10.

Name	Amount	Industry	Age
● Bill Gates (USA)	$75.9 bn	Software	58
● Carlos Slim Helú (MEX)	$71 bn	Telecoms	73
Amancio Ortega (ESP)	$62.7 bn	Textiles	77
● Warren Buffett (USA)	$58.6 bn	Investment	83
Ingvar Kamprad (SWE)	$51.9 bn	Retail	87
Charles Koch (USA)	$46.9 bn	Engineering	78
David Koch (USA)			73
Larry Ellison (USA)	$43 bn	Software	69
Christy Walton (USA)	$36.9 bn	Retail	59
Sheldon Adelson (USA)	$35.4 bn	Casinos	80

Wealth average taken from: bloomberg.com, celebritynetworth.com, citywire.co.uk, forbes.com, londonlovesbusiness.com, and nationaljournal.com

FACT

If Bill Gates were still worth $120 bn today, his wealth would be greater than the GDP of 134 of the world's 192 countries.

Key

Each bar represents the dollar value of each person in a given year; bars are shown to scale based on their *actual* known wealth at the time, plus this figure *adjusted* for inflation to the value at today's figures.

inflation adjusted ———

actual ———

i Who wants to be a quadrillionaire?

In Jun 2013, it was reported that Christopher Reynolds (USA) became the **first trillionaire** and **first quadrillionaire** when a (brief) bank error in his favor resulted in a balance of $92,233,720,368,547,800 in his PayPal account. Reportedly, when asked what he would have spent the money on, Reynolds said, "I probably would have paid down the national debt." He would have been able to do that and then some, given that his balance was 1,200 times greater than the GDP of every country in the world combined!

1980　1985　1990　1995　2000　2005　2010

Gordon Getty
(USA, b. 1933)
Record: 1986
Industry: Father's oil empire, selling to Texaco in contentious deal for $10 bn in 1984
Peak: $4.1 bn
Adjusted: $9.06 bn

Sam Walton
(USA, 1918–92)
Record: 1987–88
Industry: Retailing empire based around Walmart chain stores, founded 1962
Peak: $21 bn
Adjusted: $42.4 bn

Yoshiaki Tsutsumi
(JPN, b. 1934)
Record: 1989–1992
Industry: Developing and expanding father's property-base business empire
Peak: $21 bn
Adjusted: $38.9 bn

S. Robson Walton
(USA, b. 1944)
Record: 1993
Industry: Oldest son of Sam Walton, chairman of Walmart (biggest retailer in 2013)
Peak: $10 bn
Adjusted: $15.9 bn

John Werner Kluge (DEU, 1914–2010)
Record: 1994
Industry: Mainly media, including TV, radio, and advertising
Peak: $8.1 bn
Adjusted: $12.5 bn

Warren Buffett
(USA, b. 1930)
Record: 1995–96, 2009
Industry: Investing in a diverse range of companies all over the world
Peak: $62 bn
Adjusted: $66.1 bn

Bill Gates
(USA, b. 1955)
Record: 1997–2008, 2010, 2014
Industry: Software engineering, founder of Microsoft
Peak: $90 bn
Adjusted: $120 bn

Carlos Slim Helú
(MEX, b. 1940)
Record: 2011–13
Industry: Telecoms, after stockbroking, investment, and general business
Peak: $74 bn
Adjusted: $74 bn

World at war

There has not been a 25-year period without war since **1495**

Least peaceful country

Created by the Institute for Economics and Peace, the Global Peace Index ranks countries by the safety of their citizens, the extent of conflict, and the degree of militarization. The index runs from 1 to 5, where 1 represents peace. As of 2013, Afghanistan was rated least at peace (3.440), with Somalia second-least peaceful, and Syria third.

Least secure nation in relation to nuclear weapons
In 2012, the Economist Intelligence Unit and the Nuclear Threat Initiative (a nongovernmental organization) reported that of the 32 nations with more than 2.2 lb (1 kg) of weapons-grade nuclear material, North Korea is the least secure. The state's leader, Kim Jong-un—at the age of 31, according to official reports—is the **youngest state leader to control nuclear weapons**.
As of 2012, these sources rank Australia as the **most secure nation in relation to nuclear weapons**.

Largest refugee camp

According to the humanitarian aid charity Cooperative for Assistance and Relief Everywhere (CARE), the Dadaab refugee camp in Kenya, Africa, is the largest in the world. On Apr 29, 2013, its registered refugee population stood at 423,496—nearly five times the size the camp was originally built to accommodate. Most of the refugees are from neighboring Somalia.

Most peaceful country
As of 2013, Iceland was No. 1 on the Global Peace Index (see above) with a score of 1.162. Denmark was second and New Zealand was ranked third.

Highest defense budget
The USA had a defense budget totaling $645.7 bn in 2012.

Longest civil war of modern times

The civil war in Myanmar started shortly after the country—formerly known as Burma—achieved independence from the UK on Jan 4, 1948, and it continues to the present day. Small armed groups are active in the west and, according to Amnesty International, clashes in Rakhine State started in Jun 2012 and have continued since.

Most civilian deaths in an undeclared civil war
Accurately recording deaths in any conflict is difficult and subject to variation of numbers. However, the United Nations estimated on Jul 24, 2013 that 100,000 people had died in Syria since the start of hostilities in Mar 2011. On Sep 24, 2013, France is reported to have told the UN General Assembly that 120,000 people had been killed in Syria. In Oct 2013, the Syrian Observatory for Human Rights, based in the UK, also reported 120,000 fatalities.

Deadliest conflict for children (current)
In the Nov 2013 report "Stolen Futures" (spanning Mar 2011 to Aug 2013) by the Oxford Research Group, 11,420 victims 17 years old and under are believed to have been killed in the Syrian civil war. Of these, more than 112 were tortured, 389 were killed by sniper fire, and some 764 were summarily executed.

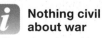

HIGHEST DEATH TOLLS IN CONFLICTS SINCE 1955

Second Congo War 2.5–5.4 million, 1998–2003

Vietnam War 800,000–3.8 million, 1955–75

Nigerian Civil War 1–3 million, 1967–70

Soviet War in Afghanistan ca. 960,000–1.6 million, 1979–89

Iran-Iraq War ca. 1 million, 1980–88

Second Sudanese Civil War ca. 1 million, 1983–2005

Mozambican Civil War 900,000–1 million, 1975–94

Rwandan Civil War 800,000–1 million, 1990–93

First Congo War 800,000, 1996–97

Eritrean War of Independence 570,000, 1961–91

KEY:
† x1 = 100,000 deaths
††††††††††
= lowest estimate
††††††††††
= highest estimate

FACT
During World War I, the average life expectancy of soldiers in the trenches was around six weeks.

i Nothing civil about war
Civil wars have brought about the death of around 25 million people since the conclusion of the last global conflict in 1945.

⚡ Casualties of war
The first *Guinness Book of Records* was published only 10 years after the end of World War II. That conflict featured in our debut edition as the **bloodiest war**, with overall casualties of around 56.4 million. Poland suffered most in proportion to its population, with 6,028,000 (or 17.2%) of its 35,100,000 citizens killed. It is a measure of the magnitude of this loss of life that it still represents history's **highest wartime death toll**.

Most terrorist attacks per country

The survey "Country Reports on Terrorism 2012," published in May 2013 by the US National Consortium for the Study of Terrorism and Responses to Terrorism, identified Pakistan as the country with the most terrorist attacks during 2012. It saw 1,404 attacks during that 12-month period, in which 1,848 people were killed and 3,643 injured. Iraq was placed second in the survey and Afghanistan third.

The number of Syrian child refugees is now 1 million (the **most refugee children**), most of whom are under the age of 11.

Most refugees by country of origin
According to UNHCR, the UN refugee agency, a combined total of 2,585,605 refugees had escaped from Afghanistan as of Jan 2013, the greatest number from any country.

The **country with the largest population of refugees** is Pakistan. In Jan 2013, it housed 1,638,456 refugees, nearly all of whom have fled from Afghanistan.

Largest peace-keeping force (one operation)
A United Nations Protection Force (UNPROFOR) peace-keeping mission was deployed in the former Yugoslavia from Feb 1992 to Mar 1995. In Sep 1994, the mission reached a strength of 39,922 military personnel, including a "Rapid Reaction Force."

At present, the UN is undertaking 15 peace-keeping operations worldwide, with one special political mission in Afghanistan. The **largest peace-keeping force deployed on one operation (present day)** is the stabilization mission in the Democratic Republic of the Congo. Of the 26,024 UN personnel deployed there, 19,557 are military troops.

Lowest score on the Press Freedom Index
Based on data for deaths, violence, censorship, media independence, and other factors, the African dictatorship of Eritrea is rated as the country with the least press freedom, according to the 2013 Press Freedom Index.

According to the Committee to Protect Journalists, as of Dec 19, 2013 the **most dangerous country for the media (current year)** was Syria: 21 journalists were killed there in 2013. In all, 52 journalists were killed in 2013 worldwide with a "confirmed" motive—i.e., where a murder is in direct reprisal for their work, or in crossfire, combat, or during dangerous assignments, such as coverage of a street protest.

First post-World War II head of state convicted by an international war crimes court
The international Special Court for Sierra Leone based in the Hague, Netherlands, found Charles Taylor, the ex-President of Liberia, Africa, guilty of 11 crimes. These included rape, murder, and the use of child soldiers during the civil war in Sierra Leone between 1991 and 2002, in which around 50,000 people died. He was sentenced to 50 years' imprisonment in May 2012 for aiding the rebels who committed atrocities.

Largest special forces

Special forces are trained military units with non-conventional tasks. North Korea has the largest such force, with around 60,000 operatives and some 130,000 personnel with special forces-like characteristics, according to US military officials.

Largest emergency aid appeal

On Jun 7, 2013, the United Nations launched an appeal for $5 bn in humanitarian aid for Syria to help more than 10 million people by the end of that year. The UN estimates that 4 million children are in need of humanitarian assistance as a result of the three-year conflict. The war has forced more than 6 million people out of their homes and caused 2 million to flee the country.

❌ Military hardware? Turn to p. 194

Remote-controlled death: striking drones

Drones are remotely controlled, armed, and unmanned aerial vehicles. According to nongovernmental organizations and Pakistan government sources cited by Amnesty International in its "Will I Be Next?" report on US drone strikes in Pakistan, the USA launched some 330–374 drone strikes in that country between 2004 and Sep 2013. Another estimate, from the New America Foundation public policy institute, puts the figure at 364 US drone strikes in Pakistan as of Jul 2013. Either estimate represents the **most drone strikes**.

👁 Waging warfare

Shortest war: Between Britain and Zanzibar (now part of Tanzania); lasted from 9:00 a.m. to 9:45 a.m. on Aug 27, 1896

Longest continuous international war: Thirty Years War (1618–48), between various European countries; ended with Peace of Westphalia

Highest death toll from a civil war: Russian Civil War (1917–22), with the death of ca. 1.5 million soldiers and more than 8 million civilians ○ ○ ○

Hot spots

The **average life expectancy in 1955** was 48 years; today, it is 67.2

Most murders per country

There were 47,106 murders in Brazil during 2012, corresponding to 24.5 homicides per 100,000 of the population. In Nov 2012, protesters concerned by these figures amassed outside the Brasilia National Congress, where more than 900 blood red bricks were laid out: one for each victim in a typical week.

Most dangerous place to fly

The 2012 Annual Review of the International Air Transport Association (IATA) reported that the most dangerous place to fly is Africa—nine times more dangerous than the global average. In 2011, Africa suffered 3.27 aircraft destroyed or written off for every million flights taken. Reasons included an aging fleet of turbo-prop aircraft, and inadequate air-traffic control.

Country with the highest percentage of the poor

Despite India's growing economy, its borders contain 41.01% of the world's poor. China comes second with 22.12%. The UN Department of Economic and Social Affairs defines poverty as "equating to those who earn $1.25 a day or less."

Deadliest place to travel by road

The World Health Organization (WHO) in 2013 reported that the Dominican Republic recorded 41.7 road deaths per 100,000 population during the year 2010, the highest rate of nations with a population of more than 1 million. Globally, 1.24 million people died on the road in 2010.

Lowest GDP per head

Gross Domestic Product (GDP) reflects all the goods and services produced by a nation in a year, stated as a value per head of population. The citizens of Malawi, an East African country with an undeveloped economy, have a GDP per head of $223. Luxembourg has the **highest GDP** (excluding the tiny principalities of Monaco and Lichtenstein) at $110,424.

Largest global toxic threat

According to a report from 2010 by the Blacksmith Institute (USA), 10 million people are at risk from lead poisoning. The next most toxic global pollutants, in order, are: mercury, chromium, arsenic, pesticides, and radionuclides. These can cause mental and physical disabilities, cancers, and even death.

Most murders per capita
While Brazil has the most murders in an absolute sense (see above), per capita the record is held by Honduras. The Central American country has 82.1 murders per 100,000 people, according to research by *The Economist*.

Most prisoners per capita
According to the International Center for Prison Studies, in 2011 the USA had a record prison population of 2,239,751, and a rate of 716 prisoners for every 100,000 residents—the most prisoners per capita. By comparison, the micro-state of San Marino had just two prisoners—or 6 prisoners per 100,000.

Most fatal snakebites per country

India reports a greater number of fatalities from snakebites than any country, recording 81,000 "envenomings" annually. Of these, 11,000 eventually prove to be fatal, according to conservative estimates published in *The Global Burden of Snakebite* (2008).

GLOBAL PEACE INDEX: THE LEAST PEACEFUL COUNTRIES

The Global Peace Index 2013 ranks 162 nations on a scale of 1 to 5 (1=most peaceful), using 22 indicators ranging from military expenditure to relations with neighboring countries and the percentage of prison population.

Russia **3.060**
Iraq **3.245**
Afghanistan **3.440**
Syria **3.393**
North Korea **3.044**
Sudan **3.242**
Pakistan **3.106**
Central African Republic **3.03**
Somalia **3.394**
Dem. Rep. of the Congo **3.085**

Source: Institute for Economics and Peace

Country comparisons

Highest death rate: Ukraine, with 16.2 deaths per 1,000 population projected for 2010–15.

Highest cancer death rate: Hungary, with 316 deaths per 100,000 population in 2009.

Highest heart disease death rate: Ukraine, with 1,070.5 deaths per 100,000 population in 2011.

Highest obesity rate: The island state of Nauru in the South Pacific, with 71.1% of people in 2008.

Most polluted major city

A 2011 report by the WHO measured air pollution by the mass of particles smaller than 10 microns in diameter per cubic meter of air (known as PM_{10}). Ahwaz in Iran was the main offender, with a PM_{10} of 372 micrograms per cubic meter.

average of only 3 micrograms of PM_{10}, making it the **least polluted city**.

Worst land pollution

In Nov 1994, thousands of tons of crude oil flowed across the pristine Arctic tundra of the Komi Republic near Usinsk, Russia. Estimates of the amount of oil lost vary from about 15,400 to 220,000 tons, and the total contaminated area measured 227.11 million sq ft (21.1 million m²), almost the same area occupied by El Salvador. The cost of the accident was estimated at more than 311 billion roubles ($11 bn).

Worst air pollution

In 2011, the World Health Organization (WHO) reported that the air in Mongolia had an annual average of 279 micrograms of PM_{10} per cubic meter (see Glossary below right). Many of the country's factories burn coal and many people live in *gers*: yurtlike felt-lined tents with central stoves. See above for the **most polluted major city**.

On a lighter note, the WHO report also stated that Whitehorse in Yukon, Canada, has an annual

Unhappiest country

According to a survey of 156 nations conducted in 2013 by the UN Sustainable Development Solutions Network, the citizens of the West African nation of Togo are the unhappiest, with a score of 2.936 out of 10. The survey looked at factors such as quality and quantity of life, mental health, and personal liberty. At the other end of the scale was Denmark with a score of 7.693—making it the **happiest country**.

Most tornadoes by area

The Netherlands has one twister for every 769 sq mi (1,991 km²) of land. The USA has one per 3,161 sq mi (8,187 km²).

Most deaths from natural disasters

In 2013, the Centre for Research on the Epidemiology of Disasters, Belgium, provided a report of fatalities from disasters such as earthquakes, floods, and hurricanes during 2012. The most deaths—2,385—occurred in the Philippines, with China in second place with 802. In Dec 2012, almost 2,000 people in the Philippines were killed by Typhoon Bopha alone.

Most robberies per capita

In 2013, *The Economist* reported that Belgium has 1,714 robberies for every 100,000 people in a population of 10.8 million. The figures include an audacious heist on Feb 18, 2013, when cars with police markings were used to steal $50 m of diamonds from a plane at Brussels Airport—without a shot being fired.

Most dangerous resort for shark attacks

New Smyrna Beach in Florida, USA, has recorded 238 attacks, and the beach has become known as the shark attack capital of the world, although most of the bites have been nibbles from hungry juveniles. Pictured here are surfers with a blacktip shark not far behind them—a photo snapped in 2008 by Kem McNair, who had finished surfing for the day.

FACT

Experts believe New Smyrna's reputation as a shark diner is simply down to the large numbers of people in the water who venture in despite frequent shark sightings.

State of danger

From our first edition: "Taking figures for the decade (1940–1950) that part of the world with the highest annual average murder rate is the state of Georgia, USA, with 167.3 per million." By 2012, the figure had dropped to 59 per million, according to the FBI. The record holder per capita is now Honduras (see main text).

Hard news: journalists in danger

The **most dangerous country for journalists** is Iraq, with 153 killed since 1992. A total of 1,014 journalists have been killed worldwide since 1992, according to the Committee to Protect Journalists (CPJ). The problem is compounded by impunity—when governments deliberately don't investigate murders because they don't want to have abuses of power and human rights violations reported. The second most dangerous country is the Philippines, with 73 journalists killed since 1992.

Glossary

PM_{10}: Used to assess the extent of air pollution, this refers to "particulate matter" smaller than 10 micrometers wide. (The period at the end of this sentence is about 1,000 micrometers wide.) At this size, particulate matter such as dust, salts, and the products of industrial processes are small enough to penetrate into the deepest part of the lungs and cause a range of health problems, such as asthma and lung cancer.

Travel & tourism

Mexico City is sinking by 3 ft 3 in per year—**10 times faster** than Venice

Most northerly ski resort

The Tromsø Alpinsenter ski resort is located in Kroken, Norway, more than 186 mi (300 km) inside the Arctic Circle. The resort has two drag lifts, a 1,640-ft (500-m) children's tow, and four slopes with varying levels of difficulty. The longest run extends for some 1.2 mi (2 km).

Highest earnings from tourism
According to the UNWTO, tourism in the USA was worth $126.2 bn in 2012 and single-handedly accounted for 8.5% of international tourism takings. Spain was second, with $56 bn, and France third, with $54 bn.

Most international tourist arrivals in one year
In 2012, according to a UNWTO report, the number of international tourist arrivals was 1.035 billion.

The same source reports that the **most popular country for tourism** is France, with 83 million international arrivals. The country accounts for just over 8% of the global

Fastest-growing tourist region

Tourist arrivals in Asia and the Pacific rose 7% in 2012, the equivalent of 15 million more international tourist visitors than in 2011. Among Asian subregions, southeast Asia posted the highest growth, with 9% more arrivals than the previous year, and Thailand saw a growth of 16% in absolute terms over 2011. This was the second year in a row that this region posted a record increase, according to the UNWTO.

Highest tourist receipts
In 2011, global receipts (earnings) from tourism topped $1 tr for the first time in history, according to the United Nations World Tourism Organization (UNWTO). In 2012, however, total exports from international tourism rose once again, to reach an unprecedented level of $1.3 tr.

Greatest spending on tourism (country)
The Chinese spent $102 bn on tourism in 2012—an increase of 37% on the country's 2011 spending and an eightfold increase from the $13 bn spent in 2000. Germany's tourists spent the next largest amount internationally—$83.8 bn— with the USA third, spending $83.5 bn.

Largest apartment ship

Launched in 2002, MS *The World* incorporates 165 residential units comprising 106 apartments, 19 studio apartments, and 40 studios. While it continuously circumnavigates the world, its residents are able to conduct their professional lives while living and relaxing onboard. The average stay lasts for around three to four months of the year and average occupancy is 150 residents (with an average age of 65).

tourism market. Its nearest rivals are the USA (with 67 million visitors) and China (with 57.7 million).

Europe remains the **most-visited tourism region**, with 534.2 million arrivals in 2012, according to the UNWTO. Asia and the Pacific are its nearest rivals, with 233.6 million arrivals. In third place are the Americas, with 163.1 million.

Most continents visited in one calendar day
Gunnar Garfors (NOR) and Adrian Butterworth (UK) visited five continents in one calendar day, taking scheduled transport between the east side of Istanbul in Turkey (Asia), Casablanca in

For truly epic journeys, see p. 156

THE WORLD

WANDERERS OF THE WORLD: INTERNATIONAL TOURISM

Changing trends in 60 years of globe-trotting:

International Tourist Arrivals (million)

- Africa
- Middle East
- Americas
- Asia and the Pacific
- Europe

1,200 1,000 800 600 400 200 0

1960 1970 1980 1990 2000 2010

Source: UNWTO Tourism Highlights 2013 Edition

Transportation mode

- Air 52%
- Road 40%
- Rail 2%
- Water 6%

Purpose of visit

- Leisure 52%
- Health; religion; friends/ family; other 27%
- Business 14%
- Not specified 7%

Plus ça change ...

China has overtaken the USA in terms of tourist spending, and over the years London and Paris have vied for the honor of being the most-visited city. But for years now, one country has consistently proved to be the most popular for tourists: France. Back in 1999, it welcomed 73 million visitors. As of 2012, 83 million of us chose France for its rich cultural heritage, beautiful countryside, beaches, ski resorts, culinary delights, historic castles, and cathedrals … and, of course, to see the "city of light," Paris.

FACT

Only an estimated 1,000th of 1% of the world's population has visited Antarctica.

Towering achievement

Every seven years, the Eiffel Tower receives a fresh coat of paint. In all, 132,275 lb of paint are required to cover its 2.69 million-sq-ft surface area.

Largest marina

In terms of inhabitants, Marina del Rey in Los Angeles County, California, USA, is the largest marina, with a population of 8,866 according to a 2010 census. It is home to 6,500 boats. The Dubai Marina, however—a 2-mi-long (3-km) canal city in Dubai, UAE, inaugurated in 2003—will accommodate approximately 120,000 people. It has a provisional completion date of 2015.

Morocco (Africa), Paris in France (Europe), Punta Cana in the Dominican Republic (North America), and Caracas in Venezuela (South America) on May 18, 2012. The entire trip took 28 hr 25 min, but the changing time zones ensured that Garfors and documentary filmmaker Butterworth cleared customs in each country on the same day.

Most international visits by a US president

Two US presidents have each visited 74 unique nations in office. The first was Bill Clinton, whose trips began on Apr 3–4, 1993 in Vancouver, Canada, where he had a summit meeting with President Yeltsin (RUS) and a meeting with Canadian Prime Minister Brian Mulroney. His final trip was to the UK on Dec 12–14, 2000, and included meetings with Prime Minister Tony Blair and Queen Elizabeth II. In all, Clinton made 133 trips.

George W. Bush, the 43rd president, visited 74 unique nations during 140 trips in his two terms. The first, on Feb 16, 2001, was to San Cristóbal in Mexico, where he met with President Fox. The final visit was to Kabul in Afghanistan, from Dec 14 to 15, 2008, to meet President Karzai and visit US military personnel.

Most national capitals visited in 24 hours by scheduled transport

Sarah Warwick and Lucy Warwick (both UK) visited London, Brussels, Prague, Paris, Bratislava, and Vienna from Sep 24 to 25, 2013.

Most popular city for tourism

According to the MasterCard Global Destination Cities index, the city that attracted the greatest number of tourists in 2012 was London, UK, with an estimated 16.9 million international visitors. The same report noted that tourists to London spent $21.1 bn, a 10.3% increase on 2011. No doubt the city's role as host of the 2012 Olympics played a part in this achievement.

Largest national park

The Northeast Greenland National Park covers 375,290 sq mi (972,000 km²), from Liverpool Land in the south to the northernmost island, Oodaaq, off Peary Land. Established in 1974 and enlarged in 1988, much of the park is covered by ice and is home to a variety of protected flora and fauna, including polar bears, musk ox, and birds of prey.

The **oldest national park** is Yellowstone National Park, USA. It was given its status in 1872 by US president Ulysses S. Grant, who declared that it would always be "dedicated and set apart as a public park or pleasuring ground for the benefit and enjoyment of the people." It covers 3,470 sq mi (8,980 km²), mostly in the state of Wyoming.

Most-visited art gallery

The Louvre Museum in Paris, France, attracted 9,720,260 visitors in 2012. Housed in the Palais du Louvre on the Right Bank of the Seine, the museum first opened in 1793. In 1989, a glass pyramid designed by architect I. M. Pei was controversially added to its main courtyard (below).

According to *The Economist*, the Tate Modern in London, UK, remains the **most-visited modern art gallery**. In 2012, it drew 5,300,000 art lovers.

Water resistance: Venice in peril

The historic Italian city of Venice, a UNESCO World Heritage Site, is increasingly threatened with settlement and serious flooding of its lagoon and canals. In 2002, a plan was inaugurated to control water surges from the Adriatic Sea into the lagoon. Named the Moses Project, it envisages building 78 giant steel gates across three inlets to the lagoon, and sinking 660,000-lb hinged gates (see bottom left)—each around 88 ft wide—into huge concrete bases dug into the seabed. This represents the **largest project to save a tourist resort**.

👁 The final frontier

First space tourist: Businessman Dennis Tito (USA), trip to *International Space Station* (*ISS*), Apr 28 to May 6, 2001

First space tourist (female): Anousheh Ansari (IRN), trip to *ISS*, Sep 18 to 29, 2006

Most trips into space by a tourist: Charles Simonyi (USA, b. HUN) embarked on first trip to *ISS* on Apr 7, 2007; made second trip, at the age of 60, on Mar 26, 2009

○ ○ ○

In a year, the average container ship will cover the distance of a trip to the **Moon and halfway back**

Greatest lifting capacity for a ship

The MV *Fairplayer* and MV *Javelin*, operated by Jumbo Shipping of Rotterdam (NLD), are J-class mega ships. Equipped with two Huisman mast cranes, each can carry a load of 2 million lb (900 metric tons), giving a maximum lifting capacity of 4 million lb (1,800 metric tons).

Busiest shipping lane

The Dover Strait marks the narrowest part of the English Channel between the UK and continental Europe. Through its shipping lane pass 500–600 ships a day.

First container ships

Shipborne containers were employed—usually on short sea routes—from the early 20th century. Modern containerization started in the 1950s, one of the first vessels being the former tanker *Ideal X*, modified by Sea-Land Service (USA) in 1955. Standard container sizes were adopted in the 1960s alongside the introduction of purpose-built ships. A unit of cargo capacity can be measured by TEU—Twenty-foot Equivalent Unit—based on the volume of one standard, 20-ft-long (6.1-m) container.

Largest container shipping line

Maersk (DNK) runs more than 600 vessels that make a total of 3.4 million

Busiest ocean trade route

A total of 7.52 million cargo containers were transported from North America to Asia in 2012, and 14.42 million containers shipped in the opposite direction. In all, the route saw 21.94 million units.

container moves annually. The company reported that they call at 35,000 ports annually and, in 2012, their work included shipping 8.4 billion bananas.

Largest ship ever

The oil tanker *Mont* (formerly *Jahre Viking*, *Happy Giant*, and *Seawise Giant*) had a deadweight tonnage of 622,544 tons (564,763 tonnes). She was 1,504 ft (458.45 m) long, 226 ft (68.8 m) wide, and had a draft of 80 ft 9 in (24.61 m). In 2010, she became the **largest ship to be scrapped**.

Fastest shipbuilding

The World War II shipbuilding program at Kaiser's yard in Portland, Oregon, USA, built 22-million-lb (10,000-metric-ton) ships in as little as

Longest container ship

The Maersk (DNK) Triple E-class ships are each 1,312 ft (400 m) long and 20 have been ordered. The lead, *Maersk Mc-Kinney Møller*, was launched in Geoje, South Korea, on Feb 24, 2013. Each of the ships will contain as much steel as eight Eiffel Towers and, placed in Times Square, New York City, USA, would tower above the billboards and most of the buildings. Each ship has enough space to accommodate 36,000 cars or 863 million cans of beans.

LARGEST SHIPS

For comparison:
Eiffel Tower, 1,062 ft tall

Largest privately owned yacht:
Azzam, owned by Sheikh Khalifa bin Zayed Al Nahyan (UAE), 590 ft (cost: approx. $654 m)

Largest passenger liner: Royal Caribbean International Oasis class, 1,187 ft, DWT (deadweight tonnage) 33 million lb

Largest oil tanker: Daewoo Shipbuilding & Marine Engineering T1 class, 1,243 ft, DWT 973.5 million lb

Longest container ship: Maersk Triple E class, 1,312 ft, DWT 432 million lb

Largest ship ever: *Mont*, 1,504 ft, DWT 1.24 billion lb

i Modeling big ships

For the ship enthusiast who needs a Maersk in their life, LEGO® have created a model version of the Triple E-class ship (see **longest container ship**). It comes in 1,519 pieces and measures 1 ft high, 2 ft 1.5 in long, and is 3.5 in wide.

👁 Deadweight tonnage (DWT)

Largest oil tanker—current:
Hellespont Alhambra, Daewoo Shipbuilding & Marine Engineering (KOR), Jun 11, 2001, 973 million lb

Largest bulk carrier ship:
Vale Beijing (Dec 2011) and *Vale Qingdao* (Jun 2012), STX Offshore & Shipbuilding (KOR), 891 million lb

Largest dry bulk carrier ship: *Berge Stahl*, Bergesen (NOR), 1986, 804 million lb

Largest pipe-laying ship:
Solitaire, Allseas Group (NDL), 1998, 280 million lb

Busiest port for cargo volume

The Port of Shanghai turned over 811 million tons (736 million metric tons) of cargo in 2012, handling more than 32 million containers. It has a total quay length of around 12.43 mi (20 km), with 125 berths for container ships.

11 million lb (5,000 metric tons). The *Seven Borealis* crane extends a record 492 ft (150 m) above deck level, although other cranes lift heavier weights. The structure revolves on a bearing that is 36 ft (11 m) in diameter. The ship began work in 2012.

Largest open-deck transport ship

The semi-submersible *Dockwise Vanguard* is 902 ft (275 m) long and has a flat deck measuring 230 x 902 ft (70 x 275 m). It can carry oversize cargo weighing 242.5 million lb (110,000 metric tons). The carrier, operated by Dockwise (NLD), submerges its deck to a depth of 52 ft (16 m) to allow it to load cargoes, such as oil and gas platforms, by floating underneath them.

Most powerful nuclear-powered cargo ship

The Russian *Sevmorput* is not only the most powerful but is now the only nuclear-powered cargo ship left of the four that were originally produced. Nuclear power has not been widely adopted in shipping, and *Sevmorput* itself was to be scrapped until it was announced in Dec 2013 that it is to be restored by 2016.

SHIPWRECKS

Deepest

The *Rio Grande* was a German World War II blockade runner, evading enemies to deliver cargo. In Jan 1944, she was sunk by American ships and was discovered in 1996 by Blue Water Recoveries (UK) at a depth of 18,904 ft (5,762 m).

Another World War II casualty was UK merchant ship SS *Gairsoppa*, from which was retrieved the **deepest salvage of cargo from a shipwreck**. She was sunk by a German U-boat submarine and lay at a depth of 15,420 ft (4,700 m). In 2011, the ship was discovered by Odyssey Marine Exploration (USA), who had retrieved 105,821 lb (48 metric tons) of silver by Jul 2013.

Largest

The 708-million-lb (321,186-metric-ton) deadweight crude oil carrier *Energy Determination* broke in two in the Strait of Hormuz, Persian Gulf, on Dec 12, 1979. She was not carrying any cargo but had a hull value of $58 m.

Oldest

A single-mast sailing ship, discovered in 1912, was wrecked off Uluburun, near Kaş in southern Turkey, in the 14th century BC.

---

4 days 15 hr 30 min. In 1942, the SS *Robert E. Peary* had her keel laid on Nov 8, launched on Nov 12, and was operational on Nov 15. Prefabrication speeded up production.

Largest ship builder

Hyundai Heavy Industries (KOR) is said to account for 15% of total world ship production. According to a report from a South Korean news agency in

Feb 2014, a fall in ship prices meant that the giant's profits were down 86% in 2013, at 146.3 bn South Korean Won ($136 m). In Jan 2014, it began work on a container ship with a capacity of 19,000 TEU.

Largest offshore mast crane

Onboard the *Seven Borealis* is a crane, built by Huisman (NLD), that lifts payloads of up to

Longest big ship canal

The Suez Canal has allowed ships to navigate from the Red Sea to the Mediterranean Sea, without sailing around Africa, since opening on Nov 17, 1869. Ten years in the making, it is 100.8 mi (162.2 km) in length and varies in width between 984 ft (300 m) and 1,198 ft (365 m).

Spinning around: a propeller with a twist

The *Emma Maersk* was launched in 2006 and featured the world's **largest propeller**. Made by Mecklenburger Metallguss GmbH (DEU), the single-piece, 286,600-lb propeller has six blades and measures 31 ft 6 in in diameter. Because of its size, the metal alloy from which it's made required two weeks to cool after casting. The blades are turned by a 14-cylinder Wärtsilä-Sulzer RTA96C two-stroke engine, the world's **largest diesel engine**. In Feb 2013, however, as the ship entered the Suez Canal, an engine-room flood put it out of service for some months.

Glossary

Deadweight tonnage: The total weight that a ship can carry, including crew, passengers, supplies, etc.

Gross tonnage: The total enclosed space within a ship (i.e., not a weight measurement).

Displacement tonnage: The weight of the water that a ship displaces when floating with full fuel tanks and stores. It is the actual weight of the ship, as a floating body displaces its own weight in water.

World of chance

Most money lost by a nation to gambling per capita

According to international gambling organization H2 Gambling Capital, during 2010 the average Australian 17 years old or over lost US$1,199. Around 70% of Australians are believed to participate in some form of gambling.

Greatest winning streak

In Dec 1992, Greek-American Archie Karas arrived in Las Vegas, USA, with $50 in his pocket. By early 1995, he had turned this sum into $40 m by playing pool, poker, and dice. It's the largest winning streak in history, and even has its own name in gambling lore: "The Run." Karas's love of dice and (later) baccarat were his downfall: by mid-1995, he had lost all of the money.

First bookmaker

The first person to turn a profit as a bookmaker is thought to have been Harry Ogden (UK), who operated on Newmarket Heath, Suffolk, UK, during the mid-1790s. Prior to this, people who wanted to bet on horse racing would simply make bets against one another. Ogden was the first to look at the entire field and offer different odds on every horse, calculating its chance of winning so that he would make a profit.

First offshore bookmaker

Victor Chandler International, now trading as BetVictor, decided to move its entire operation offshore in 1997 to evade the UK gambling tax, a move that was completed in 1999. The company relocated to Gibraltar—where the betting tax is zero. Many other bookmakers now also have a presence on the "Rock."

Largest horse-racing win

Scottish race horse owner Harry Findlay scooped £1.85 m ($3 m) over the British May Bank Holiday weekend in 2007. Findlay had placed bets of £140,000 ($276,000) with online pool betting firm RaceO. He ended up with 16 winners, comprising two eight-horse accumulators (a multiple, high-risk bet that only pays out if every horse wins).

Most successful horse-racing gambler

William Benter (USA) makes some $10 m per year betting on horses at the two tracks

Largest win in a televised poker game

Tom Dwan (USA) picked up £0.6 m ($1.1 m) from one hand of televised poker against fellow American Phil Ivey during Full Tilt Poker's Million Dollar Cash Game, filmed in London, UK, in Sep 2009. Both players had drawn a "straight" (five cards of any suit ranked in order), but Dwan's 3-4-5-6-7 beat Ivey's ace-2-3-4-5.

Largest lottery win donated to charity

In Jul 2010, Canadians Allen and Violet Large won CAN$11.2 m ($10.8 m) on the Lotto 6/49 draw. They gave away some 98%—CAN$10.9 m ($10.5 m)—to local groups, including the Red Cross and hospitals where Violet had cancer treatment.

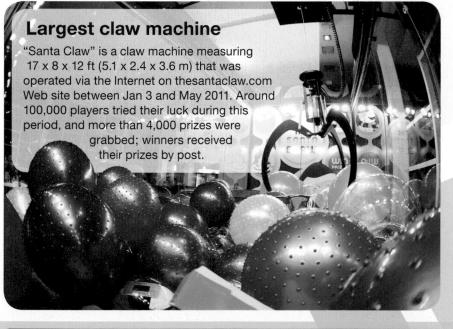

Largest claw machine

"Santa Claw" is a claw machine measuring 17 x 8 x 12 ft (5.1 x 2.4 x 3.6 m) that was operated via the Internet on thesantaclaw.com Web site between Jan 3 and May 2011. Around 100,000 players tried their luck during this period, and more than 4,000 prizes were grabbed; winners received their prizes by post.

TOP 10 BIGGEST GAMBLING LOSSES PER ADULT (PER ANNUM)

In absolute terms, populations of larger countries, such as the USA and China, naturally lose more money to gambling than smaller countries. (Macau in China is the **largest gambling city by revenue**—more than $38 bn was generated by its casinos and other gaming services in 2012.) But measured in proportion to their overall population, gambling's biggest losers tend to be the smaller nations:

Source: H2 Gambling Capital, 2011; all figures quoted in US$

- $1,000
- $500
- $0
- Spain: $389
- Greece: $391
- Norway: $416
- Hong Kong: $468
- Italy: $481
- Finland: $514
- Canada: $528
- Ireland: $547
- Singapore: $1,093
- Australia: $1,199

FACT

The chances of winning the jackpot in a 6/49 lottery (i.e., selecting six numbers correctly out of a choice of 49) are 1 in 13,983,816.

AZ Glossary

Jackpot: Maximum prize; the name originates from a type of poker in which the stakes built up until a player could open with a pair of jacks or better.

First Facebook game to offer cash prizes

On Aug 7, 2012, British online gaming company Gamesys launched the first Facebook game to offer real cash prizes. Titled *Bingo Friendzy*, it featured 90 mini games. Only Facebook users over the age of 18 are legally allowed to play the game.

in Hong Kong, China. Benter trained as a physicist, and he used his scientific skills to build a computer model that takes into account more than 100 statistics—quantifying horses, jockeys, trainers, tracks, and race conditions— to calculate each runner's exact chance of winning.

Longest craps roll

On May 23, 2009, at the Borgata Hotel Casino in Atlantic City, New Jersey, USA, craps player Patricia Demauro (USA) threw a pair of dice 154 times before a 7 ended her winning streak. It took her 4 hr 18 min, beating odds of 1,560 billion to 1.

Largest win in a poker competition

Antonio Esfandiari (USA, b. Iran) won $18,346,673 at the World Series of Poker tournament (WSOP2012) in Las Vegas, Nevada, USA, on Jul 3, 2012.

Largest online poker tournament

PokerStars (UK) organized an online poker tournament with 225,000 participants on Jun 16, 2013. Each player paid 60p ($1), with a £15,000 ($25,000) top prize.

Largest slot machine tournament

A total of 3,001 players attended a slot machine event organized by Bally Technologies (USA) at Mohegan Sun in Uncasville, Connecticut, USA, on Apr 27, 2013.

Most lottery prizes given in a year

Pronósticos para la Asistencia Pública (MEX) awarded 97,909,447 lottery prizes during 2008, distributed across eight different games.

Most members of a family to win a national lottery

In Sep 2012, teenager Tord Oksnes

became the third member of his family to hit the jackpot in the Norwegian National Lottery when he won 12.2 m kroncr ($2.1 m). Three years previously, Tord's sister Hege Jeanette claimed 8.2 m kroner ($1.27 m). Three years before that, Tord and Hege's father Leif scooped a win of 8.4 m kroner ($1.5 m).

Greatest national lottery jackpot

By Mar 30, 2012, the American Mega Millions lottery jackpot reached an annuity value of $656 m, or $474 m in cash. The three unidentified winners (all USA) split the cash sum between them.

Largest Tote betting win

Sixty-one-year-old Steve Whiteley (UK) won an incredible £1,445,671.71 ($2,356,444.89) on a £2 ($3.25) Tote Jackpot accumulator bet in which he successfully predicted the winner of all six races from the meeting at Exeter, UK, on Mar 8, 2011. Afterward, he was quoted as saying: "I'm a heating engineer—well, I was."

Lottery winners: what do they spend it on?

Source: Camelot Group

As of Mar 2012, the **largest national lottery** (see Lottery legends, right) had created 3,000 millionaires, each winning an average of $4.68 m. So how did they choose to spend their windfalls?

Property: $5.5 bn

Investments: $3.5 bn

Future needs (inc. provisions for children): $2.67 bn

Dream vacations: $35 m

Cars: $774 m

Lottery legends

Highest prize pot for a lottery: *El Gordo* ("The Fat One") in Spain is an annual lottery that, in 2013, had a total prize pool of 2.6 bn euros ($3.59 bn).

Largest lottery win: $314.9 m, by Andrew "Jack" Whittaker, Jr. (USA) for a Powerball jackpot on Dec 24, 2002.

Largest national lottery: The UK National Lottery had total ticket sales of £95 bn ($158.8 bn) as of Mar 31, 2013.

Fakes, frauds, & forgeries

In 1496, the young **Michelangelo** faked an "ancient" statue of Cupid

Most expensive fake diaries

In 1983, *Stern* magazine paid some 9 million German marks ($5 m) for 62 diaries allegedly written by Adolf Hitler, Germany's leader during World War II. US expert Kenneth W. Rendell later proved that they were forged. The forger, Konrad Kujau (DEU), was jailed for 3 years 6 months, as was the man who had "uncovered" the diaries, Gerd Heidemann (DEU, above).

Most lucrative art fraud by a woman

On Sep 16, 2013, Glafira Rosales (MEX) pleaded guilty in New York City, USA, to nine counts of fraud. She had taken part in a scheme to sell more than 60 fakes of abstract and Impressionist art, allegedly by 73-year-old American-Chinese artist Pei-Shen Qian, for more than $80 m. The forgeries included copies of works by Mark Rothko and Jackson Pollock.

Most prolific forger of Shakespearean work

In 1794–95, manuscripts appeared in London, UK, supposedly written by William Shakespeare (1564–1616), among them a love poem to his wife, a letter

Largest collection of fake masterpieces

French artist Christophe Petyt owns just over 2,500 fake paintings of some of the world's most famous artworks. His company, L'Art du Faux, employs a selection of highly talented artists to copy masterpieces, which are then officially registered as a reproduction and sold.

from Queen Elizabeth I, revisions to his work, and two new plays. They were, in fact, forgeries by William Henry Ireland (UK). One of the new dramas, *Vortigern and Rowena*, was performed in 1796.

Most lucrative wine fraud

On Oct 16, 2013, two Italian wine merchants suspected of faking at least 400 bottles of the exclusive Romanée-Conti burgundy wine were arrested. The fraudsters may have made some $2.75 m from the scheme.

Most prolific art forger

At his trial in 1979, Thomas Keating (UK, 1917–84) put his output of fake pictures at more than 2,000 works, representing 121 different artists across a 25-year period.

Highest career earnings for a forger

Han van Meegeren (NLD, 1889–1947) is often cited as the most successful and influential art forger of all time. Estimates of his earnings vary, but by 1943 he had made the equivalent today of $25–30 m, and also had property investments in the region of $500 m. He focused on forgeries of work by the artists Johannes Vermeer and Pieter de Hooch.

Most successful defense equipment faker

On May 2, 2013, James McCormick (UK) received a 10-year sentence for selling devices that he claimed could detect explosives and drugs, but which were actually modified novelty golf-ball finders. He sold them for around £27,000 ($40,000) each, making an estimated £50 m ($77 m) overall.

Largest ATM fraud

In May 2013, it was reported that cyber criminals had stolen $45 m by hacking into a database of prepaid credit cards in a scheme dubbed "PIN cashing" or "carding." Seven US citizens were arrested and accused of removing withdrawal limits, creating access codes, and using associates to spread the data online to leaders of "cashing crews," who drained cash machines.

CONFOUNDING THE COUNTERFEITERS

The Swiss have the most secure banknotes (see right). Security features include:

Bank of Guinness World Records
Ten Dollars

10 **10**

01 777 700 555

01 777 700 555

- Color-shifting ink—changes color when viewed from different angles
- Holographic strip
- Watermark, visible when held up to the light
- Hidden numbers, visible when held up to the light
- Very fine lines—difficult to replicate
- Raised printing
- Security thread, embedded in the note
- Microprint text—difficult to replicate
- Made from multi-layer polymer plastic; changes color when tilted

⚡ Splashing the plastic

In 2006, we declared Swiss franc notes to be the **most secure banknote**. The 1,000-franc note incorporated 14 security features, including micro lettering, fluorescent ink, and braille. Several nations—including Australia, Canada, and Brunei—have now abandoned paper notes in favor of plastic film. They are also four times more durable than paper banknotes; on average, the US dollar bill lasts for only around 18 months before it wears out.

FACT

In all, 830 million UK banknotes—worth £11.4 bn ($19.1 bn)—were destroyed in 2013 due to poor condition.

ℹ Finance agents

The US Secret Service, a law-enforcement agency, was originally created at the end of the American Civil War (1861–65) to tackle counterfeit currency.

○○○

Largest bitcoin fraud

Bitcoin—a virtual monetary system based on digital tokens—was conceived in 2008, and by Nov 2013, its value had soared to $1,000 per bitcoin. The currency has already suffered from fraud losses, the worst being that of the Bitcoin Savings and Trust. By the time it was shut down in 2012, the savings scheme had reportedly lost the equivalent of $5.6 m.

Largest fine for pharmaceutical fraud

In Jul 2012, British company GlaxoSmithKline received a £1.9-bn ($3-bn) penalty after admitting to history's biggest healthcare fraud. From 1997 to 2004, the company was alleged to have bribed doctors to prescribe drugs linked with safety concerns and promoted drugs that were not approved for their intended purpose.

Greatest goldsmith fraud

In 1896, the Louvre Museum in Paris, France, exhibited a large gold helmet weighing more than 1 lb 12 oz (800 g). The "Tiara of Saitaphernes" allegedly dated from either the late third or second century BC. The Louvre bought the object for 200,000 gold French francs, but it was later shown to be a fake that had been crafted by Russian goldsmith Israel Rouchomovsky.

Largest fine for mortgage fraud

On Nov 19, 2013, the largest US bank—JPMorgan Chase—concluded a settlement with officials from the US Justice Department. This included a fine that amounted to $13 bn—the largest civil settlement with any one company resulting from the sale and misrepresentation of residential mortgage-backed securities (RMBS).

Largest fake army

Before allied forces invaded Europe, via Normandy in France, on "D-Day" (Jun 6, 1944), a ruse was invented. Operation Bodyguard gave the illusion of two field armies, one set to menace Pas-de-Calais, comprising 1 million men. As a result, many German troops stayed in Pas-de-Calais instead of Normandy—preserving many allied lives on the day of the invasion.

Largest fraud by a rogue trader

On Jan 24, 2008, French bank Société Générale declared that it had uncovered 4.9 bn euros ($7.16 bn) of losses following rogue trading by a member of its staff. Bank trader Jérôme Kerviel (FRA) was taken into police custody and was said to have admitted hiding his activities from his superiors. He was sentenced to five years in prison, with two years suspended. In 2010, however, he published a memoir entitled *Downward Spiral: Memoirs of a Trader* in which he claims that his employers were aware of his trading activity.

Longest time under an assumed identity

In 1914, newspaper editor Anton Ekström (SWE) had a breakdown after the death of his wife and the loss of his wealth.

He became a hermit in the countryside under the name Magnusson. In 1955, after 41 years, he was exposed and reunited with his bewildered children.

The Wi-Fi network "GWROFFICE" requires a WPA password.

Password: Password123
☑ Show password
☑ Remember this network

Cancel   Join

Highest annual cost of cybercrime

Stolen identities, raided bank accounts, and hacked e-mails are all forms of cybercrime. The 2013 Norton Report puts the annual cost of consumer cybercrime at $113 bn, or $298 per victim, of which there are more than 1 million every day or one every 3 sec.

For genuine works of art, view p. 170

For genuine works of art, view p. 170

Worrying signs: the rogue interpreter

Nelson Mandela's memorial service took place on Dec 10, 2013 in the 95,000-capacity FNB Stadium in Soweto, South Africa. It was attended by leaders and dignitaries from more than 100 countries and some 60,000 South Africans. As US President Barack Obama and South African President Jacob Zuma spoke, the official interpreter for the deaf stood beside them and made signs. These were later described by experts as childish hand gestures relating neither to the signs associated with the country's 11 official languages, nor to any of the related facial gestures. According to one international expert, the man—identified as Thamsanqa Jantjie—had also falsely interpreted at a military event in 2012.

👁 Financial finagling

Longest prison sentence for fraud: 141,078 years, for Chamoy Thipyaso (THA) and seven associates in 1989, for swindling some 16,000 Thai citizens out of their life savings.

Greatest banknote forgery: the Third Reich's Operation Bernhard, during World War II, produced approximately 9 million counterfeit British notes valued at around £130 m ($520 m).

Money & economics

1,781 tons of gold was recycled in 2012, generating **$23.5 bn**

Largest gender gap

According to the World Economic Forum's 2013 Global Gender Gap Index, Yemen has the largest gender gap of any country. The measurement is made by scoring four indicators: economic participation and opportunity, educational attainment, health and survival, and political empowerment. Yemen scored 0.5128 (with 1 as the highest possible score). The country with the **smallest gender gap** was Iceland, scoring 0.8731. The USA scored 0.7392 and the UK 0.7440.

WPP reported record revenues of $16.8 bn in the same period.

Greatest economic freedom

With a score of 89.3 (out of 100), Hong Kong, China, enjoys the greatest economic freedom according to the Heritage Foundation's Index of Freedom. Economic freedom is a measurement of the right of workers to control their own labor, consumption, investments, and property.

Highest economic growth

Sierra Leone ended a decade of often barbaric civil war in 2002, and growth has

Most unequal society

According to World Bank data from 2009 (the most recent figures available), South Africa is the economy in which disparities of income between richest and poorest are at their worst. The country with the **most equal distribution of income** is Slovakia.

been relatively speedy given how poor its citizens are in absolute terms. The country saw a 15.2% increase in GDP (Gross Domestic Product) in 2011–12. However, citizens also have the lowest **average life expectancy**, at 45 years.

In 2011, South Sudan gained independence from Sudan after another long civil war. The fledgling country went on to experience the **lowest economic growth**, with an enormous drop of 55.8% in 2011–12. Next door, Sudan recorded the second lowest growth with -10.1%.

Most innovative economy

As of Jul 2013, Switzerland had a score of 66.59 in the annual Global

Fastest rising brand

Facebook's brand value increased by 43% to take it to No. 52 in the Interbrand list of 2013, the only social media brand to claim a place on the Top 100 Best Global Brands. Its global user base increased by 26% to an incredible 1.19 billion MAU (monthly active users), and its mobile user base went up by 51% to 751 million in the year to Sep 2013.

Largest advertising agency

In Jul 2013, Publicis (FRA) and Omnicom (USA) announced that they would merge to create the Publicis Omnicom Group, which would have had $23 bn in revenue had it been in existence during 2012. As it stands,

> **FACT**
>
> Big givers: The Bill and Melinda Gates Foundation has given away $28 bn since its instigation in 1997.

Highest annual earnings by a CEO

John H. Hammergren (USA), chief executive of the pharmaceutical firm McKesson, received $131.19 m in 2012. Of this, "just" $1.66 m was earned as salary; $4.65 m was a bonus, $112.12 m was given as stock options, and the remaining $12.76 m came under the heading of "other."

Richest media tycoon

Former mayor of New York City Michael Bloomberg (USA) is the richest media mogul. His Bloomberg LP empire, which includes the Bloomberg financial news firm, is worth $27 bn according to Forbes' list of billionaires from Mar 2013.

ECONOMY SIZES: LARGEST GDP

Source: worldbank.org

USA $16.24 tr

China $8.22 tr

Japan $5.95 tr

Germany $3.42 tr

France $2.61 tr

UK $2.47 tr

Brazil $2.25 tr

Russia $2.01 tr

Italy $2.01 tr

India $1.84 tr

> **FACT**
>
> The GDP of the USA is $16.24 tr. But how long would it take you to count this out in $1 bills? Fast (human) money counters can count 200 notes in a minute; at 12,000 per hr, that's more than 154,000 years—nonstop—to count all 16.24 trillion bills!

Prosperous people

Richest person (ever): John D. Rockefeller (USA, 1839–1937), $189 bn—if adjusted to 2013 figures.

Richest person (current): Bill Gates (USA), $75.9 bn, Feb 2014.

Richest investor: Warren Buffett (USA), $58.6 bn, Feb 2014.

Richest woman: Christy Walton (USA), $36.9 bn, Feb 2014.

Most valuable brand

According to the 2013 Interbrand Top 100 Best Global Brands rankings, Apple is worth $98.31 bn—which is a 28% rise over the previous year. The record ends 13 years of domination by Coca-Cola, which dropped to third behind Google. There are 72 million Mac computers in use, and 9 million iPhone 5s and 5c models were sold in launch weekend alone. In 2013, the App Store reached the 50-billion download mark after just five years.

The Economist.

Highest budgetary expenditure

The USA spent $3.53 tr in 2012, a figure that excludes social benefits of approximately $2.3 tr. The USA accounts for more than 15% of worldwide budgetary expenditure and also brings in the **highest revenue**, with an estimated $2.44 tr in 2012. This excludes social contributions revenue of approximately $1 tr.

Highest cost of living

According to a Dec 2012 survey by the Economist Intelligence Unit, Japan is the most expensive nation to live in for expatriate executives and their families. Prices for products of international comparable quality in stores in New York City, USA, are used as a base, with the USA scoring 100. Japan is the priciest, with a score of 152, followed by Australia (137). The country with the **lowest cost of living** is Pakistan, with a rating of 44.

Largest municipal bankruptcy

On Jul 18, 2013, Detroit in Michigan, USA, filed for the largest bankruptcy in modern times, with debts estimated at $18–20 bn. Up to 40% of streetlights are broken in the city that is home to more than 150,000 deserted buildings. Among them is the former Packard car factory (pictured), a 3.5-million-sq-ft (325,160-m^2) property that is the **largest abandoned factory**. Closed since 1956, Packard once produced 75% of the world's cars in Detroit—known as "Motor City."

Innovation Index, published by Cornell University, the business school INSEAD, and the World Intellectual Property Organization. Measurements are taken in such areas as institutions, infrastructure, research, the sophistication of the market, and in business, creativity, and technology.

Highest budget for ...

• **Defense:** According to *The Economist*, Iraq spent 11.3% of its GDP on defense in 2012.
• **Health:** World Bank figures from 2011 put Liberia top of spending on health with 19.5% of its GDP.
• **Education:** In 2012, Lesotho put 13% of its GDP toward education, according to figures from

Worst modern recession

The ongoing downturn in Greece has been more severe than in any other country in the developed world since World War II. In 2013, the economy shrank by 23–25%, compared with 20% in 2012. The jobless rate increased from 25% to 27% and youth unemployment leaped from 50% to 60%.

Costly quaffs

As an indicator of how our spending habits have changed since 1955, the **most expensive bottle of wine** then was a 1949 Feinste Trockenbeerenauslese priced at $22; adjusting for inflation means that it would cost $294 today. But the most expensive wines commercially available now sell for ca. $52,900— that's 180 times more than the adjusted figure!

Starship enterprise: high transactions

Russian cosmonaut Pavel Vinogradov was in the *International Space Station* orbiting at 260 mi (419 km) above Earth when he made the **highest-altitude financial transaction**, a land tax payment of 616 roubles ($18.51) on Apr 22, 2013. The money was transferred to the Federal Tax Service of Russia in an event organized by Mikhail Mishustin and Vladimir Bezrukov. This transaction represents the first time that anyone has paid their tax bill—or, indeed, any kind of bill—from space!

Gross world product

Totaling the gross domestic product (GDP) of every country gives you the "gross world product"—i.e., the value of all goods and services in the world. Sixty years ago, this figure stood at $5.43 tr (or $1,966 per person); in 2014, this is an estimated $72.21 tr (or $10,316 per person). This means our economy today is more than 13 times bigger than it was back in 1955.

Internet

By 2015, **44%** of the world will have Internet access at home

Most viewed online video advertisement

"Dove Real Beauty Sketches" was watched 134,265,061 times—in 25 languages in more than 110 countries—as of May 1, 2014, by which date it had been shared 4,517,422 times. The video was posted on Apr 14, 2013, and data was collected by Unruly for their Viral Video Chart.

FACT

Google's Trekker helped collect images for the **southernmost Street View** (right). Trekker is a backpack with a battery-powered camera on a mast. Its 15 lenses are differently angled and their images were later joined into a 360-degree panorama.

to download the spacecraft's entire 1-gigabyte science data in less than five min—an operation that would have taken three days if conventional radio waves were used.

Southernmost location on Google Street View

On Jul 17, 2012, Google released images on its ground-level perspective Street View service showing the South Pole. Other areas of Antarctica available on Street View include penguin colonies, Ernest Shackleton's hut, and Robert Falcon Scott's supply hut. Users can guide their cursors inside the buildings and take a virtual tour of these shrines of exploration.

First Google hoax

On Apr 1, 2000, Google perpetrated the "MentalPlex" hoax to mark April Fool's Day. It invited users of its search engine to stare at an animated gif on its home page and think of what they wanted to find on the net.

First Webcam

In 1991, computer scientists at Cambridge University, UK, set up a camera and a computer to monitor the status of their coffeepot without having to leave their room. The system was upgraded in Nov 1993, when it was linked to the net, and live images of the famous coffeepot were broadcast until the feed was turned off in 2000.

Highest Earth–Moon bandwidth

In Oct 2013, NASA and the Massachusetts Institute of Technology successfully demonstrated the first two-way communications laser link to the Moon. They sent signals to a spacecraft orbiting the Moon, and achieved a download data rate of 622 megabits per second. Mission engineers were able

Most Facebook "likes" on an item

On Nov 30, 2013, *Fast & Furious* star Paul Walker (USA, far left) died in a car crash in California, USA. Friend Vin Diesel, aka Mark Vincent (USA, left), posted a photo of them together on Facebook (below), where it had received 6,817,898 "likes" as of May 7, 2014. The previous record holder was a 2012 photo on Barack Obama's Facebook page showing his embrace with wife Michelle after being elected US president for a second term. As of May 7, 2014, it had 4,433,487 "likes".

Most mentions of a brand name on Twitter in 24 hours

A chocolate-coated cookie stick called Pocky was mentioned 3,710,044 times on Twitter on Nov 11, 2013. That works out at slightly over 4,294 mentions per sec for the Ezaki Glico Co., Ltd. (JPN) snack. Everything from emojis (Japanese smileys) to straight retweets were counted in the attempt.

WHAT HAPPENS IN AN INTERNET MINUTE

e-mail
204 million e-mails sent

flickr
20 million photo views

Google
2 million searches

facebook
1.8 million "likes"

skype
1.4 million connection minutes

twitter
278,000 tweets

You Tube
3 days of video uploaded

tumblr.
20,000 new photos

iTunes
15,000 tracks downloaded

Pinterest
11,000 active users

Source: Intel and qmee.com, 2013

E-mail spamming

Anyone who has ever used e-mail has received spam—unsolicited messages. Billions of the nuisances are sent daily but, before the phenomenon had a name, Gary Thuerk (USA) sent the **first spam**, on May 3, 1978. His memo was quite innocent—a message to 397 e-mail accounts on the ARPAnet of the US Department of Defense, with an invitation to attend a product demonstration.

FACT

Tim Berners-Lee had the idea for the **first hypertext browser**—what became the World Wide Web—in Mar 1989. Marking its 25th anniversary, in 2014 Berners-Lee called for a bill of rights to keep the Web free and open. "Our rights are being infringed ... on every side and the danger is that we get used to it ... the key thing is getting people to fight for the Web."

First Instagram from space

"Back on *ISS*, life is good" wrote Steve Swanson (USA) from the *International Space Station* on Apr 7, 2014, posing in a T-shirt from cult TV sci-fi show *Firefly* (USA, 2002).

The **most "liked" image on Instagram** (inset) shows actor Will Smith (USA) and Justin Bieber (CAN), posted in Aug 2013. "Me and uncle Will," noted the pop star, who posted the image. It has been "liked" more than 1.5 million times.

exists only online—belonged to Ross Ulbricht (USA), who is accused of running the Silk Road, an online marketplace for drugs.

Northernmost underwater communications cable

Longyearbyen in Norway, at a latitude of 78.22°N, is the landing point of the Svalbard Undersea Cable System, which provides a fiber-optic Internet connection with the Norwegian mainland. The two-cable system is 1,686 mi (2,714 km) long and provides fast access to data from Svalbard's SvalSat. This is one of only two ground

Most retweeted message on Twitter

The selfie organized by 2014 Oscars host Ellen DeGeneres (USA) exceeded 1 million retweets within about an hour of being tweeted on Oscars night, Mar 3, 2014. Smiling alongside stars such as Bradley Cooper, Jennifer Lawrence, Brad Pitt, Kevin Spacey, and Meryl Streep, DeGeneres tweeted, "If only Bradley's arm was longer. Best photo ever. #oscars." As of May 5, 2014, the message had been retweeted 3,428,897 times.

Largest Internet census by a botnet

A botnet ("ro**bot net**work") consists of many computers linked together to run services. In 2012, an anonymous hacker hijacked 420,000 devices that had only default passwords and used them to conduct an illegal mapping of the Internet, particularly insecure devices. His control program was called the Carna Botnet.

Largest seizure of virtual currency

On Oct 25, 2013, the US Federal Bureau of Investigation (FBI) revealed that it had seized a total of 144,000 bitcoins worth around $28.5 m. The FBI allege that the tranche of bitcoins—a currency that

Fastest time to reach 1 million followers on Twitter

On Apr 11, 2014, Twitter was a-flutter to learn that Robert Downey Jr (USA) had joined the site with a "Talk to me, Twitter" (@robertdowneyjr). Within a day, the star had attracted 1,017,322 fans, but he still lags behind the **most followers on Twitter for an actor**. Ashton Kutcher (USA; @aplusk) had 16,022,147 followers as of May 6, 2014.

❌ For more top tech turn to pp. 206–207

stations optimally located to download data from all 14 polar-orbiting satellites.

Most consecutive daily personal video blogs on YouTube

As of May 6, 2014, Charles Trippy (USA) had posted 1,831 vlogs consecutively, without missing a day, on his YouTube channel Internet Killed Television.

In Apr 2014, he documented his split from wife and fellow vlogger Alli.

Most expensive property sold at online auction

A plot of land in the same area of Dubai as the Burj Khalifa sold for 94,176,000 United Arab Emirates dirham ($25,634,707) on Feb 19, 2013, through Emirates Auction (UAE).

Most subscribers on YouTube

As of May 6, 2014, "PewDiePie," aka Felix Arvid Ulf Kjellberg (SWE), had 26,540,250 YouTube subscribers for his comedic video-gaming highlights.

FACT
Robert Downey Jr also operates a Facebook account that had been "liked" by 16,373,295 fans as of May 7, 2014.

Turn it off and on again: rebooting the net

Seven experts—including Moussa Guebre (BFA), left—form the **first international group capable of rebooting the World Wide Web**, or at least certain aspects of it, in the event of a major catastrophe such as a cyber attack. They are the backup for a security system called DNSSEC that adds a digital signature to Web site names, helping in the battle to stop hackers redirecting surfers to fake sites. Should a disaster take out DNSSEC, five of the seven global keyholders would be summoned to a secure US location to save the day. Each of the team has a swipe card that provides one-fifth of the reboot key.

🅰🆉 Glossary

DNS: Stands for Domain Name System. It manages navigation of the Internet by resolving proper names used by Web sites into the strings of numbers understood by computers.

DNSSEC: Stands for Domain Name System Security Extensions, a set of standards to ensure that our browsers are not being sent to fake sites with malicious code.

○ ○ ○

Crowdsourcing

A bank robber used crowdsourcing to hire a team of identically dressed workmen, aiding his escape

Most money pledged for a Kickstarter comic project

Graphic designer Rich Burlew (USA) couldn't afford to reprint *The Order of the Stick* himself, so turned to his fans. Almost 15,000 people had pledged $1,254,120 by the time the project closed on Feb 21, 2012.

in the Jun 2006 edition of *Wired* under the title "The Rise of Crowdsourcing."

Largest platform for crowdfunding

From Kickstarter's launch on Apr 28, 2009 until Mar 4, 2014, 5.7 million people pledged a total of $1,001,567,335. This support has aided 57,171 projects to meet their funding goals.

First crowdsourced military vehicle design

The XC2V FLYPMode, made by Local Motors and the US Defense Advanced Research Projects Agency (DARPA), used design ideas

Most money pledged for a Kickstarter project

The Pebble (USA) is a customizable watch with Internet connectivity, message and e-mail alerts, and access to sports and fitness apps. The watch received pledges of $10,266,845 by May 19, 2012, surpassing its goal 10-fold.

from more than 150 people. Built to replace the Humvee, the prototype was presented to President Obama in 2011.

First use of the term "crowdsourcing"

In 2005, US journalist Jeff Howe coined the term "crowdsourcing" while pitching an article about how the Internet was being used to outsource work to the general public, or "crowd." The article appeared

First crowdsourced car design

The Rally Fighter, an off-road racer produced by Local Motors (USA), represents the culmination of 35,000 designs by 2,900 people from more than 100 countries. The car made its debut at the Specialty Equipment Market Association Show in Las Vegas, Nevada, USA, on Nov 3, 2009.

Highest chart placing by a crowdfunded album

Theatre is Evil, an album by Amanda Palmer and The Grand Theft Orchestra (USA, see above right), achieved a top 10 placing on the *Billboard* 200 on its release in Sep 2012—the highest position achieved by a crowdfunded music release.

Fastest Kickstarter project to reach $1 m

On Oct 27, 2013, "Reaper Miniatures Bones II" (USA)— a project created to fund an expansion of the miniatures range—sped to a pledge total of $1 m in just 2 hr 41 min 51 sec.

Most money pledged on Kickstarter for photography

On Jul 1, 2013, US-based Planetary Resources raised more than $1.5 m for "A Space Telescope for Everyone." The project aims to launch a publicly accessible telescope that can take photos of space or allow people to have their photo displayed above Earth (artist's impression above).

⊗ For more on cars, turn to p. 186

Group efforts: the history of crowdsourcing

Crowdsourcing is nothing new. In the UK, the Oxford English Dictionary (left) received six million suggestions from the public when it first solicited entries in the 1850s, while Nelson's Column (below left, erected 1843) was paid for in part from public subscriptions (crowdfunding). In 1567, England's Queen Elizabeth I effectively crowdfunded the enlarging of the Navy by initiating the first national lottery. Competitions can also be considered a form of crowdsourcing; the Longitude Prize in the 1700s, for example, sought to find a solution to determining a ship's longitude at sea—a problem finally solved in 1756 by John Harrison (right).

i What is Kickstarter?

Kickstarter was founded by Perry Chen, Yancey Strickler, and Charles Adler (all USA) in New York, USA, and launched on Apr 28, 2009. The concept allows investors to pledge money toward creative projects in return for rewards and experiences. However, the funds are only handed over if the project's entire funding goal is met. ○ ○ ○

Most crowdfunded music project

Amanda Palmer (USA) initiated a Kickstarter appeal to fund her album with the aim of raising $100,000. By the time the appeal closed on Jun 1, 2012, she had received pledges of $1,192,793, making hers the most successful crowdfunded music project of any kind.

MOST MONEY PLEDGED FOR A KICKSTARTER ...

Art project
The Marina Abramović Institute, a performance and education center in New York City, USA, aimed to raise $600,000. The goal was surpassed on Aug 25, 2013 with pledges of $661,452.

Dance project
STREB Extreme Action (USA) beat their $45,000 goal on Nov 25, 2013 with pledges of $45,512.

FORCES is described as a theatrical show centered on "action."

Fashion project
Jake Bronstein (USA) is so sure of his lifetime-lasting hoodie that he provides a 10-year free mending service. He passed his funding goal on Apr 21, 2013 with pledges of $1,053,830.

Food project
Scott Heimendinger's (USA) "Sansaire Circulator" uses *sous vide*—a method of cooking using exact temperature control—in a product designed for the home cook. Final pledges reached $823,003 on Sep 6, 2013.

Publishing project
Planet Money's (USA) project leads the consumer on an innovative journey through a T-shirt's creation. Each T-shirt has a bar code linking to a Web page featuring photos of the people who made it, from cotton growers to factory workers. Pledges of $590,807 were received by May 14, 2013.

Theater project
Tim O'Connor (USA) raised $175,395 by Sep 24, 2012 to upgrade Catlow Theater in Barrington, Illinois, USA, with modern audio and visual equipment.

Most crowdfunded stage project

The story of serial killer Patrick Bateman may seem an unlikely source for a musical, but *American Psycho* opened in London, UK, in Dec 2013 with ex-*Doctor Who* star Matt Smith as the lead. Producer Jesse Singer of Act 4 Entertainment (USA) had raised pledges of $154,929 in May 2013 to help fund the production.

Most crowdfunded video-game console

The Kickstarter appeal to back the OUYA (USA) raised $8,596,474 by Aug 9, 2012. The $99 eighth-generation console is an Android-base device that connects to a standard modern TV set and allows users to play free-to-try games.

Most crowdfunded project (overall)

Efforts to fund *Star Citizen*, a space-base trading and combat adventure video game, resulted in the largest single amount ever raised via crowdsourcing. As of Mar 4, 2014, publisher Cloud Imperium Games (USA) had raised $39,680,576 via its own Web site appeal alone. Chris Roberts designed the game, scheduled for release in 2015.

KICKSTARTER CATEGORIES WITH THE MOST SUCCESSFUL PROJECTS

Category	Total	Funded	Unfunded
Music	$94.20 m	15,011	12,208
Movie/Video	$163.95 m	13,096	19,594
Art	$30.24 m	5,613	5,101
Publishing	$40.42 m	5,125	10,755
Theater	$19.69 m	3,556	1,974
Games	$189.97 m	2,948	5,435
Design	$125.13 m	2,537	4,040
Food	$30.69 m	2,089	3,121
Comics	$22.96 m	1,762	1,814

Source: kickstarter.com, Mar 4, 2014

Kickstarter's most funded ...

- **Art book:** *Masters of Anatomy* (CAN); $532,614; Nov 20, 2013
- **Children's book:** *Hello Ruby* by Linda Liukas (USA); $380,74; Feb 22, 2014
- **Fiction:** *The Warden and the Wolf King* by Andrew Peterson (USA); $118,188; Oct 31, 2013
- **Poetry:** *A Bruise on Light* by Shane Koyczan (CAN); $91,154; Feb 26, 2014

Great journeys

Each continent has a **Pole of Inaccessibility**—its farthest point from an ocean

First 360-degree panorama filmed on the summit of Mount Everest

The first fully spherical 360-degree video from the summit of Mount Everest was recorded in May 2013. The footage was captured with 360Heros' 360-degree video gear for a documentary by Everest Media Productions about Nepalese climber Apa Sherpa, who was a consultant for the shoot. The veteran sherpa summited the mountain 21 times between 1990 and 2011, the **most conquests of Mount Everest**.

Slipping into place
The 3D-printed H3PRO6 holder was invented by Michael Kintner (USA), CEO of 360Heros. On Everest, six GoPro cameras were slipped into the holder and software was later used to create the final footage.

Contents

"Little Planet" mode
As well as being available as a fully interactive 3D video, the panorama can also be viewed in "little planet" or "miniplanet" mode, which creates a spherical or "stereographic" projection.

FACT
In Nepal, the name of Everest is *Sagarmatha* ("forehead of the sky"), and in Tibet it is *Chomolungma* ("mother goddess of the world").

North Pole

The ocean at the North Pole is more than **13,100 ft deep**

First traverse of the North Pole by wheeled vehicle

The Russian Marine Live-Ice Automobile Expedition MLAE 2013 (Sergey Isayev, Nikolay Kozlov, Afanasy Makovnev, Vladimir Obikhod, Alexey Shkrabkin, and Andrey Vankov, led by Vasily Elagin) left Golomyanny Island, Russia, on Mar 1, 2013. Driving two 6 x 6 low-pressure-tire ATVs, the team arrived at the North Pole on Apr 6, then continued to the Canadian coast, which they reached on Apr 30. The 60-day journey covered approximately 2,480 mi (4,000 km) in all.

Most polar expeditions completed by an individual
Richard Weber (CAN) has successfully completed eight polar expeditions. He reached the geographic North Pole from the coast six times between May 2, 1986 and Apr 14, 2010, and the geographic South Pole twice from the coast on Jan 7, 2009 and Dec 29, 2011.

First solo expedition to the North Pole
At 4:45 a.m. GMT on May 1, 1978, Japanese explorer and mountaineer Naomi Uemura became the first person to reach the North Pole in a solo expedition across the Arctic sea ice. He had traveled 478 mi (770 km), setting out on Mar 7, 1978 from Ellesmere Island in Canada.

The expedition was supported by dogs, and Uemura had access to resupplies.

First person to ski to both poles (unassisted and unsupported)
Polish-born Marek Kamiński (USA) reached the North Pole from Cape Columbia on May 23, 1995 and the South Pole from Berkner Island on Dec 27, 1995. He completed both trips under his own power and without any external assistance.

FASTEST ...

Surface journey to the North Pole
On Mar 21, 2005, Tom Avery and George Wells (both UK), Matty McNair and Hugh Dale-Harris (both CAN), Andrew Gerber (ZAF), and a team of 16 husky dogs left Cape Columbia on Ellesmere Island in Canada. They reached the North Pole 36 days 22 hr 11 min later on Apr 26, 2005. Their journey was an attempt to re-create as closely as possible the disputed 1909 expedition of explorer Robert Peary.

Ski journey to the North Pole by a women's team
Catharine Hartley and Fiona Thornewill (both UK) skied to the North Pole (with support in the form of resupplies en route) in 55 days between Mar 11 and May 5, 2001. They began their expedition from Ward Hunt Island in Nunavut, Canada.

Trek to the North Pole
David J.P. Pierce Jones (UK), Richard Weber and Tessum Weber (both CAN), and Howard Fairbanks (ZAF) took 41 days 18 hr 52 min to trek to the North Pole, from Mar 3 to Apr 14, 2010. The team set out from 82°58'02"N and 77°23'3"W and were picked up after reaching the North Pole, at 90°N, on Apr 14, 2010.

Solo trek to the North Pole (unsupported)
Børge Ousland (NOR) skied his way to the North Pole from Cape Arkticheskiy on the archipelago of Severnaya Zemlya in the Russian Federation. He undertook the trip without external assistance in 52 days, from Mar 2 to Apr 23, 1994. This also makes him the **first person to make a solo journey to the North Pole from land (unassisted and unsupported)**.

The **fastest trek to the North Pole by a woman (unsupported)** was achieved by Cecilie Skog (NOR). She left Ward Hunt Island with Rolf Bae and Per Henry Borch (both NOR) on Mar 6, 2006, reaching the Pole 48 days 22 hr later.

Marathon on each continent and the North Pole (male)
From Feb 26 to Apr 9, 2013, Ziyad Tariq Rahim (PAK) ran a marathon on each continent and one at the North Pole, taking 41 days 20 hr 38 min 58 sec in all.

Youngest female to ski to the North Pole (unsupported, unassisted)

Amelia Darley (née Russell, UK, b. Aug 29, 1982) was 27 years 239 days old when she reached the geographic North Pole on Apr 25, 2010. Her journey of 484 mi (780 km) began at Cape Discovery, McClintock Inlet, on Ward Hunt Island, Canada. Amelia traveled in a two-person expedition accompanied by her boyfriend, Dan Darley (UK).

Three Poles Challenge

The **first person to complete the Three Poles Challenge** was Erling Kagge (NOR), who reached the North on May 8, 1990, the South on Jan 7, 1993, and Everest on May 8, 1994. The latest challenger was Johan Ernst Nilson (SWE, right), who topped Everest in May 2007. He began the polar stages by being dropped at the North Pole on Jun 22, 2011 and walking to land, and completed a South Pole trek on Jan 19, 2012. Having left from 90°N, Nilson achieved the **first Three Poles Challenge—North Pole to land**.

> ### i The "Three Poles"
> Adventurers consider Earth to have three poles: the North and South poles and Mount Everest. The latter is regarded as a "pole" in this context, due to its relative inaccessibility.

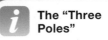

Magnetic North Pole: Unlike the geographic North Pole, this is not a fixed point; it moves by some 37 mi each year, driven by fluctuations in Earth's magnetic field. This is the "north" to which magnetic compasses align themselves.

Canada

Greenland

Svalbard archipelago

Norway

Geographic North Pole: Also known as "True North," this is located at 90°N. All the lines of longitude on Earth converge at this point.

"Our carbon paddles were lightweight, but durable. The sharp blade helped us to cut through thin ice layers and make a channel."

"This small outdoor weather station allowed us to measure wind speed, temperature, air pressure, and humidity. It was also of some help to us in predicting the weather."

"A very simple and ordinary GPS. It's lightweight and consumes less energy than those with color maps. In the Arctic Ocean, there is no need for GPS maps: there is nothing to be mapped."

"Ski goggles protect the eyes and part of the face in harsh weather conditions. The yellow and red lenses also enhance contrast and give a better definition in overcast and white-out conditions."

"A waterproof 'spray skirt' covers the cockpit and prevents water from getting in when we paddle in high winds and heavy waves."

"To protect our hands from the wind and cold, weatherproof mittens are a must."

"Waterproof Gore-Tex dry suits made paddling through the freezing cold Arctic waters both comfortable and safe."

"For some reason, we managed to break all our plastic spoons. So we had to improvise and combine new ones from the leftovers."

"This type of camping stove is simple and sturdy—exactly what you need in the Arctic Ocean. It is such a crucial part of our gear that we had a spare."

"A sled, rather than this kayak, would have been more appropriate to pull across the sea ice of the Arctic Ocean. But we needed it to cross the large open areas of water at the later stages of the expedition in order to get on land and continue along the fjords."

THREE POLES CHALLENGE

First woman to complete the Three Poles Challenge

Sweden's Tina Sjögren reached the North Pole on May 29, 2002 with her husband Thomas. She had summited Everest on May 26, 1999, and reached the South Pole on Feb 1, 2002. The couple's two polar journeys also mark the **fastest time to reach both poles unsupported**.

First person to complete the Three Poles Challenge without the use of oxygen on Everest

As of Mar 2014, the only person to complete the Three Poles Challenge unsupported and without the use of supplementary oxygen on Everest is Antoine de Choudens (FRA), who achieved this breathtaking feat from Apr 25, 1996 to Jan 10, 1999.

Fastest time to complete the Three Poles Challenge

The shortest time taken to reach the three extreme points on Earth is 1 year 217 days by Adrian Hayes (UK). He summited Everest on May 25, 2006, reached the North Pole on Apr 25, 2007 (from Ward Hunt Island, Canada), and claimed the South Pole, journeying from the Hercules Inlet in western Antarctica, on Dec 28, 2007.

The **fastest time to complete the Three Poles challenge by a woman** is 1 year 336 days, and was accomplished by Cecilie Skog (NOR). She summited Mount Everest on May 23, 2004, reached the South Pole on Dec 27, 2005, and got to the North Pole on Apr 24, 2006.

Fastest journey from the North Pole to land (unsupported, unassisted)

In 1895, Fridtjof Nansen and Hjalmar Johansen (both NOR) almost became the first people to reach the North Pole, but were forced to retreat at 86°14'N. In 2012, Audun Tholfsen (NOR) and Timo Palo (EST), pictured right, set out on what would have been Nansen and Johansen's return route. The duo left the North Pole on Apr 23, 2012. Using skis and kayaks, but no external support or resupplies, they negotiated about 715 mi (1,150 km) of drifting ice and curious polar bears to reach Phippsøya island, in Norway's Svalbard archipelago, 55 days later. They arrived at Longyearbyen, Svalbard, on Jul 3, having covered 1,060 mi (1,620 km) in all.

:South Pole

Approximately **90% of the ice on Earth** is located in Antarctica

Fastest trek to the South Pole by a team (unsupported)

Norwegians Mads Agerup (main picture, above), Christian Eide (photographer, reflected), Morten Andvig, and Rune Midtgaard skied from the Messner Start on the Filchner Ice Shelf to the geographic South Pole in 24 days 8 hr 57 min between Dec 2 and Dec 26, 2008.

First expedition to reach the South Pole
The South Pole was conquered on Dec 14, 1911 by a Norwegian party of five men led by Captain Roald Amundsen, after a 53-day march with dog sleds from the Bay of Whales, then part of Antarctica's Ross Ice Shelf.

A total of 19 expeditions in Antarctica were undertaken in 2011, the **most expeditions to the South Pole in a single year**. Most of the expeditions were launched with the aim of marking the centenary of Captain Robert Scott (UK) and Roald Amundsen's race to the South Pole. Around 500 people were involved in the various attempts,

either as participants or working as support staff.

The **first person to walk to both poles** was Robert Swan OBE (UK). He led the three-man "In the Footsteps of Scott" expedition, which reached the South Pole on Jan 11, 1986, and three years later headed the eight-man "Icewalk" expedition, which arrived at the North Pole on May 14, 1989.

First solo expedition to the South Pole
Erling Kagge (NOR) became the first person to reach the South Pole after a solo and unsupported surface trek

on Jan 7, 1993. His 870-mi (1,400-km) journey from Berkner Island took 50 days.

The **first woman to complete a journey to the South Pole solo (unsupported)** was Liv Arnesen (NOR), who trekked solo from the Hercules Inlet on Nov 4, 1994, arriving at the pole 50 days later on Dec 24.

Fastest journey to the South Pole overland
Two-man team Jason De Carteret and Kieron Bradley (both UK) set off from Patriot Hills in western Antarctica on Dec 18, 2011 in their Thomson Reuters polar vehicle. They arrived at their destination 1 day 15 hr 54 min later. Having

Farthest distance skied by a team (unsupported)

James Castrission and Justin Jones (both AUS, above left and right) skied 1,410 mi (2,270 km) from the Hercules Inlet to the South Pole and back, finishing on Jan 27, 2012 after an 89-day trek. They crossed the finish line with Aleksander Gamme (NOR, center), who had completed the trip solo (see opposite).

Youngest person to trek to the South Pole

Lewis Clarke (UK, b. Nov 18, 1997) was 16 years 61 days old when he reached the geographic South Pole on Jan 18, 2014. He had skied 698.18 mi (1,123.61 km) from Hercules Inlet on the Ronne Ice Shelf with guide Carl Alvey (30 years old). The duo were unsupported but were assisted with three resupplies by air.

covered 692 mi (1,114 km) at an average speed of 17.34 mph (27.9 km/h), they also recorded the **fastest average speed to the South Pole overland**.

Fastest walk to the South Pole (unsupported, unassisted)
Ray Zahab, Kevin Vallely, and Richard Weber (all CAN) reached the South Pole from the Hercules Inlet, on the southwestern edge of the Ronne Ice Shelf, on Jan 7, 2009 after just 33 days 23 hr 30 min.

Farthest distance skied solo (unsupported)
Aleksander Gamme (NOR) skied solo for 1,410 mi (2,270 km) across Antarctica, completing his epic journey on Jan 25, 2012 (local time). He set off from the Hercules Inlet and traveled to the South Pole, then returned to

First person to cycle to the South Pole (supported, assisted)

British cyclist Maria Leijerstam (left) departed from the Russian Novo air-force base on Antarctica on Dec 16, 2013, on her recumbent tricycle. She reached the South Pole 10 days 14 hr 56 min later, despite a knee injury.

Records for the **first** and **fastest person to reach the South Pole by bicycle**—that is, a two-wheel cycle—are currently in research. Two expeditions were attempted during the winter of 2013/14 but evidence has yet to be collated.

Ronne-Filchner Ice Shelf: second-largest ice shelf in Antarctica, covering 11,580 sq mi.

Hercules Inlet: Located on the southwest edge of the Ronne Ice Shelf, this ice-packed inlet is frequently chosen as a starting point for Antarctic treks.

Ross Ice Shelf: Earth's most southerly navigable point. It is some 182,240 sq mi in size.

South Pole: Located at 90°S. Ice is about 9,180 ft thick here. As with the North Pole, there is also a magnetic South Pole, which fluctuates with Earth's magnetic field. It is presently in the Southern Ocean, some 1,755 mi from the geographic South Pole.

"Antarctica is right beneath the ozone hole, so there is little or no natural protection from the Sun's harmful UV rays. Without these ski goggles for eye protection, I would quickly have gone snow-blind."

"These mittens have both a fleece inner glove and down outer glove for extra warmth and are completely windproof."

"In the extreme cold, my face had to be covered at all times. This face mask has a clever system that allows me to breathe freely without losing too much heat."

"This jacket is lightweight but it is a very effective wind barrier and so keeps me warm when I am skiing. It has deep, well-placed pockets so that I had easy access to the equipment I needed while skiing."

"These meals were made especially for me, with added carbohydrate and fat for energy. Once cooked, the meals are dehydrated to make them light to carry. To eat them, I simply had to pour hot water into the bag and wait a few minutes."

"The sleds were made of strengthened plastic that was lightweight and resilient. I dragged two sleds, one behind the other, together containing all my equipment."

"These boots are handmade in Norway, based on a traditional design. Inside the canvas and leather outer boot is an inner liner made of pressed wool surrounded by a fleece sock."

FACT
Antarctica is larger than the USA (and bigger than the entire continent of Europe), and is nearly twice the size of Australia.

0.6 mi (1 km) from his start. There, he waited two days to cross the finish line with two other skiers—James Castrission and Justin Jones (both AUS)—who had traveled a similar route.

On Jan 27, 2012, the three men returned to their starting point at the Hercules Inlet. They had traveled without food drops, snowmobiles, kites, or other means of assistance, thereby setting the record for the **first ski trip to the South Pole and back (unassisted)**.

First solo Antarctic traverse by a woman

In Nov 2011, Felicity Aston (UK) skied solo from the Ross Ice Shelf to the South Pole, then carried on across Antarctica to the Hercules Inlet on the Ronne Ice Shelf, arriving 59 days later on Jan 23, 2012. Aston made the 1,084-mile (1,744-km) journey—with resupplies—on Nordic cross-country skis, dragging 187 lb (85 kg) of provisions on two sleds in temperatures as low as -40°F (-40°C).

Youngest person to traverse Antarctica (wind-supported, assisted)
Teodor Johansen (NOR, b. Aug 14, 1991) traversed Antarctica at the age of 20 years 151 days. Johansen started out on his journey from the Axel Heiberg Glacier on Nov 26, 2011, reaching the South Pole on Dec 18, 2011, and completing the trip at the Hercules Inlet on Jan 12, 2012. In all, Johansen covered 1,034 mi (1,665 km).

First circumnavigation via both poles (surface)
Sir Ranulph Fiennes (UK)— named in 1984 by GWR's Founding Editor Norris McWhirter as the greatest living explorer—traveled south with Charles Burton (UK) from Greenwich in London, UK, on Sep 2, 1979. They reached the South Pole on Dec 15, 1980, the North on Apr 10, 1982, and returned to Greenwich on Aug 29, 1982, after a 35,000-mi (56,000-km) journey.

Most expeditions to the South Pole
Hannah McKeand (UK) made six expeditions to the South Pole from Nov 4, 2004 to Jan 9, 2013. By skiing to the pole in 39 days 9 hr 33 min from Nov 19 to Dec 28, 2006, she also made the **fastest solo journey to the South Pole by a woman (unsupported, unassisted)**.

"The highlight of my day was crawling into the tent when I had finished skiing, taking off my ski boots, and slipping my feet into my treasured down booties. Warm and comfortable, I often slept in them too!"

"This shovel was a vital piece of kit. At the end of each day, the tent has to be dug into the snow for protection against high winds. And in the morning, all the snow that has accumulated overnight has to be dug away."

"One of the major hazards in Antarctica are crevasses that are hidden from the surface by a thin layer of snow. Skis, especially long ones, spread out the skier's weight and reduce the likelihood of falling through the snow into an unseen crevasse."

Mount Everest

It took **16 attempts** before the highest peak was finally conquered

First astronaut to summit Everest

On May 20, 2009, former NASA astronaut Scott Parazynski (USA) successfully topped Mount Everest, becoming the first person to travel in space and climb Earth's highest peak. According to NASA, Parazynski participated in five space flights and spent more than 1,380 hr in space. Once at the top of Everest, he left a small Moon rock that he had collected during one of his seven space walks.

Most ascents of Everest (female)

Lakpa Sherpa (NPL) reached the 29,029-ft-high (8,848-m) summit of Mount Everest for the sixth time on May 11, 2006. She made the climb accompanied by her husband, Gheorghe "George" Dijmarescu (ROM/USA), who was completing his eighth ascent of Everest. For the **most conquests of Everest** overall, see p. 142.

First woman to climb Everest twice in a season

Chhurim Dolma Sherpa of Nepal conquered Mount Everest twice in the same climbing season. She reached the peak from the Nepalese side for the first time on May 12, 2011, and again seven days later as leader of the same expedition.

Most ascents of Everest in one day

On May 19, 2012, a total of 243 climbers summitted Everest—the most on a single day. The **most ascents of Everest in one year** came in 2013, with 658 ascents, up from 623 in 2007.

Tragically, an avalanche near Everest's base camp on Apr 18, 2014 killed 16 Nepalese climbers, the **most deaths on Mount Everest in one day**.

Longest stay on the summit of Everest

Babu Chhiri Sherpa (NPL) completed a stay of 21 hr at the summit of Mount Everest, without the use of bottled oxygen, in May 1999.

Oldest man to climb Everest

Yuichiro Miura (JPN, b. Oct 12, 1932) reached the top of Everest on May 23, 2013 at the age of 80 years 223 days. This is the third time that he has held this record: he previously climbed to the highest point on Earth as the world's oldest summiteer in 2003 and again during 2008. The achievement also makes Miura the **oldest man to climb any mountain over 8,000 m (26,246 ft)**.

Tamae Watanabe (JPN, b. Nov 21, 1938) climbed Everest for the second time

on May 19, 2012 at the age of 73 years 180 days, making her the **oldest woman to climb Everest**.

Fastest time to ski down Everest

Slovenian ski instructor Davo Karničar skied from the summit of Everest to Base Camp (located at an altitude of 17,550 ft, or 5,350 m) in just 5 hr on Oct 7, 2000. By contrast, it took him a whole month to get to the mountaintop, as he was obliged to stop at several camps to acclimatize to the extreme altitude.

Youngest woman to climb Everest (south side)

Ngim Chhamji Sherpa (NPL, b. Nov 14, 1995) reached the summit from the Nepali side on May 19, 2012 aged 16 years 187 days. She and her father, Dendi Sherpa (NPL), are the **first father and daughter to climb Everest together**. The **youngest woman to climb from the north side** (Tibet) was 15-year-old Mingkipa Sherpa (NPL, b. 1987) on May 22, 2003.

Fastest ascent of Everest (south side)

Pemba Dorje Sherpa (NPL) climbed from Base Camp to the peak of Mount Everest in a time of 8 hr 10 min on May 21, 2004.

FIRST ...

Ascent of Everest

At 11:30 a.m. on May 29, 1953, Edmund Percival Hillary (NZ) and Tenzing Norgay (IND/Tibet) became the first people to conquer Mount Everest. The successful expedition was led by Colonel (later Honorary Brigadier) Henry Cecil John Hunt. Hillary was knighted by Queen Elizabeth II and Norgay awarded the George Medal.

First twins to summit Everest

On May 23, 2010, Damián and Willie Benegas (b. ARG, now USA) became the first twins to climb Mount Everest. They set out from the South Col—a pass located between Everest and Lhotse (the world's fourth-highest mountain, at 27,940 ft; 8,516 m)—situated on Nepalese territory.

Junko Tabei (JPN) achieved the **first ascent of Everest by a woman**, reaching the summit on May 16, 1975.

Ascent of Everest without oxygen

Reinhold Messner (ITA) and Peter Habeler (AUT) made the first successful ascent of Mount Everest without supplemental oxygen on May 8, 1978. This feat is regarded by some purist mountaineers as the first "true" ascent of Everest, because overcoming the effects of altitude (i.e., the low oxygen content of the air) is the greatest challenge facing high-altitude climbers.

Highest-altitude cricket match

The Everest Test 2009 (UK) was played 16,942 ft (5,164 m) above sea level at the Gorak Shep plateau near Everest on Apr 21, 2009. This epic feat saw two 15-man squads, three qualified cricket umpires, four medics, two members of the press, and 10 spectators scale the heights to the plateau. Team Hillary defeated Team Tenzing.

First female twins to summit Everest

Tashi and Nungshi Malik (both IND) are the first twin sisters to have climbed Everest, doing so on May 19, 2013. They reached the peak alongside Samina Baig, the first Pakistani woman to complete the climb. All three successful climbers raised the flags of both countries in a symbolic gesture of peace.

On Aug 20, 1980, Messner also became the **first person to ascend Everest solo**. It took him three days to make the ascent from his base camp at 21,325 ft (6,500 m), again without bottled oxygen.

Blind person to climb Everest

Erik Weihenmayer (USA) was born with retinoschisis, an eye condition that left him blind by the age of 13. Despite this, on May 25, 2001 he topped Everest, the first—and so far only—blind person to have done so.

Erik's other notable feats include his 2008 completion of the Seven Summits—climbing the highest mountain on each of the seven continents of the world. This makes him the **first blind person to climb the Seven Summits including Carstensz**.

Married couple to climb Everest

Andrej and Marija Štremfelj (both SVN) became the first married couple to conquer Mount Everest, on Oct 7, 1990.

On the same day, Jean-Noël and his son Bertrand "Zébulon" Roche (both FRA) became the **first father and son team to summit Everest**.

First person to climb Everest from both sides in one season

David Liaño González (MEX) reached the peak of Mount Everest from Nepal on the south side on May 11, 2013, and returned to the peak on May 19, 2013, climbing from Tibet on the north side. This is the first time that any climber has scaled the mountain from both sides in one climbing season.

FASTEST TIME TO CLIMB HEIGHT OF EVEREST BY ...		
Machine (such as a Versaclimber stepping machine). Requires climbing the equivalent of 29,029 ft		
Individual	2 hr 53 min 47 sec	Richard Pemberton (AUS)
Male (team)	1 hr 56 min 8 sec	Richard Saville, Edward Kerry, Steve Wilson, Chris Grimshaw, Charlie Boyes, Dan Levy, Dave Rome, and Kevin Williams (all UK)
Female (team)	2 hr 45 min 53 sec	Bridget Funnell, Victoria Brown, Natasha Jones, Sarah Ruscombe-King, Sandra Heard, Margaret Reeve, Sandra Cann, and Nicola Hammond (all UK)
Indoor climbing wall		
Individual	13 hr 25 min	Tom Lancaster (UK)
Team	4 hr 24 min 33 sec	The Climbing Society at Texas A&M University-Commerce (USA)

"Oxygen levels at the summit of Everest are approximately one-third of those available at sea level. This mask mixes pure oxygen from a tank with ambient air."

"These goggles protect my eyes from hurricane-speed winds and the Sun reflected on the snow, which can cause blindness. The LED head lamp illuminates my way when I'm climbing at night."

"I use this ice axe for self-arrest in case I have a fall and for additional support while climbing."

"The outermost layer of this suit is filled with goose down, which is still one of the best materials for insulation while climbing."

"For nourishment at high altitudes, I rehydrate freeze-dried food by adding water to it from melting ice."

"This is an ascender: a safety device that allows climbers to clip into ropes and anchors already set up on the route. It's attached to the mountaineering harness by a length of climbing cord."

"Fingers are one of the first body parts to get injured because of extreme cold. These mittens are filled with goose down to protect my hands against frostbite."

"The backpack is expandable, to accommodate big loads—such as those carried to the lower camps—and small loads—such as those carried on summit day."

"This solar panel provides clean energy to power electronics, such as radios, satellite phones, and cameras on the mountain."

"The double-layer boots protect the toes against frostbite and are comfortable enough to be worn for hours and hours. The crampons are easily attached to the boots, and allow climbers to ascend steep ice sections where boots alone would slip."

Mountaineering

The Seven Summits' combined height is the equivalent of **113 Eiffel Towers**

First ascent of Nanga Parbat via the Mazeno Ridge

In 1953, Hermann Buhl (AUT) became the **first person to climb Nanga Parbat**—the ninth-highest mountain, situated in the Himalayas at 26,656 ft (8,125 m). It was not until Jul 15, 2012 that it was ascended via the technically difficult Mazeno Ridge or west-southwest route—one of the most demanding challenges in alpinism—by Sandy Allan and Rick Allen (both UK).

FIRST …

Person to climb the Seven Summits
The highest mountains on each of the continents are collectively known as the "Seven Summits" (see table). Two lists have been compiled: the "Bass list," which includes Mount Kosciuszko in New South Wales, Australia, and the more difficult "Messner list," which recognizes Oceania's highest point as Puncak Jaya in Indonesia. Patrick Morrow (CAN) completed the Messner list on Aug 5, 1986 with a summit of Puncak Jaya.

Woman to climb the Seven Summits
On Jun 28, 1992, Junko Tabei (JPN) topped Puncak Jaya, completing Messner's list. Tabei also recorded the **first ascent of Everest by a woman**, when she climbed it on May 16, 1975.

It took Vanessa O'Brien (USA) 295 days to climb both Messner's and Bass's list—the **fastest Seven Summits ascent (female)**. She began with Everest on May 19, 2012 and finished on Kilimanjaro on Mar 10, 2013.

Person to climb all 8,000er mountains
Reinhold Messner (ITA) began his quest to climb each of the 14 mountains higher than 8,000 m—or 26,246 ft—in Jun 1970. He ended the feat with a summit of Lhotse, on the Nepal-Tibet border, on Oct 16, 1986. The feat is so difficult that as of Apr 25, 2014—nearly 30 years later—only 32 people had climbed all 14 mountains.

Woman to climb all 8,000er mountains
On May 17, 2010, Edurne Pasaban Lizarribar (ESP) completed her climb of the 14 mountains over 8,000 m (undisputed) by summiting Shisha Pangma in Tibet. A month earlier, Korea's Oh Eun-Sun had claimed this title, but doubt was cast on her summit of Kangchenjunga and her record remains disputed.

The **first woman to summit all 8,000ers without bottled oxygen** was Gerlinde Kaltenbrunner (AUT) on Aug 23, 2011.

Person to complete the Explorers' Grand Slam
The Explorers' Grand Slam comprises climbing the Seven Summits, the 14 mountains over 8,000 m, and trekking to the North and South poles on foot. Park Young-Seok (KOR) began by climbing Everest on May 16, 1993,

First ascent of Puncak Jaya

The 16,024-ft-high (4,884-m) peak of Puncak Jaya, aka Carstensz Pyramid, in Indonesia was first ascended by Heinrich Harrer (AUT), Philip Temple, Russell Kippax (both NZ), and Albertus Huizenga (NLD). The team reached the summit on Feb 13, 1962. It is considered the most difficult of the Seven Summits to climb.

and finished the slam when he reached the North Pole on Apr 30, 2005. Sadly, Park died in Oct 2011 on Annapurna, the **deadliest mountain**.

Ascent of K2
On Jul 31, 1954, Italy's Achille Compagnoni and Lino Lacedelli completed the first ascent of K2, which at 28,251 ft (8,611 m) is the world's second-highest mountain. K2 is situated in the Karakoram range, on the border between Pakistan and China.

Wanda Rutkiewicz (POL) became the **first woman to climb K2**, on Jun 23, 1986.

Russia's Andrew Mariev and Vadim Popovich completed the **first ascent of K2's west face**, on Aug 21, 2007, after a grueling 10-week climb.

Fastest time to climb the Seven Summits (both lists)

Vernon Tejas (USA) climbed the combined Kosciuszko and Carstensz lists of summits, beginning with Vinson Massif on Jan 18, 2010 and ending with McKinley, aka Denali, on May 31, 2010. This musically minded climber has also played guitar on top of each of the summits and at the North and South poles.

The pair—led by Viktor Kozlov (RUS)—conquered this notoriously vicious face and reached the peak without the use of bottled oxygen.

Ascent of Kangchenjunga
The third-highest mountain (28,169 ft; 8,586 m) was first climbed on May 25, 1955 by George Band and Joe

First to summit Annapurna via the south face (female)

Wanda Rutkiewicz (POL) reached the peak of Annapurna (26,545 ft; 8,091 m) from the south face in the Himalayas, Nepal, on Oct 22, 1991. Rutkiewicz was also the **first woman to ascend K2**, doing so on Jun 23, 1986.

THE SEVEN SUMMITS

As with many mountaineering distinctions, the definition of the "Seven Summits" is disputed. Some climbers include Kosciuszko in Australia instead of Carstensz. Others place Elbrus within the borders of Asia, and thus regard Mount Blanc as Europe's highest mountain.

Continent	Mountain	Location	Height	First climbed
Africa	Kilimanjaro	Tanzania	19,350 ft	Oct 6, 1889
Antarctica	Vinson Massif	Antarctica	16,049 ft	Dec 18, 1966
Asia	Everest	Nepal/China	29,029 ft	May 29, 1953
Australasia	Puncak Jaya, aka Carstensz	Indonesia	16,024 ft	Feb 13, 1962
Europe	Elbrus	Russia	18,510 ft	Jul 27, 1874
North America	McKinley, aka Denali	USA	20,321 ft	Jun 7, 1913
South America	Aconcagua	Argentina	22,841 ft	Jan 14, 1897

Source: www.8000ers.com

FACT
Kim Chang-Ho made a sea-to-summit ascent of Everest, starting from sea level at the Bay of Bengal.

"Helmet: To protect the head from falling rocks and chunks of ice."

"Glasses: To protect the eyes from the Sun's UV radiation and wind."

"Gloves: To protect against the cold."

Fastest time to climb all 8,000ers

Kim Chang-Ho (KOR) climbed the 14 mountains over 26,246 ft (8,000 m) in 7 years 310 days, starting with his successful summit of Nanga Parbat on Jul 14, 2005 and ending with Everest on May 20, 2013. Significantly, he completed all climbs without supplemental oxygen.

"Ice ax: To climb on icy terrain."

"Rope: For protection in case of a fall and to rappel [abseil]."

Brown (both UK).

The **first female to climb Kangchenjunga** was Ginette Harrison (UK), who summited via the northwest face on May 18, 1998.

OLDEST ...

Person to climb the Seven Summits (Messner list)
Male: Takao Arayama (JPN, b. Oct 4, 1935) completed his final Seven Summits climb on Kilimanjaro in Tanzania on Feb 18, 2010, at the age of 74 years 138 days.
Female: Carol Masheter (USA, b. Oct 10, 1946) completed her last Seven Summits climb by ascending Carstensz Pyramid on Jul 12, 2012, aged 65 years 276 days.

Masheter also climbed Kosciuszko on Mar 17, 2012, thus becoming the **oldest female to climb the Bass list of the Seven Summits**.

Person to climb the Seven Summits (Bass list)
Ramón Blanco (ESP, b. Apr 30, 1933) completed the last mountain on the Bass list on Dec 29, 2003, at 70 years 244 days old.

Person to climb an 8,000er without bottled oxygen
Only five people older than 65 have summited an 8,000er without the use of supplementary oxygen. The oldest of these was Boris Korshunov (RUS, b. Aug 31, 1935), who climbed Cho Oyu on Oct 2, 2007 aged 72 years 32 days. However, as some

alpinists dispute Korshunov's claim, the undisputed record goes to Carlos Soria (ESP, b. Feb 5, 1939), who summited Manaslu on Oct 1, 2010, aged 71 years 238 days.

"Harness: Provides the link between your body and the rope."

First person to climb the Triple Seven Summits

Building on the idea of the Seven Summits, the Triple Seven Summits refers to climbing the three highest mountains on each continent. Christian Stangl (AUT) was the first to achieve the feat when he finished with Europe's third-highest mountain, Shkhara, on Aug 23, 2013.

While achieving this hat trick, Stangl also became the **first person to climb the Seven Second Summits** and the **Seven Third Summits**, having conquered the second-highest mountain on each continent by Jan 15, 2013.

"Carabiners and quickdraws: For safety and to provide quick connection to the rope while climbing."

"Pants and jacket: Waterproofed and with insulation."

Continent	Second Summits	Third Summits
Africa	Batian (17,057 ft)	Mawenzi (16,889 ft)
Antarctica	Tyree (15,918 ft)	Shinn (15,288 ft)
Asia	K2 (28,251 ft)	Kangchenjunga (28,169 ft)
Australasia	Sumantri (15,977 ft)	Puncak Mandala (15,610 ft)
Europe	Dykh-tau (17,076 ft)	Shkhara (17,037 ft)
North America	Logan (19,550 ft)	Orizaba (18,490 ft)
South America	Ojos del Salado (22,614 ft)	Pissis (22,293 ft)

"Crampons: Steel frame with spikes, essential to get a grip on icy ground."

"Boots: Waterproofed and with good insulation."

Crossing the seas

As of Sep 2013, a total of **340 ocean rows** had been successfully completed

Youngest person to row across any ocean (nonsolo)

Eoin Hartwright (UK, b. Jan 17, 1997) was 16 years 340 days old when he left La Gomera in the Canary Islands, Spain, to row the Atlantic Ocean east to west. The team, also consisting of Simon Hartwright (Eoin's uncle), Matthew Collier, and Tom Alden, reached Antigua in the *Trilogy Extra* on Feb 4, 2013, in just under 44 days.

Fastest single-handed trans-Atlantic sailing

Francis Joyon (FRA) sailed from New York City, USA, to Cornwall, UK, in 5 days 2 hr 56 min. He arrived on Jun 16, 2013, after a trip of 2,880 nautical mi (3,314 mi; 5,333 km). Joyon still holds the **fastest global solo circumnavigation sailing** record, set back in 2008 at 57 days 13 hr 34 min. He sailed 21,600 nautical mi (24,170 mi; 38,900 km).

Fastest row across the Indian Ocean, east to west

Maxime Chaya (LBN), Livar Nysted (DNK), and Stuart Kershaw (UK) rowed from Geraldton, Australia, to Mauritius onboard *tRIO*.

First person to row across two different oceans in a year

Livar Nysted (DNK) rowed the Atlantic east to west in a team of eight from Gran Canaria to Barbados from Jan 17 to Feb 22, 2013. After a few months' rest, on Jun 9, he rowed a second ocean, crossing the Indian Ocean east to west in a team of three from Australia to Mauritius (see left), arriving on Aug 5, 2013. He spent a total of 93 days 4 hr at sea during the two voyages.

Fastest single-handed sail from Cádiz to San Salvador

Following a similar route to that of Christopher Columbus (leading to its name "The Discovery Route"), Armel Le Cléac'h (FRA) sailed from Cádiz in Spain to San Salvador in The Bahamas in 6 days 23 hr 42 min. Le Cléac'h sailed in his 103-ft (31.4-m) trimaran *Banque Populaire 7* and completed the 3,884-nautical-mi (4,469.62-mi; 7,193.17-km) route on Jan 23–30, 2014, at an average speed of 23.16 knots (26.65 mph; 42.89 km/h).

On Jan 26–27, during the voyage, veteran sailor Le Cléac'h also achieved the **greatest distance sailed in 24 hours single-handedly**, covering 682.85 nautical mi (785.81 mi; 1,264.64 km).

Longest unsupported open ocean journey by jet ski

Frederico Rezende (PRT) jet-skied 598.4 mi (963 km) in the Atlantic Ocean between the Portuguese cities of Lisbon and Funchal on Sep 11–13, 2013. The voyage took him 48 hr 55 min, during which time he was the sole pilot and had no sleep.

Their trip—which took 57 days 15 hr 49 min, from Jun 9 to Aug 5, 2013—also represents the **first team of three to row an ocean**.

First person to row mid-Pacific west to east solo

Sarah Outen (UK) rowed onboard *Happy Socks* from Chōshi in Japan to Adak in Alaska, USA, taking 149 days 13 hr between Apr 27 and Sep 23, 2013.

Prior to this, at the age of 23 years 310 days, Outen (b. May 26, 1985) had become the **youngest female to row the Indian Ocean solo**. She made her epic east-to-west crossing between Apr 1 and Aug 3, 2009.

Longest distance rowed solo nonstop in the Atlantic (female)

Janice Jakait (DEU) rowed 3,545 mi (5,705 km) as the crow flies, east to west from Portugal to Barbados, from Nov 23, 2011 to Feb 21, 2012. This also makes her the **first woman to row across the Atlantic east to west from mainland Europe to the West Indies solo**, a feat unmatched as of Apr 2014.

Youngest tandem row across an ocean

UK rowers Jamie Sparks (b. Jan 11, 1992) and Luke Birch (b. Jul 4, 1992) set off on Dec 4, 2013 in the *Maple Leaf* from La Gomera, Spain, on the Talisker Whisky Atlantic Challenge. At, respectively, 21 years 327 days and 21 years 153 days old on departure, they reached English Harbour in Antigua 54 days 5 hr 56 min later, on Jan 27, 2014, having covered 2,934.48 mi (4,722.6 km).

Youngest person to row solo across an ocean

On Mar 14, 2010, Katie Spotz (USA, b. Apr 18, 1987) completed her 70-day row across the Atlantic, east to west from Senegal to Guyana. When she set off on Jan 3, 2010, she was at the age of 22 years 260 days.

Tommy Tippetts (UK, b. Mar 26, 1989) was 22 years 301 days old at the start of his trip east to west across the Atlantic, making him the **youngest male to row solo across an ocean**. His trip took place from Jan 21 to Apr 12, 2012.

Fastest monohull solo circumnavigation (40-ft class)

Guo Chuan (CHN, above left) sailed the world in 137 days 20 hr 1 min, finishing on Apr 4, 2013. In 2005–06, he was the first Chinese sailor to take part in the Clipper Round the World Yacht Race, founded by Sir Robin Knox-Johnston (UK, above right, with GWR's Frank Chambers). Sir Robin became the **first person to sail solo around the world (nonstop)** on Apr 22, 1969, as the only finisher of the Golden Globe Race.

"A tracking beacon charts the boat's progress every step of the way and relays data to team members on dry land."

"The sun hat provides neck protection, which is vital in temperatures exceeding 104°F on the mid-Atlantic route."

"An offshore life jacket with spray hood, whistle, and reflective tape; this is designed to keep a rower's head above water in case of becoming unconscious."

"White flares are set off to avoid collision and red flares are to ask for help."

"A safety harness keeps the rower attached to the rowing boat at all times."

First crossing of the Tasman Sea by kayak

James Castrission and Justin Jones (both AUS) traveled from Australia to New Zealand across the Tasman Sea in *Lot 41*. They left Foster in Victoria on Nov 13, 2007 and rowed 2,061.7 mi (3,318 km) over 62 days, reaching New Plymouth in New Zealand on Jan 13, 2008.

TASMAN SEA

First solo row

From Feb 6 to Apr 10, 1977, Colin Quincey (NZ) rowed solo in the *Tasman Trespasser* across the Tasman Sea—a stretch of water approximately 1,200 mi (2,000 km) wide and known locally as "The Ditch." Quincey rowed from Hokianga in New Zealand to Marcus Beach in Queensland, Australia, taking 63 days 7 hr.

The **first person to row across the Tasman Sea west to east** (from the mainland) is Shaun Quincey (NZ)—Colin's son. He rowed in *Tasman Trespasser 2* from New South Wales in Australia to Ninety Mile Beach in New Zealand. The trip took him 53 days, between Jan 20 and Mar 14, 2010.

First team to row east to west

Steven Gates, Andrew Johnson, Kerry Tozer, and Sally Macready (all AUS) rowed from Hokianga in New Zealand to Sydney Harbour, Australia, between Nov 29 and Dec 30, 2007.

The **first team to row west to east** was Nigel Cherrie, Martin Berka, James Blake, and Andrew McCowan (all NZ), from Sydney to the Bay of Islands, between Nov 26, 2011 and Jan 16, 2012.

"The satellite phone is for safety first and foremost but it's good to hear news from back at home and tell loved ones how the rowers are getting on."

"Fenders are only used in port and not taken on the trip. They prevent damage to the boat when moored."

"Specifically designed for ocean rowing, the oars provide the only means of propelling the boat."

"Desalinated water is heated in the Jetboil cooker to rehydrate the freeze-dried food rations—and is good for making the odd cup of tea, too!"

Most ocean rows by one person

Simon Chalk (UK, b. Sep 12, 1972) has made a total of eight ocean rows. He rowed east to west across the Atlantic Ocean in teams of two (1997), five (2007/08), six (2013), eight (2012 and 2014), and 14 (2011). He rowed the Indian Ocean east to west, solo, in 2003—making him the **youngest male rower to cross the Indian Ocean**—and in a team of eight in 2009.

"The throwing line is used as a first rescue attempt in the event of man overboard."

Endurance

We can survive for about two months without food, but only around five days **without water**

Fastest speed in a human-powered vehicle (single rider)

Sebastiaan Bowier (NLD) notched up a speed of 83.13 mph (133.78 km/h) in his streamlined recumbent bicycle *VeloX3* at the World Human Powered Speed Challenge near Battle Mountain in Nevada, USA, on Sep 14, 2013. Sebastiaan is pictured left, with teammate Wil Baselmans.

Fastest speed in a human-powered vehicle (multiple riders)

On Sep 14, 2013, Tom Amick and Phil Plath (both USA) reached 73.08 mph (117.61 km/h) in their streamlined recumbent bicycle *Glowworm* on a flat road surface at the World Human Powered Speed Challenge near Battle Mountain in Nevada, USA.

Fastest circumnavigation by bicycle (female)

In just 152 days 1 hr, Juliana Buhring (DEU) cycled a total distance of 18,063 mi (29,069 km). The journey started and finished at Piazza Plebiscito in Naples, Italy, and lasted from Jul 23 until Dec 22, 2012.

Fastest human-powered propeller submarine

In Jun 2007, the two-person, propeller-driven submarine *OMER 5* reached 8.035 knots (9.2 mph; 14.9 km/h) at the 9th International Submarine Races held at the David Taylor Model Basin in Bethesda, Maryland, USA. It was piloted by Sebastien Brisebois and Joel Brunet (both CAN) of the École de Technologie Supérieure at the University of Quebec, Canada.

Most countries visited by bicycle in seven days

Between Apr 29 and May 5, 2013, Glen Burmeister (UK) cycled through 11 countries, from Břeclav in the Czech Republic to Shkodër in Albania. Burmeister passed through Austria, Slovakia, Hungary, Slovenia, Croatia, Romania, Serbia, Bosnia and Herzegovina, and Montenegro.

Longest time flying in a human-powered vehicle

Kanellos Kanellopoulos (GRC) kept his *Daedalus 88* aircraft aloft for 3 hr 54 min 59 sec on Apr 23, 1988, while pedaling the 71.93 mi (115.11 km) between Heraklion, Crete, and the Greek island of Santorini. Unfortunately, a gust of wind broke off the plane's tail and it crashed just before reaching shore.

Farthest distance to swim under ice with breath held

Wearing fins and a diving suit, Stig Åvall Severinsen (DNK) swam 500 ft (152 m) under ice, with his breath held, at Qorlortoq Lake on Ammassalik Island, Greenland, on Apr 16, 2013. He returned the next day to make the **farthest swim under ice with breath held (no fins, no diving suit)**: 250 ft (76 m).

LONGEST JOURNEY ...

By bicycle (individual)

The greatest mileage amassed in a cycle tour was more than 402,000 mi (646,960 km), by the itinerant lecturer Walter Stolle (CZE) from Jan 24, 1959 to Dec 12, 1976. He

Longest walk on flower petals

Between Jan 2 and 27, 2013, a group of 1,128 Buddhist monks walked 278.6 mi (448.4 km) between temples, across eight provinces in Thailand, stepping on marigold petals. The walk was part of the Second Dhammachai Dhutanga pilgrimage to welcome in the year 2013.

Farthest distance barefoot (24 hours)

Peter Wayne Botha (NZ, b. ZAF) ran 131.43 mi (211.51 km) barefoot on Oct 5–6, 2013, in the 16th annual Sri Chinmoy 24-hour race in Auckland, New Zealand. En route, he clocked the **fastest 100 km barefoot**, in 8 hr 49 min 42 sec.

Fastest crossing of the USA by bicycle

During the Race Across America in 2013, Christoph Strasser (AUT) cycled across the USA in 7 days 22 hr 11 min, completing the trip on Jun 19. In doing so, the indefatigable cyclist also became the first person to cross the USA coast to coast in under 8 days.

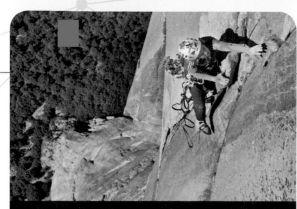

Fastest time to climb El Capitan (female)

Mayan Smith-Gobat (NZ, above) and Libby Sauter (USA) successfully climbed the "Nose" route of El Capitan in Yosemite National Park in California, USA, on Sep 29, 2013. The duo took 5 hr 39 min to complete the ascent, beating the previous record by almost two hours.

visited 159 countries, starting out from Romford in Essex, UK.

On crutches
From Mar 21 to Jul 27, 2011, Guy Amalfitano (FRA) journeyed 2,488 mi (4,004 km) through France on crutches. His journey took him from Salies-de-Béarn to the Centre Hospitalier in Orthez.

On roller skis
Between May 11 and Jul 5, 2012, César Baena (VEN) traveled 1,395.73 mi (2,246.21 km) on roller skis from Stockholm in Sweden to Oslo in Norway.

On inline skates
Khoo Swee Chiow (SGP) covered a distance of 3,782 mi (6,088 km) on inline skates. Khoo departed from Hanoi in Vietnam on Oct 20, 2007 and arrived in Singapore on Jan 21, 2008.

Swimming in open water
Martin Strel (SVN) swam 3,273 mi (5,268 km) down the length of the Amazon River in Peru and Brazil from Feb 1 to Apr 8, 2007.

Walking backward
To date, the greatest exponent of reverse pedestrianism is Plennie L. Wingo (USA). From Apr 15, 1931 to Oct 24, 1932, he walked 8,000 mi (12,875 km) from Santa Monica in California, USA, to Istanbul in Turkey at a rate of 15.47 mi (24.89 km) per day.

Fastest speed in a human-powered vehicle (female)

On Sep 15, 2010, Barbara Buatois (FRA) reached a speed of 75.69 mph (121.81 km/h) pedaling her streamlined recumbent bicycle *Varna Tempest*. She achieved the feat on a flat road surface at the World Human Powered Speed Challenge near Battle Mountain in Nevada, USA.

"I used these beat-up binoculars for 20–30 years. They were small but clear for finding a way over difficult mountains or ravines. Also, to see in wars, where the shooting and bombing was."

"I wore these sunglasses out in two years across Africa. The dust on dirt roads from passing trucks rose up in huge clouds. I also wore contact lenses. These were almost priceless."

"My greatest treasure and necessity. When faced with dangers, death, and struggles I pull it out and hold it in my hand."

Longest ongoing pilgrimage

As of Apr 24, 2013, the greatest distance claimed for an "around the world" pilgrimage is 40,235 mi (64,752 km) by Arthur Blessitt (USA), who has been walking on a mission since Dec 25, 1969. He has visited all seven continents, including Antarctica, having traversed 321 nations, island groups, and territories carrying a 12-ft-tall (3.7-m) wooden cross and preaching from the Bible throughout.

"I've used this hipster for 20 years. It carries my small Bible and sometimes my passport. Sometimes I have food snacks in it, too. It's like a small backpack. I still use it."

"A true pleasure, these utensils fit inside a plastic holder with a salt and pepper shaker. So even with dirty hands on the road and awful food at least I have something clean to eat with."

"My army knife is one thing that always goes with me. It fits right on my belt with its bottle and can opener, sewing kit, paper, writing pen, magnifying glass, saw, wrench, scissors, screwdriver, and stone for sharpening."

"My water canteen, last used in the Darién Gap in Panama/Colombia in 1978. I've never gotten sick from the water sources I used on the roads of the world. Jesus did it. It is very emotional to see this …"

"Keep the passport dry, out of sight, and away from sticky fingers— some border police of remote areas would hold the passport for a bribe. Interestingly, it's the smallest countries that have a full-page stamp!"

"In 1969, there were only working boots—it was years before specialty walking shoes became developed. I learned the hard way to get walking shoes that were larger than my typical shoe size; I would have to cut holes on the side for my toes. I tighten my shoe laces in the morning and loosen them as my feet expand."

"The wheel for my cross, this one used on my trip across southern Africa in 1985–86 and China in 1987. The cross wood wears away as it drags on the rocks and pavement, and I'd have to replace the cross every few weeks without the wheel."

Epic journeys

We walk the equivalent of about **four times** around Earth in a lifetime

Youngest person to circumnavigate by aircraft

Between May 2 and Jun 29, 2013, Jack Wiegand (USA, b. Jun 22, 1992) flew around the world in a Mooney M20R Ovation aircraft, covering approximately 24,000 mi (38,600 km) in all, and making 22 stops en route. Jack was 21 years 7 days old when he touched down in Fresno, California, USA, at the end of his trip.

applicable in 1989 and 1991 embracing more than an equator's length of driving (24,901 road miles; 40,075 km), is held by Saloo Choudhury and his wife Neena Choudhury (both India). The journey took 69 days 19 hours 5 minutes from September 9 to November 17, 1989. The couple drove a 1989 Hindustan "Contessa Classic" starting and finishing in Delhi, India.

Longest journey ...
• **Barefoot:** Michael Essing (DEU) walked 924.65 mi (1,488.09 km) on his bare feet between the German towns of Flensburg and Efringen-Kirchen from May 30 to Sep 5, 2013.

Longest journey by 50-cc scooter

Theodore Rezvoy and Evgeniy Stoyanov (both UKR) rode 8,968 mi (14,434 km) from Odessa in Ukraine to Ulan-Ude in Russia on two 50-cc Honda Zoomer scooters between Jul 11 and Sep 11, 2013. In doing so, they surpassed the previous record, set in 2010, by approximately 1,240 mi (2,000 km).

BY AIR

Fastest circumnavigation by microlight

Colin Bodill (UK) circled the globe in his Mainair Blade 912 Flexwing microlight aircraft in 99 days from May 31 to Sep 6, 2000, starting and landing at Brooklands airfield in Weybridge, Surrey, UK. Accompanying him was Jennifer Murray (UK), who made the **fastest circumnavigation by helicopter (female)** on the trip, flying in a Robinson R44. The pair covered some 21,750 mi (35,000 km).

Longest journey ...
• **By ultralight aircraft:** Roberto Bisa and Antonio Forato (both ITA) of ASD Riding the Skies flew an ultralight aircraft 12,505 mi (20,126 km) from Cassola in Italy to Southport in Queensland, Australia, from Oct 8 to 31, 2013.

• **Kite surfing in 24 hours:** On Feb 26, 2012, Rimas Kinka (LTU) covered 401.2 mi (645.6 km) off the coast of Islamorada in Florida, USA.

• **Kitesurfing (female):** No woman has kitesurfed for longer than Germany's

Anke Brandt, who covered 135.16 nautical mi (155.54 mi; 250.32 km) between Amwaj Marina and Al Dar Island, Bahrain, on Mar 1, 2014.

BY LAND

Fastest circumnavigation by car

The record for the first and fastest man and woman to have circumnavigated the Earth by car covering six continents under the rules

Longest journey by solar-powered car

A team from SolarCar Projekt Hochschule Bochum (DEU) carried out an 18,487-mi (29,753-km) trip by electric vehicle, leaving Adelaide in Australia on Oct 26, 2011 and arriving in Mount Barker, Australia, on Dec 15, 2012. They spent a total of 168 days driving. Eight days were devoted to recharging the vehicle; the remaining days were spent exhibiting the SolarCar at various locations, events, and universities and being transported between continents.

• **By car:** As of Apr 3, 2013, Emil and Liliana Schmid (both CHE) had covered 420,842 mi (677,281 km) in a Toyota Land Cruiser. Their trip began on Oct 16, 1984.

• **By nonsolar electric vehicle:** Duane Leffel (USA) drove 3,534.77 mi (5,688.68 km) from Charleston in South Carolina to Laguna Hills in California, USA, from Jul 4 to Aug 24, 2013.

• **By motorcycle in one country:** Buck Perley (USA) and Amy Mathieson (UK) rode 20,727.13 mi (33,357.15 km) across China from Jul 19 to Dec 11, 2013.

• **By motorized bicycle:** From Jul 14 to Sep 4, 2012, Danny Halmo (CAN) rode

LONGEST JOURNEY BY ...			
Vehicle	**Distance**	**Record holders**	**Dates**
Bus	54,287 mi	Hughie Thompson, John Weston, and Richard Steel (all UK)	Nov 6, 1988–Dec 3, 1989
Fire engine	31,663 mi	Stephen Moore (UK)	Jul 18, 2010–Apr 10, 2011
Hovercraft	4,970 mi	British Trans-African Hovercraft Expedition, led by David Smithers (UK)	Oct 15, 1969–Jan 3, 1970
Motorcycle	456,707 mi	Emilio Scotto (ARG)	Jan 17, 1985–Apr 2, 1995
Quad bike	34,945 mi	Valerio De Simoni, Kristopher "Ted" Davant, and James Kenyon (all AUS)	Aug 10, 2010–Oct 22, 2011
Skateboard	7,555 mi	Rob Thomson (NZ)	Jun 24, 2007–Sep 28, 2008
Tandem	23,700 mi	Phil and Louise Shambrook (UK)	Dec 17, 1994–Oct 1, 1997
Tractor	13,172 mi	Vasilii Hazkevich (RUS)	Apr 25–Aug 6, 2005
Wheelchair	24,901 mi	Rick Hansen (CAN)	Mar 21, 1985–May 22, 1987

4,176 mi (6,721 km) within Canada, from English Bay in Vancouver, British Columbia, to Halifax Harbour, Nova Scotia.

• **By rickshaw:** Tim Moss (UK) rode a rickshaw 856.22 mi (1,377.96 km) from Aviemore to West Molesey, UK, between Apr 26 and May 19, 2010.

BY WATER

First person to swim from Cuba to Florida without a shark cage
Diana Nyad (USA, b. Aug 22, 1949) swam from Havana, Cuba, to Key West, Florida, USA, in 52 hr 54 min 18.6 sec on Aug 31—Sep 2, 2013, aged 64 years 11 days.

Longest journey ...
• **Swimming nonstop in open water (male):** Martin Strel (SVN) swam 313.1 mi (504.5 km) down the Danube, from Melk in Austria to Paks in Hungary, in 84 hr 10 min on July 3–6, 2001. He was escorted by four kayakers, a safety escort boat, and six road vehicles.

• **Rowed in 24 hours by a team (men):** On Jun 14–15, 2013, Dutch rowers Ansgar John Brenninkmeijer, Gert Jan Keizer, Oscar Dinkelaar, Jacques Klok, Jeroen van Renesse, and Hans-Jan Rijbering covered 183.4 mi (295.2 km) up- and downstream on the Amstel River in the Netherlands.

Longest journey by electric motorcycle

As part of the Meneghina Express event—a project to investigate global food nutrition and sustainability—Nicola Colombo and Valerio Fumagalli (both ITA) covered 7,691 mi (12,379 km) on electric motorcycles. The duo rode from Shanghai, China, to Milan, Italy, between Jun 10 and Jul 23, 2013.

First row of the navigable length of the Amazon

Embarking from Nauta in Peru on Sep 13, 2013, Anton Wright (UK, below left) and Dr. Mark de Rond (NLD, below right) rowed down the Amazon River to Macapá in Brazil, arriving on Oct 14, 2013. Altogether, they covered more than 2,000 mi (3,200 km) in their Woodvale Pairs-class ocean rowing boat, made out of plywood and reinforced with glass fiber and resins.

"Tropical storms can whip up quickly in the Amazon basin. These JL splash jackets provided ideal protection from the torrential rain."

"Wearing a sun hat is a must when rowing the Amazon to prevent sunstroke and provide protection from the blistering Sun."

"One of our most important pieces of equipment by far was this GPS device. It would indicate where we were on the river, how much progress we'd made, and what we could expect ahead."

"A life vest is a non-optional accessory, and for good reason: tropical storms and strong currents have claimed the lives of plenty of strong swimmers in the past."

"Oars made of reinforced carbon fiber are ideal for their durability and strength. They are also surprisingly lightweight."

The top 10 most visited museums had a total of **52.9 million visits** in 2012

Highest-grossing action-movie heroine

The phenomenal success of the first two *Hunger Games* movies (USA, 2012 and 2013) means that the character of Katniss Everdeen—portrayed by Jennifer Lawrence (USA)—is the movie industry's most successful action heroine at the box office, with both movies grossing a total of $1.55 bn internationally. *The Hunger Games: Catching Fire* was the **highest-grossing post-apocalypse movie**, taking $424,668,047 in the USA and grossing $864,565,663 worldwide.

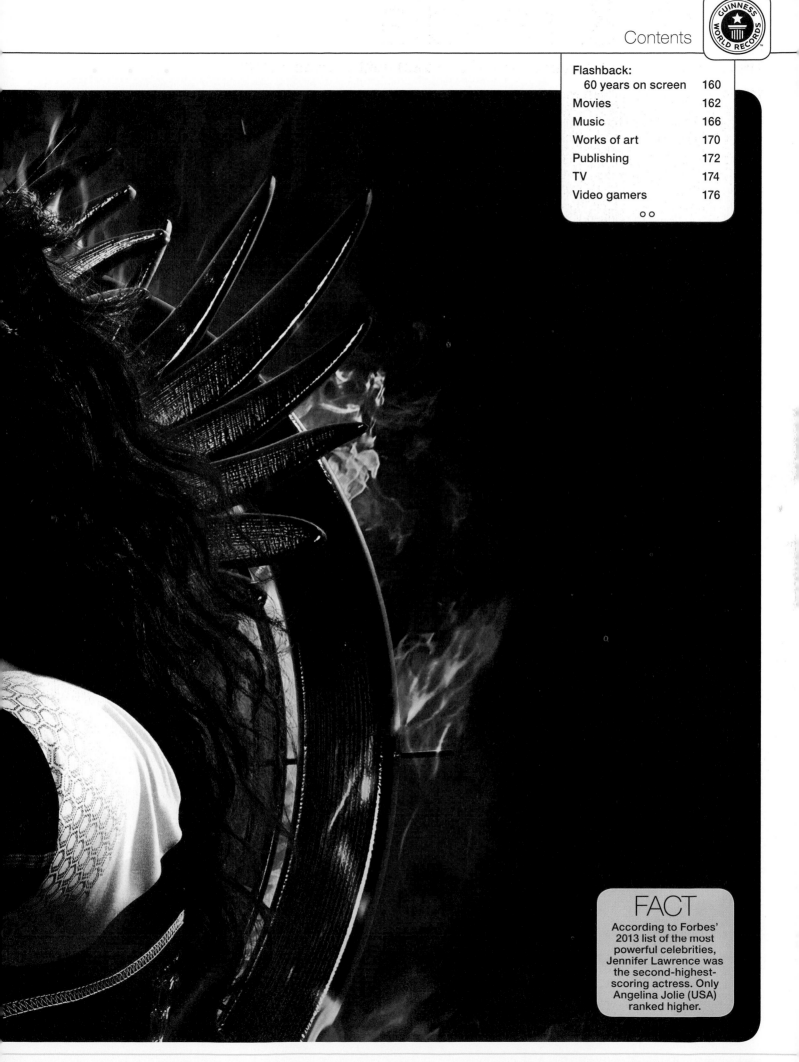

FACT

According to Forbes' 2013 list of the most powerful celebrities, Jennifer Lawrence was the second-highest-scoring actress. Only Angelina Jolie (USA) ranked higher.

⚡ 60 years on screen

The movie industry has seen a huge increase in technological sophistication over the past six decades, but how has this affected our appetite for movies? Are we going to the movies more than ever? Are we releasing as many movies? And are new releases just as successful if you account for inflation?

All figures in US$

In the past 60 years on screen, everything has changed, and yet nothing has changed. In 1955, the highest-grossing movie of all time was *Gone with the Wind* (USA, 1939). Adjusting for current inflation, it seems probable it will still be the highest-grossing movie of all time at the end of 2015.

American movie houses made today's equivalent $10.68 billion in 1954, and $10.90 billion in 2012. Does this mean that movies are as popular as they've ever been? Well, it's estimated that US movie houses sold about 2.5 billion tickets in 1955, compared with 1.3 billion in 2012. While

most people go to the movies less regularly than they did in 1955, the rise of blockbusters—with their ever-spiraling budgets and technical breakthroughs—means that the public is prepared to pay more when they do.

The rise of affordable video technology has also helped the total number of movies made around the world each year to spiral, creating grass-roots industries such as Nigeria's Nollywood, which now produces over 1,000 movies each year, beating the USA into third place on the list of the most prolific moviemaking countries.

NUMBER OF FEATURE MOVIES RELEASED PER YEAR (WORLDWIDE)

There has been a steady increase in the number of movies released annually, from 1,904 in 1955 to 10,048 in 2013. The affordability of high-end film-making technology has led to a rapid rise in the past 10 years.

12,000
10,000
8,000
6,000
4,000
2,000
0

Cleopatra (USA, 1963)
Most expensive movie produced (adjusted): $306.86 m in today's money

Peak of 3,248 releases in 1968; not surpassed until 1990

AVERAGE PRICE OF A US MOVIE TICKET

$10
$9
$8
$7
$6
$5
$4
$3
$2
$1
$0

Prices have crept up over the last six decades, as you would expect, but when adjusted for inflation (the lighter color), there is plenty of variation over the years, peaking in 1971. Of course, this is just the cost of the seat, not the parking, the popcorn, the drinks, the 3D glasses ...

Average ticket price peaks in 1971 at $9.3 (in today's money)

Doctor Zhivago (USA, 1965)
First movie to win five Golden Globe awards: Best Film, Director, Actor, Screenplay, and Score; five Globes is also a record, shared with four other movies

US MOVIE HOUSE ADMISSIONS

3,000,000,000
2,500,000,000
2,000,000,000
1,500,000,000
1,000,000,000
500,000,000
0

It's been a bumpy ride when it comes to movie house admissions. As ticket prices grew, so the number of visits to the movies dropped drastically, reaching a low at the start of the 1970s. The advent of the blockbuster and multiplexes has seen this trend reverse, but not back to the glory days of the 1940s and 50s.

Jaws (USA, 1975)
First blockbuster movie: The first movie to earn $100 m at the box office

Record low of 709 million admissions in 1971

The Golden Age of Hollywood peaked at 4.7 billion admissions in 1947; by 1964, with the rise of TV, the figure had dropped below 1 billion

Blockbusters pre-1955

Below is a list of the highest-grossing movies since 1955. Only two movies in the all-time top 10 list of **most successful movies** predate 1955: *Gone with the Wind* (1939) and *Snow White and the Seven Dwarfs* (1937). When adjusted to today's ticket prices, the former remains at the No. 1 slot, with a gross of $3.44 bn.

TOTAL US BOX-OFFICE GROSS

$12,000,000,000
$10,000,000,000
$8,000,000,000
$6,000,000,000
$4,000,000,000
$2,000,000,000

The money earned by the theaters has fluctuated annually between a high of ca. $12 bn and a low of $6 bn.

Adjusted peak of $11.98 bn in 1956; remains unbeaten until 2002

2001: A Space Odyssey (USA/UK, 1968)
Largest movie budget for special effects: Stanley Kubrick's mind-altering sci-fi classic spends more than 60% of its budget on special effects

1955   1960   1965   1970

TOP 10 MOVIES OF THE PAST 60 YEARS ...

1956
The Ten Commandments
Chart position: 6
Ticket sales: 262.0 m
Adjusted gross: $2.187 bn
Biblical epic starring Charlton Heston as Moses, tasked with freeing the Hebrew slaves

1961
101 Dalmatians
Chart position: 10
Ticket sales: 199.8 m
Adjusted: $1.003 bn
A litter of dalmatian dogs must be rescued before they become the fashion victims of Cruella de Vil

1965
Doctor Zhivago
Chart position: 7
Ticket sales: 248.2 m
Adjusted: $2.073 bn
A doctor/poet experiences illicit love and hardship during the Bolshevik Revolution

1965
The Sound of Music
Chart position: 4
Ticket sales: 283.3 m
Adjusted: $2.366 bn
The hills are alive with the sound of children and their nanny fleeing Nazi-occupied Austria

1973
The Exorcist
Chart position: 9
Ticket sales: 214.9 m
Adjusted: $1.794 bn
The Church is called in after a demonic entity takes possession of a young girl

Ranking based on number of tickets sold, seat prices, and box-office gross

Most prolific movie industry

India continues to be the source of more movies than any other country: 1,255 releases in 2011, compared with 819 in the USA. In May 2013—during Bollywood's 100th anniversary year—Vijay Krishna Acharya (IND) released *Dhoom 3*, the **highest-grossing Bollywood movie**, which raked in $88 m internationally.

FACT

More Americans went to the movies in 2011 than attended sporting events or theme parks combined. But in the same year, India recorded twice as many theater visits as the USA.

E.T.: The Extra-Terrestrial (USA, 1982)
Most weekends at No. 1: Enjoys 16 (nonconsecutive) weekends as the highest-ranking movie; seen by an estimated 161 million people in the USA alone

The Rescuers Down Under (USA, 1990)
First fully digital feature movie: Made using a digital ink system developed by Disney and Pixar (both USA)

Peak of 3,482 releases in 1990; not surpassed until 1999

Releases exceed 4,000 for first time; 1,041 of them originate in India

Avatar (USA, 2009)
First movie to gross $2 bn: Surpasses $2 bn globally by the weekend of Jan 29–31, 2010

FACT

The average spend in a US movie house in 2013 was $20 per person, of which only $8.12 was for the seat.

True Lies (USA, 1994)
First movie to have a $100-m budget: James Cameron ups the ante on the spectacle of moviemaking; it ends up making back $378 m

FACT

The Japanese pay the most for their movie tickets, as of 2013—the equivalent of $22 per seat.

The Twilight Saga: Eclipse (USA, 2010)
Widest movie release: Opens in 4,468 movie houses in USA on Jun 30

Tron (USA, 1982)
First major motion picture to use CGI: Producers desperate to keep movie audiences growing discover the benefits of computer-generated imagery

Attendances peak at 1.6 billion in 2002, with *The Lord of the Rings*, *Harry Potter*, *Men in Black*, and *Star Wars* all enjoying chart-topping sequels

Titanic (USA, 1997)
Most consecutive weekends at No. 1: 15 weekends as the highest-ranking movie

The Avengers (USA, 2012)
Fastest time to gross $100 m at the domestic box office: Two days (May 4–5)

Star Wars helps annual grosses to peak at $9.5 bn in 1978—a figure not surpassed for another 20 years

Super Mario Bros. (USA, 1993)
First live-action movie based on a video game: Movie producers, looking for inspiration from popular licenses, turn to video-gaming for the first time

US box-office takings peak in 2003, with combined adjusted earnings of $12.06 tr

The 12 biggest movies of 2009's Christmas weekend (Dec 25–27) earn a combined $259.9 m in three days at the domestic (US) box office—the **biggest weekend at the movies**

Star Wars (USA, 1977)
Highest-grossing sci-fi series: George Lucas's blockbuster and its sequels (and prequels) go on to gross an adjusted $2.65 bn

Titanic (see above) becomes the **first movie to gross $1 bn**

Harry Potter and the Deathly Hallows Part 2 (UK/USA, 2011)
Highest-grossing movie—single day: Earns $91 m on Jul 15 in the USA alone

1980 | 1985 | 1990 | 1995 | 2000 | 2005 | 2010 | 2015

1975
Jaws
Chart position: 8
Ticket sales: 242.8 m
Adjusted: $2.027 bn
A man-eating great white shark terrorizes a US tourist hotspot at the height of the summer season

1977
Star Wars
Chart position: 2
Ticket sales: 338.4 m
Adjusted: $2.825 bn
Swashbuckling adventure set a long time ago in a galaxy far, far away …

1982
E.T.: The Extra-Terrestrial
Chart position: 5
Ticket sales: 276.7 m
Adjusted: $2.310 bn
An alien visitor to Earth is left stranded and befriends a young boy, who helps him "phone home"

1997
Titanic
Chart position: 3
Ticket sales: 301.3 m
Adjusted: $2.516 bn
James Cameron's epic tale of the sinking of the "unsinkable" ocean liner

2009
Avatar
Chart position: 1
Ticket sales: 238.6 m
Adjusted: $3.02 bn
Cameron again, this time setting the sci-fi action on the distant planet Pandora

:Movies

Movie theater visits in Senegal cost the **equivalent of 63¢**

Highest box office film gross for an animation

Frozen (USA, 2013) surpassed *Toy Story 3* (USA, 2010) as the most successful animated movie at the global box office, earning $1.112 bn (£664.7 m)—and counting—as of Apr 14, 2014. The Disney musical, inspired by Hans Christian Andersen's fairy tale *The Snow Queen*, broke the record while still on general release.

Most expensive year in Hollywood

The 50 biggest blockbusters released by major Hollywood studios in 2010 cost a combined total of $5.2 bn—the highest total in one year in US cinematic history.

In 2013, the USA experienced the **highest box-office summer gross**, with movie theaters taking a total of $4.76 bn between May 1 and Aug 31.

Most extensive digital object

For the final battle sequence in *Ender's Game* (USA, 2013), US effects studio Digital Domain created 333,443 individual spaceships, all of which appeared simultaneously in shots comprising more than 27 billion polygons.

Largest total movie theater attendance (current)

There were some 3.17 billion trips made to movie theaters in India in 2011. The **largest annual movie theater attendance** in a given year occurred in 1929, when 4.49 billion admissions were made to US movie theaters.

Largest international movie market

North America represents the largest market for movies, with box-office receipts in USA and Canada totaling $10.8 bn in 2012.

Largest annual movie output

According to UNESCO, India is the most prolific movie-making nation. The Bollywood industry produces up to 1,000 feature movies a year, and in 2011

Longest continuously running movie franchise

Despite several significant gaps in production, the scheduled release of *Godzilla* (USA/JPN) on May 16, 2014 means that Japan's Toho studios have owned and promoted the *Godzilla* (*Gojira*) franchise for nearly 60 years. The original movie by Ishirō Honda (JPN) was released in Nov 1954.

1,255 movies were made, in 24 languages, compared with 819 movies made in the USA.

Most movies made in one language

The most recent UNESCO cinematic survey found that in 2011, 1,302 movies

Highest box-office gross for a zombie movie

The 2013 blockbuster *World War Z* (UK/USA) took a worldwide box-office gross of more than $540 m by the time it closed in movie theaters on Oct 10, 2013. The movie is based on a book of the same name by Max Brooks and stars Brad Pitt. In Jun 2013, it was announced that there would be a *World War Z* sequel.

FACT

Max Brooks, author of *World War Z*, is the son of comedy director Mel Brooks, whose movies include horror spoofs *Young Frankenstein* (USA, 1974) and *Dracula: Dead and Loving It* (USA, 1995).

BUDGET vs. BOX OFFICE: BIGGEST RETURNS ON INVESTMENT

Charted here are the top 10 most profitable movies, as identified by the-numbers.com as of May 14, 2014. Profit is estimated from global box-office figures and domestic video/DVD sales. At the top is *Paranormal Activity* (USA, 2009), which cost $450,000 to make but netted $89.7 m.

Legend:
- Budget
- Gross
- Return

Budget	Profit (estimated)	Return on investment (%)
	Paranormal Activity (2009)	19,850%
	The Devil Inside (2012)	3,644%
	Peter Pan (1953)	3,443%
	Grease (1978)	3,056%
	Paranormal Activity 2 (2010)	2,474%
	Insidious (2011)	2,079%
	Jaws (1975)	1,730%
	Reservoir Dogs (1992)	1,632%
	The King's Speech (2010)	1,154%
	Beauty and the Beast (1991)	1,148%

Just the ticket

In our 1955 book, we reported that the Brits were the most prolific moviegoers: "The people of the United Kingdom go to the cinema more often than any other country in the world. Each week on average half the total population visit a cinema, of which there are a total of 4,595." Fast forward to the present day and Iceland has the **largest annual cinema attendance per capita**, with an average of 5.24 trips per person per year according to a 2011 survey by UNESCO. (See above for **largest total attendance**.)

Source: www.the-numbers.com/Nash Information Services; budget and profit scales are not proportional

162 **Arts & media**

Most times an actor has played themselves

Legendary *lucha libre* wrestler El Santo (MEX) starred as himself in 50 action-adventure movies made over 24 years, beginning with *Santo contra el cerebro del mal* in 1958 and concluding with *Santo en la furia de los karatekas* in 1982.

were made exclusively in English. French came second with 293 movies and Spanish was third with 263. Although India makes the most movies, a range of languages were featured including Hindi, Tamil, and Telugu.

Most expensive movie

Pirates of the Caribbean: At World's End (USA) had a production budget of $300 m in 2007. Even if movie budgets are adjusted for inflation to 2014 prices, *At World's End* remains the most expensive production of all time. Its $339-m budget narrowly beats *Cleopatra* (1963, USA), starring Elizabeth Taylor and Richard Burton (both UK), which

cost $44 m in 1963—the equivalent of $337 m today.

Most expensive movie series

The eight *Harry Potter* movies (USA/UK, 2001–09) had a combined production budget of $1.15 bn. However, it is *James Bond* that takes the record of **most expensive movie series adjusted for inflation**, with costs of around $2.07 bn across 23 movies and 50 years.

HIGHEST GROSSING …

- **Movie:** *Avatar* (USA, 2009), $2.78 bn
- **Bollywood movie:** *Dhoom: 3* (IND, 2013), $88 m
- ***James Bond* movie:** *Skyfall* (UK/USA, 2012), $1.10 bn
- **Post-apocalypse movie:** *The Hunger Games: Catching Fire* (USA, 2013), $864 m

Highest-grossing superhero movie

Marvel's *The Avengers* (USA, 2012) took $1.51 bn at the international box office in its 22 weeks on general release between May 4 and Oct 4, 2012. The movie, directed by Joss Whedon (USA), accounted for 52% of all domestic box-office takings in the USA for the month of May.

Most extensive lighting on a movie set

"Zero-gravity" footage for the movie *Gravity* (USA, 2013) was filmed within a custom-built light box containing 1.8 million high-powered LEDs. The LEDs were individually controlled by the movie's effects team to help re-create the natural light and shade of outer-space photography. The light box took the form of a hollow cube, within which the actors were suspended.

✕ For more movies, turn the page

Crowdfunded: Veronica Mars

Veronica Mars (right) is the **most crowdfunded movie**, having received $5,702,153 via the Kickstarter crowdfunding site as of Apr 13, 2013. The appeal, which began in response to the cancellation of the *Veronica Mars* TV show, funded the movie, which premiered on Mar 14, 2014, a year and a day after the appeal launch.

The **first crowdfunded Oscar winner**, *Inocente* (left), won the Best Documentary (short feature) award on Feb 24, 2013. The movie, about a homeless Californian girl's efforts to become an artist, was directed by Sean Fine and Andrea Nix.

FACT

Pledges totaling $52,527 were raised on Kickstarter to help fund *Inocente* (2012).

Standout studios

Most billion-dollar movies by a studio: Buena Vista International (USA), seven (*Pirates of the Caribbean: Dead Man's Chest*, *Alice in Wonderland*, *Toy Story 3*, *Pirates of the Caribbean: On Stranger Tides*, *The Avengers*, *Iron Man 3*, and *Frozen*)

Highest average gross for a studio: Pixar (USA) has earned an average of $252.6 m across 14 movies ○ ○ ○

Johnny Depp once worked for a **telemarketing** firm, selling pens

Bollywood big-hitters

Topping the *Forbes* list as the **highest-earning Bollywood actor** is Shah Rukh Khan (IND), with estimated earnings in 2013 of 220.5 crore (2.2 bn rupees; $37.06 m). Khan is pictured here in the 2012 romantic drama *Jab Tak Hai Jaan* (*As Long as I Live*) with Katrina Kaif (HKG/UK), the **highest-earning Bollywood actress**, with earnings of 63.75 crore (637 m rupees; $10.7 m) during the same period.

Highest box-office movie gross for a director
The 27 theatrically released movies thus far directed by Steven Spielberg (USA)—from *The Sugarland Express* (USA, 1974) to *Lincoln* (USA, 2012)—have grossed a total of $9.01 bn worldwide.

Most billion-dollar movies at the box office for a director
Three directors have each made two movies that have grossed at least $1 bn at the box office. They are: Canada's James Cameron, for *Titanic* (USA, 1997) and *Avatar* (USA/UK, 2009); New Zealand's Sir Peter Jackson, for *The Lord of the Rings: The Return*

of the King (USA/NZL, 2003) and *The Hobbit: An Unexpected Journey* (USA/NL, 2012); and the UK's Christopher Nolan, for *The Dark Knight* (USA/UK, 2008) and *The Dark Knight Rises* (USA/UK, 2012).

Most overpaid actor
According to business magazine *Forbes*, Adam Sandler (USA) returned an average of $3.40 for every $1 he was paid, based on the last three movies he starred in to Jun 1, 2013. For the same period, *Forbes* ranked Katherine Heigl (USA) as the **most overpaid actress**, with an average return of $3.50 for every $1 earned. (See also: "Payback with interest," below.)

Highest box-office gross for a female director

With a total worldwide box-office gross of $1,152,567,728 for her six movies as director, including *What Women Want* (USA, 2000) and *It's Complicated* (USA, 2009), US moviemaker Nancy Meyers remains the highest-grossing female movie director of all time.

Most powerful actor

Best known for his role as Wolverine, Hugh Jackman (AUS) topped Forbes' 2013 list of most powerful actors and is 11th overall in the list of most powerful celebrities. The list measures fame in terms of factors such as earnings, media exposure, and Internet presence.

Oldest actress in a leading role
Lillian Gish (USA, b. Oct 14, 1893) was 93 years old when she starred in *The Whales of August* (USA), released on Oct 16, 1987.

The **oldest actress to debut in a leading role** is Harue Akagi (JPN, b. Mar 14, 1924), who was 88 years 175 days old when she starred in *Pekorosu no Haha ni Ai ni Iku* (JPN), released on Nov 9, 2013.

HIGHEST ...

Annual earnings for a producer
Steven Spielberg (USA) earned $100 m from Jun 2012 to Jun 2013 according to Forbes' Celebrity 100 list. The total gross of Spielberg-produced movies stands at more than $6.4 bn.

Highest average box-office gross for a leading role

Harry Potter star Emma Watson (UK) has an average box-office gross of $775,303,380. Her *Harry Potter* costar Daniel Radcliffe (UK) took top billing in one more non-*Harry Potter* movie than Watson, which has reduced his per-movie lead role average slightly to $712,856,021.

HOLLYWOOD ROYALTY: THE MOST INDIVIDUAL OSCAR WINS

Most Oscars won in a lifetime: Walt Disney (USA), 26

Most Oscars won in a lifetime (female): Edith Head (USA), eight

Most Best Director Oscars won: John Ford (USA), four

Most Best Actress Oscars won: Katharine Hepburn (USA), four

Most Best Actor Oscars won: Daniel Day-Lewis (UK), three

⚡ Walt and Oscar

In 1955, *The Guinness Book of Records* noted that "Walt Disney has won more 'Oscars'—awards of the United States Academy of Motion Picture Arts and Sciences instituted 1929—than any other person." Back to the present day … and Disney (USA) still holds the record for **most Oscars awarded in a lifetime**: a career total of 26. His final Academy Award—Best Short Subject (Cartoon) for *Winnie the Pooh and the Blustery Day* (1968)—was awarded posthumously.

👁 Payback with interest

Best investment return for an actress: According to Forbes, as of Dec 2010, Emma Stone (USA) returned an average of $80.70 for every $1 she was paid. Other actors with a supercompetitive rate of return include Mila Kunis (USA), at $68.70 for every $1 paid, and Jennifer Lawrence (USA), at $68.60. The **best investment return for an actor** was that of The Rock aka Dwayne Johnson (USA), with $31.10 in returns for every $1 paid.

Most billion-dollar movies at the box office for an actor

Johnny Depp achieved three billion-dollar box-office smashes with *Pirates of the Caribbean* movies *On Stranger Tides* and *Dead Man's Chest*, and *Alice in Wonderland*. Hugo Weaving (AUS, top inset) matches him with *The Hobbit: An Unexpected Journey*, *Transformers: Dark of the Moon*, and *The Lord of the Rings: The Return of the King*. Gary Oldman (UK, bottom inset) scores for *Harry Potter and the Deathly Hallows: Part 2*, *The Dark Knight*, and *The Dark Knight Rises*.

Box-office gross for an actor

Samuel L. Jackson (USA) has a career worldwide gross of $12,126,213,694 from the 94 movies in which he has appeared. These include supporting roles in box-office record breakers *The Avengers* and *Iron Man 2* (USA, 2010).

Average box-office gross for a director (male)

Lee Unkrich (USA) has an average US gross of $332.9 m as a director, with a worldwide overall gross of $2.97 bn as of Nov 8, 2013. His highest-grossing movie is *Toy Story 3* (USA, 2010).

Average earnings for a movie composer

John Williams (USA) has written scores for 76 movies, each grossing an average of $289.6 m at the box office. They include

Most bankable Hollywood figure

Steven Spielberg (USA) contributed the equivalent of $26,344,040 annually to the movie industry as of Feb 2014, according to the-numbers.com. His annual earnings (see **highest earnings for a producer**, p. 164) also make Spielberg the **highest-earning director**.

Highest annual earnings for an actor

According to Forbes, two actors share the record for the highest earnings over a 12-month period. Robert Downey Jr. (USA, main picture) earned around $75 m from Jun 2012 to Jun 2013, benefiting from the success of *The Avengers* and *Iron Man 3*. Tom Cruise (USA, below right) earned a similar figure from May 2011 to May 2012, during which *Mission: Impossible: Ghost Protocol* (USA/UAE/CZE, 2011) grossed some $700 m.

the six *Star Wars* movies and several of the *Harry Potter* movies. The **highest career box-office movie gross for a composer** is $22.48 bn by Hans Zimmer (DEU), nearly $4 bn more than John Williams, his nearest rival. His credits include *The Dark Knight Rises* and three *Pirates of the Caribbean* movies.

> **ⓘ Cruising to success**
>
> In the past eight years, Tom Cruise, seen here as Jack Reacher, has been the highest-earning movie actor three times. His big-screen debut came back in 1981.

Supercameo-Man: Stan Lee

With movies based on his creations breaking box-office records around the world, it's perhaps unsurprising that Marvel Comics mastermind Stan Lee (USA), at 91 years 68 days old as of March 5, 2014, would want to play his part in the action. The 19 movies in which he has made cameo appearances since his cinematic debut in *Mallrats* (USA, 1995)—including *X-Men 3: The Last Stand* (USA, 2006; above left), *Spider-Man 3* (USA, 2007; center left), and *Fantastic Four* (USA, 2005; bottom left)—have grossed $10,077,831,163 at the global box office, making Stan Lee the **highest-grossing actor from cameo appearances**.

> **✋ And finally ...**
>
> • **Most appearances in $100-m-grossing movies:** Bruce Willis (USA), with 25 such movies as of Jan 21, 2014.
> • **Most powerful actress:** Angelina Jolie (USA), ranked 41 in Forbes' 2012–13 Celebrity 100 list.
> • **Most screenwriters credited:** 51, for *50 Kisses* (UK, 2014), produced by the London Screenwriters' Festival (UK).
> ○ ○ ○

:Pop music

There are more than **26 million songs** in the iTunes catalog

Most traveled musician in one year

According to research carried out by the live music events Web site Songkick, electro-house musician, DJ, and producer Steve Aoki (USA) traveled 241,850 mi (389,221 km) performing a total of 168 shows in 41 countries in 2012.

Most consecutive years with a UK No. 1 single

Three acts in the 62-year history of the UK's Official Singles Chart have achieved No. 1 singles in seven consecutive years: Elvis Presley (USA) in 1957–63, The Beatles (UK) in 1963–69, and in 2007–13 Rihanna, whose latest chart-topper, "The Monster," debuted at No. 1 on Nov 9, 2013.

First act to play a concert on every continent

Metallica (USA) became the first music act to play on all seven continents when they entertained 120 scientists and competition winners at Antarctica's Carlini Station on Dec 8, 2013. The show was dubbed "Freeze 'Em All."

First act to debut at No. 1 in USA with first three albums

One Direction (UK) completed a hat-trick of No. 1 debuts on the *Billboard* 200 albums chart when *Midnight Memories* entered in pole position with first-week sales of 546,000 on Dec 14, 2013. It followed the chart-topping success of *Up All Night* and *Take Me Home* in 2012.

Longest officially released song

"Zwei Jahre" ("Two Years"), performed by German band Phrasenmäher, lasts 1 hr 30 min 10 sec. It was released via iTunes, Amazon, and Spotify on Jan 10, 2014.

Most Facebook "likes" for a musician

As of Apr 25, 2014, Shakira (COL) had the most "likes" with 90,938,442. Not far behind was Rihanna (BRB) with 87,042,153, and at No. 3 was Eminem (USA) with 86,136,651.

Over on Twitter, the **musician with the most followers** is Katy Perry (USA) with 52,463,838. Next up are Justin Bieber (CAN) with 51,140,907 and Lady Gaga (USA) with 41,297,293.

Highest-earning dead celebrity

American singer Michael Jackson earned $160 m from Oct 2012 to Oct 2013. If Forbes included the dead, he would top the 2013 list of highest-earning celebs.

Fastest-selling iTunes album

On Dec 13, 2013, Beyoncé (USA) unexpectedly released self-titled studio album *BEYONCÉ*—with 14 new tracks and 17 videos—exclusively on iTunes. In its first three days of availability as a download, it sold 828,773 copies worldwide.

Longest-running album series

There have been 87 albums in the *NOW That's What I Call Music!* series (Virgin/EMI). The first was released in 1983 and the most recent on 7 Apr 2014.

- **First:** *NOW That's What I Call Music!*, 28 Nov 1983
- **Editions:** 87
- **Songs:** 3,440
- **Units sold:** more than 100 million
- **Most appearances:** Robbie Williams (33)
- **Most appearances on one album:** Calvin Harris (3)

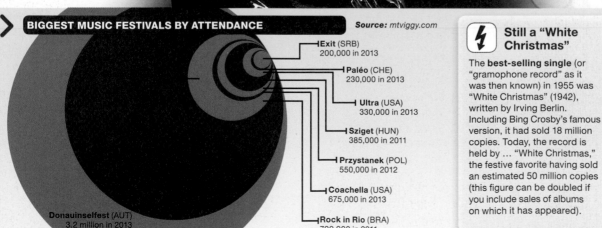

> **BIGGEST MUSIC FESTIVALS BY ATTENDANCE**   *Source: mtviggy.com*

Exit (SRB) 200,000 in 2013

Paléo (CHE) 230,000 in 2013

Ultra (USA) 330,000 in 2013

Sziget (HUN) 385,000 in 2011

Przystanek (POL) 550,000 in 2012

Coachella (USA) 675,000 in 2013

Rock in Rio (BRA) 700,000 in 2011

Donauinselfest (AUT) 3.2 million in 2013

Still a "White Christmas"

The **best-selling single** (or "gramophone record" as it was then known) in 1955 was "White Christmas" (1942), written by Irving Berlin. Including Bing Crosby's famous version, it had sold 18 million copies. Today, the record is held by … "White Christmas," the festive favorite having sold an estimated 50 million copies (this figure can be doubled if you include sales of albums on which it has appeared).

Silver stars

Oldest US Hot 100 entrant: Fred Stobaugh (USA), 96 years 23 days ("Oh Sweet Lorraine," No. 42, Sep 14, 2013).

Oldest UK albums chart-topper: Dame Vera Lynn (UK), 92 years 183 days (*The Very Best of Vera Lynn—We'll Meet Again*, Sep 19, 2009).

Oldest UK singles chart-topper: Robert "Bobby" Elliott (UK, Hollies drummer), 71 years 21 days ("He Ain't Heavy, He's My Brother" by The Justice Collective, Dec 29, 2012).

Most words in a hit single

"Rap God" by Eminem (USA) packs 1,560 words into a fast and furious 6 min 4 sec—that's a tongue-twisting average of 4.28 words every second! In one 15-second segment alone, "Slim Shady" spits out 97 words (6.46 words per sec) at supersonic speed.

Longest time between UK No. 1 albums

On Jun 22, 2013, British rock band Black Sabbath returned to the top of the UK albums chart with their 19th studio set, *13*, some 42 years 255 days after first topping the chart with their second album, *Paranoid*, on Oct 10, 1970.

Most cover versions of a single charted before the original

Seven cover versions of "I Love It," by Swedish duo Icona Pop and singer-songwriter Charli XCX, aka Charlotte Aitchison (UK), made the Top 200 of the UK's Official Singles Chart before the original debuted at No. 1 on Jul 6, 2013.

Largest TV audience for a Super Bowl half-time performance

The half-time show by Bruno Mars and the Red Hot Chili Peppers (both USA) at Super Bowl XLVIII attracted 115.3 million US viewers, according to data supplied by Nielsen. The 2014 Super Bowl was contested by the Denver Broncos and the Seattle Seahawks at MetLife Stadium in East Rutherford, New Jersey, USA, on Feb 2. The game itself was watched by an average of 111.5 million—the **largest TV audience for a Super Bowl**.

Best-selling album ever

Thriller by Michael Jackson (USA), released in Nov 1982, has sold more than 65 million copies worldwide. *Thriller* and the Eagles' (USA) *Their Greatest Hits (1971–1975)* have been certified 29x platinum by the Recording Industry Association of America (RIAA) and are joint holders of the **best-selling album in the USA**.

According to the Official Charts Company, the **best-selling album in the UK** is Queen's *Greatest Hits* (1981). In 2014, it became the first album to sell 6 million copies in the UK.

GWR'S POP MUSIC POWER INDEX

	Name	Power rating
1	Lady Gaga (USA)	100
2	Justin Bieber (CAN)	75.5
3	Taylor Swift (USA)	66.8
4	Katy Perry (USA)	66.2
5	Rihanna (BRB)	64.2
6	Shakira (COL)	62.9
7	One Direction (UK/IRL)	56.2
8	Madonna (USA)	49.0
9	Britney Spears (USA)	47.0
10	Miley Cyrus (USA)	46.3

Index accounts for earnings, social media presence, video views, and search hits, as of Mar 6, 2014; benchmarked to Lady Gaga = 100.

Best-selling female artist

Madonna has sold more than 300 million albums in her career. Her earnings of $125 m for Jun 2012–Jun 2013 were also the **highest annual earnings ever for a female pop star**, dwarfing those of record holder Celine Dion for 1998—$56 m ($80 m today).

Most searched-for pop star

According to Google, Miley Cyrus (USA) was the most searched-for pop star in 2013. No. 5 on the overall list, her Internet popularity peaked after she "twerked" with Robin Thicke at the 2013 MTV Video Music Awards.

Most weeks on US singles chart (one single)

"Radioactive," by US rock band Imagine Dragons, spent a total of 86 non-consecutive weeks on the US Hot 100 singles chart between Aug 18, 2012 and May 3, 2014. It reached a peak chart position of No. 3.

Most weekly radio impressions

Robin Thicke's (USA/CAN) controversial single "Blurred Lines" had 228.9 million audience impressions on *Billboard*'s Radio Songs chart on Aug 24, 2013. Impressions are calculated according to the number of times a song is played and the radio station's audience size.

Calvin climbs: superstar DJ

The **highest-paid DJ in one year** is Calvin Harris (UK), with earnings of $46 m in the 12 months to Jun 2013, according to Forbes, including up to $300,000 for one night's work in Las Vegas, USA. Electronic dance music has become very popular in the USA in the last decade and is worth more than $4 bn a year. Harris proved his worth on May 16, 2013 when he was named Songwriter of the Year at the 58th Ivor Novello Awards. Harris has collaborated with artists such as Rihanna, Dizzee Rascal, Kylie Minogue, and Tinchy Stryder.

FACT

The UK's Glastonbury festival began in 1970, attracting 1,500 fans. Fast forward to 2013: All 135,000 tickets were sold in just 1 hr 40 min.

Pop videos

After Robin Thicke performed "Give it 2 U" at 2013's MTV MVAs, the single's sales **leaped by 251%**

1958: First music videos
The Big Bopper, aka Jiles Perry Richardson (USA), booms "Hello, baby!" in his "Chantilly Lace" video of 1958, miming into a prop phone. He was the first to use the term "music video," only weeks before he died in the plane crash that also claimed Buddy Holly. The Bopper filmed clips for three songs on the same day.

1981: First music video shown on MTV
On Aug 1, 1981, MTV used "Video Killed the Radio Star" by The Buggles (UK duo Geoff Downes and Trevor Horn) as its opening track. On Feb 27, 2000, the same video was the millionth to be broadcast by the channel.

1982: First music video banned by MTV
Tame by today's standards, Queen's "Body Language" was full of sweaty, writhing, Lycra-clad bodies in a dimly lit steam room. While the band was fully clothed, the flesh and alleged "homoerotic undertones" worried MTV.

1982: First Grammy for Video of the Year
Elephant Parts (Pacific Arts, 1981) was an hour-long mix of five songs with comedy by former Monkee Michael Nesmith (USA) that won at the 1982 Grammys. Short- and long-form video awards were separated in 1984.

1986–99: Most wins at the MTV Music Video Awards
Madonna (USA) has won a total of 20 MTV Music Video Awards (MVAs): Video Vanguard Award (1986); one for "Papa Don't Preach" (1987); three for "Express Yourself" (1989); one for "Like a Prayer" (1989); three for "Vogue" (1990); one for *The Immaculate Collection* (1991); two for "Rain" (1993); one for "Take a Bow" (1995); five for "Ray of Light" (1998); one for "Frozen" (1998); and one for "Beautiful Stranger" (1999).

1987: Most MTV MVAs for a single video
In 1987, Peter Gabriel's (UK) "Sledgehammer" (1986) won nine awards,

1982
Queen
"Body Language"

1982
Michael Nesmith
Elephant Parts

1990
Madonna
"Vogue"

1958
The Big Bopper
"Chantilly Lace"

1981
The Buggles
"Video Killed the Radio Star"

1987
Peter Gabriel
"Sledgehammer"

TOP OF THE POPS: MOST VIEWED AND TOP TRENDING MUSIC VIDEOS OF 2013

1
PSY—"Gentleman M/V" **598 million**
Ylvis—"The Fox (What Does The Fox Say?)" **265 million**

2
Miley Cyrus—"Wrecking Ball" **393 million**
Kenneth Håkonsen—"Harlem Shake (Original Army Edition)" **95 million**

3
Miley Cyrus—"We Can't Stop" **304 million**
SteveKardynal—"Wrecking Ball (Chatroulette Version)" **67 million**

4
Katy Perry—"Roar (Official)" **251 million**
thelonelyisland—"YOLO (feat. Adam Levine & Kendrick Lamar)" **53 million**

5
P!nk—"Just Give Me A Reason ft. Nate Ruess" **236 million**
ERB—"Mozart vs Skrillex: Epic Rap Battles of History Season 2" **41 million**

■ **Most viewed music videos of 2013**
■ **Top trending music videos of 2013**

Listed here are the top five most viewed music videos of 2013 alongside the year's top five trending music videos. Both sets of figures represent the total viewing figures for each video as of Dec 2013.

Video firsts

First video featuring unauthorized use of an act's music: "Up All Night" (2011), Blink-182, compiled from clips taken from fan-made videos

First video in Simlish: "Smile" (2007), Lily Allen in *The Sims 2: Seasons* (2007)

First video to receive one billion views on YouTube: "Gangnam Style", PSY, Dec 2012

including Best Special Effects and Video of the Year. Lady Gaga, aka Stefani Germanotta (USA), is second with seven awards for "Bad Romance" (2009).

1991: Largest TV audience for a music video premiere

An estimated 500 million people in 27 countries watched "Black or White" by Michael Jackson (USA) on Nov 14, 1991. The 11-min clip was filmed by "Thriller" director and movie maker John Landis.

2010
Lady Gaga and Beyoncé
"Telephone"

2004: First official fan-made music video

Placebo (BEL/SWE/UK) were so impressed by fan Grégoire Pinard's (ZAF) claymation clip for "English Summer Rain" that they adopted it as the official promo video for the song.

2010: Most product placement in a video

Lady Gaga has approximately a dozen brands on show in "Telephone" (featuring Beyoncé), including Virgin Mobile, Beats Electronics, Polaroid, Chanel sunglasses, Wonder bread, Kraft salad dressing, and Diet Coke cans imaginatively utilized as her hair rollers.

2013: First video in space

On May 12, 2013, Commander Chris Hadfield (CAN) posted a video of himself singing David Bowie's "Space Oddity" onboard the *International Space Station*. Read an interview with Chris on p. 17.

2013: Longest video

Pharrell Williams (USA) released the "world's first 24-hour music video." *Happy* features fans dancing to the four-min track of the same name, which is looped 360 times. Pharrell appears in the video on the hour every hour.

2013: Longest wait for an official video

An interactive video for Bob Dylan's (USA) "Like a Rolling Stone" appeared on his Web site on Nov 19, 2013, more than 48 years after the song was a hit. Viewers could flick through different "channels" to watch artists lip sync the song.

2004
Placebo
"English Summer Rain"

2013
Chris Hadfield
"Space Oddity"

1991
Michael Jackson
"Black or White"

2013
Pharrell Williams
"Happy"

2013
Bob Dylan
"Like a Rolling Stone"

Take your partners: biggest dances

Record attempts can be inspired by music videos. Pictured right is the **largest "Thriller" dance**, in which 13,597 "zombies" pulled Michael Jackson moves in Mexico City, Mexico, on Aug 29, 2009. "Harlem Shake" by Baauer inspired the **highest Harlem Shake** (below left), danced at an altitude of 62,300 ft on a British Airways plane on Mar 10, 2013. "Cha Cha Slide" (DJ Casper, 2000) prompted 3,231 dancers to achieve the **largest Cha Cha Slide** (above left) at the Pleasure Beach in Blackpool, UK, on Oct 8, 2011.

Distinctive Dylan

Described by one Web site as "a Dylan cable network with 16 channels of mindless entertainment," the star-studded interactive video (see above) features a host of celebrities and musicians including vintage footage of Dylan himself performing "Like a Rolling Stone." According to the video's creator, Interlude, no viewer will see the same video twice.

Works of art

On Aug 21, 1911, the **Mona Lisa** was stolen from Paris's Louvre

Most expensive sculpture (living artist)

On Nov 12, 2013, the 12-ft-tall (3.6-m) stainless steel sculpture entitled *Balloon Dog (Orange)* by Jeff Koons (USA) sold for $58.4 m at Christie's in New York City, USA.

Most frequently stolen painting

The Ghent Altarpiece—also known as *The Adoration of the Mystic Lamb*—is a large, early-15th-century Flemish panel painting by Hubert and Jan van Eyck. It has been stolen seven times since it was first unveiled. Police are still searching for one missing panel.

Most expensive sculpture

A 6-ft-tall (1.8-m) bronze sculpture entitled *L'Homme qui marche I (The Walking Man I)* (1960), created by Alberto Giacometti (CHE), sold to an anonymous bidder at Sotheby's in London, UK, for £65 m ($104 m) on Feb 3, 2010.

Actual Size

Oldest sculpture

In Sep 2008, excavations at Hohle Fels Cave in southwest Germany uncovered a 35,000–40,000-year-old female figurine carved from a mammoth's tusk.

Most expensive painting

The Card Players, painted by Paul Cézanne (FRA), was sold to the royal family of Qatar for $250 m in 2011. The painting, which was created in the early 1890s, is one of five in a series by the renowned post-Impressionist artist.

Oldest painting

Discovered in the 1870s, paintings of animals and handprints from a cave called El Castillo in Puente Viesgo in the province of Cantabria, Spain, have now been proved to be at least 40,800 years old.

Most expensive painting sold at auction

On Nov 12, 2013, *Three Studies of Lucian Freud* (1969), a triptych by Francis Bacon (UK), was sold to an unnamed client for $142.4 m at Christie's in New York City, USA.

Largest horse-head sculptures

In Nov 2013, two 100-ft-tall (30-m) equine sculptures were unveiled in Falkirk, UK. *The Kelpies* were designed by artist Andy Scott (UK) as a tribute to the local tradition of working horses.

Largest Rubik's Cube mosaic

Created by Josh Chalom (USA), the largest mosaic made out of Rubik's Cubes measured 225 ft 7 in (68.78 m) long by 13 ft 2 in (4.03 m) high and was unveiled at One Central Macau, China, on Dec 7, 2012. The mosaic depicted famous views in Macau and comprised 85,626 cubes.

Anamorphic art: seeing is believing

Anamorphic art is two-dimensional but appears to have three dimensions when viewed from one point. The **largest anamorphic sidewalk art** (above) covers 16,899 sq ft (1,570 m²) and was created to promote tourism in Wilhelmshaven, Germany, on Aug 4, 2012. Above left is the **largest anamorphic print**: a 45,504-sq-ft (4,227.5-m²) image commissioned by Renault Trucks (FRA) and realized by François Abélanet (FRA) in Lyon, France, on Jul 6, 2013.

Smallest handmade sculpture

Golden Journey is a gold sculpture measuring just 0.006 in (0.1603 mm) long. It was crafted by hand by artist Willard Wigan (UK) and sits in a hollowed-out section of a single hair. The measurement was verified in Birmingham, UK, on Jun 19, 2013.

Longest wood sculpture

Designed by Zheng Chunhui (CHN), the lengthiest wooden carving measures 40 ft 3 in (12.28 m) and was unveiled in Putian, Fujian, China, on Nov 14, 2013. It took the record holder and his 20 coworkers four years to complete the highly intricate work from camphor wood.

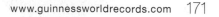

Publishing

Harry Potter creator J. K. Rowling **does not have a middle name**

BEST-SELLING ...

Fiction book
Due to a lack of audited figures, it is impossible to state categorically which single work of fiction has the highest sales. However, Charles Dickens' (UK) *A Tale of Two Cities* (1859) is believed to have sold in excess of 200 million copies.

Children's book series
J. K. Rowling's (UK) seven-part *Harry Potter* saga began in 1997 and ended in 2007, with *Harry Potter* and the Deathly Hallows. By 2008, the series had sold a combined total of ca. 400 million copies.

The **best-selling children's trilogy** is Suzanne Collins' (USA) *Hunger Games*; during 2012 alone, the three books—*Hunger Games* (2008), *Catching Fire* (2009), and *Mockingjay* (2010)—sold a total of 27.7 million copies across both printed and digital formats.

Nonfiction book
Even without exact sales numbers, there is little doubt that the Bible is the world's best-selling and most widely distributed book. A survey by the Bible Society concluded that around 2.5 billion copies were printed between 1815 and 1975, but more recent estimates put the number at more than 5 billion.

Regularly updated book
The *Xinhua Zidian* (New China Character Dictionary) is the world's most popular reference work. Originally published in 1953, the dictionary has been revised 11 times, had more than 200 print runs, and sold well in excess of 400 million copies.

Highest *New York Times* ranking for a "mash-up"

A "mash-up" is a work of fiction that combines preexisting text—often a literary classic—and new text written by a contemporary author. *Pride and Prejudice and Zombies*—a hybrid of Jane Austen's 19th-century period romance and Seth Grahame-Smith's (left) alternative-universe zombie horror—reached No. 3 on the *New York Times* best-seller list in 2009.

FACT
Bob's collection weighs an estimated 16,800 lb—about the same as 118 adult men!

FIRST ...

Encyclopedia
Speusippus compiled the earliest known encyclopedia in Athens, Greece, in ca. 370 BC. As of 2014, it would have been compiled 2,384 years ago.

Detective novel
According to the British Library, *The Notting Hill Mystery* (1863) by Charles Felix (UK) was the first detective novel. Starting with a murder, the plot reveals the twists and turns leading up to the crime, establishing many features of the now-ubiquitous detective genre.

Digital library
Currently offering around 133,000 free eBooks, Project Gutenberg was established in 1971 with the aim of

Largest comic book collection

Bob Bretall (USA) has amassed a collection of 94,268 comic books. The tally was made at his home in Mission Viejo, California, USA, on May 1, 2014 and includes only unique comic books. Bretall began collecting comics when he was eight years old, when he purchased *The Amazing Spider-Man* #88.

HIGHEST-GROSSING LITERARY CREATIONS AT THE MOVIES

Based on total movie gross of each creation, measured in billions of dollars

- Harry Potter (J. K. Rowling)
- James Bond (Ian Fleming)
- *The Lord of the Rings* (J. R. R. Tolkien)
- Shrek (William Steig)
- *The Twilight Saga* (Stephenie Meyer) — 4.72
- Jurassic Park (Michael Crichton) — 3.51
- *The Chronicles of Narnia* (C. S. Lewis) — 3.34
- The Hunger Games (Suzanne Collins) — 2.01
- John McClane/ *Die Hard* (based on Detective Joe Leland in *Nothing Lasts Forever* (Roderick Thorp)) — 1.58
- Robert Langdon/ *The Da Vinci Code* (Dan Brown) — 1.52
- 1.43
- 1.24

Lucrative literature

Highest annual earnings for an author: $95 m, E. L. James (UK), *Fifty Shades ...* trilogy.

Highest annual earnings for a children's author: $55 m, Suzanne Collins (USA), *Hunger Games* trilogy.

Largest advance for a nonfiction book: $15 m, US President Bill Clinton for his memoir, *My Life*.

FACT
Self-published author John Locke (USA) has sold more than 2 million Kindle-formatted eBooks on Amazon using the Kindle Direct Publishing service. He passed the 1-million milestone in Jun 2011, and to date has published 21 novels plus one non-fiction book, entitled —appropriately enough —*How I Sold 1 Million eBooks in 5 Months*.

Smallest printed book

The illustrated reference book *Flowers of the Four Seasons* measures 0.02 x 0.02 in (0.74 x 0.75 mm) and was printed by Toppan Printing Co. Printing Museum in Bunkyo, Tokyo, Japan.

making 10,000 of the most consulted books available to the public at little or no cost.

Graphic novel
The term "graphic novel" first appeared in 1976 on the dust jacket of *Bloodstar* by Richard Corben and Robert E. Howard (both USA).

Author to earn $1 bn
In 2004, J. K. Rowling (UK)—one of only five self-made female billionaires—became the first author to earn

$1 bn. Her *Harry Potter* books have been published in at least 55 languages.

Author to sell one million eBooks
By Jul 6, 2010, James Patterson (USA), creator of *Alex Cross* and *Women's Murder Club*, had exceeded sales of one million eBooks.

MOST ...

Prolific computer-assisted author
With a little help from computers, a team of programmers, and a clever software algorithm that he designed, Philip M. Parker (USA) has "written" in excess of 200,000 books. His algorithm gathers information freely available in the public domain and compiles it into book form. Digital files are produced in around 13 min and printed on demand. Given the specialized nature of the content, cover prices are

often high—for example, $1,300 in the case of *The 2007–2012 World Outlook for Floor Lamps*.

Booker Prize wins
Awarded since 1969, the Booker Prize has been won twice by four authors as of 2013: J. G. Farrell (UK), J. M. Coetzee (ZAF), Peter Carey (AUS), and Hilary Mantel (UK).

Pseudonyms
A total of 325 pen names were listed for humorist Konstantin

Arsenievich Mikhailov (RUS) in the 1960 *Dictionary of Pseudonyms*. Most were abbreviations of his real name.

Translated author
According to the Index Translationum—UNESCO's book translation inventory—Agatha Christie (UK) has had an astonishing 6,598 translations of her novels, short stories, and plays.

Blank pages in a published book
Sheridan Simove's (UK) book *What Every Man Thinks About Apart from Sex ...* (2011) contains 196 blank pages.

Youngest Booker Prize winner

Eleanor Catton (NZ, b. Sep 24, 1985) was 28 years 22 days old when she won the Booker Prize on Oct 15, 2013 for her novel *The Luminaries*.

Largest book

A photo book measuring 16 ft 5 in x 26 ft 6 in (5.01 x 8.08 m) was created by Samsung Electronics in Berlin, Germany, on Sep 7, 2013. The 16-page book consists of 28,000 photos sent via Facebook to Samsung. It was unveiled in the Museum für Kommunikation Berlin.

Diamond seller: the record-breaking record book

The 100-millionth copy of *Guinness World Records* was sold in 2004, although the book by then had already earned its own entry in the records archive. In the edition published in 1975 (right), our founding editors Norris and Ross McWhirter announced that, in Nov 1974, the *Guinness Book of Records* "first sold in October 1955 and [with] total sales in 14 languages now running at 60,000 a week, surpassed the 23,916,000 of *The Common Sense Book of Baby and Child Care* by Dr Benjamin Spock." We continue to be the **biggest-selling annual book**.

GUINNESS BOOK OF RECORDS

Nobel Prize in Literature
The Nobel Prize in Literature has been awarded to 110 authors since 1901. According to Alfred Nobel's will, the winner should have produced "... the most outstanding work in an ideal direction ..." Doris Lessing (UK, 1919–2013) was the **oldest recipient of the Literature Prize**, winning it in 2007 at the age of 87 years 355 days.

And finally ...
- **Fastest-selling nonfiction book (UK):** *My Autobiography*, by retired soccer manager Sir Alex Ferguson (UK), published on Oct 24, 2013—first week sales of 115,547 copies.
- **Fastest-selling video game guide (UK):** *Grand Theft Auto V Signature Series Strategy Guide*, published on Sep 17, 2013—first week sales of 21,530 copies.

TV

Bermuda has **more TV sets per capita** than any other country (1,024 per 1,000)

First 3D television
We often think of 3D TV as a modern invention, but stereoscopic 3D television was first demonstrated by Scottish inventor John Logie Baird at his company's premises at 133 Long Acre in London, UK, on Aug 10, 1928. Baird pioneered a variety of 3D TV systems using electromechanical and cathode-ray tube techniques, including simultaneous left- and right-eye images for true stereoscope viewing. It took until Apr 12, 2008, however, for the **first commercially available 3D TV set** to go on sale, made by Hyundai in Japan.

Most pirated TV program

Game of Thrones retains the No. 1 spot in Torrent Freak's top 10 list of most pirated TV shows, with 5,900,000 downloads per episode in 2013. One reason is HBO's refusal to license the series to Netflix; HBO and Warner Bros. executives also stated, controversially, that "receiving the title of 'most-pirated' was better than an Emmy," creating a "much-needed cultural buzz."

Highest-rated TV series (current)

As of the 2013–14 season, the first series of Canal+'s *The Returned* (aka *Les Revenants*, FRA) had a rating of 92 out of 100 on Metacritic. Based on the French 2004 movie *Les Revenants*, the creepy story revolves around a French village where the dead start to return from the grave.

Most powerful person in television
According to Forbes, Oprah Winfrey (USA) tops the list of most powerful celebrities. The list assesses fame by taking into account income, exposure in print and on TV, Internet presence, public opinion, and marketability. Her estimated earnings from Jun 2012 to Jun 2013 were $77 m, the **highest annual earnings for a TV personality (female)**.

Ashton Kutcher (USA), who joined sitcom Two and a Half Men (CBS, 2003–present) in 2011, earned an estimated $24 m from Jun 2012 to Jun 2013, the **highest annual earnings for a TV actor (current)**.

Highest annual earnings for a TV chef
Gordon Ramsay (UK) earned $38 m between

Jun 2012 and Jun 2013, according to Forbes. He is known for TV shows such as *Hell's Kitchen* and *The F Word*.

Highest box-office gross for a TV simulcast
The *Doctor Who: The Day of the Doctor* simulcast on Nov 23, 2013 (see below) grossed $10.2 m at the global movie-theater box office. In the USA alone, 320,000 tickets were sold, earning $4.7 m at more than 650 sites. That made it the second biggest attraction of the day after *The Hunger Games: Catching Fire* (USA, 2013), but the per-screen average for *Doctor Who* was higher at $13,607, compared with $12,300.

Longest career as a TV news anchor (same program)
Guillermo José Torres (USA) worked on WAPA-TV's *Noticentro* in Guaynabo, Puerto Rico, for 43 years 303 days until Aug 5, 2013. He was awarded his GWR certificate as a surprise during his final telecast.

Largest TV drama simulcast

At 7:50 p.m. (GMT) on Nov 23, 2013, the 50th-anniversary episode of *Doctor Who* (BBC, UK) was broadcast in 98 countries across six continents. Themed around a Time War between Timelords and Daleks, the episode featured three Doctors, played by Matt Smith, David Tennant, and John Hurt (main picture, right). The inset picture shows (left to right) Executive Producer Steven Moffat, Matt Smith, and Jenna-Louise Coleman, who plays the Doctor's companion Clara.

FACT

The first US president to appear on television was Franklin D. Roosevelt, on Apr 30, 1939.

ℹ️ TV gets a cool reception

There were no television broadcasts in Iceland during July until 1983. And Icelanders had to wait until 1987 before state television broadcast on Thursdays.

A dose of reality: *Got Talent*

The **most successful reality television format** is *Got Talent* (Fremantle Media/Syco), sold to 58 countries—including India, below left—since debuting as *Britain's Got Talent* in the UK in Jun 2007. Simon Cowell (UK, right) and Howard Stern (USA, top left)—judges on the UK and US editions respectively—enjoy the **highest annual earnings by a TV celebrity**. Each earned $95 m for the year ending Jun 2013. In Forbes' annual list of the most powerful celebrities, however, Cowell (No. 17) outranks Stern (No. 45), factoring in areas such as marketability and social media ranking.

Most Primetime Emmy Awards for a TV series

Saturday Night Live (NBC, USA, 1975–present) won four trophies at the 2013 Primetime Emmy Awards, bringing its overall haul to 40 awards. The late-night comedy sketch show, which was created by Lorne Michaels and developed by Dick Ebersol, is in its 39th season as of 2014.

As of the 2013 ceremony, *Saturday Night Live* had also received the **most Primetime Emmy Award nominations** (171).

Highest-rated reality-competition series

As of Feb 2014, *Project Runway: Season 2* (Lifetime/Bravo, USA, 2005–06) boasted a Metacritic rating of 86. The 14-week show, fronted by model Heidi Klum, saw designers compete to have their work selected for the catwalk in New York Fashion Week.

Most Emmy Awards won by an individual

Producer Sheila Nevins (USA), President of Documentary and Family Programming for HBO and Cinemax, has won 25 Primetime Emmy Awards. Most recently, she took home two statuettes in 2013: Outstanding Documentary or Nonfiction Special for *Manhunt* (2013) and Exceptional Merit in Documentary Filmmaking for *Mea Maxima Culpa: Silence in the House of God* (2012).

Camera operator Hector Ramirez (USA) has been nominated for an Emmy Award

Highest annual earnings for a TV actress (current)

Modern Family star Sofía Vergara (COL) celebrates her second year as the best-paid actress on TV, with earnings estimated at $30 m by Forbes. This makes her the **highest paid actor in absolute terms**—earning more than her male counterpart, Ashton Kutcher (see left).

71 times in his 40-year career, the **most Emmy Award nominations received by an individual**. His first nod came in 1978 for *CBS: On the Air*. As of the 2013 ceremony, he had won 17 awards.

The **most nominations for a game-show producer** is 37 for Harry Friedman (USA), Executive Producer of *Wheel of Fortune* and *Jeopardy!*

Most BAFTA Children's Awards won by a TV series

The BBC's educational sketch series *Horrible Histories* (UK) is the first program to win four successive BAFTAs at the Children's Awards (2010–13). Commissioned by CBBC and produced by Richard Bradley of Lion TV, it is based on Terry Deary's award-winning books.

LONGEST-RUNNING TV SERIES BY CATEGORY

Category		
Documentary series: *Meet the Press* (NBC, USA), Nov 6, 1947–present	66 years 119 days	
Sports program: *Hockey Night in Canada* (CBC, CAN), Oct 11, 1952–present	61 years 145 days	
Children's magazine program: *Blue Peter* (BBC, UK), Oct 16, 1958–present	55 years 140 days	
Cooking show: *Hasta La Cocina* (Canal 4, MEX), Dec 1, 1960–present	53 years 94 days	
Soap opera: *Coronation Street* (ITV, UK), Dec 9, 1960–present	53 years 86 days	
Quiz show: *It's Academic* (NBC4, USA), Oct 7, 1961–present	52 years 149 days	
Variety show: *Sábado Gigante* (Univision Television Network, CHL/USA), Aug 8, 1962–present	51 years 209 days	
Educational show: *Teleclub* (Canal 13, CRI), Feb 8, 1963–present	51 years 25 days	
Animated series: *Sazae-san* (Fuji Television Network, JPN), Oct 5, 1969–present	44 years 151 days	
Medical drama: *Casualty* (BBC, UK), Sep 6, 1986–present	27 years 180 days	

1945 | 1950 | 1955 | 1960 | 1965 | 1970 | 1975 | 1980 | 1985 | 1990 | 1995 | 2000 | 2005 | 2010

 "D'oh!"

Longest running sitcom (episodes): *The Simpsons* (FOX, USA), 546 episodes, Dec 17, 1989–Mar 30, 2014

Most guest stars in a TV series: *The Simpsons*, 671 guest stars, Dec 17, 1989–Mar 30, 2014

Most Emmy Awards won by an animated TV series: *The Simpsons*, 29 awards, 1990–2013

○ ○ ○

Small-screen millionaires

In 1954, US comedian Jackie Gleason signed the most lucrative TV contract up to that date: $65,000 per episode for CBS's *The Honeymooners*, a half-hour, once-weekly TV show. Even though this is worth a cool $555,000 in today's money, it still doesn't beat Ashton Kutcher (USA), currently the **highest-paid TV actor per episode**, who picks up $750,000 for each installment of *Two and a Half Men*.

⌖ Video gamers

According to the ESA, **58% of Americans** play video games

Longest marathon on a dance video game
Carrie Swidecki (USA) danced herself into the record books with a body-pumping 49-hr 3-min 22-sec session on *Just Dance 4* (Ubisoft, 2012) at Otto's Video Games & More! in Bakersfield, California, USA, between Jun 15 and 17, 2013.

Longest NHL video game marathon
Hockey-mad Canadians James Evans (left) and Bruce Ashton (right) racked up a thumb-numbing 24-hr 2-min game of *NHL 10* (EA, 2009) in Orillia, Ontario, Canada, from Jul 30 to 31, 2011. Bruce's Winnipeg Jets fantasy team won the 45-game series against James and his Detroit Red Wings by a score of 32–13.

Youngest pro gamer
Born on May 6, 1998, "Lil Poison," aka Victor De Leon III (USA), picked up a Dreamcast Controller at the age of just two to play *NBA 2K* (Sega). In 2005, at seven, he signed an exclusive deal with the organizers of Major League Gaming.

Largest competitive *Pokémon* gaming family
Pokémon's family-friendly charm is amply affirmed by the five-strong Arnold family from Frankfort, Illinois, USA, who take part in official *Pokémon* video game world championships. Pictured from left to right are Ryan, mom Linda, Ryan's twin David, dad Glenn, and youngest child Grace.

Most international *Street Fighter* competition wins
Ryan Hart (UK) won more than 450 *Street Fighter* events from 1998 to 2011. On Mar 27, 2010, he also set the record for the **longest winning streak on *Street Fighter IV*** with 169 unbeaten matches at GAME in Hull, UK. Hart is pictured here with "Kayane," aka Marie-Laure Norindr (FRA)—the **first woman to win a pro-*Street Fighter* event**.

Arts & media

Highest score at Level 1-1 of "Poached Eggs" on *Angry Birds* for Chrome

Stephen Kish (UK) notched up 37,510 points at this level on *Angry Birds* for Chrome (Rovio, 2011) in East Sussex, UK, on Aug 23, 2011.

On the same day, he also ran up the **highest score on World's Biggest PAC-Man** (Soap Creative, 2011), with 5,555,552 points.

Fastest completion of *Batman: Arkham City*

On May 27, 2012, Sean "DarthKnight" Grayson (USA) flew through *Batman: Arkham City* in just 2 hr 3 min 19 sec. The game settings were single-segment (played without stopping) and "normal" difficulty (including Catwoman DLC story-driven episodes).

FACT

The Joker is voiced in the game by Mark Hamill, who played Luke Skywalker in the original *Star Wars* trilogy.

Fastest completion of *Super Mario Kart* Circuit 1

Speedy Sami Çetin (UK) took the checkered flag for the fastest completion of the iconic Circuit 1 on the first game in the series, *Super Mario Kart* (Nintendo, 1992). Sami holds the record on both the PAL and NTSC versions of the game, with times of 58.34 sec and 56.45 sec respectively.

FACT

Sami's niece Leyla Hasso (UK) is also an *SMK* star, having held 30 time-trial records.

Highest score on *Guitar Hero III* (female)

On Sep 30, 2010, at her home in San Francisco, California, USA, Annie Leung achieved a record score of 789,349—the highest by a female gamer—playing the DragonForce track "Through the Fire and Flames" on *Guitar Hero III: Legends of Rock* (Neversoft, 2007).

Largest joy pad

Officially verified in Aug 2011 as the largest console game pad, this fully functional NES pad measures 12 ft x 5 ft 3 in x 1 ft 8 in (3.66 x 1.59 x 0.51 m). Its main creator is engineering student Ben Allen (right), who was helped by Stephen van't Hof and Michel Verhulst, all students at Delft University of Technology in the Netherlands at the time.

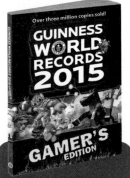

Guinness World Records Gamer's Edition

All these gamers were photographed for our record book dedicated to video gaming. Look out for *Gamer's Edition 2015*—packed with new gaming achievements and coming soon!

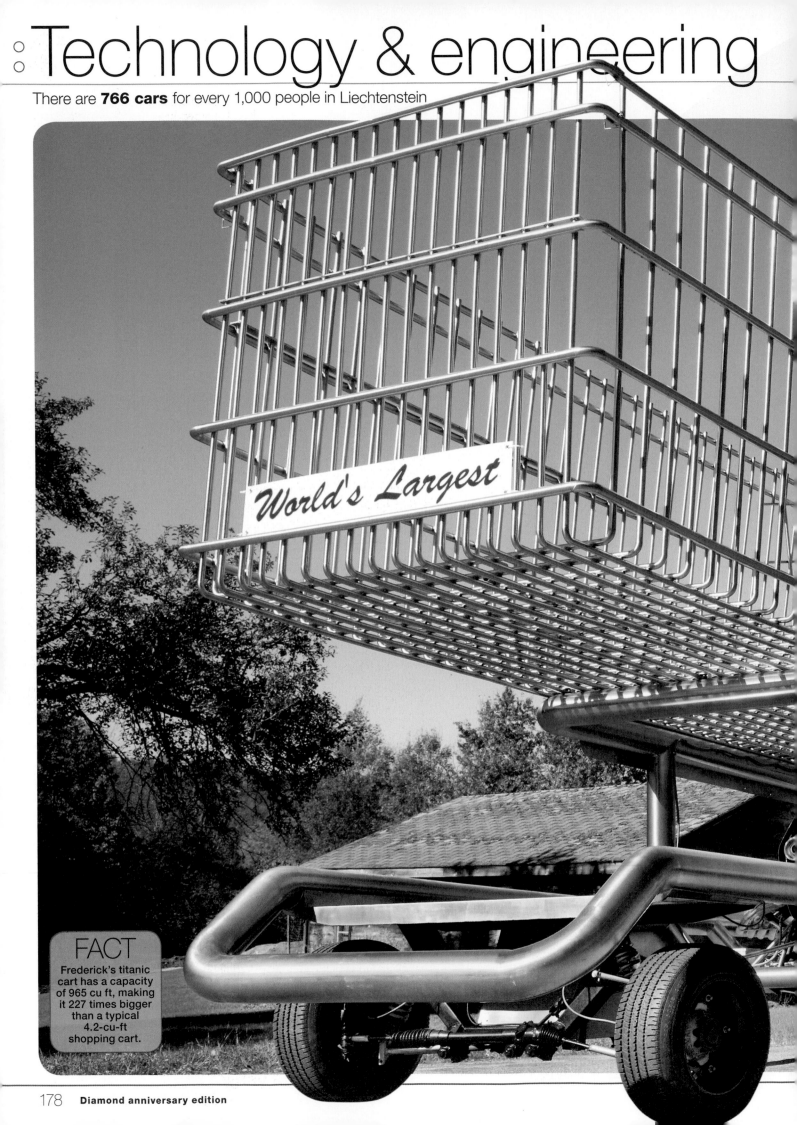

Technology & engineering

There are **766 cars** for every 1,000 people in Liechtenstein

World's Largest

FACT
Frederick's titanic cart has a capacity of 965 cu ft, making it 227 times bigger than a typical 4.2-cu-ft shopping cart.

Largest motorized shopping cart

Powered by a 7,439-cc engine, this mammoth cart measures 27 ft (8.23 m) long, 15 ft (4.57 m) tall, and 8 ft (2.43 m) wide and incorporates 7,200 lb (3,265 kg) of stainless steel. Built by Frederick Reifsteck (USA), it was displayed in South Wales, New York, USA, on Apr 20, 2012.

However, it's not the **largest shopping cart** overall. That honor goes to a 31-ft 5-in-long (9.6-m), 44-ft 7-in-tall (13.6-m), 27-ft-wide (8.23-m) behemoth created by Migros Ticaret A.Ş. (TUR) in Istanbul, Turkey, and unveiled on Jun 14, 2012.

...about the satellite strawberry

1979 First true laptop is the GRiD Compass, designed by William Moggridge (UK) for GRiD Systems (USA); boasts 512 K of RAM

1981 Oldest archived Usenet post, written by Mark Horton (USA), describes how the bulletin board forerunner should be run; unlike forums, Usenet content is sent between servers as news feeds

1972 First all-in-one desktop computer is the HP 9830, launched by Hewlett-Packard

1962 First active direct relay communications satellite is *Telstar 1*, launched on Jul 10; transmits intercontinental TV, phone, and telegram signals

1955/56 First transatlantic telephone call becomes possible after TAT-1 cable is laid between Gallanach Bay in Scotland, UK, and Clarenville, Canada, in 1955; public phone service starts on Sep 25, 1956

1963 First touch-tone telephone used at Bell Labs (USA) on Nov 18, replacing "pulse" dialing

1973 First cellular phone invented by Motorola's Martin Cooper (USA), who first uses it to call his rival at Bell Labs, Joel Engel

1981 First IBM Personal Computer (model 5150) launches, operating with Microsoft's MS-DOS; becomes the first "true" home PC

1955 | 1965 | 1975 | 1985

1974 First Voice over Internet Protocol (VoIP) carried out in Aug 1974, using Network Voice Protocol (NVP) over the ARPANET; enables multiple computers to "talk" to each other over a single wire connection

1957 First artificial satellite, *Sputnik 1*, put in orbit from Kazakhstan on Oct 4; transmits signals for three weeks to Soviet scientists and radio enthusiasts

1982 First digital emoticons entered by Scott Fahlman (USA) on a bulletin board to signify emotion and avoid misunderstandings in e-mails: :-) and :-(

1964 First fax machine or Long Distance Xerography (LDX) is launched by Xerox

1984 First successful PC using a graphical user interface (GUI) is the Apple Macintosh; Microsoft's DOS interface is text-only

1969 First remote computer connection made from the University of California, USA, to Stanford Research Institute

1976 First public fiber-optic cable network installed in Hastings, UK, by Rediffusion (UK), leading to faster and farther telecommunications

1958 First monolithic integrated circuit (microchip) patented by Jack Kilby (USA, pictured). He and Robert Noyce (USA) etch transistors and connections onto silicon, key to modern telecoms

1988 First ISDN (Integrated Services Digital Network) standard defined by the International Telecommunication Union to allow digital transmission over copper telephone wires

FACT

It was Ray Tomlinson, sender of the first e-mail (see right), who decided to use the @ symbol to separate the recipient's name and location.

1971 First e-mail sent is the somewhat unimaginative "QWERTYUIOP" by Ray Tomlinson (USA), who programs a system to exchange messages between computers in the same office (above) linked through the US Department of Defense's ARPANET

1977 *Voyager 1* launches; in 2014, it is still sending back data, from 11.8 billion mi away—the **longest communications distance**

1987 First MMORPG (multiplayer online video game) with graphics, *Air Warrior*, is released by Kesmai on the GEnie (USA) service

2006 **First tweet** sent by Twitter founder Jack Dorsey (USA, above) at 9:50 p.m. PST on Mar 21, 2006: "just setting up my twittr"

1990 **First hypertext browser** launched by Tim Berners-Lee (UK, above) and released on the Internet as the World Wide Web in 1991

2007 **First land-base cell phone call from the summit of Mount Everest** is made, at 29,028 ft, by Rod Baber (UK) on a Motorola MOTO Z8 satellite phone

1991 **First e-mail sent from space** by Shannon Lucid (inset) and James C. Adamson (both USA) on an Apple Macintosh Portable on the Space Shuttle

2007 **Best-selling smartphone** is the original Apple iPhone; in its first month on sale, 2.31 million units were sold

1993 **First Internet radio show**, "Geek of the Week," produced by Internet Talk Radio (USA)

2012 First neutrino message

On Mar 13, 2012, it was announced that scientists working at Fermilab in Batavia, Illinois, USA, had used a beam of neutrinos to send a message to a detector for the very first time. The word "neutrino" was sent across 1.6 mi—262 yd of which was solid rock—at a data rate of 0.1 bits per sec. Subatomic neutrinos pass through matter easily, because they rarely interact with it, but they require huge equipment to be detected so are unlikely to replace e-mail any time soon.

2011 **Highest-capacity communications satellite**, with a throughput of 134 gigabits per sec, is *ViaSat-1* in geostationary orbit above North America

2014 Facebook buys the instant messaging service WhatsApp for $19 bn—**the largest acquisition of a venture-backed company**

2012 **Fastest Internet connection** reaches 200 Gbit per sec at The Gathering IT event in Norway, meaning users can download a BluRay movie in 2 sec

1995

2005

2015

2008 **First online legal summons** served by lawyers Mark MacCormack and Jason Oliver (both AUS) on Facebook

1996 **First public GPS network** introduced, although already used by the US government since the 1980s

2009 **First video phone watch** is LG's GD910 Watch Phone, with color screen, voice recognition, and video-call capability

2012 **Largest e-mail service provider** becomes Google's Gmail, with 425 million users, surpassing previous record holders Yahoo! Mail and Microsoft Hotmail

2000 **Longest submarine fiber-optic cable**, the Sea-Me-We 3. It is 24,233 mi long and connects users in Europe, Australia, and Japan

2002 Scientists at Essex University, UK, transmit data at a rate of 1.02 terabits per sec (equivalent to 15.9 million phone calls), becoming the **first fiber transmission system to exceed 1 terabit per sec**

2009 **First 3D broadcast on the Internet** is a 20-min set by rock band Keane (UK) from Abbey Road Studios in London, UK

2012 **First Google+ Hangout in space** conducted with Akihiko Hoshide (JPN) of the Japan Aerospace Exploration Agency (JAXA) onboard the *International Space Station*

2010 **Fastest-selling consumer electronics device** is the iPad (pictured with Apple's Steve Jobs), 3 million of which are sold in the first 80 days of its launch; the iPad 2, launched in Mar 2011, sells at a rate of 311,666 per day

Do not print the Internet...

In May 2013, the TechHive Web site calculated that if you wanted to print out the entirety of the Internet, you would need 4.73 billion sheets of paper—creating a stack 305.7 mi high. If you factored in just one year of e-mails, the stack of paper would grow to nearly 3.4 million mi tall!

2005 Facebook—originally known as thefacebook—launches worldwide to become the **largest social network**, with 1.19 billion monthly active users by late 2013

Roller coasters

There are **3,360 roller coasters** in the world: 3,186 steel and 174 wood

FACT
When looping the loop, acceleration is stronger than gravity at the top, keeping you in your seat.

Largest roller coaster loop

Full Throttle at Six Flags Magic Mountain in Valencia, California, USA, has the largest loop, at 127 ft 1 in (38.75 m). Its name doesn't lie. Riders accelerate into the record-breaking loop at a fearsome 70 mph (110 km/h) and are turned upside down twice in less than a minute.

Most roller coasters in one country

The nation with the greatest number of coasters of any kind is China, which has 824. Next up is the USA with 653 and then Japan with 212.

Most roller coasters in one theme park

As of Jan 20, 2014, Six Flags Magic Mountain in Valencia, California, USA, has 18 operating roller coasters. The theme park opened on May 29, 1971.

Most roller coasters ridden in 24 hours

The greatest number of different roller coasters

Highest thrill ride

The aptly named *Sky Drop* sits at the top of the 1,591-ft (485-m) mast of the Canton Tower in Guangzhou, Guangdong, China. Visitors are dropped 101 ft 8 in (31 m) back to the top deck at 48 ft/s (16 m/s).

ridden in one 24-hour period is 74. On Aug 9, 2001, Philip A. Guarno, Adam Spivak, John R. Kirkwood, and Aaron Monroe Rye (all USA) rode cars in 10 parks in four US states, using helicopters to travel between them.

Most naked people on a theme park ride

On Aug 8, 2010, 102 coaster fans bared all on the *Green Scream* roller coaster at Adventure Island in Southend-on-Sea, UK.

Most track inversions on a roller coaster

The Smiler at Alton Towers Resort in Staffordshire, UK, inverts its riders 14 times. The (possibly misleadingly named) ride also includes optical illusions, blinding lights, and near misses as it reaches speeds of 52.82 mph (85 km/h) through drops of up to 98 ft (30 m).

Most costumed riders on a theme park ride

Dorney Park & Wildwater Kingdom in Allentown, Pennsylvania, USA, saw 330 costumed riders—all dressed as zombies—enjoy the *Steel Force* roller coaster on Aug 18, 2011.

Longest marathon on a roller coaster

Richard Rodriguez (USA) rode the *Pepsi Max Big One* and *Big Dipper* roller coasters at the Pleasure

Steepest steel roller coaster

The *Takabisha* ride at Fujikyu (aka Fuji-Q) Highland amusement park, Fujiyoshida City, Japan, stands 141 ft (43 m) at its highest. Its steepest drop—at a 121-degree angle down an 11-ft 2-in (3.4-m) stretch—takes a mere 0.38 sec.

THE FORCE IS WITH YOU: WHAT A ROLLER COASTER DOES TO YOUR BODY

In 2013, the *Washington Post* provided a fascinating step-by-step guide to what happens to your body during a roller coaster ride.

1: A linear G-force (G for gravity) launch of 0–120 mph in under 5 sec pushes riders back, and fear and adrenaline kick in.

2: The drop makes riders feel extra-heavy—positive G-force, anything up to 5G, briefly.

3: Upside-down riders stay in their seats through centripetal force exerted over the course of the loop. Riders may feel queasy, though, as gravity isn't keeping their lunch where it should be.

4: Just the right amount of negative G-force makes your insides float momentarily (too much would make your eyeballs explode).

5: Bumpy corners make you feel the lateral G-force that—when uncontrolled, such as in car crashes—can result in whiplash injuries.

Largest pleasure beach

Stretching 27 mi along the Atlantic Ocean is Virginia Beach in Virginia, USA, which offers 147 hotels and 2,323 campsites. Back in 1955, the record was held by Coney Island in New York, USA. "As well as its five-mile beach, it features more than 350 business and amusement places ... An estimated 50 million visit Coney Island and each spends about $1.25."

Source: "Roller coasters: feeling loopy," washingtonpost.com, Jul 1, 2013

Biggest drop on a wooden roller coaster

El Toro at Six Flags Great Adventure near Jackson, New Jersey, USA, is 188 ft (57.3 m) tall and features a drop of 176 ft (54 m). As if that weren't enough, this heart-stopping plunge is tilted at a 76-degree angle and is taken at 70 mph (110 km/h).

built at Lakemont Park in Altoona, Pennsylvania, USA, in 1902. It closed, seemingly for good, in 1985, but funds were raised for its restoration and it reopened in 1999.

Most expensive roller coaster

Expedition Everest at Walt Disney World Resort in Florida, USA, opened in 2006 at a cost of $100 m. The concept is a train journey through the Himalayas via Forbidden Mountain, wherein lies a huge Yeti: a 22-ft-tall (6.7-m) audio-animatronic beast covered in around 1,000 sq ft (93 m²) of fur.

Steepest wooden roller coaster

Outlaw Run at Silver Dollar City in Branson, Missouri, USA, has a drop at an 81-degree angle. The coaster—which can achieve a reported speed of 68 mph (109 km/h)—has been open since Mar 15, 2013 and is estimated to have cost more than $10 m to build.

Beach in Blackpool, UK, for 405 hr 40 min from Jul 27 to Aug 13, 2007.

Fastest accelerating roller-coaster

Dodonpa, the 170-ft 7-in-tall (52-m) steel roller coaster at Fuji-Q Highland in Fujiyoshida, Yamanashi Prefecture, Japan, accelerates its eight riders from 0 to 106.9 mph (172.03 km/h) in 1.8 sec.

Oldest roller coaster operating continuously

The Scenic Railway, a traditional wooden coaster at Luna Park in St. Kilda, Victoria, Australia, opened on Dec 13, 1912 and has been running ever since.

Oldest roller coaster fully restored

Leap-the-Dips, another old wooden ride, was

Fastest roller coaster

After going from 0–62 mph (100 km/h) in 2 sec, the steel *Formula Rossa* at Ferrari World Abu Dhabi, in the UAE, can accelerate to 149 mph (240 km/h) and move 170 ft (52 m) upward—higher than the Statue of Liberty—in as little as 4.9 sec.

Biggest roller coaster drop

Kingda Ka at Six Flags Great Adventure near Jackson, New Jersey, USA, includes a drop of 418 ft (127.4 m) and sees riders reach 128 mph (206 km/h) just seconds after launch. *Kingda Ka* is no ordinary ride —at 456 ft (139 m), it's the world's **tallest roller coaster**.

LONGEST ...

Roller coaster

Don't hold your breath on *Steel Dragon 2000* at Nagashima Spa Land in Kuwana, Mie, Japan—it's 1.54 mi (2.48 km) long.

Flying roller coaster

Six Flags Magic Mountain in Valencia, California, USA, has the longest flying coaster, *Tatsu*, measuring 0.68 mi (1.09 km), as well as the **longest stand-up coaster**, *The Riddler's Revenge*, which is 0.82 mi (1.33 km) long.

Floorless roller coaster

The Dominator at Kings Dominion in Doswell, Virginia, USA, continues for 0.79 mi (1.28 km).

Wooden roller coaster

The 1.40-mi (2.28-km) *Beast*, at Kings Island in Ohio, USA, lasts for 3 min 40 sec.

Track records: coasters identified

In addition to the typical "sit down" coaster (which you ride above the track in a seated position), look out for:

Flying: riders are strapped parallel to the track, as if flying (top left: *Tatsu*, Six Flags, Valencia, California, USA).

Fourth dimension: riders sit either side of the track, allowing seats to rotate (bottom left: *Eejanaika*, Fuji-Q, Yamanashi, Japan).

Floorless: riders are seated above the track but with their legs dangling (top right: *Griffon*, Busch Gardens, Williamsburg, Virginia, USA).

Inverted: seats are suspended under the track (bottom right: *Wicked Twister*, Cedar Point, Ohio, USA).

i Steel versus wood

The first roller coasters were made out of wood, with tubular-steel coasters appearing in the 1950s. Steel coasters are stronger and more flexible than wooden ones, so can include more complex twists and turns, require fewer supports, and give a smoother ride. Wooden roller coasters sway more than steel versions and generally give a bumpier ride—although for many people this simply adds to the thrill of the experience.

Bridges & tunnels

The bridge that inspired Winnie the Pooh's **Pooh sticks** cost $47,280 to renovate

Largest ferris wheel bridge

The Tianjin Eye on the Yongle Bridge is 394 ft (120 m) high. Opened on Apr 5, 2009 in Tianjin, China, the wheel bisects the bridge and road itself. The bridge has two layers: the upper for six lanes of traffic and the lower for pedestrians and the entrance to the Eye.

Most bridges in a city

Hamburg in Germany has between 2,300 and 2,500 bridges—more than Venice, Amsterdam, and London combined. The oldest is Zollenbrücke (1663). A more accurate figure is hard to find, partly because bridges are added and destroyed all the time and partly because sources disagree on how big a river, stream, or channel has to be to qualify for needing a bridge.

First Leonardo da Vinci bridge to be built

Italy's master artist and inventor Leonardo da Vinci designed the Golden Horn bridge in 1502 to cross the Bosphorus in Istanbul, Turkey. It would have been the longest bridge in the world, but Ottoman Empire ruler Sultan Bayezid II believed the bridge wouldn't work and it was not until 2001 that the design was realized. It was finally built as a footbridge, measuring 328 ft (100 m) long and 26 ft 3 in (8 m) wide, over the E18 highway in Ås, Norway. It was created by artist Vebjørn Sand (NOR) with Norway's National Roads Authority.

Highest sky bridge

A double-decker bridge connects the Petronas Twin Towers in Kuala Lumpur, Malaysia, at the 41st and 42nd floors. (The buildings are distinct, instead of one structure as with other contenders.) The bridge is 558 ft (170 m) above the ground, 190 ft (58 m) long, and weighs 1.65 million lb (750 metric tons).

Largest double helix bridge

Taking inspiration from the structure of DNA, the Helix Bridge in Singapore was designed by Cox Architecture and Architects 61. If the steel that created its complex tubular truss was to be stretched out, it would measure 1.4 mi (2.25 km)—but the bridge still uses five times less steel than its regular box girder equivalent.

Largest spiral bridge access

Traffic approaches the Nanpu Bridge over the Huangpu River in Shanghai, China, via a sweeping swirl of an elevated road section that minimizes the steepness of the gradient. The final section is 590 ft (180 m) in diameter and 4.66 mi (7.5 km) long, and cars complete two full rotations on the way up. The road, opened in 1991, was designed by the Shanghai Municipal Engineering Design Institute and Tongji Architectural Design and Research Institute.

Longest canal bridge

The Mittellandkanal and Elbe-Havel canals in Germany are joined by the Magdeburg Water Bridge over the Elbe river. The bridge is 3,012 ft (918 m) long and was opened on Oct 10, 2003. The 142-ft-wide (43-m) structure contains 52.9 million lb (24,000 metric tons) of steel and carries ships of up to 2.9 million lb (1,350 metric tons).

Longest bridge over water (continuous)

The Lake Pontchartrain Causeway joins Mandeville and Metairie in Louisiana, USA. It is 23.87 mi (38.42 km) long and was completed in 1969. It runs alongside a slightly shorter bridge that was opened in 1956—each has two lanes for traffic.

FACT
The Causeway withstood the effects of Hurricane Katrina in 2005, when nearby bridges were destroyed.

RECORD BREAKING BRIDGES AND TUNNELS

Longest bridge: 102.4 mi
Danyang–Kunshan Grand Bridge, Beijing–Shanghai High-Speed Railway, China

Longest road bridge: 33.5 mi
Bang Na Expressway, Bang Na–Bang Pakong Highway, Thailand

Longest bridge over water (aggregate): 26.4 mi
Qingdao Haiwan road bridge, Jiaozhou Bay, Shandong, China

Longest *Minecraft* tunnel: 6.2 mi
Eric McCowan's (USA) tunnel in the *Minecraft* video game covered 10,001 blocks, equating to 6.2 mi

Longest rail tunnel: 35.4 mi
Gotthard Rail Tunnel, Switzerland

Longest road tunnel: 15.2 mi
Lærdal Tunnel, Aurland–Lærdal, Norway

Longest tunnel

The 1955 *Guinness Book of Records* suggested that the **longest road tunnel** was the 2.8-mi-long Birkenhead (aka Queensway or Mersey) Tunnel joining Liverpool and Birkenhead in Merseyside, UK. It was later determined that between 1948 and 1964 the record was, in fact, held by the Vielha Tunnel in Catalonia, Spain, at 3.24 mi. (The Birkenhead Tunnel, however, was the **longest underwater tunnel** as of 1955.)

Longest multicolor light tunnel

The Bund Sightseeing Tunnel connects East Nanjing Road and Pudong in Shanghai, China: a distance of 2,121 ft (646 m). Tourists ride on driverless trains through the tunnel, illuminated with different colored lights and accompanied by sound effects.

Longest self-anchored suspension span bridge
While a suspension bridge is anchored in the ground, a self-anchored bridge is secured to the road deck ends. The latter form was chosen to replace the eastern span of the San Francisco–Oakland Bay Bridge, USA, which centers on Yerba Buena Island. The span is 2,047 ft (624 m) long, supported from a 525-ft-high (160-m) tower.

Largest system of military infiltration tunnels
The tunnels of Cu Chi in Ho Chi Minh City, Vietnam, became a key part of the Viet Cong insurgency fight against a South Vietnamese government backed by the USA in the 1960s. At their peak, the claustrophobic, snake-and-spider-infested tunnels stretched for 150 mi (250 km), an extent of which has been preserved to be explored by tourists.

First tunnel under a navigable waterway
The Thames Tunnel was 1,300 ft (365 m) long and completed in 1843 by engineer Sir Marc Brunel (FRA) to connect Rotherhithe and Wapping in London, UK. On the opening day, 50,000 people paid a penny each to wander through the attraction and within 10 weeks one million had visited it, although it was never used for traffic. It is today part of the London rail network. The tunnel used the **first tunneling shield**, also developed by Brunel, to act as a temporary support structure. The basic idea is still used to allow workers to install permanent support systems in unstable conditions.

Most expensive rail tunnel
The rail link underneath the English Channel between the UK and France was opened in 1994 at a total cost of around £12 bn ($20 bn), including train stock. The link consists of two 31-mi (50-km) rail tunnels, each 25 ft (7.6 m) in diameter, and one 16-ft-diameter (4.8-m) service tunnel that runs between them.

First tilting bridge

The Millennium or "Winking" Bridge was opened on Jun 28, 2001 over the River Tyne in Newcastle upon Tyne, UK. The bridge rotates instead of lifting up, turning on pivots on both sides of the river. Its nickname comes from the way it mimics a (very slow) blink of an eye when opening to allow for boats to pass underneath.

First curling bridge

Instead of opening up rigidly, the Rolling Bridge curls up its eight segments, like a scorpion's tail, to let boats pass. Thomas Heatherwick (UK) designed the pedestrian bridge and it was built in 2004 in London's Paddington Basin, UK.

Longest bridge-supported airport runway

A runway extension to accommodate larger aircraft at Madeira Airport was built partly over the sea. A bridge supporting this section is 3,346 ft (1,020 m) long and 591 ft (180 m) wide, and it sits on 180 pillars. It cost 520 m euros ($707.76 m) to build and was opened in Dec 2011.

Changing channels: bridge tunnels

The **longest bridge tunnel** is the Chesapeake Bay Bridge Tunnel, which was opened to traffic on Apr 15, 1964, extending 17.6 mi from the Eastern Shore region of the Virginia Peninsula to Virginia Beach, Virginia, USA. Bridges on each side give way to a tunnel, allowing ships access from the Atlantic along the Thimble Shoals and Chesapeake shipping channels. The longest bridge section is Trestle C at 4.56 mi and the longest tunnel is the Thimble Shoal Channel Tunnel at 1.08 mi.

FACT

The Channel Tunnel between England and France was first proposed in 1802 by French engineer Albert Mathieu-Favier. It was finally completed in 1994.

Tunnel vision

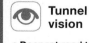

- **Deepest road tunnel:** Eiksund road tunnel, Norway, 941 ft below sea level
- **Most expensive road tunnel:** Central Artery/Tunnel Project, Boston, USA, $14.6 bn
- **Longest sewage tunnel:** Chicago TARP (Tunnels and Reservoir Plan), currently 109 mi (extending to 131 mi when completed in 2029)

Cars

Fastest vehicle drift

Regular drivers might react with panic when taking a turn so fast that their back wheels swing out and their car slides into an uncontrolled drift. For others, it's a skill and a sport. Jakub Przygoński (POL) drifted at a speed of 135.44 mph (217.97 km/h) at Biała Podlaska Airport near Warsaw, Poland, on Sep 3, 2013.

Largest producer of vehicles

Toyota (JPN) ended General Motors' 77-year winning streak as the biggest maker of cars in 2008, and the two companies have traded places twice since. In 2013, Toyota sold 9.98 million vehicles across all its divisions, again ahead of General Motors (9.71 million) and just short of 10 million units—a figure as yet never reached by a manufacturer in a single year.

Best-selling two-seater sports car

The Mazda MX-5 (known as the Miata in North America) has held the record for best-selling two-seater since 1999. By the first half of 2014, it had sold over 940,000 units.

First folding car

An electric car with a chassis that folds itself up, the Hiriko Fold shrinks from a length of 8 ft 7 in (2.63 m) to 6 ft 9 in (2.07 m). Three Hirikos can park in the same space as one four-door sedan. The two-seater car was invented by the Massachusetts Institute of Technology (USA) and developed by Denokinn (ESP), but as of Apr 2014 this model is yet to be launched commercially.

First hydrogen-powered production car

Hydrogen-powered cars are good for the environment in that they create no carbon emissions once they are on the move. The Honda FCX, introduced in 2002, was the first hydrogen-powered production car. Although only a handful are currently on the road, manufacturers such as Toyota and Honda

Cheapest consumer car

The 1922 Briggs & Stratton Flyer, known as the "Red Bug" for its paint job and small size, was built by Briggs & Stratton of Wisconsin, USA, and listed at $125–150 (today's price would be $1,600–1,920). Following close behind is the Nano car, made by Tata Motors of India and launched in 2009 at a cost of 100,000 rupees ($1,900).

Most expensive car commercially available

Prices for cars in Bugatti's six-part "Legends" series range from 2.09 m euros ($2.84 m) for the "Meo Costantini" to 2.35 m euros ($3.2 m) for the "Ettore Bugatti", the final edition to be unveiled. The Legends series—based on the Veyron 16.4 Grand Sport Vitesse—is limited to just three cars per edition. Prices exclude tax and transportation.

are planning to have more affordable versions available by 2016.

Highest vehicle mileage

On Sep 18, 2013, Irvin Gordon (USA) clocked up his three-millionth mile (4.28 million km) in the 1966 Volvo P1800S that he had driven continuously for 48 years. By May 1, 2014, the retired science teacher had driven 3,039,122 mi (4.89 million km). Irv now has a brand-new XC60R AWD, and plans to "give my 1800 a bit of a break."

TOP 10 LARGEST PARADES OF ...

1.	VWs (Beetle) 2,728
2.	Porsches 2,325
3.	Minis 1,450
4.	Ferraris 964
5.	Jaguars (E-Type, 1961 model) 767
6.	Mazdas (MX-5) 683
7.	Renaults 678
8.	Fords (Mustang) 620
9.	Volvos 570
10.	Hondas (Beat) 569

KEY:

x1 = 400 cars

Oldest "horseless carriage"

The Grenville Steam Carriage was a three-wheeled vehicle built in 1875. More than 45 years after featuring in our first edition as the oldest "horseless carriage" still in working order, it completed the 54-mi London to Brighton Veteran Car Run of 2000 in under 9 hr. In 2009, it was moved from Bristol to the Beaulieu National Motor Museum—and, as of Apr 2014, is still in working order. Robert Neville Grenville of Somerset, UK, designed the self-propelled vehicle, which holds four passengers and boasts a top speed of 14.9 mph.

Most expensive car at auction

A 1963 Ferrari 250 GTO racer was sold to a private buyer in Oct 2013 for $52 m. The competition car was formerly owned by US collector and racer Paul Pappalardo. Only 39 of the GTO cars were made, with an original retail price of around $18,000 (today's equivalent would be $135,000).

Longest fuel range (standard tank)
Marko Tomac and Ivan Cvetković (both HRV) drove a Volkswagen Passat 1.6 TDI BlueMotion for 1,581.88 mi (2,545.8 km) on one tank of fuel between Jun 27 and 30, 2011 in Croatia.

Longest journey by car in a single country
Durga Charan Mishra and Jotshna Mishra (both IND) toured continuously throughout India between Feb 23 and Apr 1, 2014, driving 11,469 mi (18,458 km). They started and finished their epic 38-day road trip in Puri in the state of Odisha, averaging 301.7 mi (485.7 km) per day.

Most expensive veteran car
Only cars built before 1905 are classed as "veteran"—qualifying for entry in the UK's annual London to Brighton Veteran Car Run. A Rolls-Royce built in 1904 was sold for £3.52 m ($7.24 m) in the UK on Dec 3, 2007. It has the serial number 20154 and is the oldest existing Rolls-Royce.

Largest production car engine (ever)

Three cars had engines of 823.8-cu-in-capacity (13.5-liter): the Pierce-Arrow 6-66 Raceabout (1912–18, above), the Peerless 6-60 of 1912–14, and a 1918 Fageol (all USA). But big is not always better. Their power output was 65.7 hp (49 kW), roughly the same as a typical modern family car with a capacity of 79.3–122 cu in (1.3–2 liters).

Tightest parallel parking of two cars
On Jan 9, 2014, in the city of Jiangyin, China, Tian Linwen and Xia Hongjun (both CHN) drove into a parking space that was just 16.5 in (42 cm) longer than their two cars combined. This was less than the length of a sheet of tabloid paper.

Fastest automated parking facility
At Volkswagen's Autostadt in Wolfsburg, Germany, cars fresh from the production line are retrieved and delivered by an automated system that travels at up to 3 ft 3 in per sec (2 m/sec). The parking process from the entrance of the Autostadt to the farthest parking box takes 1 min 44 sec.

Largest automated parking facility
The parking lot at Emirates Financial Towers in Dubai, UAE, stores up to 1,191 cars in an area of 297,150 sq ft (27,606.14 m²).

First 10-million-selling car
On Jun 4, 1924, the 10-millionth Model T rolled off the assembly line at Ford (USA). Henry Ford (USA) had done much to innovate—his Model T production line lowered costs, enabling him to sell 15 million units in total.

First 20-million-selling car
On May 15, 1981, Volkswagen's iconic Beetle—originally designed in 1938 for the Nazis as a cheap option for the German masses—hit the 20-million milestone. By the time that production ceased in 2003, around 22 million Beetles had been made.

First 30-million-selling car
In 2005, the Toyota Corolla sold its 30-millionth car, and in 2013, as reported by the manufacturer, was the **first car to sell 40 million units**, making the Corolla overall the **best-selling car**.

Largest production car engine (current)

Chrysler's (USA) 2014 SRT Viper has a 512-cu-in (8.39-liter) V10 engine. Even Bugatti's mighty Veyron has only a 488-cu-in (8-liter) engine. The Viper can produce 640 hp (477 kW) of power, 600 lb/ft (814 Nm) of torque, and accelerates from 0 to 60 mph (96.5 km/h) in 3.3 sec.

Driving seat: big producers

China was the **largest producer of cars** in 2013, making 18,085,213 of a total of 65,386,596 automobiles (excluding commercial vehicles). This contributes to 2013 being the **biggest year on record for car sales**, according to data from the International Organization of Motor Vehicle Manufacturers. Japan was in second place, with 8,189,323 sales, and Germany came in third with 5,439,904. According to industry experts WardsAuto, the number of vehicles on the road (including commercial traffic) hit 1 billion in 2010, rising from 250 million in 1970.

Most people crammed in ...

an original Fiat 500: 14 students from ESSCA business school in Paris, France, on Apr 2, 2011.

a classic model Mini Cooper: 25 people organized by Virgin Mobile in Johannesburg, South Africa, on Oct 2, 2013.

a new model Mini: 28 people organized by Dani Maynard and the David Lloyd Divas (UK) in London, UK, on Nov 15, 2012.

a Smart car: 20 people organized by Glendale College Cheerleading Team (USA) in Los Angeles, USA, on Sep 28, 2011.

Urban transport

Japan is home to **45 of the 51 busiest train stations** in the world; almost half are in Tokyo alone

Longest driverless metro network

The two lines of the driverless Dubai Metro have a combined length of 46.41 mi (74.69 km). They were constructed by the Roads & Transport Authority in Dubai, UAE, and officially inaugurated on Sep 9, 2011.

At 32.3 mi (52.1 km) in length, the Dubai Metro Red Line is the **longest driverless metro line**. The second line, Green Line, is 13.9 mi (22.5 km) long.

The **longest metro system by total length** is the Seoul Metropolitan Subway in South Korea, with 580 mi (940 km) of routes across 17 lines as of 2013.

Largest underground train depot (metro)

Singapore's Kim Chuan Depot, which opened in 2009, measures 2,624 ft (800 m) long, 524 ft (160 m) wide, and 75 ft (23 m) high, and has a volume of 1,057 million cu ft (2.9 million m³).

The depot took five years and 295 million Singapore dollars (US $209 m) to construct. It houses equipment and stabling,

First congestion program In 1975, Singapore implemented the Area Licensing Scheme (ALS). Owners of vehicles entering the Central Business District or the "Restricted Zone" had to buy a special paper licence. In 1998, the system was upgraded to the Electronic Road Pricing (ERP) program.

Busiest underground network (current) The Tokyo Metro served a ridership of 3.102 billion passengers in 2012. The underground system runs for 190 mi (310 km) altogether and serves a metropolitan area of 35 million residents. It incorporates 13 lines and 290 stations in total.

The Moscow Metro is the **busiest underground network ever**, with 3.3 billion passenger journeys in a year at its peak, although by 1998 the figure had declined to 2.55 billion. The system has been serving the Russian capital since 1935, and incorporates 3,135 coaches covering 159 stations and 132 mi (212 km) of track.

Most cycle rickshaws in one city

There are some 500,000 cycle rickshaws in Dhaka, Bangladesh (above). In this city of 15 million people, they account for nearly 40% of all trips.

As of 2012, an estimated 120,000–160,000 autorickshaws were active in Mumbai, India (inset), the **most autorickshaws in one city**. They are used by up to 85% of residents.

Longest buses

Currently trialing in Germany is the AutoTram Extra Grand (pictured), a bi-articulated (three-section) bus 100 ft 9 in (30.7 m) long that is designed to carry 256 passengers. In China, meanwhile, the Youngman JNP6250G bus is being piloted: an 82-ft-long (25-m) vehicle that will transport 300 passengers.

Neither will beat the **longest buses ever**, though: the 105-ft 7-in-long (32.2-m) articulated DAF Super CityTrain buses in the Democratic Republic of the Congo.

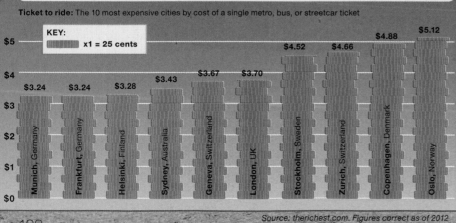

MOST EXPENSIVE PUBLIC TRANSPORT SYSTEMS

Ticket to ride: The 10 most expensive cities by cost of a single metro, bus, or streetcar ticket

KEY: ▮▮▮ x1 = 25 cents

City	Cost
Munich, Germany	$3.24
Frankfurt, Germany	$3.24
Helsinki, Finland	$3.28
Sydney, Australia	$3.43
Geneva, Switzerland	$3.67
London, UK	$3.70
Stockholm, Sweden	$4.52
Zurich, Switzerland	$4.66
Copenhagen, Denmark	$4.88
Oslo, Norway	$5.12

⚡ Tram-packed

The **largest urban streetcar network ever** was in Argentina's capital Buenos Aires. Inaugurated in 1897, by the 1960s it had 532 mi of streetcar lines, including some underground. The lines were discontinued to save money and make way for buses. Today's **most extensive streetcar system** is more than three times smaller. Located in Melbourne, Victoria, Australia, it runs "just" 155 mi, with 487 streetcars, 1,763 stops, and 30 routes.

FACT

In Japan, some metro cars are set aside for women to provide greater personal safety.

ℹ Test drive

All of London's black cab drivers have to pass "The Knowledge," to test their familiarity with 320 routes, across 25,000 streets, in the capital. The training can take four years to complete.

Source: therichest.com. Figures correct as of 2012

Largest ships by capacity

Although other ships can potentially carry more passengers, the vessels with the largest "standard" passenger loads are the Staten Island Ferry sister ships *Andrew J. Barberi* and *Samuel I. Newhouse* in New York City, USA, each of which can carry 6,000 passengers. They are 310 ft (95 m) long and 69 ft 10 in (21 m) wide, with a service speed of 16 knots (19 mph; 30 km/h).

and provides maintenance facilities for up to 70 three-car driverless trains.

Most expensive public transit commute

According to the UBS Price and Earnings Report 2012, which assessed 72 cities in 58 countries, Oslo in Norway has the most expensive transit ticket fare (based on a 10-stop bus, streetcar, or subway trip): $5.12.

The same report also noted that Zurich in Switzerland offers the **most expensive taxi ride**, at $28.93. This calculation is based on a taxi journey over a distance of 3 mi (5 km), taken during the day within the city limits.

Farthest distance by a battery-powered streetcar (one charge) in 24 hours

Stadler Pankow GmbH (DEU)

ran the battery-powered Variobahn streetcar 11.79 mi (18.98 km) on a single charge at Velten/Hennigsdorf rail-test track near Berlin, Germany, on May 25, 2011.

The **most southerly streetcar terminus** is at Brighton East in Melbourne, Victoria, Australia, on route

Largest bicycle-share program

The Hangzhou Public Bicycle program in Hangzhou, China, is the largest bicycle-sharing system. In 2013, its fleet included 69,750 bicycles, with 2,965 stations spread across the city. Users can easily access the system as stations are placed less than 0.6 mi (1 km) apart.

number 64 at the junction of Hawthorn Road and Nepean Highway.

The **longest streetcar route** is the Kusttram service; it runs along the Belgian coast from Knokke in the north to Adinkerke in the south—a distance of 42 mi (68 km).

Largest bus rapid transit (BRT) system

The TransJakarta bus rapid transit system in Jakarta, Indonesia, boasts some 120 mi (194 km) of dedicated busways. It carries more than 300,000 passengers daily on 12 "corridors."

Longest intracity streetcar route

The 501 Queen route in Toronto, Canada, is 15.2 mi (24.5 km) long, and averages 52,000 passengers daily, 24 hr a day, seven days a week. It runs from Long Branch in the west to Neville Park in the east.

Oldest railroad tunnel

British engineer Benjamin Outram (UK) built an 88-ft-long (27-m) railroad tunnel at Fritchley near Crich in Derbyshire, UK, in 1793. It remained in use until 1933. Both ends were sealed in the 1960s.

As of Jan 2014, the **oldest railroad workshop in continuous operation** is the Boston Lodge Works of the Ffestiniog Railway near Minffordd, UK. Wagon maintenance began there in 1838 with a blacksmith's shop, from which the current complex has grown.

Liverpool Road station in Manchester, UK, is the **oldest railroad station**. It opened on Sep 15, 1830 and closed on Sep 30, 1975.

Largest rail freight yard

Bailey Yard in North Platte, Nebraska, USA, is 8 mi (12.8 km) long and covers an area of 4.4 sq mi (11.5 km²). It is operated by the Union Pacific Railroad.

Metro mania: station masters

For some, going underground provides a direct route to breaking records. Chris Solarz and Matthew Ferrisi (both USA, top left) achieved the **fastest time to travel to all New York City Subway stations** (22 hr 52 min 36 sec) from Jan 22 to 23, 2010. Tim Littlechild and Chantel Shafie (both UK; Chantel seen bottom left) recorded the **fastest time to travel to all Hong Kong metro stations** (8 hr 18 min 8 sec) on Dec 30, 2013. Geoff Marshall and Anthony Smith (both UK, right) set the **fastest time to travel to all London Underground stations** (16 hr 20 min 27 sec) on Aug 16, 2013.

Premier service

First regular passenger railroad service: The Oystermouth Railway, later the Swansea and Mumbles Railway, in Swansea, UK, began on Mar 25, 1807.

First motorized taxicab service: Operated by the Daimler Motorized Cab Company in Stuttgart, Germany, in 1897. The taxi was able to travel 43 mi a day. The fleet was increased to seven vehicles just two years later.

Alternative transport

As of 2013, around 95.4% of the USA's energy needs are still met by **fossil fuels**

Highest cable car above ground

The Peak 2 Peak Gondola in Whistler, British Columbia, Canada, rises to 1,430 ft (436 m). The three-cable gondola lift runs for around 2.7 mi (4.4 km) and connects the peaks of the Whistler and Blackcomb mountains. The vertiginous ride also incorporates the **longest unsupported span between two cable-car towers**—a length of 9,921 ft (3,024 m).

Longest funicular

The Sierre to Crans-Montana funicular is 2.604 mi (4.192 km) long. It connects passengers to the ski resort of Crans-Montana from the Swiss city of Sierre and was built in 1911 as two separate funiculars. The two lines were merged and rebuilt as one system in 1997. The funicular travels at speeds of 26 ft per sec (8 m/sec) and completes the journey in 12 min.

Longest cable car beneath sea level

A 4,359-ft-long (1,328-m), 12-cabin cable car connects Elisha's Spring with the Mount of Temptation in Jericho, Palestine. The lower station is 721 ft 3 in (219.86 m) below sea level; the upper station is 164 ft 11 in (50.29 m) below sea level.

Longest cable car ever

A cable car of approximately 60 mi (96 km) in length was first opened in 1943 to transport ore from Kristenberg to Boliden in Sweden. Constructed in lieu of a road, due to the shortage of rubber and gasoline during World War II, the system was only decommissioned for ore transport as late as 1987. Still in operation today, it is now used as an 8.2-mi-long (13.2-km) tourist ride.

Longest nonstop aerial tram

Wings of Tatev, constructed in collaboration with the National Competitiveness Foundation of Armenia, is a nonstop cable-car line measuring 18,871 ft (5,752 m) long. It links the Tatev monastery and Halidzor, Armenia.

Highest ascent by a nonstop cable car

The Bà Nà Hills single-track cable car in Da Nang, Vietnam, opened on Mar 29, 2013, takes 15 min to rise 4,488 ft (1,368 m) between its start and end stations.

Steepest railroad gradient

The Katoomba Scenic Railway in the Blue Mountains of New South Wales, Australia, has a 52-degree-angle slope. The 1,017-ft-long (310-m) funicular was built in 1878, originally for mining purposes, but was converted into a tourist ride in 1945.

Longest monorail

The most extensive monorail system is 46.2 mi (74.4 km) long and forms part of the Chongqing Rail Transit. The most recent stretch of line was completed in Dec 2012. The **longest monorail line** is line 3 of the Chongqing Rail Transit system. It is 34 mi (55 km) in length.

First maglev train to enter public service

A 1,970-ft (600-m) maglev line operated between

Busiest public-transit cable car

Line K of the Metrocable system in Medellín, Colombia, is the busiest cable-car line built for public transportation, with a ridership of 6,330,713 passengers in 2012. The 1.2-mi (2-km) line, opened in 2004, was designed to connect the impoverished hillside communities to the city's metro network.

(X) For cutting-edge science, see p. 202

ECO TRANSPORT: THE FUTURE OF TRAVEL

The latest developments in public transport may mark the beginning of the end for fossil fuels:

Backpack helicopter: Motor and rotor from helicopter strapped to the back

Zeppelin: Fuel efficient and does not require a runway

SkyTran: Automated cabins, running on nonstop aerial "guideways"

Electric bicycles: Eco-friendly version of conventional bicycle

Driverless pods: Automated four-seater that runs on a guideway

Segway: Two-wheeled, electric-powered, scooterlike vehicle

Slidewalk: Moving walkway for public sidewalks; allows for faster movement and helps reduce pedestrian congestion

Maglev train: Faster, quieter, and less CO$_2$-hungry than conventional trains

(⚡) Rise of the zeppelins

The **largest airships** were the 800-ft-long, 471,500-lb German *Hindenburg* (LZ 129) and *Graf Zeppelin II* (LZ 130). Although their heyday had passed by 1940, our 1955 edition included the **longest nonrigid airship**, the US Navy anti-submarine airship ZP2N, with a capacity of 970,000 cu ft (27,400 m³) of helium. Interest in these eco-friendly giants revived with such designs as Germany's Zeppelin Luftschifftechnik and Worldwide Aeros (USA).

FACT

The first flight of a zeppelin took place on Jul 2, 1900 over Lake Constance in Germany.

(i) Aerial survey

All cable-car records on this spread refer to aerial carriages propelled by a steel cable. The term "cable car" is also sometimes used to refer to cable-drawn cars at street level.

Source: EU Infrastructure

Longest suspended monorail

Measuring 9.45 mi (15.2 km), the Chiba Urban Monorail near Tokyo, Japan, is the longest suspended monorail train system. The first 1.98-mi (3.2-km) stretch opened on Mar 20, 1979, but the line has been expanded three times since then. The monorail has 18 stations, and an average of 120 trains run on the system per day.

Birmingham International Airport and the nearby Birmingham International Interchange in West Midlands, UK, from 1984 to 1995. It was taken out of service due to the high cost of replacing worn parts and succeeded by a conventional cable-drawn shuttle system.

Fastest maglev train
A MLX01 maglev train operated by the Central Japan Railway Company and Railway Technical Research Institute attained a speed of 361 mph (581 km/h) on the Yamanashi Maglev Test Line in Yamanashi Prefecture, Japan, on Dec 2, 2003.

The **fastest maglev train in public service** links China's Shanghai International Airport and the city's financial district and reaches a speed of 267 mph (431 km/h) on each 18-mi (30-km) trip. Built by Germany's Transrapid

International, the train had its official maiden run on Dec 31, 2002.

Highest-capacity funicular
The Funicular de Montjuïc in Barcelona, Spain, can transport 16,000 people per hr (8,000 people each way). It can hold 400 people

at a time and reach a speed of 32 ft per sec (10 m/sec) or 22 mph (36 km/h).

First public electric railroad
The earliest public electric railroad opened on May 12, 1881 in Lichterfelde near Berlin, Germany. It was 1.5 mi (2.5 km) long, ran on 100-V current, and carried 26 passengers at 30 mph (48 km/h).

The Volk's Electric Railway, which runs along the seafront at Brighton, UK, between the pier and the marina, is the **oldest electric railroad in operation**. Designed

Shortest funicular

The Fisherman's Walk Cliff Railway in Bournemouth, UK, is 128 ft (39 m) long. Built in 1935 by borough engineer F. P. Dolamore, the system travels on a 5-ft 10-in-gauge (1.77-m) railway track with a 45-degree incline. It has transported more than 4 million passengers.

by Magnus Volk (UK), the railroad first opened for business on Aug 4, 1883.

Largest fleet of electric taxis
Shenzhen in China is home to a fleet of 800 "e6" model electric taxis built

by the Chinese automobile manufacturer BYD. Each taxi can travel 185 mi (300 km) on one charge. The fleet's total mileage is estimated to have now exceeded 62 million mi (100 million km).

First "duck" tour

"Ducks" are amphibious vehicles widely used in sight-seeing tours. The first ever duck tour company was established in 1946 by Mel Flath and Bob Unger (both USA) in Wisconsin Dells, Wisconsin, USA. The original company has changed ownership since then, and today operates under the name Original Wisconsin Ducks. Flath's family also owns another duck tour company, bearing the name Dells Army Ducks.

Who's driving this? Driverless cars

For several years now, Google has been testing driverless cars (below), controlled by onboard computers that also keep track of the cars' locations. A qualified driver would still be required to sit at the wheel—but only to take over in emergencies. To date, Google's autonomous automobiles have racked up more than 186,000 mi on the road without any major incidents, and the company claims that they could be safer than human drivers. Above left: Children peer inside a self-driving car at Google's HQ in California, USA. Below left: A street as interpreted by a driverless car.

Glossary

Funicular: A cable railroad, enabling travel on gradients too steep for conventional trains. The word is derived from the Latin *funiculus*, meaning "rope" or "cord."

Maglev: Abbreviation of "magnetic levitation." Maglev vehicles are propelled by magnets—supported by a magnetic field that runs around the train tracks—instead of fuel-powered wheels.

Wacky wheels

Wheels were first used for transport more than **5,500 years** ago, but not like this!

Fastest motorized shopping cart

Bringing a whole new meaning to the words "fast food," Matt McKeown (UK) reached 70.4 mph (113.2 km/h) in a shopping cart at Elvington Airfield in North Yorkshire, UK, on Aug 18, 2013.

Fastest bathroom

The *Bog Standard* consists of a motorcycle and sidecar hidden under a bathroom set comprising a Victorian-style throne toilet, bathtub, sink, and laundry bin. Created by Edd China (UK), this mobile restroom can reach a speed of 42.25 mph (68 km/h).

A past master in mobile furniture, Edd has also made the **fastest garden shed** (58 mph; 94 km/h), **bed** (69 mph; 111 km/h), and **office** (87 mph; 140 km/h).

Lowest roadworthy car

The *Mirai* car measures just 1 ft 5 in (45.2 cm) from the ground to its highest part. Students and teachers of the Automobile Engineering Course of Okayama Sanyo High School in Asakuchi, Japan, unveiled it on Nov 15, 2010. *Mirai* means "future" in Japanese.

Heaviest ridable tricycle

Wouter van den Bosch (NLD) has constructed a tricycle that's truly off the scale, weighing in at a colossal 1,650 lb (750 kg). Wouter took his heavyweight creation for a ride in Arnhem, Netherlands, in May 2010.

Smallest caravan

The QTvan is just 7 ft 10 in (2.39 m) long, 5 ft (1.53 m) high, and 2 ft 7 in (79 cm) wide. It was manufactured by the Environmental Transport Association (UK) and measured in Aylesbury, UK, on Jun 5, 2013. Below, designer Yannick Read (UK) shows off his compact creation.

Smallest roadworthy car

The ideal complement for the smallest caravan, this diminutive car measures 2 ft 1 in (63.5 cm) high, 2 ft 1.75 in (65.4 cm) wide, and 4 ft 1.75 in (1.26 m) long. It was made by Austin Coulson (USA) and measured in Carrollton, Texas, USA, on Sep 7, 2012.

Largest monster truck

Bigfoot 5 is 15 ft 6 in (4.7 m) tall with 10-ft-high (3-m) tires and weighs in at more than 38,000 lb (17 tonnes). It is one of a fleet of 17 Bigfoot trucks created by Bob Chandler (USA) and was built in 1986. Permanently parked in St. Louis, Missouri, USA, *Bigfoot 5* makes occasional exhibition appearances at local shows.

Tallest limousine car

Gary and Shirley Duval (both AUS) have made a lofty limo that measures 10 ft 11 in (3.33 m) tall. The record-breaking car has an eight-wheel independent suspension system and sits on eight monster truck tires. It has eight-wheel steering, two engines, and took a little more than 4,000 hours (166 days) to complete.

FACT

The Hornster was built to highlight the dangers cyclists face on busy roads. It's louder than a clap of thunder!

Loudest bicycle horn

Not content simply with creating the **smallest caravan** (left), the Environmental Transport Association has developed a bicycle horn capable of emitting a honk measuring 136.2 dB(A) (decibels) from a distance of 8 ft 2 in (2.5 m). *The Hornster* uses a modified freight train horn powered by a scuba-diving tank and was demonstrated by Yannick Read on Feb 13, 2013 in Weybridge, Surrey, UK.

 For wild wheel skills, flip to p. 114

Longest golf cart

From bumper to bumper, the longest golf cart stretches an impressive 31 ft 6 in (9.62 m) and was created by Mike's Golf Carts (USA). The cart was measured in Perry, Georgia, USA, on May 30, 2013.

Military hardware

On average, there are **88.8 firearms per 100 people** in the USA

First 3D-printed pistol

In 2013, Solid Concepts, based in Austin, Texas, USA, produced a 3D-printed gun using "laser-sintering"—a process that creates objects from powders, in this case metal powders. The gun is a replica of the 1911 Browning pistol and has fired 50 rounds successfully. The purpose of the project was to demonstrate that 3D metal printing provides strong, reliable, and accurate products.

ON LAND

First javelin
A study published by the journal *PLOS ONE* on Nov 13, 2013 dated the use of projectile weapons akin to javelins to more than 279,000 years ago. An examination of fossils indicated that pointed stone artifacts were used on throwing weapons. The stone-tipped weapons were found at Gademotta in Ethiopia, suggesting that eastern Africa was a source of more modern culture and biology than previously thought. The weapons ultimately allowed humans to leave Africa and out-compete Neanderthals.

First hand grenades
Grenades appeared in the Eastern Roman (Byzantine) Empire in ca. AD 741, when soldiers realized that Greek fire—a buoyant incendiary weapon—could be thrown at the enemy in stone, ceramic, or glass containers. The use of grenades spread, with evidence found in a Chinese military writing from 1044, *Wujing Zongyao* (*Compilation of Military Classics*).

IN THE AIR

First air-to-air refueling by hose
On Jun 27, 1923, at Rockwell Field in San Diego, California, USA, a successful refueling of one aircraft from another took place. An Airco DH.4B passed 75 gal (284 L) of gasoline through a hose to a craft of the same type.

Newest deployable chemical weapon destroyer

The US Defense Threat Reduction Agency commissioned a mobile unit that can destroy chemical weapons, following Syria's agreement to surrender them. The Field Deployable Hydrolysis System works by splitting chemical weapon molecules into small fragments that can then be disposed of like normal hazardous waste.

Most expensive supercarrier

The USS *Gerald R. Ford*, a 1,092-ft-long (332-m) carrier, is scheduled for service in 2016. It has capacity for 75 fighter and strike aircraft, and comes equipped with a new type of catapult—the Electromagnetic Aircraft Launch System—which can launch up to 220 air strikes a day. It cost $13 bn to build, but will save $4 bn over its lifetime compared with the current Nimitz-class carriers.

First manned missile
In 1944, during World War II, German V1 missiles were found to lack accuracy. This led the German Research Institute for Sailplane Flight to design a manned missile. The Fieseler Fi 103R-4 Reichenberg could be guided to its target by a pilot, who would bail out. The plan was abandoned, because getting out of a 400-mph (650-km/h) speeding missile was impossible without death or serious injury.

MILITARY MIGHT—GLOBAL FIRE POWER 2014

	manpower	land vehicles	aircraft	seacraft
USA	145,212,012	39,162	13,683	473
Russia	69,117,271	57,503	3,082	352
China	749,610,775	23,664	2,788	520
India	615,201,057	15,681	1,785	184
UK	29,164,233	6,935	908	66
France	28,802,096	8,672	1,203	120
Germany	36,417,842	5,124	710	82
Turkey	41,637,773	15,948	989	115
South Korea	25,609,290	13,158	1,393	166
10. Japan	53,608,446	4,611	1,595	131

KEY:
x1 = 30,000,000 manpower
x1 = 5,000 land vehicles
x1 = 1,000 aircraft
x1 = 100 seacraft

Source: globalfirepower.com

Submarine spotlight

Largest non-nuclear submarine: 396.9-ft-long World War II I-400 Japanese submarines of the Sen-Toku class (1946)

Longest-range stealth mini-submarine: Torpedo SEAL, 2013, capable of transporting two divers and equipment at 4 knots (4.5 mph) over a range of 10 nautical mi (11.5 mi)

Newest class of submarine: Iran's Fateh class, 2013, a diesel-electric submarine

FACT
The total known land area occupied by US nuclear weapons bases and facilities is 15,654 sq mi.

Glossary

SEALs: SEa, Air, and Land—the US Navy's main operations force
UAS/UAV: Unmanned Aerial System/Vehicle

Most expensive military aircraft program

By 2012, the Lockheed Martin F-35 Lightning Joint Strike Fighter had costs of $336 bn—a 52.8% increase from 2001—with some reports putting it as high as $392 bn, for the USA. This 50-year, multinational program has an estimated sustainment cost for the USA of $0.85–1.5 tr over its lifetime.

Most expensive UAV

A US General Accountability Office Report in Mar 2013 gave the Northrop Grumman Global Hawk a unit cost of $222 m, making it the most expensive UAV yet.

IN THE SEA

First sea mine

A reference to sea mines can be found in *Huolongjing*, a Chinese military manual from the early Ming dynasty (1368–1644). It describes the "Submarine Dragon King"—a wrought-iron mine weighed by stones with an explosive contained in an ox bladder, ignited via a joss stick enclosed in a goat's intestine.

First successful combat submarine

On Feb 17, 1864, during the American Civil War, the *H. L. Hunley* became the first combat submarine to sink an enemy warship when it sunk the USS *Housatonic* off Charleston in South Carolina. The 40-ft-long (12-m) *H. L. Hunley*—which sank minutes after engagement—was recovered in 2000 and, after restoration work, displayed in Jan 2013.

First self-propelled torpedo

In 1866, Robert Whitehead (UK) developed a new weapon in the shape of a self-propelled underwater torpedo, which was fired via compressed air. Whitehead's weapon could hit a target as far away as 2,100 ft (640 m) with an 18-lb (8-kg) charge of explosive, at a speed of 7 knots (8 mph; 13 km/h).

The **first ship sunk by a self-propelled torpedo** was *Intibah* in Jan 1878. Whitehead torpedoes launched from Russian torpedo boats sank the Turkish ship during the 1877–78 Russo-Turkish War.

First drone launch from a submerged combat submarine

On Dec 5, 2013, the XFC (eXperimental Fuel Cell) unmanned aerial system was launched from a submerged submarine. It can undertake video reconnaissance and intelligence missions, and relay its output to its command center.

First pilotless aircraft to cross the Pacific Ocean

On Apr 23, 2001, the Northrop Grumman RQ-4A began its flight at the Edwards Air Force Base in California, USA. The unmanned aerial vehicle (UAV) flew for 22 hr nonstop across the Pacific Ocean before landing at the Royal Australian Air Force Base in Edinburgh, Adelaide, Australia.

Largest anti-mine naval exercise

On May 13, 2013, a fleet of 34 ships, 100 divers, and 18 unmanned submarines began an anti-mine exercise in the Persian Gulf. The aim was to show how the strategically important Strait of Hormuz—a critical route for the world's oil supplies—could be kept open in the event that a hostile nation would seek to block it.

Longest-serving bomber

The Boeing B-52 jet bomber, which entered service with the US Air Force in 1954, is the longest-serving currently operational bomber aircraft. With 60 years of service already, it is scheduled to remain in use until 2044 and will receive a further $24.6 m of upgrades to increase its ability to carry smart weapons.

Mouse droppings: aerial assault

The snake population on the island of Guam in the Pacific grew to some 2–3 million following their arrival in freight from Australia and Papua New Guinea. The snakes threatened native fauna and cost the Guam Power Authority up to $4 m annually in repairs. The solution? The **largest aerial assault by paramice**. On Dec 1, 2013, 2,000 dead mice tied to miniature parachutes (left) were air-dropped onto Guam by US authorities. Each mouse contained 80 mg of the over-the-counter painkiller acetaminophen: a fatal dose for snakes.

And finally ...

- **Most common fighter aircraft (current):** US F-16 Fighting Falcon, made by US General Dynamics and Lockheed Martin: 2,281 combat aircraft (15% of global total)
- **Largest air force by number of fighter aircraft (current):** USA: 2,271 active fighters/interceptors, according to globalfirepower.com (see full table, left) ○ ○ ○

Architecture

"Skyscraper" originally referred to a triangular sail at the top of a ship's mast

Largest planetarium

The planetarium of Nagoya City Science Museum in Japan has a hemispherical dome with an internal diameter of 114 ft 10 in (35 m). The almost perfectly spherical section that houses the planetarium measures 129 ft (39.2 m) tall and is suspended 37 ft (11.4 m) above the ground.

OLDEST ...

Continuously inhabited city

Archaeologists have discovered settlements in Jericho, part of the Palestinian territories, that date back to 9000 BC. The city, located near the Jordan River in the West Bank, is today home to approximately 20,000 people. Its population in 8000 BC is thought to have numbered 2,000 to 3,000.

Minaret

The Great Mosque of Kairouan in Tunisia houses a minaret that was largely built in the ninth century and completed by AD 836. It is 103 ft 4 in (31.5 m) high and rests on a square base measuring 35 ft 1 in x 35 ft 1 in (10.7 x 10.7 m).

Surviving skatepark

The Albany Skate Track in Albany, Western Australia, was completed in Mar 1976. It consists of a 459-ft-long

Tallest art nouveau church

La Sagrada Família in Barcelona, Spain, was begun in 1882 under architect Francisco de Paula del Villar y Lozano and taken over in 1883 by Antoni Gaudí (both ESP). It is not expected to be completed until at least 2026. Currently 351 ft (107 m) high, the tallest of the 18 towers will reach 560 ft (170 m) when finished.

(140-m) concrete "snake run" with steeply banked sides, varying from 19 ft 8 in to 26 ft 2 in (6–8 m) wide. The facility cost AUS$15,000 ($18,600).

LARGEST ...

Airport passenger terminal roof

The roof of the Hajj terminal at King Abdulaziz International Airport near Jeddah, Saudi Arabia, covers 2.8 million sq ft (260,129 m²). Designed by Skidmore, Owings & Merrill, the Teflon-

Largest architectural practice (employees)

According to the "2013 World Architecture 100" survey by the UK's *Building Design* magazine, the largest firm of architects in terms of the number of employees is Gensler, with a 1,468-strong workforce on its books. Gensler's headquarters are in San Francisco, USA, but it also has 43 offices in 14 countries worldwide.

Logically enough, according to the "Top 300 Architecture Firms" list compiled by US magazine *Architectural Record*, the **largest firm of architects by revenue** is also Gensler, with earnings of $807 m in 2012.

Largest glass greenhouse

The Flower Dome greenhouse at Gardens by the Bay in Singapore covers 3.16 acres (1.28 ha) under its glass roof. Designed by architects Wilkinson Eyre, the column-free grid shell and arch shape allow for maximum sunlight and climate control. Along with the smaller Cloud Forest conservatory, it was completed in Jun 2012.

Tallest building

Developed by Emaar Properties, the 2,716-ft-tall (828-m) Burj Khalifa opened in Dubai, UAE, on Jan 4, 2010. Almost 26,000 hand-cut glass panels were used in the exterior cladding of the building, which has residential, office, and hotel use.

Dome grown: Eden Project

The Eden Project, near St. Austell in Cornwall, UK, is the **largest greenhouse**. It comprises two giant transparent domes ("biomes"), the larger of which—the humid tropics, or rain forest biome—is 180 ft tall, covers 273,295 sq ft, and has a volume of 14,681,365 cu ft. The smaller warm temperate, or Mediterranean, biome has 70,395 sq ft of floor space and a volume of 3,023,640 cu ft. Both are made of steel frames carrying hexagons and pentagons of flourine-base plastic. The site also features an unroofed outdoor biome.

coated roof modules are supported by 147-ft-high (45-m) pylons.

Basket-shape building

Completed in 1997, the seven-story headquarters of the Longaberger basket company in Ohio, USA,

Largest building shaped like a musical instrument

The Piano House in Huainan, China, is around 52 ft (16 m) tall. It was designed by students of Hefei University of Technology in 2007. Visitors enter through a "violin," then proceed via an escalator that takes them into the main, piano-shape section of the building.

resembles a giant basket and has 180,000 sq ft (16,722 m²) of floor space. With a maximum length of 208 ft (63.4 m) and a width of 142 ft (43.3 m), it is 160 times larger than Longaberger's "Medium Market Basket."

Opera house

Designed by architect Wallace K. Harrison, the Metropolitan Opera House at the Lincoln Center in New York City, USA, can accommodate an audience of 3,975, based on it having 3,800 seats and 175 standing-room places. It cost $45.7 m and was opened on Sep 16, 1966.

Television building

The China Central Television building in Beijing is 768 ft (234 m) tall, contains 54 floors, and cost 850 million euros ($1.17 bn) to construct. It was designed by architects Office for Metropolitan Architecture (NDL) with engineers

Arup (UK), and officially completed on May 16, 2012. The total floor space measures 5,091,300 sq ft (473,000 m²)—equivalent to more than 85 football fields—and includes areas for news and program production, TV broadcasting, and parking. Beijing residents have nicknamed the building the "giant shorts" due to its unique shape.

Vertical garden

Keppel Land Limited completed a 22,879.33-sq-ft (2,125.56-m²) green wall in Singapore's Ocean Financial Centre on Sep 13, 2013. It took three years to create the garden, which features 25 plant species.

Tallest twisted tower

The Cayan Tower in Dubai, UAE, stands 1,008 ft (307.3 m) tall and features a 90-degree twist. Each floor has a 1.2-degree rotation, which creates a helix shape. It was developed by Cayan Real Estate Investment & Development and opened on Jun 10, 2013.

The **first twisted skyscraper** was the HSB Turning Torso in Malmö, Sweden (2005).

Highest building jack-up

The Main Yuzhen Palace Gate, East Palace Gate, and West Palace Gate of the Ancient Building Complex in Hubei Province, China, were lifted 50 ft (15 m)—from an elevation of 524 ft (160 m) to 574 ft (175 m)—between Aug 15, 2012 and Jan 16, 2013 to avoid the risk of flooding from a water-diversion project.

Tallest summit cross

Built in 1926–28 to honor the dead of World War I, Heroes' Cross (aka the Caraiman Cross) is 129 ft 7 in (39.5 m) tall with its concrete base. It sits 7,516 ft (2,291 m) up Mount Caraiman in Romania's Bucegi Mountains.

---

i Kingdom Tower

So far, work has only begun on its foundations, but when completed—possibly by 2019, and at a cost of around $1.2 bn—the Kingdom Tower will become the first building ever to break the 1-km (0.6-mi) barrier. Its sloping exterior and triangle-shape footprint are designed to help reduce the impact of wind on the supertall building.

TALLEST BUILDINGS AROUND THE WORLD

Under construction: Kingdom Tower, Jeddah, Saudi Arabia: **3,280 ft 10 in**

Building: Burj Khalifa, Dubai, UAE: **2,716 ft 6 in**

Tower: Tokyo Skytree, Japan: **6,080 ft**

In North America: One World Trade Center, New York, USA: **1,776 ft**

Office: Taipei 101, Chinese Taipei, China: **1,666 ft 8 in**

Residence: Princess Tower, Dubai, UAE: **1,356 ft**

Hotel: J. W. Marriott Marquis Hotel Dubai Towers 1 and 2, Dubai, UAE: **1,164 ft 8 in**

In Oceania: Q1, Queensland, Australia: **1,058 ft**

In Europe: Eurasia, Moscow, Russia: **1,013 ft 5 in**

Twisted building: Cayan Tower, Dubai, UAE: **1,008 ft**

In South America: Torre Costanera, Santiago, Chile: **984 ft**

In Africa: Carlton Centre, Johannesburg, South Africa: **730 ft**

⚡ Scraping the sky

In 1955, the **tallest building** was the Empire State Building in New York City, USA, measuring "1,472 feet [488.6 m] high to the top of the television tower." A succession of buildings have held that coveted title since, the latest being the Burj Khalifa, which is nearly twice as tall as that 1955 record holder. The Sky City skyscraper in Changsha, China, was to top out at 32 ft 9 in taller but, by 2013, work stalled on the challenging prefabricated design.

Castles

Castle stairwells usually turn **clockwise**, giving right-handed swordsmen an advantage in attacks

Largest cave castle

More than 115 ft (35 m) in height, Predjama Castle near Postojna, Slovenia, is built in the entrance to a cave system (inset). Set halfway up a 403-ft-high (123-m) cliff face, the castle dates back to at least the 13th century, and was rebuilt in a Renaissance style in 1570.

FACT

Predjama's most famous resident was a "robber baron" named Erazem. The castle's defensive advantages enabled him to withstand a siege by Austrian Habsburg troops for a whole year before a servant betrayed him.

Oldest castle

The earliest recorded castle is located in the old city of Sana'a, Yemen. Known as Gomdan or Gumdan Castle, it dates from before AD 200 and is believed to have originally comprised 20 stories.

Largest inhabited castle

The royal residence of Windsor Castle at Windsor, Berkshire, UK, is originally of 12th-century construction and takes the form of a waisted parallelogram measuring 1,890 x 540 ft (576 x 164 m). The entire site covers 570,000 sq ft (53,000 m²)—the area of nearly 10 football fields—in the center of which stands the iconic 214-ft-tall (65.5-m) Round Tower topped off with gothic-style battlements.

Largest nonpalatial residence

St. Emmeram Castle (or Abbey) in Regensburg, Germany, has 517 rooms and a floor area of 231,000 sq ft (21,460 m²). Originally a Benedictine monastery (founded in AD 739), it was acquired in 1812

Largest brick castle

Poland's Malbork Castle was built largely in the 13th and 14th centuries by Teutonic Order crusader knights. It encompasses a 52-acre (21-ha) site and is built almost entirely from locally made bricks of a distinctive red hue. Its grandiose Knights' Hall refectory could house up to 400 visiting knights and guests.

by the Thurn und Taxis family, who built up a fortune from their exclusive control of the mail service in Bavaria over the course of 200 years. Princess Gloria von Thurn und Taxis still uses the castle as her primary residence.

Longest castle siege

The cathedral fort of Ishiyama Hongan-ji, in what is today Osaka, Japan, first came under attack from the renowned warrior Oda Nobunaga in Aug 1570, but the defending Ikkō-ikki warrior monks under Abbot Kōsa held out for a decade until Aug 1580, when the complex was finally burned to the ground. Osaka Castle was constructed on the site and continues to be a popular tourist destination.

Northernmost castle

The small Kajaani Castle in Finland, at a latitude of 64.2295 degrees, is the most northerly castle. It was built on a small river island between 1604 and 1619 and first used as a prison. It survives only as stone ruins today.

Longest castle

Constructed mainly between ca. 1255 and 1490, the Burg zu Burghausen measures 3,448 ft (1,051 m) long and is built on a ridge that runs above the town of Burghausen in Germany. It was once a residence of the dukes of Bavaria, and it is composed of a main inner courtyard—where the family lived—and five large outer courtyards, all of which would have been protected by portcullises, moats, and drawbridges.

Glossary

Castle: Specifically, a defensively constructed residence for rulers, often with state-of-the-art military hardware. Sometimes a generic term for fortified structures.

Citadel: A fort or fortress used to defend a town or city.

Fort: A heavily defended military outpost but not always designed as a residence for royalty or aristocracy.

Palace: The non-fortified residence of a leader.

ANATOMY OF A CASTLE

Drawbridge

Lower bailey

Watchtower

Moat

Gateway to middle bailey

Round mural tower

Middle bailey

Forebuilding

Keep

Gateway to upper bailey

Upper bailey

Siege engine tower

Arsenal tower

Rocky cliff

Mill tower

Curtain wall

FACT

In all, 40 monarchs have lived in Windsor Castle, from Henry I to the present British queen, Elizabeth II.

Narrow advantage

The term "loophole" originally referred to the narrow slit in a castle wall through which arrows could be fired.

Largest ancient castle

Prague Castle in the Czech Republic was constructed in the ninth century. It is an oblong irregular polygon with an axis of 1,870 ft (570 m) and an average transverse diameter of 420 ft (128 m), resulting in a total surface area of 18 acres (7.28 ha).

Largest inflatable (bouncy) castle

Designed by Dana Caspersen and William Forsythe (both USA) and produced in three weeks by Southern Inflatables, UK, the largest inflatable castle stands 39 ft (12 m) tall and is 62 sq ft (19 m²) at the base. Made from 29,330 sq ft (2,725 m²) of white-PVC-coated polyester, it takes 6 hr to fully construct and 15 min to fill with 13,500 cu ft (385 m³) of air. Between Mar 24 and May 11, 1997, it served as an architectural

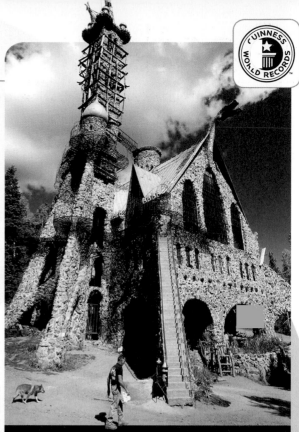

Oldest museum

The Royal Armouries museum in the Tower of London (UK)—the city's most famous castle—is the oldest museum. It first opened its doors to the public in 1660, although it was possible to view the collection by appointment for up to eight years prior to this date.

Tallest theme-park castle

The Cinderella Castle at Disney's Magic Kingdom in Florida, USA, is 189 ft (57.3 m) high. Partly based on picturesque real-life castles, such as those at Neuschwanstein (Germany), Segovia (Spain), and Moszna (Poland), the "forced-perspective" design of the steel, concrete, and fiber-glass structure makes it seem even taller than it is. It opened in 1971.

FACT
Wewelsburg Castle has been claimed as the inspiration for the video game *Wolfenstein 3D* (iD Software, 1992).

Largest triangular castle

Wewelsburg Castle in Büren, Germany, was constructed between 1603 and 1609. The Renaissance-style structure has a total perimeter of 787 ft (240 m). Originally used by the Prince-Bishopric of Paderborn, it later became notorious as one of the centers for the Nazi SS under Heinrich Himmler.

Tallest self-built castle

The 160-ft-tall (48.75-m) stone-and-steel Bishop Castle in Colorado, USA, has been a work in progress by American welder Jim Bishop since Jun 1969. It features stained-glass windows, three towers, a grand ballroom and a sculpture of a fire-breathing dragon.

installation in Camden, London, UK. Since then, it has been used at a range of events worldwide.

A more modest inflatable, measuring 12 x 15 ft (3.6 x 4.5 m) at the base, was used for the **longest marathon on a bouncy castle by a team**. Eight bouncers from the logistics company Wincanton and the Tesco supermarket in Rugby, Warwickshire, UK, clocked a time of 37 hr 14 sec on Aug 30–31, 2013.

Largest can sculpture

An 18-ft-tall (5.5-m) reproduction of Yoshida Castle in Toyohashi, Japan, was built from 104,840 aluminum drinks cans by Junior Chamber International in Toyohashi Park, Aichi, Japan, on Sep 21, 2013.

Spellbinding school: Hogwarts

One of the most instantly recognizable castles is Hogwarts School of Witchcraft and Wizardry from J. K. Rowling's *Harry Potter* series. The **largest model of Hogwarts castle** was made by the art department of Warner Bros. (UK) in 2011. The 1:24-scale model (pictured right, with model supervisor José Granell) is 50 ft wide and can be visited at the Warner Bros. studio tour in London.
The **largest model of Hogwarts made from LEGO®** was created by Alice Finch (USA, left) in 2012; 13 ft long, it used around 400,000 bricks.

Armored division

Largest suit of armor made for an animal: Adult Asian elephant suit, weighing 260 lb, in Royal Armouries museum, Leeds, UK

Most expensive suit of armor sold at auction: Suit of armor made for Henri II in 1545 by Giovanni Negroli, sold for £1,925,000 ($3,032,800) on May 5, 1983, from Hever Castle collection, Kent, UK

Tallest suit of armor: 6.7 ft high, dated to ca. 1535, in the White Tower at HM Tower of London, UK

Sports architecture

A UK home valued at $117.39 m in 2005 boasted a **squash court, bowling alley, and five pools**

Largest tensile stadium roof

Tensile structures are held in place using tension, anchored by cables instead of bent or compressed with poles. The King Fahd International Stadium in Riyadh, Saudi Arabia, covers 505,900 sq ft (47,000 m²) and was completed in 1987 from a design by Ian Fraser Associates. Its 24 masts support an 807-ft-wide (246-m) roof shaped like Bedouin tents. The roof protects more than 67,000 spectators from the desert climate.

of Rome's temples. First begun in the 6th century BC, the Circus Maximus reached its largest form under Trajan in AD 103. It remains most famous for the chariot races that were re-created in *Ben-Hur* (USA, 1959), as well as for track and field events and gladiator combat. The last race in the Circus Maximus was recorded in AD 550.

Largest marble stadium
The Panathenaic Stadium is unique in being constructed almost entirely out of white marble. It was first built in the 6th century BC in Athens, Greece, rebuilt in marble in

Largest soccer stadium

The Rungnado May Day Stadium is on an island in the middle of the Taedong River in Pyongyang, North Korea. It was inaugurated on May 1, 1989, and is also used for the Arirang Festival (inset, the 2013 event) that celebrates the country's late leaders. It has a current capacity of 150,000.

Largest ancient stadium
The Circus Maximus in Rome, Italy, could accommodate 255,000 spectators in a triple-bank structure measuring some 2,000 ft (610 m) long and 650 ft (200 m) wide. Writer Pliny the Younger said it rivaled the beauty

329 BC by Lycurgus, and has been enlarged and renovated many times since. It hosted the first modern Olympic Games in 1896.

Highest-capacity Olympic stadium
Stadium Australia was constructed to hold approximately 110,000 people for the Sydney Olympics of 2000, but more than 114,000 spectators crammed into the stadium for the closing ceremony. Also known as the ANZ Stadium, the venue is still used, although with a reduced capacity of 83,500. Four other Olympic cities have had stadia with

Largest floating sports platform

The Float at Marina Bay, Singapore, was completed in 2007 and has 214,847 sq ft (19,960 m²) of usable space plus a grandstand for 27,000 fans on the shore. The platform is secured by six pylons and can support the weight of 9,000 people.

Largest solar-powered stadium

The National Stadium in Kaohsiung, Chinese Taipei, is topped with 8,844 solar panels covering 152,362 sq ft (14,155 m²). They can generate 1.14 million kWh of electricity every year: 80% of the venue's needs. If it were powered by traditional power stations, 1.45 million lb (660 metric tons) of carbon dioxide would be released annually. Designed by Toyo Ito (JPN), the stadium's shape is said to be based on that of a curled dragon.

TOP 10 LARGEST STADIA BY CAPACITY

1. Indianapolis Speedway: 257,325 USA
2. Tokyo Racecourse: 223,000 Japan
3. Shanghai International Circuit: 200,000 China
4. Nakayama Racecourse: 165,676 Japan
5. Bristol Motor Speedway: 160,000 USA
=6. Istanbul Park: 155,000 Turkey
=6. Suzuka Circuit: 155,000 Japan
=8. Rungnado May Day Stadium: 150,000 North Korea
=8. Nürburgring: 150,000 Germany
10. Daytona International Speedway: 147,000 USA

Supersize stadia

Building for top sports comes at a cost. Portugal spent 536.5 m euros ($745.4 m) to host soccer's Euro 2004, with seven new stadia in a country about the size of Indiana, USA. For the 2002 soccer World Cup, Japan spent ¥526 bn ($5.1 bn) on new venues and renovations. For the Olympics, Greece's 2004 Games cost 9.4 bn euros ($13 bn) and China spent ¥293 bn ($47.8 bn) in 2008.

Source: World Stadiums

Largest stadium

The **largest stadium** in 1955 was the Strahov Stadium in Prague, Czechoslovakia. Completed in 1934, it could house 240,000 fans, typically watching more than 40,000 gymnasts. Today, the Strahov's grand gymnastic displays are a distant memory and the record holder is the Indianapolis Motor Speedway in Indiana, USA, with 257,325 seated. The future for Prague's striking monolith of the Communist era remains uncertain.

Largest floating golf green

To play the 14th hole of the Coeur d'Alene golf course in Idaho, USA, you have to take a boat trip. Measuring some 15,000 sq ft (1,390 m²), the green is on a computer-controlled island that can be moved between 246 ft (75 m) and 574 ft (175 m) from the shore. Golfers reach the island by an electrically powered water taxi in a course that was completed in 1991.

capacities of more than 100,000: Los Angeles, USA (101,574 in 1932); Berlin, Germany (110,000 in 1936); Melbourne, Australia (100,000 in 1956); and Moscow, Soviet Union (103,000 in 1980).

Largest sumo stadium
The Ryōgoku Kokugikan in Tokyo, Japan, has a capacity of 11,908. Spectators in the *suna-aburi-seki* ringside seats are so close to the action in the *dohyō* central ring that they are often sprayed with sand during bouts. The venue opened in Jan 1985 and holds three of the country's six official sumo tournaments.

Longest bobsled track
The 2014 Winter Olympics track at the Sliding Center Sanki in Sochi, Russia, is the most fiendish yet. It has a competition length of 0.93 mi (1.5 km) and drops 432 ft 8 in (131.9 m) at an average grade of 9.3% over

its 18 curves. Riders can reach speeds as high as 83.9 mph (135 km/h).

Tallest ski-flying hill
Ski flying is a more extreme version of ski jumping. The ski-jump facility at Vikersundbakken in Vikersund, Norway, is partly manmade and partly modified natural hill. It reaches a dizzying height of 738 ft (225 m)—almost two-and-a-half times the height of the Statue of Liberty. Begun in 1935, Vikersundbakken had been modified into its current form by 2011. On Feb 11 of that year, Johan Remen Evensen (NOR) set the **longest competitive ski jump** on the hill, with a distance of 809 ft (246.5 m).

Newest real tennis court
The court may be new, but the game is old. Real tennis is a precursor of modern

Longest motor-racing circuit

The longest purpose-designed circuit in use is Nürburgring in Nürburg, Germany. Built in 1927, the "Nordschleife" ("north loop") measures 12.93 mi (20.81 km) and the "Südschleife" ("south loop"), which was rebuilt in 1984, is 3.199 mi (5.148 km) long. When combined for the annual 24-hr endurance event, the track is 16.129 mi (25.958 km) long, with more than 180 corners.

tennis, played on a hard court surrounded by four walls. Fewer than 50 courts exist today; their numbers were swelled in 2012 by the Racquet Club of Chicago, Illinois, USA.

The **oldest surviving real tennis court** is at Falkland Palace in Fife,

UK. It was constructed for James V of Scotland between Apr 1539 and late 1541 and is home to the Falkland Palace Royal Tennis Club, which was founded in 1975.

First retractable grass pitch

The GelreDome in Arnhem, Netherlands, opened on Mar 25, 1998. Home to soccer club Vitesse Arnhem, its playing surface sits in a concrete tray that takes 5 hr to slide outside the stadium (inset) to prepare for concerts.

The **largest retractable roof** covers the Toronto Blue Jays' Rogers Center (formerly SkyDome) in Toronto, Canada. It spans 685 ft (209 m) and covers 8 acres (3.2 ha).

Sky-high sports: top courts

You'd need serious danger money to be a ball boy on the **highest tennis court**, 692 ft above the ground. The court was temporarily installed on the helipad of the Burj Al Arab hotel in Dubai, UAE, on Feb 22, 2005 as Roger Federer (CHE) and Andre Agassi (USA) played a friendly game to promote the ATP's Dubai Duty Free Men's Open. "Do you think I can knock this guy off his boat?," joked Agassi as they paused to peer over the side of the sheer drop to the shallows far below. If you were ever on the beach in Dubai and wondered where that tennis ball came from—it was from former world No. 1 Andre Agassi!

Motor sports venues
First motor-racing circuit: Brooklands in Weybridge, UK, opened Jun 17, 1907
Longest Formula One circuit (all time): Pescara Circuit (used for F1 racing 1959–61), at 15.9 mi
Shortest Formula One circuit (all time): Circuit de Monaco, Monte Carlo (used for F1 racing since 1929), 1.8 mi (1929–79)

As helium was first **discovered on the Sun**, it was named after Helios, the Greek sun god

Most accurate clock

Researchers at the Joint Institute for Laboratory Astrophysics (JILA)—a project initiated by the University of Colorado and the US National Institute of Standards and Technology—have used the element strontium to create an atomic clock that will neither gain nor lose a second in 4.5 billion years. The research was announced on Jan 22, 2014. Because the SI definition of the second is based on the caesium atom, caesium clocks were previously regarded as the most accurate.

First country to mine gas hydrates

Gas hydrates, aka "flammable ice," are a solid resembling water ice. They contain methane gas trapped in a crystalline structure and occur beneath sediments on the ocean floor. In Mar 2013, Japan announced that it had successfully extracted methane gas from hydrate deposits in

the Nankai Trough, 30 mi (50 km) offshore from Japan. Scientists estimate that there could be enough hydrate deposits in the Nankai Trough to meet Japan's energy needs for a decade.

First photon interaction

In Sep 2013, researchers from Harvard University and the Massachusetts Institute of Technology (both USA) completed an experiment that compared the interaction of protons to the behavior of light sabers, the fictional weapons used in *Star Wars*. Researchers observed an attractive force between two photons—the basic particles that form light—which interacted to form a joined, two-photon molecule. This indicated that photons could be manipulated to create a solid "blade" of light, like a light saber.

Highest manmade RPM

Scientists at the University of St. Andrews in the UK created a tiny sphere of calcium just 4 micrometers (0.00015 in; 0.004 mm) across, around 10 times narrower than a human hair. They suspended the sphere using laser light inside a vacuum and made it spin by altering the polarity of the light. On Aug 28, 2013, the team published the results of their research, which observed the calcium sphere reaching 600 million revolutions per min (RPM) before disintegrating.

Thinnest manmade material

In Oct 2004, British and Russian scientists announced the discovery of the nanofabric graphene. With a thickness of just one single atom

Most accurate electron mass measurement

On Feb 19, 2014, the Max Planck Institute for Nuclear Physics (DEU) announced the mass of an electron measured at 0.000548579909067 of an atomic mass unit. It was measured by binding a single electron to a bare carbon nucleus in a Penning trap (above) and manipulating it with electric and magnetic fields. The result is ca. 13 times more accurate than previous efforts.

Fastest computer

The supercomputer "Tianhe-2," developed by China's National University of Defense Technology, performs at 33.86 petaFLOPS on the Linpack benchmark (see below). The list of the most powerful supercomputers was announced on Jun 17 during the opening session of the 2013 International Supercomputing Conference.

天河二号

COMPUTING EFFICIENCY

Computations per kilowatt-hour

- SiCortex SC5832
- Apple Macintosh
- Dell Dimension 2400
- Compaq Deskpro 386/20e
- SDS 920
- Altair 8800
- UNIVAC III
- Commodore 64
- UNIVAC II

1e+16
1e+15
1e+14
1e+13
1e+12
1e+11
1e+10
1e+9
1e+8
1e+7
1e+6
1e+5
1e+4
1e+3
1e+2
1e+1
1e+0

1955 1960 1965 1970 1975 1980 1985 1990 1995 2000 2005 2010 2015

⚡ Enormous instruments

In 1955, the **largest scientific instrument** was the Radio Telescope of the Manchester University Experimental Station in Cheshire, UK. "The filigree skeletal bowl and 180-ft [54-m] high supports weigh 1,500 tons [1,524 metric tons]." Today, the record is held by the Large Electron-Positron storage ring collider at CERN in Geneva, Switzerland, which was built to examine the smallest and most fundamental particles of matter. This huge device is a circular tube with an overall circumference of 16.77 mi.

FACT

A supercomputer's performance is measured in FLOPS—FLoating-point Operations Per Second. A floating-point operation is the calculation of a mathematical equation, so a petaFLOP, as used to measure the fastest supercomputer (above), means 1,000,000,000,000,000 calculations per sec.

First proof of the Higgs boson

On Mar 14, 2013, it was confirmed that an experiment performed at the Large Hadron Collider (above) at CERN in Geneva, Switzerland, had revealed the existence of the Higgs boson. The confirmation of this elementary particle—known as the "God particle"—is the most important discovery in physics for decades. It strengthens the idea of the Standard Model, a unified theory about the nature of the universe that connects fundamental particles and the forces acting between them.

Thinnest transistor
A transistor is a device that opens or closes an electrical circuit, or amplifies a signal. On Feb 19, 2012, scientists from the Centre for Quantum Computation & Communication Technology (AUS) unveiled a transistor less than 1 nanometer (0.000001 mm) high—the same height as one atom. The active element in this transistor is a single phosphorus (P) atom set within a silicon (Si) crystal. All elements of the device are fabricated on a single atomic plane, so the entire transistor is only one atomic layer in height. It is termed a "single atom transistor."

Highest projectile velocity
Scientists at the Naval Research Laboratory in Washington, D.C., USA, have used the Nike krypton fluoride laser to propel a sphere

First earthquake detected from orbit

On Mar 17, 2009, the European Space Agency launched *GOCE*, a satellite that can map Earth's gravitational field from an orbit of 158.3 mi (254.9 km). On Mar 11, 2011, as it passed through the weak sound waves of Earth's thermosphere, the spacecraft detected the devastating earthquake that struck Japan.

of carbon, graphene can exist as a single sheet of a theoretically infinite size.

In Jan 2012, researchers from the University of California in Riverside (USA) showed that when just 10% graphene was added to other materials, a 23-fold increase in thermal conductivity was seen— the **highest increase in thermal conductivity by a material**. These composite materials have potential for use as thermal interface materials; for example, they are used in electronic devices to avoid overheating, by absorbing the heat generated.

less than 12-thousandths of an inch (300 micrometers) in size to velocities in excess of 621 mi/s (1,000 km/s). This figure is some 186 mi/s (300 km/s) faster than previous attempts.

Largest neutrino detector
IceCube is a US-led international telescope designed to detect neutrinos, subatomic particles with almost no mass. Located at the Amundsen-Scott South Pole Station in Antarctica, it consists of 5,160 detectors in 86 vertical cables buried 4,750–8,050 ft (1,450–2,450 m) below sea level, where the ice is optically clear.

Airy aerogel: least dense solid

Professor Gao Chao and his team from the Department of Polymer Science and Engineering at Zhejiang University in China have created graphene aerogel with a density of just 0.00009 oz/cu in. The team freeze-dried solutions of carbon nanotubes and large sheets of graphene oxide, then chemically removed oxygen to leave a conductive, elastic, solid foam. Aerogel is lighter than air and has numerous applications, from mopping up oil spills to capturing dust from comet tails. The breakthrough was announced in *Nature* magazine on Feb 27, 2013.

Glossary

Caesium: An alkali metal element ($_{55}$Cs) that provides the basis of the SI unit of measurement for the second; one second equals 9,192,631,770 oscillations of a caesium atom with an atomic weight of 133 atomic units ($^{133}_{55}$Cs).

Carbon nanotube: An allotrope of carbon ($_6$C) in which the molecules are in the shape of a cylinder 50,000 times smaller than a human hair.

Robots & AI

In the Middle East, **robot jockeys** are replacing children in camel racing

First robot trumpeter

A bipedal robot made by Toyota (JPN) in 2004 mastered the embouchure (complex coordination of mouth, lips, and tongue) to play the trumpet. Fellow robots were constructed to play tuba and drums.

First public reference to robots

The word "robot" was introduced into English by Karel Čapek (CZE) in his 1921 play *R.U.R. (Rossum's Universal Robots)*. The story features "artificial people" who have been designed to enjoy hard work. The word, suggested by the playwright's brother Josef, derives from the Czech word *robota*, which means "slave labor."

First computer to play in the Checkers World Championship

Chinook, a computer program designed to play checkers, was developed at the University of Alberta, Canada, in 1989. In 1990, it won the right to compete in the Checkers World Championship by being rated second in the US nationals behind Marion Tinsley (USA), one of the greatest checkers players of all time. Chinook won the World Championship in 1994, following Tinsley's retirement due to ill health.

Most dexterous robot band

Z-Machines is a band created by engineers at the University of Tokyo, Japan, in 2013. As well as keyboardist Cosmo, the group consists of guitarist Mach (who boasts 78 "fingers") and drummer Ashura (who can play with 22 drumsticks). The group released their debut album,

composed by the UK electronic music artist Squarepusher, in Apr 2013.

Longest journey by an unmanned autonomous surface vehicle

On Feb 14, 2013, "Benjamin Franklin" the Wave Glider®—developed by Liquid Robotics (USA)—finished a 7,939-nautical mile (14,703-km) journey across the Pacific Ocean from San Francisco in California, USA, to Lady Musgrave Island in Queensland, Australia. It is one of four Wave Gliders; they convert wave energy into thrust and use solar energy to generate electricity for sensors, communications, and navigation.

Largest planetary rover

The *Curiosity* rover landed on Mars on Aug 6, 2012 as part of NASA's Mars Science Laboratory mission. It is 9 ft (3 m) long and weighs 1,900 lb (900 kg), including 176 lb (80 kg) of scientific instruments. As of Mar 2014, the rover had traveled

First bionic hand with real-time sensory feedback

Dennis Aabo Sørensen (DNK) was the test subject for a prosthetic hand that was wired into his nerves. According to a report issued on Feb 5, 2014 by École Polytechnique Fédérale de Lausanne in Switzerland, he was able to tell how hard he was grasping and to distinguish between objects, including their shape and softness.

First self-organizing robot construction swarm

TERMES robots are the size of a shoe and their design, by Harvard University, USA, was inspired by termites. As reported on Feb 14, 2014, TERMES robots are able to use blocks to construct towers, pyramids, and other structures. They require no centralized command, operating as a swarm to complete the task collectively.

almost 3 mi (5 km). *Curiosity* uses an arm and "hand" to collect samples; having analyzed them, it sends the resulting data back to Earth. Scientists believe that its current location may have once been a riverbed.

Glossary

Artificial narrow intelligence: Typically focused on a narrow task, such as playing chess or fulfilling requests, as Apple's Siri does in iOS.

Artificial general intelligence: Theory of humanlike intelligence, including the ability to display reason, strategy, planning, and make complex judgments.

Hello, world: machines answer back

In 2011, IBM's *Watson* (right) responded in real time to questions to record the **highest score by a computer on *Jeopardy!*** (USA, 1964–present). Its $77,147 total beat the show's two human contestants. IBM also built *Deep Blue*, the **first computer to beat a world chess champion under regular time controls**, defeating Garry Kasparov (RUS) on May 11, 1997 (below right). Mike Dobson and David Gilday (both UK) built *CUBESTORMER 3* (left), which achieved the **fastest time to solve a Rubik's Cube by a robot**, taking just 3.253 sec on Mar 15, 2014.

Actual Size

Head-mounted stereo cameras, sensors, and perception algorithms

First person to control a robot hand with the mind

Matthew Nagle (USA), who had been paralyzed from the neck down, had a BrainGate—an experimental brain-computer interface—attached to the surface of his motor cortex in 2004 in Massachusetts, USA. The implant was linked to a computer and used his brain waves to allow him to open and close a robotic hand.

Lightest flying robot

RoboBee is a flylike robot weighing only 0.0028 oz (80 mg), with wafer-thin, 1-in-wide (3-cm) wings that can flap 120 times per sec. Harvard University, USA, published details of the first flight of the RoboBee in 2013, saying future uses for the penny-size robot may include artificial crop pollination.

Deadliest anti-personnel robot

South Korea deploys Super aEgis 2 robot sentries that can lock on to targets up to 1.8 mi (3 km) away. They are deployed in the demilitarized zone between North and South Korea, picking off intruders on sight using heavy-duty machine guns and grenade launchers.

A computer on its chest checks sensors, controls actuators (devices that activate a mechanism or system), collects data, and can communicate with a remote user

Materials are mostly aluminum, steel, and titanium—which helps in crash protection

Boston Dynamics: rise of the robots

Boston Dynamics (USA) is one of the world's most advanced robotics companies and was bought by Google in Dec 2013. Their *Atlas* robot (right) is the **most agile humanoid robot**, able to run over rocky terrain and stay balanced when hit with a 20-lb (9-kg) medicine ball (above left). Boston Dynamics' *WildCat* is the **fastest-running untethered, quadruped robot** (below left), running up to 16 mph (25 km/h) on flat terrain.

Wrist accessories can be swapped for different units by third-party manufacturers

Farthest distance by a quadruped robot

BigDog, developed by Boston Dynamics (above), is a four-legged robot designed to be a "pack mule" for soldiers. In Feb 2009 it was announced that BigDog had walked 12.8 mi (20.5 km) autonomously by following a GPS tracking system.

Largest automated factory

In 2011, Grupo Modelo (MEX) opened a fully automated bottling factory that uses robots and laser-guided trolleys to achieve production capabilities of 6,000 or 144,000 bottles per hr.

Largest stock market crash caused by automated trading

"Algorithmic trading" refers to AI computers executing thousands of trades per sec. On May 6, 2010, the US Dow Jones plunged by more than 600 points, with algorithmic trading thought to be to blame. The index recovered 20 min later, leading to the event being nicknamed the "flash crash."

Atlas stays upright with the help of 28 hydraulically actuated joints, which allow it to crouch, kneel, and jump down

Atlas is 6 ft 2 in tall and has been designed to resemble a full-size adult with joints that facilitate near-human movement

Crumple-zone cages around limbs protect the sensors in case of collision

HIGHEST-GROSSING MOVIES FEATURING ROBOTS

Source: www.boxofficemojo.com; scale relative to box-office gross

Transformers: Dark of the Moon (USA, 2011) $1.12 bn

Transformers: Revenge of the Fallen (USA, 2009) $836.3 m

Transformers (USA, 2007) $709.7 m

WALL-E (USA, 2008) $521.31 m

Terminator 2: Judgment Day (USA, 1991) $519.84 m

Terminator 3: Rise of the Machines (USA, 2003) $433.37 m

Pacific Rim (USA, 2013) $411 m

Prometheus (USA, 2012) $403.35 m

Terminator Salvation (USA, 2009) $371.35 m

I, Robot (USA, 2004) $347.2 m

No robot job too small

Smallest robotic lunar rover: *Jade Rabbit* (CHN), 4 ft 11 in long, landed on Dec 14, 2013.

Smallest robotic minesweeper: *RoboClam*, designed by Massachusetts Institute of Technology, USA, based on Atlantic razor clam, burrows 0.39 in per sec and can dig to a mine to detonate it.

Smallest robotic tweezers: University of Toronto, Canada, developed tweezers that can sense how to move a 10-micrometer heart cell with the correct force.

○ ○ ○

Top tech

"Gadget": may originate from French, *gâchette* ("lock tumbler") or *gagée* ("tool")

Highest power drawn from a fruit battery
Da Vinci Media (DEU), an educational TV channel, generated 1.21 watts by connecting 1,500 lemons together in Budapest, Hungary, on Apr 27, 2013.

Largest animated cell phone mosaic
At the inaugural China Smart Device Games—held at the National Olympic Sports Centre in Beijing on Jul 13, 2013—China Unicom, Sohu IT, and HTC created an animated cell phone mosaic using 400 smartphones. The devices were linked via China Unicom's WCDMA HSPA+ network; each screen showed a different video that, in combination with the others, formed a video ad.

Fastest-selling portable gaming system

Apple reported opening-weekend sales of the iPhone 5c and 5s in Sep 2013 of 9 million units, breaking its own record of 5 million for the iPhone 5 in 2012 and becoming the fastest-selling device capable of playing video games. Apple's sales were boosted by releasing two models instead of one, and for the first time debuting in China on the same day as the USA.

Fastest time to type a text message blindfolded

Mark Encarnación (USA) used a smartphone to type a specified text message in 25.9 sec in Redmond, Washington, USA, on Apr 24, 2013. Without a blindfold, the **fastest time to type a text message on a smartphone** is 18.44 sec, achieved by Gaurav Sharma (USA), who was also in Redmond, on Jan 16, 2014.

Most consumer electronics recycled in 24 hours
Sims Recycling Solutions (USA) recycled electronics weighing a total of 126,344 lb (57,308 kg) at seven locations in the USA and Canada on Apr 20, 2013. The event, staged as part of Earth Day 2013, saw the company collecting unwanted electronics from locations in California, Hawaii, Illinois, Nevada, New Jersey, and Ontario.

First bluetooth gloves commercially available
In Oct 2012, Italian company hi-Fun released a range of knitted and leather gloves with built-in bluetooth communication for cell phones. Users can make calls by speaking into the glove's pinkie finger and listening via the thumb.

Largest loop-the-loop by a remote-controlled vehicle

On Jun 15, 2013, Jason Bradbury—host of *The Gadget Show* (Channel 5, UK) and pictured left with cohost Rachel Riley— guided a remote-controlled car in a 10-ft 5-in-wide (3.18-m) loop-the-loop. Other records from the show include the **heaviest machines moved using a brain-control interface** (in which cranes weighing 123,899 lb (56.2 metric tons) were used to move a car with an electromagnet in 2011, bottom left) and the **largest architectural projection-mapped game** (a game of *PAC-Man* covering 23,881 sq ft (2,218.65 m²) played in London, UK, in 2013, below right).

⊗ **For cutting-edge science, turn to p. 202**

For cutting-edge science, turn to p. 202

TOP 10 MOST FREQUENTLY USED SMARTPHONE APPS

Google Maps 54%	**Facebook** 44%	**YouTube** 35%	**Google+** 30%	**WeChat** 27%
Facebook Messenger 22%	**Skype** 22%	**Twitter** 22%	**WhatsApp** 17%	**Instagram** 1%

⚡ Phone alone
When we first published in 1955, the country with the most telephones was deemed to be the USA, with approximately 50 million. We calculated that this provided 31 phones per 100 population, adding that Canada made the most calls, with an annual average of 459. By 2011, according to the International Telecommunication Union (ITU), the world had gone mobile, with 6 billion subscriptions (these were for sim cards instead of phones).

FACT
The Oxford Dictionary recognized "selfie" as 2013's word of the year, defining this as "a photograph that one has taken of oneself, typically one taken with a smartphone or Webcam, and uploaded to a social media Web site." It beat competition from "twerk," "binge-watch," "whackadoodle," and "showrooming."

Source: GlobalWebIndex survey, Aug 2013

First 3D-printed titanium alloy bicycle frame

Empire Cycles (UK) designed a bike frame that was constructed by UK manufacturing firm Renishaw from titanium. The 3D laser melting process ensured that there was less waste, and made it easier to create a more organic form. The MX-6 Evo prototype frame of 2014 weighs 3 lb (1.4 kg), making it 33% lighter than conventional frames.

3D PRINTING

Fastest ultrahigh-resolution 3D printer

Researchers have developed a printer that can make models the size of a grain of sand. The superfast nano printer at the Vienna University of Technology in Austria uses a liquid resin, which is hardened by a laser beam. The applications for the printer's nano models in the future include biomedical technology and nanotechnology.

Largest 3D object from a desktop 3D printer

Skylar Tibbits, Marcelo Coelho (both USA), Natan Linder, and Yoav Reches (both ISL) used a desktop 3D printer to create "folded" items within a print chamber measuring 4.9 x 4.9 x 6.5 in (12.4 x 12.4 x 16.5 cm). The 2013 project linked each part of the larger structure in a chain and the team created a chandelier approximately five times larger in volume than the printer's chamber.

Most 3D printers operating simultaneously

Students of Dr. Jesse French (USA) in 2013 were required to make a 3D printer as part of their engineering course at LeTourneau University in Longview, Texas, USA. A total of 102 undergraduates assembled with their printers on Apr 4, 2014 and printed a special coin designed for the event.

Most money pledged for a Kickstarter 3D-printer project

As of May 1, 2014, the Micro printer by M3D had attracted pledges of $3.15 m—toward an initial goal of $50,000—on the crowdsourcing Web site kickstarter.com. As 3D printing is becoming increasingly popular, it is used to create everything from plastic ornaments to whole houses, and the price of printers has been coming down. The Micro is aimed at the consumer market, with a cube-shape printer chamber measuring 7.3 in (18.5 cm) on each side. It costs $299.

Most used smartphone app

A global study of smartphone owners 16–64 years old (below left) asked them to complete an online questionnaire that found 54% use Google Maps. The GlobalWebIndex data was published in Aug 2013, showing users opened the app at least once in the previous month. In second place (44%) was the Facebook mobile app.

First 3D-printed complete lower-jaw implant

In Jun 2011, an 83-year-old woman underwent surgery at the Orbis medical center in the Netherlands, during which she was implanted with a lower jaw "printed" from titanium powder fused together using a laser. It was created by LayerWise in collaboration with scientists at Hasselt University (both BEL)

First selfie
In Oct 1839, Robert Cornelius (USA) took a self-portrait using the daguerreotype technique: a photographic process employing a polished silver plate that is afterward exposed to mercury vapor. He sat for the shot—which typically would need 3–15 min to expose—in the backyard of his family's store in Philadelphia.

First selfie in space
On Jul 18, 1966, *Gemini 10* launched with astronauts John Young and Michael Collins (both USA). A day later, while in orbit, Collins took this picture of himself sitting in the capsule.

First selfie in open space
On Nov 13, 1966, Edwin "Buzz" Aldrin, Jr. (USA) started the second of three spacewalks during the *Gemini 12* mission. During the 2-hr 6-min tethered walk in open space, he took photos of the visible star fields and of himself.

Need for 3D: real printing

The **first 3D-printed football cleat shoes** (left) were tailored by Nike in 2013 for NFL footballers. Nike's Vapor Laser Talon boots have soles made by "selective laser sintering," in which lasers fuse small particles of plastic. The **first 3D-printed record** (above right) was made in 2013 by researcher Amanda Ghassaei (USA), who wrote code to transform audio files into 3D files. And Blizzident (ESP) produced the **first 3D-printed toothbrush** (right) in 2013, in which 400 bristles are mounted in a plastic mold made from scans of your mouth; you brush using a chewing motion.

Remote-control model vehicles

Fastest speed by a jet-powered aircraft: 439.29 mph on Sep 14, 2013, by a turbine-powered 4-ft 3-in-long plane built by Niels Herbrich (DEU).

Fastest speed by a battery-powered car: 171.95 mph on Dec 19, 2012, by the R/C Bullet, designed, built, and driven by Nic Case (USA).

Longest ramp jump by a remote-control car: 121 ft by a Carson Specter 6S, controlled by Thomas Strobel (DEU) on Jul 30, 2011.

Sports

On average, a tennis game lasts for two-and-a-half hours—of which the ball is in action for just **20 min**

Most "powerful" sports star (female)

The highest-ranked female athlete in Forbes' "most powerful" list is tennis player Serena Williams (USA). The list measures fame by taking into account celebrity earnings, exposure in print and on television, the strength of a star's Internet presence, public opinion, and marketability.

Serena also became the **first female athlete to win $50 million in prize money** when she won the US Open at Flushing Meadows in New York, USA, on Sep 8, 2013. And on Oct 27, 2013, at the age of 32 years 31 days, she became the **oldest female tennis player to be ranked world No. 1**.

What's more, she has enjoyed the **longest span of Grand Slam titles in the open era**, male or female. Her win over Victoria Azarenka at the US Open on Sep 8, 2013 came 13 years 362 days after her maiden Slam against Martina Hingis, in the same tournament, on Sep 11, 1999.

Contents

FACT

Serena's sister Venus shares a world record with Brenda Schultz-McCarthy (NLD) for the **fastest tennis serve (female)**—an incredible 129 mph.

Football

The 2013 Super Bowl was watched on TV by **164.1 million people**

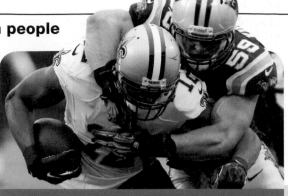

Longest NFL touchdown run by a quarterback

Terrelle Pryor of the Oakland Raiders ran for 93 yards before scoring a touchdown. The record run was set during an NFL (National Football League) game against the Pittsburgh Steelers on Oct 27, 2013.

Kansas City Chiefs, and Minnesota Vikings.

Andersen also scored records for the **most points** (2,544), **most successful field goals** (565), and **most attempted field goals** (709) in an NFL career.

Most consecutive games played

Jeff Feagles appeared in 352 consecutive games between 1988 and 2009 while playing for the New England Patriots, Philadelphia Eagles, Arizona Cardinals, Seattle Seahawks, and New York Giants.

Most tackles in an NFL game

Luke Kuechly of the Carolina Panthers made 24 tackles in a game against the New Orleans Saints on Dec 22, 2013, tying the single-game NFL record set by David Harris of the New York Jets, playing against the Washington Redskins, on Nov 4, 2007.

NFL

Most seasons played

George Blanda played for four different teams across 26 NFL seasons. He first played in 1949 and ended his career with the Oakland Raiders in 1967–75.

Most seasons played for the same team

Jason Hanson spent 21 seasons (1992 to 2012) with the Detroit Lions.

Most games played

Between 1982 and 2007, place kicker Morten Andersen (DNK) played in 382 games with the New Orleans Saints, Atlanta Falcons, New York Giants,

Most points by a player in a season

San Diego Chargers' LaDainian Tomlinson scored 186 points in 2006. In the same year, the running back secured the **most touchdowns in a season**, with 31.

Most points by a team in a season

Colorado's Denver Broncos scored 606 points during the 2013 season.

Most points in a game

Ernie Nevers scored 40 points for the Chicago (now Arizona) Cardinals on Nov 28, 1929. Also in 1929, Nevers racked up the **most touchdowns in an NFL game** (six), a feat matched by William "Dub" Jones in 1951 and Gale Sayers in 1965.

Most consecutive games scoring a touchdown

Two footballers managed at least one touchdown in 18 consecutive games: Lenny Moore from 1963 to 1965 and LaDainian Tomlinson in 2004–05.

Most field goals in a season

David Akers kicked 44 field goals in the 2011 season for the San Francisco 49ers. In the same year, he recorded the **most field goals attempted in a season** (52).

Most NFL career yards gained by interception return

Baltimore Ravens, Houston Texans, and New York Jets star Ed Reed accumulated 1,590 interception return yards from 2002 to 2013. He also recorded the **longest interception return for a touchdown**, with 107 yards while playing for the Ravens against the Philadelphia Eagles on Nov 23, 2008. He broke his own record of 106 yards, set against the Cleveland Browns on Nov 7, 2004.

Most NFL career interception returns for touchdown

Rod Woodson scored 12 touchdowns after intercepting a pass during an NFL career played with the Pittsburgh Steelers, Baltimore Ravens, and Oakland Raiders from 1987 to 2003.

Most yards rushing in a game

On Nov 4, 2007, Minnesota Vikings running back Adrian Peterson gained 296 yards rushing in a game. The 2007 season saw Peterson named NFL Offensive Rookie of the Year.

Most pass completions in a playoff game

Drew Brees completed 40 passes for the New Orleans Saints in a playoff game against the San Francisco 49ers on Jan 12, 2014.

SUPER BOWL GAME RECORDS

Most yards gained passing	407	St. Louis Rams (2000)
Most yards gained rushing	280	Washington Redskins (1988)
Most yards gained by interceptions	172	Tampa Bay Buccaneers (2003)
Most rushing attempts	57	Pittsburgh Steelers (1975)
Most points	55	San Francisco 49ers (1990)
Largest margin of victory	45	San Francisco 49ers vs. Denver Broncos, 55–10 (1990)
Most passes completed	34	Denver Broncos (2014)
Most first downs	31	San Francisco 49ers (1985)
Most penalties	12	Dallas Cowboys (1978)
		Carolina Panthers (2004)
Most punts	11	New York Giants (2001)
Most kickoff returns	9	Denver Broncos (1990)
		Oakland Raiders (2003)
Most turnovers	9	Buffalo Bills (1993)
Most fumbles	8	Buffalo Bills (1993)
Most touchdowns	8	San Francisco 49ers (1990)
Most punt returns	6	Washington Redskins (1983)
		Green Bay Packers (1997)
Most interceptions	5	Tampa Bay Buccaneers (2003)
Most field goals	4	Green Bay Packers (1968)
		San Francisco 49ers (1982)

Correct as of Feb 3, 2014

Most career return touchdowns
Devin Hester and Deion Sanders have achieved 19 return touchdowns each.

Most career receiving yards by a tight end
Tony Gonzalez gained 15,127 receiving yards for the Kansas City Chiefs and the Atlanta Falcons from 1997 to 2013.

SUPER BOWL

Most games played
Mike Lodish has played in six Super Bowl games: four for the Buffalo Bills in 1991–94 and two for the Denver Broncos in 1998–99.

Most points in a game
Four players have scored 18 points in a Super Bowl game: Roger Craig in 1985; Jerry Rice twice, in 1990 and 1995; Ricky Watters in 1995; and Terrell Davis in 1998.

Most career touchdowns
Jerry Rice racked up eight touchdowns in Super Bowl games, as well as the **most career NFL touchdowns** (208) in 1985–2004.

Most career field goals
Adam Vinatieri scored seven field goals in Super Bowl games in 2001–06.

Most yards rushing in a game
During Super Bowl XXII (1988), the Washington Redskins' Timmy Smith gained 204 yards rushing.

Longest NFL field goal
Denver Broncos' Matt Prater set the NFL field goal record by kicking a 64-yard goal in a game against the Tennessee Titans on Dec 8, 2013. The previous mark of 63 yards was set by New Orleans Saints' Tom Dempsey in 1970 and had later been tied three times.

CFL

Most touchdown passes in a career
Anthony Calvillo has thrown 455 touchdown passes in his CFL (Canadian Football League) career. He played for the Las Vegas Posse and Canada's Hamilton Tiger-Cats and Montreal Alouettes from 1994 to 2013.

Highest pass completion percentage in a season
Ricky Ray completed 77.23% of his passes (234 of 303) for the Toronto Argonauts (CAN) in 2013.

Most career pass completions
From 1994 to 2013, Anthony Calvillo set many CFL records, including 5,892 pass completions and the **most pass attempts in a career** (9,437).

Most yards rushing in a Grey Cup game
The 101st CFL Grey Cup on Nov 24, 2013 saw Kory Sheets run for 197 yards while leading the Saskatchewan Roughriders (CAN).

First player to record 200 receiving yards in consecutive NFL games
Josh Gordon of the Cleveland Browns recorded 237 receiving yards on Nov 24, 2013, and then 267 receiving yards on Dec 1, 2013. It marked the first time in NFL history that a player had logged consecutive 200-yard receiving games.

For soccer, see pp. 236–39

Pig in a blanket
American footballs were originally made from natural materials, most commonly a pig's bladder wrapped in leather.

All players and teams USA unless otherwise stated.

Track & field

If he could sustain his peak speed, it would take Usain Bolt **44 days** to sprint around the globe

Most IAAF Athlete of the Year trophies won
Male: Usain Bolt (JAM) has won the International Association of Athletics Federations' (IAAF) Athlete of the Year trophy five times, in 2008–09 and 2011–13.
Female: The women's record belongs to Yelena Isinbayeva (RUS) with three wins, in 2004–05 and 2008.

DIAMOND LEAGUE

Youngest meeting winner
Male: Conseslus Kipruto (KEN, b. Dec 8, 1994) won the 3,000-m steeplechase Diamond League title in 2012 aged 17 years 225 days old.
Female: Francine Niyonsaba (BDI, b. May 5, 1993) is the youngest female winner, taking the 800-m crown on Sep 7, 2012 at the age of 19 years 126 days.

Oldest meeting winner
Male: Discus thrower Virgilijus Alekna (LTU, b. Feb 13, 1972) was 39 years 175 days old when he won the London meet in 2011. Female: Brigitte Foster-Hylton (JAM, b. Nov 7, 1974) took the 100-m hurdles crown in Doha, Qatar, at the age of 37 years 187 days in 2012.

Most titles won
A man and a woman have each won four Diamond Race titles. Renaud Lavillenie (FRA,

above) won the pole vault from 2010 to 2013 and Milcah Chemos Cheywa (KEN) won four 3,000-m steeplechase events between 2010 and 2013.

OLYMPICS

Most northerly Summer Games
The XV Olympiad (1952) in Helsinki, Finland, was located at 60.1-degree latitude and 24.6-degree longitude. By contrast, the 1956 Summer Games in Melbourne, Australia, were the **most southerly**, at a 37.5-degree latitude and 144.6-degree longitude. The **highest altitude Summer Games** were

Highest indoors pole vault (male)
Renaud Lavillenie (FRA) achieved 20 ft 2.5 in (6.16 m) in the indoors pole vault at Pole Vault Stars in Donetsk, Ukraine, on Feb 15, 2014. The previous record of 20 ft 2.12 in (6.15 m), set by pole vault legend Sergey Bubka, had stood for almost 21 years.

the 1968 Games in Mexico City, Mexico, at 7,380 ft (2,250 m) above sea level.

Most track & field golds
Male: Paavo Nurmi (FIN) won nine track & field golds in 1920–28. Carl Lewis (USA) matched his feat between 1984 and 1996.
Female: Six women have four golds to their name, the

Sprinting hat-trick

Shelly-Ann Fraser-Pryce (JAM) became the **first woman to win three sprint golds at one World Championships** when she won the 100 m, 200 m, and 4 x 100 m relay at the 2013 IAAF event on Aug 12–18. Maurice Greene (USA) was the **first athlete** to achieve the feat, doing so at the 1999 World Championships in the same three events.

OUTDOOR TRACK EVENTS (MALE)

Event	Time	Name (Nationality)	Date
100 m	9.58	Usain Bolt (JAM)	Aug 16, 2009
200 m	19.19	Usain Bolt (JAM)	Aug 20, 2009
400 m	43.18	Michael Johnson (USA)	Aug 26, 1999
800 m	1:40.91	David Lekuta Rudisha (KEN)	Aug 9, 2012
1,000 m	2:11.96	Noah Ngeny (KEN)	Sep 5, 1999
1,500 m	3:26.00	Hicham El Guerrouj (MAR)	Jul 14, 1998
1 mile	3:43.13	Hicham El Guerrouj (MAR)	Jul 7, 1999
2,000 m	4:44.79	Hicham El Guerrouj (MAR)	Sep 7, 1999
3,000 m	7:20.67	Daniel Komen (KEN)	Sep 1, 1996
5,000 m	12:37.35	Kenenisa Bekele (ETH)	May 31, 2004
10,000 m	26:17.53	Kenenisa Bekele (ETH)	Aug 26, 2005
20,000 m	56:26.00	Haile Gebrselassie (ETH)	Jun 27, 2007
25,000 m	1:12:25.4	Moses Cheruiyot Mosop (KEN)	Jun 3, 2011
30,000 m	1:26:47.4	Moses Cheruiyot Mosop (KEN)	Jun 3, 2011
3,000 m steeple-chase	7:53.63	Saif Saaeed Shaheen (QAT)	Sep 3, 2004
110 m hurdles	12.80	Aries Merritt (USA)	Sep 7, 2012
400 m hurdles	46.78	Kevin Young (USA)	Aug 6, 1992
4 x 100 m relay	36.84	Jamaica	Aug 11, 2012
4 x 200 m relay	1:18.68	Santa Monica Track Club (USA)	Apr 17, 1994
4 x 400 m relay	2:54.29	USA	Aug 22, 1993
4 x 800 m relay	7:02.43	Kenya	Aug 25, 2006
4 x 1,500 m relay	14:36.23	Kenya	Sep 4, 2009

OUTDOOR FIELD EVENTS (MALE)

Event	Meters	Name (Nationality)	Date
High jump	2.45	Javier Sotomayor (CUB)	Jul 27, 1993
Pole vault	6.14	Sergey Bubka (UKR)	Jul 31, 1994
Long jump	8.95	Mike Powell (USA)	Aug 30, 1991
Triple jump	18.29	Jonathan Edwards (UK)	Aug 7, 1995
Shot put	23.12	Randy Barnes (USA)	May 20, 1990
Discus	74.08	Jürgen Schult (GDR)	Jun 6, 1986
Hammer	86.74	Yuriy Sedykh (USSR)	Aug 30, 1986
Javelin	98.48	Jan Železný (CZE)	May 25, 1996
Event	**Points**	**Name (Nationality)**	**Date**
Decathlon	9,039	Ashton Eaton (USA)	Jun 23, 2012

Statistics correct as of Mar 12, 2014

OUTDOOR TRACK EVENTS (FEMALE)

Event	Time	Name (Nationality)	Date
100 m	10.49	Florence Griffith-Joyner (USA)	Jul 16, 1988
200 m	21.34	Florence Griffith-Joyner (USA)	Sep 29, 1988
400 m	47.60	Marita Koch (GDR)	Oct 6, 1985
800 m	1:53.28	Jarmila Kratochvílová (TCH)	Jul 26, 1983
1,000 m	2:28.98	Svetlana Masterkova (RUS)	Aug 23, 1996
1,500 m	3:50.46	Yunxia Qu (CHN)	Sep 11, 1993
1 mile	4:12.56	Svetlana Masterkova (RUS)	Aug 14, 1996
2,000 m	5:25.36	Sonia O'Sullivan (IRL)	Jul 8, 1994
3,000 m	8:06.11	Junxia Wang (CHN)	Sep 13, 1993
5,000 m	14:11.15	Tirunesh Dibaba (ETH)	Jun 6, 2008
10,000 m	29:31.78	Junxia Wang (CHN)	Sep 8, 1993
20,000 m	1:05:26.6	Tegla Loroupe (KEN)	Sep 3, 2000
25,000 m	1:27:05.9	Tegla Loroupe (KEN)	Sep 21, 2002
30,000 m	1:45:50.0	Tegla Loroupe (KEN)	Jun 6, 2003
3,000 m steeple-chase	8:58.81	Gulnara Samitova-Galkina (RUS)	Aug 17, 2008
100 m hurdles	12.21	Yordanka Donkova (BGR)	Aug 20, 1988
400 m hurdles	52.34	Yuliya Pechenkina (RUS)	Aug 8, 2003
4 x 100 m relay	40.82	USA	Aug 10, 2012
4 x 200 m relay	1:27.46	USA "Blue"	Apr 29, 2000
4 x 400 m relay	3:15.17	USSR	Oct 1, 1988
4 x 800 m relay	7:50.17	USSR	Aug 5, 1984
4 x 1,500 m relay	17:09.75	Australia	Jun 25, 2000

OUTDOOR FIELD EVENTS (FEMALE)

Event	Meters	Name (Nationality)	Date
High jump	2.09	Stefka Kostadinova (BGR)	Aug 30, 1987
Pole vault	5.06	Yelena Isinbayeva (RUS)	Aug 28, 2009
Long jump	7.52	Galina Chistyakova (USSR)	Jun 11, 1988
Triple jump	15.50	Inessa Kravets (UKR)	Aug 10, 1995
Shot put	22.63	Natalya Lisovskaya (USSR)	Jun 7, 1987
Discus	76.80	Gabriele Reinsch (GDR)	Jul 9, 1988
Hammer	79.42	Betty Heidler (DEU)	May 21, 2011
Javelin	72.28	Barbora Špotáková (CZE)	Sep 13, 2008

Event	Points	Name (Nationality)	Date
Heptathlon	7,291	Jackie Joyner-Kersee (USA)	Sep 24, 1988
Decathlon	8,358	Austra Skujytė (LTU)	Apr 15, 2005

Statistics correct as of Mar 12, 2014

most recent being Sanya Richards-Ross (USA) and Allyson Felix, who added to their tallies in 2012.

PARALYMPICS

Most track & field medals
Male: Heinz Frei (CHE) competed in 14 Paralympic competitions between 1984 and 2012—both Winter and Summer Games. He won 22 track & field medals in total.

Youngest World Championships relay medalist
Female: Dina Asher-Smith (UK, b. Dec 4, 1995) won 4 x 100-m bronze at 17 years 247 days old in 2013.
Male: Darrel Brown (TTO, b. Oct 11, 1984) was 16 years 305 days old when he won 4 x 100-m silver in 2001.

Female: Chantal Petitclerc (CAN) won 21 Paralympic track & field medals between 1992 and 2008 in distances between 100 m and 1,500 m.
Chantal also holds the record for the **most Paralympic track & field gold medals** (14), a record she shares with male athlete Franz Nietlispach (CHE).

IAAF WORLD CHAMPIONSHIPS

Most appearances
Male: Spanish 50-km walker Jesús Ángel García competed in 11 IAAF World Championships between 1993 and 2013.
Female: Susana Feitór (POR) also appeared 11 times, contesting three different events

between 1991 and 2011: the 10,000-m walk, 10-km walk, and 20-km walk.

Most gold medals
Four athletes—three men and one woman—have won eight gold medals at the World Championships. Carl Lewis was the first in 1983–91, a feat matched by Michael Johnson (1991–99), Allyson Felix (all USA, 2005–11), and Usain Bolt (JAM, 2009–13).

Most 200-m wins
Female: Allyson Felix won three consecutive 200-m golds, in 2005–09.
Male: Usain Bolt matched her record in 2009–13.

Most consecutive 4 x 400-m relay wins
LaShawn Merritt (USA) won gold in four World Championships in a row in 2007–13.

Most points in Diamond League track & field meetings

Female: The most points scored in a Diamond League career is 94, by Valerie Adams (NZ, above) in the shot put in 2010–13. An athlete scores points by finishing in the top three at a meeting.
Male: Renaud Lavillenie (see left) has scored the most points for a man. By the end of the 2013 Diamond League season, he had 86 points.

Most medals won at the IAAF World Championships

Male: The most medals accumulated by a man at the World Championships is 10, by Carl Lewis (below), who won eight gold, one silver, and one bronze between 1983 and 1993. His feat was equaled by Usain Bolt (left), who won eight gold and two silver medals between 2007 and 2013.
Female: Merlene Ottey (JAM) won 14 medals—three gold, four silver, and seven bronze—from 1983 to 1997.

Ball sports

A brutal Mayan ball game played 3,000 years ago may have used **severed human heads**

Highest team score in a Netball World series final

New Zealand scored the most points in a final of netball's top competition, aka Netball Fast5, when they beat Australia on Nov 10, 2013. The Ferns won by 29, with a final score of 56–27.

Largest attendance for a netball match
The Allphones Arena in Sydney, Australia, recorded an official attendance of 14,339 for the Australia vs New Zealand international game on Nov 13, 2004. Australia won 54–49.

Highest total score in a women's World Handball Championship final
On Dec 14, 2003, France and Hungary met in the World Championship final in Croatia. France won by 32 points to 29 for an aggregate score of 61.

Most World Polo Championships
Argentina have won the World Championships four times since its inauguration in 1987, taking the crown in 1987, 1992, 1998, and 2011.

FIELD HOCKEY

Most World Cups
Female: The Dutch women's team won the field hockey World Cup six times between 1974 and 2006.
Male: Pakistan hold the record for the most men's World Cup wins with four between 1971 and 1994.

Most international goals scored
Defender Sohail Abbas (PAK) scored 348 goals between Mar 1, 1998 and Aug 5, 2012.

Largest winning margin in a men's World Handball Championship final

The biggest score difference in an International Handball Federation men's World Championship final is 16 goals. It was achieved by Spain, who beat Denmark 35–19 in the 2013 final at the Palau Sant Jordi stadium in Barcelona, Spain, on Jan 27. Pictured is pivot Julen Aguinagalde (ESP, left) vying with Denmark's left back Mikkel Hansen.

Most wins of the men's African Cup for Nations
The field hockey African Cup for Nations is a qualifier for the World Cup and in some years the Olympic Games. The greatest number of wins is seven, by South Africa between 1993 and 2013.

Largest margin of victory in an Olympic match
Male: The third men's field hockey match at the 1932 Olympics in Los Angeles, California, USA, saw India beat the home team 24–1.
Female: South Africa beat the USA 7–0 at London 2012 on Aug 6.

GAA

Most All-Ireland Hurling championships won
The GAA (Gaelic Athletic Association) sport of hurling is a fast-moving Irish stick-and-ball sport (not unlike a free-form version of hockey). Kilkenny won its top competition—contested by intercounty teams—34 times between 1904 and 2012.

Most All-Ireland Senior Camogie championships
Camogie is hurling, but played by women. Dublin have the greatest number of All-Ireland titles with 26.

Most All-Ireland Hurling championships won (individual)

Henry Shefflin (IRL) secured nine medals— and countless battle scars—while playing for Kilkenny in 2000, 2002–03, 2006–09, 2011, and 2012. One of the game's greats, Waterford-born Shefflin (nicknamed "King Henry") is a center forward—and works as a bank official when not winning trophies.

Most All-Ireland Gaelic Football championships
Gaelic football is roughly a cross between rugby and soccer. Kerry have won 36 championships—more than any other side.

KORFBALL

Highest score in a mixed World Championship final
Korfball is a mixed-gender sport similar to netball and basketball. The final on Nov 5, 2011 saw the Netherlands score 32 points against Belgium in Shaoxing, China.

Most Europa Cup titles
Dutch team PKC won the Europa Cup seven times, in 1985, 1990, 1999–2000, 2002, 2006, and 2014.
The Dutch national team have the **most World Games titles** (8) having won

FACT
A type of handball was played by the ancient Greeks in Homer's *Odyssey*, using a ball made of purple wool.

Most women's Volleyball World Grand Champions Cups

Brazil became the first women's team to win the FIVB World Grand Champions Cup twice when they triumphed in Tokyo, Japan, on Nov 17, 2013. The first five editions were won by different countries; Brazil had previously won it in 2005.

every korfball tournament at the World Games between 1985 and 2013.

LACROSSE

Most men's World Championship titles
Between 1967 and 2010, the men's USA team won nine World Lacrosse Championship titles. The USA also hold the record

for **most women's Lacrosse World Cup titles**, with seven golds between 1982 and 2013.

Fastest shot
Mike Sawyer (USA) recorded 114 mph (183 km/h) in Charlotte, North Carolina, USA, on Jul 13, 2013.

VOLLEYBALL

Most men's FIVB Volleyball World League titles
The Fédération Internationale de Volleyball World League is an annual event in which teams compete in pools before the best sides progress to the final round. The most men's World League wins is nine, by Brazil in 1993, 2001, 2003–07, and 2009–10.

Most FIVB Volleyball World League participants (men)
In 2013, 18 countries from four continents took part in the FIVB Volleyball World League. Russia were the eventual winners, seeing off Brazil 3-0 in the final.

Most appearances by a pair in men's FIVB beach volleyball events
Norwegian duo Vegard Høidalen and Jørre Kjemperud recorded

135 appearances in FIVB beach volleyball events between 1987 and 2010.

> **FACT**
> In 1363, hockey was banned in England by King Edward III, along with soccer and other "idle games."

Most goals by an individual in the Euro Hockey League

The top scorer in the Euro Hockey League (field hockey's top competition) is Jeroen Hertzberger (NLD). The striker notched up 32 goals for HC Rotterdam between Oct 27, 2007 and Oct 25, 2013.

Most points scored in a lacrosse season

The highest points tally accumulated in a single Major League Lacrosse season is 72, by Paul Rabil (USA) while playing for the Boston Cannons in the 2012 season.

AUSTRALIAN RULES FOOTBALL: Most...

Career games	426	Michael Tuck (1972–91)
Consecutive games	244	Jim Stynes (1987–98)
Career goals	1,360	Tony Lockett (1983–2002)
Goals in a season	150	Bob Pratt (1934)
		Peter Hudson (1971)
Goals in a game	18	Fred Fanning (1947)

CANADIAN FOOTBALL: Most...

Career games	408	Lui Passaglia (1976–2000)
Consecutive games	353	Bob Cameron (1980–2000)
Career touchdowns	147	Milt Stegall (1992–2008)
Touchdowns (season)	23	Milt Stegall (2002)
Touchdowns (game)	6	Eddie James (1932)
		Bob McNamara (1956)

Most tournament titles in women's beach volleyball

Kerri Walsh Jennings (USA) has the most tournament wins with 113. This total comprises 67 domestic and 46 international wins from May 2001 to Oct 28, 2013. Walsh Jennings has won 113 (60%) of the 189 tournaments she has entered, mostly alongside Misty May-Treanor (USA), whose record she broke on Oct 28, 2013.

Baseball

To improve grip for pitchers, every MLB baseball is rubbed in **mud from a secret site** in New Jersey

Most grand slam home runs in a MLB career

A grand slam home run is a homer hit with batters on all the bases. Since 1994, Alex Rodriguez has hit 24 of them for the Seattle Mariners, Texas Rangers, and New York Yankees.

MOST GAMES ...

Finished in a career
Playing for the New York Yankees between 1995 and 2013, Mariano Rivera (PAN) was the last pitcher for his team in 952 games. With the Yankees, he also recorded the **most games pitched with one team**: 1,115.

Won consecutively by a pitcher
Masahiro Tanaka (JPN) won 30 successive games pitching for Japan's Tohoku Rakuten Golden Eagles from Aug 26, 2012 to Oct 27, 2013. Tanaka also recorded the **most consecutive baseball games won by a pitcher during regular-season play** (28), again for the Tohoku Rakuten Golden Eagles, from Aug 26, 2012 to Oct 8, 2013. For the same team, Tanaka registered the **most consecutive baseball games won by a pitcher in a season** (24), from Apr 2 to Oct 8, 2013.

Won consecutively by a pitcher in the MLB
Roger Clemens (USA) won 20 consecutive games for the Toronto Blue Jays and New York Yankees from Jun 3, 1998 to Jun 1, 1999.

Most strikeouts by a pitching staff in a season

Detroit Tigers pitchers struck out 1,428 batters during the 2013 season. Their achievement surpasses the previous record of 1,404 by the Chicago Cubs' pitching staff in 2003.

MOST HOME RUNS ...

By a catcher
Mike Piazza (USA) hit 396 home runs (with an overall total of 427) while playing for the Los Angeles Dodgers, Florida Marlins, New York Mets, San Diego Padres, and Oakland Athletics from 1992 to 2007.

By a switch hitter
Playing for the New York Yankees from 1951 to 1968, Mickey Mantle (USA) hit 536 home runs.

Most home runs in a career by a designated hitter

David Ortiz (DOM) has hit 381 career home runs—a Major League Baseball (MLB) record for a designated hitter—from an overall total of 431 home runs, playing for the Minnesota Twins and the Boston Red Sox since 1997. His 47 home runs for the Red Sox in 2006 represent the **most home runs by a designated hitter in a season**. His overall home run total was 54.

Most combined wins and saves
Andy Pettitte (USA) and Mariano Rivera (PAN) combined for a win and a save 72 times while pitching for the New York Yankees from 1996 to 2013.

Oldest player to hit a walk-off home run
A walk-off home run is a game-ending homer on the final pitch of the game that results in a victory for the home team. At 42 years 202 days old, Jason Giambi (USA, b. Jan 8, 1971) is the oldest player in MLB history to perform such a feat. Giambi accomplished the record with a pinch-hit homer in the ninth inning to defeat the Chicago White Sox on Jul 29, 2013.

Most doubles hit in a season
Earl Webb (USA) hit 67 doubles playing for the Boston Red Sox

in 1931. The **most triples hit in a season by an individual player** is 36, by "Chief" Wilson (USA) for the Pittsburgh Pirates in 1912.

Youngest player to hit 30 home runs and steal 30 bases in a season

At the age of 21 years 53 days, Mike Trout (USA, b. Aug 7, 1991, left) became the youngest MLB player ever to hit 30 or more home runs and steal 30 or more bases within just one season. He accomplished this feat while playing for the Los Angeles Angels of Anaheim in 2013. Before Trout, the youngest person to do this had been 22-year-old Alex Rodriguez, while playing for the Seattle Mariners in 1998.

Most consecutive baseball crowd sellouts

The longest home sellout streak in major pro sports history (i.e., Major League Baseball, the National Basketball Association, the National Football League, and the National Hockey League) lasted 820 games. The Boston Red Sox set it with every home game at Fenway Park in Boston, USA, from May 15, 2003 to Apr 10, 2013.

By a second baseman
Jeff Kent (USA) scored 351 home runs as a second baseman (with an overall total of 377) with the Toronto Blue Jays, New York Mets, Cleveland Indians, San Francisco Giants, Houston Astros, and LA Dodgers from 1992 to 2008.

The **most home runs in one season hit by a third baseman** stands at 52 (with an overall total that season of 54), scored by Alex Rodriguez (USA) for the New York Yankees in 2007.

First father-and-son home runs in sequential at bats

Ken Griffey and his son Ken, Jr. (USA) hit back-to-back home runs for the Seattle Mariners on Sep 14, 1990. They also became the **first father-son duo to play on the same team at the same time**, on Aug 31, 1990.

MOST STRIKEOUTS ...

By a batter in a postseason
Alfonso Soriano (DOM) struck out 26 times in 17 games while playing for the New York Yankees in the 2003 postseason.

By a pitching staff in a postseason series
Detroit Tigers pitchers struck out 73 Boston Red Sox batters over the course of the six-game American League Championship Series in 2013.

By a batter in a season
The MLB record for most strikeouts by a batter in a season is 223, by Mark Reynolds (USA) for the Arizona Diamondbacks in 2009. In doing so, he surpassed his own mark of 204, established in 2008.

By a pitcher in a career
Nolan Ryan (USA) recorded 5,714 strikeouts while playing for the New York Mets, California Angels, Houston Astros, and Texas Rangers from 1966 to 1993.

By a team in a season
Houston Astros (USA) batters struck out 1,535 times during the 2013 season, surpassing the previous mark of 1,529 by the Arizona Diamondbacks in 2010.

By batters in a postseason (team)
Boston Red Sox (USA) batters struck out 165 times in 16 playoff games during the 2013 postseason.

Across all teams in a season
Major league batters struck out 36,710 times in the 2013 regular season.

First siblings to hit home runs in successive at bats

On Apr 23, 2013, B. J. Upton and his brother Justin (USA, above) struck back-to-back home runs for the Atlanta Braves against the Colorado Rockies, becoming only the second pair of siblings to do so. The first were Lloyd and Paul Waner (USA) of the Pittsburgh Pirates, who hit successive homers on Sep 15, 1938. The Uptons' feat marked the 27th time in MLB history that brothers had homered in the same game.

Most saves in a career

The MLB record for most career saves is 652, achieved by Mariano "Sandman" Rivera (PAN) playing for 19 seasons with the New York Yankees from 1995—when he made his MLB debut—to his retirement in 2013. New York mayor Michael Bloomberg declared Sep 22, 2013 "Mariano Rivera Day" in his honor.

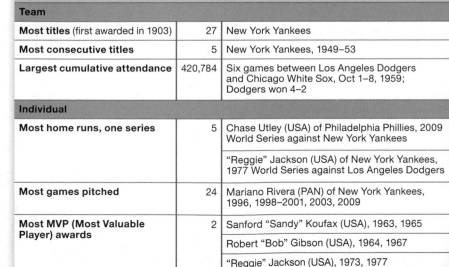

> ### *i* The last 42 in history
>
> Rivera was the last baseball player to wear a number 42 shirt in baseball history. The shirt was retired across the major leagues on Apr 15, 1997 in memory of baseball legend Jackie Robinson of MLB's Brooklyn Dodgers.

MAJOR LEAGUE BASEBALL (MLB) WORLD SERIES RECORDS

Team		
Most titles (first awarded in 1903)	27	New York Yankees
Most consecutive titles	5	New York Yankees, 1949–53
Largest cumulative attendance	420,784	Six games between Los Angeles Dodgers and Chicago White Sox, Oct 1–8, 1959; Dodgers won 4–2

Individual		
Most home runs, one series	5	Chase Utley (USA) of Philadelphia Phillies, 2009 World Series against New York Yankees
		"Reggie" Jackson (USA) of New York Yankees, 1977 World Series against Los Angeles Dodgers
Most games pitched	24	Mariano Rivera (PAN) of New York Yankees, 1996, 1998–2001, 2003, 2009
Most MVP (Most Valuable Player) awards	2	Sanford "Sandy" Koufax (USA), 1963, 1965
		Robert "Bob" Gibson (USA), 1964, 1967
		"Reggie" Jackson (USA), 1973, 1977

Statistics correct as of the end of the 2013 season

Basketball

The late "Chick" Hearn is credited with coining the phrase **"slam dunk"**

Most games in an NBA career

Robert Parish played 1,611 NBA (National Basketball Association) regular-season games from 1976 to 1997. His 21-season career saw him play for the Golden State Warriors (1976–80), Boston Celtics (1980–94), Charlotte Hornets (1994–96), and Chicago Bulls (1996–97).

rebounds at just 27 years 130 days old. He took the record while playing for the Los Angeles Lakers in a game against the Houston Rockets on Apr 17, 2013.

Oldest player to record 20 rebounds in a game
On Mar 2, 2007, at the age of 40 years 251 days, Dikembe Mutombo (COD, b. Jun 25, 1966) of the Houston Rockets became the oldest player in NBA history to get more than 20 rebounds in a game, with 22.

Most free throws attempted in a game
Dwight Howard equaled his own record of 39 while playing for the Los Angeles Lakers on Mar 12, 2013.

Most free throws in a WNBA career

As of Feb 12, 2014, Tamika Catchings had made 1,709 free throws in Women's National Basketball Association (WNBA) games. Catchings—who has played for the Indiana Fever since 2002—also holds the record for **most steals in a WNBA career**, with 930.

NBA

Most career minutes
During Kareem Abdul-Jabbar's 20-year NBA pro career, he spent 57,446 min on court for the Milwaukee Bucks and the Los Angeles Lakers (1969–89)—that's almost 40 days!

First players to win an NBA and Olympic title in one year
In 1992, Michael Jordan and Scottie Pippen won the NBA finals playing with the Chicago Bulls, then won an Olympic basketball gold as part of the USA team.

Most consecutive games played
A. C. Green played in 1,192 consecutive games for the Los Angeles Lakers, Phoenix Suns, Dallas Mavericks, and Miami Heat from Nov 19, 1986 to Apr 18, 2001.

Youngest player to reach 9,000 rebounds
Dwight Howard (b. Dec 8, 1985) had recorded 9,000

> ## FACT
> The NBA three-point line is 23 ft 9 in from the middle of the basket, while the WNBA line is 22 ft 1.75 in from the top of the key.

Most three-pointers attempted by a team in an NBA season

The New York Knicks attempted 2,371 three-point field goals during the 2012/13 season, 891 of which were successful—the **most three-pointers scored in a season**. The Knicks also hold the record for the **longest postseason losing streak**, with 13 consecutive playoff games lost from 2001 to 2012.

Most consecutive games scoring a three-pointer
Kyle Korver's run of scoring a three-pointer per game hit 127, ending on Mar 5, 2014. It began on Nov 4, 2012, and beat Dana Barros' 89-game record on Dec 6, 2013.

Most three-pointers in a game
Kobe Bryant (Los Angeles Lakers) and Donyell Marshall (Toronto Raptors) each scored 12 three-pointers, on Jan 7, 2003 and Mar 13, 2005 respectively.

Most wins of Defensive Player of the Year

Two players have been named NBA Defensive Player of the Year four times, as of the end of the 2014 season. Dikembe Mutombo (COD) won for the Denver Nuggets, Atlanta Hawks, and Philadelphia 76ers between 1994 and 2001, and Ben Wallace (above left) was awarded the title for the Detroit Pistons between 2001 and 2006.

Most three-pointers in a season
Stephen Curry accumulated 272 three-point field goals while playing for the Golden State Warriors during the 2012–13 season, surpassing the 269 recorded by Ray Allen in 2005–06.

As of Apr 16, 2014, Allen still holds the record for the **most three-point field goals in a career**, with 2,973 sunk since 1996. Allen joined Miami Heat in 2012.

Most three-pointers in an NBA Finals

Danny Green scored 27 three-point field goals in the 2013 NBA Finals. Green was playing for the San Antonio Spurs against Miami Heat in the Finals, which lasted seven games. He beat Ray Allen's 22 with the Boston Celtics in 2008.

NBA & WNBA—CAREER RECORDS

Individual	NBA		WNBA	
Most points	Kareem Abdul-Jabbar (1969–89)	38,387	Tina Thompson (1997–present)	7,488
Most rebounds	Wilt Chamberlain (1959–73)	23,924	Lisa Leslie (1997–2009)	3,307
Most field goals made	Kareem Abdul-Jabbar (1969–89)	15,837	Tina Thompson (1997–present)	2,630
Most assists	John Stockton (1984–2003)	15,806	Ticha Penicheiro (PRT, 1998–2012)	2,599
Most free throws made	Karl Malone (1985–2004)	9,787	Tamika Catchings (2002–present)	1,709
Most blocks	Hakeem Olajuwon (NGA, 1984–2002)	3,830	Margo Dydek (POL, 1998–2008)	877
Most steals	John Stockton (1984–2003)	3,265	Tamika Catchings (2002–present)	930
Team	**NBA**		**WNBA**	
Most Championship titles	Boston Celtics (1957, 1959–66, 1968–69, 1974, 1976, 1981, 1984, 1986, and 2008)	17	Houston Comets (1997–2000)	4
Most Finals appearances	Los Angeles Lakers (1949–50, 1952–54, 1959, 1962–63, 1965–66, 1968–70, 1972–73, 1980, 1982–85, 1987–89, 1991, 2000–02, 2004, and 2008–10)	31	Houston Comets (1997–2000)	4
			Detroit Shock (2003, and 2006–08)	
			New York Liberty (1997, 1999, 2000, and 2002)	

Correct as of 12 Feb 2014

Longest basketball shot

On Nov 11, 2013, Corey "Thunder" Law of the Harlem Globetrotters threw a basketball 109 ft 9 in (33.45 m) into the net. His record-breaking basket occurred at the US Airways Center in Phoenix, Arizona, USA, in celebration of GWR Day 2013. Three fellow Globetrotters gave it their best shot, but they fell short of Law's length.

The **most three-pointers in a game by a team** is 23, a record shared by the Orlando Magic (Jan 13, 2009) and the Houston Rockets (Feb 5, 2013).

Most three-pointers in a quarter

Joe Johnson scored eight three-pointers for the Brooklyn Nets on Dec 16, 2013, equaling Michael Redd's 2002 record.

WNBA

Most games in a career

As of Dec 20, 2013, Tina Thompson had played in 496 Women's National Basketball Association (WNBA) games. Her career began in 1997 with the Houston Comets; she has since played with the Los Angeles Sparks and is currently with Seattle Storm.

Thompson has also clocked up the **most minutes played in a WNBA career**, with 16,088—the equivalent of more than 11 days on court.

Most free throws attempted in a game

Two women have attempted 24 free throws in a game: Cynthia Cooper did so on Jul 3, 1998, and Tina Charles followed suit on Jun 29, 2013.

Highest rebounds per game average

Tina Charles—playing for the Connecticut Sun since 2010—also holds the record for rebounds per game: an unrivaled average of 10.8.

Most three-pointers in a career

Katie Smith had scored 906 three-pointers as of Feb 12, 2014, since her career began in 1999. Smith has played for five teams: Minnesota Lynx, Detroit Shock, Washington Mystics, Seattle Storm, and New York Liberty.

On Sep 8, 2013, Riquna Williams scored the **most three-pointers in a game**, with eight for the Tulsa Shock. Williams equaled the mark set twice by Diana Taurasi for Phoenix Mercury, on Aug 10, 2006 and May 25, 2010.

Largest half-time lead

Connecticut Sun led New York Liberty by a massive 34 points (61–27) at half-time on Jun 15, 2012. The Suns went on to win the match with a comfortable 97–55 victory. Their half-time lead bested Seattle Storm's 33-point margin against Tulsa Shock on Aug 7, 2010.

Fewest turnovers in an NBA game

The Oklahoma City Thunder committed just two turnovers against the Los Angeles Lakers on Mar 5, 2013, equaling the mark set by the Milwaukee Bucks in 2006 and Cleveland Cavaliers in 2009.

The **fewest turnovers in an NBA Finals game** is four, by the Detroit Pistons on Jun 16, 2005 and San Antonio Spurs on Jun 6, 2013.

All players and teams USA unless otherwise stated.

Most points scored in an NBA career

Kareem Abdul-Jabbar scored 38,387 points (at an average of 24.6 points per game) in his regular-season career from 1969 to 1989. He also scored 5,762 points in playoff games, which ranks second to 5,987 by Michael Jordan from 1984 to 1998.

Combat sports

Size matters: There are **no weight divisions** in pro sumo wrestling

WRESTLING

Most freestyle wrestling world titles (male)
Two men have won seven freestyle wrestling world titles: Aleksandr Medved (BLR) in the over-100-kg class between 1962 and 1971, and Valentin Jordanov (BGR) in the 55-kg class between 1983 and 1995.

Most siblings to win world boxing titles

As of Aug 1, 2013, brothers Kōki, Daiki, and Tomoki Kameda (JPN) had each won a world boxing title. Tomoki won the WBO bantamweight title, Kōki secured the WBA bantamweight crown, and Daiki started the brothers' success by winning the WBA flyweight title.

Most freestyle wrestling world titles

Between 2002 and 2013, Saori Yoshida (JPN) won a record 11 championships in the 55-kg wrestling class. This achievement—unmatched by any man or woman in Japan or anywhere else—saw Yoshida receive a Japanese People's Honour Award in Nov 2013.

BOXING

Most world title fights
Julio César Chávez (MEX) won 31 of his 37 fights contested between 1984 and 2000 in the super featherweight, lightweight, and light welterweight divisions.

Most flash KOs in a pro career
Mike Tyson (USA) managed nine under-60-sec knockouts during his career.

Shortest world title fight
Just 17 sec was all it took for Daniel Jiménez (PRI) to knock out Harold Geier. Jiménez was defending his WBO super bantamweight title at Wiener Neustadt in Austria on Sep 3, 1994.

Most career matches won by a sumo wrestler
Kaiō Hiroyuki (JPN) won 1,047 (of 1,731) bouts between Mar 1988 and Jul 2011. Remarkably, Kaiō initially doubted if he was good enough to make it as a sumo wrestler.

Heaviest living athlete
Sumo wrestler Emmanuel "Manny" Yarborough of Rahway, New Jersey, USA, stands 6 ft 8 in (203 cm) tall and weighs 704 lb (319.3 kg).

Most arm wrestling matches in 24 hours
On Feb 12, 2012, world champion Ion Oncescu (ROM) contested 1,024 arm wrestles in Bucharest, Romania. He won every match.

FENCING

Most individual world fencing titles
Male: Christian d'Oriola (FRA) won six foil titles in World Championships and Olympics between 1947 and 1956. Russian Stanislav Pozdnyakov matched this feat with six saber wins from 1996 to 2007.

Highest-selling pay-per-view boxing match

The junior middleweight fight between Saúl "El Canelo" Álvarez (MEX, left) and Floyd Mayweather Jr. (USA, right) on Sep 14, 2013 grossed $150 m from 2.2 million TV viewers. In addition, the venue in Las Vegas, Nevada, USA, sold out and another $20 m was taken in gate receipts.

Most siblings to win gold at a taekwondo championships

The López family (USA) won three gold medals at the World Taekwondo Championships in Madrid, Spain, in Apr 2005. Steven won the welterweight title, younger brother Mark the featherweight crown, and sister Diana took featherweight gold. Their coach was dad Jean.

Female: Valentina Vezzali (ITA) won nine individual foil titles: three Olympic golds and six at the World Fencing Championships. She won the titles in 1999–2011.

Most golds at the World Championships (country)
In 2013, Italy became the first nation to win more than 100 golds at the Fencing World Championships. As of the end of 2013, their tally stood at 101 gold, 97 silver, and 114 bronze medals.

MARTIAL ARTS

Most World Taekwondo Championships wins
Male: Steven López (USA) won five Championships: lightweight in 2001 and four welterweights in 2003–09.
Female: Jung Myung-suk's (KOR) three heavyweight wins came in 1993–97, a feat equaled by Brigitte Yagüe (ESP), who won finweight in 2003 and flyweight in 2007 and 2009.

Most single-leg martial arts kicks in one minute
Raul Meza (USA) performed 335 single-leg kicks at Meza's Karate America in Sioux Falls, South Dakota, USA, on Nov 17, 2011.

Most gold medals won at the World Combat Games
Russia's tally from 2010 in Beijing, China, and 2013 in St. Petersburg, Russia, is 65. The latter featured 97 nations and 135 events. Shown here is Nikita Selyanskiy in the 71-kg full-contact kickboxing category.

Most men's team kumite World Karate Championships wins
The first World Karate Championships were held in 1970. Since then, the French men's team have won the kumite title seven times, in 1972, 1994, 1996, 1998, 2000, 2004, and 2012.

UFC

Most fights won by decision
Georges St-Pierre (CAN) won 12 Ultimate Fighting Championship (UFC) fights by decision from Apr 16, 2005 to Nov 16, 2013. St-Pierre also holds the record for the **most UFC wins**—19—from Jan 31, 2004 to Nov 16, 2013.

Most fights won by KO
Anderson "The Spider" Silva (BRA) secured 20 knockout wins between 2000 and 2012. Silva also has the **most consecutive UFC wins**—17—in 2006–12.

Most World Judo Championships wins

Male: Teddy Riner (FRA) has won six titles—five at heavyweight (over-100 kg) in 2007, 2009–11, and 2013, and one with the French men's team in 2011.
Female: Ryoko Tani (JPN) won seven titles in the under-48-kg category in 1993–2007.

Shortest average contest time
The shortest average UFC contest time is 2 min 20 sec, achieved by Drew McFedries (USA) in 17 fights from Sep 8, 2001 to Jan 25, 2013.

Tallest UFC fighter
Stefan "Skyscraper" Struve (NLD), who competes as a heavyweight in the UFC, measures 6 ft 11 in (211 cm); he also reportedly has a phenomenal 7-ft (2.13-m) reach.

BOXING WINS—OLDEST AND YOUNGEST

Record	Age	Boxer	Title (date)
Oldest …			
World champion (male)	48 years 53 days	Bernard Hopkins (USA, b. Jan 15, 1965)	IBF light heavyweight (Mar 9, 2013)
World champion (female)	46 years 61 days	Alicia Ashley (USA/JAM, b. Aug 23, 1967)	WBC super bantamweight (Oct 23, 2013)
Youngest …			
World champion (male)	17 years 176 days	Wilfred Benítez (USA, b. Sep 12, 1958)	WBA light welterweight (Mar 6, 1976)
World champion (female)	18 years 342 days	Ju Hee Kim (KOR, b. Jan 13, 1986)	IFBA light flyweight (Dec 19, 2004)

Correct as of Jan 23, 2014

❌ For more strength, turn to p. 104

FACT

The only rules for the freestyle combat sport of pankration (recorded in the Olympic Games of 648 BC) were no biting and no eye gouging.

Longest total fight time in a UFC career

The longest overall time spent in the octagon (the eight-side enclosure where Ultimate Fighting Championship bouts take place) is 5 hr 28 min 21 sec, achieved by Georges St-Pierre (CAN) between Jan 25, 2002 and Nov 16, 2013. Pictured is St-Pierre (left)—fighting Jake Shields—on his way to successfully defending the welterweight title on Apr 30, 2011.

Cricket

With ca. 3 billion fans, cricket is the world's **second most popular sport**

Longest cricket ban
In Sep 2013, Indian bowler Shanthakumaran Sreesanth was handed a lifetime ban from cricket. He was found guilty of "spot-fixing," or fixing the game, in the Indian Premier League match between Rajasthan Royals and Kings XI Punjab on May 9, 2013.

Fastest delivery of a cricket ball
Shoaib Akhtar (PAK) bowled a ball at 100.23 mph (161.3 km/h) on Feb 22, 2003, during a World Cup match against England in Cape Town, South Africa.

Most wins of a domestic first-class cricket competition
New South Wales won Australia's Sheffield Shield 45 times between 1895–96 and 2007–08.

WICKETS

Most wickets without conceding a run in a women's ODI
Two women have taken three wickets without conceding a run in an ODI (One-Day International). Olivia Magno (AUS) snapped up three tail-end wickets in 1.4 overs on

FACT
Cricketers batting in positions 8 to 11 are known as the lower order or "tail."

Most wickets in a T20 International career (female)

Spin bowler Anisa Mohammed (TTO) is the leading wicket taker in women's Twenty20 Internationals. As of Mar 9, 2014, she had claimed 74 wickets in 59 matches playing for the West Indies, at an average of 13.68 runs conceded per wicket.

Most Champions League Twenty20 wins
The annual Champions League Twenty20 (T20) is contested by leading domestic teams from seven countries. Mumbai Indians (IND) are the only team to have won the title twice. Their first win came on Oct 9, 2011, and most recently they claimed a 33-run win against Rajasthan Royals (IND) in Delhi, India, on Oct 6, 2013.

Highest single-day Test match attendance
A crowd of 91,092 people packed out the Melbourne Cricket Ground in Australia on day one of the fourth Ashes Test between Australia and England on Dec 26, 2013.

Most runs scored by a player in a T20 International

The highest individual score in a Twenty20 International is 156 runs, by Australian Aaron Finch against England at the Ageas Bowl in Southampton, UK, on Aug 29, 2013. Opening batsman Finch hit 14 sixes in his 63-ball innings to guide Australia to a formidable 248 for 6.

Most runs by a No. 11 batsman in a Test match innings

Test match debutant Ashton Agar (AUS) rewrote the record books when he scored 98 runs in the opening Test of the 2013 Ashes series against England at Trent Bridge in Nottingham, UK, on Jul 11. Agar's astonishing 101-ball knock featured 12 fours and two sixes and rescued Australia from a perilous 117 for 9.

Dec 14, 1997, a feat matched by England's Arran Brindle in two maiden overs in Mumbai, India, on Feb 5, 2013.

RUNS

Highest Test match 10th-wicket partnership
Australians Ashton Agar (98) and Phillip Hughes (81 not out), batting at 11 and 6 respectively, made 163 runs in 31.1 overs in the 2013 Ashes at Trent Bridge in the UK on Jul 11.

Most runs in a T20 match
Chris Gayle (JAM) finished on 175 not out—the highest score by a player in any professional T20 innings—for Royal Challengers Bangalore in the Indian Premier League on Apr 23, 2013. Gayle hit 100 runs in 30 balls—the **fastest T20 century**—and 13 fours and 17 sixes, the **most T20 runs scored in boundaries** (154).

Fastest international century
Corey Anderson (NZ) hit a century from just 36 balls in an ODI against the West Indies on Jan 1, 2014. Anderson struck 14 sixes and six fours in an unbeaten 131 from 47 balls.

Most catches by a wicket keeper in a Test series

Australia gloveman Brad Haddin broke a 30-year-old Test record when he claimed 29 catches in the 2013 Ashes series between hosts England and Australia—despite his team losing the five-match series 3–0. Haddin pouched the record on Aug 25, 2013—day five of the fifth Test—from another Australian wicket keeper, Rod Marsh, who took 28 catches in five Test matches in 1982–83.

RUNS, WICKETS, AND CATCHES

Test matches (men)

Most runs	15,921	Sachin Tendulkar (IND), 1989–2013
Most wickets	800	Muttiah Muralitharan (LKA), 1992–2010
Most catches	210	Rahul Dravid (IND), 1996–2012

Test matches (women)

Most runs	1,935	Janette Brittin (ENG), 1979–98
Most wickets	77	Mary Duggan (ENG), 1949–63
Most catches	25	Carole Hodges (ENG), 1984–92

One-Day Internationals (men)

Most runs	18,426	Sachin Tendulkar (IND), 1989–2012
Most wickets	534	Muttiah Muralitharan (LKA), 1993–2011
Most catches	201	Mahela Jayawardene (LKA), 1998–2013

One-Day Internationals (women)

Most runs	5,432	Charlotte Edwards (ENG), 1997–2014
Most wickets	180	Cathryn Fitzpatrick (AUS), 1993–2007
Most catches	50	Jhulan Goswami (IND), 2002–14

Source: www.espncricinfo.com, as of Feb 4, 2014
(catches excluding wicket keepers)

Highest match aggregate in a T20 International

England made 209 for 6 in reply to Australia's 248 for 6 at the Ageas Bowl in Hampshire, UK, on Aug 29, 2013, for a match aggregate of 457 runs.

SIXES

Highest aggregate in a Test match series

In the five-match 2013–14 Ashes series between Australia and England, 65 sixes were recorded. Australia, who won the series 5–0, contributed 40 maximums—the **most sixes by one team in a Test match series**. Chief contributions came from Aussies Brad Haddin (nine) and George Bailey (eight), with six each from Shane Watson (AUS), Ian Bell, and Stuart Broad (both ENG).

Bailey hit three of his sixes in one over during the third Test in Perth on Dec 16, 2013, when he equaled the 28-run record for the **most runs scored off an over in a Test match**. West Indies batsman Brian Lara had achieved the feat on Dec 14, 2003.

Most in an ODI

Rohit Sharma (IND) hit 16 sixes in Bangalore, India, on Nov 2, 2013. Opening batsman Sharma made 209—the second highest score in ODI history—off 158 balls.

Most sixes by a player in a first-class innings

Jamaican cricketer Chris Gayle cleared the boundary 17 times on his way to a Twenty20 record of 175 not out. His set of sixes came in the record breaking Indian Premier League match on Apr 23, 2013 (see left).

Most in a Test match innings

Wasim Akram (PAK) scored 12 sixes in an innings of 257 not out against Zimbabwe in Sheikhupura, Pakistan, on Oct 19–20, 1996.

Most in an IPL career

At the conclusion of the 2013 Indian Premier League tournament on May 26, 2013, Chris Gayle (JAM) had scored a total of 180 maximums in his five-season career (2009–13).

Origin of the "Ashes"

The Sporting Times mourned the death of English cricket in 1882, when England lost to Australia on home soil for the first time. The mock obituary of English cricket read: "The body will be cremated and the ashes taken to Australia."

First multi-format series in international cricket

A Test match, three Twenty20 Internationals, and three One-Day Internationals determined the winner of the multi-format women's Ashes series between England and Australia in Aug 2013. Captained by Charlotte Edwards, hosts England clinched the series by 12 points to 4 and regained the Ashes crown that they had lost on Australian soil in 2011.

For sports architecture, see pp. 200–01

THE CENTURION OF CRICKET

Sachin Tendulkar's career totals (1989–2013)	
Most centuries in internationals	100
Most centuries in Test matches	51
Most centuries in One-Day Internationals	49
Most international centuries scored in a partnership (career)—with Sourav Ganguly (IND)	38

Source: www.espncricinfo.com

Most Test matches played

Batsman Sachin Tendulkar (IND)—known by his fans as the "God of Cricket"—retired on Nov 16, 2013 after a 24-year career, but not before playing a record 200th Test, against the West Indies at Mumbai's Wankhede Stadium. Tendulkar has 20 Guinness World Records titles to his credit, the highlights of which are listed in the tables above.

Most by a team in a T20 International

The Netherlands struck 19 sixes in a World T20 group match against Ireland at Sylhet Stadium, Bangladesh, on Mar 21, 2014, reaching their target of 190 with 37 balls to spare to progress to the Super 10 stage of the tournament.

Cycling

Most **bicycles are "right-handed"**: the chain is typically located on the right of the frame

Oldest Olympic road cycling gold medalist

When Kristin Armstrong (USA, b. Aug 11, 1973) successfully defended her time trial title at the 2012 Games in London, UK, on Aug 1, she became the oldest road cycling winner. At the age of 38 years 356 days, Kristin rode the 18-mi (29-km) course in 37 min 34.82 sec.

Greatest distance cycled in 12 hours

Marko Baloh (SVN) cycled 295.31 mi (475.26 km) solo and unpaced in 12 hr at the Montichiari Velodrome in Brescia, Italy, on Oct 8, 2010. He completed 1,901 full laps of the 820-ft (250-m) course in the allotted time.

Baloh continued his solo, unpaced cycling for another 12 hr and went on to achieve the **greatest distance cycled in 24 hours** with 561.57 mi (903.76 km), or 3,615 full laps.

Largest cycling race

The 2004 Cape Argus Pick n Pay Cycle Tour held in Cape Town, South Africa, on Mar 14, 2004 began with 42,614 entrants, 31,219 of whom finished the race.

Most riders to finish a Grand Tour

The greatest number of cyclists to complete an edition of a Grand Tour is

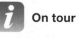 **On tour**

The cycling Grand Tours are: the Tour de France, the Giro d'Italia, and the Vuelta a España, which date from 1903, 1909, and 1935 respectively.

175, during the 2012 Vuelta a España (Tour of Spain) from Aug 18 to Sep 9, 2012.

Fastest 4-km pursuit (women)

The Great Britain team consisting of Katie Archibald, Elinor Barker, Danielle King, and Joanna Rowsell completed the 4-km team pursuit in 4 min 16.552 sec to win gold at the Union Cycliste Internationale (UCI) Track Cycling World Cup in Aguascalientes, Mexico, on Dec 5, 2013.

OLYMPICS

Most cycling medals

The greatest number of Olympic cycling medals won by an individual is seven, by Bradley Wiggins and Chris Hoy (both UK). Wiggins won four gold, one silver,

Oldest person to win a cycling Grand Tour

Chris Horner (USA, b. Oct 23, 1971) won the 2013 Vuelta a España at the age of 41 years 327 days in Madrid, Spain, on Sep 15, 2013. He also became the **oldest winner of a stage in a Grand Tour** when he took stage 10 of the race at the age of 41 years 314 days in Alto de Hazallanas, Spain, on Sep 2, 2013.

Most Olympic cycling medals won (female)

Leontien Zijlaard-van Moorsel (NLD) won six Olympic cycling medals including four golds. Her medals were won at Sydney 2000 and Athens 2004.

and two bronze medals in 2000–12. Hoy's seven came from six golds and one silver, also between 2000 and 2012.

Chris Hoy's six golds give him the record for the **most Olympic track cycling gold medals**. He picked up gold in the 1-km time trial at Athens 2004, the individual sprint, team sprint, and Keirin at Beijing 2008, and the team sprint and Keirin at London 2012.

Most cycling gold medals won at one Olympic Games

On Aug 5, 1904, at the Olympic Games in St. Louis, USA, Marcus Hurley (USA) won four gold medals, in the quarter mile, third mile, half mile, and 1 mile events.

Most medals won at both Summer and Winter Olympics (female)

Canadian athlete Clara Hughes won a total of six medals across both Summer and Winter Games. She won two bronze medals in cycling events at the 1996 Summer Games in Atlanta, USA, before switching to speed skating. In this new discipline, Hughes won a bronze medal at the 2002 Winter Olympics in Salt Lake City, USA, a gold and silver medal at the 2006 Games in Turin, Italy, and another bronze medal at the 2010 Winter Olympics in Vancouver, Canada.

FACT

Prior to Horner's victory, the oldest Grand Tour winner was Firmin Lambot (BEL), who won the Tour de France in 1922 at 36 years old.

First to win the Tour de France and Olympic gold in the same year

Bradley Wiggins capped a memorable summer for British cycling when he eased to victory in the men's time

Most podium finishes in the Tour de France

Raymond Poulidor (FRA) finished in the top three of the Tour de France eight times. He came second on three occasions (1964, 1965, and 1974) and third five times (1962, 1966, 1969, 1972, and 1976).

TRACK CYCLING—ABSOLUTE

Men	Start	Time/Distance	Name & Nationality	Place	Date
200 m	flying	9.347	François Pervis (FRA)	Aguascalientes, Mexico	Dec 6, 2013
500 m	flying	24.758	Chris Hoy (UK)	La Paz, Bolivia	May 13, 2007
1 km	standing	56.303	François Pervis (FRA)	Aguascalientes, Mexico	Dec 7, 2013
4 km	standing	4:10.534	Jack Bobridge (AUS)	Sydney, Australia	Feb 2, 2011
Team 4 km	standing	3:51.659	Great Britain (Steven Burke, Ed Clancy, Peter Kennaugh, and Geraint Thomas)	London, UK	Aug 3, 2012
1 hour	standing	49.7 km	Ondřej Sosenka (CZE)	Moscow, Russia	Jul 19, 2005

Women	Start	Time/Distance	Name & Nationality	Place	Date
200 m	flying	10.384	Kristina Vogel (DEU)	Aguascalientes, Mexico	Dec 7, 2013
500 m	flying	29.481	Olga Streltsova (RUS)	Moscow, Russia	May 29, 2011
3 km	standing	3:22.269	Sarah Hammer (USA)	Aguascalientes, Mexico	May 11, 2010
1 hour	standing	46.065 km	Leontien Zijlaard-van Moorsel (NLD)	Mexico City, Mexico	Oct 1, 2003

Statistics correct as of Dec 7, 2013

Most UCI Mountain Bike Marathon World Championships

Christoph Sauser (CHE) has won the UCI Mountain Bike Marathon World Championships a total of three times, in 2007, 2011, and 2013.

Most World Championships in cyclo-cross (female)

Marianne Vos (NLD) has won six cyclo-cross World Championships, in 2006 and consecutively in 2009–13. The championships began in 2000. She also won Olympic gold in different cycling events at the Beijing and London games.

and 1974; Bernard Hinault (FRA) in 1978–79, 1981–82, and 1985; and Miguel Indurain (ESP) in 1991–95. With 34 victories, Merckx also enjoyed the **most Tour de France stage wins**, between 1969 and 1978.

Closest

In the 1989 Tour de France, after 2,030 mi (3,267 km) ridden over a period of 23 days (July 1–23), Greg LeMond (USA) finished the race in 87 hr 38 min 35 sec, beating Laurent Fignon (FRA) by only 8 sec.

Largest attendance at a sporting event

The most spectators at any sporting event is an estimated 12 million people over a three-week period for the 2012 Tour de France. The Tour took place in Belgium, Switzerland, and France from Jun 30 to Jul 22. The organizers estimate that 80% of spectators were French and that 70% were men.

BMX

Most World Championships won

Male: The most UCI BMX World Championships won by an individual is three, by Kyle Bennett (USA) in 2002–03 and 2007.

Female: Two women have won three titles: Gabriela Diaz (ARG)

in 2001–02 and 2004, and Shanaze Reade (UK) in 2007–08 and 2010.

Most Olympic medals

BMX was first incorporated into the Olympics in 2008. Since then, only one rider has won two medals. Mãris Štrombergs (LVA) won the individual men's event in 2008 and 2012.

trial in 50 min 39 sec at the London Olympics on Aug 1, 2012—just 10 days after becoming the first Brit to win the Tour de France.

TOUR DE FRANCE

Longest

In 1926, the Tour de France totaled 3,569 mi (5,745 km) and was won by Lucien Buysse (BEL).

Most wins

Four riders have won the Tour five times: Jacques Anquetil (FRA) in 1957 and 1961–64; Eddy Merckx (BEL) in 1969–72

Most UCI Trials World Championships won

Male: Benito Ros Charral (ESP) won nine elite men's UCI Trials World Championships, in 2003–05 and 2007–12.
Female: Karin Moor (CHE) won the women's title nine times between 2001 and 2011.

A bit too slow? Try Motorsports, p. 232

First person to win the cycling Triple Crown

The inaugural winner of cycling's Triple Crown was Eddy Merckx (BEL), who won the Tour de France, Giro d'Italia, and UCI Road World Cycling Championships in 1974. The only other person to achieve this feat was Stephen Roche (IRL) in 1987.

The word **"caddy"** comes from the French *cadet*, meaning junior or student

First winner of the FedEx Cup and Race to Dubai in one year

Henrik Stenson (SWE) won the US Professional Golfers' Association (PGA) Tour's FedEx Cup (inset) on Sep 22, 2013, and the PGA European Tour's Race to Dubai (main picture) on Nov 17, 2013. The scale of his achievement is indicated by the fact that no player has even won both tours in *different* years before.

was part of the 18 Tour titles that Nelson won in the same year. He turned professional in 1932 and retired from full-time golf in the 1946 season, by which time he had amassed a career total of 52 PGA titles.

Most PGA Player of the Year awards
The greatest number of PGA Player of the Year awards won by an individual golfer is 11, by Tiger Woods (USA) in 1997, 1999–2003, 2005–07, 2009, and 2013. Inaugurated in 1948, this award is based on a points system, including variables such as wins, top 10 finishes, performances in major

Longest hole in one in the Ryder Cup

Paul Casey (UK, above) holed a 213-yd (194-m) drive at the 14th hole (par 3) at the K Club in Straffan, County Kildare, Ireland, on Sep 23, 2006. Incredibly, the feat was repeated by Scott Verplank (USA) the next day at the same hole on the final day of the tournament. The Ryder Cup is contested every two years between the USA and Europe.

Longest golf hole
The seventh hole (par 7) of the Satsuki gold course in Sano, Japan, measures 964 yd (881 m) long.

Longest hole in one in a PGA Tour event
On Jan 25, 2001, Andrew Magee (USA) shot a 332-yd (303-m) hole in one on the 17th hole (par 4) in the first round of the Phoenix Open at TPC of Scottsdale in Arizona, USA.

The **longest hole in one in the US Masters** is 213 yd (194 m), by Jeff Sluman (USA) at the par-3 fourth hole at Augusta National Golf Club in Georgia, USA, on Apr 9, 1992.

Most consecutive PGA Tour titles won
Byron Nelson (USA) won 11 PGA Tour titles in a row in 1945. The run, commonly referred to as "The Streak,"

tournaments, and scoring average. Woods has almost twice as many awards as his nearest rival, Tom Watson (USA), who won the award on six occasions.

LOWEST ROUNDS

Lowest single-round score (18 holes) in the US Masters
Two players have each recorded a single-round score of 63 at the US Masters, which is played at the Augusta National Golf Club. They are Nick Price (ZWE) in 1986 and Greg Norman (AUS) in 1996.

Lowest score at the British Open
Eight players have played a round of 63 at the British Open golf championships:

FACT
The 2014 Humana Challenge had a total prize purse of $5.7 m, with $1.026 m going to Patrick Reed for winning the event.

MOST WINS AND LOWEST SCORES (72 HOLES)

British Open		
Most wins	6	Harry Vardon (UK)
Lowest total score	267	Greg Norman (AUS), 1993
US Open		
Most wins	4	Willie Anderson (USA)
		Bobby Jones Jr. (USA)
		Ben Hogan (USA)
		Jack Nicklaus (USA)
Lowest total score	268	Rory McIlroy (UK), 2011
US PGA		
Most wins	5	Walter Hagen (USA)
		Jack Nicklaus (USA)
Lowest total score	265	David Toms (USA), 2001
US Masters		
Most wins	6	Jack Nicklaus (USA)
Lowest total score	270	Tiger Woods (USA), 2007

Statistics correct as of Feb 24, 2014

Lowest score below par after 54 holes in a PGA Tour event

Patrick Reed (USA) scored 27 under par after 54 holes during the 2014 Humana Challenge on the PGA West course in La Quinta, California, USA, on Jan 16–18. Reed received a congratulatory call afterward from former US President Bill Clinton. The tournament is held in partnership with the Clinton Foundation.

Most appearances by a pair in the Ryder Cup

The most frequent pairing in Ryder Cup history is that of Spaniards Severiano "Seve" Ballesteros (above right) and José María Olazábal (above left), who played together 15 times for Europe in foursomes and four-ball from 1987 to 1993. The duo ended with an overall record of 11 wins, 2 draws, and 2 losses.

Mark Hayes (USA) at Turnberry, South Ayrshire, in 1977; Isao Aoki (JPN) at Muirfield, East Lothian, in 1980; Greg Norman (AUS) at Turnberry in 1986; Paul Broadhurst (UK) at St. Andrews, Fife, in 1990; Jodie Mudd (USA) at Royal Birkdale, Southport, in 1991; Nick Faldo (UK) and Payne Stewart (USA), both at Royal St. George's, Sandwich, in 1993; and Rory McIlroy (UK) at St. Andrews in 2010.

Lowest score under par in a pro golf tournament (single round)
Richard Wallis (UK) shot 59 at the PGA Southern Open Championship OOM Pro-Am on the par-73 course at The Drift Golf Club, East Horsley, Surrey, UK, on Jun 2, 2013. This represents a score of 14 under par.

Lowest below-age score
Two golfers have had a score of 17 below their ages. James D. Morton (USA) hit a 72 at Valleybrook Golf and Country Club, Hixson, Tennessee, USA, on Apr 21, 2001, at 89 years years old, and Keith Plowman (NZ) hit 72 at Maungakiekie Golf Club, Auckland, New Zealand, also at 89 years old, on Nov 20, 2007.

YOUNGEST AND OLDEST

Youngest golfer to make the cut at the US Masters
At the age of 14 years 171 days, Guan Tianlang (CHN, b. Oct 25, 1998) made the cut with 4 over par after 18 holes at the 77th US Masters on Apr 13, 2013. The tournament was staged at Augusta National Golf Club in Georgia, USA.
Guan had already become the **youngest golfer to play at the US Masters** when he teed off at the

Highest annual earnings from golf
Released in 2013, Forbes' Celebrity 100 list ranked Tiger Woods (USA) as both the highest-earning golfer and the **highest-earning athlete**. His earnings for 2012–13 came to an estimated $78 m.

---

same tournament two days beforehand, at 14 years 169 days old. His final score was 300 (73, 75, 77, 75).

Youngest golfer to score their age
Tsugio Uemoto (JPN, b. Jul 3, 1928) scored 68 at the Higashi Hiroshima Country Club, Hiroshima, Japan, on Oct 22, 1996.
The **oldest player to score their age** is C. Arthur Thompson (CAN, 1869–1975), who scored 103 on the 6,215-yd (5,682-m) Uplands Golf Club course in Victoria, British Columbia, Canada, in 1973.

Youngest Ryder Cup captain
Arnold Palmer (USA) was 34 years 31 days old when he captained the US Ryder Cup team at East Lake Golf Club in Atlanta, Georgia, USA, in 1963.

The **oldest Ryder Cup captain** is Tom Watson (USA, b. Sep 4, 1949), who was selected on Dec 13, 2012, at the age of 63 years 100 days, to lead the US team. The 2014 Ryder Cup at Gleneagles in Scotland,

Most consecutive golf majors won in a single year (female)

Mildred Ella "Babe" Didrikson Zaharias (USA, main picture) won three successive majors in 1950, a feat matched by Inbee Park (KOR, inset) in 2013. Their three wins also represent the **most majors won in a year (female)**, a record shared with Mary "Mickey" Wright (USA, 1961) and Pat Bradley (USA, 1986).

UK, begins on Sep 26, 2014, at which point Watson will be 65 years 22 days old.

Youngest golfer to play in the Ryder Cup
Sergio García (ESP, b. Jan 9, 1980) competed for Europe in the Ryder Cup in 1999, at 19 years 229 days old.

The **oldest golfer to play in the Ryder Cup** is Raymond Floyd (USA, b. Sep 4, 1942), who competed in the 1993 tournament at 51 years 20 days old. Floyd retired from professional golf in 2010, but Tom Watson recruited him as a vice-captain for his 2014 Ryder Cup team.

Oldest golfer to score a hole in one
Switzerland's Otto Bucher (b. May 12, 1885) hit a hole in one on the 130-yd (119-m) 12th hole at La Manga in Spain on Jan 13, 1985, at the age of 99 years 244 days.

Oldest golf club president
Jack Miles (UK, b. Mar 10, 1913), the president of Wimbledon Common Golf Club, celebrated his 101st birthday in 2014. Jack has been an active playing member of the club since 1947.

Most LPGA Player of the Year awards

Sweden's Annika Sörenstam has won a total of eight Ladies Professional Golfers' Association (LPGA) Player of the Year awards. Her victories came in 1995, 1997–98, and 2001–05.

> **i** Solheim Cup
>
> The female equivalent of the Ryder Cup is the Solheim Cup, held every two years since 1990. The USA has won eight times to Europe's five.

Ice hockey

Pucks used to be made from **frozen cow dung**

FACT

Jágr started playing ice hockey at the age of three.

Most game-winning goals in an NHL career

As of Dec 30, 2013, the Czech Republic's Jaromír Jágr had scored 122 game-winning goals in his National Hockey League (NHL) career. He has also scored the **most regular-season NHL career goals in overtime**, with 18 for the Pittsburgh Penguins, Washington Capitals, New York Rangers, Philadelphia Flyers, and New Jersey Devils from 1990 to 2013.

Longest undefeated run by an NHL team
From Oct 14, 1979 to Jan 6, 1980, the USA's Philadelphia Flyers had an unbeaten run of 35 games, with 25 wins and 10 ties. (For the **longest NHL winning streak**, see the table below right.)

Most career games in professional ice hockey
Canadian right winger Gordon "Gordie" Howe (b. Mar 31, 1928) featured in 2,421 professional games over 26 seasons from 1946 to 1980, including NHL and WHA (World Hockey Association) games. When Howe retired in 1980, he was 52 years old, an age that made him the **oldest player in NHL history**.

Oldest goalscorer in Olympic ice hockey

At the age of 43 years 234 days, Teemu Selänne (FIN, b. Jul 3, 1970) scored twice in the Olympic bronze medal match against the USA in Sochi, Russia, on Feb 22, 2014. Selänne's goals helped Finland to a 5–0 victory over the Americans, and also made him the **oldest medalist in Olympic ice hockey**.

Most wins in an NHL season
The Detroit Red Wings (USA) won 62 times in the 1995/96 NHL season.

Most assists in an NHL season
Wayne Gretzky (CAN) carried out 163 assists playing for the Edmonton Oilers during the 1985/86 NHL season.
Gretzky also recorded the **most assists in an NHL career**, with 1,963 for the Edmonton Oilers, Los Angeles Kings, St. Louis Blues, and New York Rangers from 1979 to 1999.

Most penalty minutes in an NHL game
Playing for the Los Angeles Kings in a game against the Philadelphia Flyers on Mar 11, 1979, Canadian Randy Holt racked up 67 penalty minutes.
The player with the **most penalty minutes in NHL history**, however, is Dave "Tiger" Williams (CAN), with 3,966 in 17 seasons between 1974 and 1988, playing for the Toronto Maple Leafs, Vancouver Canucks, Detroit Red Wings, Los Angeles Kings, and Hartford Whalers.

Fastest coach to reach 200 NHL wins
Pittsburgh Penguins' 3–1 win over the Ottawa Senators on Apr 22, 2013 gave Dan Bylsma (USA) his 200th win from 316 games coached.

Fastest NHL hat-trick
On Mar 23, 1952, Canadian right winger Bill Mosienko scored a hat-trick in 21 sec for the Chicago Blackhawks vs. the New York Rangers at Madison Square Garden, New York City, USA. The Blackhawks went on to triumph 7–6.

Most consecutive NHL games played
Doug Jarvis (CAN) played 964 games for the Montreal Canadiens, Washington Capitals, and Hartford Whalers from Oct 1975 to Oct 1987.

Most consecutive games played by an NHL defenseman
Jay Bouwmeester (CAN) had featured in 635 consecutive NHL regular-season games as of the end of the 2012/13 season. Chris Chelios (USA) played the **most career regular-season games by an NHL defenseman**, with 1,651 for various teams from 1983 to 2010.

Most shootout wins by an NHL goalkeeper
Henrik Lundqvist (SWE) achieved 44 shootout wins while playing for the New York Rangers—more than any other NHL goalie.

Most tickets sold for an NHL match

A total of 105,491 tickets were sold for the 2014 Bridgestone NHL Winter Classic game between the Detroit Red Wings (USA) and the Toronto Maple Leafs (CAN). The match was held at the University of Michigan Football Stadium in Ann Arbor, Michigan, USA, on Jan 1, 2014.

Highest save percentage by a goalkeeper in an NHL season

Craig Anderson (USA) recorded a .941 save percentage while playing for the Ottawa Senators during the 2012/13 season, surpassing the previous mark of .940 set by Brian Elliott (CAN) of the St. Louis Blues in 2011–12.

Most overtime goals in an NHL season

The NHL record for overtime goals in a season is five, by Steven Stamkos (CAN) in the 2011/12 season for Tampa Bay Lightning.

Most shootout goals in an NHL career

Zach Parise (USA) has scored 34 shootout goals in the service of the New Jersey Devils and Minnesota Wild since 2005.

Most goals by a rookie in an NHL season

In the 1992/93 NHL season, Finland's Teemu Selänne racked up 76 goals for the Winnipeg Jets.

Most goals on an NHL debut

On Oct 9, 2010, Derek Stepan (USA) became only the fourth player to score a hat-trick on his NHL debut, playing for the New York Rangers in a 6–3 victory over the Buffalo Sabres. The others are: Alex Smart (CAN) on Jan 14, 1943, Réal Cloutier (CAN) on Oct 10, 1979, and Fabian Brunnström (SWE) on Oct 15, 2008.

Most men's ice hockey World Championships

The men's IIHF (International Ice Hockey Federation) World Championships were first held in 1920. The Soviet Union/Russia have won more times than any other nation, with 22 victories as the Soviet Union (in 1954, 1956, 1963–71, 1973–75, 1978–79, 1981–83, 1986, and 1989–90) and four wins as Russia (in 1993, 2008–09, and 2012).

Most women's ice hockey World Championships

The women's IIHF World Championships was first held in 1990 and has been staged annually since then, apart from Olympic years and in 2003, during the SARS outbreak. The Canadian team have won 10 titles in total: in 1990, 1992, 1994, 1997, 1999–2001, 2004, 2007, and 2012. The USA has won five times, most recently in 2013.

Most individual wins of the Stanley Cup

Henri Richard (CAN) won the Stanley Cup 11 times with the Montreal Canadiens from 1956 to 1975. The shorter sibling of legendary right winger Maurice "The Rocket" Richard, Henri was nicknamed "The Pocket Rocket."

Most NHL career points

Wayne Gretzky (CAN) scored a remarkable 2,857 points for the Edmonton Oilers, Los Angeles Kings, St. Louis Blues, and New York Rangers between 1979 and 1999. This total comprises 894 goals and 1,963 assists in 1,487 games. In addition to these regular-season goals and 122 Stanley Cup goals, Gretzky scored 56 goals in the World Hockey Association (WHA) in 1978–79.

Youngest captain of a Stanley Cup-winning team

At 21 years 309 days, Sidney Crosby (CAN, b. Aug 7, 1987) became the youngest captain of any team to win the Stanley Cup when the Pittsburgh Penguins beat the Detroit Red Wings in the 2009 finals.

Fewest goals conceded in a Stanley Cup finals series

The fewest goals conceded by a goalkeeper in a Stanley Cup finals series is eight, by Tim Thomas (USA) for the Boston Bruins vs. the Vancouver Canucks in 2011.

NATIONAL HOCKEY LEAGUE

Most Stanley Cup Final appearances	34	Montreal Canadiens (CAN), 1916–93
Most Stanley Cup wins	24	Montreal Canadiens (CAN), 1916–93
Most games played in a career	1,767	Gordie Howe (CAN), for the Detroit Red Wings and Hartford Whalers, 1946–80
Longest winning streak	17	Pittsburgh Penguins (USA), from Mar 9 to Apr 10, 1993
Most goals scored	894	Wayne Gretzky (CAN), for the Edmonton Oilers, Los Angeles Kings, St. Louis Blues, and New York Rangers
Most goals in a game by a player	7	Joe Malone (CAN), for the Quebec Bulldogs vs. Toronto St. Patricks on Jan 31, 1920
Most goals in a game by a team	16	Montreal Canadiens, in a 16–3 victory over the Quebec Bulldogs (both CAN) on Mar 3, 1920
Most goals in a season by a player	92	Wayne Gretzky (CAN), for the Edmonton Oilers in 1981–82
Most goals in a season by a team	446	Edmonton Oilers (CAN), 1983–84
Most saves by a goalkeeper	27,312	Martin Brodeur (CAN), for the New Jersey Devils, 1993–present

All statistics correct as of Jan 29, 2014

Marathons

London Marathon runners have raised some **$1.1 bn** for charity

Deepest marathon
The Crystal Mine Underground Marathon is run in an old salt mine located 1,640 ft (500 m) below sea level. It has taken place in Sondershausen, Thuringia, Germany, annually since 2002.

Coldest marathon
In 2001, the Siberian Ice Marathon in Omsk, Russia, registered a temperature of -38°F (-39°C), making it the coldest regular marathon.
Some 169°F (94°C) warmer, the **hottest marathon** is the Badwater Ultramarathon held between Death Valley and Mount Whitney in California, USA, which registers temperatures of 131°F (55°C).

Most northerly marathon
The North Pole Marathon held at the geographic North Pole has been run annually since 2002. In 2007, Thomas Maguire (IRL) ran the **fastest men's North Pole marathon** in 3 hr 36 min 10 sec. A year later, Cathrine Due (DNK) recorded the **fastest women's** in 5 hr 37 min 14 sec.
The **most southerly marathon** is the Antarctic Ice Marathon, held on the Antarctic mainland at a latitude of 80 degrees south.

Fastest marathon (female)
Paula Radcliffe (UK) finished the London Marathon on Apr 13, 2003 in 2 hr 15 min 25 sec, making her the fastest female marathon runner of all time. She also ran the **fastest Chicago Marathon (female)**, on Oct 13, 2002, finishing in 2 hr 17 min 18 sec.

Fastest aggregate World Marathon Majors time
The "World Marathon Majors" comprise the Olympic and World Championship marathons as well as those held in Berlin, Boston, Chicago, London, and New York City. Kjell-Erik Ståhl (SWE) completed the seven Majors in an aggregate time of 15 hr 36 min 47 sec. His record-breaking sequence began at the Moscow 1980 Olympic Games and ended in Berlin in 1991.

Fastest marathon
The Berlin Marathon in Germany was the setting for the fastest marathon ever. It took Wilson Kipsang (KEN) just 2 hr 3 min 23 sec to complete the course on Sep 29, 2013. Kipsang has also won the Frankfurt Marathon twice (2010–11) and the London Marathon twice (2012 and 2014).

Fastest Olympic marathon
Female: On Aug 5, 2012, Tiki Gelana (ETH) clocked 2 hr 23 min 7 sec to take gold in the women's marathon at the London 2012 Games. However, the Olympic record isn't her personal best. She ran the Rotterdam Marathon in the Netherlands in 2 hr 18 min 58 sec on Apr 15, 2012.
Male: Samuel Wanjiru (KEN) won the marathon in Beijing in 2 hr 6 min 32 sec on Aug 24, 2008.

Most World Marathon Majors races won
Female: Grete Waitz (NOR) won 12 Majors: nine in New York, two in London, and one World Championship between 1978 and 1987.
Male: Bill Rodgers (USA) won eight Majors: four in Boston and four in New York from 1975 to 1980.

Most ITU World Triathlon Series medals
Female: Michellie Jones (AUS) won two gold, two silver, and four bronze medals at the International Triathlon Union World Championships. She won her eight medals in 1991–2003.
Male: Simon Lessing (UK) collected seven World Championship medals: four

2014 VIRGIN MONEY LONDON MARATHON: NEW WORLD RECORDS

While marathon running is a serious business for elite athletes, such as those featured above, for others it is a great excuse to have some fun and raise money for charity—and where better to have it than at the world's premier marathon event: the London Marathon! Pictured below are some of the colorful characters who took part this year, listed in order of their running times.

Animal
Alex Collins (UK)
2 hr 48 min 29 sec

Television character
David Stone (UK)
2 hr 49 min 51 sec

Schoolboy
Steven Nimmo (UK)
2 hr 50 min 17 sec

Baby
Ali King (UK)
2 hr 51 min 18 sec

Toilet
Marcus Mumford (UK)
2 hr 57 min 28 sec

Bride (male)
Lee Goodwin (UK)
3 hr 0 min 54 sec

Jockey
Ross Birkett (UK)
3 hr 8 min 30 sec

Astronaut
Simon Couchman (UK)
3 hr 8 min 45 sec

Cowboy
Rik Vercoe (UK)
3 hr 9 min 9 sec

Nurse (female)
Caroline Pleasence (UK)
3 hr 13 min 58 sec

Bride (female)
Sarah Dudgeon (UK)
3 hr 16 min 44 sec

Monk
Tom Collins (UK)
3 hr 29 min 32 sec

Bottle
Paul Simons (UK)
3 hr 31 min 57 sec

Organ (male)
Adam Giangreco (UK)
3 hr 36 min 42 sec

Logo
Kevin Hunt (UK)
3 hr 37 min 14 sec

BIGGEST MARATHONS

Marathon	Most finishers	Fastest (male)	Fastest (female)
Berlin, Germany	36,544 Sep 29, 2013	Wilson Kipsang (KEN), 2:03:23, Sep 29, 2013	Mizuki Noguchi (JPN), 2:19:12, Sep 25, 2005
Boston, Massachusetts, USA	35,868 Apr 15, 1996	Geoffrey Mutai (KEN), 2:03:02, Apr 18, 2011	Rita Jeptoo (KEN), 2:18:57, Apr 21, 2014
Chicago, Illinois, USA	39,122 Oct 13, 2013	Dennis Kimetto (KEN), 2:03:45, Oct 13, 2013	Paula Radcliffe (UK), 2:17:18, Oct 13, 2002
London, UK	36,672 Apr 22, 2012	Wilson Kipsang (KEN), 2:04:29, Apr 13, 2014	Paula Radcliffe (UK), 2:15:25, Apr 13, 2003
New York City, New York, USA	50,062 Nov 3, 2013	Geoffrey Mutai (KEN), 2:05:06, Nov 6, 2011	Margaret Okayo (KEN), 2:22:31, Nov 2, 2003
Osaka, Japan	27,674 Oct 27, 2013	Ser-Od Bat-Ochir (MNG), 2:11:52, Nov 25, 2012	Lidia Şimon (ROM), 2:32:48, Oct 30, 2011
Paris, France	38,690 Apr 7, 2013	Kenenisa Bekele (ETH), 2:05:04, Apr 6, 2014	Feyse Tadese (ETH), 2:21:06, Apr 7, 2013
Tokyo, Japan	35,308 Feb 24, 2013	Dickson Chumba (KEN), 2:05:42, Feb 23, 2014	Tirfi Tsegaye (ETH), 2:22:23, Feb 23, 2014

Statistics correct as of Apr 30, 2014. The IAAF rules the Boston course ineligible to set world records

gold, two silver, and one bronze from 1992 to 1999. The record was equalled by Javier Gómez (ESP), with three golds, three silvers, and one bronze in 2007–13.

Fastest time to complete the Hawaiian Ironman

Male: The Ironman World Championship, aka the "Hawaiian Ironman", was first held on Feb 18, 1978 in Kailua-Kona, Hawaii, USA. It was described as "Swim 2.4 miles! Bike 112 miles! Run 26.2 miles! Brag for the rest of your life!" Craig Alexander (AUS) holds the course record of 8 hr 3 min 56 sec, which he set on Oct 8, 2011 with a 3.8-km swim in 51 min 56 sec, a 180-km cycle in 4 hr 24 min 5 sec, and a marathon run in 2 hr 44 min 2 sec.

First winner of the wheelchair marathon Grand Slam

Tatyana McFadden (USA) completed the wheelchair marathon "Grand Slam" in 2013. The feat comprises wins of the wheelchair marathons in Boston, London, Chicago, and New York in a single year. Tatyana also recorded the **fastest women's wheelchair London Marathon** in a time of 1 hr 46 min 2 sec on Apr 21, 2013.

Female: On Oct 12, 2013, Australia's Mirinda Carfrae recorded the fastest women's time, in 8 hr 52 min 14 sec. Her nearest rival was more than 5 min behind.

The **oldest person to complete the Hawaiian Ironman** is Lew Hollander (USA, b. Jun 6, 1930), who was 82 years 129 days old when he crossed the finish line on Oct 13, 2012.

Fastest time to run an ultramarathon on each continent

Ziyad Tariq Rahim (PAK) ran seven 50-km (36.6-mi) ultramarathons—one on each continent from Jan 26 to Mar 8, 2014. The timing for this record began when Ziyad started his first ultramarathon in Antarctica and ended when he crossed the line of his last ultramarathon in South Africa, with a total time of 41 days 3 hr 23 min 40 sec.

Andrei Rosu (ROM) set the **fastest time to run a marathon and an ultramarathon on each continent** in 1 year 217 days. He started with the Australian Outback Marathon on Jul 31, 2010 and ended with the Supermaratona Cidade do Rio Grande ultramarathon in Brazil on Mar 4, 2012.

Fastest time to complete 10 marathons in 10 days

Male: Adam Holland (UK) ran the 2010 Brathay 10 in 10 challenge in Cumbria, UK, from May 7–16. His total time was 30 hr 20 min 54 sec.

Female: Sally Ford (UK) ran the same challenge two years later on May 11–20, taking 36 hr 38 min 53 sec.

Fastest marathon barefoot

Male: Abebe Bikila (ETH) ran the 1960 Olympic marathon in his bare feet. He set a time of 2 hr 15 min 16.2 sec in Rome, Italy, on Sep 10, 1960.

Female: It took just 2 hr 29 min 45 sec for barefooted Kenyan Tegla Loroupe to run the Olympic marathon in Sydney, Australia, on Sep 24, 2000.

![Virgin money LONDON MARATHON 2014]

Mailman Pete Waumsley (UK) 3 hr 47 min 35 sec

Mascot Francis Gilroy (UK) 3 hr 51 min 50 sec

Organ (female) Emma Denton (UK) 3 hr 52 min 2 sec

Faucet Richard Quartermaine (UK) 3 hr 52 min 9 sec

Doctor Naomi Garrick (UK) 3 hr 54 min 6 sec

Crustacean Oliver Johnson (UK) 3 hr 55 min 13 sec

Playing card Lisa Wright (UK) 4 hr 23 min 57 sec

Nut Spenser Lane (UK) 4 hr 29 min 36 sec

Fireman James Dajlid (UK) 4 hr 39 min 13 sec

Carrying a 20-lb backpack Gill Begnor (UK) 5 hr 7 min 56 sec

Longest crochet chain while running a marathon Susie Hewer (UK) 139.4 m (time of 5 hr 40 min 47 sec)

Knight in chainmail Michael Dodd (UK) 5 hr 49 min 7 sec

Telephone booth Sid Keyte (UK) 5 hr 54 min 52 sec

Four-person costume Andy Newman (back) and, from front left, Earl Edwards, Adam James, and Stuart Bailey (all UK) 6 hr 29 min 44 sec

Marching band Huddersfield Marathon Band (UK) 6 hr 56 min 48 sec

Motor sports

There are approximately **80,000 components** in every Formula One car

Most finishers in the Baja 1000 off-road race

The 620-mi (1,000-km) Baja 1000 is staged on Mexico's Baja California peninsula. The off-road race allows motorcycles, cars, and trucks to compete together. Unmarked challenges include harsh desert conditions, wandering animals, and traps made by spectators for their own amusement. The most drivers to complete the race is 237, out of the 424 starters in 2007.

on to win the 2013 MotoGP World Championship at Circuit Ricardo Tormo in Spain, becoming the **youngest MotoGP world champion**, at 20 years 266 days old on Nov 10, 2013.

Fastest Isle of Man TT Superbike race

Michael Dunlop (UK) set a time of 1 hr 45 min 29.98 sec on his 1000-cc TT Legends Honda in a six-lap Isle of Man TT Superbike race in Douglas, Isle of Man, UK, on Jun 2, 2013.

Most wins of the Motocross des Nations

Staged on off-road circuits, the Motocross des Nations,

Most consecutive NASCAR Sprint Cup Series wins

Jimmie Johnson (USA) won five successive National Association for Stock Car Auto Racing (NASCAR) Sprint Cup Series championships between 2006 and 2010. His streak ended when Tony Stewart (USA) won in 2011, but Johnson regained the title in the 2013 series. This brings his total to six series titles overall in 2006–13.

BIKES

Most MotoGP championships won

MotoGP is one of the three classes in the Road Racing World Championship Grand Prix, motorcycling's premier road-racing competition since it replaced the 500-cc class in 2002. The greatest number of victories in the MotoGP championships is six and was achieved by Valentino Rossi (ITA) in 2002–05 and 2008–09.

The **most wins of the MotoGP championships by a constructor** is seven,

achieved by Honda (JPN) in 2002–04, 2006, and 2011–13.

Youngest rider to achieve a MotoGP pole position

On Apr 20, 2013, Marc Márquez (ESP, b. Feb 17, 1993) took pole position at the 2013 Motorcycle Grand Prix of the Americas at the Circuit of the Americas in Austin, Texas, USA, at the age of 20 years 62 days.

The next day, Márquez won the race, becoming the **youngest MotoGP race winner**, at the age of 20 years 63 days. He went

also known as the "Olympics of Motocross," has been contested annually since 1947. The team with the most wins is the USA, with 22 between 1981 and 2011.

CARS

Most F1 victories by a constructor

The greatest number of Formula One (F1) Grand Prix wins by one manufacturer is 221, by Italian constructor Ferrari between 1951 and 2013. The team's first victory came at the 1951 British Grand Prix held at Silverstone, Northamptonshire, UK, which was won by Argentinian driver José Froilán González. Ferrari has also recorded the **most consecutive F1 Grand**

Most leaders in an Indianapolis 500 race

There were 14 different leaders of the 2013 edition of the Indianapolis 500 race at Indianapolis Motor Speedway in Indiana, USA, on May 26, 2013. In order, they were: Carpenter, Kanaan, Andretti, Hunter-Reay, Power, Jakes, Viso, Muñoz, Allmendinger, Tagliani, Bell, Hinchcliffe, Castroneves, and Dixon. The race was won by Tony Kanaan.

Fastest lap for a TT superbike at the Isle of Man TT

In a TT Superbike-class race in Douglas, Isle of Man, UK, on Jun 2, 2013, John McGuinness (UK) completed a lap on a Honda CBR1000RR in just 17 min 11.57 sec. McGuinness set the record with his sixth and final lap of the Mountain Course, during which he maintained an average speed of 131.67 mph (211.90 km/h).

MOST WINS OF THE ...

Competition	Wins	Champion
International Isle of Man TT (Tourist Trophy) Race	26	Joey Dunlop (UK) in 1977, 1980, 1983–88, 1992–98, and 2000
Motocross des Nations	22	USA in 1981–93, 1996, 2000, and 2005–11
Formula One World Constructors' Championship	16	Ferrari (ITA) in 1961, 1964, 1975–77, 1979, 1982–83, 1999–2004, and 2007–08
Road Racing World Championship Grand Prix	15	Giacomo Agostini (ITA) 500-cc in 1966–72 and 1975; and 350-cc in 1968–74
Motocross World Championship	10	Stefan Everts (DEU) 125-cc in 1991; 250-cc in 1995–97; 500-cc in 2001–02; MXGP in 2003; and MX1 in 2004–06
World Rally Championship	9	Sébastien Loeb (FRA) in 2004–12
Formula One World Drivers' Championship	7	Michael Schumacher (DEU) in 1994–95 and 2000–04
NASCAR Sprint Cup Series Drivers' Championship	7	Richard Petty (USA) in 1964, 1967, 1971–72, 1974–75, and 1979
		Dale Earnhardt, Sr. (USA) in 1980, 1986–87, 1990–91, and 1993–94
Karting World Championship	6	Mike Wilson (UK) in 1981–83, 1985, and 1988–89
MotoGP Championship	6	Valentino Rossi (ITA) in 2002–05 and 2008–09
Dakar Rally	5	Stéphane Peterhansel and Jean-Paul Cottret (both FRA) in 2004–05, 2007, and 2012–13
Superbike World Championship	4	Carl Fogarty (UK) in 1994–95 and 1998–99

Statistics correct as of Mar 25, 2014

Most consecutive Formula One Grand Prix wins

Sebastian Vettel (DEU) won nine Formula One Grands Prix driving for Red Bull in the 2013 season from Aug 25 to Nov 24, 2013. Vettel also became the **youngest F1 world champion** when he won the 2010 Abu Dhabi Grand Prix at the age of 23 years 134 days on Nov 14, 2010

to win at least one Grand Prix in the eight successive seasons up to and including his victory at the Grand Prix in Sepang, Malaysia, on Mar 30, 2014.

Most wins in a NASCAR Sprint Cup Series season
In the 1967 season, Richard Petty (USA) recorded 27 wins in the NASCAR Sprint Cup Series. In the same year, he set the mark for the **most consecutive NASCAR race wins**, with 10 victories from Aug 12 to Oct 1, 1967.

First F1 driver to finish every debut season Grand Prix

Max Chilton (UK) completed all 19 races during his debut season in 2013, driving for Marussia. True, he didn't secure a single point, but he became the first rookie in the 64-year history of the F1 championship to finish every race.

Prix points finishes by a constructor.
The team enjoyed 71 successive points finishes between the German Grand Prix staged on Jul 25, 2010 and the Chinese Grand Prix on Apr 20, 2014. Since 2010, a driver must finish in the top 10 to earn points for both themselves and their constructor.

Most points by a driver in an F1 career
The greatest number of points in an F1 career is 1,647, by Fernando Alonso (ESP) between Mar 9, 2003 and Apr 20, 2014.

Most F1 Grand Prix wins by a driver in a season
Michael Schumacher (DEU) won 13 Grands Prix in the 2004 season. His feat was equaled by Sebastian Vettel (DEU) in 2013.

Most consecutive seasons to win an F1 Grand Prix from debut
British driver Lewis Hamilton made his F1 Grand Prix debut in 2007 and his first win was in Canada that year. He went on

Most NASCAR race victories in a career
Richard Petty (USA) enjoyed 200 wins during his NASCAR career from 1958 to 1992. He also had the **most NASCAR pole positions** (126) and **most NASCAR race wins from pole position** (61).

Most WRC points in a season by a driver

Sébastien Ogier (FRA) scored 290 points driving for Volkswagen during the 2013 World Rally Championship (WRC) season. Ogier ended Sébastien Loeb's record run of nine consecutive championships by winning the 2013 season, and in the process scored 14 more points than Loeb amassed in 2010.

Rugby

Scotland beat England in the first international rugby match

Most international appearances in rugby union

Brian O'Driscoll (IRL, above with daughter Sadie) made 141 international appearances from Jun 12, 1999 to Mar 15, 2014, playing for Ireland 133 times and 8 times for the British and Irish Lions (2001, 2005, 2009, and 2013 tours). He scored 47 international tries and won 81 matches, ending with the 22–20 victory over France that secured the 2014 Six Nations trophy.

Bernard Norman (all AUS), playing for Annandale in the New South Wales Rugby League (the predecessor of the NRL) in the 1910 season. More than 100 years later, the feat was equaled by Sam, Luke, Tom, and George Burgess (all UK), who played for South Sydney Rabbitohs against Wests Tigers at the Allianz Stadium in Sydney, Australia, on Aug 30, 2013.

Longest dropkick
Joseph "Joe" Lydon (UK) scored a 183-ft (56-m) dropkick for Wigan against Warrington in a Challenge Cup semifinal held at Maine Road in Manchester, UK, on Mar 25, 1989.

Most points scored in a Super League career

Kevin Sinfield (UK) scored 3,498 points for Leeds Rhinos from Sep 13, 1998 to Mar 14, 2014. In 2012, the loose forward won the coveted *Rugby League World* Golden Boot Award, given to the player judged to be the best in the world.

LEAGUE

Fastest try
Tim Spears (UK) scored for Featherstone Rovers just 7.75 sec into a game against Wakefield Trinity Wildcats at Post Office Road in Featherstone, West Yorkshire, UK, on Jan 12, 2014. This (just) beat the previous record of 7.9 sec set by Rochdale Hornets' Danny Samuel (UK) in 2010.

Largest attendance at a World Cup final
A crowd of 74,468 fans watched the Rugby League World Cup final between Australia and New Zealand at Old Trafford in Manchester, UK, on Nov 30, 2013 (see right).

Most siblings to play in the same NRL team
Four brothers have played for the same National Rugby League (NRL) team twice in history. The first set of brothers to achieve this was Ray, Roy, Rex, and

Highest margin of victory in a World Cup final

Australia's 32-point win over New Zealand in the 2013 Rugby League World Cup final on Nov 30, 2013 represents the greatest victory margin ever recorded in this competition, which has been held since 1954.

Most points in an international career
Between May 5, 2006 and Nov 30, 2013, Australia's Johnathan Thurston scored 318 points in international rugby league matches. He finally surpassed Mick Cronin's long-standing record of 309 points when he kicked seven goals for 14 points in the 2013 World Cup final against New Zealand.

Oldest player with an international cap in union and league
Tom Calnan (b. Oct 22, 1976) is the oldest person to have won a "double cap" in international rugby, by playing in both codes. Calnan was 36 years 50 days old when he made his debut for the UAE rugby union side against Hong Kong in Dubai, UAE, on Dec 11, 2012. He had previously represented the UAE rugby league side in a match on Mar 30, 2012.

Youngest international player
Gavin Gordon (b. Feb 28, 1978) played for Ireland vs. Moldova on Oct 16, 1995 at Spotland in Rochdale, UK, at the age of 17 years 229 days. He scored a hat trick of tries in this debut game, which Ireland won 48–26.

MOST INTERNATIONAL ...

Rugby union		
Caps	141	Brian O'Driscoll (IRL, 1999–2014)
Points	1,442	Dan Carter (NZ, 2003–13)
Tries	69	Daisuke Ohata (JPN, 1996–2006)
Rugby league		
Caps	59	Darren Lockyer (AUS, 1998–2011)
Points	318	Johnathan Thurston (AUS, 2006–13)
Tries	41	Mick Sullivan (GB, 1954–63)

Statistics correct as of Mar 15, 2014

Bloemfontein in South Africa. During this match, the All Blacks scored 21 tries.

Youngest World Cup player

On Sep 30, 2007, Thretton Palamo (b. Sep 22, 1988) played for the USA vs. South Africa, at 19 years 8 days old, at Stade de la Mosson in Montpellier, France.

Most tries scored in Rugby Union World Cup tournaments by a player

Jonah Lomu (NZ) scored 15 tries in the 1995 and 1999 Rugby Union World Cups. His top tally in a single match was four tries in a 45–29 win against England on Jun 18, 1995. Above, Lomu is shown playing in the 1999 World Cup, in what proved to be a commanding 101–3 win over Italy.

FACT

Farrell's debut, at the age of 17, for Saracens against the Llanelli Scarlets in 2008 made him the youngest player in English professional rugby at that time.

Most penalties scored in the Heineken Cup by a player

Owen Farrell (UK) kicked 10 penalties for Saracens vs. Racing Métro 92 in the Heineken Cup match held at Stade de la Beaujoire in Nantes, France, on Jan 12, 2013.

UNION

Fastest try

Just 7.24 sec into a game on Nov 23, 2013, Tyson Lewis (UK) scored a try for Doncaster Knights vs. Old Albanians at Woollam Playing Fields in St. Albans, UK.

Fastest sending off in an English Premiership match

London Scottish player Mike Watson (UK) was sent off after 42 sec against Bath at the Recreation Ground in Bath, UK, on May 15, 1999.

Most consecutive international wins

Cyprus had 21 successive victories from Nov 29, 2008 to Nov 30, 2013.

Most consecutive World Cup defeats

Namibia suffered 15 Rugby Union World Cup losses in a row between Oct 1, 1999 and Sep 26, 2011.

Highest aggregate score in a World Cup match

New Zealand beat Japan 145–17 on Jun 4, 1995 at

First person to play Australian rules, rugby league, and rugby union

Karmichael Hunt (AUS) began his career in the NRL with Brisbane Broncos in 2004, switching to rugby union with Biarritz in 2009/10. In 2011, he played in the AFL for the Gold Coast Suns.

Most successive matches to score a try in the English Premiership

Mark Cueto (UK) scored tries in eight consecutive games for Sale Sharks from Apr 9 to Sep 25, 2005.

Most Heineken Cup points scored by a player

Ronan O'Gara (IRL) scored 1,365 points in Heineken Cup matches for Munster from Sep 7, 1997 to Apr 27, 2013.

The **most Heineken Cup tries scored by a player** is 35, by Vincent Clerc (FRA) for Stade Toulousain from Oct 13, 2002 to Jan 13, 2013.

Most tries in a Super Rugby career

Doug Howlett (NZ) scored 59 tries for the Auckland Blues from 1999 to 2007.

Oldest international player

Mark Spencer (b. May 21, 1954) was 57 years 340 days old when he played for Qatar in the Asian 5 Nations competition against Uzbekistan in Dubai, UAE, on Apr 25, 2012. Mark was born in the USA but took up Qatari residency, allowing him to represent the national side.

Most consecutive international rugby union matches unbeaten in a calendar year

New Zealand's All Blacks remained unbeaten for 14 international matches during 2013, from Jun 8 to Nov 24. Not only was the team undefeated, but it also won all of the 14 matches played. In 2003, England won more games (16) but were not unbeaten, having lost one match.

Club soccer

More than **265 million people** play soccer worldwide

First player to score a hat trick in the Copa Libertadores and the Champions League

On Dec 11, 2013, Barcelona's Neymar (BRA) scored a hat trick in a Champions League game at the Nou Camp in Spain. Having previously achieved the feat in the Copa Libertadores on Mar 7, 2012, for Brazilian side Santos, he became the first player to score hat tricks in both contests.

Most valuable soccer club
According to Forbes, as of Apr 17, 2013, Real Madrid was valued at $3.3 bn. The Spanish side, who won a 32nd La Liga title in 2011/12, ended Manchester United's run at the top of the rich list.

Most red cards in a game
In an Argentine Primera D match between Club Atlético Claypole and Victoriano Arenas on Feb 27, 2011, 36 players (both sides and all substitutes) were sent off by Damián Rubino (ARG).

First player to hold four major continental trophies simultaneously
When Chelsea won the Europa League on May 15, 2013, Fernando Torres and Juan Mata (both ESP) held four of soccer's most prestigious titles:

by 4.7 billion people across 212 territories. The total was boosted by its broadcast on terrestrial TV in China.

Most goals in a single national top-division season by an individual
Archibald Stark (UK) scored 67 times for Bethlehem Steel in the American Soccer League between Sep 15, 1924 and May 18, 1925.

Most consecutive top-division league titles
Skonto FC, from capital city Riga, won the Latvian Higher League 14 consecutive times from 1991 to 2004.

Most hat tricks in La Liga
Telmo Zarra (ESP) scored 22 hat tricks for Athletic Bilbao from 1940 to 1953. Alfredo Di Stéfano (ARG/ESP) matched the feat playing for Real Madrid and Espanyol from 1953 to 1966.

Most MLS championships
Two teams have won the USA's Major League Soccer Cup four times: Washington's DC United (1996–97, 1999, and 2004) and LA Galaxy from California (2002, 2005, and 2011–12).

Most consecutive losses
A home defeat by Rothwell Corinthians saw Woodford United FC (UK) record

the World Cup, European Championship, Champions League, and Europa League.

DOMESTIC

Most viewed domestic soccer league (global)
In 2010/11, the English Premier League was viewed

Most appearances for the same club

Rogério Ceni (BRA) appeared in 1,081 competitive matches for São Paulo Futebol Clube between Jul 7, 1993 and Nov 27, 2013. Keeper Ceni regularly takes free kicks and penalties, securing him the record for **most goals by a goalkeeper** (113) as of Nov 13, 2013.

Longest unbeaten streak in the Bundesliga

Bayern Munich were unbeaten in the Bundesliga—the top division in German soccer—for 53 matches from Nov 3, 2012 to Mar 29, 2014. The run finally ended on Apr 5, 2014 against Augsburg, who beat them 1–0. The previous record of 36 matches unbeaten had been set by Hamburg in 1983.

62 consecutive losses. The United Counties League match finished 6–2 at Byfield Road stadium in Woodford Halse, UK, on Oct 26, 2013.

Youngest man to play in all four English Football League divisions
Jack Hobbs (UK, b. Aug 18, 1988) made his debut for League One side Leicester City on Aug 9, 2008, at the age of 19 years 357 days. Hobbs had previously played for Lincoln City in League Two, Liverpool in the Premier League, and Scunthorpe in the Championship.

Most appearances in the English top division
Goalkeeper Peter Shilton (UK) recorded 848 appearances for Leicester City, Stoke City, Nottingham Forest, Southampton, and Derby County from May 3, 1966 to May 11, 1991.

Most expensive player
The transfer fee for winger Gareth Bale (UK) from Tottenham Hotspur (UK) to Real Madrid (ESP) on Sep 1, 2013 was a reported £85.3 m ($132 m), eclipsing the £80 m ($132 m) Real Madrid paid for Cristiano Ronaldo on Jul 1, 2009.

MOST WINS OF A MAJOR CONTINENTAL TROPHY

Team	Country	Trophy	Wins
Real Madrid	Spain	European Cup/Champions League	9
Al Ahly	Egypt	African/CAF Champions League	8
AC Milan	Italy	European Cup/Champions League	7
Independiente	Argentina	Copa Libertadores	7
Boca Juniors	Argentina	Copa Libertadores	6
Cruz Azul	Mexico	CONCACAF Champions' Cup/League	6
América	Mexico	CONCACAF Champions' Cup/League	5
Auckland City	New Zealand	OFC Champions League	5
Bayern Munich	Germany	European Cup/Champions League	5
Liverpool	England	European Cup/Champions League	5
Peñarol	Uruguay	Copa Libertadores	5
Zamalek	Egypt	African/CAF Champions League	5

Statistics correct as of Apr 25, 2014

Longest goal scored

On Nov 2, 2013, when Stoke City's goalie Asmir Begović (BIH) cleared the ball 13 sec into a Premier League game, something very unusual happened. The ball, caught by the wind, flew over the head of the Southampton keeper, scoring Begović a goal from 301 ft 6 in (91.9 m) away. Only Ledley King has scored faster in the Premier League, his goal coming after just 10 sec.

League match is 11, and was achieved when Monaco (FRA) beat the Spanish side Deportivo La Coruña 8–3 at home on Nov 5, 2003.

Most consecutive weeks leading La Liga

Barcelona spent 59 weeks at the top of La Liga, the Spanish top division, from Aug 19, 2012 to Jan 27, 2014. Barcelona also hold the record for the **most consecutive La Liga victories**. They racked up 16 wins in a row between Oct 16, 2010 and Feb 5, 2011, outscoring their opponents by 60 goals to 6 during the streak.

Most Champions League wins by an individual
Spanish midfielder Xavi won 83 matches playing for Barcelona from Sep 16, 1998 to Mar 12, 2014.

Most consecutive Champions League matches with a goal
Real Madrid scored in 35 consecutive Champions League games from May 3, 2011 to Apr 2, 2014.

Highest total score in a European Cup match
A first-round European Cup match between Feyenoord (NLD) and KR Reykjavík (ISL) saw a total of 14 goals scored. The match, which took place on Sep 17, 1969, saw a Dutch 12–2 victory.

The **most goals in a single Champions**

EUROPEAN

Oldest player to make a Champions League debut
Mark Schwarzer (AUS, b. Oct 6, 1972) took to the pitch at the age of 41 years 66 days in his Champions League debut for Chelsea against Steaua Bucharest at Stamford Bridge in London, UK, on Dec 11, 2013.

Tottenham keeper Brad Friedel (USA, b. May 18, 1971) was 42 years 305 days old when he played against Benfica on Mar 20, 2014, making him the **oldest player in the UEFA Europa League**.

Most appearances in the Champions League
Ryan Giggs (UK) has racked up 151 appearances for Manchester United in the UEFA Champions League. His debut came in Sep 1993, and more than 20 years later, on Apr 1, 2014, he played in a quarter-final match against Bayern Munich.

Most Europa League appearances
Ola Toivonen (SWE) appeared in 36 UEFA Europa League games for PSV Eindhoven between Jul 30, 2009 and Dec 12, 2013.

FACT

Ronaldo is a record breaker off the pitch too. He has the **most Twitter followers for an athlete**, with 25,229,560 as of Apr 1, 2014.

Most Champions League goals in a calendar year

Cristiano Ronaldo (POR) found the back of the net 15 times for Real Madrid between Feb 13 and Dec 10, 2013, beating the record of 13 goals set by his Barcelona rival Lionel Messi in 2012.

International soccer

The average soccer player **runs 7 mi** in a 90-min match

SPAIN 10 - 0 TAHITI
89:36
TORRES 5' 33' 57' 78'
DAVID SILVA 31' 89'
VILLA 39' 49' 64'
MATA 66'

Youngest player to reach 100 caps
South Korea's Cha Bum-Kun (b. May 22, 1953) was 24 years 139 days old playing his 100th game on Oct 9, 1977 against Kuwait.

Oldest international player
On Mar 31, 2004, MacDonald Taylor Sr (VIR, b. Aug 27, 1957) played for the US Virgin Islands at the age of 46 years 217 days.

Most teams in UEFA European Championship qualifying
Following Gibraltar's addition to the Union of European Football Associations (UEFA) in 2013, a record 53 teams will try to qualify for the 2016 European Championship.

Most international goals
No soccer player—male or female—has scored more international goals than American striker Abby Wambach (left). As of Mar 12, 2014, she had 167 goals to her name, scored since Sep 9, 2001. Wambach surpassed her old teammate Mia Hamm's record of 158 goals, taking the record in Jun 2013 with four goals against South Korea in Harrison, New Jersey, USA.

Highest margin of victory in a FIFA tournament (men)
A Confederations Cup match on Jun 20, 2013 saw Spain put 10 goals past Tahiti at the Estádio do Maracanã in Rio de Janeiro, Brazil. Tahiti—a team of amateur players—had been surprise qualifiers following their victory in the 2012 Oceania Football Confederation Nations Cup.

Most international caps
Kristine Lilly (USA) won 352 caps during her international career—more than any other man or woman. Her first cap came in 1987 and her last on Nov 5, 2010.

The record for the **most international caps by a man** belongs to Ahmed Hassan (EGY), who won 184 caps between Dec 29, 1995 and May 22, 2012.

Most international wins by a player
Goalkeeper Iker Casillas racked up 112 wins playing in 153 games for Spain between Jun 3, 2000 and Mar 5, 2014.

Most consecutive losses
On Sep 4, 2004, San Marino began a losing streak of 57 matches in a row. Their most recent match, on Oct 15, 2013, saw an 8–0 hammering by Ukraine. Prior to Gibraltar joining UEFA, San Marino was the smallest side competing in European soccer, with a population of just 30,000.

Most hat-tricks in the Confederations Cup
Fernando Torres (ESP) is the only player to have scored two hat-tricks in the FIFA (Fédération Internationale de Football Association) Confederations Cup. Torres scored them on Jun 14, 2009 and Jun 20, 2013.

FIFA WORLD CUP

Most tournaments won
The Brazilian men's team have won five World Cups, taking the crown in 1958–62, 1970, 1994, and 2002.

The **most Women's World Cup wins** is two, first achieved by the USA in 1991 and 1999 and then matched by Germany in 2003–07.

Longest unbeaten run in competitive internationals
Spain went unbeaten for 29 games between Jun 21, 2010 and Jun 27, 2013. Their winning streak came to an end at the hands of Brazil in the 2013 Confederations Cup final. If friendly matches were included, Spain and Brazil would share the record.

Most international goals (men)
Ali Daei earned 149 caps for Iran in his career. He scored in more than half of the matches—109 goals in total—between Jun 25, 1993 and Mar 1, 2006. In second place is Hungarian Ferenc Puskás, who scored 84 goals in 85 matches.

MOST CONFEDERATION CHAMPIONSHIP WINS

Men's competition	No.	Country
Asian Football Confederation (AFC): Asian Cup	4	Japan
Confederation of African Football (CAF): African Cup of Nations	7	Egypt
Confederation of North, Central American and Caribbean Association Football (CONCACAF): Gold Cup	6	Mexico
Union of European Football Associations (UEFA): European Championship	3	Spain
		Germany
Confederación Sudamericana de Fútbol/Confederação Sul-Americana de Futebol (CONMEBOL): Copa América	15	Uruguay
Oceania Football Confederation (OFC): Nations Cup	4	New Zealand
		Australia

Women's competition	No.	Country
AFC: Asian Cup	8	China
CAF: African Women's Championship	8	Nigeria
CONCACAF: Gold Cup	4	USA
UEFA: European Championship	8	Germany
CONMEBOL: Sudamericano Femenino	5	Brazil
OFC: Oceania Cup	4	New Zealand

Statistics correct as of Mar 11, 2014

Oldest coach to win the European Championship

Luis Aragonés (ESP, 1938–2014) was at the age of 69 years 337 days when he coached Spain to a UEFA European Championship title. The win came at the Ernst-Happel Stadium in Vienna, Austria, on Jun 29, 2008.

Highest goal average at a World Cup finals
The 1954 World Cup in Switzerland saw an average of 5.38 goals scored per match. The **lowest goal average at a World Cup finals** was 2.21 per game in 1990.

Most goals scored
Men: Brazilian striker Ronaldo, aka Ronaldo Luís Nazário de Lima, scored 15 goals across three World Cup tournaments in 1998–2006.

Women: Birgit Prinz (DEU) scored 14 goals at four World Cups between 1995 and 2007. Marta (BRA) matched the feat over three World Cups in 2003–11.

Highest margin of victory
Women: The very first match at the Women's World Cup on Sep 10, 2007 saw Germany put 11 goals past the Argentinian defense. Germany went on to lift the trophy, beating Brazil 2–0.
Men: On Jun 17, 1954, five Hungarians scored in a 9–0 thrashing of South Korea. Subsequently, Yugoslavia defeated Zaire 9–0 in 1974 and Hungary beat El Salvador 10–1 in 1982.

Most players sent off in one finals match
Nicknamed "The Battle of Nuremberg," a match between the Netherlands and Portugal at the 2006 World Cup had four players seeing red, two from each side, in Nuremberg, Germany, on Jun 25.

Most teams represented at the FIFA World Cup

FIFA rules prohibit players from switching nationalities at senior level; however, Dejan Stanković has represented three Balkan countries because political borders have shifted. He played in three World Cups, representing Yugoslavia in 1998 (above), Serbia and Montenegro in 2006 (above inset), and Serbia in 2010 (right).

Most qualifiers played
Between Mar 4, 1934 and Nov 20, 2013, the Mexican men's team participated in 141 World Cup qualifying matches. Mexico won 92 of the games—the **most World Cup qualifiers won**.

West Germany recorded the **most consecutive World Cup qualifiers won**, with 16 between May 10, 1969 and Apr 30, 1985.

Most wins of the FIFA World Cup by a player

The only soccer player to have won the FIFA World Cup three times is Pelé (BRA), who won the 1958, 1962, and 1970 titles with Brazil.

From Sep 7, 1956 to Oct 1, 1977, Pelé scored 1,279 goals in 1,363 games—the **most career goals**.

Most wins of the Confederations Cup

The Brazilians have won the FIFA Confederations Cup four times, in 1997 and 2005–13. They also have the **most consecutive Confederations Cup match wins**, with 12, from Jun 25, 2005 to Jun 30, 2013.

ℹ Cup competitors

The Confederations Cup is contested every four years by the winners of the six FIFA confederation championships (see table above), the FIFA World Cup holder, and the host nation.

Tennis & racket sports

FACT

Graf won 22 Grand Slam singles titles, starting and ending with the French Open in 1987 and 1999.

First tennis player to win a "Career Super Slam"

A "Career Super Slam" involves winning all four Grand Slams, the Davis Cup (male)/Fed Cup (female), the ATP World Tour Finals (male)/WTA Tour Championships (female), and an Olympic gold medal. In 1988, Steffi Graf (DEU) became the first tennis player to achieve this. Her husband, Andre Agassi (USA), became the **first male tennis player to win a "Career Super Slam,"** doing so in 1999.

BADMINTON

Most Sudirman Cup wins
The Sudirman Cup—held every two years since 1989—is the mixed-team world championship. China accumulated nine wins between 1995 and 2013. The 2013 final also saw China record the **most consecutive Sudirman Cup wins**: five triumphs in a row (2005–13).

Most Thomas Cup wins
Also known as the World Men's Team Championships, the Thomas Cup was won 13 times by Indonesia between 1958 and 2002.

Most singles BWF World Championships titles
Male: When China's Dan Lin won the singles title at the Badminton World Federation (BWF) World Championships on Aug 11, 2013, he did so for the fifth time.

Female: Four Chinese women have won the singles title twice: Li Lingwei, Han Aiping, Ye Zhaoying, and, most recently, Xie Xingfang in 2005 and 2006.

Longest rally in competition
On Mar 18, 2010, during the third set of a Swiss Open match in Basel, 154 strokes were played by Petya Nedelcheva (BGR) and Anastasia Russkikh (RUS) vs. Shizuka Matsuo and Mami Naito (both JPN).

SQUASH

Most European Team Championships won
England hold both the **male** and **female** records for this competition with 38 and 35 wins respectively.

Most World Open wins
Male: Jansher Khan (PAK) won a record eight

World Open titles: in 1987, 1989–90, and 1992–96.
Female: The women's title has been won seven times by Nicol David (MYS), in 2005–06 and 2008–12.

Most World Series Finals
Male: Jansher Khan has had the most wins of the World Series Finals, with four titles between 1993 and 1998.

FACT

Jahangir Khan and Jansher Khan were fierce rivals. However, they are not related.

Longest unbeaten squash run

Male: The longest unbeaten run in men's squash is 555 games, by Jahangir Khan (PAK) from Nov 1981 to Nov 1986.
Female: Heather McKay (AUS) was unbeaten in 1962–81, and lost just two matches in her career.

Female: The women's World Series Finals have been held twice. Nicol David won both times, in 2012 and 2013.

Longest singles marathon
Guy Fotherby and Darren Withey (both UK) endured 31 hr 35 min 34 sec playing squash singles at Racquets Fitness Centre in Thame, Oxfordshire, UK, on Jan 13–14, 2012. Darren won 422 of 465 games.

TENNIS

Most prize money for a Grand Slam
Total prize money for the US Open rose to $34.3 m for the 2013 tournament. The singles champions, Rafael Nadal and Serena Williams, each collected $2.6 m.

Most retirements in one day at a Grand Slam
On Jun 26, 2013, at the Wimbledon Championships in London, UK, seven players retired mid-match or withdrew before making it onto court. Dubbed "Wipeout Wednesday," the day saw injuries to one shoulder, one arm, one hamstring, and four knees.

Most "powerful" athlete

Swiss sensation Roger Federer is the top sports star on Forbes' list of the world's most powerful celebrities, ranking No. 8 overall. Federer holds a wealth of men's tennis records, including **most Grand Slam singles titles (17)**, **most Grand Slam matches won (265)**, and **most weeks ranked world No. 1 (302)**. Forbes' list measures fame by considering earnings, TV and print exposure, strength of Internet presence, public opinion, and marketability.

108 mph

FACT

Federer earned an estimated $71 m from Jun 2012 to Jun 2013, according to Forbes.

First duo to win each Grand Slam together

Serena Williams (USA) and Rafael Nadal (ESP) are the only duo to win each tennis Grand Slam singles tournament together, both claiming titles at the 2009 Australian Open, Wimbledon in 2010, and Roland Garros in 2013. They completed their set at the US Open on Sep 8–9, 2013.

Most ITTF World Tour Grand Finals singles titles
Female: Zhang Yining (CHN) claimed four International Table Tennis Federation (ITTF) World Tours, taking the singles crown in 2000, 2002, and 2005–06.
Male: Two Chinese men have won three ITTF singles titles: Wang Liqin (1998, 2000, and 2004) and Ma Long (2008–09 and 2011).

Most Olympic golds
Male: Ma Lin (CHN) has won three table tennis golds, winning doubles in 2004, and singles and team in 2008.
Female: Three Chinese women have won four Olympic golds: Yaping Deng at the 1992 and 1996 Games; Nan Wang in 2000, 2004, and 2008; and Yining Zhang in 2004 and 2008.

Most singles titles won at one Grand Slam
Female: No one, male or female, has won more open era (since 1968) singles titles at one Grand Slam than Martina Navratilova (USA). Between 1978 and 1990, she won Wimbledon nine times.
Male: Rafael Nadal won an eighth French Open title when he defeated David Ferrer in straight sets on Jun 9, 2013.

MOST TENNIS GRAND SLAM SINGLES WINS

Australian Open		
Female	11	Margaret Court (AUS, 1960–73)
Male	6	Roy Emerson (AUS, 1961–67)
French Open (Roland Garros)		
Male	8	Rafael Nadal (ESP, 2005–13)
Female	7	Chris Evert (USA, 1974–86)
Wimbledon		
Female	9	Martina Navratilova (USA, 1978–90)
Male	7	W. C. Renshaw (UK, 1881–89)
		Pete Sampras (USA, 1993–2000)
		Roger Federer (CHE, 2003–12)
US Open		
Female	8	Molla Mallory (NOR, 1915–26)
Male	7	Richard Sears (USA, 1881–87)
		William Larned (USA, 1901–11)
		Bill Tilden (USA, 1920–29)

TABLE TENNIS

Most World Table Tennis Championships singles
Female: Angelica Rozeanu (ROM) won six consecutive singles titles in 1950–55.
Male: The men's singles crown was won five times by Viktor Barna (HUN), in 1930 and 1932–35.

Youngest Olympic table tennis gold medalist
On Aug 21, 2004, Chen Qi (CHN, b. Apr 15, 1984)— one of the few top-ranked Chinese left-handers—won the men's doubles at the age of 20 years 128 days, with his partner Ma Lin (CHN).

Most consecutive wins of the ITTF World Tour Grand Finals
Female: Liu Shiwen (CHN, left) won consecutively from 2011–13.
Male: Two Chinese men have won two consecutive ITTF Grand finals: Ma Long (2008–09) and Xu Xin (2012–13).

Most IRF World Championships won (male)
Americans Rocky Carson (above) and Jack Huczek have each won the International Racquetball Federation (IRF) World Championships three consecutive times: Huczek in 2002–06, and Carson in 2008–12.

Fastest serve
On May 9, 2012, Samuel Groth (AUS) served an ace at 163.4 mph (263 km/h).

Most Grand Slams before first title win (female)
Frenchwoman Marion Bartoli won her first Grand Slam title at her 47th attempt, defeating Germany's Sabine Lisicki in the Wimbledon final on Jul 6, 2013. Her Grand Slam debut was at the 2001 French Open.

Water sports

Michael Phelps eats a mammoth **12,000 calories a day** during training

First open-water swimmer to win a World Championships gold in every discipline (male)

Thomas Lurz (DEU) was the first man to win a FINA World Championships gold in every open-water event, winning the 5, 10, and 25-km races between 2005 and 2013. The **first female** to achieve the same feat was Viola Valli (ITA), between 2001 and 2003.

Most nations in a FINA World Championships
The 15th FINA (Fédération Internationale de Natation) World Championships included participants from 181 nations. It was held in Barcelona, Spain, in 2013.

DIVING

Most consecutive FINA World Championships titles
Guo Jingjing (CHN) won five 3-m diving titles in both individual and synchronized events from 2001 to 2009.

Youngest Summer Olympic medalist in an individual event
Nils Skoglund (SWE, 1906–80) was just 14 years 11 days old when he won silver in the plain high-diving event at the 1920 Olympics.

Most Olympic medals
Male: Dmitri Sautin (RUS) won eight Olympic medals, including two golds, in 1992–2008.
Female: Two Chinese divers have six Olympic medals: Guo Jingjing (2000–08) and Wu Minxia (2004–12).

Most America's Cup wins

US teams have won 30 of the 35 America's Cup sailing competitions held between 1851 and 2013. The America's Cup is a yacht race held between two clubs—the reigning champion and the challenger. The trophy was first won in 1851, making this the **oldest international yacht race**. The 2013 winners, Golden Gate Yacht Club, are pictured.

SWIMMING

Most individual Olympic medals (male)
Michael Phelps (USA) has won more individual medals than any other man across any discipline. He swam his way to 13 medals in individual events at Athens 2004, Beijing 2008, and London 2012. Only one athlete has won more individual medals than him: gymnast Larisa Latynina (USSR/UKR), who won 14.

Phelps also holds Olympic men's records for **most individual event golds** (11), **most golds** (18), and **most swimming medals** (22), as well as seven speed records (see table below).

Most Olympic golds at one Games (female)
Kristin Otto (GDR) won a sensational six swimming gold medals at the 1988 Olympic Games in Seoul.

Most consecutive golds in synchronized swimming at the FINA World Championships

From Jul 23, 2009 to Jul 27, 2013, Russia won 17 synchronized swimming golds at the FINA World Championships, with their latest clean sweep of seven golds in Barcelona, Spain. Russia hope to add to their medal run on home soil at the 2015 Championships in Kazan.

MEN'S SWIMMING—FASTEST ...

Event	Time	Name (Nationality)	Time	Name (Nationality)
Freestyle	**Short course**		**Long course**	
50 m	20.30	Roland Schoeman (ZAF)	20.91	Cesar Filho Cielo (BRA)
100 m	44.94	Amaury Leveaux (FRA)	46.91	Cesar Filho Cielo (BRA)
200 m	1:39.37	Paul Biedermann (DEU)	1:42.00	Paul Biedermann (DEU)
400 m	3:32.25	Yannick Agnel (FRA)	3:40.07	Paul Biedermann (DEU)
800 m	7:23.42	Grant Hackett (AUS)	7:32.12	Zhang Lin (CHN)
1,500 m	14:10.10	Grant Hackett (AUS)	14:31.02	Sun Yang (CHN)
4 x 100 m	3:03.30	USA	3:08.24	USA
4 x 200 m	6:49.04	Russia	6:58.55	USA
Butterfly	**Short course**		**Long course**	
50 m	21.80	Steffen Deibler (DEU)	22.43	Rafael Muñoz (ESP)
100 m	48.48	Evgeny Korotyshkin (RUS)	49.82	Michael Phelps (USA)
200 m	*1:48.56	Chad le Clos (ZAF)	1:51.51	Michael Phelps (USA)
Backstroke	**Short course**		**Long course**	
50 m	22.61	Peter Marshall (USA)	24.04	Liam Tancock (UK)
100 m	48.94	Nicholas Thoman (USA)	51.94	Aaron Peirsol (USA)
200 m	1:46.11	Arkady Vyatchanin (RUS)	1:51.92	Aaron Peirsol (USA)
Breaststroke	**Short course**		**Long course**	
50 m	25.25	Cameron van der Burgh (ZAF)	26.67	Cameron van der Burgh (ZAF)
100 m	55.61	Cameron van der Burgh (ZAF)	58.46	Cameron van der Burgh (ZAF)
200 m	2:00.67	Dániel Gyurta (HUN)	2:07.01	Akihiro Yamaguchi (JPN)
Medley	**Short course**		**Long course**	
200 m	1:49.63	Ryan Lochte (USA)	1:54.00	Ryan Lochte (USA)
400 m	3:55.50	Ryan Lochte (USA)	4:03.84	Michael Phelps (USA)
4 x 100 m	3:19.16	Russia	3:27.28	USA

As of Mar 19, 2014 (*pending FINA approval)

WOMEN'S SWIMMING—FASTEST ...

Event	Time	Name (Nationality)	Time	Name (Nationality)
Freestyle	**Short course**		**Long course**	
50 m	23.24	Ranomi Kromowidjojo (NLD)	23.73	Britta Steffen (DEU)
100 m	51.01	Lisbeth Trickett (AUS)	52.07	Britta Steffen (DEU)
200 m	1:51.17	Federica Pellegrini (ITA)	1:52.98	Federica Pellegrini (ITA)
400 m	3:54.52	Mireia Belmonte (ESP)	3:59.15	Federica Pellegrini (ITA)
800 m	7:59.34	Mireia Belmonte (ESP)	8:13.86	Katie Ledecky (USA)
1,500 m	*15:26.95	Mireia Belmonte (ESP)	15:36.53	Katie Ledecky (USA)
4 x 100 m	3:28.22	Netherlands	3:31.72	Netherlands
4 x 200 m	7:35.94	China	7:42.08	China
Butterfly	**Short course**		**Long course**	
50 m	24.38	Therese Alshammar (SWE)	25.07	Therese Alshammar (SWE)
100 m	55.05	Diane Bui Duyet (FRA)	55.98	Dana Vollmer (USA)
200 m	2:00.78	Liu Zige (CHN)	2:01.81	Liu Zige (CHN)
Backstroke	**Short course**		**Long course**	
50 m	25.70	Sanja Jovanović (CRO)	27.06	Zhao Jing (CHN)
100 m	55.23	Shiho Sakai (JPN)	58.12	Gemma Spofforth (UK)
200 m	2:00.03	"Missy" Franklin (USA)	2:04.06	"Missy" Franklin (USA)
Breaststroke	**Short course**		**Long course**	
50 m	*28.71	Yulia Efimova (RUS)	29.48	Rúta Meilutyté (LTU)
100 m	*1:02.36	Rúta Meilutyté (LTU)	1:04.35	Rúta Meilutyté (LTU)
200 m	2:14.57	Rebecca Soni (USA)	2:19.11	Rikke Moeller-Pederson (DNK)
Medley	**Short course**		**Long course**	
200 m	2:03.20	Katinka Hosszú (HUN)	2:06.15	Ariana Kukors (USA)
400 m	4:20.85	Katinka Hosszú (HUN)	4:28.43	Ye Shiwen (CHN)
4 x 100 m	3:45.56	USA	3:52.05	USA

*As of Mar 19, 2014 (*pending FINA approval)*

Fastest short-course 100-m medley (female)

Hungarian swimmer Katinka Hosszú completed the 100-m short-course medley in 57.45 sec. She set the record at the FINA Swimming World Cup in Berlin, Germany, on Aug 11, 2013. Hosszú also holds two other short-course speed records (see table left).

World League titles (two as Serbia and Montenegro), between 2005 and 2013. The competition was inaugurated in 2002. **Female:** The women's competition was added in 2004 and has seen the USA score seven titles in 2004, 2006–07, and 2009–12.

SURFING

Most ASP World Tour event wins
The surfer with the most ASP (Association of Surfing Professionals) World Tour event wins is Kelly Slater (USA), with 54 titles between 1992 and 2014.

Slater also boarded his way to the **most ASP World Championship Tour titles**, won by the surfer with the most points at the end of the year. Slater's 11 wins between 1992 and 2011 put him seven ahead of the man in second place: Mark Richards (AUS). Layne Beachley (AUS) has the **most women's ASP**

World Championship Tour titles, winning six consecutively from 1998 to 2003 and a seventh in 2006.

CANOEING

Most Olympic appearances (female)
Josefa Idem (ITA, b. FRG) has participated in eight Olympic Games in the canoe sprint—the most for any female athlete. Idem competed for West Germany in 1984 to 1988 and Italy from 1992 to 2012. During her Olympic career, she won five medals, including gold in the K-1 500-m event at Sydney 2000.

Most individual canoe slalom Olympic medals
Michal Martikán (SVK) won five Olympic canoe slalom medals. He picked up two gold, two silver, and a bronze between 1996 and 2012.

Most canoe slalom Olympic golds
Tony Estanguet (FRA) claimed his third Olympic gold medal in canoe slalom on Jul 31, 2012.

WATER POLO

Most Olympic golds
Hungary won gold on nine occasions, including consecutive wins in 2000, 2004, and 2008. Eleven men have recorded three Olympic water polo golds. Women's water polo was introduced into the Olympics in 2000, but no country has won gold more than once.

Most Water Polo World League wins
Male: The Serbian national team have collected seven FINA Water Polo

Fastest short-course 800-m freestyle (female)

On Aug 10, 2013, Mireia Belmonte (ESP) finished the 800-m short-course freestyle in a time of 7 min 59.34 sec—the first woman to break the 8-min barrier—in Berlin, Germany. Belmonte was awarded the title of Best Spanish Athlete of 2013, alongside tennis star Rafael Nadal.

ⓘ Surf's up
Garrett McNamara (USA) caught a wave measuring 78 ft off the coast of Praia do Norte in Portugal on Nov 1, 2011, the **largest unlimited wave surfed**.

Youngest ASP World Tour champion (female)

Carissa Moore (USA, b. Aug 27, 1992) became the youngest female ASP World Tour champion when she won the 2011 Tour at the age of 18 years 322 days on Jul 15, 2011. Hawaiian-born Carissa won the title on her second attempt, having finished third in 2010. She broke the 27-year-old record held by Frieda Zamba (USA), who won the 1984 title as a teenager, at the age of 19 years 164 days.

Winter sports

Downhill skiers can attain speeds of up to **155 mph**

Highest score in free dance figure skating

US gold medalists Meryl Davis and Charlie White achieved a score of 116.63 at the XXII Winter Olympics in Sochi, Russia, on Feb 17, 2014. Their high score was set in the free dance section of the ice dancing event, which they performed to Rimsky-Korsakov's "Scheherazade."

First shared gold medal in alpine skiing

The women's downhill skiing event at the 2014 Games saw Tina Maze (SVN) and Dominique Gisin (CHE) record the exact same time, 41.57 sec, on Feb 12.

FASTEST ...

Ski-bob
On Apr 19, 2006, during the Pro Mondial speed skiing event at Les Arcs, Rhône-Alpes, France, Romuald Bonvin (CHE) attained a speed of 127.03 mph (204.43 km/h) on a ski-bob.

Oldest ski jump Olympic medalist

Noriaki Kasai (JPN, b. Jun 6, 1972) won bronze in the men's ski jump team event at 41 years 256 days old in Sochi, Russia, on Feb 17, 2014. He's also the **oldest ski jump World Cup winner**, taking gold in the ski flying event at 41 years 219 days old in Tauplitz, Austria, on Jan 11, 2014.

MOST ...

Skiing Nations' Cup wins
The skiing Nations' Cup is based on the combined men's and women's results at the Alpine Ski World Cup. It was won 35 times by Austria between 1969 and 2014.

> **FACT**
> Snowboarding was first included in the Winter Olympics in 1998.

Youngest Olympic snowboard medalist

Ayumu Hirano (JPN, b. Nov 29, 1998) was just 15 years 74 days old when he won silver in the snowboard halfpipe in Sochi, Russia, on Feb 11, 2014. The record for the **youngest Olympic freestyle skiing medalist (female)** was also set in Sochi, by Justine Dufour-Lapointe (CAN, b. Mar 25, 1994), who won gold in the moguls event at 19 years 321 days old on Feb 8, 2014.

WINTER OLYMPICS

Most expensive Olympics (Winter or Summer)

The 2014 Winter Olympics in Sochi, Russia, were widely reported to have cost $50 bn to stage, including all sports-related and infrastructure costs.

The Sochi Games also set the record for the **most participating countries at a Winter Olympics**: 87 National Olympic Committees entered athletes. Of these, the **largest Winter Olympics team** was the USA, with 230 athletes.

Most medals won by a country

By the close of the 2014 Sochi Games, Norway's all-time haul of Winter Olympics medals had grown to 329: 118 gold (the **most Winter Olympics gold medals won by a country**), 111 silver, and 100 bronze.

Most gold medals won by an individual

Male: Two Norwegian Olympians have each won eight golds: Ole Einar Bjørndalen (see opposite page) in the biathlon in 1998–2014, and cross-country skier Bjørn Dæhlie in 1992–98.

Female: Three Olympians share this record with six gold medals apiece: speed skater Lydia Skoblikova (USSR) in 1960–64, and cross-country skiers Lyubov Yegorova (EUN/RUS) in 1992–94 and Marit Bjørgen (NOR) in 2010–14.

First women's Olympic curling team to win every first-round game

The round-robin format was introduced to curling at the 1998 Winter Olympics in Nagano, Japan. Canada is the only women's team to have won every first-round game, with nine wins in Sochi from Feb 10 to 18, 2014.

Speed skating 500 m
Male: Jeremy Wotherspoon (CAN) skated 500 m in 34.03 sec in Salt Lake City, Utah, USA, on Nov 9, 2007.
Female: Lee Sang-Hwa (KOR) took 36.36 sec to skate 500 m, also in Salt Lake City, on Nov 16, 2013.

Speed skating 1,000 m
Male: On Mar 7, 2009, multiple record holder Shani Davis (USA) skated 1,000 m in 1 min 6.42 sec in Salt Lake City, Utah, USA.

Female: Brittany Bowe (USA) skated 1,000 m in 1 min 12.58 sec, also in Salt Lake City on Nov 17, 2013.

Bobsled skeleton
Male: Alexander Tretyakov (RUS) and Sandro Stielicke (DEU) both reached 90.96 mph (146.4 km/h) during the Winter Olympics in British Columbia, Canada, on 19 Feb 2010.
Female: Marion Trott (DEU) recorded a speed of 89.78 mph (144.5 km/h), also during the 2010 Winter Olympics competition at Whistler, on Feb 19.

Most appearances at the Winter Olympics

Two athletes have competed in seven consecutive Winter Olympics: ski-jumper Noriaki Kasai (JPN) and luger Albert Demchenko (RUS, above) appeared in every Winter Games from Albertville 1992 to Sochi 2014.

Most consecutive individual Olympic medals

Armin Zöggeler (ITA) won six consecutive individual Olympic medals from 1994 to 2014: two gold, one silver, and three bronze, all in the men's singles luge. The previous record was also held by a luger, Georg Hackl (DEU), who won five consecutive individual medals from 1988 to 2002.

Most ...	Total	Athlete	Dates
Medals (female)	27	Ragnhild Myklebust (NOR)	1988–2002
Medals (male)	22	Gerd Schönfelder (DEU)	1992–2010
Gold medals (female)	22	Ragnhild Myklebust (NOR)	1988–2002
Gold medals (male)	16	Gerd Schönfelder (DEU)	1992–2010
Most medals in ...	**Total**	**Athlete**	
Alpine skiing (male)	22	Gerd Schönfelder (DEU)	1992–2010
Alpine skiing (female)	19	Reinhild Möller (DEU)	1980–98, 2006
Cross-country skiing (male)	17	Frank Höfle (DEU)	1988–2006
Cross-country skiing (female)	16	Ragnhild Myklebust (NOR)	1988–2002
Ice sled speed racing (male)	12	Knut Lundstrøm (NOR)	1988, 1994–98
Ice sled speed racing (female)	11	Brit Mjaasund Øjen (NOR)	1980–84, 1994
		Sylva Olsen (NOR)	1980–88
Biathlon (male)	7	Vitaliy Lukyanenko (UKR)	2002–14
Biathlon (female)	7	Olena Iurkovska (UKR)	2002–14

Most Paralympic cross-country skiing gold medals

Male: Frank Höfle (DEU), Terje Loevaas (NOR), and Brian McKeever (CAN, above) have each won 10 golds in Paralympic cross-country skiing. McKeever added three golds to his tally in 2014.
Female: Norway's Ragnhild Myklebust won 16 Paralympic gold medals in cross-country skiing between 1988 and 2002.

Individual (male): Eduard Khrennikov (RUS) has won 11 WSOC medals, including seven golds.
Individual (female): Fellow Russian Tatiana Vlasova has taken 10 individual medals.

Bobsled Skeleton World Cup race wins (male)
Martins Dukurs (LVA) won 31 bobsled Skeleton World Cup races between Feb 8, 2008 and Jan 25, 2014.

Most Winter Olympics medals
Male: Ole Einar Bjørndalen (NOR) won 13 Olympic biathlon medals between 1998 and 2014.
Female: Three women have won 10 cross-country skiing medals: Raisa Smetanina (USSR/EUN), Stefania Belmondo (ITA), and Marit Bjørgen (NOR).

WSOC medals
Relay: Finland has won 38 World Ski Orienteering Championships (WSOC) medals across the three relay categories (men, women, and mixed).

YOUNGEST ...

Curling rink (team) to win an Olympic medal (female)
The Great Britain side of Eve Muirhead, Anna Sloan, Vicki Adams, Claire Hamilton, and Lauren Gray had an average age of

Most points in a single end of an Olympic curling match

An "end" in curling is complete when both teams have delivered all eight rocks. The most points scored by a team in a single end of an Olympic match is seven, by Great Britain against the USA in Sochi, Russia, on Feb 11, 2014. Great Britain won the game 12–3, needing only 6 of the 10 possible ends to do so.

23 years 255 days when they won bronze in Sochi, Russia, on Feb 20, 2014.

World Women's Curling Championship winning skip
Scottish skip Eve Muirhead (UK, b. Apr 22, 1990) led her team to victory at the age of 22 years 336 days in Riga, Latvia, on Mar 24, 2013.

OLDEST ...

Individual Winter Olympics medalist
Luge silver-medalist Albert Demchenko (RUS, b. Nov 27, 1971) was 42 years 74 days old when he won in Sochi, Russia, on Feb 9, 2014. The **oldest individual Winter Olympics gold medalist** is Ole Einar Bjørndalen (NOR, b. Jan 27, 1974), who was 40 years 12 days old when he won the 10-km biathlon sprint on Feb 8, 2014.

Skiing World Cup slalom race winner (male)
Mario Matt (AUT, b. Apr 9, 1979) finished first at the age of 34 years 250 days in Val d'Isère, France, on Dec 15, 2013.

Most Olympic short track speed skating golds (male)

Viktor Ahn (KOR/RUS, b. Ahn Hyun-Soo) won three short track speed skating gold medals for South Korea at the 2006 Olympics in Turin, Italy, and another three golds for Russia at the 2014 Games in Sochi. Ahn represented South Korea at the 2006 Games, but in 2011 he became a Russian citizen and so represented Russia at the Sochi Olympics.

Sports roundup

In 1927, the first world snooker champion received **prize money of $10**

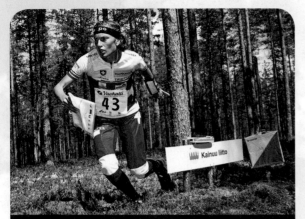

Most wins of the individual long-distance World Orienteering Championships

The World Orienteering Championships long-distance event has been contested annually since 1966. Simone Niggli-Luder (CHE) has taken the crown eight times, more than any other person—man or woman. Her wins came in 2001, 2003, 2005–06, 2009–10, and 2012–13.

Most competitive 147 breaks in snooker
Ronnie O'Sullivan (UK) has racked up 12 maximum breaks in competitive snooker matches. He achieved his 147s from Apr 21, 1997 to Mar 2, 2014.

O'Sullivan has also made the **most century breaks at the World Snooker Championship** (144), from Apr 15, 1995 to May 5, 2014.

First female snooker player to qualify for the final stages of a ranking event
Reanne Evans (UK)— 10-time ladies' world champion—qualified for the televised stages of China's Wuxi Classic with a 5–4 victory over male snooker player Thepchaiya Un-Nooh (THA) in a qualifying match at the South West Snooker Academy in Gloucester, UK, on May 28, 2013.

Most century breaks in a season
Neil Robertson (AUS) made 103 century breaks in 22 tournaments in the 2013–14 season that ran from Jun 7, 2013 to May 5, 2014. As of May 3, 2014, Robertson had made 361 century breaks as a professional. He is the fifth best all-time century maker, on a list that is headed by Stephen Hendry (UK) with 775.

Longest snooker ban
On Sep 25, 2013, an independent tribunal found professional snooker player Stephen Lee (UK) guilty of fixing seven matches in 2008 and 2009. Lee was banned from playing in any match sanctioned by the World Professional Billiards and Snooker Association for 12 years.

Most Professional Bowlers Association tour event appearances
Between 1976 and 2013, Tom Baker (USA) competed in 840 Professional Bowlers Association (PBA) ten-pin bowling tour events.

Carmen Salvino (USA, b. Nov 23, 1933) is the **oldest ten-pin tour bowler**. He played in the 2014 PBA Tournament of Champions at the age of 80 years 58 days at Thunderbowl Lanes in Michigan, USA, on Jan 20.

Walter Ray Williams, Jr. (USA) has the **most PBA ten-pin bowling titles**. His tally stands at 47 titles; the latest was won at the USBC Masters on Feb 14, 2010.

Most players to score a televised nine-dart finish in one day
The fewest throws needed to score 501 points in a game of darts is nine, aka the nine-dart finish. Two players achieved this feat during the televised 2014 PDC World Darts Championship in London, UK: Terry Jenkins (UK) and Kyle Anderson (AUS), in different matches, on Dec 14, 2013.

First woman to win the Mongol Derby
When Lara Prior-Palmer (UK, b. Jun 24, 1994) won the Mongol Derby on Aug 10, 2013, she became the first woman to do so. The competition takes place over a grueling 621-mi (1,000-km) course and is the

Most 180s in a World Darts Championship

At the 2014 Professional Darts Corporation (PDC) World Championship, held at Alexandra Palace in London, UK, from Dec 13, 2013 to Jan 1, 2014, a total of 603 maximums (180s) were recorded, beating the 588 achieved in the 2012 competition. The title was eventually won by Michael van Gerwen (NLD, pictured), who hit 16 of the maximums.

Youngest X Games medalist
Alana Smith (USA, b. Oct 20, 2000) was 12 years 210 days old when she won a silver medal in the Women's Skateboard Park competition at the X Games in Barcelona, Spain, on May 18, 2013.

Tom Schaar (USA, b. Sep 14, 1999) is the **youngest X Games gold medalist**. He was 12 years 229 days old when he won the Mini Mega category on Apr 30, 2012.

longest multihorse race. Lara's 2013 title also made her the youngest **Mongol Derby winner**, at the age of 19 years 47 days.

Most Grade 1 victories by a horse
Hurricane Fly (IRL) won 19 Grade 1 races—the premium class of horse racing—from Nov 30, 2008 to Jan 26, 2014.

Most Archery World Cup recurve wins

Female: Yun Ok-Hee (KOR) has won the women's recurve competition twice at the Archery World Cup. Ok-Hee's wins came in 2010 and 2013. The World Cup was instituted in 2006 and comprises four separate events in different locations before a final competition.
Male: Brady Ellison (USA) has also scored two recurve World Cup wins, in 2010–11.

Most USASF Cheerleading Worlds international titles

Cheer Athletics of Kentucky, USA, had won 15 international All Star Federation Cheerleading Worlds titles as of the end of 2013. Their wins include both all-girl and co-ed, levels 5 and 6.

• 200-m road (female): Jersy Puello (COL) skated 200 m on the road in 17.677 sec on Aug 27, 2013 in Ostend, Belgium.

• 1,000-m track (male): Bart Swings (BEL) skated 1,000 m on a track in 1 min 20.923 sec on Aug 25, 2013 in Ostend, Belgium.

• 1,000-m track (female): Barbara Fischer (DEU) set a track time of 1 min 27.06 sec in Inzell, Germany, on Aug 27, 1988.

Youngest World Artistic Gymnastics Championships floor gold medalist (male)

Kenzo Shirai (JPN, b. Aug 24, 1996) won the floor event at the World Artistic Gymnastics Championships at the age of 17 years 43 days in Antwerp, Belgium, on Oct 6, 2013. Shirai also became the **first person to perform a quadruple twist in a major final** (pictured above).

Most jump racing wins

Tony "AP" McCoy (UK) rode 4,106 jump-racing winners in his career between Mar 26, 1992 and Apr 26, 2014. McCoy also has the **most jump racing wins in a season** (289 in 2001/02) and the **most jump racing Champion Jockey titles** (19, awarded from 1996 to 2014).

Fastest speed skating
• 200-m road (male):
On Dec 9, 2012 in San Benedetto del Tronto, Italy, Ioseba Fernandez (ESP) finished the 200-m individual time trial in 15.879 sec.

• 10,000-m track (male): On Aug 23, 2013, inline skating world champion Fabio Francolini (ITA) covered 10,000 m on a track in Ostend, Belgium, in just 14 min 23.54 sec.

• 10,000-m track (female): Yang Hochen (TWN) recorded a time of 15 min 26.970 sec in a 10,000-m track skate in Ostend, Belgium, on Aug 24, 2013.

Most appearances in the World Equestrian Games
Anky van Grunsven (NLD) appeared in the Fédération Equestre Internationale (FEI) World Equestrian Games six times between 1990 and 2010. She is the only rider to have appeared in every edition of the tournament since its inception in 1990.

Longest raft race
The Great River Amazon Raft Race has been staged annually since 1999 between the Peruvian locations of Pescadores Island and the Club de Caza y Pesca in Bella Vista. The race, which covers some 112 mi (180 km), was created by Mike Collis (UK). It challenges four-person teams to build a log raft and paddle the course in three stages over three days.

FACT
The All-Around title is awarded to the leading money winner in a single season in two or more events.

Most Rodeo World Championships

Between 2002 and 2013, Trevor Brazile (USA) won 19 titles at the Professional Rodeo Cowboys Association World Championships. His titles were won across four events: All-Around, Tie-Down Roping (individual and team), and Steer Wrestling. Brazile also has the **most All-Around Rodeo World Championships titles**, with 11 wins in 12 years.

PARALYMPIC (IPC) POWERLIFTING			
Category	Weight	Name	Year
Male			
<49 kg	181 kg	Yakubu Adesokan (NGR)	2014
<59 kg	190 kg	Ali Jawad (UK, b. LBN)	2014
<80 kg	236 kg	Xiao Fei Gu (CHN)	2014
<97 kg	240 kg	Mohamed Eldib (EGY)	2013
107+ kg	285 kg	Siamand Rahman (IRN)	2014
Female			
<41 kg	103 kg	Nazmiye Muslu (TUR)	2014
<50 kg	122 kg	Olesya Lafina (RUS)	2014
<61 kg	135.5 kg	Fatma Omar (EGY)	2014
<73 kg	150 kg	Souhad Ghazouani (FRA)	2013
86+ kg	151 kg	Precious Orji (NGR)	2014

Statistics correct as of Apr 21, 2014

Index

Acknowledgments

Guinness World Records would like to thank the following for their help in compiling this edition:

Across the Pond (Rob, Aaron, Julie, Karen, Katie and all their colleagues); API Laminates Ltd (Simon Thompson); Asatsu-DK Inc. (Motonori Iwasaki, Shinsuke Sakuma); Charlotte Atkins; Eric Atkins; Freya Atkins; Simon Atkins; BAFTA; Alexander Balandin; Elle Bartlett; BBC; Oliver Beatson; Sarah Bebbington; Andrew Benson (Carnegie Institution for Science); BFI; Anisa Bhatti; Alexander Boatfield; Joseph Boatfield; Luke Boatfield; Bodyflight Bedford (Bryony Doughty, Ged Parker); Sam Borden; Chiara Bragato; Patrick Bragato; Veronica Bridges (Featherstone Rovers RLFC); Broadcast; Colin Burgess (Stoke City FC); Nicola Campbell (Camelot Group); Canton Classic Car Museum, Ohio, USA; Carousel Candies, California, USA; CCTV (Guo Tong, Wang Wei and all their colleagues); Frank Chambers; Richard M Christensen (Professor Research Emeritus, Stanford University); The Chunichi Shimbun (Tetsuya Okamura, Tadao Sawada); Adam Cloke; Collaboration Inc. Japan

(Mr Suzuki, Miho, Kyoto and all their colleagues); Connexion Cars (Rob and Tracey); Ken Cook (Caboose Hobbies, Denver, Colorado, USA); Anne Cowne (Information Officer, Information Centre, Lloyd's Register); Pietro D'Angelo; Panos Datskos; Anastassia Davidzenka; Martyn Davis; Denmaur Independent Papers Limited (Julian Townsend); Frank Dimroth; Gemma Doherty; Emmys (Academy of Television Arts & Sciences); Europroduzione (Renato, Gabriela, Carlo, Paola and all their colleagues); Toby and Amelia Ewen; Eyeworks/Warner Bros. Germany (Michael, Martin, Käthe and all their colleagues); Benjamin Fall; Rebecca Fall; Daniel Fernandez; Jonathan de Ferranti; FJT Logistics Limited (Ray Harper, Gavin Hennessy); Forbes; Martin Fuechsle; Gemological Institute of America (Kristin Mahan, Shane McClure, Stephen Morisseau, Gwen Travis); Damien Gildea; Andrew Goodwin; Brandon Greenwood; Jordan Greenwood; Ryan Greenwood; Victoria Grimsell; GWRJ internship students (Jiani Xie, Natsumi Kawakami, Chisaki Iijima, Maho Miyamoto, Yumina Murata); Carmen Alfonzo de Hannah; Alexia Hannah Alfonzo;

Amy Hannah Alfonzo; Rod Hansen (Museum of Idaho, Idaho Falls, Idaho, USA); Ellie Hayward; Dr Haze (Circus of Horrors); Bob Headland; Matilda and Max Heaton; High Noon (Brad, Jim, Dana and all their colleagues); The Himalayan Database; Hololens Technology Co., Ltd; Stephen J Holroyd (US Soccer Archives); Claire Holzman (Houghton Mifflin Harcourt); Marsha K Hoover; Dora Howard; Tilly Howard; Colin Hughes; Cynthia Hunt; Sarah Icken (Camelot Group); Integrated Colour Editions Europe (Roger Hawkins, Susie Hawkins, Clare Merryfield); Richard Johnston, Barbara Jones (Information Centre Manager, Lloyd's Register); Stephanie Jones (Great British Racing); Raymond S Jordan, Drogheda, Ireland; Justin Kazmark (Kickstarter); Harry Kikstra; Laleham Camping Club, UK; Orla Langton; Thea Langton; Sophie Lawrenson (Royal Collection Trust); Frederick Horace Lazell; Sydney Leleux; Lion Television (Simon, Jeremy, Tom and all their colleagues); Lloyd's Insurance (Oonagh Bates, Jonathan Thomas); London Pet Show; London Wonderground; Rüdiger Lorenz; Luci Producciones (Maria, Shaun, Stefano); Ciara Mackey; Sarah & Martin Mackey;

Theresa Mackey; Christian de Marliave; Missy Matilda; Dave McAleer; Chelsea McGuffin; Clare Merryfield; Metacritic; Jeremy Michell, Historic Photographs and Ships Plans Manager, Royal Museums Greenwich; Miditech (Niret, Nivedith, Nikhil and all their colleagues); John Jackson Miller; Tamsin Mitchell; Harriet Molloy; Sophie, Joshua and Florence Molloy; Colin Monteath; Dan Morrison; Steven Munatones (Open Water Source); Museum of the Weird, Austin, Texas, USA; Anikó Németh-Móra (International Weightlifting Federation); James Ng; Jim Nicholls; David Oberlink; Caitlin Penny; Periscoop (Peri, Elsy and all their colleagues); Karen Perkins (World Alternative Games); Tom Pierce; Sophie Procter (British Airways); Robert Pullar; Miriam Randall; John Reed (World Speed Sailing Records Council); Kevin Rochfort (FISB); Dan Roddick (World Flying Disc Association); Roller Coaster Database; Kate Rushworth (YouTube); Nick Ryan (Xpogo); Nick Ryuan (Xpogo); Eric Sakowski; Paolo Scarabaggio; Rob Schweitzer (Historic Hudson Valley); Nellie Scott (Brick Artist); Michael Serra (São Paulo Futebol Clube); Bill Sharp (Billabong XXL

Big Wave Awards); Ang Tsering Sherpa; Dawa Sherpa; Patrice Simon; Athena Simpson; Chris Skone-Roberts; Katy Smith (John Wiley & Sons, Inc.); Spectratek Technologies, Inc (Terry Conway, Mike Foster); Glenn Speer; Bill Spindler; St Mary's University, UK; Ray Stevenson; Stephen Sutton; Charlie, Holly and Daisy Taylor; Terry and Jan Todd (H J Lutcher Stark Center for Physical Culture and Sports, University of Texas, USA); Matthew Tole; Anaelle Torres; Cliff Towne (Professional Disc Golf Association); truTV (Michael, Chris, Stephen, Angel, Marissa and all their colleagues); Sheryl Twigg, Press & PR Manager, Royal Museums Greenwich; UPM Plattling, Germany; Kripa Varanasi; Variety; Virgin (Charmaine Clarke, Philippa Russ); Craig Walter; Lara and Sevgi White; Oli White; Robert White; Paul Winston (Zippos Circus); Robert Wood; Daniel Woods; Madeleine Wuschech; Hayley Wylie-Deacon; Rueben George Wylie-Deacon; Tobias Hugh Wylie-Deacon; Zodiak Clips (Sandra, David, Dom, Cath and all their colleagues); Zodiak Kids (Karen, Gary and all their colleagues); Zodiak Rights (Andreas, Tim, Barney and all their colleagues)

Picture credits

PA, Kem McNair/Getty Images **127:** Global Times, Onur Coban/Getty Images, Wim Scheire/Getty Images, Mahmoud Raouf Mahmoud/Reuters **128:** Ragnhild Gustad, Chaiwat Subprasom/Reuters **129:** United States Geological Survey, Alamy, Oleksandr Rupeta/Alamy, Pascal Ducept/Alamy, Giorgio Marcoaldi/CVN, Reuters, Manuel Silvestri/Reuters **130:** Kristijan Vuckovic, National Center for Ecological Analysis and Synthesis, Jahre-Wallern, Michael Kooren/Reuters **131:** Aly Song/Reuters, Marine Traffic, Reuters **132:** Cameron Laird/Rex, Pablo Blazquez Dominguez/Getty Images **133:** Mark Bialek/Alamy, Phil Mingo/Pinnacle **134:** Thomas Grimm/AP/PA, Michael Urban/Getty Images, Paul Cooper/Rex, Alamy, Alamy **135:** Alamy, RMN-Grand Palais/Musée du Louvre/Hervé Lewandowski, Roger Viollet/Getty Images, Alamy **136:** Tina Hager/Getty Images, Chao-Yang Chan/Alamy, George Nikitin/AP/PA, Craig Barritt/Getty Images **137:** Toru Hanai/Reuters, Alamy, Rebecca Cook/Reuters, Yorgos Karahalis/Reuters, NASA **138:** Dove, Google Maps, Universal Pictures/Alamy, Facebook, Alamy **139:** Instagram, Instagram, AP, Lucy Nicholson/Reuters, Andrew Kelly/Reuters, Laurence Mathieu/The Guardian **140:** Mike Goldwater/Alamy, Alamy **141:** Alastair Muir/Rex **142:** Everest Media Productions **144:** Afanassi Makovnev, Getty Images **145:** Jarek Jõepera/GWR **147:** Getty Images, Paul Michael Hughes/GWR **148:** Will Wintercross **149:** James Ellerker/GWR **150:** British Nanga Parbat 2012 Expedition, Philip Temple, Paul A Souders/Corbis, Frieder Blickle/Camera Press **151:** Paul Michael Hughes/GWR **152:** Felipe Souza, Ben Duffy **153:** Daniel Deme/GWR, Torsten Blackwood/Getty Images, Paul Michael Hughes/GWR **154:** Bas de Meijer, Lars Stenholt Kirkegaard, Lupi_Spuma, Shutterstock **155:** John Dickey, Claudia Marcelloni, James Ellerker/GWR, James Ellerker/GWR **157:** Paul Michael Hughes/GWR **158:** Lionsgate/Alamy **160:** MGM/Alamy, Walt Disney Productions, Twentieth Century Fox, MGM/Alamy, Universal, MGM/Alamy, Paramount, Walt Disney Productions/Rex, MGM, Twentieth Century Fox, Warner Bros. **161:** Universal/Alamy, Yash Raj Films, Walt Disney Pictures, Twentieth Century Fox/Alamy, Twentieth Century Fox, Summit Entertainment, Walt Disney Productions, Twentieth Century Fox, Marvel, Lucasfilm, Hollywood Pictures, Warner Bros., MGM/Alamy, Lucasfilm, Universal, Twentieth Century Fox, Twentieth Century Fox **162:** Lionsgate, Warner Bros., Paramount Pictures **163:** Paramount Pictures, Warner Bros., Salty Features, Warner Bros. **164:** Yashraj Films, Twentieth Century Fox, Alamy, Cross Creek Pictures, Alamy **165:** Alamy, Mario Anzuoni/Reuters, Alamy, Walt Disney Pictures, Karen Ballard/Paramount Pictures, Fred Prouser/Reuters **166:** Getty Images, Brian Snyder/Reuters **167:** Lucy Nicholson/Reuters, Steven Klein, Terry Richardson, Isaac Brekken/Getty Images **168:** YouTube **169:** Girlguiding North West, Matt Crossick/GWR **170:** Don Emmert/Getty Images, Alamy, PA, Marijan

Murat/PA, Alamy, Rodrigo de Balbin Behrmann **171:** WENN, WENN, Russell Cheyne/Reuters, Alain Perus/L'Oeil du Diaph **172:** Ryan Schude/GWR, Alamy **173:** Olivia Harris/Reuters, Benjamin Pritzkuleit **174:** Rex Features, Haut et Court, Virginia Sherwood/Getty Images, Yogen Shah/Getty Images, Samir Hussein/Getty Images **175:** A & E Networks, Bob D'Amico/Getty Images, BBC **176:** Ryan Schude/GWR, Kevin Scott Ramos/GWR, Paul Michael Hughes/GWR, Ryan Schude/GWR, Richard Bradbury/GWR **177:** Ranald Mackechnie/GWR, Richard Bradbury/GWR, Ryan Schude/GWR **178:** Kevin Scott Ramos/GWR **180:** Alcatel-Lucent, Topfoto, HP Museum, Eric Risberg/AP/PA, Getty Images, AP/PA, NASA, Getty Images, Gene J Puskar/AP/PA, Science Photo Library **181:** Elise Amendola/AP/PA, Getty Images, Rebecca Cook/Reuters, Fabrizio Bensch/Reuters, Reidar Hahn, Getty Images, Kimberly White/Reuters, Denis Closon/Rex **182:** Mathew Imaging, Ho New/Reuters, Justin Garvanovic/Coaster Club **183:** Iain Masterton/Alamy, Stan Honda/Getty Images, Craig T Mathew/Mathew Imaging, Kazuhiro Nogi/Getty Images **184:** Corbis, J S Callahan/Alamy, Alamy **185:** Rex Features, Alamy, Getty Images, Ray Roberts/Rex **186:** Damian Kramski, Max Earey/Newspress **187:** Alamy, Canton Classic Car Museum, Chrysler Group LLC, Alamy, Alamy, Kim Kyung Hoon/Reuters, Tobias Schwarz/Reuters, Reuters **188:** Maciej Dakowicz/Alamy, iStock **189:** Peter Brogden/Alamy, Robert Nickelsberg/Alamy, PA **190:** Andy Clark/Reuters, Alison Thompson/Alamy, Colombia Travel, Alamy **191:** Shadow Fox, Mark L Simpson/Electric Lemonade Photography, Wisconsin Duck Tours, Marcio Jose Sanchez/AP/PA, Rex **192:** Paul Michael Hughes/GWR, Paul Michael Hughes/GWR, Shinsuke Kamioka/GWR, Paul Michael Hughes/GWR, Ranald Mackechnie/GWR, James Ellerker/GWR **193:** Paul Michael Hughes/GWR, Richard Bradbury/GWR, Drew Gardner/GWR, Kevin Scott Ramos/GWR **194:** Solid Concepts, US Navy, Reuters, USAF **195:** US Navy, Alamy, USDA **196:** Sean Pavone/Alamy, Gustau Nacarino/Reuters, Rory Daniel, Rex Features, Alamy, Alamy, Alamy **197:** Jianan Yu/Reuters, Rex Features, iStock **198:** iStock, Postojna Cave, Jim Zuckerman/Alamy **199:** Jorge Royan, Glenn Asakawa/Getty Images, Alice Finch, Alamy **200:** Khaled Al-Sayyed/Getty Images, Dominique Debaralle/Corbis, Ed Jones/Getty Images, Chi Po-lin, Pichi Chuang/Reuters, Christian Haugen **201:** Joel Riner, Hans Blossey/Corbis, Cor Mulder/EPA, Reuters, David Cannon/Getty Images, David Cannon/Getty Images, Getty Images **202:** Baxley/JILA, Baxley/JILA, Long Hongtao/Rex, Long Hongtao/Rex, Sven Sturm/MPI for Nuclear Physics **203:** ESA, Felipe Pedreros/IceCube/NSF, Jim Haugen/IceCube/NSF, Alamy **204:** Alamy, Iberpress, Harvard School of Engineering and Applied Sciences, Seth Wenig/AP/PA, Peter Morgan/Reuters **205:** Kevin Ma and Pakpong Chirarattananon/Harvard Microrobotics Lab, Boston Dynamics **206:** Kumar Sriskandan/Alamy **207:** Alamy,

NASA, NASA **208:** Stephane Mahe/Reuters **210:** Ezra Shaw/Getty Images, Jeremy Brevard/Reuters, Lucy Nicholson/Reuters, Reuters **211:** Alamy, Jack Dempsey/AP/PA, John Leyba/Getty Images **212:** John Thys/Getty Images, Dylan Martinez/Reuters, Pascal Lauener/Reuters **213:** Ian Walton/Getty Images, Alamy, Alamy **214:** Hannah Johnston/Getty Images, Lorraine O'Sullivan/Inpho, Lluis Gene/Getty Images, Toshifumi Kitamura/Getty Images **215:** Alamy, Marco Garcia/Getty Images **216:** Ray Stubblebine/Reuters, Alamy, Mike Cassese/Reuters **217:** Martin Thomas/Alamy, Keith Charles/Getty Images, Getty Images, Mike Blake/Reuters **218:** Dick Raphael/Getty Images, Ron Hoskins/Getty Images, Joe Skipper/Reuters, Reuters, Mike Segar/Reuters **219:** Layne Murdoch Jr/Getty Images, Getty Images **220:** Getty Images, Alamy, Al Bello/Getty Images, Kristian Dowling/Getty Images **221:** David Finch/Getty Images, Nathan Denette/PA **222:** Christopher Lee/Getty Images, Philip Brown/Reuters, Philip Brown/Reuters, David Gray/Reuters **223:** Aijaz Rahi/AP/PA, Alamy, Philip Brown/Reuters **224:** Stefano Rellandini/Reuters, Reuters **225:** Javier Lizon/Alamy, Getty Images, John Sommers/Corbis, PA, Corbis, Leo Mason/Corbis **226:** Caren Firouz/Reuters, Tami Chappell/Reuters, Daren Staples/Reuters, Alamy, Alamy **227:** Phil Sheldon/Getty Images, Andy Lyons/Getty Images, Jim Young/Reuters, Harry Warnecke/Getty Images, Denis Balibouse/Reuters **228:** Reuters, Antti Aimo-Koivisto/PA, B Bennett/Getty Images, Reuters, Alamy, Reuters **229:** Dick Raphael/Getty Images **230:** Reuters, Tobias Schwarz/Reuters, Chris Helgren/Reuters **231:** Reuters, Reuters, Alamy, Reuters, Alamy **232:** Cody Duncan/Alamy, Alamy, Tannen Maury/Alamy, Mervyn McClelland/Presseye **233:** Adrees Latif/Reuters, Lars Baron/Getty Images, Dozier Mobley/Getty Images, Lehtikuva/Reuters **234:** Cathal McNaughton/Reuters, Alamy, Alamy **235:** Jean Sebastien Evrard/Getty Images, Alamy, Reuters, Eddie Keogh/Reuters **236:** Josep Lago/Getty Images, Michaela Rehle/Reuters, Paul Hanna/Reuters, Alamy **237:** Alamy, Paul Burrows/Action Images, Alex Morton/Action Images, Susana Vera/Reuters **238:** Reuters, Christophe Simon/Getty Images, Wolfgang Rattay/Reuters, Getty Images, Juan Medina/Reuters **239:** Alamy, Clive Brunskill/Getty Images, Goran Tomasevic/Reuters, Alamy, Jorge Silva/Reuters **240:** Adam Stoltman/Corbis, Bob Thomas/Getty Images, Mike Hewitt/Getty Images **241:** Darren Carroll/Getty Images, Stan Honda/Getty Images, Charles Platiau/Reuters **242:** Albert Gea/Reuters, Matthias Oesterle/Alamy, Alamy **243:** Alamy, Alamy, Alex Laurel/Red Bull **244:** Lucy Nicholson/Reuters, Michael Dalder/Reuters, Alamy, Fabrizio Bensch/Reuters, Alamy **245:** Alamy, Sergei Karpukhin/Reuters, Alamy, Alexander Demianchuk/Reuters **246:** Lehtikuva Lehtikuva/Reuters, Bryce Kanights/ESPN Images, Alamy, Franck Fife/Getty Images, Getty Images, Alamy, Dan Abraham, Isaac Brekken/AP/PA **254:** Derek Wade Alamy **255:** Birmingham Mail, Kevin Scott Ramos/GWR

Country codes

Code	Country
ABW	Aruba
AFG	Afghanistan
AGO	Angola
AIA	Anguilla
ALB	Albania
AND	Andorra
ANT	Netherlands Antilles
ARG	Argentina
ARM	Armenia
ASM	American Samoa
ATA	Antarctica
ATF	French Southern Territories
ATG	Antigua and Barbuda
AUS	Australia
AUT	Austria
AZE	Azerbaijan
BDI	Burundi
BEL	Belgium
BEN	Benin
BFA	Burkina Faso
BGD	Bangladesh
BGR	Bulgaria
BHR	Bahrain
BHS	The Bahamas
BIH	Bosnia and Herzegovina
BLR	Belarus
BLZ	Belize
BMU	Bermuda
BOL	Bolivia
BRA	Brazil
BRB	Barbados
BRN	Brunei Darussalam
BTN	Bhutan
BVT	Bouvet Island
BWA	Botswana
CAF	Central African Republic
CAN	Canada
CCK	Cocos (Keeling) Islands
CHE	Switzerland
CHL	Chile
CHN	China
CIV	Côte d'Ivoire
CMR	Cameroon
COD	Congo, DR of
COG	Congo
COK	Cook Islands
COL	Colombia
COM	Comoros
CPV	Cape Verde
CRI	Costa Rica
CUB	Cuba
CXR	Christmas Island
CYM	Cayman Islands
CYP	Cyprus
CZE	Czech Republic
DEU	Germany
DJI	Djibouti
DMA	Dominica
DNK	Denmark
DOM	Dominican Republic
DZA	Algeria
ECU	Ecuador
EGY	Egypt
ERI	Eritrea
ESH	Western Sahara
ESP	Spain
EST	Estonia
ETH	Ethiopia
FIN	Finland
FJI	Fiji
FLK	Falkland Islands (Malvinas)
FRA	France
FRG	West Germany
FRO	Faroe Islands
FSM	Micronesia, Federated States of
FXX	France, Metropolitan
GAB	Gabon
GEO	Georgia
GHA	Ghana
GIB	Gibraltar
GIN	Guinea
GLP	Guadeloupe
GMB	Gambia
GNB	Guinea-Bissau
GNQ	Equatorial Guinea
GRC	Greece
GRD	Grenada
GRL	Greenland
GTM	Guatemala
GUF	French Guiana
GUM	Guam
GUY	Guyana
HKG	Hong Kong
HMD	Heard and McDonald Islands
HND	Honduras
HRV	Croatia (Hrvatska)
HTI	Haiti
HUN	Hungary
IDN	Indonesia
IND	India
IOT	British Indian Ocean Territory
IRL	Ireland
IRN	Iran
IRQ	Iraq
ISL	Iceland
ISR	Israel
ITA	Italy
JAM	Jamaica
JOR	Jordan
JPN	Japan
KAZ	Kazakhstan
KEN	Kenya
KGZ	Kyrgyzstan
KHM	Cambodia
KIR	Kiribati
KNA	Saint Kitts and Nevis
KOR	Korea, Republic of
KWT	Kuwait
LAO	Laos
LBN	Lebanon
LBR	Liberia
LBY	Libyan Arab Jamahiriya
LCA	Saint Lucia
LIE	Liechtenstein
LKA	Sri Lanka
LSO	Lesotho
LTU	Lithuania
LUX	Luxembourg
LVA	Latvia
MAC	Macau
MAR	Morocco
MCO	Monaco
MDA	Moldova
MDG	Madagascar
MDV	Maldives
MEX	Mexico
MHL	Marshall Islands
MKD	Macedonia
MLI	Mali
MLT	Malta
MMR	Myanmar (Burma)
MNE	Montenegro
MNG	Mongolia
MNP	Northern Mariana Islands
MOZ	Mozambique
MRT	Mauritania
MSR	Montserrat
MTQ	Martinique
MUS	Mauritius
MWI	Malawi
MYS	Malaysia
MYT	Mayotte
NAM	Namibia
NCL	New Caledonia
NER	Niger
NFK	Norfolk Island
NGA	Nigeria
NIC	Nicaragua
NIU	Niue
NLD	Netherlands
NOR	Norway
NPL	Nepal
NRU	Nauru
NZ	New Zealand
OMN	Oman
PAK	Pakistan
PAN	Panama
PCN	Pitcairn Islands
PER	Peru
PHL	Philippines
PLW	Palau
PNG	Papua New Guinea
POL	Poland
PRI	Puerto Rico
PRK	Korea, DPRO
PRT	Portugal
PRY	Paraguay
PYF	French Polynesia
QAT	Qatar
REU	Réunion
ROM	Romania
RUS	Russian Federation
RWA	Rwanda
SAU	Saudi Arabia
SDN	Sudan
SEN	Senegal
SGP	Singapore
SGS	South Georgia and South SS
SHN	Saint Helena
SJM	Svalbard and Jan Mayen Islands
SLB	Solomon Islands
SLE	Sierra Leone
SLV	El Salvador
SMR	San Marino
SOM	Somalia
SPM	Saint Pierre and Miquelon
SRB	Serbia
SSD	South Sudan
STP	São Tomé and Príncipe
SUR	Suriname
SVK	Slovakia
SVN	Slovenia
SWE	Sweden
SWZ	Swaziland
SYC	Seychelles
SYR	Syrian Arab Republic
TCA	Turks and Caicos Islands
TCD	Chad
TGO	Togo
THA	Thailand
TJK	Tajikistan
TKL	Tokelau
TKM	Turkmenistan
TMP	East Timor
TON	Tonga
TPE	Chinese Taipei
TTO	Trinidad and Tobago
TUN	Tunisia
TUR	Turkey
TUV	Tuvalu
TZA	Tanzania
UAE	United Arab Emirates
UGA	Uganda
UK	United Kingdom
UKR	Ukraine
UMI	US Minor Islands
URY	Uruguay
USA	United States of America
UZB	Uzbekistan
VAT	Holy See (Vatican City)
VCT	Saint Vincent and the Grenadines
VEN	Venezuela
VGB	Virgin Islands (British)
VIR	Virgin Islands (US)
VNM	Vietnam
VUT	Vanuatu
WLF	Wallis and Futuna Islands
WSM	Samoa
YEM	Yemen
ZAF	South Africa
ZMB	Zambia
ZWE	Zimbabwe

Stop press

Largest Garfield collection

Cathy Kothe (USA) has 6,190 unique Garfield items, as listed by her official cataloger—husband Robert—and verified in Huntington Station, New York, USA, on Apr 10, 2014. The collection includes three slot machines and an inflatable measuring 25 ft (7.6 m) tall—higher than the couple's house!

Most haikus about one town
As of Apr 29, 2014, 1,663 haikus had been written about Luton in Bedfordshire, UK, by the local *Clod Magazine*. The Luton Haiku team—Andrew Kingston, Tim Kingston, Andrew Whiting, and Stephen Whiting—began posting haikus online each weekday from Jan 23, 2007.

Most pubs visited
As of Jan 29, 2014, Bruce Masters (UK) had visited 46,495 pubs and drinking establishments, sampling local beers where available. He began his tour in 1960, and visited 936 pubs in 2013 alone. The most popular UK pub name so far, says Bruce, is the Red Lion.

Longest group drum roll

To celebrate the 350th anniversary of the Royal Marines (founded in 1664), the Corps of Drums of Her Majesty's Royal Marines Band Service (UK) achieved a group drum roll lasting 64 hr 27 min 59 sec. Beginning on Apr 30, 2014, 40 members of the Corps took it in turns to drum on the same snare drum at the Tower of London, London, UK, finishing on May 3, 2014.

Largest game of "What's the time, Mr. Wolf?"
The playground favorite was played by 494 staff of Royal London (UK) at the EICC in Edinburgh, UK, on Feb 6, 2014.

Largest charity walk
Iglesia Ni Cristo (PHL) organized a walk with 175,509 people, starting at the Quirino Grandstand in Manila, Philippines, on Feb 15, 2014. Money was raised for victims of 2013's Typhoon Haiyan.

Most southerly navigation
On Jan 27, 2014, the *Arctic P*, skippered by Russell Pugh and owned by the Packer family (both AUS), reached the Bay of Whales in the Ross Ice Shelf of Antarctica. An instrument on the bow recorded 78°43.042'S 163°42.069'W, the most southerly point. The latitude of the shelf is dynamic due to the ice calving—when ice melts and breaks off the shelf.

Telmex triple certification

Telmex (MEX) achieved a GWR treble at Aldea Digital in Mexico City, Mexico, from Apr 11 to 27, 2014. CEO Héctor Slim (center) receives the certificate for **largest digital inclusion event**, (258,896 people), plus those for **most people trained in IT in one month** (177,517, at the same event) and for **most scans of an Augmented Reality app in eight hours** (49,273, on Apr 26).

Most consecutive rolls by an aircraft
Kingsley Just (AUS) rolled his Pitts Special biplane 987 times at Lethbridge Airpark in Victoria, Australia, on Mar 1, 2014. Kingsley rolled his aircraft continuously for just under an hour without any break.

Largest observation wheel
The Las Vegas High Roller is 549 ft 8 in (167.5 m) tall. Opened on Mar 31, 2014 in Las Vegas, Nevada, USA, it has 28 cabins, each holding 40 people. One full revolution of the wheel takes 30 min.

Rumeysa Gelgi
The new record holder tells us: "I'm adapting everything to my height. It has good and bad sides but, anyway, I feel lucky myself."

Oldest boxing world champion
Bernard Hopkins (USA, b. Jan 15, 1965) broke his own record when, at 49 years 94 days old, he outpointed Beibut Shumenov (KAZ) for the WBA (super) light heavyweight, IBA light heavyweight, and IBF light heavyweight titles on Apr 19, 2014.

Largest greetings card
A Mother's Day card measuring 33 ft 5 in (10.19 m) tall and 23 ft 3 in (7.09 m) wide was unveiled by Nestlé Middle East FZE (UAE) at Dubai Mall, United Arab Emirates, on Mar 21, 2014.

Tallest teenager (female)

Measuring 7 ft 0.09 in (213.6 cm) at full standing height, Rumeysa Gelgi (TUR, b. Jan 1, 1997) is the tallest female under the age of 18. Rumeysa, pictured left with niece Zeynep Ravza Yakut, was diagnosed with Weaver syndrome, a rare genetic disorder that causes rapid growth. She was measured by Dr. Ömer Hakan Yavaşoğlu (inset) in Karabük, Turkey, on Mar 19, 2014.

Most siblings to celebrate diamond wedding anniversaries

Edward Thomas and Ellen Jane Howell (UK) had five children, all of whom had celebrated 60 years of marriage as of Mar 4, 2014:
• Gwendoline Jean Howell and Douglas Derek Bennett: 61 years
• John Edward Howell and Sylvia Beryl (née Winter): 61 years
• Doris Winifred Howell and Donald Street: 66 years
• Stanley Frederick Howell and Margaret Elizabeth (née Sharpe): 65 years
• William George Howell and Hazel Pauline (née Freeman): 60 years.

Largest underwater viewing dome

The whale shark tank at Chimelong Ocean Kingdom in Hengqin, Guangdong, China, has a dome with a diameter of 39 ft 4 in (12 m). The attraction opened on Jan 28, 2014 and set five world records, including **largest underwater viewing dome** (above). It uses 12.87 million gal (48.75 million liters) of salt and fresh water.

Most people people making heart-shaped hand gestures

Stephen Sutton (UK, 1994–2014) and 553 friends gathered to make a heart symbol with their hands on May 4, 2014 in Staffordshire, UK. Stephen, diagnosed with terminal cancer, made headlines in 2014 with his fund-raising efforts, and stated that one of his dreams was to secure a Guinness World Records title.

Longest time ranked as chess world No. 1 (female)

As confirmed by the International Chess Federation, Judit Polgár (HUN) has been the world No. 1 female player since Feb 1, 1989, and retains the spot as of Apr 17, 2014.

Most valuable life-insurance policy

The identity of the Silicon Valley billionaire who holds an insurance policy worth $201 m remains anonymous, but with more than 100 billionaires resident in the famous strip of California, USA, there is no shortage of candidates. The policy was brokered by Dovi Frances (ISR) of the advisory firm SG, LLC (USA), and certified by a public notary in Santa Barbara, California, USA, on Feb 28, 2014. This beats the long-standing record for a $100-m policy sold by Peter Rosengard (UK) for US media mogul David Geffen back in 1990.

Fastest lawn mower

The *Mean Mower* can cut grass while moving at a speed of 116.57 mph (187.61 km/h) and was constructed and raced by Honda and Team Dynamics (both UK) at Applus+ IDIADA's test track in Tarragona, Spain, on Mar 8, 2014. *Top Gear* journalist Piers Ward drove the mower.

Most bungee jumps in 24 hours

Fitness coach Colin Phillips (UK) recorded 151 bungee jumps from a 328-ft-tall (100-m) crane in aid of charity Breast Cancer Arabia. His attempt was set with Gravity Zone at Dubai Autodrome in the United Arab Emirates on Mar 21, 2014. He dislocated a finger and afterward admitted to feeling "a bit beaten up, to be honest."

Most weight lifted by dumbbell rows in one minute with one arm

Strongman Robert Natoli (USA) set five records in an hour at the Pacific Health Club in Liverpool, New York, USA, on Mar 22, 2014, to raise money for the Patterson family, whose three children had been badly injured in a car crash that claimed the life of their mother. He lifted 4,356 lb (1,975.85 kg) with dumbbell rows and recorded the **most pull-ups in one minute with a 40-lb pack** (23); the **most step-ups in one minute with an 80-lb pack** (41); the **most step-ups in one minute with a 100-lb pack** (38); and the **most knuckle push-ups in one minute** (58).

In a separate charity event in Oswego, New York, USA, on Apr 4, 2013, Natoli achieved two further records: the **most step-ups in one minute with a 40-lb pack** (52) and the **most step-ups in one minute with a 60-lb pack** (47).

Highest 2D movie box-office gross (opening weekend)

Shortly before we went to press, we were delighted to have the chance to present Tom Hardy (UK) with a GWR certificate. Tom played Batman's enemy Bane, who terrorizes the caped crusader and Gotham City in *The Dark Knight Rises* (USA/UK, 2012). The hit movie grossed $160,887,295 from Jul 20 to 22, 2012.